MEDICINE

LAW

&

PUBLIC POLICY

MEDICINE

LAW

&

PUBLIC POLICY

Volume I

with a foreword by **Senator Walter F. Mondale**

Edited by

Nicholas N. Kittrie
Harold L. Hirsh
Glen Wegner

AMS Press, Inc. New York

Library of Congress Cataloging in Publication Data
Main entry under title:

Medicine, Law, and Public Policy.

   1. Medical jurisprudence – United States – Congresses. 2. Medical laws and legislation – United States – Congresses. 3. Medical policy – United States – Congresses. I. Kittrie, Nicholas N., 1928- II. Hirsh, Harold L. III. Wegner, Glen.
RA1016.M42   ISBN 0-404-10426-6   75-793

TABLE
OF
CONTENTS

ACKNOWLEDGMENTS

Acknowledgment is made to the authors and publishers below who have granted permission to reprint material and who reserve all rights in the articles appearing in this anthology.

Adler, "Malicious Prosecution Suits as Counterbalance to Medical Malpractice Suits," *Cleveland State Law Review,* Vol. 21, No. 1, January 1972, pp. 51-57.

Brook and Appel, "Quality-of-Care Assessment," *The New England Journal of Medicine,* Vol. 288, June 21, 1973, pp. 1323-1328.

Bryant, "International Trends toward Humanization of Health Services," *Journal of the American Medical Association,* Vol. 224, June 25, 1973, pp. 1772-1775.

Carlson, "Health Manpower Licensing and Emerging Institutional Responsibility for the Quality of Care," reprinted, with permission, from a symposium on Health Care: Part II appearing in *Law and Contemporary Problems,* Vol. 35, No. 4, Autumn, 1970, published by the Duke University School of Law, Durham, North Carolina. Copyright, 1970-71, by Duke University.

Chappel, "Attitudinal Barriers to Physician Involvement with Drug Abusers," *Journal of the American Medical Association,* Vol. 224, May 14, 1973, pp. 1011-1013.

Clouser, "Some Things Medical Ethics Is Not," *Journal of the American Medical Association,* Vol. 223, February 12, 1973, pp. 787-789.

Cohrssen and Lieberman, "Cannabis," *Southwestern Law Journal,* Vol. 24, August, 1970, pp. 446-462.

Cross, "Privileged Communications between Participants in Group Psychotherapy," *Law and the Social Order,* 1970, pp. 191-211.

Curran, "The Medicolegal Autopsy and Medicolegal Investigation," *Bulletin of the New York Academy of Medicine,* Vol. 47, July, 1971, pp. 766-775.

Dornette, "Medical Injury Insurance," *The Journal of Legal Medicine,* March-April, 1973, pp. 28-34.

Dunne, "Here's What H.M.O. Is All About," *Medical Times*, Vol. 100, December, 1972, pp. 79-100.

Ehrenreich, "Empires at Work," from *The American Health Empire: Power, Profits, and Politics*, 1970. Random House, Copyright 1970. Health Policy Advisory Center.

Fletcher, "Ethical Aspects of Genetic Controls," *The New England Journal of Medicine,* Vol. 285, September 30, 1971, pp. 776-783.

Gunn, "Sentencing As Seen by a Psychiatrist," *Medicine, Science, and the Law*, July, 1971, Vol. 11, No. 3, pp. 95-103.

Halleck, "The Power of Psychiatric Excuse," from *The Politics of Therapy*, Science House, Inc., New York, 1971, pp. 135-156.

Heese, "Thoughts on the Ethics of Treating or Operating on Newborns and Infants with Congenital Abnormalities," *South African Medical Journal*, Vol. 45, June, 1971, pp. 631-632.

Hirsh, "Dying, Death, and Dead," *Case and Comment*, Vol. 79, No. 5, September-October, 1974, pp. 27-36.

Hirsh, "Educational Opportunities in Law and Medicine in Law and Medical Schools," *Journal of Legal Medicine*, Vol. 2, No. 2, March-April, 1974, pp. 41-46.

Hirsh, "Impact of the Supreme Court Decisions on the Performance of Abortions in the United States," *Forensic Science*, Vol. 3, March, 1974, pp. 209-223.

Kittrie, "Prisons or Behavior Control?" *Congressional Record*, January 18, 1972, pp. E123-E127.

Knox, "Attitudes of Psychiatrists and Psychologists toward Alcoholism," *American Journal of Psychiatry*, Vol. 127, June, 1971, pp. 1675-1679. Copyright © 1971 The American Psychiatric Association.

McGarry and Greenblatt, "Conditional Voluntary Mental-Hospital Admission," *The New England Journal of Medicine*, Vol. 287, August 10, 1972, pp. 279-280.

McNerney, "Health Care Financing and Delivery in the Decade Ahead," presented at the American Medical Association, San Francisco, California, June 18, 1972.

Medical World News, "Comprehensive Health Planning," *Medical World News*, February 16, 1973, pp. 54-64.

Morris, "Voluntary Euthanasia," *Washington Law Review*, Vol. 45, April, 1970, pp. 239-266.

Muller, "The Johns Hopkins Medical Institutions," *Johns Hopkins Medical Journal*, February, 1973, Vol. 132, pp. 71-79.

Myers, "Insurance Coverage for Mental Illness," *American Journal of Public Health*, Vol. 60, No. 10, October, 1970, pp. 1921-1930.

Ramsey, "Shall We 'Reproduce'?" *Journal of the American Medical Association*, Vol. 220, June 5, 1972, pp. 1346-1350 and Vol. 220, June 12, 1972, pp. 1480-1485.

Reynolds, "What the New Peer-Review Law Says—and Doesn't Say," *Medical Economics*, December 4, 1972, pp. 35-45. Copyright © 1972 by Medical Economics Company, Oradell, New Jersey 07649. Reprinted by permission.

Robitscher, "The New Face of Legal Psychiatry," *American Journal of Legal Psychiatry*, Vol. 129, 1972, pp. 315-321. Copyright 1972, The American Psychiatric Association.

Rose, "Criminal Responsibility and Competency as Influenced by Organic Disease," *Missouri Law Review*, Vol. 35, 1970, pp. 326-348 Copyright 1970 The Curators of the University of Missouri; reprinted with permission.

Rose, "The Medical Expert and the Lawsuit," *South Dakota Law Review*, Vol. 16, Winter, 1971, pp. 1-19.

Sagall and Reed, "Legal Responsibility for Negligence of Assistants, Substitutes, Partners, Consultants, and Jointly Treating Physicians," from *The Law and Clinical Medicine*, Sagall and Reed, editors, 1970, J.B. Lippincott.

Sheridan, "New Rights for Patients, New Risks for You," *Medical Economics*, March 19, 1973, pp. 35-47. Copyright © 1973 by Medical Economics Company, Oradell, New Jersey 17649. Reprinted by permission.

Sidel, "The Consequences of Accountability to the Community," *Clinical Research*, Vol. XX, pp. 694-697.

Sidel, "Medical Ethics and Socio-Political Change," presented at the National Conference on the Teaching of Medical Ethics, Tarrytown, New York, June 1, 1972.

Slovenko, "Civil Commitment in Perspective," *Journal of Public Law*, Vol. 20, 1971, pp. 3-32. Reprinted with permission of the *Journal of Public Law* of Emory University.

Slovenko, "Everything You Wanted to Have in Sex Laws," *Journal of Forensic Sciences*, 1972, pp. 118-124.

Strauss, "Psychiatric Testimony, with Special Reference to Cases of Post-Traumatic Neurosis," *Forensic Science*, Vol. 1, 1972, pp. 77-90.

Suarez and Hunt, "The Scope of Legal Psychiatry," *Journal of Forensic Sciences*, 1972, pp. 60-68.

Szasz, "Voluntary Mental Hospitalization," *The New England Journal of Medicine*, Vol. 287, August 10, 1972, pp. 277-278.

Tanay, "Psychiatric Morbidity and Treatment of Prison Inmates," *Journal of Forensic Sciences*, 1972, pp. 53-59.

Tao, "Psychiatry and the Utility of the Traditional Criminal Law Approach to Drunkenness Offenses," *Georgetown Law Journal*, Vol. 57, 1969, pp. 818-834. Copyright © 1969 Georgetown Law Journal Association.

Wecht, "The Role of the Forensic Pathologist in Criminal Cases," *Tennessee Law Review*, Vol. 37, 1970 pp. 669-687.

Willig, "Civil Redress," *Case and Comment*, Vol. 76, November-December, 1971, pp. 30-31, 33, 34.

Worthington and Silver, "Regulation of Quality of Care in Hospitals," reprinted, with permission, from a symposium on Health Care: Part I appearing in *Law and Contemporary Problems*, Vol. 35, No. 2, Spring, 1970, published by the Duke University School of Law Durham, North Carolina. Copyright, 1970-71, by Duke University.

The health sciences have made incredible advances over the past half century. Fifty years ago tuberculosis was perhaps the most feared killer of American children and adults. Sanitariums for those afflicted by this terrible, wasting disease dotted the country. Other infectious diseases such as pneumonia and scarlet fever brought tragedy to countless families.

Today, with the discovery of antibiotics, these diseases are controlled by routine treatment. Twenty years ago polio struck 57,879 American children and adults every year. Yet, with the discovery of the Salk vaccine in 1955, polio has been virtually eliminated in this country. In 1971 only 21 cases were reported.

Since 1900 our average life expectancy has increased from 47 to 71 years. Medical science is performing incredible feats as a matter of routine. Who would have thought 30 years ago that he would live to see surgery performed by a laser?

And as impressive as the recent accomplishments of the health sciences have been, these same health sciences offer hope, and in some cases fear, that still greater accomplishments lie ahead:

——Advances in genetics and cell biology may permit us to affect the genetic make-up of human beings.

——Improvements in psychosurgery and drug therapy may give us the power to order human emotions — to call up fear, anger, anxiety, or indifference from human beings as we wish, to make fundamental, controlled changes in human personality.

——Continuing improvements in medical practice combined with expanding knowledge of human biology may give us the power to extend human life, at least for a select few, far beyond its present span.

None of these discoveries may be frightening in themselves, and all may have tremendous potential for improving human lives. But I have been deeply concerned, as I think many Americans are, about these developments. As a member of the Senate Health Subcommittee, on the Labor Committee, and now a member of the Health Subcommittee on the Senate Finance Committee, it is my view that our society is fundamentally unprepared to cope with the profound legal, moral, and ethical questions that will be forced upon us by this revolution in medical theory and technology. And I think most of my colleagues on the Subcommittee agree.

When we began hearings I was shaken by the approach of the American Medical Association. After our first proposal for the establishment of a mere study on health sciences and society, the President of the AMA insisted upon going on the "Today" show to imply that this meant a politician in every surgery room in America.

However, Dr. Daniel J. Callahan, one of our witnesses, outlined the problem bluntly and clearly in testimony two years ago:

> For better or for worse, the biological and medical decisions now being made will radically change future conditions of life . . . It would be foolish to assume that the needed ethical codes, the requisite intellectual resources, the imperative wisdom will inevitably be found. On the contrary, it is possible to imagine a permanent state of moral and social chaos, resting on jerry-built moral rules, and on ad hoc solutions and policies. That may work for our generation, but it will almost certainly mean that we will bequeath to our children a mess of pottage. They will have to live with our mistakes, which in this case may be irreversible.

And we're not talking about "science fiction" questions we'll face only in the far distant future. Let's look at a few of them that we see today, for existing medical technology raises compelling and difficult ethical questions. Each year 50,000 Americans die due to kidney failure. We presently have the resources to perform around 1500 transplants, and to put around 500 new people each year on artificial kidneys. In the course of our hearings we have received several letters from practicing doctors who have complained that in their practice they have traditionally, in effect, had to decide who is going to live and who is going to die just on the basis of the availability of transplants or kidney dialysis machines.

Now, how do we decide on the 2,000 who will live and the 48,000 who will die? Should we help the 45-year old bank executive with a family of four . . . the 70-year old composer . . . or the 17-year old high school drop-out? Should we help only those who can afford to pay $30,000 a year for a kidney machine or $25,000 for a transplant? Should the government pay for treatment for those who cannot afford it? I am pleased to say we did pass a bill in the last session to include automatically persons suffering from kidney disease under Medicare's definition of disabled for the purpose of trying to provide the financial resources needed for transplants or dialysis, but I don't think we have fully solved the problem by any means.

And these transplants raise many other questions. What are the rights of the donor? Surely we need to assure living donors that they will be fully informed of the consequences of their action. And how does a physician split his loyalty between prolonging the life of the dying and the optimum conditions for transplant to save the life of one who can surely be saved? Can these decisions be entrusted to the sole judgment of a single physician, or are procedures for peer review too cumbersome or bureaucratic?

I might say that some of the people in the medical profession now want help from the government to redefine the laws to permit any technology to be used without raising legal and criminal responsibilities on their part. What should the role of the government be? Should it seek to establish rules? Or should they be left solely to the medical community?

Other urgent questions are also before us now. For example, the ability of modern medicine to prolong life has raised wholly new questions about the definition of death, and about the duty of doctors to prolong life.

The old dilemma of "euthanasia" — the so-called "mercy killing" of the incurably ill — has become far more complicated. Is a patient alive or dead when his heart is beating but his brain has ceased to function? Is a doctor compelled to continue to maintain body functions . . . often at great economic and emotional cost to the patient's family?

Or, still more difficult, is it right or wrong to prolong the lives of the incurably sick through days and weeks of pain and humiliation for themselves and their families? They recently had a symposium in Washington sponsored by the Kennedy Institute, which has tried very hard to focus on this problem, and they presented to the participants an actual case of an infant, born with Downs Syndrome, that is, a Mongoloid child. This child had an intestinal obstruction which could easily have been cured by a routine operation. But his parents felt that raising the child would be unfair to their two other, normal children. They refused to authorize the operation. The child lay in an isolated crib for nearly two weeks before starving to death as a result of the obstruction.

Can we give a doctor and a patient's family the power to decide when all efforts to save a life should stop? Or is the danger of mistake or abuse too great? How do we decide when a patient should speak for himself, or who should speak for those, like the infant, who cannot?

This is only a sample of the questions raised during the Health Subcommittee's study. And if modern medical science poses ethical and moral questions which we are not now equipped to answer, the future promises to overwhelm us with questions that will make these seem mild.

We stand on the brink of major breakthroughs in genetic engineering — of being able to determine the genetic make-up of human beings. DNA, the basic genetic material, has been manufactured in the laboratory. Means have been found to perform "genetic surgery" by using a virus to penetrate human cells carrying with them new genetic material.

One day we may be able to select many of the characteristics of our children. And it appears likely that we will be able to create precise genetic duplicates of living human beings by a process known as "cloning," which involves the development of a human infant using the complete genetic material of a cell from a living person.

The ability to perform "genetic surgery" could be of tremendous benefit. It is estimated that one of 250 infants is born with a serious genetic defect. We might cure genetic diseases which now cause so much heartbreak — diabetes, sickle-cell anemia, hemophilia, mongolism, genetic mental retardation, Tay-Sachs disease which strikes one in 10 children from Eastern Jewish backgrounds, and others. We could control the threat of mutation which increases with the growing radioactive and chemical pollution of our environment.

But the ability to affect genetic endowment will confront us with great problems. Will we create a race of intellectual or physical supermen? How do we decide the qualities of future generations? What will be the role of government? Should we restrict the opportunity of individuals to select the genetic characteristics of their children. The problems abound.

We know that we are on the brink of revolutionary new developments in the field of genetics. We cannot tell whether they will come in five years or fifty. But if we do not begin to prepare now, we will not be ready.

And we may also be on the brink of tremendous breakthrough in our ability to control human behavior. Dr. Jose Delgado, a man who has pioneered research in the electrical stimulation of the brain through implantation of electrodes, testified before our Committee that electrical stimulation may be used to control epilepsy, cancel pain, and serve as a "pace-maker" for bodily functions. But Dr. Delgado also said that his research supports the notion that, "Emotion and behavior can be directed by electrical forces and that humans can be controlled like robots with push buttons."

We know of the work of B.F. Skinner and of his advocacy of the governmental use of behavioral conditioning to create a society without conflict which as he says, "Will be liked not by people as they are now, but by those who will live in it."

The Health Subcommittee has heard another new range of testimony that existing, cruder techniques for personality modification are now used in cases where the subject cannot be said to have given free and informed consent. For example, two psychosurgeons wrote to us:

(Thomas) agreed to the suggestion (of psychosurgery) while he was relaxed from (electrical brain stimulation). However, 12 hours later, when this effect had worn off, Thomas turned wild and unmanageable. The idea of anyone's making a destructive lesion in his brain enraged him . . . it took many weeks of patient explanation before he accepted the idea . . .

Clearly, the potential of abuse from more sophisticated methods of altering personality are great. As Herman Kahn wrote, "If a great upcoming problem in biochemical brain research is 'who is to control the mind-controllers?' a similar problem will arise in genetic research: who is to control the genetic engineer and according to what values?''

The strides that we have made in the health sciences, and the even greater advances that we may expect, are enormously encouraging. But, in my opinion, they are also enormously frightening.

Hearings before our Committee have provided us with another set of warnings, and that is in the area of experimentation without authorization.

There is, for example, the story of a group of Chicano women in San Antonio, Texas, involved in an experiment to determine whether the side-effects from birth control pills were physiological or psychological. The women weren't told about the experiment — they came to the clinic for help in contraception. Seventy-six of these women were given capsules full of glucose. Not surprisingly, a number had unwanted pregnancies. The tragic impact of this experiment on human lives is clear, and yet when controversy arose, the local medical society commended the experiment.

We've heard extremely disturbing evidence that school officials have been involved in treating children for hyperactivity with amphetamine drugs — without adequately informing the children or their families of possible side-effects and without any thorough examination of the cause or extent of the hyperactivity. I have the strong impression that hundreds of healthy, rambunctious children are presently receiving drug therapy in this country just because it makes them easier to handle.

And, of course, you are all familiar with the tragic case of the Relf children in Alabama who were induced to undergo sterilization by a federally funded family planning agency. Their mother did sign a consent form — but she signed it with an X because she couldn't read. It is pretty clear she did not understand what was going to be done to her children. And it's also pretty clear she thought she would lose her welfare benefits if she refused to consent.

What the Relf case really illustrates is the incredible power which those in authority have over those in our society who are not well-to-do, well educated, or well connected.

I think the task ahead is clear. Developments in the health sciences over the next 30 years will have profound consequences for our society, and pose legal, moral and ethical questions which we are not yet prepared to answer.

For almost seven years I have worked for the establishment of a National Commission on Health Sciences and Society. This Commission would be composed of experts from the health and behavioral sciences, law, philosophy, and religion. Its job would be a two-year study of the social and ethical implications of advances in modern medicine.

The National Protection of Human Subjects of Research Act, adopted by the Congress and signed into law earlier this year, provides for the establishment of a national commission on the protection of human subjects. This commission has been assigned the task of performing the study which I have suggested. I hope this study can lay the ground work for national public debate and for an informed public judgment.

It is past time for the American people and for those of us in public life to become concerned with these questions. As Donald Huisingh wrote:

> The time ahead is uncharted. No one has been there, so there are no experts. Each of us whose body and brain may be modified or whose descendants' characteristics may be predetermined has a vast personal stake in the outcome. We can help to insure that good will be done only by looking to it ourselves. We must be careful to retain the individuality of the individual and the personality of the person, or else the humanity of the human may be lost.

I believe strongly in programs of medical research. I think our medical profession, our great medical schools, our great medical research teams, have truly been miracle men in American life. I think I have voted for and supported practically every program they have wanted, but at the same time I am deeply concerned about the possibility that in all of this we might undermine the most precious single ingredient of humanity — respect and love for each other as human beings.

Senator Walter F. Mondale
U.S. Senate

I
ISSUES IN PUBLIC POLICY

I. ISSUES IN PUBLIC POLICY

INTRODUCTION

Regardless of their diverse professional or ideological orientations, medical experts uniformly agree that during the last quarter of a century this country has experienced a marked crisis — and possible failure — in the delivery of its health care services. This crisis has occurred despite the fact that scientifically the American health care system is one of the best, if not the best, in the world.

We have witnessed a gradual erosion of the old health care delivery system. The general practitioner and his solo practice on a fee-for-service basis has been nearing extinction in recent times. At the same time a new awareness has emerged concerning groups which are particularly deprived medically, such as the aged, the indigent, racial minorities, socially marginal groups like inmates of prisons and asylums, and those in crowded urban areas.

The crisis in American medicine has been aggravated by inertia on the part of the major professional specialties involved in health care delivery. There are those who remain blissfully oblivious of the need for drastic change, while others are inherently reluctant or resistant to changes because of vested interests.

A significant factor in the coming of the crisis have been the incredible scientific advances, resulting in the availability of more therapies for people previously untreatable, the availability of undreamed of preventive medical techniques, and the concurring need for specialization and specialized services. The new and advanced science however caused costs to escalate, in many cases making medical care prohibitive. At the same time other social factors, such as population increases and mobility, added further complexities to the crisis.

Advances in hospital and clinic services afforded only a temporary respite. In actuality hospitals found themselves to be both the suppliers and creators of new demands for health care. The growth of private and collective insurance coverage, as well as the assumption of some of the costs of health care by the government through Medicaid and other programs, similarly helped meet new needs while concurrently expanding the demand.

Another factor in the national "health crisis" has been the change in the role and status of the medical schools. In the past, schools primarily supplied medical manpower, but traditional schools have become part of new "medical center" complexes, calling for greater emphasis upon research and preventive medicine, and requiring the development of an interlocking and elaborate system of satellite facilities. All this growth requires expanded and increased massive financial planning and resources.

The changes in the various sectors of the health delivery system have had also a radical impact upon the traditional physician-patient relationship. Mobility and specialization have added new complexities to the interaction between physician and patient, posing fresh and urgent issues of public policy and medical ethics.

The articles selected include a discussion of these issues: the disappearance of the general practitioner, the financing of health care, the humanization of health services, medical injury insurance, and the physician's role in the promotion of the public interest. For the medical arts, the law and the policy sciences, these critical issues require multi-disciplinary study, discussion and efforts at resolution.

HEALTH CARE FINANCING
AND DELIVERY
IN THE DECADE AHEAD

Walter J. McNerney

One hundred and eighty-six years ago, Robert Burns pleaded that we might be given the power to see ourselves as others see us. If that plea proves anything, it is that 18th century Scotland was not blessed with the newspapers and television news broadcasts that we in the United States enjoy today. Through them, we have indeed been given the power to see ourselves through the eyes of others. All we have to do is read or listen. For example:

Rochester, New York, November, 1971 — Surveys in the area were reported to show that because of a lack of areawide planning, 30 per cent of all hospital and nursing home patients should have been cared for elsewhere.

Chicago, February, 1972 — Dr. Huntley, of the Department of HEW, said 60,000 lives could be saved annually if present knowledge about emergency care were put into effect. He added that only eight to ten communities have proper emergency services.

Toledo, Ohio, June, 1971 — The president of the local Academy of Medicine said doctors and hospitals alike are responsible for high hospital costs by keeping patients too long and by not using facilities and services in an economical way.

Washington, D.C., February, 1972 — The Kennedy health subcommittee has subpoenaed records of the JCAH and will subpoena records of the California Medical Association to evaluate the quality of hospital care.

Boston, March, 1972 — Wilbur Mills said the time is ripe for national health insurance, without confining ourselves to any one system.

Washington, D.C., December, 1971 — A reporter berated the American Medical Association for deploring the rise in malpractice suits rather than acting to reduce their causes, such as eliminating needless surgery.

San Jose, February, 1972 — Representative Roy's assistant, Dr. Biles, said there are too many specialists and not enough general practice physicians.

I call your special attention to the following two items:

Chicago, May, 1972 — The *American Medical News* reported that the President's manpower report said there will be enough MDs by 1980 to overcome shortages. In January, 1972 the *American Medical News* reported that Geoffrey Moore, U.S. Commissioner for Labor Statistics, said the total number of MDs trained in this decade will fall short of the need.

Chicago, May, 1972 — Discussing MD distribution, Chicago papers pointed out that the three states with the highest ratio of MDs to patients — states with the most attractive living conditions — receive half of all Medicaid funds and a third of all Medicare funds, even though only one-fifth of the persons eligible for both programs live there.

Washington, D.C., August, 1971 — A report submitted to the Secretary of HEW calls for a two-year moratorium on all licensing laws, more stringent standards for license renewal and representatives of consumers on licensing boards.

The next two are also interesting when seen side by side:

Chicago, May, 1972 — A *New England Journal of Medicine* article, and letters of response from readers, reflected the belief of MDs that their services should go to the highest bidder and that no one has an automatic right to be treated.

And finally . . . Washington, D.C., March, 1972 — A bill to establish a new National Institute of Health Care Delivery was introduced.

To these specific items we can add some general assertions that are made time and time again: 1. hospitals and physicians are not interested in productivity, 2. health is better in other countries than it is here, 3. prepayment plans and insurance companies have excessively high retentions and exorbitant profits, 4. prepayment and insurance fail to provide coverage for the poor, and 5. prepayment and insurance exert no influence over providers in the area of costs, but merely act as conduits of money from subscribers and policyholders to providers.

From those and many other comments and criticisms heard from every side, it is apparent that the health field is restlessly in transition. The future is not in sharp focus. The direction is not carefully laid. New issues — many of them directly contradictory — are raised almost every day. Bad news about the field heavily overshadows the good news.

It is important that all of us recognize those issues and criticisms. But it is even more important to recognize that they are not the basic issues facing voluntary hospitals and prepayment plans. Furthermore, they do not represent the key to the future. Solving all of the problems raised, and answering all of the criticisms made against us, will not guarantee the kind of future all of us want to see.

The things I have been talking about are symptoms. They are not basic illnesses. If we in the health field use up our time responding to each one, then our field will drift more than before, will become more expedient-oriented, will fragment itself further and eventually find itself at war with its own elements.

The assaults from outside are inevitable, and with them the contradictions. But there is no reason for us to accept all of them as gospel and to permit ourselves to be pushed to and fro with every change of direction of our critics.

Instead, if we truly accept responsibility for the financing and delivery of health care services; if we want to be positive; if we want to give some predictability to the 1970's and the years beyond; then we must meet certain basic conditions: First, it is essential that we develop and embrace a basic philosophy regarding the delivery and financing of health care. Second, it is essential that we understand the real issues underlying the events that take place. Without such an understanding, we lack reference points by which to set goals, judge priorities and achieve both better access and higher productivity in the field. Third, it is equally essential that we gain a broad understanding of the public policy framework within which we want to operate; and that we establish clear programs within that framework.

A PHILOSOPHY OF HEALTH CARE

First, the matter of an over-all philosophy. Without fanfare, such a philosophy has been jelling in the midst of the debate over national health insurance. The following points have come to light and have received widespread acceptance inside and outside of the health field: 1. no individual should be deprived of health care simply because of his inability to pay for it. 2. every person, regardless of his circumstances, should be able to receive high quality care, and receive it with dignity. 3. families should not suffer financial deprivation because of illness. 4. systems must be responsive to changes in medical science and management knowledge; not freeze past or present practices. 5. financing should be linked to delivery to achieve greater effectiveness and efficiency within the system. 6. programs of financing and delivery should be easy to administer. 7. programs must be so designed as to be acceptable to professionals and to the people as well. 8. physicians and other professionals must be motivated by the system to work within the system, and to accept and respect leadership other than their own in many circumstances. 9. there must be a reasonable pluralism — a diversity of methods of delivering, receiving and financing health care.

Before I go on, I would like to ask, silently, whether you as physicians can accept those points of view. Even though many of those ideas are general, and all are not unanimously accepted, they represent progress and a significant momentum that should not and cannot be ignored.

BASIC ISSUES UNDERLYING CURRENT DEBATE

The second essential, after establishing a basic philosophy, is to identify the underlying issues that are not always apparent in public dialogue. At the outset, we have to return to a fundamental economic truth: Health is a unique market. If there was any doubt about it, we proved it in 1966. Medicare and Medicaid made it clear that we cannot solve health problems by merely spending more money. Increased demand can and did produce marked inflation.

It is true that the health field, with its large labor component, is peculiarly vulnerable to the forces of inflation — as are all service industries. But complicating this is the fact that the basic supply and demand forces of the classic market are weak, or apply unevenly. Thus, quality, efficiency and effectiveness do not materialize in the ordinary course of events between purchasers and providers of service. They must be built in. How that can be done is a major management challenge, and the answer will not be found easily.

A second underlying force is that health is caught up in a raging revolution of rising expectations. Seeing that more can be done, people first expect more. Then they demand more. Consequently, new social policy may help solve the problem as it is today; but at the same time may well change and expand the problem itself.

It has been pointed out that Sweden — with a more moderate range of social problems than the United States — has a tax budget which takes more than 40 per cent of the GNP. And new items are emerging that will raise the percentage higher. For example, only a small proportion of the population goes on to higher education and housing is in short supply.

The point is made to indicate that even under higher taxes, social demands would continue to press on public resources — especially in the face of growing pressure for economic as well as political equality. That realization brings us firmly against the fact of limited resources and a need for hard priorities.

A third underlying consideration is the increasingly important — and usually ignored — question: What is the relation, if any, between health services and the health of the population?

That is a tough relationship to unravel. We do know that in countries where infectious diseases no longer predominate the causes of death (the U.S., for example, where they are only one of the top ten causes), it is difficult to demonstrate a strong relationship between longevity and the amount spent on health services. The amount spent can vary as much as a hundred per cent, yet longevity can vary only from five to ten per cent. The question appears to be whether the solution lies in expanding traditional health care (making more of the same available to everyone at lower cost), or in taking a broader ecological view of health.

It is worth noting that in 1951 under the British National Health Service in Scotland, there was a 300 per cent difference in infant mortality ratios between the highest and lowest social classes. In 1969, after the maturing of the national health service and the enactment of substantial social welfare programs, there was still a 266 per cent differential.

The answer seems to be that important factors in health lie outside the traditional boundaries of health care. If we are to avoid spending huge sums of money unproductively, we must attack factors such as income, housing, nutrition and education along with improving actual health care services. It is only in such an approach to total health that we shall find the answers to health problems.

Unfortunately, this whole issue is surrounded by some very popular myths. For example: 1. The greater the technology of care, the better the care provided. Actually some of the best health care is simply primary care received by a person who stays close to his family. 2. Increasing the number of MDs will automatically improve the unit cost and productivity of the field. There is no evidence so far to prove that contention. 3. In some glorious millenium, all health care must be coordinated by a controlling system. Actually, the patient must meet any system half-way or it cannot help him.

The fourth underlying issue is the relationship of private and public sectors. The two are working together now, but only awkwardly.

Unfortunately, too much of the current debate about NHI tends to set the government and private sectors against one another in regard to both delivery and financing of care. Our focus must be on results; on what works. The public has been the object of too many unfulfilled promises already — from both sides. Now we need to let everybody know how things can really be.

We have all heard attempts to discredit private prepayment and insurance in justifying the need for a totally federal financing system. However, our current health problems cannot be that easily simplified. They result from the interplay of strengths and weaknesses throughout the system, involving both sectors. Both have strengths. And both have weaknesses, which have become apparent.

The private sector, for example, has been slow to develop delivery systems such as HMOs designed to deliver comprehensive care to defined populations, with heavy accent on primary care. Areawide planning has been slow to develop. Carriers have not monitored use of services as energetically as they should have.

But the public sector also must accept its share of the responsibility for the problems as well as of the glories of considerable accomplishments. The excess number of costly beds in some sections of the country and over-preoccupation with inpatient care relate to the enthusiasm with which public programs met bed shortages by equating better health care with bricks and mortar. Failure to control costs and restructure the delivery of care can be seen in Medicare and Medicaid as clearly as they can in private financing programs.

If the private sector has been fragmented in response to a myriad of neighborhood and local pressures, the government has been equally fragmented in adding one piece of legislation on another in response to various interests — such as Comprehensive Health Planning, Regional Medical Programs, Hill-Burton, and so forth. If we are to criticize weak state regulation of health prepayment and insurance, let us recall that the McCarran Act is a federal law.

Little is gained from viewing the problems of health care from the single vantage point of either the public or private sector. Both are needed. Each has its strengths and weaknesses. It is time we got away from name-calling and down to the business of solving problems by strengthening both sectors and taking full advantage of each one's capabilities.

The health field is deeply imbedded in many subjective, as well as objective, issues; and is enmeshed in a strong tradition of professionalism. It demands as unusual degree of both sophistication and flexible administration. A monolithic posture would strain the political bonds of the system, if not its administrative structure as a whole. In another posture, however, the system could flourish.

It is government that can best set national goals; set important resource priorities; monitor and regulate over-all performance; and protect the rights of all citizens through constant pursuit of social justice. The private sector cannot come close to meeting the health needs of the country without strong government leadership and involvement. And, parenthetically, do you accept that concept? I think acceptance of it is mandatory if the private and public sectors are truly to work together effectively to get done the job that neither can do alone.

Equally important is the acceptance by government of the talents of the private sector, which can best provide managerial ability, diversity and a capacity to innovate and change. The private sector can meet accountabilities so that excessive conservatism does not result; and it can be a guard against the restricted, or restrictive, budgets of government.

Whatever the nature of the private-public relationship we should not expect it to be mutually uncritical. Ideally, it should involve honest adversary relations. Progress will come from a frank admission of differences rather than a pretense that there is none. There should be healthy conflicts of ideas, methods and perceived needs reflecting different points of view.

The Medicare contract between Blue Cross and the Social Security Administration is an outstanding example of the dynamics that can be developed to get a huge job well done. Differing viewpoints clearly stand out during current negotiations on a new Medicare contract:

On its part, the SSA wants extensive prior approval rights on contractor expenses and wants the right to change the contract during its term. In effect, in other words, the SSA wants to manage the contract functions rather than the contract.

On its own part, the Blue Cross Association wants the government to set goals; to establish expected results; and to define standards and guidelines by which the implementation of the contract can be judged. However, our view is that the contractor must manage the job, and have a decent term of contract in which to do its whole job. The final results — the signed contract — should prove to be an interesting example of just how well private and public sectors can mesh their efforts.

Having listed four underlying issues in the health debate — the uniqueness of health as a market; the revolution of rising public expectations; the relationship between health services and the health of the population; and the relationship between public and private sectors — I have three more to cover only briefly.

The fifth is the issue of consumerism. We see the effect of the consumer movement in newly shaped governing boards of Blue Cross Plans; in hospital boards; in the appointment of ombudsmen; and in the wider establishment of area planning boards. We also see its effect throughout the economy.

Since the early 1950's, we have seen life, liberty and the pursuit of happiness joined by demands for greater equality in other areas by those who have been less than equal. Blacks agitate for racial equality. Students demonstrate for more power in running their high schools and colleges. Teenagers are seeking sexual freedom; younger children are seeking more equality in the family. Women demand equality with men. Patients want decision powers over their doctors. Consumers want more power over what products are made and sold.

The movement is affecting every institution — profit and nonprofit; private and governmental. It cannot be ignored. And it is moving more and more into the health field as young citizens cite health care as a right and demand that medicine become a public service. It must be incorporated. Our response to the consumerism movement is one of the most important issues we face in the months ahead.

The sixth underlying issue is profit versus nonprofit in the health field. Which way should we go? The health field is filled with 19th century idealists who proclaim that profit has no place in it. At the same time, the more pragmatic see a shortage of capital for building facilities and increasing the numbers of services needed to provide more care to more people than ever before.

Finally, there is the issue of competition — of jockeying for position — among physicians, hospitals, government agencies and private carriers for definition of their roles and their responsibilities, as well as of their privileges, in the total field.

Some promote HMOs and some protest them. Some favor PSRO type plans and others vigorously oppose them. What it all boils down to is that each of us — as an individual or as an institution — is protecting his own turf, and demanding "no trespassing" by the others.

We must face these controversies, and we must negotiate our way out of them if we are to succeed in building and maintaining a strong private sector. If we spend our time shooting at one another in our little battles of selfishness, we leave the field wide open for occupation by others who might prove to be enemies of all of us.

NEED FOR PUBLIC POLICY FRAMEWORK

The shadow of national health insurance, which grows longer and touches more of us every day, brings into sharp focus the need for a public policy framework and careful consideration of programs to be carried out within that framework.

NHI itself can be divided into two major parts — the framework and the programs.

With regard to the framework, three patterns are emerging: 1. Build more incentive into the present system (such as the proposals of the AMA and the commercial insurance industry). 2. moderated pluralism, with varying approaches to varying needs (the Byrnes proposal). 3. public utility (exemplified with respect to financing by the Kennedy bill; with respect to delivery by the Ullman bill).

The first seems to be losing favor because it lacks the power to improve access or productivity and because it ducks some of the real issues. I can foresee a day when the AMA will move its position away from its present proposal toward a more far-reaching program. Regarding the other two, hard decisions must be made.

The public utility approach has its advantages and disadvantages. In its favor are the fact that we see it working well in the telephone, water and electric fields; that it can provide a high level of access, with minimum standards for participation; and that it can reduce wasteful competition by eliminating overlap.

Against it, however, is the fact that it can be a captive of its own constituents and detailed regulations. Those regulations cover such areas as exclusionary licensing, franchising, proper financing and the complications of regulating the resulting monopolies. Such a system in the health field could bog down.

In its favor, moderated pluralism can have a greater orientation toward goals, make full use of the private sector as well as the public sector, capitalize on what each one does best and provide options both to the public and to professionals.

It tends to focus on results more than on techniques, using the contract as a device for getting the job done. And it more neatly fits into complex situations and services, offering consumer choice among controlled alternatives rather than a bureaucracy or the wellspring of innovation and adaptation to changing environments. On the minus side, it can involve excessive overlap and fragmentation; and it is less geared to the guarantee of access than the public utility form.

Difficult decisions must be made, and they must be made with one cardinal principal in mind: The choices must be tailored to the field of health care. Concepts and ideas can neither be uncritically adopted nor automatically rejected because they have proved successful or unsuccessful in other areas. The health field is not a port authority; it is not a telecommunications industry; it is not a Tennessee Valley Authority.

While franchisement of health facilities may have merit, territorial exclusivity may or may not. More energetic regulation of financing mechanisms — for example, Blue Cross — may strengthen the market without destroying its resolve — with or without line-by-line regulation of providers.

During the months ahead, the issues must be debated among the best minds available — both inside and outside of the field of health care. Currently, major forces seem to favor a compromise between the two schools of public-utility or pluralistic approaches. What finally happens will depend to a significant extent on your collective — your unified, clearly designed and clearly stated — resolve.

In any event, HEW must be reorganized to give leadership in the areas of both delivery and finance. Areawide planning must be strengthened. And the market must be freed of constraints placed upon it now by restrictive licensure laws, group practice laws and the like.

Given a framework within which to operate under national health insurance, effectiveness will be achieved only through carefully conceived programs expertly carried out. Naturally, the programs would change according to the framework.

IMPORTANT PROGRAMS IN ANY FRAMEWORK

Keeping in mind that we do not have all of the answers — nor do we know all of the questions, for that matter — let me give you some views on the kinds of programs that must be carried out. I want to mention only six:

First is reimbursement. There are many different forms now in use, and active experiments are underway to devise newer and better ones. The consensus seems to be that providers must begin sharing financial risk to a larger extent, rather than simply being paid for whatever services they provide, regardless of cost.

We still see more experimentation and more evaluation of systems of reimbursement, with some states going one way on regulation, and other states or the federal government going another. NHI will undoubtedly lead to more unity of method, but how much unity is a question that remains to be answered. Clearly there is a danger in settling on one. The ultimate validation of any method is comparison with another method.

Second is benefits. Here we must put greater accent on primary care and unrestricted choice to avoid excessive use of expensive acute care facilities and services.

Third is the HMO — the group practice, prepaid approach to primary and all other health care. There is no stampede toward this form of practice, but its use is slowly growing. The Congress is moving toward a practical bill to facilitate its growth. The AHA and the BCA are working together to develop this kind of alternative benefit. Blue Cross now has 13 operational HMOs and will have 30 by the end of the year. By 1980 it is doubtful that more than 20 to 40 per cent of the market will involve HMO services, but it is an essential option to offer the consumer if productivity is to be achieved reasonably close to the point of care rather than at some distant point.

There are many factors to be considered in the formulation of HMO legislation, including these: 1. How comprehensive should benefits be to the subscriber? 2. Should rates be based on community or experience rating? 3. What kind of payments should be made to professionals within HMOs? 4. Should they be profit or nonprofit? 5. What quality of care should be the minimum, and how will it best be evaluated? 6. What breadth of services will be required within the HMO's subscriber area?

It appeares now that we will follow the path of reasonable flexibility rather than rigid orthodoxy, desirably if not inevitably.

Fourth is peer review, which is best illustrated, perhaps, by the growth of medical foundations. It certainly is in the interests of medical societies, specialty societies and the AMA to develop workable standards and boundaries for these programs. The conflicts that now exist regarding relative roles among foundations, hospitals and carriers must be settled amicably and effectively so that whatever is the best kind of PRO approach can be utilized for the benefit of the nation's people. Whereas areawide physician groups can contribute significantly to better quality and utilization, we don't need a duplication of claims administration, EDP capacity and other well-established mechanisms.

Fifth is areawide planning, which hardly needs any remarks from me. The ultimate approach to this program must make the best possible use of our present capital structure, and at the same time bring some kind of order out of the present chaos by addressing itself to manpower and the market as well as to bricks and mortar.

Sixth and last is the question regarding the efficacy of preventive medicine and health education.

Criticizing either of these concepts, no matter how gently, is tantamount to kicking the sacred cow off the sidewalk. But both need to be looked at carefully. Many people apparently are beginning to see that health is related deeply to lifestyle and the environment. Emphasis in some quarters has happily begun to shift from a focus on more physicians and more hospitals to a focus on a better general life, a realization of rights and an interest in protecting one's own health.

The track record for both preventive medicine and health education has been poor so far, although undertaken with enthusiasm in selected instances by hospitals, carriers, schools, medical associations and others. We shall see renewed interest in programs in this area sparked by recommendations now being compiled by the President's Committee on Health Education. There is no single answer, of course, as to whether any given technique can work. The only possibility is to continue to experiment and then evaluate.

CONCLUSION

By way of conclusion, I would emphasize that heat will continue on the subjects of health delivery and financing. It will come from consumers, from management, from labor and — certainly not least — from government. The issues are complex and are not amenable to easy solutions. In trying to develop our own solutions, we must learn to live in a brilliantly illuminated goldfish bowl.

Those of us in the health field must accept the fact that we need a viable NHI bill. Not that we should acquiesce to the proposals of others; but that we should realize that piecemeal approaches will not work. A middle ground between the extreme proposals now before the Congress holds promise as a rallying point for the sound exploitation of the massive skills in both the public and private sectors. Key decisions will revolve around how much public and how much private sector involvement and what framework and what tools will be available to us.

The AMA and its constituent societies have a key role to play in building the future. If I were to list do's and don't's, I would list them roughly as follows. Do orient programs more toward the public than has been the case in the past. Work from facts rather than wishes, to a greater extent. Stay close to your own area of competence — the practice of medicine, its quality and its essence. Your integrity here will produce the right pressures on the political and economic environment. Be consistent. Can you preach a free market, yet not provide wide options in methods of delivery? Can you say that only physicians can judge their peers, yet say it is too difficult to do? Can you fight proprietary exploitation by insurance or drug companies, yet sanction conflict of interest within proprietary hospitals? Do become committed to participation in hospital management rather than taking shots from the sidelines. Make sure that the AMA, state societies, AAMC, specialty societies, foundations, etc., don't become widely fragmented and antagonistic. Develop effective liaison to reinforce all of them and give them direction toward a successful, broad end result.

Don't be fearful. Support what you really believe in, even if it gives you control of a lesser empire. Avoid producing the mechanics of public relations without a sound product behind it. Don't over-react. Learn to spot posturing and harrassment in contrast to a really substantive issue.

The AMA is doing things well today, attempting to broaden its membership and supporting various federal programs. But your ultimate strength will come through productivity, not through vocalizing; through meeting demonstrable need, not generating your self-image.

The AMA must learn to be responsive and to negotiate well. Busy MDs can't address all complex issues effectively. The real key is the spirit that animates the organism and stimulates organized medicine's participation in a series of public policy decisions that will involve consumers as well as providers in a reasonably sophisticated merger of specific interests.

In my view, if we make reasonable responses to the basic issues we face, there will be ample opportunity for solo as well as group practice; for fee schedules as well as per capita payments; for various arrangements within HMOs, etc. The practicalities of financing and delivering health care point this way. Only an unthinking response would make it different.

INTERNATIONAL
TRENDS TOWARD
HUMANIZATION OF HEALTH SERVICES

John H. Bryant

Recent years have brought a number of areas of newness to the international health scene: new insights into the interrelationships between health and national development; the emergence of new disciplines, such as systems analysis and operations research, with potential applications to health; new initiatives in the education of health personnel; and new approaches to planning and implementing health services, to name but a few. Woven through all of these has been an increasing concern for the ways in which human values should be taken into account in the development of health related technology and health services.

CHANGING CONCEPTS OF THE ROLE OF HEALTH

The late 1960's and early 70's have seen the emergence of striking changes in concepts of national development and the role of health in that process. According to development concepts that dominated the 1960's, economic stagnation of the poor countries was due to a low ratio of capital to labor, and what was needed was a big push of new capital to get countries on the way to self-sustained growth. Thus, the key policy tool for economic progress of the poorer countries became investment in large physical projects such as roads, dams, and heavy industry.(1)

Unhappily, the promised development did not occur and the economically defined gap between the rich nations and the poor has been widening. The difference in per capita incomes between rich and poor nations is already more general population is increasing in importance, with strong implications for both political and social values. Perhaps the most important health issue that confronts every nation is how to reach all, or nearly all of the population with health care, recognizing that resources will always be limited relative to need.

It is frequently said that *health care is a human right*. What is meant by that? Does it mean that everyone has a right to a clean water supply? To a blood count? To renal dialysis? Clearly, what one might have a right to depends on one's needs relative to the needs of others and to resources available. Providing a clean water supply for a rural population is beyond the resources of most of the poorer nations. How then are we to interpret the injunction, health care is a human right? Or is this a pie-in-the-sky statement without practical applications?

This issue puts us in the middle of a socio-technical dilemma. A nation wishes to serve all its people. Resources are inadequate, and some will be served and some neglected. Now we add the precept: health care is a human right. Have we deepened the dilemma impossibly? I think not. I believe that precept is valid both as a social imperative and a practical principle, largely because what makes sense in terms of human right also makes sense in terms of the wise use of limited health care resources.

Thus, what one has a right to is to have one's needs taken into account as decisions are made on whom to serve and whom to leave unserved. Social injustice lies not in not receiving health care, but in not being taken into account as health care decisions are made.

This precept calls for conceptual extension of health care beyond its usual mode of operation. It requires, first, that the system accepts responsibility for all the people — not to serve all, but to take the needs of all into account. This, in turn, calls for the capability for searching through the population, identifying priority problems and, when possible, serving those most in need. Nor does this have to be an inordinately complex or costly burden for the health care system. Auxiliary midwives and trained community women could evaluate the nutritional status of children by determining their weight or height for age and see that the most seriously malnourished children are identified. Similarly, those women most at risk with respect to complications of pregnancy and childbirth could be identified through a series of simple criteria.

Here, then, is an area where our technical competence in planning and delivering health care can be brought together with our concern for human values in a manner that is sensible in the uses of limited resources.

PARTICIPATION OF COMMUNITIES IN HEALTH CARE

While communities have participated in health care planning and programs for a long time, the wide-spread emphasis on community participation is relatively recent. Impetus for this trend was probably the crumbling of colonialism and the emergence of independent nations. Neocolonialism, paternalism, and cultural imperialism were words that marked the change to a new set of ground rules for cross-national relationships. A similar set of forces went into play intra-nationally, between majority and minority groups in many countries, and also between the providers and receivers of services. It is clear, of course, that the recipients of assistance or services — nations or communities — have more going for them than the social principle of participatory democracy. They have political and, at times, physical power. Generally speaking, most nations are skilled in the use of such power, but many communities are not. A prominent testing ground for community participation has been the United States. While original expectations may not have been realized, the United States is contributing substantially to international understanding of provider-consumer interaction in the provision of health care.

From purely technical considerations of how to improve and maintain the health of populations, intimate involvement of communities is essential. Health care cannot be "delivered" to a passively awaiting population. Some of the most important health care decisions must be made by individuals and families — to feed their children differently, to be concerned about the source of their water, to limit the number of their children, or to space them differently. If health care fails to enlist at least the interest if not the support of the population, then there is little chance that those essential changes in behavior will occur.

The interface between the health care effort and families and communities needs to be identified as an essential link in the chain that connects modern biomedical technology and the needs of populations. It is often weak or missing. Thus, substantial investments in the education of professional personnel, biomedical research, and hospitals may have little impact on the health of the population. The forging of this connection stands as a prominent challenge in health care.

To go on, human value issues are involved in communities sharing in health care decisions. Aside from the problem of professionals and consumers finding ways of working together, is the importance to the community of participating in making decisions that will affect their own destiny, helping them gain a sense of what they are on the way to, and of controlling what they are becoming. Important examples are under way in many parts of the world, including the United States and, certainly, China.

Here we see a coming together of decisions that fulfill a human need for self determination, are essential for meeting some of the most pressing health problems, and have the chance of contributing to those motivational changes that are a part of increased economic productivity.

TRENDS IN THE EDUCATION OF HEALTH PERSONNEL

In universities, there is increased emphasis on bringing together educational programs for a variety of health personnel; thus, isolated medical schools are giving way to health sciences centers. Universities are experimenting with new structural relationships, both internally and externally, for relating their teaching and research programs to health care settings. The trend has been away from departments of preventive medicine to the somewhat broader concept of departments of community medicine and, in some instances, beyond to interdepartmental, even interinstitutional, programs in community health or health care systems.

Focusing on medical education for the moment, the resistance of clinical and often basic science medical faculties to curriculum innovations in health care seems to be a world-wide phenomenon. That resistance, coupled with the difficulties of developing effective teaching programs in the area, have led to what is often an embattled, or at least circumscribed, position for these programs within medical schools. Such educational programs have had limited impact on the attitudes and interests of the medical students. Few graduates choose to work in rural areas, and when they are there, by choice or compulsion, they often cannot provide the leadership that is needed. There are splendid exceptions, but thus far they are exceptions.

The record of medical schools in terms of commitment, pedagogical methodologies, and technical competence is not impressive, and we have reason to wonder if they will develop the programs and graduate the physicians who can fill the vacuum of leadership these countries so desperately need. This is another expression of disappointed expectations.

One's sense of pessimism deepens when costs are put alongside production figures. Given that one of the leading objectives of national expenditures on health, including medical education, is to provide health care for a nation's population, it is reasonable to look at the costs of getting health personnel into the areas where they are needed as well as into the areas where they are not needed. It is not unusual in some countries for only a few percent of a graduating class to opt to work for the government in a rural setting. Taking ten percent for the sake of discussion, and a cost of medical education at $25,000 (costs of medical education are notoriously difficult to identify. In a recent study, the cost per medical graduate ranged from $1,200 to $84,000 among a selection of institutions around the world; $25,000 per graduate is taken here as an intermediate figure.(5)), a conservative figure, the cost to the nation of getting a physician into a rural setting is $250,000. How long he would remain there is problematic. In some countries, the figure would approach $1,000,000.

Consider, too, the loss of physicians through migration. Looking from the United States' viewpoint, this country has a net gain of more than 5,000 foreign medical graduates per year — the output of about 50 medical schools, at a cost to these nations of roughly $125 million annually. That rate of immigration is projected to maintain a similar level over the next 20 years.

Most countries are willing to spend scarce resources on medical education on the assumption that those funds will yield an important return. One has a sense of precious resources being lost like water running into dry sand. There are no easy answers, but to be fiscally responsible, at the least, calls for rethinking both the orientation of medical education and the options open to its graduates.

Our concern must go beyond that of fiscal responsibility. We have spoken of the trend towards humanizing development and health services. That will amount to little if the health personnel who operate, particularly those who lead, the health care effort are not also caught up in this move toward humanization. To speak of the humanization of health care becomes a mockery if we talk about it and teach about it but in the end health care itself is unchanged. Just as the effectiveness of a health care system needs to be judged in part in terms of provision of services at the periphery, so it is appropriate to judge medical education in terms of its end product — physicians providing care and leadership in the places where their country needs them. Without such end-points for assessment, we risk overlooking the fact that large, expensive, even highly sophisticated and attractive enterprises may be only thinly connected with national need, which is human need.

DEVELOPMENTS IN THE PROVISION OF HEALTH SERVICES

A decade ago, there was a sense of optimism about the possibilities of gaining substantial improvements in health services within a reasonable period of time. Advances in health planning, the application of techniques of systems analysis and operations research, the strong emphasis on the development of health services by the World Health Organization, the growth of departments of preventive and community medicine in universities, and often increased allocations of national funds to the health sector, collectively lent strength to expectations of improvements in both the quality of care and the proportion of the population reached by that care. These expectation have largely not been realized. While there are splendid examples of improved care particularly in major hospitals, health care for urban slums and distant rural areas has improved modestly if at all. We can wonder if there is some fundamental flaw in the way health services are conceptualized, designed, and implemented.

A cluster of problems is involved.

There are shortages of health-related sources, absolute shortages plus maldistribution, and limited capabilities for using the resources that are there most effectively.

Health planning has either not matured enough technically or has not been given adequate opportunities in administrative hierarchies to contribute substantially to improvements in health services.

Despite increased production of physicians and nurses from the universities, the number that serve in rural areas and their competence for working there is limited.

Health services are often designed to reach to the periphery of a country with emphasis on the use of paramedical and auxiliary personnel, but the resources that trickle down to the periphery are exceedingly thin.

The trend to use medical assistants deserves special emphasis because they represent the possibility of sparing physicians from the burden of primary care so that they might assume more of the leadership role that is seriously needed. This works well in parts of Africa, Asia, Papua New Guinea, China, and, increasingly, the United States, to name a few. But at least two obstacles remain. One is the widespread reluctance of the medical profession to allow the training of such personnel. The second obstacle is the poor quality of supervision and ongoing training. Ideally, professional personnel should lead, or at least provide guidance for the health team and community participants in planning, implementing and evaluating programs, coaching and supervising them on an ongoing basis. Unhappily, the ideal seldom obtains. Again, the vacuum of leadership.

One so often hears that the problems of health care in the poorer nations can be met by using large numbers of paramedical personnel. That simplistic answer ignores the complexity of health problems and of the health care programs required to meet these problems, as well as the plainly human limitations of such personnel. Paramedical personnel can do many important things very well, but effectiveness does not follow simply from their presence. Their skills must be addressed to selected problems in appropriate ways or little will come of it. Again, leadership and supervision are essential — not necessarily on the spot and not necessarily by a physician.

To go on, governmental health services have tended to isolate themselves from others involved in health care, such as the private sector, industry, church-related programs, and so forth; conversely, others have tended to isolate themselves from one another and from government. Health services, whatever the source of their support, need to be considered as a whole and efforts made to coordinate the use of these resources. Such coordination can be technically difficult and politically sensitive; nonetheless, there are good examples of it, and the trend is there for others to follow.

Governmental health systems also tend to ignore the so-called informal health care system — pharmacists, traditional healers, injectionists, and so forth — which often flourishes because the population finds it accessible and satisfying, even though the cost may be many times that of governmental medical care. When governmental resources are scarce, it is sensible to take advantage of the useful aspects of the informal sector and to attempt to influence public spending on health in constructive directions.

While the record to date for the successful development of basic health services has been sparse, it is essential that there be a continued and vigorous effort to improve their development. Basic health services are the means for reaching most of the people and for providing a framework within which, or at least associated with which, special programs, such as those for malaria, family planning, tuberculosis and nutrition, can function.

In searching for the ingredients of improved basic health services, we may find some new, as yet undiscovered, concept from which success will follow. While searches for newness should not be discouraged, there are already sound ideas at hand that have not yet been well implemented. A few can be listed:

Planning that is central and also reaches to regional and local levels with freedom for initiative at the periphery.

An information and management system, rigorously simple so as to be economical and useful at central and peripheral levels.

Integrated, rather than fragmented programs, with all, or most, health care activities in an area coordinated by a single authority.

Use of paramedical and auxiliary personnel throughout the health care system, particularly in the periphery, for a variety of functions under professional supervision and with continuous training.

Attempt to reach all people in a geographical area, at the least to assess their condition with respect to priority problems and see that those most seriously afflicted or most at risk receive care — treatment, prevention or education — when feasible.

Participation of communities in planning, implementing, and evaluating health care programs.

What is new in this formulation?

Nothing dramatically new and not much drama in trying to make it work, but intensive attention is needed to details that heretofore have been glossed over, particularly to training for leadership, techniques of planning including evaluation and management, and supervision. Special attention has to be given to the interface between communities and health care programs, for it is largely there that the fundamental encounter of health care occurs.

REFLECTIONS ON TRENDS

These trends in international health can be summarized as follows:

There has been a disappointment in expectations in several areas. Perhaps our expectations have been unrealistic. Still our earlier optimism does not seem to be giving way to pessimism, but realism.

There is increasing conviction of the importance of developing health services that reach to the level of communities, families, and individuals.

There is a greater realism about the usefulness of technological methods, such as systems analysis, operations research, computer techniques and mathematical formulations for the provision of health care.

There is a greater humility in the face of the complexity of health and factors that influence it and a lessened inclination to reach for quick and simple answers.

While sophisticated planning methods are important, there is an increasing willingness to use more intuitive and even political approaches to planning and decision-making.

Human value considerations are emerging in many sectors and are held in balance with technological values.

There appears to be a greater willingness to respect the concerns and priorities of individuals, nations and communities and persons in defining problems, formulating solutions, allocating resources.

There is a growing appreciation that some of the most important gains are to be made at the level of the individual — the individual as a member of a family and a community and as a motivated participant in events that connect with national development; the individual who has intrinsic value simply as an individual human being.

Finally, as an overall trend that emerges from these individual trends, we appear to be moving into a period of humanization of health services and of health-related technology.

NOTES

(1) Malenbaum W: Health and economic expansion in poor lands. *Int J Health Services* May 1973.

(2) Ward B. Runnalls JD, D'Anjou L (eds): *The Widening Gap.* New York. Columbia University Press, 1971, pp 23-24.

(3) Ruderman PA: *The Relationship Between Health and Development as seen by a Health Economist.* First Regional Conference on National Health Planning, Manila, November 1972. World Health Organization, WPR/NHP/1.

(4) Tejada D: *Health Planning Methodologies: Concepts and Problems.* First Regional Conference on National Health Planning, Manila. November 1972. World Health Organization, WPR/NHP/8.

(5) Bryant J: *Health and the Developing World.* Ithaca, Cornell University Press. 1969, p 267.

(6) *The Supply of Health Manpower 1970 Profiles and Projections to 1990 (Interim Report).* Report No. 73-44 BHME/DMI/MRR. US Dept of Health, Education and Welfare, Public Health Service, National Institutes of Health, Bureau of Health Manpower Education, Division of Manpower Intelligence, October, 1972, pp 93-95.

MEDICAL INJURY INSURANCE –
A POSSIBLE REMEDY FOR
THE MALPRACTICE PROBLEM

William H.L. Dornette

The malpractice problem has reached nearly epidemic proportions in this country. Allegations of negligence are being leveled against both physicians and hospitals with apparently ever-increasing frequency. Costs of defending against claims – whether spurious or real – and payment of judgments has been forcing upward rapidly the cost of liability insurance (Figure 1) and making it harder and harder to obtain in some areas of the country.(1) The malpractice problem stems from increased exposure to liability. The causes of this exposure are complex and interrelated(1-4)

1. Modern medical practice is highly sophisticated. Patients who are older, or younger, and of poorer physical status than ever before are being treated, usually successfully, with therapeutic modalities that offer both greater potential benefit and significantly more risk than heretofore. As a result, iatrogenic complications, not related in any way to "malpractice," are much more likely.

2. With increasing medical knowledge has come increasing specialization, in the practice of both physicians and hospitals, and a consequent loss of the ability of health care personnel to maintain close rapport with their patients.

3. The attitude of the American public has been changing. Interpersonal relationships in general have deteriorated, as is often reflected in the individual patient's overly critical attitude toward the health care provider. Members of the public also expect that the delivery of all goods and services will be accompanied by a form of warranty; in the health care field, patients expect a cure.

4. The American public is becoming knowledgeable in matters pertaining to medicine. This knowledge reinforces the belief that anything short of a cure has

resulted from negligence.

5. Finally, not all physicians recognize fully their legal duties to their patients under the contract for medical care. This contract, and the ensuing duties, are recognized in courts of law, however.

It is not easy to resolve a problem of such magnitude that has been developing for so many years. Yet a solution must be found, and, to be satisfactory, must above all else be beneficial to the patient. Benefitting our patients is, after all, the primary goal of all of us in the field of health care.

The search for a solution begins with the premise that the patient who is injured through negligence deserves to be made whole; that is, he should be compensated for the medical expense and loss of earnings caused by the injury. The present system of tort (fault) liability recognizes this premise: fault = liability = recovery. If the error is glaring, the negligence is patent and generally settlement with the patient is effected. But negligence rarely is patent. If it is not admitted, negligence can only be established under our jurisprudential system by trial of the issues. And the determination of fault by this method is both costly and time consuming. Cases may remain on the docket for as long as five years in some jurisdictions.

Analysis, partially projected,(1) of the costs of the professional liability insurance dollar for one year (1968) reveals that over 50¢ of it was consumed by the process of fault determination and that injured patients received in compensation only about 27¢ (Figure 2).

The costs and protracted nature of the fault determination process are perhaps somewhat inherent to it. But to point to this process – the jury system – as the culprit seems to me to be looking in the wrong direction. Trial by jury under the adversary system, although not perfect, is far better for the determination of fault than any other legal system developed prior to it. The real question is not whether one should abolish the trial but rather whether one should abolish the *need* for the trial, by eliminating the determination of fault. If one is to abolish fault determination, it is necessary to substitute some form of compensation. This takes the form cf a no-fault type of insurance; in the case of medical injuries, medical injury insurance.

The concept of "no fault" is not new to the field of negligence law. Workmen's Compensation statutes embody a form of such insurance. The injured employee is compensated for medical expenses and loss of wages for all employment-related injuries, regardless of whether his employer, a fellow employee, or he himself was negligent, or whether the injury occurred in the absence of any negligence. Workmen's Compensation protection has been available for many years, and is in effect in all U.S. jurisdictions.

During the past several years, a very similar concept has been adopted in several states to afford protection to motorists and pedestrians injured in automobile accidents. No-fault automobile insurance laws are on the books in Delaware, Florida, Massachusetts, Oregon, and South Dakota.(5) The legislatures of the majority of the remaining states are at present at least considering the adoption of such legislation.

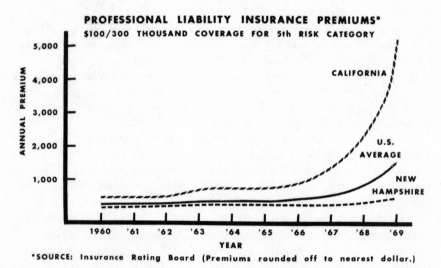

PROFESSIONAL LIABILITY INSURANCE PREMIUMS*
$100/300 THOUSAND COVERAGE FOR 5th RISK CATEGORY

*SOURCE: Insurance Rating Board (Premiums rounded off to nearest dollar.)

Figure 1. Plotting the cost of professional liability insurance premiums for the 5th risk category reveals states with the highest and lowest average premiums over a ten-year period, as well as the U.S. average. Taken from *Legal Aspects of Anesthesia*, with permission of F.A. Davis Company, Philadelphia.

Although the specific provisions of these bills or statutes differ widely among the several states, certain provisions are common to all. Medical expenses, and at least partial compensation for lost earnings or the equivalent, of injured parties are paid by the carrier insuring the automobile in which they were riding. Under some of these plans, the power to sue is abolished for minor or relatively minor injuries. Massachusetts was the first state to adopt such a law. It has been upheld by the Supreme Judicial Court of that state.(6) During the first six months of operation of this law the "number of incurred claims" and the "average paid claim cost" each fell more than 50 per cent below the level of the comparable period one year earlier.(7)

Striking similarities exist between conventional automobile insurance and medical malpractice insurance. The injuries for which coverage is obtained may be severe and incapacitating. The litigation required to assess blame and effect compensation is long and costly and crowds court calendars. The insurance is carried by a party other than the one injured and is escalating in cost for a variety of reasons that are similar in both types of insurance. There are, likewise, similarities between automobile no-fault and medical injury insurance. But there are also several significant differences. The most important of these dissimilarities lies in the mode of defining the compensable event.

At the moment an automobile strikes an immovable object, another automobile or a pedestrian, the compensable event has occurred. The ensuing bodily injury and property damage inevitably can be attributed to the impact. In health care, however, the "impact" rarely is definable with such clarity. For example, a progression of the patient's disease, a complication of it, or the presence of a condition that cannot be diagnosed initially could be mistaken for an iatrogenic complication.

Since the purpose of medical injury insurance would be to cover only iatrogenic complications (i.e.,those caused by treatment and without regard to the existence of fault), it is obvious that a system must be developed to verify with a reasonable degree of certainty the fact that the complication was caused by the treatment. This system should function before the fact, if at all possible. That is, the procedure for separating iatrogenic complications from the other causes, such as those just mentioned, should be established when the insurance is put into effect. It should function in the absence of a review board in the large majority of instances and thus abrogate the need for case by case evaluation.

To be effective, the plan must include the following: 1. Each patient must purchase, or have purchased for him, a policy of medical injury insurance; 2. The patient's power to sue a physician or hospital for alleged medical negligence must be abolished, at least in most instances; 3. Recovery for "pain and suffering" must be abolished in most instances; 4. Recovery for "wrongful death" should be limited in amount; 5. A method of determining the "compensable event" short of review by a commission or board must be established; 6. An agency must be created to review those instances in which the compensable event cannot be determined by the method mentioned above; 7. Effective professional standards review must become an accomplished fact, at the county level or on a state-wide basis; 8. An iatrogenic complications registry should be established, together with methods for dissemination of information concerning causes of injuries; and 9. Medical injury prevention programs must be established at local, state, and even national levels, with attendance at such programs compulsory.

A program such as this abolishes certain rights held by individuals under the common law, i.e. the right to sue for negligently caused injuries. The program also requires that each individual carry compulsory medical injury insurance. To abolish these rights or freedoms, a statute is required, just as in the case of no-fault automobile insurance.

Such a statute lies within the province of the states rather than the federal government. The desirability of state action goes beyond the traditional "state's rights" argument. State action is easier to achieve than legislation by the Congress, and the plan itself lends itself more to state than to national application. The plan envisions that the insurance will be underwritten by private carriers, possibly within the structure of Blue Cross-Blue Shield, and it would be easier for these carriers to shoulder this burden on a state by state basis. Loss experiences, as reflected in professional liability insurance premiums(1) (Figure 1), vary widely among the several states, and it is likely that medical injury insurance costs would also vary across the country, at least initially. Finally, the programs would not — and should not — be adopted simultaneously in all states. Deficiencies in the plans enacted initially, thus, could be reviewed by the legislative committees of other states still drafting their own legislation.

DISTRIBUTION OF THE MALPRACTICE INSURANCE PREMIUM DOLLAR

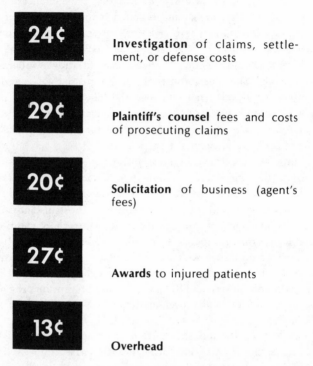

Investigation of claims, settle- ment, or defense costs

Plaintiff's counsel fees and costs of prosecuting claims

Solicitation of business (agent's fees)

Awards to injured patients

Overhead

Figure 2. Data, partially projected, show distribution of the malpractice insurance premium dollar in 1968. Adverse loss ratio reported by carriers accounts for total being greater than a dollar.

Application of the insurance must be universal. Each patient must be protected. Premiums of 25¢ to $1.00 per day of hospitalization, and 10¢ per office visit or house call, could be charged. The cost of insurance for inhospital treatment might vary with the severity of the illness or the nature of any contemplated procedure.

The realistic nature of these proposed premiums becomes obvious if one considers what might have resulted had a plan such as the one proposed been in effect in the entire U.S. in 1968. Of the projected $75 million spent on professional liability insurance during that year, injured patients received 28 per cent, or $21 million. Hospital utilization data indicate that there were 450,965,802 days of patient care in American hospitals during that year.(8) Deducting 20 per cent for overhead, and depending on the premium charged, $90 million (at 25¢/day) and $360 million (at $1.00/day) would have been available to satisfy these claims, plus others resulting from iatrogenic complications that developed in the absence of any "fault."

While any amounts paid out under such a medical insurance plan would be deductible from any awards won at a trial for alleged malpractice, it seems clear that for the proposed plan to be effective, the patient's right to sue the physician or hospital must, at the least, be markedly curtailed. In order to deprive a patient of such rights, the statute must afford the patient or next of kin "due process" that would take the form of an adequate substitute, i.e., adequate compensation under the plan. If the plan assures that all iatrogenic complications (and only these) will be compensated, sets a reasonable level of compensation, and provides an impartial board of review if the compensable event is in doubt, then the due process requirement will have been met.

The reasonable level of compensation would cover all medical expenses, plus a certain percentage of the loss of wages, earning capacity, or equivalent (for homemakers, for example). A level of compensation similar to a state Workmen's Compensation or the Federal General Employees Compensation Act(9) could be adopted. The compensation for loss of wages or earning capacity could be set at 60-70 per cent of the actual wages or earning capacity, with both a floor and ceiling on minimum and maximum amounts. Patients would be given the option of taking out additional insurance to cover loss of earning capacity in addition to the statutory minimum (as in the case of airline trip insurance). In those instances in which permanent disability ensues, formulae similar to those adopted by the Social Security Administration could be employed.(10)

In the usual civil case involving personal injuries, the plaintiff seeks both special damages — for medical expenses and loss of income — and general damages — for pain and suffering. Since the plaintiff must pay the costs of prosecuting his claim (legal services, witness fees, depositions, and the like) from his award, and since he cannot ask for these costs as part of his "damages," this sum must come from any general damages.

Medical injury insurance covers special damages, in toto or almost so; but the right to sue for pain and suffering under a medical injury insurance plan would be drastically curtailed. It might be limited to those injuries that produced permanent disability or resulted in medical expenses in excess of a given amount, for example, $20,000. Plaintiffs' lawyers argue strongly that this right should be retained in any case of serious injuries.

From a practical standpoint, however, depriving the injured patient of the right to sue for pain and suffering in reality eliminates money the patient would not retain anyway under the traditional fault system. The patient, who will be compensated for all his medical costs, and in large measure for his loss of income (or equivalent) would gain relatively little by filing a lawsuit since a significant part of any award would be absorbed by the costs of prosecuting the suit.

Some states now have statutes that limit recovery in any action for wrongful — that is, negligently caused — death. Such a limitation must be adopted if indemnification for medical injuries is to be carried out on a financially sound basis.

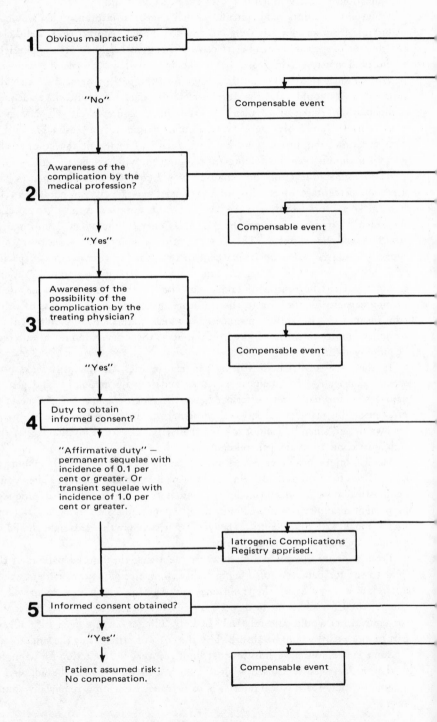

Figure 3. Proposed method for determining whether a given complication of medical treatment is a compensable event involves asking questions in the sequence diagrammed.

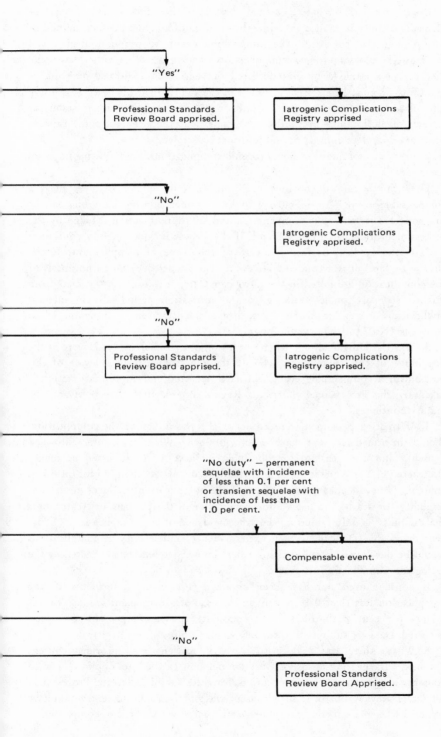

Undoubtably the greatest potential obstacle to the establishment of a system of medical injury insurance would be the creation of a before-the-fact method of determining what constitutes the compensable event. My proposal, diagrammed in Figure 3, involves posing certain questions. The answers then either determine that a compensable event has occurred or suggest an additional question or questions. It must be stressed, as noted in the figure, that this process is closely interrelated with the doctrine of informed consent, professional standards review, medical injury prevention programs, and the need for some type of medical injury data correlating and information service.

In every case of questionable iatrogenic complications, the following inquiries are made.

1. Is this a case of obvious negligence? If the answer is "yes," it is a compensable event. (An example would be an operation on the wrong part of the body.) The patient is compensated and appropriate action is taken by the Professional Standards Review Board. If the answer is "no," inquiry continues.

2. Is the medical profession aware of that type of complication? If the answer is "no," it is a compensable event. The occurrence and pathogenesis of the complication are noted in the Iatrogenic Complications Registry. Data from this registry are made available to the profession periodically in medical publications or other media and by medical accident prevention programs. If the answer is "yes," the inquiry continues.

3. Was the individual practitioner or hospital personnel involved aware of the possibility of this type of sequela? If these personnel were unaware of this possibility, a compensable event will have occurred and appropriate action is taken by the Professional Standards Review Board. If they were aware, the inquiry continues.

4. If treating personnel were aware of the possibility of the complication, should informed consent have been obtained? What constitutes informed consent, and the reasons for obtaining it, have been discussed at length elsewhere.(11-14) While it might be difficult to quantitate the need for informed consent, I suggest that it be obtained if the complication produces permanent disability (or death) and has a known incidence of 0.1 per cent or greater, or if the disability is only temporary but the incidence of the complication is 1 per cent or greater. Data on incidence, permanence, and severity of complications would be developed from existing medical knowledge and data collected by the Iatrogenic Complications Registry.

If consent need not have been obtained (for example, incidence of the complication less than 0.1 per cent in the case of a permanent sequela, or less than 1 per cent if the disability is transient), then a compensable event has occurred. Data are submitted to the Iatrogenic Complications Registry.

5. Where there was a duty to warn the patient, was informed consent obtained? If the physicians or hospital personnel failed to obtain informed consent, a compensable event occurred. Data are submitted to the Professional Standards Review Board. If such consent was obtained, the patient would have assumed the risk of the procedure and there would be no compensation

(informed consent has been likened to obtaining consent after the patient has been apprised of the risk/benefit ratio(11) i.e., what are the risks entailed by the proposed treatment as compared to the expected benefits: do the latter outweigh the former?).

This procedure for determining the compensable event is intended to eliminate the need for a board or agency to review questions of compensability on a case-by-case basis. It is probable, nevertheless, that a few situations would arise in which such individual determination will be necessary. Individual problems could be settled by arbitration, conducted under the rules of the American Arbitration Association, with the costs and any award being met by the insurance program. Or, an impartial board could be established. The composition of such a board might include physicians with degrees in law, for example fellows in the American College of Legal Medicine. The findings of any such individual case evaluations would be incorporated within the overall program, to establish before-the-fact determinations of compensable events in future, similar cases.

Advocates of no-fault automobile insurance recognize the importance of highway engineering, driver safety programs, and steps to get the alcoholic driver and chronic traffic offender off the road. If a medical injury insurance program is to become a continuing, effective reality, professional standards review likewise must become a continuing, effective reality. There are those who feel that it is not a reality at present(16-18) and that only by suing members of the medical profession can negligent practices be brought to a halt.(19-20)

It is apparent that while there are lawyers who are "ambulance chasers" and who bring unfounded suits against physicians and hospitals, there are also physicians who are chronically negligent. Some may simply fail to keep up with medical progress, incurring "educational obsolescence" in the words of one writer(16). Medical injury insurance is neither intended, nor would it be fiscally able, to compensate for repeated mistakes and recurring dangerous practices.

Professional Standards Review, accompanied by an effective mechanism to prevent repetition of such mistakes and dangerous practices, therefore, *must become an accomplished fact.* Such a review agency is necessary to receive and act upon data received in the processing of a medical injury claim (Figure 3) to determine the existence of a compensable event. It should be pointed out, however, that hospital governing boards even today are compelled by the *Darling*(21) decision to take a long, hard look at practices within their own institutions.

Another essential component of this proposal is the presentation of injury prevention programs on national, regional, and local levels. These programs would be similar in purpose and format to the one held in Chicago in May 1971 under the auspices of the American Hospital Association and the AMA. Such programs would serve to alert all members of health care teams, throughout the country, to the need for medical injury prevention and the methods by which it could be accomplished. Data from the Iatrogenic Complications Registry could be one source of information to effectuate such programs.

Some type of national clearing house for compiling and disseminating data on iatrogenic complications should be established. Input would be from all institutions and agencies obtaining knowledge of individual complications (cf. Figure 3). These data, in turn, would be correlated and disseminated to physicians and hospitals via medical and hospital journals and other media or communications.

The concept of insuring against future injury is fundamental to our present way of life. Compulsory insurance via statute does exist in America today, for example in the Social Security system and — in most states — automobile liability insurance. Requiring each patient to insure himself against medical injuries from whatever cause, therefore, does not appear to be a deprivation of one's fundamental rights. Such a program, coupled with all of its necessary ramifications, would markedly enhance patient care. It would also help assure that such care, together with the insurance program, would remain principally a responsibility of private enterprise.

All concerned with health care including health and liability insurance carriers have a stake in preserving, and strengthening, the American system of medical care. The system can no longer afford the costly liability problems that threaten to engulf it. A new approach is required. "No-fault" medical injury insurance deserves implementation now.

NOTES

(1) Dornette WHL: Professional liability insurance. *Anesthesiology* 33:535, 1970.

(2) *Medical Malpractice: The Patient v. the Physician.* U.S. Senate Subcommittee on Executive Reorganization, 91st Congress, 1st Session, Committee Print. Washington Gov't. Printing Office, 1969.

(3) Morris RC, Moritz AR: *Doctor and Patient and the Law.* St. Louis, C. V. Mosby 1971, p. 325-353.

(4) Goldsmith LS: Medical malpractice trends. Chap. 22 in Wecht, CH, ed., *Legal Medicine Annual* New York, Appleton-Century-Crofts, 1971, p. 447-464.

(5) 42 A.L.R. 3d 194 (1972).

(6) *Pinnick v. Cleary,* 271 N.E. 2d 592 (Sup. Ct. Mass. 1971).

(7) Sabbagh MJ: Memorandum to Commissioner of Insurance, Commonwealth of Massachusetts, July 27, 1971.

(8) *Hospitals, J of Amer Hosp Assn* 43: 480, 1969.

(9) 5 U.S.C. § 751 (1958).

(10) Medical Advisory Committee to the Social Security Administration: Disability Evaluation under Social Security. Washington, Government Printing Office, 1969.

(11) Dornette WHL, ed.: *Legal Aspects of Anesthesia.* Philadelphia, I. A. Davis, 1972 p 33, 183, 467.

(12) Holder AR: Informed consent I. Its evolution. *JAMA* 214 1181-1182, 1970.

(13) Holder AR: Informed consent II. The obligation. *JAMA* 214 1383-1384, 1970.

(14) Holder AR: Informed consent III. Limitations *JAMA* 214 1611-1612, 1970.

(15) Morris RC: Essay [on Malpractice] reference 2, p. 476.

(16) Harney D: Response to the Senate Subcommittee investigating Medical Malpractice, reference 2, p. 25.

(17) Harney D: The price of incompetency. *Trial* 6:17, 1970.

(18) Quirin IM: Physician licensing and educational obsolescence; a medical-legal dilemma. *Albany L Rev* 36-503, 1972.

(19) Kelner J: The conspiracy of silence. *Trial* 6:17, 1970.

(20) Durant IS: A four step program. *Trial* 6:26, 1970.

(21) *Darling v. Charleston Community Memorial Hosp.* 50 Ill. App. 2d 253 200 N.E. 2nd 149 (App. Ct., 4th Dist., 1964): att'd 33 Ill. 2nd 326, 211 N.L. 2nd 253 (Sup. Ct. 1965).

II
PUBLIC
HEALTH
SERVICES
AND
INSTITUTIONS

II. PUBLIC HEALTH SERVICES AND INSTITUTIONS

INTRODUCTION

In an effort to secure improved medical services for those most adversely affected by the inadequacies of the health care delivery system, the federal government has intervened through Medicare and Medicaid legislation, as well as through the Public Health Service Acts which made funds available for direct medical care. The goal was to provide better health care for children, the indigent, the elderly, and the disabled, but these early legislative efforts have proven insufficient and inadequate.

This section is intended to highten the public awareness of the health plight of deprived groups and their demands for increased health services. Seeking to understand the failure of existing delivery of health care, one soon becomes aware of the politics and power struggles among the various sectors and institutions of the health system. Many of the proposals for the improvement of available medical services stress the need for the reorganization of the health care system.

In such restructuring what roles are to be played by the public vis-á-vis the private sectors of the medical arts? Where is the motivation for change to originate, and to what extent can public health and public institutions not only meet growing needs but also affect the structure and functioning of the private health sector?

Related to these broader issues are specific questions regarding available manpower and resources. One of the most heated debates concerns medical manpower. Is there a physician shortage? Many have suggested that instead of increasing the number of physicians, the reorganization of health care should include expanding the functions of physicians' assistants, paramedicals and nurse practitioners.

Another suggestion for improving the delivery of health care services calls for greater regulation and control of physicians through utilization review and evaluation by peers. These proposals have been discussed and debated in the past, but little professional self-regulation has resulted. The government has now introduced or taken over some of these regulatory mechanisms, but it remains to be seen how effective governmental intervention is and whether it can accomplish what physicians would not do by themselves.

The quality of medical care in the future will greatly depend on the links and cooperation between the public and private health sectors. Recently new efforts have been made to increase cooperation among medical schools, practicing physicians and hospitals in the medical profession. For example, the practicing physician has been reintroduced to the medical school faculty, especially in the clinical ward, and the students have been "farmed out" to community hospitals manned primarily by practicing physicians.

The articles in this section are intended to explore the experiences and developments within the public health services and institutions. Yet our broader goal is to permit the reader to gain insights into the changing balance between private and public health now taking place in this country.

EMPIRES AT WORK:
THE CASE OF THE COMMUNITY
MENTAL HEALTH CENTERS

Barbara Ehrenreich
John Ehrenreich

The mental health marketplace looks, at first glance, strikingly similar to the medical care marketplace. Much of the manpower is still scattered in private offices, though increasingly it is becoming concentrated in the psychiatry departments of medical schools and in major voluntary hospitals. For most people, basic ambulatory and preventive services are financially, if not geographically, inaccessible, although free hospitalization awaits at the terminal stages of illness. The analogy to the medical marketplace is particularly clear in New York City. The city mental health agency, the Community Mental Health Board (C.M.H.B.), in a caricature of the City Hospital Department's affiliation program, confines its activities to writing contracts with private providers, and provides no services itself. The few mental health services that are operated directly by the city, like those in the city hospitals, serve chiefly the poor and the acute emergencies. In fact, both city hospitals and city-run mental hospitals hark back to a common ancestor — the town lunatic asylum.

This, then, is the mental health care scene today in New York City and many other urban centers: For the poor, there are no mental health services — only various degrees of detention and isolation. For the middle-class patient, facilities exist, but it is questionable whether any of them will be interested in the particular set of problems the patient presents at the time he presents them. From a public policy point of view, the system is irrational, expensive, and grossly wasteful of manpower.

As in the physical health field, there is growing government concern about the disorganization of mental health services in the face of mounting demand.

And, as in physical health, public efforts to spread mental health services around rely almost wholly on the imagination and good will of the private strongholds of professional manpower. At the federal level, wellspring of much corporate medicine, vast sums were earmarked in the mid-1960s for local experiments in mental health — community mental health centers.

President Kennedy's Community Mental Health Center Act of 1963 was heralded as a bold new approach to mental illness. Actually, it represented little more than the application of some common-sense principles of public health to the traditionally murky area of mental health. The idea was that mental illness, like other illnesses, could be checked by intervention at early stages. By making comprehensive mental health services available in residential communities, millions of people could potentially be headed off from lengthy incarcerations in state institutions. The federal government would provide a share of construction and staffing money, asking only that the centers provide a full range of services (inpatient, outpatient, emergency, etc.) and relate to a community somewhere between 75,000 and 200,000 in population. Community participation in the planning and operation of the centers was also mandated, not so much as an invitation to community control, but as a public relations measure. Questions about what kinds of illnesses the centers would deal with, how they would be staffed, what degree of community participation they would feature, etc. were all left to local public health agencies to resolve.

C.M.H.B. was the New York City agency which found itself charged with the task of translating the community mental health center concept into a brick-and-mortar program. C.M.H.B. is the most reticent, least publicized of New York City's health agencies. It presents no public profile of buildings or programs, operates with a small and relatively placid staff, and has usually remained aloof from the routine crises common to other city agencies, including other health agencies. Unlike the appointed commissioners of other city agencies, who report directly to the Mayor, the Commissioner of Mental Health reports to an unpaid nine-member board, which in turn is responsible to the Mayor and to the State Department of Mental Hygiene. The reason for this unusual arrangement was that C.M.H.B. was created through State legislation rather than directly by the city government. The 1954 State Mental Hygiene Law had made available state matching funds for local public and private mental health services, and authorized the establishment of local city and county C.M.H.B.s to administer the funds.

There was no reason why C.M.H.B. could not have used state monies to operate its own programs, but an early Board decision established the policy of contracting out for all direct services. Thus C.M.H.B. is essentially no more than a conduit, passing on government funds to a wide range of uncoordinated private mental health facilities.

From top to bottom, C.M.H.B. is characterized by a severe case of conflict-of-interest. Except for two *ex officio* public officials, C.M.H.B.'s elite Board is fairly evenly divided between representatives of the city's two major philanthropic organizations, Catholic Charities and the Federation of Jewish

Philanthropies, which together dominate the city's sectarian health and hospital facilities. All of the mental health facilities under the egis of these two philanthropic organizations receive public funds through C.M.H.B. and collectively absorb a large percentage of C.M.H.B.'s total outlay for private agencies. Other affiliations of C.M.H.B. members include the institutional centers of some of the city's most patrician empires — the Columbia University Medical Center and the Cornell University Medical Center. Ties to the private, C.M.H.B.-funded mental health sector are just as tight at the staff level in C.M.H.B. Several middle-echelon C.M.H.B. staffers interviewed in late 1968 were found to work part-time for private agencies receiving C.M.H.B. funds. Not surprisingly, considering these sources of recruitment, C.M.H.B.'s staff presents a white, middle-aged, well-fed face. In mid-1968, C.M.H.B. had only three nonwhite employees (out of 170) above the clerical level.

C.M.H.B.'s overall policies have been generally consistent with the interests of the staff and Board, and with the interests of the institutions which they represent. A disproportionate share of funds goes to voluntary agencies — which usually charge fees, and employ other, even more direct mechanisms of selecting middle-class, articulate patients — as compared to city-run services which serve only the indigent. For instance, in 1961, city-run clinics were handling seventy-eight percent of the city's total psychiatric outpatient admissions and receiving forty-five percent of the C.M.H.B. funds for clinic care. Voluntary agencies under contract to C.M.H.B. were handling twenty-two percent of the admissions and receiving fifty-four percent of the funds. The disproportion has, if anything, increased since that time. Voluntary agencies receiving C.M.H.B. funds have been virtually unregulated, with contracts specifying little more than the name of the agency and its budget. About five new voluntary agencies have gained C.M.H.B. contracts each year, amounting to a total of sixty-six such fortunate agencies in 1968, but it has proved nearly impossible for a black- or Puerto Rican-run agency to gain C.M.H.B. support.

From the start, C.M.H.B.'s interpretation of the Community Mental Health Centers Act clearly reflected the needs and interests of the city's medical empires. First, C.M.H.B. required that all community mental health centers had to be "affiliated with a teaching hospital or medical school, closely related and located within a reasonable distance to a general hospital," i.e., community mental health centers had to fall administratively and geographically within one of the city's medical empires. Secondly, C.M.H.B. tended to see mental health centers almost exclusively as new buildings, although the cheaper and more flexible interpretation of them as networks of services was well within the law, and would have required about ten years less to implement. But nothing, of course, could have been more attractive to an expansionist medical empire than a new, ten- or twenty-million-dollar, publicly-financed building.

In 1965, C.M.H.B. staff came up with a "master plan" for covering the entire city with community mental health centers. The city was divided into fifty-one areas tailored to fit federal population requirements (between 75,000 and 200,000 residents). Each of the fifty-one catchment areas, as they were called, was designed to cover the widest possible range of socioeconomic conditions — a feature which not only pleased the integrationists in C.M.H.B., but also assured that no community mental health center would be too heavily burdened with "inarticulate," "deprived" patients. Once the maps were drawn, C.M.H.B. saw no further need for planning: all catchment areas were to have community mental health centers, but in no particular order of priority. The only task was to find the institutions to staff them.

In its early efforts to sell community mental health centers, C.M.H.B. never strayed far from the centers of the city's seven medical empires. With maps in hand, C.M.H.B. staff dashed out to promote the program to medical schools and teaching hospitals — as a first step, Columbia was asked to take Washington Heights, Einstein to take the Bronx, and New York University was asked to take the Bellevue area on the lower east side. C.M.H.B.'s promotion of centers was reminiscent of the Department of Hospitals' earlier efforts to enlist private institutions for the hospital affiliation program: the private institutions were sometimes reticent but yielded to the promise of staff salaries, a new building, and the unbeatable argument, "only *you* have the expertise to do it."

The Columbia and Einstein empires each bought the community mental health center idea for their own, very different reasons. Columbia wanted space to expand its existing Freudian analytical-training and drug-oriented research programs. Einstein leaped at the chance for federal funds to enable bright young staff men to do their thing in "the community." If their thing meant new, socially oriented "demonstration" projects, so much the better, since these in turn could be the basis for further grant-hustling and talent recruitment. Programmatic considerations aside, Einstein was interested in any new public funds, no matter how earmarked, which could be siphoned off to shore up existing mental health programs in the empire — at Einstein, Montefiore, Bronx Municipal, and Bronx State hospitals.

Einstein College of Medicine-Yeshiva University didn't even wait for new buildings to be constructed before setting up its two centers in the Bronx: Soundview-Throgs Neck-Tremont Community Mental Health Center and the Lincoln Hospital Community Mental Health Services. Both centers are linked for staffing and backup services to other institutions within the empire — primarily to the psychiatric wards at Bronx Municipal Hospital and Bronx State (mental) Hospital. The empire has encouraged, in its own words, a global approach to psychiatry which includes centrally-controlled shifts of staff and funds from institution to institution.

The Einstein venture in Soundview-Throgs Neck-Tremont was never a bold, new approach, but a continuation of a pre-1963 program, dressed up to meet the requirements for federal community mental health centers money. The center is not a building, but a concept — an administrative network linking Einstein-run mental health services in the catchment area with the wards in Einstein-affiliated hospitals. If there is any difference between the Soundview-Throgs Neck program before and after it became a community mental health center, it is probably that as a center, it is more smoothly managed. Patients and patients' medical records are not as likely to be lost in transit between the three mental health clinics in the Soundview-Throgs Neck area and the distant wards at Bronx State.

Are the people of Soundview-Throgs Neck-Tremont grateful for this new convenience? It is unlikely that very many of the residents are even aware of the two million dollar program in their midst. The center has minimized preventive services, out-reach, and special action programs, preferring to concentrate on the few "really sick" persons who surface from the population. The center's director, an Einstein man, regards "community controlniks," socially oriented professionals, and the like as poachers. If the community wants to get involved in mental health, it should get a grant to do its own thing — far from his medical show.

Einstein reserved its showcase community mental health center for Lincoln Hospital, a municipal hospital which, along with the blighted south Bronx area which surrounds it, has been rapidly decaying for two decades. The south Bronx, a transposed and expanded version of the waterfront slums of San Juan, is distinguished by the highest crime and addiction rates in New York. Mental health services may not be what the south Bronx needed most, but it got them, starting in 1963, to the tune of $1.5 million, expanding to $4.5 million in 1968. On paper, the Lincoln community mental health center was the most lavish, most socially oriented mental health program in the city, if not the nation. Einstein boasted of the center's innovative projects in addiction, rehabilitation services, community action, and out-reach. Not until the center's workers revolted in 1969 was it revealed by a federal investigation that much of this program was non-existent — the money had been drained off to sponsor other imperial enterprises.

In June, 1969, investigations by Lincoln mental health workers and federal investigators from the National Institute of Mental Health demonstrated that Einstein's global approach was a one-way street leading directly to the empire's coffers.

The empire had skimmed off over $500,000 in overhead alone since 1965. Hidden benefits in the form of (unrelated) staff salaries, new positions, and additional facilities were accumulated through padding. Not only did Einstein not pour personnel time into the Lincoln program, but they took an additional $45,000 per year to pay for a battery of accountants, bookkeepers, etc. to work at Einstein.

It was not unusual for Lincoln Mental Health Center to wait for up to six months for its money to be passed on by Einstein. An administrator working closely with Einstein says the reason for the delay was not the work load or lack of administrative capacity, but that Einstein had greatly underestimated the deficit to be incurred from its own College Hospital; and Einstein simply preferred to use the Lincoln money, rather than dig into its own capital funds.

Bronx State Hospital, another affiliate of Einstein, also took its share. During fiscal year 1968-69, $25,000 went to supplement the drug addiction ward at Bronx State where Lincoln Mental Health Center was to be allotted twenty-four beds for detoxification. The doctor in charge of the service allowed only four beds to be utilized. More outrageous, was the disappearance of an additional $137,000 which was to be used to hire a "liaison staff" for Bronx State's eighty-bed Lincoln ward. Only one psychiatrist was hired, and even he did not relate directly to Lincoln Mental Health Center.

Three neighborhood mental health units at $70,000 each were to have been established, and only one was in existence by mid-1969. Similarly, a mandated $64,000 staff for outpatient care was nonexistent. Even more spectacular was the case of the phantom $372,000 partial hospitalization program which was supposed to provide weekend, evening, and daytime services.

Though $136,000 was provided for establishing a psychiatric emergency room service, sporadic emergency care was provided through the general Lincoln hospital emergency room. One need only realize that the Lincoln emergency room is the second busiest in the nation to appreciate the insanity of the situation. When a government investigating team visited the emergency room, it found that the psychiatric staff was not even present — only available on call. The mental health emergency service had neither a telephone listing nor a telephone answering service.

The official document prepared by the federal investigating team, an open letter from the National Institute of Mental Health to New York City's Commissioner of Mental Health, dated July 9, 1969, found that "an identifiable community mental health center . . . does not exist fiscally, administratively or programmatically." But after scolding Yeshiva University (and its fiscal intermediary, Albert Einstein) for the most blatant breaches of contract, the officials made no move to fund a more responsible, alternative structure. In the meantime, the Einstein Department of Psychiatry — which would like to preserve its year-old residency program at Lincoln — made its position more secure by creating a Lincoln Hospital Department of Psychiatry. With this arrangement, if the community mental health center fails, only the community can lose. Traditional, teaching-oriented inpatient services will go on at the Lincoln Department of Psychiatry. As have been the empire's paternalistic attitude toward its Lincoln colony in the past — he who giveth, can taketh away.

The Columbia University College of Physicians and Surgeons empire will probably never be charged with malfeasance as was the Einstein empire, because its elaborate plan for a community mental health center never got off the drawing boards. The public can only speculate that, had the black and Puerto Rican community not stood in its way, Columbia would be well on its way to developing a human laboratory for its own research and training priorities — with mental health services to the surrounding Washington Heights-West Harlem community running a very poor third.

In 1967, when Columbia first began to discuss the prospect of a community mental health center with C.M.H.B., probably few residents of the catchment area were even aware that the Columbia Medical Center offered mental health services. In the academic psychiatric world, however, Columbia is internationally famous as the best. Columbia's psychiatric resources consist of a loose complex of four separate and discrete elements, linked administratively and through personnel overlap. At the core is the Department of Psychiatry, which trains medical students and offers psychiatric residencies, and is headed by a recent past president of the American Psychiatric Association. For higher training, there is the Psychoanalytic Clinic for Research and Training, which is not a clinic at all, but one of the three top psychoanalytic institutes in New York City, well-known for its hard-line Freudian orientation. Access to patients for these two training and research centers is provided by Presbyterian Hospital's clinic and the Psychiatric Institute, an affiliated 182-bed state research and training hospital.

As in the medical center generally, psychiatric research and training come first, while service admittedly takes lower priority. Even C.M.H.B. acknowledged that Columbia "has been able to provide only limited service facilities to the people of Washington Heights." Since much of the training is aimed at the production of psychiatrists and analysts for private practice, what service is offered tends to be selective for the kind of middle-class, articulate patients who are believed to be susceptible to conventional individual therapy. Thus at the Psychiatric Institute, only one sixty-bed floor is reserved for community people, while the rest serve mainly middle-class patients from throughout the city. Therapy on the community floor is heavily drug-dependent, in line with the Psychiatric Institute's active involvement in testing for drug companies. As for the low-income Washington Heights community, a high-ranking faculty member in the Columbia Department of Psychiatry wrote in 1964: "A local community adjacent to the medical center has been delineated as a lab for long term studies of various therapeutic techniques . . . The population of the Washington Heights Health District, with a population of 269,000 (sic), constitutes the 'laboratory community.' "

Long before the community mental health center issue surfaced, Columbia's relationship to the Washington Heights-West Harlem community had been growing tenser, while its relationship to C.M.H.B. had been growing more intimate. Community resentment focussed on Columbia's expansionist real estate policies in the over-crowded slum areas, and was in no way softened by the empire's medical policies, which favored research, education, and private patient care over community service. But to the downtown offices of C.M.H.B., Columbia was a close friend and colleague. A Columbia faculty member has, since 1964, held a seat on C.M.H.B.'s elite, non-salaried board, while a Columbia associate professor held (until 1967) the top staff position (commissioner) at C.M.H.B. The Columbia-C.M.H.B. relationship was further cemented in the mid-sixties by joint research and education projects, such as survey of the public image of mental health, and a C.M.H.B. residency program for Columbia trainees in administrative psychiatry.

When the community mental center program got underway in 1966, Columbia was not only assured a center, but one to be built entirely with public funds. (Two other voluntary hospitals in New York put up much of their own construction money for centers.) After working out an informal agreement with

Columbia's Division of Community Psychiatry, C.M.H.B.'s commissioner proceeded to enter the project — the city's first — into C.M.H.B.'s 1966-67 budget for new construction. Lest the C.M.H.B. board balk at the eighteen-million-dollar request, city Hospital Commissioner Trussell made an unprecedented personal appearance before the board to plead for the community mental health center. His efforts were instrumental in pushing the Columbia center over the wire. (Three weeks after his appeal to C.M.H.B.'s board, the Commissioner resigned his city post and headed back to the deanship of the Columbia School of Public Health, which, along with the Columbia Department of Psychiatry, jointly administers the Division of Community Psychiatry.)

Within months, the architects (a private firm under contract to the city) and Columbia planners unveiled their plan for what was heralded by C.M.H.B. as a model community mental health center. The plan was never made public and was, in fact, later suppressed by both Columbia and C.M.H.B. But because of its sumptuous proportions, it has become legendary in city planning and budgeting circles. It included 407 offices for the private use of Columbia psychiatrists! The actual services, if not an afterthought, were at best far from innovative. At the core was a good-sized hospital — two hundred patient beds. The other federally mandated services appeared to have been designed from a federal how-to-do-it guidebook with little attention to whatever special needs or tastes the community might have. There were a token ten beds for drug addicts, a slightly smaller service for alcoholics, and no program whatever to utilize the supportive services of existing local social service agencies.

Struck by the probable expense of this monumental community mental health center, the state's Department of Mental Hygiene did not challenge the 407 private offices, but only suggested that two hundred beds (which in theory justified the office space) were more than enough for two catchment areas. The state proposed that the Inwood catchment area be attached to Washington Heights-West Harlem for a total catchment area population of 281,330, more than enough to stock the two hundred beds. In order to conform to the federal law limiting catchment populations to 200,000, the Columbia community mental health center's plans were revised to provide for two separate but equal sets of services under the one roof: one set for the predominantly black and Puerto Rican southern Washington Heights and West Harlem, and another for the mostly white northern Washington Heights and Inwood.

Columbia jumped at the chance to redefine its catchment area. From the beginning of the discussion of the mental health center, Columbia had expressed a preference for reaching northward to the white areas, rather than serving the black and Puerto Rican Washington Heights-West Harlem. If C.M.H.B. were going to insist that the mental health center serve the blacks and Puerto Ricans of southern Washington Heights and West Harlem, the lower-class clientele would at least be counterbalanced by white Inwoodites. And, most important of all, the move preserved the 407 offices which could easily house a couch for every therapist in Columbia's Department of Psychiatry, as well as provide room for research. Black and Puerto Rican leaders of the Washington Heights-West Harlem community greeted the idea of a Columbia-run community mental health center with immediate hostility. Community activists countered Columbia's plans with a vision of a mental health center as a street-level beachhead against addiction and alcholism, and as springboard for an attack on all the environmental and institutional causes of distress. When the Columbia two-entrance plan leaked out, resentment mounted and became more widespread. The final blow was the announcement of the location Columbia and C.M.H.B. had selected for the center — the site of the Audubon Ballroom, scene of Malcolm X's assassination and, to blacks, a national shrine. At a 1968 community meeting called by Columbia to satisfy federal requirements for community involvement in mental health center planning, black and Puerto Rican residents seized the podium, denounced Columbia's plans, and declared that henceforth the community would plan for its own mental health services.

This incident came close to becoming a severe political embarrassment to C.M.H.B., and hence to the mayor. In the weeks that followed the community "takeover", as it was called, C.M.H.B. went through some painful introspection. First, it hired a black social worker to fill the new post of community liaison. Then, impressed by the evident urgency of community demand for mental health services, C.M.H.B. reversed its former policy and decided to encourage the development of new community mental health centers which were not new buildings, but "integrated networks of services." However, C.M.H.B. did not alter its on-going plans for construction of fifteen new centers. Without them, it is doubtful whether C.M.H.B. would have had any notion of how to lure most of the city's medical empires into community mental health center programs.

Columbia, for one, was not going to step down into the streets with any loose network of services. Its response to the community revolt and to the less cooperative stance of C.M.H.B. was to gradually disentangle itself from any commitment to mental health services in the Washington Heights-West Harlem area. In an October 1968 speech at a meeting of the American Psychiatric Association, Columbia's director of psychiatry questioned whether psychiatrists should support continued federal funding to the community mental health centers program. He further questioned whether it was realistic to ever hope for the kind of redistribution of services implied by the Community Mental Health Centers Act, given the priorities of the empires. "There are clinical and organizational patterns, not always recognized, that militate against what we might consider the rational distribution of medical care of any kind, and perhaps especially of mental health care," he was quoted as saying.

Later, in his 1969 Presidential Address to the American Psychiatric Association, Kolb stated that if the mental health establishment had a social responsibility at all, it was to prevent, rather than to foment, community action. "Adminiatrators and deliverers of mental health services will have to sharpen their perception and recognition of their responsibilities in maintaing social homeostasis. They bear a social responsibility much in the same way as the courts *and other law enforcement agencies* do in the support of a healthy community environment for all." (Emphasis added.)

By mid-1969, Columbia had withdrawn all its plans for a community mental health center and made it known to C.M.H.B. that it would take much more than a 407-room office building to reawaken its interest.

The bloom is off the community mental health centers program in New York City. After the confrontation in Washington Heights, Columbia simply picked up its academic robes and retreated to its fortress-like domain on the edge of the Hudson River. And, after its embarrassment at Lincoln, Einstein has begun to retrench to the safety of its more established hospital outposts. Other private institutions in the city are reevaluating their plans for community mental health centers or, like New York University Medical Center, are gerrymandering their catchment areas to exclude potentially demanding black and Puerto Rican neighborhoods. C.M.H.B., recently brought under more careful government scrutiny, and renamed Department of Mental Health, has become more cautious about its projections of high quality, convenient mental health services for all.

Yet at the outset of the community mental health center planning, New York had everything in its favor — a largesse of psychiatric resources, a powerful public mental health agency, and a galaxy of willing medical empires. The program in New York was entrusted by the government to some of the most prestigious medical empires in the nation, and to the extent that the program has failed, they have failed. Columbia and Einstein molded the flexible community mental health centers concept to fit their institutional needs — for space, for funds, for grant-worthy "demonstrations." If these needs did not correspond to the needs of the service-starved "target populations," so much the worse for the target populations. The empires had other things on their agendas.

REGULATION OF QUALITY OF CARE
IN HOSPITALS:
THE NEED FOR CHANGE

William Worthington
Laurens H. Silver

Public concern has recently been focused upon the quality of care provided patients in the nation's public hospitals. Many of the nation's poor are treated in county or city hospitals, yet during the last year both the Boston City Hospital and the St. Louis City Hospital failed to meet the accreditation standards of the Joint Commission on Accreditation of Hospitals (JCAH).(1) The D.C. Hospital in the District of Columbia was confronted with allegations from its own house staff that it was rendering inadequate and inferior patient care.(2) In January 1970, a group of seventy residents in internal medicine at Los Angeles County-University of Southern California Medical Center filed suit in the Superior Court of Los Angeles County in an attempt to enjoin overcrowding at that hospital which resulted in patient beds being placed in corridors.(3) While these latter two confrontations arose independently, they reflect a nationwide crisis in the system which purports to deliver hospital care to the nation's poor.

The quality of care alleged by these doctors to exist at two of the nation's largest hospitals(4) can only be described as dangerously inadequate and tragically inhuman. Yet their descriptions are consistent with findings of other recent studies of hospital care in America.(5)

Explanations for the inadequacies of these hospitals can be readily advanced. They are publicly owned institutions.(6) They treat many patients whose personal financial resources are insufficient to pay for the care received.(7) Although third-party insurers and the federal Medicare and Medicaid programs enable some patients to have payments made on their behalf, not all medically indigent patients(8) are eligible for such coverage.(9) The result is that the government entity which operates the hospital must make up a substantial operating deficit out of general tax revenue. In light of the lack of sufficient revenues for many city governments it is hardly surprising that the public hospitals are forced to operate on a less than adequate budget.

While these factors provide an explanation for the deficiences of the nation's public hospitals, they do not provide a satisfactory justification. The fact that these institutions are caught in a political and economic squeeze(10) does not entitle them to endanger the health and destroy the dignity of their indigent patients. While the hospital administrators may be powerless to do anything about the inadequacies of hospital appropriations, there are regulatory bodies charged with ensuring that health care is administered in accordance with minimal professional standards. The underlying question raised by the dissident doctors in Los Angeles and Washington, D.C., is why these regulatory bodies have failed to see that professional and humane medical care is administered in the nation's hospitals.

While that question is now being raised in the context of the public institution, its implications extend to all providers of medical care, whether they be public, voluntary, or proprietary. In this article we will examine this larger question. We will examine the major agencies which regulate the quality of hospital care at the state and national level. We will examine how these agencies are affected by federal health benefits legislation (Medicare and Medicaid) and the role that the federal government is (and is not) playing in maintaining minimum standards of care in the nation's hospitals.

REGULATION AT THE STATE LEVEL

Hospital regulation at the state level is a rather recent phenomenon. Prior to World War II, fewer than a dozen states had any laws regulating hospitals.(11) However, following the passage of the Hill-Burton Hospital Construction Act(12) in 1946, almost every state adopted a hospital licensing act, since such a law was required for participation in the federal program.(13) The resulting statutes were neither strongly worded nor comprehensively conceived; the states were only required to demonstrate the existence of maintenance and operation standards which could be enforced, if necessary. The impact of these state licensing laws on the quality of care rendered in hospitals has been limited.

Although most state regulatory agencies presently have the legal authority to set standards for medical care as well as the physical plant and safety aspects of hospitals,(14) the latter are more specific and more easily developed and applied than the former. Physical plant attributes are still almost exclusively emphasized at the inspection level. This emphasis is partly the result of the enactment of the state laws contemporaneously with the early stages of implementation of the federal Hill-Burton program. Both were enacted at a time when legislators felt that is was beyond their competence to attempt to establish standards for the quality of medical care rendered in hospitals. To allay fear that the federal government would gain excessive control over the regulation of health facilities, the powers of the federal government were restricted mainly to establishing construction standards, while operational standard-setting and enforcement were left to the individual states.

The major weakness of the state regulations as they now exist, in addition to their general failure to establish adequate standards relating to the quality of care, is general laxity in enforcement.(15) Few states have attempted to establish machinery to see that standards are met.(16) Often the regulations are worded as recommendations rather than requirements;(17) words like *sufficient, adequate,* and *reasonable* are common, especially in standards dealing with patient care. These words cannot be uniformly understood by most people, nor do they set meaningful guidelines. Low budget appropriations in state regulatory agencies have caused staffing deficiencies and sporadic enforcement, and low pay scales dissuade highly qualified persons from becoming employed as inspectors.(18) It is often financially necessary to use other offices and state agencies in the enforcement procedure. This creates organizational conflicts which make it even more difficult to attain the objectives of hospital licensure. Finally, education and consultation activities are severely lacking in the programs, in part from a dearth of guidance from voluntary or governmental agencies. The U.S. Public Health Service, for example, has been very reluctant to interfere with state hospital regulations.(19)

With a few exceptions, states have not assumed the responsibility for supervising the quality of medical care rendered in hospitals. Whether by default or design, they have chosen to delegate the responsibility to the medical profession and/or the federal government, neither of which, unfortunately, has adequately provided the needed regulation. Two states, however, New York and Michigan, have recently taken steps to improve their licensing laws and to coordinate planning of health facilities with state licensure programs. These innovative departures will be discussed below.(20)

CERTIFICATION AND ACCREDITATION AT THE NATIONAL LEVEL

In addition to licensure by the states, hospitals may be subject to accreditation or certification under national standards promulgated either by a voluntary accrediting body or by the Department of Health, Education, and Welfare. Certification and accreditation are both voluntary evaluations, however, and thus do not have the direct regulatory force of the state licensing standards.

Accreditation of hospitals is a term used to signify that a hospital has met the standards of some recognized group whose sole or primary function is to promulgate and apply standards to hospitals. A variety of accreditational bodies exists for a variety of purposes,(21) but only one, the Joint Commission on Accreditation of Hospitals, has national recognition and extensive scope. Founded in 1952 out of a precursor organization established by the American College of Surgeons, the JCAH is presently a private, nonprofit body composed of representatives from six organized segments of American medicine.(22) It inspects hospitals on a voluntary basis and grants accreditation upon a finding that the hospital complies with JCAH's self-imposed "standards" of hospital adequacy.(23) Lack of accreditation, however, places only a limited constraint on the ability of a hospital to operate.(24) Until recently, JCAH accreditation was primarily a matter of prestige within the medical community and had no effect on a hospital's attractiveness to patients.(25)

Since 1965, JCAH accreditation has gained more significance, in that accreditation enables a hospital automatically to be certified as a provider under Medicare if it complies with federal utilization review requirements.(26) However, this linkage of JCAH to federal funding has not necessarily meant any improvement in the quality of hospital care.

In 1965, at the time of adoption of the federal Medicare and Medicaid programs, JCAH standards were weak in many respects, primarily stressing maintenance of medical records and medical staff organization.(27) With regard to other areas and functions of the hospital, such as the emergency room and outpatient department, the standards were grossly inadequate. Moreover, JCAH's method of enforcing these standards — usually by sending out a single surveyor once every three years after at least several weeks' notice to the hospital — allowed many hospitals to relax their vigilance, even with respect to these inadequate norms. New standards, however, were drafted by JCAH in October 1969 and approved in April 1970.(28) These standards, to be effective January 1, 1971 fail to prescribe standards for outpatient services, fail to consider the adequacy of the hospital staff to meet the patient load, do not articulate a clear responsibility of the hospital to serve effectively a particular patient community, and do not consider patient rights with regard to privacy, choice of accommodation, subjection to experimentation, and participation in clinical teaching programs, for example. Moreover, the JCAH standards fail to examine the quality of care "output" of a hospital. So long as medical staff organization comports with the standards, surveyors are not to be concerned with the substantive findings of tissue review or necropsy committees, no matter how horrendous. Thus even though the quality of care in an institution may be bad, a hospital which has the organizational appearance of peer group review will be accredited. Finally, the Standards and Interpretations do not specify what constitutes substantial compliance with the standards for the purpose of accreditation. These and other issues have been the point of recent criticism by a welfare recipient health-consumer organization.(29)

The best indication of the ineffectiveness of the JCAH accreditation survey — and the tendency toward perfunctory re-accreditation — is supplied by the fact that in 1968, of 130 state and local governmental hospitals registered with the American Hospital Association, 128 were accredited.(30) Included among the latter were D.C. General Hospital, Boston City Hospital, and such other problem-ridden institutions as Cook County Hospital and Newark City Hospital. All but the last have come under public scrutiny in recent months regarding the deterioration of patient care and staffing. The fact that such institutions are accredited despite obvious and admitted deficiencies attests to the inadequacy of the standards applied by the JCAH and the ineffectiveness of the accreditation program in maintaining hospital quality. Under considerable public pressure, JCAH has recently exercised long overdue responsibility by revoking the accreditations of St. Louis City Hospital and Boston City Hospital, and granting one-year provisional accreditations to Cook County Hospital and Detroit General Hospital;(31) later, one-year probationary accreditations were given to St. Louis City Hospital, Boston City Hospital, and D.C. General Hospital.(32)

Certification of hospitals as providers for the purpose of reimbursement for services rendered to Medicare beneficiaries is performed by the federal government pursuant to the Medicare legislation. Section 1861(e) of the Social Security Act of 1965 sets forth certain requirements that must be met by participating hospitals(33) and empowers the Secretary of Health, Education, and Welfare to establish "such other requirements as the Secretary finds necessary in the interest of the health and safety of individuals who are furnished services in the institution . . . "(34) Pursuant to this provision, the Secretary has established a detailed set of regulations entitled "Conditions of Participation for Hospitals."(35)

The fundamental weakness of the certification program is its interrelationship with JCAH accreditation. The statutory provision which empowers the Secretary to establish requirements for certification goes on to say that "such other requirements may not be higher than the comparable requirements prescribed for the accreditation of hospitals by the Joint Commission on Accreditation of Hospitals . . . ."(36) Thus the statute adopts the inadequate JCAH standards as the ceiling for federal requirements for participation and effectively prohibits the federal government from playing an active role in upgrading hospital quality through the Medicare program.

This subordination of federal standards to JCAH standards is further accomplished by another provision in the statute. Section 1865 of the act provides in part as follows:

> [A]n institution shall be deemed to meet the requirements of the numbered paragraphs of Section 1395x(e) of this title . . . if such institution is accredited as a hospital by the Joint Commission on Accreditation of Hospitals.(37)

The federal government has interpreted this section to mean that hospitals which are JCAH accredited may not be inspected or evaluated by state agencies under contract with the federal government to see if they also meet the Medicare Conditions of Participation.(38) Any hospital which attains JCAH's accreditation can participate in Medicare without ever having been surveyed by those state agencies to determine their compliance with the Conditions of Participation.(39)

Of course, not all hospitals wishing to participate in Medicare are JCAH-accredited. Those without accreditations must be inspected to determine their compliance with the federal Conditions of Participation. However, under current HEW practice, these inspections are conducted by an agency of the hospital's own state, not by employees of HEW.(40) In almost every state, the agency which conducts the Medicare inspection is the same agency which conducts the state licensing inspections. Thus any weakness in personnel or inspection methods which exist in the state hospital licensing programs are carried over to the federal Medicare program. Further, the application of the federal Conditions of Participation will vary, according to the varying interpretations and competencies of the state licensing authorities.(41)

Finally, a major difficulty in the application of the Conditions of Participation to non-JCAH-accredited hospitals lies in the interpretation of the "substantial compliance" provisions of the regulations. One of these provisions, section 405.1002, provides,

> For an institution to be eligible for participation in the program, it must meet the statutory requirements of section 1861(e) and there must be a finding of substantial compliance on the part of the institution with all the other conditions. . . . Variations in the type and size of hospitals and the nature and scope of services offered will be reflected in differences in the details of organization, staffing, and facilities. However, the test is whether there is substantial compliance with each of the conditions.(42)

A hospital is considered to be in substantial compliance if

> [It] meets the specific statutory requirements of section 1861(e) but is found to have deficiencies with respect to one or more Conditions of Participation which: 1. It is making reasonable plans and efforts to correct, and 2. Notwithstanding the deficiencies, is rendering adequate care and without hazard to the health and safety of individuals being served, taking into account special procedures or precautionary measures which have been or are being instituted.(43)

Hospitals which cannot meet the test of "substantial compliance," as broad and flexible as the Conditions may be, can yet qualify under a special certification category.(44) This provision was adopted largely out of fear that many eligible recipients living in isolated areas which lacked sufficient facilities would not otherwise have needed hospital services available to them. In addition, hospitals which cannot be certified in any category may be reimbursed by HEW for emergency services rendered to eligible patients.(45)

"Substantial compliance" has been interpreted to mean that the hospital must be in "general" conformity with each of the sixteen Conditions of Participation.(46) The only standards which must be satisfied for certification are the statutory requirements in section 1861(e); no limit has been set on the number of conditions in which the hospital may be deficient, though in "substantial compliance," so long as the deficiencies are not preventing the hospital from rendering care without hazard to the health and safety of patients and plans are being made to correct the deficiencies. The determination of substantial compliance is thus made by individual state agencies.(47)

These mandates are, at best, very basic; at worst, they are ambiguous and open to variation in interpretation. Again, a look at the federal government's statistics can be an indication of its effectiveness in monitoring hospital quality. Recent data indicates that as of June 30, 1970, there were 1704 hospitals (190,916 beds) certified as providers but with deficiencies.(48) Another 411 (13,376 beds) were given special "access" certification even though they could not meet the Conditions of Participation because of geographic isolation.(49) A total of 6799 hospitals are certified. Thus twenty-five per cent are not fully in compliance with the Conditions of Participation.(50) Recent tabulations by the Social Security Administration indicate there are ninety-eight hospitals (eighty-two general hospitals, six TB, and ten psychiatric) that have applied for participation in Medicare since the program began and are still not participating. None of these hospitals is JCAH-accredited. The mean bed size of the eighty-two general hospitals is fifty-four. The figure does not include hospitals initially denied which later upgraded and were certified. Almost all of the denials were based on applications filed in 1966.(51)

Since the inception of the program fifty-seven hospitals (1627 beds) have been terminated (decertified) for noncompliance with the Conditions of Participation, and are still not participating. Ninety-nine hospitals have voluntarily withdrawn from Medicare, in some instances apparently to avoid involuntary termination.(52) This data makes it uncertain as to whether or not HEW has followed through with its plan "to take a look at our certification experience and to work with state agencies to devise ways and means to upgrade the standards in these hospitals."(53)

Certification and accreditation are closely related. Both are voluntary, and neither establishes a sufficient standard of care to make up for the deficiencies in the state licensing laws. Certification is in effect dominated by the JCAH so that the federal government is powerless to set its own standards for Medicare participation. The JCAH is controlled by the medical profession and hospital administrators, and thus far it has failed to take an effective stand with regard to critical aspects of hospital quality. Given this interrelationship of national accrediting and certifying bodies, it seems unlikely that either will take any dramatic steps to raise hospital standards in the immediate future.(54)

IMPROVING HOSPITAL REGULATION THROUGH STATE LAWS

Effective steps could be taken for improving hospital regulation in the area of state licensing laws. Two states, New York and Michigan, have already taken steps in this direction, and others would do well to follow their example.

New York has reorganized and extended its hospital regulatory machinery. Under the new Public Health Law,(55) the Health Department was given broad powers to develop a new hospital code. The new code contains comprehensive language covering quality of patient care as well as regulation of construction and financial reporting. In a number of respects the code imposes requirements stricter than JCAH standards or imposes requirements with respect to subjects not covered by JCAH, such as outpatient facility standards.(56)

Also, the inspections in New York are now carried out by five-man interdisciplinary teams made up of full-time, board-certified physicians, hospital administrators, and allied health professionals. The inspectors are well paid and well qualified. Finally, prior to construction of all hospitals, the approval of the state commissioner must be obtained to insure that the public need exists and to prevent duplication of facilities.(57)

Michigan has also adopted a comprehensive hospital licensing law.(58) Under this statute, broad power is conferred on the state director of public health to set standards for quality of care in all hospitals.(59) The statute further provides for the establishment of a state health council to advise and consult with the director of public health in carrying out his responsibilities under the hospital licensure law.(60) This twelve-member council is appointed for four-year staggered terms by the governor with the approval of the state senate. A prestigious, high-level policy-setting body is thus provided to which representatives of consumer interests may be appointed. The state statute further provides that "standards ... for the operation and maintenance of hospitals shall be not less than is required for the certification of hospitals under Public Law 89-97,"(61) thus incorporating by reference the federal standards for certification for Medicare discussed above. The Michigan statute in effect requires all Michigan hospitals to comply with JCAH standards. The statute also provides for flexibility in enforcement of the standards. The state director has the power to revoke or deny hospital licenses and to suspend issued licenses at any time.(62) Furthermore, licenses, when issued, are generally valid for only one year, thus insuring frequent inspection for compliance. Finally, the statute takes steps to clarify the lines of authority between a hospital's governing board and its medical staff by placing responsibility for the operation of the hospital on the governing body and requiring that body to ensure an adequate system of medical review among the medical staff.(63) Medical review plans may be submitted for the approval of the state director, although this is apparently not mandatory.

CHANGING THE ROLE OF JCAH

In addition to strengthening the state licensing laws and their enforcement,(64) it is necessary to re-evaluate the role of the federal government in establishing quality of care standards. In particular, a careful examination must be made of the relationship between JCAH accreditation and Medicare certification.

JCAH considers itself a private accrediting body responsive to the needs of its subscribers. More significantly, it represents a particular interest group in the medical care field. It is true that both doctors and hospital administrators are represented on the Governing Body, and that these two groups have quite divergent views on many quality of care issues. However, this diversity does not make up for the fact that the consuming public is not represented in JCAH. The internecine disputes of doctors and hospital administrators may be negatively correlated to the most critical public interests in hospital quality.(65) It cannot be said that the voting members of JCAH represent an adequate cross section of informed opinion on the quality of care so as to properly protect the public interest in this area.(66)

This lack of public accountability on the part of JCAH would not be so critical were it not for the fact that JCAH standards have been imposed as ceilings for the purpose of Medicare participation by provider hospitals. Yet the nature of its voting membership may prevent it from setting standards at a level which is beneficial to the consuming public.(67) There is a great danger that JCAH will tend to favor the interests of physicians and hospitals at the expense of the public.

Though JCAH does not have power to exclude a hospital from Medicare participation, it does have the effective power to include hospitals that the federal government might otherwise choose to exclude. This power is very critical when quality of care is at issue.(68) Even more critical is the fact that JCAH has control over what type of quality standards will be applied.(69) So long as the doctors and hospital administrators believe that low standards are beneficial from their point of view, the federal government is powerless to require higher standards as a condition to reimbursement under Medicare. The result is that a hospital can be certified for participation in Medicare even though the Bureau of Health Insurance may suspect or know that the hospital is not a safe place for the treatment of elderly patients.(70)

The most effective step that could be taken to improve the Medicare certification scheme would be to make the Medicare program independent of JCAH. This very step has been strongly recommended by the Health Insurance Benefits Advisory Council (HIBAC) in its 1967 report to Congress.(71) Its report contained the following language:

> The Council believes ..., that it is inappropriate to continue statutory delegation to a private agency of all the Government's authority to safeguard quality of care paid for by a government program. The authority to establish policy on minimum quality should be retained by the Government. Quality standards under Medicare should not be controlled by a private agency's standards. Furthermore, the power of oversight and assurance that standards are applied adequately in individual situations should and must remain within both the responsibility and authority of the Government. In the case of Medicare, the Council has found reason for concern that JCAH standards are not applied with the frequency of inspection and range of inspector skills necessary to assure a high degree of effectiveness. Furthermore, because of present statutory provisions ... the JCAH standards in some cases impose an undesirably low ceiling on the maximum level at which health and safety standards under Medicare may be set.(72)

However, Congress has taken no steps in that direction.

Some of the difficulty with the present Medicare legislation could be avoided by an alternative interpretation of the statute. The power of JCAH is established in the statute by the following language:

> The term "hospital" [as used in this statute] means an institution which
> ... (8) meets such other requirements as the Secretary finds necessary in the
> interest of health and safety of individuals who are furnished services in the
> institution, except that such other requirements may not be higher than the
> comparable requirements prescribed for the accreditation of hospitals by the
> Joint Commission on Accreditation of Hospitals (subject to the second
> sentence of section 1395z of this title).(73)

The federal government has interpreted this section very narrowly. The
Department of Health, Education, and Welfare has drafted the federal
Conditions of Participation to follow very closely the 1965 JCAH standards.
They cover no areas not covered by the JCAH standards. Apparently, HEW has
taken the position that the statute prohibits it from establishing any more
comprehensive standards.(74) Thus, in effect, HEW has read the statutory
language to mean that the JCAH standards shall be adopted by the federal
government practically word for word.

The statute does not require this interpretation. It only prohibits the
adoption of federal standards which are higher than *comparable* JCAH
standards. It contains no prohibition against the federal government
promulgating standards in areas not covered by the JCAH standards (such as
outpatient clinic standards, standards relating to patient privacy, and so forth).
Given the narrow scope of the JCAH standards, it would seem that the statute
would permit federal regulation in areas not covered by the JCAH standards.
Such regulation could have a significant effect on quality of care within a
number of critical areas.

We have already noted, however, that hospitals which are JCAH-accredited
need not satisfy the Secretary's Conditions of Participation and must only
comply with the utilization review standards.(75) Thus, even though one might
argue that the statute does not bar the Secretary from developing Conditions of
Participation with regard to those matters not addressed in the JCAH standards
(for example, outpatient care), such standards would be applicable only to the
distinct minority of smaller hospitals that are not JCAH-accredited. It is clear,
then, that the Secretary is effectively dependent upon the standards
promulgated by the JCAH. To the extent he has any authority to promulgate
higher standards in noncomparable areas they would be applicable only to a very
limited number of hospitals.

Another critical section of the statute is the second sentence of section 1863
which provides,

> Such conditions prescribed [by the Secretary under section 1395x] may be
> varied for different areas or different classes of institutions or agencies and
> may, at the request of a State, provide higher requirements for such State
> than for other States: except that, in the case of any State or political
> subdivision of a State which imposes higher requirements on institutions as a
> condition to the purchase of services (or of certain specified services) in such
> institutions under a State plan approved under subchapter I, XVI, or XIX of

this chapter, the Secretary shall impose like requirements as a condition to the payment for services (or for the services specified by the State or subdivision) in such institution in such State or subdivision.(76)

This provision allows the states to apply higher standards to hospitals for the purpose of Medicare certification if they so choose. The statute provides two mechanisms to accomplish this. First, the states may request the Secretary to apply higher standards in certifying Medicare hospitals; alternatively, if the states have higher standards for their title XIX (Medicaid) program, the title XIX standards will be applied for the purpose of Medicare certification. At the present time, no state has either sought permission from the Secretary to apply higher standards, nor has any state prescribed higher standards for its title XIX program.(77) Moreover, the statute clearly excepts the situation where there are higher state standards from the general rule that JCAH accreditation is sufficient for the purpose of certification:

> Except as provided in the second sentence of section 1395z of this title, an institution shall be deemed to meet the requirements of the numbered paragraphs of section 1395x(e) of this title (except paragraph (6) thereof) if such institution is accredited as a hospital by the Joint Commission on Accreditation of Hospitals.(78)

Where there are higher state standards, the hospital must comply with those standards regardless of accreditation status. Thus, while it may be true that HEW may not ordinarily contract with a state agency to inspect a JCAH-accredited hospital, it is *required* to arrange for the inspection of all hospitals in a state which has either requested the Secretary to apply higher standards for Medicare certification or which has established higher standards for participation in a title XIX program. In a state with a title XIX program, the federal government is required to apply any higher title XIX standards to all hospitals which seek to participate in title XVIII even though those hospitals may be JCAH-accredited. This is an important power which the states have not chosen to utilize.

Title XVIII must be amended to provide the Secretary with greater power to promulgate appropriate standards for hospitals participating in Medicare, thereby removing the JCAH ceiling on Conditions of Participation. The Health Insurance Benefits Advisory Council's Recommendation 3 provides that

> The Council recommends legislation which would remove the present limitations on the Secretary's authority to establish health and safety standards for hospitals, contained in Section 1865 of the Social Security Act, so that: The Secretary would have the authority to establish health and safety standards for hospitals commensurate with his authority to establish such standards for other providers of services and for independent laboratories. The Secretary may, in the case of any national accrediting body with standards and certification procedures equal to or higher than those established by the Secretary for a class of providers or independent laboratories, find that such accreditation provides reasonable assurance that

the conditions of participation are met.(79)

It would further appear necessary, in light of the recommendations of the Health Insurance Benefits Advisory Council, first to amend section 1865 of the statute, which provides that JCAH accreditation shall constitute compliance with the Conditions of Participation. At a minimum, the statute should be amended to provide that JCAH accreditation shall constitute only prima facie evidence of compliance with the Conditions of Participation. The Secretary should have the authority to instruct the state agency performing the certification inspection function to apply the Conditions of Participation even though a hospital is accredited. This power is particularly necessary in view of the fact that JCAH accreditation has been until recently for a three-year period. Even though a hospital might be applying for certification as a Medicare provider over two years from its last accreditation, under present law the Secretary has no power to apply the Conditions of Participation or seek any inspection of the hospital by the state agency. Likewise, even though section 1007 of the Secretary's regulations gives the Secretary power to find that an institution is no longer in compliance with the Conditions of Participation if

> The institution has deficiencies of such character as to seriously limit the capacity of the institution to render adequate care or which place health and safety of individuals in jeopardy, and consultation to the institution has demonstrated that there is no early prospect of such significant improvement as to establish substantial compliance as of a later beginning date . . . (80)

This section applies only to unaccredited hospitals. A hospital which has had ample opportunity to prepare for the JCAH accreditation team visit and is consequently accredited may, soon after the accreditation visit, be in a state of noncompliance with JCAH standards and the Secretary's Conditions of Participation. Under the Secretary's current powers, he would have no power to reinvestigate the hospital after it had been certified as a Medicare provider — even if as much as two years had elapsed since the initial accreditation. Such a situation was illustrated at the time of the events which took place at D.C. General Hospital in the District of Columbia, for the conditions complained of at that institution had become manifest near the end of the three-year accreditation period. Any amendment in title XVIII must make it clear that the powers which the Secretary has under section 1007 of the regulations to find a hospital in noncompliance with the Conditions of Participation applies regardless of the accreditation status of the hospital.

As indicated earlier, there are a number of reasons for eliminating the virtually exclusive power of the Joint Commission on Accreditation of Hospitals to promulgate standards for the participation of hospitals in title XVIII by repealing that part of section 1861e which makes JCAH standards the ceiling for hospital providers under Medicare. First of all, the Joint Commission is entirely dominated by producer groups. Nineteen of the twenty members of its executive body, including representatives of the American Hospital Association, are doctors. The Joint Commission has primarily consulted producer groups in the articulation of its standards. Further, the Joint Commission's policy with regard to inspection reports has been to treat them as a confidential document to be released only to the hospital which has contracted for the accreditation. Inspection reports have not been made available even to the Department of Health, Education, and Welfare.(81) In sum, though functioning in a quasi-public status by virtue of the substantial standard-setting functions delegated to it by Congress under title XVIII, the Joint Commission has operated as a totally private body unaccountable to the public or to the government.(83)

Thus, while the Secretary should be guided to some extent by JCAH standards, as revised in October 1969, he should be left free to develop his own standards with regard both to areas pertaining to quality of care comparable with JCAH standards and to noncomparable quality of care criteria. To the extent that the Secretary arguably already has the power to promulgate noncomparable standards, as argued earlier, amendment would not be necessary, but clarification still desirable.

OTHER RECOMMENDATIONS FOR REFORM

Other areas of reform include building into the certification process adequate mechanisms for the processing and consideration of consumer and staff complaints concerning the quality of care being offered by the hospital. During the course of the crisis at D.C. General Hospital during the winter of 1969-70, house staff of the hospital requested a hearing both before the state agency and the Secretary of Health, Education, and Welfare wherein they could present evidence under section 1007 of the regulations to prove that the hospital had deficiencies "of such a character as to seriously limit the capacity of the institution to render adequate care or which place health and safety of individuals in jeopardy."

Such requests for a section 1007 "hearing" were denied both by the state agency and by HEW on the ground that the hospital was already accredited and therefore section 1007 did not apply. Neither agency in its reply addressed the question of providing a forum to dissident medical staff or the community for the presentation of evidence concerning quality of care at the hospital. No "hearing" appears to be provided for either under the agreement by the Secretary with the state agency to perform title XVIII certification monitoring or in the Secretary's regulations, or in the statute itself.(84) It would appear appropriate to make explicit statutory provision for the submission by consumers and hospital staff of evidence to the Secretary for the purpose of either supplementing the recommendations of the state agency with regard to certification or providing evidence upon which the Secretary could exercise his powers to decertify under section 1007 of the regulations. Of further critical importance would be a statutory mechanism whereby adequately documented consumer and/or staff complaints could trigger a section 1007 proceeding by the

Secretary.(85)

Further, the Secretary should be required, in performing his certification function, to make explicit findings on the evidence presented to him. Of course, an amendment of the statute would be required so as to provide for the applicability of section 1007 despite JCAH accreditation and to provide further that JCAH accreditation shall be only prima facie evidence of compliance with the Conditions of Participation.

CONCLUSION

Since there would appear to be growing interest by consumer groups in the quality of care in municipal and voluntary hospital settings, and an increasing interest on the part of house staff, particularly at large urban and county public hospitals, in quality of care issues, it would seem to be of critical importance to provide institutional mechanisms to address the questions raised as to quality of care. Since many of these issues affect the elderly, Medicare would appear to be an appropriate program for the hearing of and resolution of complaints concerning quality of care in hospitals. In order, however, for there to be effective redress mechanisms and adequate quality-of-care standards, the power of the Department of Health, Education, and Welfare with regard to certification of hospitals as providers under Medicare must be augmented. This would require amendment of the Social Security Act in the manner recommended by the Health Insurance Benefits Advisory Council. In view of the extensive powers granted by Congress to the producer-doctor dominated Joint Commission on Accreditation of Hospitals under title XVIII, it would appear that the HIBAC recommendations should be implemented.

NOTES

(1) For a chronicle of the conditions existing at Boston City Hospital, see Worsley *et al.,* Recommendations and Comments on Boston City Hospital 4 (JCAH survey, June 2-4, 1969). The surveyors made the following summary of their findings:

> The attention of the medical staff and administration is directed to the major deficiencies which include failure to properly maintain existing automatic sprinklering systems; lack of automatic fire extinguishing systems . . . ; delay in completion of medical records; lack of a sufficient number of graduate registered nurses for full patient coverage; need for additional qualified therapeutic dietitians; need to revise medical staff by-laws; need for relocation of surgeon's dressing room to reduce potential of outside contamination; need for architectural segregation of the labor delivery room and newborn nursery and urgent need for adequate facilities to allow for proper separation of infected gynecological patients from the obstetrical-newborn area. A concerted effort should be made to promptly correct these and other deficiencies in order that accreditation may be attained.

Similar problems exist at the Veterans Administration Center's Wadsworth

Hospital in West Los Angeles. *See* Los Angeles Times, May 11, 1970, at 3, Apr. 29, 1970, at 3 and May 26, 1970, at 3. Cook County Hospital in Chicago was recently on the verge of complete shut-down as a result of political interference in the running of the hospital and deplorable patient care conditions. *See* Chicago Daily News, May 20, 1970. It was given a provisional one-year accreditation by the JCAH on April 26, 1970. The St. Louis City Hospital was disaccredited in September 1969, and the Boston City Hospital lost its accreditation January 1, 1970. A few months later the latter was accredited provisionally for one year. *See* 27 MED. CARE REV. 584-85 (1970). Recently, D.C. General Hospital was also given a one-year provisional accreditation. *See* HOSPITAL WEEK, Sept. 4, 1970, at 36.

(2) For conditions at D.C. General, see generally 26 MED. CARE REV. 996-1009 (1969). The residents at D.C. General prepared a "Statement of the House Staff Association of the District of Columbia General Hospital Before the Survey Team of the Joint Commission on Accreditation of Hospitals" in May 1970 in anticipation of a JCAH accreditation survey of D.C. General Hospital for at least one week during the last year:

Potassium Chloride (treatment for hypertension); Primaquine (treatment for malaria); Aldomet (treatment for high lood pressure); Quinidine (treatment for heart disease); Ampicillin (treatment for urinary infections); Phenoxymethol Penicillin Potassium Salt (treatment for pneumonia and strep throat); Certain types of insulin (U 80 and U 40) (treatment for diabetes); Hydralazine (treatment for high blood pressure); Mylanta (antacid); Gylceryl Guaiacolate Elixir (treatment for coughs); Quadrinol (relieves asthmatic wheezing); Steroid Preparations (four months, treatment for inflammations); Phenylephrine (preparation for dilation); Neosporin (antibiotic); Homatropine (one month, eye drops).

Statement at 33-34. With regard to medical records, the Statement charged that

In a recent sampling of 55 requests for patient records made to the medical records department, only one out of six could be retrieved. In another sampling 15 out of 30 were missing. Because past records often cannot be found, the medical staff is unable to properly evaluate the patient's previous care, properly plan future care, communicate with other physicians and professionals contributing to the patient's care, or provide data for use in research and education.

Id. at 23. As for x-ray facilities, the Statement alleged that

First, there are considerable delays in scheduling routine x-rays, commonly as long as 10-14 days. This is because there are not sufficient competent technical personnel to conduct the services . . . . In addition, x-ray pictures are lost with astounding regularity. One physician recently reported the loss of three repeated x-ray studies on one patient within a 24 hour period . . . .

Id. at 36. Additional comments were made concerning laboratory facilities:

The laboratory at D.C. General Hospital has recently announced that it will throw away all specimens submitted for analysis after 9:00 a.m. . . . because, it is maintained, there are not sufficient personnel to do such analysis before the specimens are too old to work with . . . . Even as to specimens submitted before the deadline, it is sometimes several days before laboratory reports can be obtained, and some house staff physicians maintain they get reports back only 50% of the time.

Id. at 26.

(3)Fisher v. County of Los Angeles, No. 68621 (Los Angeles County Super. Ct., filed Jan. 12, 1970). In a press release accompanying the filing of the litigation, the doctors explained their plight:

Right now the residents are trying to care for 90 new patients a day. The medicine wards constantly run 75-100 beds over capacity. We are turning sick people out in the streets to make room for people who are even more ill. At the same time, this heavy load puts a great strain on the ancillary facilities, the nurses, the labs and others, making proper treatment that much more difficult . . . .

We residents are here to work and learn, but we can do neither with any success under these conditions.

Residents in Internal Medicine, L.A. County Hospital, Press Release, Jan. 12, 1970.

The doctors further pointed out that the primary source of overcrowding was from private hospitals in the county, which transfer approximately 1300 patients per month to County-USC Hospital. Many of these are simply unwanted, often critically ill persons who show up in ambulances, unannounced, many times without complete medical records. The suit seeks an injunction against the hospital and county to limit patient load to a number that can be adequately cared for, and to eliminate the practice of putting patients in the hallways and overcrowding wards in violation of state health laws. *See* CAL. ADMIN. CODE tit. 17, § § 157(a), 348, 353, 454. The suit contends, *inter alia*, that patients are being deprived of life and health without due process of law, that the county is forcing its doctors to practice medicine in a manner which does not comport with medical ethics, and that the county has broken its contract with the doctors to provide a suitable environment for the practice of medicine during their residencies pursuant to the Essentials of Approved Residencies of the AMA Council on Medical Education. With regard to violations of medical ethics, see AMERICAN MEDICAL ASSOCIATION, PRINCIPLES OF MEDICAL ETHICS (1957).

(4) Los Angeles County—USC Medical Center ranks first in the nation in outpatient visits (933,576) second in short-term beds (2105), and third in total beds (2105). D.C. General ranks eighteenth, eighth, and twelfth, respectively. AMERICAN HOSPITAL ASSOCIATION, ANNUAL SURVEY OF HOSPITALS (1968) data tape).

(5) R. DUFF & A. HOLLINSHEAD, SICKNESS AND SOCIETY (1968), discusses the attitudes of hospital staff and the quality of care rendered to patients of different social status, as related to the different classes of accommodations within a large teaching hospital. Sparling, *Measuring Medical Care Quality: A Comparative Study*, HOSPITALS, Mar. 16, 1962, at 62, found that the frequency of necessary appendectomy operations — medically justified on the basis of tissue examinations — and the adequacy of the preoperative examination varied with the type of hospital (teaching versus community) and the source of payment. A broad discussion of the inadequacies of U.S. hospitals is well presented in E. HOYT, CONDITION CRITICAL: OUR HOSPITAL CRISIS (1966).

(6) Of the 7137 AHA-registered hospitals in the United States in 1968, 2606, or 26.7%. were publicly owned and operated. In terms of beds, 33.1% of U.S. short-term and 95.4% of U.S. long-term beds were publicly owned. HOSPITALS (GUIDE ISSUE), Aug. 1, 1969, pt. 2, at 476.

(7) Many states impose an obligation upon their county or municipal hospitals to provide medical care for those unable to pay. *See, e.g.,* CAL. WELFARE & INSTITUTIONS CODE § 17000 (West 1966); ANN. IND. STAT. § 52-1131 (1964).

(8) A medical indigent is a person who cannot afford to provide himself or his dependents with adequate medical care without being deprived of food, clothing shelter, and other basic essentials of living.

(9) Only Social Security recipients who are 65 years of age or older are

eligible for hospital benefits under Medicare. 42 U.S.C. § 1395c (Supp. I, 1965). Medicaid, 42 U.S.C. § 1396 *et seq.* (Supp. I, 1965), eligibility varies from state to state. Only those individuals who meet stringent means tests and other eligibility criteria are eligible. Since it is closely linked to the categorical assistance programs, Medicaid shares all of the glaring faults of our welfare system. In most states, for example, children living at home with both parents, who are needy by virtue of their father's unemployment or under-employment are ineligible for Medicaid benefits. Most states have not exercised their option under 42 U.S.C. § 1396d(a)(i) (Supp. I, 1965) to provide medical assistance to all needy children. In most states medical assistance if furnished only to children whose families are already receiving categorical assistance payments. 42 U.S.C. § 1396a(10) (Supp. I, 1965). Persons who are not categorically "linked" to the federal programs — Aid to the Blind, Old Age Assistance, Aid to the Permanently and Totally Disabled, or Aid to Families with Dependent Children — are not entitled to receive medical benefits under Medicaid. *See* Stevens & Stevens, *Medicaid: Anatomy of a Dilemma,* in this symposium, p. 348.

(10) The average hospital expense per patient day has increased radically. The increases are primarily attributable to rising salaries and increased equipment, facilities, and maintenance expenditures. HOSPITALS (GUIDE ISSUE), Aug. 1, 1969, pt. 2, at 469. An indication of the extent of the increase is given in the chart below:

	expenses/patient day		*percentage*
	1960	*1968*	*increase*
State and local governmental short-term hospitals	$29.43	$60.25	105
Voluntary nonprofit short-term hospitals	33.23	62.18	86

Similarly, in the decade ending in 1968, admissions increased by 33% for state and local governmental hospitals and 24% for voluntary nonprofit hospitals. *Id.* at 474-475. In large community teaching hospitals, where many indigent and/or welfare patients are treated, costs have risen to an even greater extent. At Massachusetts General Hospital in Boston, for example, average costs per patient day have risen from $36.50 in 1959 to %103.00 in 1969 — an increase of 182%. *Hospitals Need Management Even More Than Money,* FORTUNE, Jan. 1970, at 96, 99.

(11) *See* H. FRY, THE OPERATION OF STATE HOSPITAL PLANNING AND LICENSING PROGRAMS 23 (AHA Hospital Monograph Series No. 15, 1965).

(12) 42 U.S.C. § 291 *et seq.* (1964).

(13) Section 623(d) of the Hill-Burton Act provided, "If any State, prior to July 1, 1948, has not enacted legislation providing that compliance with minimum standards of maintenance and operation shall be required in the case of hospitals which shall have received Federal aid under this title, such State shall not be entitled to any further allotments . . . ." 42 U.S.C. § 291f(d) (1946).

(14) The purpose of some state hospital licensing statutes is limited to "prescribing minimum standards of safety and sanitation in the physical plant . . . ." CAL. HEALTH & SAFETY CODE § 1411 (West 1955). Other hospital licensing statutes confer broad rule-making authority on state agencies, though aspects of physical environment are stressed. *See* ILL. STAT. ANN. ch. 111½, § 147 (1966). Some hospital licensing statutes contain express language oriented to quality of care. In Massachusetts, the hospital must meet "requirements for diagnostic and therapeutic facilities for the study, diagnosis and treatment of patients . . . ." MASS. ANN. LAWS ch. 111, § 72 (Supp. 1966). However, even where a state's hospital licensing statute contains language arguably limited to

safety and sanitation of facilities, as in California, rule-making authority may be exercised in a broader manner to set standards relating to methods of care, such as proper medical records. *Cf.* CAL. ADMIN. CODE tit. 17, § 280.

(15) A survey conducted in 1965 reported that only 37 of the 50 states inspected their hospitals at least once a year; the most common reason for not doing so was "lack of adequate staff." Foster, *States Are Stiffening Licensure Standards, Study Shows,* MODERN HOSPITAL, Aug. 1965 at 128, 129.

According to a recent survey of state licensing laws conducted for the Public Health Service's National Center for Health Statistics, 47 states had provisions in their law for suspension or revocation of hospital licensure. In 1968 there were reported 10 formal hearings to show cause why licenses should not be revoked. Twenty-three hospitals had renewal of their licenses refused or had their licenses revoked. In 1968 states reporting revocations or refusal to renew were: Alabama (3); Arizona (2); Indiana (2); Michigan (6); Mississippi (1); Nebraska (2); Utah (2); West Virginia (4); and Wyoming (1). Data as to the mean numbers of beds in these hospitals is not reported. SURVEYS & RESEARCH CORPORATION, STATE LAWS & REGULATIONS FOR LICENSING HOSPITALS, NURSING HOMES, & OTHER MEDICAL CARE AND RESIDENT CARE FACILITIES table 8A (1969) (report prepared for the National Center for Health Statistics).

(16) In 1965, Fry pointed out that not one institution of higher education offered any program for the training of directors of licensing agencies. Consequently, directors of licensing bureaus − and their subordinates − derived most of their knowledge and experience from the program itself. H. FRY, *supra* note 11, at 88. Moreover, the persons who do the inspection of health facilities are typically nurses, sanitarians, and engineers.

(17) *Id.* at 43.

(18) *Id.* at 38. *See also* A. SOMERS, HOSPITAL REGULATION: THE DILEMMA OF PUBLIC POLICY (1969).

(19) A. Somers, *These Are the Questions About Regulation. What Kind? How Much? By Whom? Why?,* MODERN HOSPITAL, Sept. 1969, at 137, 141.

(20) *See, e.g.,* MICH. COMP. LAWS ANN. § 331.411 *et seq.* (Supp. 1970); N.Y. PUB. HEALTH LAW § 2800 *et seq.* (McKinney Supp. 1969), discussed in text accompanying notes 56-64 *infra.*

(21) The major sources of accreditation, in addition to JCAH, are AMA approval for internship and residency programs; cancer program approved by the American College of Surgeons; medical school accreditation by the Liaison Committee of the AMA and Association of American Medical Colleges; professional nursing school approved by the National League for Nursing; practical nurse training program approved by the National League for Nursing; membership in Council of Teaching Hospitals of the Association of American Medical Colleges: and classification as a participating hospital by Blue Cross.

(22) The original founding members were the American Medical Association, the American Hospital Association, the American College of Physicians, the American College of Surgeons, and the Canadian Medical Association. The Canadian Medical Association has since dropped out to form its own accrediting body in Canada. Recently, JCAH has added one representative each from the American Association of Homes for the Aging and the American Nursing Home Association.

(23) Any hospital listed with the American Hospital Association and containing a specified minimum of beds can request to be accredited by the JCAH. The hospital is notified several weeks before the visit that an accreditation survey is going to take place. If there is failure to meet the Standards of Accreditation, a hospital may still be granted provisional accreditation. Unfortunately, the Standards do not establish criteria as to when

provisional accreditation is appropriate. Current practice is to grant provisional accreditation for one year only, after which the hospital is resurveyed.

(24) Only a few states have incorporated JCAH standards into their licensing laws and have made JCAH accreditation a condition of licensure; withdrawal of accreditation would have serious implications in such states. Withdrawal of accreditation would also seriously impair a hospital's ability to attract capable residents and interns.

(25) While a list is published annually containing names of accredited hospitals, a patient would have no direct way of knowing a hospital had been refused accreditation. The JCAH will not release information concerning which hospitals have had accreditation withdrawn or have been refused accreditation. It will inform the public only whether a hospital is accredited and, if not accredited, whether the hospital applied for accreditation. From this information, it is possible to conjecture which hospitals have failed, but it is first necessary for an astute "consumer" of hospital services to ask the right questions.

(26) 42 U.S.C. § 139bb (Supp. I, 1965).

(27) JCAH, *Standards for Hospital Accreditation*, in FIVE BASIC PUBLICATIONS OF THE JOINT COMMISSION ON HOSPITAL ACCREDITATION (1964).

(28) JCAH, Standards for Accreditation of Hospitals (1969). It should be noted that in at least one very significant respect the revision of JCAH Standards may have resulted in lower standards. With regard to the important subject of required consultations, the revised draft only states that "the use of consultations, and the qualifications of the consultant should be reviewed as part of medical care evaluation." *Id.* at 22 (Interpretation section to Standard III). The New York licensing provisions discussed in note 56, *infra,* contain detailed provisions relating to surgical consultations, particularly in complicated obstetric cases. The former JCAH standards required consultation in such cases and in all cases in which the patient was not a good medical or surgical risk, the diagnosis was obscure, or there was doubt as to the best therapeutic measures to be utilized. *Standards, supra* note 27, at 6.

(29) A list of 26 demands was presented to JCAH by the National Welfare Rights Organization in Chicago on June 18, 1970. These demands are set forth in Appendix A. *See also* MODERN HOSPITAL, July 1970, at 29-32.

(30) HOSPITALS (GUIDE ISSUE), Aug. 1, 1969, pt. 2, at 494-95. Hospitals may be registered by the AHA when an application form is submitted stating that the hospital 1. has at least six beds, and the average length of stay is at least 24 hours; 2. is constructed, equipped, and maintained to insure patient safety and uncrowded and sanitary facilities; 3. will allow physicians to admit patients; 4. has an organized medical staff and bylaws approved by the governing body; 5. shall submit evidence of regular care of the patient by a physician; 6. maintains medical records on all patients; 7. shall make available nursing services; 8. shall offer services more intensive than those required merely for room and board, personal services, and general nursing care; 9. shall make available minimal surgical or obstetrical facilities, relatively complete diagnostic and treatment facilities, diagnostic x-ray services, and clinical laboratory services for all patients. AHA, Requirements for Accepting Hospitals for Registration (approved Feb. 4-5, 1965). For a summary of hospitals approved by JCAH by number of beds in each state, compared with non-JCAH hospitals in each state by number of beds, see Appendix C.

(31) *See* MODERN HOSPITAL, June 1968, at 36, Feb. 1969, at 47-48, Feb. 1970, at 36B. *See also* note 1 *supra.*

(32) HOSPITALS, May 16, 1970, at 119; HOSPITAL WEEK, Sept. 4, 1970,

at 36. *See* note 1 *supra.*

(33) The act defines a hospital as eligible to participate in the program when it

"(1) is primarily engaged in providing, by or under the supervision of physicians, to inpatients (A) diagnostic services and therapeutic services for medical diagnosis, treatment, and care of injured, disabled, or sick persons;
(2) maintains clinical records on all patients;
(3) has bylaws in effect with respect to its staff of physicians;
(4) has a requirement that every patient must be under the care of a physician;
(5) provides 24-hour nursing service rendered or supervised by a registered professional nurse, and has a licensed practical nurse or registered professional nurse on duty at all times;
(6) has in effect a hospital utilization review plan which meets the requirements of subsection (k) of this section;
(7) in the case of an institution in any State in which State or applicable local law provides for the licensing of hospitals, (A) is licensed pursuant to such law or (B) is approved, by the agency of such State or locality responsible for licensing hospitals, as meeting the standards established for such licensing
. . . ."

42 U.S.C. § 1395x(e)(1-7) (Supp. I, 1965). This and subsequent footnotes refer to the sections as numbered in the codification rather than in the Act.

(34) *Id.* § 1395x(e)(8).

(35) 20 C.F.R. § 405.1001 *et seq.* (1970). Similar Conditions of Participation or Coverage have been established for extended care facilities, *id.* § 405.1101 *et seq.,* home health services, *id.* § 405.1201 *et seq.,* clinical laboratories, *id.* § 405.1301 *et seq.,* and portable x-ray services, *id.* § 405.1401 *et seq.*

(36) 42 U.S.C. § 1395x(e)(8) (Supp. I, 1965). This provision is subject to an important exception which will be discussed at p. 322 *infra.*

(37) *Id.* R 1395bb.

(38) Interview with Pearl Bierman, Bureau of Health Standards, Health Services and Manpower Administration, Dec. 12, 1969. Legislative history sustains this interpretation. The Senate Finance Committee Report accompanying the 1965 Ammendments to the Social Security Act states that "Hospitals accredited by the Joint Commission on Accreditation of Hospitals would be conclusively presumed to meet all the conditions for participation, except for the requirement of utilization review." S. REP. No. 404, 89th Cong., 1st Sess. 29 (1965).

(39) The state agency, however, must determine compliance with the utilization review requirements. 42 U.S.C. § 1395x(e)(6) (Supp. I, 1965).

(40) This practice is based on section 1864 of the act, 42 U.S.C. § 1395aa (Supp. I, 1965), which says that the Secretary must make contracts with participating states "under which the services of the State health agency or other appropriate State agency (or the appropriate local agencies) will be utilized by him for the purpose of determining whether an institution therein is a hospital
. . . ."

(41) State agency Medicare surveys are reviewed, however, by Bureau of Health Insurance and Public Health Service staff in Social Security Administration regional offices. Additionally, there are program review teams, composed of federal surveyors, who make independent surveys of Medicare facilities to evaluate the state agency's performance and to assure uniform application of the Conditions of Participation. Letter to authors from Morris B. Levy, Assistant Bureau Director, Division of State Operations, Bureau of Health

Insurance, Sept. 11, 1970.

The recently issued report of the Task Force on Medicaid and Related Programs has commented:

Minimum requirements of training, experience and education for State surveyors for Medicaid and Medicare and their immediate supervisors should be developed by HEW. The Department should also be empowered to develop equivalency criteria to be used as a measure in determining whether individuals meet the minimum requirements for surveyors.

REPORT OF THE TASK FORCE ON MEDICAID AND RELATED PROGRAMS 46 (1970).

(42) 20 C.F.R. § 405.1002 (1970).

(43) *Id.* § 405.1005(c).

(44) *Id.* § 405.1010 provides that "Where, by reason of factors such as isolated location or absence of sufficient facilities in an area, the denial of eligibility of an institution to participate would seriously limit the access of beneficiaries to participating hospitals, an institution may, upon recommendation by the State agency, be approved by the Secretary as a provider of services."

(45) *Id.* § 405.1011 provides that "An institution which has not been determined by the Secretary as being in compliance with all of the Conditions, or which is not accepted to become a participating hospital may, nevertheless, be paid under the program for emergency services furnished provided it meets requirements of section 1861(e)(1), (2), (3), (4), (5), and (7) of the Act, as amended." In 1968, 35,740 emergency bills were paid ($9 million total), but the Social Security Administration paid only 4448 emergency bills in 1969 ($1.4 million total). The decrease may be due to provider hospital compliance with title VI and stricter emergency payment criteria. Telephone converstion with Morris B. Levy, Sept. 9, 1970.

(46) Cashman, Bierman & Myers, *The "Why" of Conditions of Participation in the Medicare Program,* 83 PUB. HEALTH REP. 714, 718 (1968).

(47) It appears that state Medicare agencies have been furnished some federal guidelines for evaluating compliance with the Conditions of Participation. "These guidelines explain in detail what the state surveyors should evaluate in determining the nature and severity of each deficiency, and the relative greater significance of certain requirements as opposed to others." Letter of Morris B. Levy, *supra* note 41.

(48) Letter to authors from Morris B. Levy, Aug. 24, 1970. Detailed data as to certification status of participating hospitals are set forth in Appendix B.

(49) Hospitals may be certified as Medicare providers under special circumstances despite deficiencies where no other facility is available in a particular geographical area. *See* 20 C.F.R. § 405.1010 (1970).

(50) It should be pointed out that the sixteen Conditions of Participation are qualified by a large number of corollary standards. It may be difficult for any one hospital to comply with each Condition. There are fewer than 600 hospitals participating in Medicare (other than those accredited by JCAH) which have been determined to meet all of the requirements. Letter of Morris B. Levy, *supra* note 41.

Not all deficiencies noted by state agencies necessarily adversely affect the type of care offered patients. For example, there may be instances where a committee may fail to meet each month, or fail to produce timely minutes of its meeting. This would have to be noted as a deficiency, although it might not necessarily reflect on the quality of care offered. The Bureau of Health Insurance further believes it is easier to obtain corrections of deficiencies when a facility is participating in the program and the state agency is able to work with it to obtain uprading of conditions. *Id.*

(51) *Id.*

(52) *Id.*

(53) Cashman & Meyers, *Medicare: Standards of Service in a New Program – Licensure, Certification, Accreditation,* 57 AM. J. PUB. HEALTH 1107, 1115 (1967). It may be further noted that after Boston City Hospital lost its accreditation in early 1970, the Medicare Conditions of Participation were applied to the hospital. It was found to be in substantial compliance therewith and has never stopped receiving Medicare payments.

(54) It should be noted, however, that the 1970 JCAH standards represent a substantial improvement over the grossly inadequate 1964 version. In addition, JCAH has recently taken steps to improve its survey procedures by experimenting with three-man survey teams. Henceforth, surveys will be conducted every two years rather than every three years.

(55) N.Y. PUB. HEALTH LAW § 2800 *et seq.* (McKinney Supp. 1969).

(56) The New York Hospital Code, 10 N.Y.C.R.R. § 700.1 *et seq.* (1969), contains a number of other provisions relating to quality of care which should be noted. With regard to ambulatory services, section 703.3 provides that facilities must submit to the department a plan providing for "comprehensive medical evaluation for such patients on a periodic basis" and for "continuity of care when such patients require hospitalization, home care or emergency care when such services in the facility are not available." Further, that section provides that outpatient facilities should schedule "not more than five patients per hour with an allowance of at least 30 minutes for the first complete patient workup."

Hospitals are also required to establish written admission and discharge policies, including rules governing emergency admissions and policies concerning advance deposits, insurance agreements, and other financial considerations. *Id.* § 720.7(a). No patient is to be transferred when such transfer would create a medical hazard to the person unless such transfer is considered by a physician to be in the person's best interest despite the potential hazard of movement. A transfer may be made "only after prior notification to an appropriate medical facility." *Id.* § 720.7(j). Another provision of interest in protecting indigent patients is the requirement that no patient receiving services under Medicaid "shall be deprived the right of free choice of a duly qualified physician on the medical staff of the hospital regardless of the type of bed accommodation to which the patient may be assigned." *Id.* § 720.7(m). With regard to emergency rooms, the Code requires, *inter alia,* that hospitals "having 40,000 or more emergency room visits annually shall have a full-time attending or resident physician-in-charge and he or a physician-designee shall be accessible 24 hours a day." *Id.* § 720.17(a). A committee of the medical staff must review clinical and research work performed with the written and informed consent of the patients." *Id.* § 721.1(c)(2). Detailed rules are set forth with regard to the necessity of surgical consultations, particularly in complicated obstetric cases. *Id.* § 721.1(c)(3). Surgery and treatment of complicated obstetric cases are restricted to board-certified physicians. These regulations were promulgated pursuant to authority conferred by the state's public health law. N.Y. PUB. HEALTH LAW § 2803 (McKinney Supp. 1969).

(57) N.Y. PUB. HEALTH LAW § 2802 (McKinney Supp. 1969).

(58) MICH. COMP. LAWS ANN. § 331.411 *et seq.* (Supp. 1970).

(59) The statute provides that

[the state director] shall establish a comprehensive system of licensing for all hospitals in the state in order to protect the public through the assurance that hospitals provide the facilities and the ancillary supporting services necessary to enable a high quality of patient care by licensed physicians. All hospitals . . . shall meet the minimum standards authorized by this act . . . . *Id.* § 331.411.

(60) *Id.* § 331.413. The health council is also given the power to advise and consult with the state director of public health concerning the administration of the state's Hill-Burton program.

(61) *Id.* § 331.415.

(62) *Id.* § 331.423.

(63) *Id.* § 331.422.

(64) With respect to Medicaid, section 1902a(22)(B) of title 19, 42 U.S.C. § 1396a(22)(B) (Supp. I, 1965), requires states to describe in their state plans "the standards, for private or public institutions in which recipients of medical assistance under the plan may receive care or services, that will be utilized by the State authority or authorities responsible for establishing and maintaining such standards." No minimum federal standards or Conditions of Participation are established in Medicaid. Therefore states are completely free to prescribe their own standards. A preliminary survey of state plan material has indicated that most states have simply prescribed that hospitals be licensed under state law; a substantial number of states have further required that the hospital be a certified Medicare provider. It appears that no state has adopted a separate set of standards for regulating hospital quality of care for title XIX pruposes. The recently issued report of the Task Force on Medicaid and Related Programs has highlighted the need for uniform Medicare and Medicaid standards.

> A legislative amendment is needed requiring uniform provisions and unified State standard-setting, certification, and consultation functions with respect to providers of service under both Medicaid and Medicare. (To the extent possible, also, consistent with desired State flexibility to exceed Federal minimum standards, State-controlled licensure of health facilities and agencies should be integrated with those related functions.) The State agency with primaty responsibility for health functions in the State should be responsible for all standards functions. Incentives, guidance and assistance should be provided to the States in bringing this about.

REPORT OF THE TASK FORCE ON MEDICAID AND RELATED PROGRAMS 46 (1970). H.R. 17550, 91st Cong., 2d Sess. (1970), the proposed Social Security Amendments of 1970, would have strengthened the state agency standard-setting functions, for, as passed by the House of Representatives, section 238(a) provided that the state health agency would be responsible for establishing review of the appropriateness and *quality of care* and *services* furnished to recipients of medical assistance under the plan. H.R. 17550 did not pass finally in the 91st Congress but is scheduled to be reintroduced in some form in the 92nd Congress.

(65) These internecine disputes primarily involve responsibility for medical care in the hospital and really raise the question: Who runs the hospital? Hospital administrators and doctors have substantially varying opinions on this critical subject.

(66) Recently a coalition of consumer groups, including the National Welfare Rights Organization, American Patients Association, and Consumer Federation of America, have sought representation on the board of JCAH, and the JCAH agreed to consider the issue of consumer representation. At time of writing, no decision has been reached.

(67) For example, doctors and administrators are particularly sensitive to such questions as malpractice liability. As such, they are likely to take particular care to prevent JCAH from establishing minimum standards at a level that would tend to raise the legal standard of "due care" in a malpractice suit. Their special interest and defensive attitude in this area could prevent JCAH's adoption of a

standard which would be very desirable form the patient's point of view.

(68) This power, together with the fact that JCAH represents a particular constellation of groups with interests not identical to those of patients, raises some questions concerning whether Congress acted constitutionally when it incorporated JCAH standards into Medicare by creating a conclusive presumption that JCAH-approved hospitals complied with the Conditions of Participation and prohibited the Secretary from developing Conditions that would be higher than comparable JCAH standards. It is critical to note that Congress did not adopt by reference existing JCAH standards but in effect delegated the authority to JCAH to promulgate standards in the future with regard to accreditation of hospitals. These future standards are to be a binding ceiling on the standards set by the Secretary, and if JCAH were to lower its requirements the Secretary would have to change the Conditions of Participation. Many such delegations to a private entity of prospective rule-making authority have been invalidated in the state courts. *See, e.g.,* Group Health Ins. v. Howell, 40 N.J. 436, 193 A.2d 103 (1963); Fink v. Cole, 302 N.Y. 216, 97 N.E.2d 873 (1951); State v. Emery, 55 Ohio St. 364, 45 N.E. 319 (1896); Hillman v. Northern Wasco County People's Util. Dist., 213 Ore. 264, 323 P.2d 664 (1958); State *ex rel.* Kirschner v. Urquhart, 50 Wash. 2d 131, 310 P.2d 261 (1957).

While the delegation-of-authority doctrine has been historically suspect since Schechter Poultry Corp. v. United States, 295 U.S. 495 (1935), and Carter v. Carter Coal Co., 298 U.S. 238 (1936), it should be noted that the *Carter* case, which involved delegation of authority to a group of producers and workers in the coal industry to reach industry-wide binding agreements with regard to wages and prices, has never been expressly overruled. Commentators, of course, have been critical of *Carter. See, e.g.,* Jaffe, *Law Making by Private Groups,* 51 HARV. L. REV. 201 (1937). Substantial critiques have been made of the state delegation cases also. *See* Note, *The State Courts and Delegation of Public Authority to Private Groups,* 67 HARV. L. REV. 1398 (1954).

Federal courts which have considered delegations to private groups have sustained such delegations where the standards of the private association are subject to the approval of a federal agency. *See* R.H. Johnson & Co. v. SEC, 198 F.2d 690 (2d Cir. 1952); McManus v. CAB, 286 F.2d 414 (2d Cir. 1961). *See also* Crain v. First Nat'l Bank, 324 F.2d 532 (9th Cir. 1963), in which the court sustained a delegation by distinguishing between a delegation to a private entity of ministerial functions and a delegation of rule-making functions. The power delegated to the JCAH is tantamount to prospective rule-making power; moreover, the Secretary of HEW does not "approve" JCAH standards revisions. While the delegation argument has disturbing implications in that it might invalidate statutes that make entry into the professions conditional upon graduation from accredited schools (in effect a legislative delegation of prospective rule making), perhaps it is best to quote Professor Davis on delegation of authority: "The case law has not crystallized any consistent principles, either in the federal courts or in the state courts." I.K.DAVIS, ADMINISTRATIVE LAW TREATISE § 2.14 (1958).

(69) HEW has taken the position that it can adopt no standards which are more strict or more comprehensive than JCAH standards, even with regard to subject matter on which JCAH has not spoken. *See* note 74 *infra.*

(70) The report of the JCAH inspection team is held in the strictest confidence by JCAH and is not even released to HEW. Apparently HEW has protested this policy but has never challenged its legal validity in court.

(71) HIBAC was established by the Medicare legislation to monitor the program and make annual reports to Congress concerning the need for changes

in the legislation. *See* 42 U.S.C. § 1395dd (Supp. I, 1965).

(72) HIBAC, 1966-67 ANNUAL REPORT ON MEDICARE 9.

(73) 42 U.S.C. § 1395x(e)(8) (Supp. I, 1965). The effect of the second sentence of section 1395z will be discussed at pp. 322-23 *infra.*

(74) This was confirmed in an interview by one of the authors with Pearl Bierman, *supra* note 38. Miss Bierman indicated that it was HEW's position that if JCAH chose to lower or omit certain standards, HEW was bound to do the same. HEW's position contains the latent premise that JCAH's failure to address a particular aspect of quality of care is tantamount to an assertion by JCAH that such an aspect is not to be subject to standards. The legislative history of title XVIII lends support to neither position and does not illuminate the meaning of the word "comparable" in 42 U.S.C. § 1395x(e)(8).

(75) 42 U.S.C. § 1395x(e)(6) (Supp. I, 1965).

(76) *Id.* § 1395z.

(77) Letter of Morris B. Levy, *supra* note 41.

(78) 42 U.S.C. § 1395bb (Supp. I, 1965).

(79) HIBAC, *supra* note 72, at 10.

(80) 20 C.F.R. § 405.1007(a)(2) (1970).

(81) Contents of the JCAH inspection reports become public only when they are released by the contracting hospital.

(82) The JCAH may be in the process of officially codifying such a grievance hearing procedure with regard to accreditation inspections. Two of the consumer demands made to JCAH were that:

> . . . A formal procedure should be established for the submission of complaints to the Commission. The procedure should include provision for surprise inspections to be made by the Commission upon a showing of good course. Also, there should be a mechanism for appeal if the complaint is not acted upon.
>
> Surveyers must hold confidential interviews with selected members of the various echelons of the medical staff, as well as with any representative of any organized segment of the medical staff, allied professional health workers, or other hospital employees, whenever such meetings are requested during the course of an accreditation inspection, in order to determine their evaluation of the quality of care rendered by the hospital services with which they are most familiar. Surveyors should also, on a random basis, interview selected patients in each major service, including the emergency service. Where requested by the community served by the hospital, a hearing should be held, wherein the community can voice views and comments concerning the hospital. Notice of a pending accreditation must be posted in clear and conspicuous places throughout the hospital so that all medical staff, including house staff and other hospital employees have an opportunity to request a meeting with the surveying staff.

In fact, at the request of house staff and community groups in the District of Columbia such a public hearing was held shortly after the completion of the accreditation visit. The accreditation team heard complaints from house staff, ex-patients, and community representatives concerning conditions at the hospital. A lengthy document containing evidence of violations of JCAH standards was presented to the surveyors. It is not known to what extent JCAH has considered the allegations of staff and community. Since these inspection reports are considered confidential documents, it is doubtful that staff and community representatives will ever know whether findings were made with regard to their complaints.

(83) As to the quasi-public status of accrediting bodies like JCAH, see Note, 67 HARV. L. REV. 1398, *supra* note 67; Comment, *The Legal Status of the*

Educational Accrediting Agency: Problems in Judicial Supervision and Governmental Regulation, 52 CORNELL L.Q. 104, 117 (1966). The term *quasi-public* denotes legal obligations to perform the accrediting function fairly and objectively with procedural devices for appeal of a decision not to accredit. The extent of these procedural obligations, and the devices for achieving such objectives, have not been delineated by the courts. The U.S. Court of Appeals for the District of Columbia has recently considered the obligations of a voluntary educational accrediting body to accredit a proprietary institution and has held that because of the nature of proprietary institutions, the voluntary accrediting association need not extend its evaluation to such an institution. Marjorie Webster Junior College v. Middle States Ass'n of Colleges & Secondary Schools, 432 F.2d 650 (D.C. Cir. June 30, 1970).

(84) *See* 20 C.F.R. § 405.1502(a) (1970), which requires the Secretary to make findings of fact and conclusions as to compliance of a participating institution with the Conditons of Participation.

(85) There would appear to be no due process right for patients and dissident medical staff to participate in the Secretary's certification function by submitting evidence, even through informal hearings, on the issue of noncompliance with his Conditions of Participation. Such participation, however, would be desirable for the reasons outlined above. Recently, the U.S. Court of Appeals for the District of Columbia ruled that welfare recipients have standing to intervene in conformity hearings called by HEW against particular states on matters pertaining to the administration of federal welfare programs. National Welfare Rights Organization v. Finch, 429 F.2d 725 (D.C. Cir. 1970). In this case, however, a formal hearing was afforded by statute, and the sole question before the court was whether welfare recipients could intervene therein on the issue of nonconformity. Under Medicare no hearing is afforded to providers or other interested parties under the statute with regard to the certification of hospitals. In a similar situation, involving the right to judicial review by a competitor bank of the authorization granted by the Comptroller of Currency to establish a branch of a national bank, it was held that neither due process nor the Administrative Procedure Act required the holding of an administrative hearing for that decision. First Nat'l Bank v. Saxon, 352 F.2d 267 (4th Cir. 1965), *aff'd*, 385 U.S. 252 (1966). Dissenting, Judge Sobeloff argued,

> Rightly, I think, the majority holds that this interest is sufficient to entitle the Smithfield bank to appeal from the Comptroller's decision granting the application. Smithfield contends, however, that this right of appeal is meaningless unless it has previously been given an *effective* chance to be heard before the Comptroller reaches his final decision on the merits of the application. With this contention I agree, and would hold that such an opportunity, if requested, is a prerequisite to a valid decision on the part of the Comptroller. The right of the plaintiff to appear is of little worth to it if there is no disclosure of the pertinent data and if the Comptroller may make up his mind in a private huggermugger with the applicant.
>
> Smithfield's argument is that it should be allowed to inform itself and express its views before the Comptroller arrives at his decision which will be accorded a large measure of finality in any appeal.

352 F.2d at 273-74. *See also* Hahn v. Gottlieb, 430 F.2d 1243 (1st Cir. Aug. 14, 1970), in which it was held that tenants had no constitutional right to a hearing before FHA approval of rent increases in § 221(d)(3) housing.

THE JOHNS HOPKINS MEDICAL INSTITUTIONS:
A CASE STUDY IN ADMINISTRATION

Steven Muller

The Gilman Lecture, named after Daniel Coit Gilman, was founded by the Avalon Foundation to establish better communications between the humanities and medicine. In a lecture that bears this distinguished title, you may wonder why I am talking about administration. In order to make my peace with the Avalon Foundation and to introduce what I am going to say, I would like to begin with a favorite quote of mine from Malcolm Muggeridge's book, "Affairs of the Heart." It will tell you something about why I think that a lecture on administration is not inappropriate. He wrote:

> I have always been deeply interested in the administrative side of love, which I find more absorbing than its purely erotic aspects. What Lady Chatterley and her game-keeper did in the woods is, to me, of only passing interest compared with how they got there, what arrangements were made for a shelter in the case of inclement weather, and for refreshments, how they accounted for their absence, whether either party could recover incidental expenses, and if so how? This attitude is, after all, not so unreasonable. Most great generals have admitted that planning campaigns and winning victories in the field is relatively easy compared with arranging transport and supplies. An army, Napoleon said, in one of his most celebrated remarks, marches on its stomach. So do lovers. If the administrative arrangements are faulty, the campaign which follows cannot but be laborious, and even victory brings little satisfaction.

If you substitute medicine for love, I think you will see what I mean. I want then to talk about The John Hopkins Medical Institutions as a case study in administration. The first question is what are "The Johns Hopkins Medical Institutions"? Its components I think you all could identify more readily than I: The Johns Hopkins Hospital, The Johns Hopkins University School of Medicine. The Johns Hopkins University School of Hygiene and Public Health, a new School of Health Services, and as adjuncts, the Columbia and East Baltimore Medical Plans, the Welch Medical Library, and related units like the Kennedy Institute, and others. The large cluster of these is mostly on this East Baltimore campus, and when we say "The Johns Hopkins Medical Institutions" that is what we mean.

In administrative terms, of course. The Johns Hopkins Medical Institutions are not an entity. They still look to me like a loose federation of components living in precarious interdependence. On the other hand, these components cannot do without each other. It is quite clear that whether they are organized as a unit or not, they constitute in the aggregate one of this nation's and one of the world's, major academic health science centers. There is a unity in the making. There is a community.

The question is how do The Johns Hopkins Medical Institutions operate together? The structural arrangements now are a bit awkward. There are two different boards; the Boards of Trustees of the University and of the Hospital, representing two different corporations with two different systems of management, and, in some ways, two distinctively separate sets of operational responsibilities. There are a few trustees who serve on both boards, but essentially the two boards are separate. The real bridge, and a slender one, is a joint committee of trustees, composed of four trustees from each of the two institutions, and chaired since its establishment by the President of the University.

Because there are separate financial and accounting systems, we have developed a rather interesting device, an annual joint agreement, to bridge the financial gap. It is a very comprehensive, and to some an incomprehensible, piece of paper which regulates the dollar flow between the University and the Hospital. In the most simplified terms, the Hospital pays for the time of a lot of University people: and the University pays for the very large amount of Hospital space it uses, and for the time and efforts of a large number of nonprofessional people. The joint agreement, however, does not constitute the basis for any kind of unified administration.

There is no longer a vice-president for medical affairs, which in the past has been a position in the University but not in The Johns Hopkins Medical Institutions. For those men who held it, the position, with its limited authority, must have been very difficult to fill.

There is one other organization that should be mentioned. The Medical Planning and Development Committee represents the administrative principals of The Johns Hopkins Medical Institutions. Its membership includes the individual in charge of the Hospital, the Deans, the University President and other administrators. The Committee is either a real or a potential administrative cabinet for the Medical Institutions, and operates directly under the auspices of the joint trustees.

These are existing arrangements and at the moment they have been supplemented by the unique decision to have a dual President: one human being who serves both as the President of the University and as President of the Hospital. I do not intend to describe now how this administrative structure may look in the future. One reason is that I don't know. Another is that even if I did know, this lecture would not be the appropriate place to go into that kind of detail. I spend more of my time as the President of the University than as the President of the Hospital. This has to be understood in the context that I spend a great deal of time as President of the University on problems of East Baltimore. Responsibility for day-to-day operations of the Hospital is vested in Dr. Robert Heyssel, the Executive Vice-President and Director as of October 1. I deal on a daily basis with the Deans of the University Schools in East Baltimore: Dean Morgan, Dean Hume, Dean Peterson of the new school, and Dr. David Price whom I am going to nominate to the trustees as Executive Director of the Medical Planning and Development Committee, and who is serving now as the Senior Staff Associate of the President in East Baltimore.

Instead of going into how the two boards eventually will relate to each other and what we will do in administrative detail, I would like to share with you my perspective about The Johns Hopkins Medical Institutions. In order to do that I have to make one other qualifying remark or state a precondition. It is my assumption, not only in this lecture but in fact, that there is an entity formed by The Johns Hopkins Medical Institutions, that it is one of the major academic health science centers in the United States, and that its most fundamental mission is to be the best academic health science center in the world.

In administrative terms, The Johns Hopkins Medical Institutions are now drowning in their own growth. We have become too big and too complex to do business in the old way, and institutionally we have not yet found a new way to operate.

I will comment on this from my own point of view, but I would first like to call to your attention some analytical thoughts which I have drawn from an article by Larry E. Greiner, Associate Professor of Organizational Behavior at the Harvard Business School. This article appeared in the July-August 1972 issue of the Harvard Business Review (pp 37-46). It is entitled "Evolution and Revolution as Organizations Grow." It seems to me that it has some interesting applicability to where The Johns Hopkins Institutions are today and where they are going.

The basic argument of Greiner's article is that growing organizations move through five distinguishable phases of development. Each contains a relatively calm period of growth, and ends with a management crisis. Greiner uses the term "evolution" to describe prolonged periods of growth when no major upheaval occurs in organization practices, and the term "revolution" to describe periods of substantial tumult in organizational life. The author, I would say, is to a large extent a determinist, in that he argues that each phase is strongly influenced by the previous phase, and that a management with a sense of its own organization's history can anticipate and prepare for its next developmental crisis. In other words these crises follow a pre-determined pattern.

Mr. Greiner argues that management problems and principles are rooted in time, and that a close study of growth, over time, of a number of corporations indicates a rather precise model of organizational development. In effect, for those of you that have read Marx or Hegel, he develops a dialectic. His five phases invariably follow each other, and he argues each phase is both affected by the previous phase and is cause for the next phase.

The first phase he identifies is creativity. For Hopkins this would coincide with the period of our founding beginning nearly a hundred years ago. Summarized very briefly, this phase of creativity involves a prolonged period of growth, along the lines of creativity established by the original founders. It then results in a leadership crisis which is a direct result of the first period of successful growth, insofar as the organization simply outgrows its foundations. The first revolution then follows the evolutionary phase of creativity. The need in the first revolution is to provide direction, which in Greiner's terms means to improve business management practices and put more emphasis on the role of effective administration. Incidentally, each revolution may not be successful and the organization may fail.

In Greiner's terms, the result of that first revolution is stronger direction, and then a second prolonged evolutionary growth phase occurs. Greiner goes on to say that after the second evolutionary growth phase, marked by effective direction, there is a second revolution. The directive hierarchy has become too restrictive, and the second revolution results in very substantial delegation of authority and a more decentralized organizational structure.

If successful, this results in a prolonged third phase of evolutionary growth marked by very substantial delegation. As I reflect upon The Johns Hopkins Medical Institutions, it seems to me that we have passed through the third phase, marked by very substantial delegation, and have just come into the third crisis. The third revolutionary crisis Greiner identifies as a control crisis. He writes that when an organization reaches the end of the third evolutionary phase "top executives sense that they are losing control over a highly diversified field operation. Autonomous field managers prefer to run their own shows without coordinating plans, money, technology, and manpower with the rest of the organization. Freedom breeds a parochial attitude. Hence, the phase-three revolution is under way when top management seeks to regain control over the total company. Some top managements attempt a return to centralized management, which usually fails because of the vast scope of operations. Those companies that move ahead find a new solution in the use of special coordination techniques."

Greiner observes that in the wake of the third revolution there is a fourth evolutionary period, marked by coordination. This he says is characterized by the use of formal systems for achieving greater coordination. Then he stipulates that this fourth evolutionary phase of coordination produces a fourth crisis —

the red tape crisis — which results in the final evolutionary phase of collaboration.

As I translate this analysis into our terms, I find that we seem to be in the middle of Greiner's third revolution. This would mean that our management problem is to make a successful transition from a prolonged evolutionary phase of growth, marked by delegation, to a new evolutionary phase of growth, marked by coordination. If we do not master this transition, we will suffer and perhaps fail as an organization because of a control crisis that we cannot solve. Some of the details of Greiner's analysis are so heavily drawn in corporate, business and industrial terms that it is difficult to translate them to The Johns Hopkins Medical Institutions. I would like to suggest that it is a useful analysis from our standpoint and I would like to supplement it by one other observation. It is true that not only have we gone through a prolonged period of growth in the period between World War II and the recent past, but this was abnormal growth both in terms of the amount of growing that went on in a very short time, and in that the growth was largely caused by external factors, particularly public funds invested in health care and the health sciences after World War II.

Fundamentally in terms of administrative analysis, I think The Johns Hopkins Medical Institutions face two absolute imperatives at this time. One is to achieve coordination in Greiner's terms. We must not go back to centralized management which, as he says, usually fails, but must achieve effective coordination of a substantial amount of decentralization and delegation. The second, and equally important imperative is for The Johns Hopkins Medical Institutions to attempt again to control and master its own growth: to take charge as much as it can of its own affairs; to set its own priorities, not simply to react to others; to be in a more and more political world, accountable to all, but dictated to by none.

It is useless and mischievous, in my judgment, to equate bigness with bestness, or size with quality. They usually are not related. I am more interested in quality than I am in size. It is my view that a future evolutionary phase of growth for The Johns Hopkins Medical Institutions should be above all qualitative growth rather than quantitative growth. There is something very fundamental about the traditions of these institutions. We are a human enterprise, and there is really such a thing as human dimension. Hopkins became great because it existed on a scale that allowed the human dimension to flourish. We must find a way to restore the human dimension to our present growth and any future quantitative growth that we undertake. I do not believe that this is impossible, but it is going to take a kind of effort which I don't believe we've made yet. I think it is going to require a constellation of human universes, in which human beings can function well, and which can interact humanly and effectively with each other.

I wish I could tell you specifically how The Johns Hopkins Medical Institutions could accomplish this. At this stage, I cannot. What I can do is list eight basic principles and points in which I believe. I would not say that I am in the position to attempt to impose these on the Institutions, but in as far as I have a contribution to make they will be the guidelines by which I will orient much of my own thinking and much of my own action. These eight points, and they are quite uneven in substance and in no particular order, are as follows:

The first is that we have made as a unit, as The Johns Hopkins Medical Institutions, the decision to remain in East Baltimore. That decision was made before I came here, but I am pleased it was made because I am convinced that it was and is the right decision. It has enormous implications for us. It means above all that we must live with our neighbors because we cannot live only despite them. The effort for us to live with our neighbors is going to be a difficult challenge for us. I believe also that the decision to remain where we are is right because I do not believe that individuals or institutions can run away from problems. I think we have to face them where they are, and where we are. Obviously I suffer from the incurable disease of optimism, so I have hope, although no evidence or proof, that in the long run — some 20 or 30 years — the inner-city will be a better place to be than the suburbs. In part, this is also what the sociologists and students of administration call self-fulfilling prophesy. If we had moved out, we would be contributing to the further decay of the inner-city. Our decision to remain here forces us to act on the assumption that we are going to stay and do a good job of it. It requires an enormous new effort on our part to live up to that decision. We will try to live with our neighbors, to draw strength from them and to add strength to them.

The second point, a basic principle as far as I am concerned, is that above all The Johns Hopkins Medical Institutions are human institutions serving human health needs. I don't want to be misunderstood here, so I am going to say this twice. Patient care is only one of the things that we do in The Johns Hopkins Medical Institutions. But to the extent that we render patient care, I believe that the patient has absolute first priority. I am going to repeat that. I am not saying that patient care has first priority within The Johns Hopkins Medical Institutions as far as I am concerned. What I am saying is that patients have first priority whenever patients are involved. I am sorry to say that, as a newcomer and an outsider, in my brief encounter so far with these institutions, I have not unfailingly found this to be the case. I was mildly embarrassed that Dean Morgan in his introduction referred to my childhood experience in Germany. And yet, all of us are the products of our own experience. I grew up, unfortunately, in a society which treated people as objects. It is one thing that I find absolutely intolerable.

The third basic point is that we are now in a position, and here I speak more administratively, where we have to re-examine the internal administrative structure by which we have grown great. We must not destroy it, but make it more useful and more flexible. I am referring to the basic unit of American higher education and of American academic medicine — the department. There are two things about the departments at Johns Hopkins that are quite striking. They are desperately overloaded as administrative units, and they are organized traditionally along vertical lines on disciplines. They have fragmented into subspecialties. I don't think anyone needs to make the point any longer that we need what every institution like us needs now: interdisciplinary effort. I am not saying that there are no interdisciplinary efforts at Hopkins now. There have always been interdisciplinary efforts at Hopkins and some of the most brilliant things that have been done here have been done across disciplines. I am saying that it is terribly important for busy and brilliant people to work with institutional arrangements that facilitate rather than obstruct what is important.

The purely departmental structure is in many ways too much of an obstacle. We must find ways to make it as easy as possible administratively for people to work together, and I believe that interdisciplinary efforts can be effectively woven into the existing departmental structure. I would not ever wish to see the departments go, because I have seen nothing that works as well even when they are not working as well as we would like them to work. What I am suggesting is a two-ply approach which allows a departmental structure to be married to interdisciplinary units — we call them centers here.

Along with that goes a second problem: all enterprises require leadership. If you look coldly, analytically and administratively at the job description of the departmental chairman, you find an absolutely overloaded position. It is interesting to hear people on search committees for departmental chairmen say that they are looking for Renaissance men. I think that is an admirable ambition and probably quite an accurate description of what an excellent department chairman should be, but even Renaissance men cannot themselves bring about the entire Renaissance. It does seem from an administrative point of view that if there is to be continued effective delegation to the departments and to interdisciplinary units like centers, then there has to be effective performance at that level. There cannot be effective performance if the job is literally undoable. This isn't even administration; this is basic good sense, or basic electronics. If you overload your circuits you blow your fuses, and then the lights go out, and we can't afford that.

We have to find ways to make departmental chairmanships here viable. I have no precise prescription for that either, and I'm not sure that there is a simple formula that can be applied across the board to solve institution-wide problems. There must be effective administrative support systems in the department, to a degree that we have not achieved. We have to broaden the leadership base within our institutions, and not put too much of a leadership burden on too few people. Quite honestly, and without saying that I or others have reached a conclusion. I do believe that we will have to look at whether a term assignment for a departmental chairman is more satisfactory than the arrangement that we now have. One of the most hideous crimes that we can commit is to burn out our best people by exposing them on a semipermanent basis to an intolerable burden. This is not an easy matter to resolve, but is one we are going to have to try to solve together.

The fourth point is that we have to recognize, in using the description "academic health science center," that we are basically a university community, and that includes the Hospital, and therefore we have a unique commitment to research. At this particular time in the life of The Johns Hopkins Medical

Institutions, it may seem hardly necessary to make that point. Reasearch at Hopkins has flowered probably more than anything else in the past decade. Three or four years ago someone in my position talking about the importance of research would have sounded irrelevant because nothing was flourishing more. We face a period now where there is a shrinkage, and quite probably a continued and increasing shrinkage, of research support from external sources. Though we may have reacted in a time of affluence by building up research because external pressures encouraged it, we might seriously betray our character, our integrity and ourselves if we now cut it back in the same simple reaction to loss of outside support. We do face a period when we have to re-examine and then re-assert our commitment to the research mission here, and to its substantial support. When we talk about substantial support we will not be simply paying lip service, but we will be committing scarce dollars to keep something alive, something which has to stay alive and vigorous if this is to remain an academic health science center.

The fifth point is very important, I think, particularly for those people who are full-time faculty members in the University. We must re-evaluate and re-assert, and re-encourage the absolutely essential contributions to The Johns Hopkins Medical Institutions made by the part-time faculty. We cannot live without the part-time faculty, and there are at least two reasons why. One is, and this is something I say with deepening awareness in view of where I now sit, that it is simply foolish and untrue to pretend that The Johns Hopkins Hospital and The Johns Hopkins University faculty can always live in harmony because they always have parallel objectives. We can make no progress at all if we do not recognize that at times our priorities and objectives differ as between Hospital and full-time University faculty. It is very obvious that the Hospital has a primary service mission which operates around the clock, and the effort of the Hospital is to be always open at near full capacity. It is equally obvious, it seems to me, that full-time medical faculty who have very major and demanding academic responsibilities orient their patient care schedules around their academic responsibilities. That produces problems for the Hospital, just as the Hospital's obligations produce problems for the full-time medical faculty. This kind of gap can be bridged by a part-time faculty; it can't really be bridged by anyone else.

Even more important, the part-time faculty constitutes a reservoir of talent, a reservoir of energy and enthusiasm. It brings in a patient mix we need. It is the basis on which we have referrals. If we cease to be a national and international referral institution, we are to some extent dead as far as quality and reputation are concerned. Now we have an excellent part-time faculty, but since I've been here, I detect that some of them are not sure that their services are fully appreciated in the institution. Sometimes I don't know whether the full-time faculty is as vividly aware of the need for the part-time faculty as we all should be.

The sixth point is that I believe there is one area into which the academic divisions of the University in East Baltimore must move with much greater vigor.

The area is an inviting one; it is there for us to explore and to use. It is the area of continuing education. It seems to me obvious that at the pace at which knowledge and technology in the health sciences has expanded, what we are talking about here is not merely continuing education for adults or late bloomers or people who come on the scene late, but the consistent opportunity to retain and re-acquaint professionals with the latest development in the profession. I know a great deal of that already goes on here, but in terms of the need and the opportunity, I don't believe we are doing anywhere nearly enough of this kind of thing. I know Dean Morgan agrees. I think the development, particularly in the School of Medicine, of a more vigorous program of continuing education is something we will do.

The seventh point is one that perhaps I should have put first. It is that when I travel now and I am identified with Johns Hopkins, the echo that comes back when you mention Johns Hopkins is a respect for the quality of this institution. We are known to have high standards. The maintenance of high standards in this day and age is not always easy and it is almost never popular, but it is the single most important asset we bring with us from our past. It is the one thing to which we must be absolutely true. It is our hallmark. We should be second to none. We should always want to be the best and we should not tolerate second-rate performance within this institution. That goes not only for faculty, or for clinical practitioners, but for nurses, for orderlies, for technicians, for laboratory scientists, for doormen, janitors, everybody. Either this is the best place we can make it, or we are failing ourselves. I would like to think that we could rekindle here the kind of pride that high standards inspire. It is very difficult to live by the highest standards. The one reward you have is that you can feel pride in always attempting to do your best. That is a matter of morale, but the maintenance of high standards is something much different. It is toughness with one's self, toughness with one's colleagues, and it is the ability and the courage to continue to make judgments of performance, to insist that only the best possible performance is even adequate. If we don't do that then we will lose the reputation we have and the leadership opportunity we have. It would not only be wrong for us in selfish terms, but immoral for us to do that. God knows this country needs leadership institutions probably more than it needs anything else.

The last point, the eighth, is about the role of administration in all this. There are a couple of observations about what administration can and cannot do that may be worth making. Perhaps the most important is that administrators in The Johns Hopkins Medical Institutions — the Executive Vice-President and Director of the Hospital, the Deans, the Executive Director of the Medical Planning and Development Committee, the President — cannot make decisions effectively for the community. We do not have the collective wisdom or the collective right, or the individual wisdom or the individual right to make decisions. Our job when decisions have to be made is to force our colleagues who are involved to come to an agreement about a decision, or in effect to make the decision. Then, having forced the decision, we must see that it is implemented. In other words, our job is not to choose for others, but to compel choices to be made when choices are necessary, and to see that the choices made are effectively implemented. In my own case that has to be the way I operate. I am no health professional, and I do not intend at my age to become one. What I can contribute is an insistence that those most qualified choose, and that we then live by the best choice we can make.

Making decisions is always risky, because very seldom is one absolutely sure of the right decision. The other thing that administration perhaps can contribute is the willingness to take risks. And the willingness to take risks is important right now for The Johns Hopkins Medical Institutions. If what I have read to you from Mr. Greiner's article is correct, we are going through an organizational or management crisis. Perhaps we are on the way to resolving it, but even resolution is risky, and the new evolutionary period of growth that will follow will involve more risks. This is hardly a time for the timid. Administration is calculated risk-taking, but it means we must build a good management information system. Though I am willing to take risks and my senior colleagues are willing to take risks, we would prefer not to take risks flying by the seat of our pants with little penciled estimates on the backs of envelopes. It is intolerable to try to take sensible risks based on substantial ignorance. We need new management tools in these institutions.

I have one bit of news. At the request of Dean Morgan and myself, three students from the Massachusetts Institute of Technology Sloan School of Business Administration, actually three senior executives who are taking a year off to be M.I.T. students, will be here during this year to study decision-making processes in the medical school and the possibility of providing a management information system. If that is successful, we might try to persuade them to take a look at the larger Johns Hopkins Medical Institutions.

It is all right to take risks, but you have to coordinate the right people, make the right choices and have an information base from which intelligent people can operate. The Johns Hopkins Medical Institutions right now have a collection of individuals, but as an organization it needs the courage to choose and to act. We will rebuild our most antiquated facilities on this lot. We will solve our management problems. We will raise the funds that we need. We will achieve performance second to none. This will happen if we move; if we move together; if we move with informed judgment; and if we move with courage and confidence,   and   with   pride   in   ourselves   and   in   these   institutions.

COMPREHENSIVE HEALTH PLANNING

Medical World News

In 1903, young Dr. Robert C. McClymonds set out from College Springs, Iowa, in search of adventure on the West Coast. When the train reached Walton, Kan., he got out for a walk, liked what he saw, and fetched his bags. For more than 50 years, he practiced in the town, which never grew to much over 200 in population. At first, there was no hospital where he could send patients, but within a few years, church groups built two facilities in the county seat six miles away. From time to time, other GPs would find their way to the little town and set up practice, but when Dr. McClymonds died in 1962, Walton was again left without medical care.

Historically, provision for health care in this country has been just about that chancy. There has been little real planning. Instead, individual decisions and the uncoordinated efforts of independent organizations have often set the scene for medical feast or famine. Vast areas remain without physicians, while facilities and manpower cluster in metropolitan centers.

Can it be otherwise? Is a more systematic and sensitive approach possible? Congress set out to try. In 1966, it made Comprehensive Health Planning (CHP) a law of the land. Since then, more than $100 million in federal money has been spent to create hundreds of state and regional planning bodies, some with as many as 1,000 unsalaried members on their rolls.

Although the legislation was far from specific in stating how the planning groups should be organized and run, it laid down one stipulation of serious concern to physicians: Consumers of health care, rather than practitioners and providers of services, must make up a majority of the membership of all CHP agencies and committees. Given this built-in emphasis on consumer interests, how has the program worked out? Is Congress' CHP design fulfilling its ambitious goal?

Apparently the White House thinks so. The President's 1974 budget, which eliminated or slashed many other health programs in a crackdown on bureaucratic waste, recommended a boost in funds for CHP. The purpose of the modest increase is "to strengthen the capacity of 56 state and 208 areawide health agencies to influence the orderly and efficient development of local health services and to design their health systems more effectively."

Numerous critics in and out of CHP organizations take a less charitable view of the program. They admit that, here and there, CHP groups have already spurred the development of needed clinic services, forestalled unnecessary hospital construction, and encouraged action to correct local environmental health hazards. But according to these observers, the six-year-old program has also shown itself, in many instances, to be much the sort of ineffectual bureaucratic quagmire that the Administration condemns. While sucking up money, the planning efforts have tended to flounder in a multitude of confusions that were foreordained by CHP's vague congressional mandate. Local power struggles and conflicts of interest have hampered the organization and operation of many individual CHP councils. Moreover, excellent plans drawn up by some CHP agencies frequently haven't been adhered to because Congress failed to build any regulatory teeth or implementation apparatus into the program. Assessments of CHP vary from a few hymns of praise to a multitude of harsh indictments.

At one end of the spectrum is the claim made by Leon Kingsolver, executive director of a West Virginia CHP council, that "extraordinary things have been done here." At the other end of the spectrum is the complaint of a physician, who has sat through hours of "planning for planning" at CHP organizational meetings, that "all you get for your money is a lot of paper shuffling and immense amounts of hot air." Criticism has not stopped at words, either. In New York, a number of community groups and individual citizens have joined together to bring a court suit against administrators of the city's CHP agency as well as city, state, and federal government officials. They want to know what became of $1.25 million in federal and local funds that were allocated to set up 30 community planning boards but did not bring about the establishment of a single one.

To understand how the program could have such diverse effects, it is necessary to look at its elusive mission and amorphous structure. Comprehensive health planning would seem to be the fabrication of ideas — broad proposals for meeting present and future needs. CHP's mandate goes further. It is not only supposed to produce its own plans but also to review and comment on plans from many other sources that are put into its hopper. Yet it has no hookup to machinery for implementing approved plans.

The original Comprehensive Health Planning Act of 1966 was followed in 1967 by the Partnership for Health Act. Both were omnibus bills that amended the Public Health Service Act of 1944, the legislative fountain of authority for most public medical programs in this country. The portions amending Section 314 of the old law created CHP, which was to blanket the nation with two layers of planning bureaucracy.

As amended, Section 314(a) established state planning agencies; Section 314(b) created so-called areawide planning agencies that divide the country up into a greater number of regional subdivisions; and Section 314(c) added project grants for training, studies, and CHP demonstrations. In state as well as areawide agencies, the majority of members of the boards or advisory councils must be consumers of health services, with the rest of the rosters made up of various providers and government representatives. Generally, members serve without pay. Both types of agencies, however, may hire professional health planners and supporting staffs.

Why the two sets of agencies? The program's top administrator, Robert P. Janes, director of the Comprehensive Health Service located in Rockville, Md. gave us the following explanation: "Areawide agencies are more concerned with individual projects as they impact on a community. State agencies are more concerned with classes of institutions, groups and types of hospitals, services, and facilities."

CHP has covered the nation with state agencies. Every one of the 50 states has one, as does Guam, Puerto Rico, American Samoa, the Virgin Islands, the Trust Territory of the Pacific Islands, and the District of Columbia. Each has an advisory council, usually appointed by the governor, sometimes with concurrence of the legislature.

This fiscal year, which began on July 1, 1972, federal funding has supported approximately 200 areawide agencies, covering 70% of the nation's population and about half its geographical area. Areawide grants may go to any public or nonprofit organization whose proposal to carry out CHP functions is approved. Currently, the overwhelming majority of the regional planning groups — some 150 — have been organized as nonprofit private corporations. Sixty of these areawide agencies are in their "organizational" phase — for which federal grants generally allow two years — but well over 100 have supposedly geared up to the planning stage.

Amendments to the Public Service Act adopted in 1970 extend CHP through June 30, 1973. Its continuance after that depends on passage of further legislation. The President's 1974 budget request for a $38-million CHP appropriation helps its chances for survival.

Uncertain funding is probably not CHP's worst problem, although it hasn't always gotten as much money as seemed forthcoming and contends it could use much more. Through the end of the last fiscal year, a total of $97,612,528 in federal funds have gone into the program. The law authorized appropriations of $72 million for the current fiscal year, but subsequent to two Nixon vetoes of bills including HEW appropriations, CHP has been operating under a continuing resolution that authorizes expenditures at the fiscal 1972 level. This reduced it to a current budget of $25 million, including $7.675 million for state planning agencies, $13.2 million for areawide agencies, and $4.125 million for project grants. In addition, state and local sources must provide some matching funds. The federal share may be 50% to 75% depending on such factors as the area's population and economy. Funding decisions are not made by the central Rockville, Md., office but by ten regional federal offices. The job of just getting started organizationally to carry out CHP's broad mission has evidently been troublesome.

For instance, the 1970 act provided for a 16-member National Advisory Council on CHP programs. Its members are finally expected to be appointed shortly. As for the program's mandate, Mr. Janes' description summarizes both its breath and weakness. "Comprehensive Health Planning agencies are concerned with planning and, as the name implies, planning comprehensively — considering the relationship of services, facilities, and manpower as it impacts on environmental health, mental health, and personal health. They have not been regulatory in nature and still are not regulatory," says Mr. Janes who, before coming to Washington, was chairman of the Hennepin County Board of Commissioners in Minneapolis. (He became director of the CHS two years ago, after helping to organize testimony on the Partnership for Health Act, working with the National Association of Counties and League of Cities in developing local governments' viewpoints on health legislation, and serving on the staff of the Vice President.)

When asked how his cloutless program can get its recommendations implemented, Mr. Janes replies: "Federal requirements on many programs require our CHP agencies to provide review and comment. In providing such review and comment, the agencies must ensure that the projects are consistent with the plans they are developing. We have also held in this office that the planning agencies have a responsibility to urge the implementation of their plans. They act as a catalyst within the community. They look around for somebody to set up and operate, say, a neighborhood health center or for a group of people to submit an application for federal funds."

The system does work on occasion. Concrete accomplishments, for example, have been brought about by the Comprehensive Health Planning Council of Northwestern Pennsylvania, Inc., covering 13 counties. Gerald Farmer, its executive director, reports that when the water system in Slocum Hollow was condemned by the state's Department of Environmental Resources, people from the town of about 300 "felt they had no place to turn and came to the county CHP council." The council got funding from the Farmer's Home Administration to replace the water system. This areawide agency in its two years of planning has also initiated development of two ambulatory care units. Actually, the group managed to convince two hospitals that wanted to add traditional daytime outpatient services that what was needed instead were 24-hour primary care services with staff physicians.

In another example, the Comprehensive Health Planning Council of Maricopa County, Ariz., covering the 9,000-square-mile area that includes Phoenix and 200 other municipalities, got an OEO grant of $2.6 million in the past year to set up an "alternate health care program" for 20,000 people. Initiated by a CHP task force on the health of the poor, the project will include a prepaid care plan, a form of fee-for-service, and a "shading of the two," says executive director Milton Gan.

The Phoenix-based CHP has also been involved in setting up a medical foundation and a new prepaid insurance plan for people of all incomes – the first such plan in Phoenix. Moreover, the planning agency has "taken on the mines," says Gan, by opposing reductions in environmental quality control measures. It has also been active in programs for alcohol and drug abuse and pulled together various groups that had been working independently. Some 1,000 people work in the various Maricopa County CHP task forces and committees, including medical experts specifically recruited for the groups.

If health planning stirs such community participation, does it make sense that CHP stands apart from local planning boards or planning commissions as a separate entity? It does, according to Mr. Janes, who explains that health planning is a different type of undertaking: "It's social planning rather than physical or land-use planning, which traditionally has been the jurisdiction of local governments. We spend on the order of $70 billion a year on health. About $25 billion of that is federal and about $4 billion, city and local. This means that the health field is by and large a private endeavor and, as such, local government has never been very much a part of it.

"We're not talking necessarily about building facilities so much as trying to identify gaps in services," says Mr. Janes. "We wouldn't want the new hospital always built in the wealthiest part of town. You don't locate health services the way you put in a department store – where the dollars are. Sometimes you have to go where the need is.

"If you want a planning mechanism where you get providers and consumers together on one level and at the same time share responsibilities between the public and private sectors, many people have thought that the agencies ought to be developed in a neutral environment and not be a captive of either sector," adds Janes.

The nitty gritty of CHP's problem has been both managing to keep the environment neutral in a field where power struggles and conflicts of interest are an inevitable feature of the landscape and also getting more accomplished than merely setting up endless dialogues between many rival voices. CHP administrators think the effort is worthwhile. "Planning requires involvement of affected people as early as possible." maintains Mr. Gan of the Arizona county agency. "You plan with them, not for them. This may take longer than having a few unrepresentative people working on plans that leave a lot of people frustrated," he says. "It takes time and a philosophy that recognizes the dignity of the guy you are working with."

Mr. Janes fully subscribes to this "tremendous process of getting people together within the community, of getting the private sector together with the public sector, of getting the consumers together with the providers. I think that if anything is going to help us make sense out of the complexity of the health care scene today," says the administrator, "it is this ability of people to get together and communicate with one another. Part of the problem with the health profession historically was the way it laid a program on the community. Somebody decided that something was needed and that was it. It may or may not have been relevant to what was needed."

CHP accomplishments in a given locality are often mixed — with some recommendations carried out and others ignored. That's what has happened in Dade County, Fla. The Comprehensive Health Planning Council of South Florida, Inc., which covers the county from offices in Miami, counts as its big achievement the development of an ambulatory care system for its southern region. More sparsely populated than the north and central portions occupied by Miami and its sister cities, South Dade "has a lot of poor and near poor," according to health planner Fran Strychaz. It is the winter home of migrant farm workers. The county provides health care for the indigent at Jackson Memorial Hospital in Miami — but that would mean a 30-mile trip for the needy from South Dade. No local ambulatory care facilities existed. Taking this on as a priority, the CHP agency and its board worked with the area's cities, department of hospitals, and medical society to develop a coordinated system of primary care throughout South Dade. To do so, a nonprofit corporation, Community Health of South Dade, Inc., was set up just a year ago. Two clinics are already in operation.

On the opposite side of the coin, the Dade agency foresees a potential excess of 4,000 to 5,000 hospital beds by 1975. Four new hospitals are under construction and others are expanding. "We have reviewed about 35 proposals for additional hospital beds and have turned down on the order of 3,500 beds and approved 2,500," says health planner Strychaz. About 80% of the disapproved plans were dropped. But the other 20% that are being implemented include the construction of two more hospitals.

In truth, the facts in which CHP deals are often murky. For instance, the Government Accounting Office recently reported that Baltimore is overbuilding hospitals and nursing homes. This report, says William M. Hiscock, director of health planning for the areawide agency, was based on Hill-Burton information from 1970-1971 using "artificial statistics" that do not take into account the total region. In terms of total numbers, the area appears to be overbuilt, he admits, but the beds are badly distributed. Mr. Hiscock, whose agency is often cited as one of the best, is happy that the GAO is looking at such matters. Perhaps, he suggests, such scrutiny will "bring about recognition that the kinds of incentives now available have contributed to overbuilding in certain areas." The incentives for building nursing homes, he says, outweigh those for providing home care, and incentives for hospital construction outweigh those for setting up ambulatory care.

The relatively rare successes of individual CHP efforts have sometimes actually surprised the administrators leading them. Mr. Kingsolver, director of the CHP council of Region VII that covers 12 counties in West Virginia, cites one such case. His CHP staff was working with a subcommittee of the Greenbrier

County planning commission. Two competitive hospital projects, neither of which met the county's total needs, both got negative reviews.

Then, a year ago, the Benedum Foundation of Pittsburgh provided funds for a thorough study by the county and CHP planning group. Today, a 125-bed hospital is under construction in central Greenbrier County and an out-patient facility is being developed in the western part. The county health department has agreed to decentralize and will have an office in the western clinic. An emergency trauma unit has also been set up in the clinic and will have a working relationship with the central hospital. "If you had told me a year and a half ago that this would happen," says Kingsolver, "I would have said you were crazy."

That CHP has already helped spawn any sterling examples of comprehensive planning and development on the local level is perhaps even more surprising in view of the fact that the six-year-old national program has only recently begun to issue guidelines suggesting how the agencies might go about planning and is for the first time requiring the agencies to actually produce plans. Says Mr. Janes, "We feel this is necessary because, if they are going to recommend that something be approved or denied, they should have a good, firm yardstick by which one can judge whether or not an agency is doing a good job in relation to what other agencies are doing. We hope to have these criteria out in the next few months."

This lack of performance criteria and requirements may explain why many CHP agencies have had so much trouble getting going. "Organizational guidelines have been very broad," acknowledges a public information officer at Rockville. "There is no cookbook approach. Essentially, it is a local problem."

Since there is no set way to organize the advisory councils, one areawide agency may choose to have a board of 36 members; another, 70. Consumer representation seems to vary from the mandated 51% on up to 70%. Some agencies reserve seats on their board for representatives of the local medical societies or med schools. Others have seats for such categories as "private office practice." Some carefully proportion their racial and economic representations. Boards sometimes are chosen by popular election in community meetings or by delegate assemblies. And in some councils, a number of members may be appointed by the elected ones to "balance" the board.

Thus, costly trial and error and false starts were inevitable. In Baltimore, for example, director Hiscock reports that, at first, consumer representation was drawn from various organizations. Subsequently, geographic distribution has come to be considered a better basis than the "welfare rights" and "chamber of commerce" sort of representation they had been getting. In fact, the agency now encourages the formation of subarea coalitions for CHP. In Los Angeles and nearby counties, size proved to be a major problem. The original areawide agency, the Southern California CHP Council covering Los Angeles, Orange, and Riverside counties, proved too large geographically and was disbanded on Jan. 1, 1972. A less unwieldy Los Angeles County CHP Council came into being on April 1, 1972. In working up a health facilities plan for the county, the agency is now going by a 130-page book on how the plan is to be organized and written.

But the Los Angeles council "has not really been functiong," says Dr. Gerald Looney, associate director of the department of emergency medicine at Los Angeles County-University of Southern California Medical Center. Last year, his department "had a heck of a time finding an agency just to review a project request."

Dr. Looney has become critical of CHP in general. "Partnership for Health looks great on paper, but in practice it seems virtually unworkable," he says. "When you separate planning from implementation, that's like separating the heartbeat from the lungs."

Another problem, in Dr. Looney's view, is that "very few health professionals have training for health planning, and no consumers have it. And yet the way CHP functions, it lets passengers decide how to fly the plane. I am not being critical of consumers. I just feel that they are being given inappropriate jobs. How can you expect people who don't have any experience at all to make decisions regarding policies and programs?"

Dr. Looney also sees a problem in domination of agencies such as CHP by a latter-day phenomenon — professional consumers. "These people really represent only their own biases," he says. "But because they are vocal and crowd politicians' doorsteps, they are likely to be accepted as the voice of the people."

A New York physician, experienced in health planning, points out a basic obstacle to recruiting competent, unprejudiced members for planning councils. "It is almost impossible to find people knowledgeable about health affairs who do not have a conflict of interest. And just as surely, those who have no conflict of interest aren't likely to know much about health matters."

Dr. James Kimmey — the outspoken former executive director of the American Public Health Association and now special assistant for health policy in the Wisconsin governor's office, a post that includes directing the state CHP agency — describes one result of having special medical interests represented in the planning councils. "In many areas," he says, "it has suited the interests of a governmental agency or a hospital group to keep the local CHP organizations from doing anything except reviewing and commenting, instead of going out and identifying problems" The low profile of many CHP agencies, he charges, is by design — of hospitals that are trying to control them.

To Mr. Janes, such domination doesn't seem a problem. Asked whether his agencies tend to suffer from special-interest power struggles, he replied that the councils are "not captured by anybody." But his outgoing boss, HEW Secretary Elliot Richardson, revealed his doubts on the matter in an address last May. Among many proposals for strengthening CHP, he urged increasing the federal share of the matching formula in order to "eliminate an unhealthy dependence by planning units on the benevolence of provider organizations. Too often planning units have had to panhandle funds for their existence from the very entities that their planning efforts affect directly."

Secretary Richardson decried not only the "fragmented and irrational nonsystem" of health services in this country, which CHP was set up to rectify, but also CHP's inadequate funding and staffing and lack of any real authority to coordinate planning. "It is, again, a 'nonsystem,'" he said, "incapable of either rationally identifying shortfalls or gaps in performance, or of rationally addressing needs." But rather than scrapping CHP, Secretary Richardson wanted the program improved.

Ironically, Mr. Richardson is one of the defendants — along with New York's Governor Rockefeller, Mayor Lindsay, and other officials — in the most drastic complaint action taken against CHP, the now pending federal court suit charging that the New York City areawide agency failed to carry out the proposal that was the basis for $1.25 million in funding. During the funded year, 30 community CHP boards were to be set up, but not one was organized, says David P. Glasel, lawyer for the plaintiffs, a group including the New York City Coalition for Community Health and other organizations and individuals.

Attorney Glasel points out that on July 6 of this year the state agency was "quite negative" in its review of the city agency but six weeks later reversed itself and passed on the request for refunding to the federal regional office. The New York areawide agency's chairman, Gordon Chase, is also the city's health services administrator — and a codefendant in the suit. Mr. Glasel sees a possible conflict of interest in "vesting this much power in a single individual." One week, he says, Mr. Chase can ask the board's help in planning for the city's Health and Hospitals Corporation and, the next, return for approval of that plan, to the probable disadvantage of any community group submitting a counter proposal.

Bertram Black, executive director of the areawide agency, comments: "Actually, the same charges have been made before and were thoroughly aired, and we were cleared by the state people previously." Mr. Black indicates that plans now call for 33 subunit boards and that ten of these are almost ready to operate. The plans, he says, "have been long in the making because they were complex to develop." Moreover, the central areawide agency *is* in the operating stage, adds Mr. Black.

One of the plaintiffs in the suit — State Senator Sidney von Luther, who happens to be black and a licensed nurse — pleads for rational planning and "not just opening up the pot for everyone to reach in." He hopes the court action will help to overcome CHP's "insensitivity to community needs." But he is against appointing a minister or the "invariable community leader" to represent an area on the board. "They're too busy with all their other projects to hunt out health problems and, furthermore, probably don't have any insight into these problems."

How do health care providers and the medical profession feel about CHP? To Anne Brixner, director of health planning for Luthern Medical Center in Brooklyn, CHP has simply added another layer of bureaucracy to those that must review proposals for grants. Since the process now takes longer, submission dates must be moved up.

Says Mr. Janes: "The medical profession has indicated its support of the health planning process." He cites the AMA, the American Hospital Association, and groups such as the American Psychiatric Association and the American

Optometric Association as having expressed support for or interest in the general planning process.

But that doesn't constitute wide professional endorsement of CHP itself. In fact, the AMA has warned that "planning is seldom voluntary where federal funding of health services and facilities is involved. Built into the planning program must be a fair, equitable appeal and review mechanism for those decisions of the health planning agency that are thought to be incorrect or unreasonable."

What else might make CHP more acceptable and effective? A clearer definition of its objectives, composition, and procedures would certainly help. And last year CHP finally contracted with Community Health, Inc., a New York organization that has no formal connection with the program, for an "Expectations Project" covering these questions. To prepare the report, five three-day conferences were held with 31 providers and consumers who were also not involved in CHP. Among the results are lengthy definitions of who is a provider and who, a consumer, along with proposals for what a CHP agency should be expected to do and how it should be evaluated. These suggestions have not yet been officially adopted, but they go farther toward clarifying CHP's mission than anything has before. Moreover, the ideas are apparently being picked up, says George Olson, executive director of Community Health Inc.

Another step that would give CHP more clout is "certificate of need" legislation, which about 21 states have already enacted. These laws require that, before any service or facility can be added or changed, the applicant must apply for a certificate of need from the state. Generally, CHP agencies will be the ones that review applications to see whether or not the needs exist, says Mr. Janes.

The omnibus bill H.R. 1, passed by the last Congress, creates a similar review requirement for federally funded projects. Health-related expenditures in excess of $100,000, to which there is a federal contribution, must now be reviewed by an agency such as CHP.

Utilization of computers to store data may, in addition, cut down on some of CHP's bureaucratic red tape. For example, the Oklahoma state agency, which gathers utilization data for all its hospitals and nursing homes, stores the information electronically in a computer system with 14 terminals throughout the state. Areawide CHP agencies also feed in review and adjustment data for new plans that must undergo review in several state offices before adoption. As a result of the collaborative computer setup, "everyone is now reviewing facilities requests against the same plan," says the state agency's director.

As for the program's future. "CHP is probably now starting into its make-or-break era," observes Mr. Olson, whose organization prepared the independent expectation report. "A year or so ago, its survival seemed at stake, but now the question appears to be what form it will take." In one sense, he is concerned about "the constant availability of opportunity to change a planning group's structure. In some agencies, there is continuing tension concerning structure," says Mr. Olson. On the other hand, "the opportunity for change keeps an agency honest and on its toes." And although the performance of CHP agencies is now being questioned after $100 million has already been spent, he points out that there is also growing recognition that, if the program didn't exist, one would probably have to be created.

A troubling prospect for the efficiency-minded.

III
LEGAL REGULATION OF HEALTH SCIENCES AND THEIR PRACTITIONERS

III. LEGAL REGULATION OF HEALTH SCIENCES AND THEIR PRACTITIONERS

INTRODUCTION

The crisis in American health care during the last twenty-five years reflects a growing drive towards the legal regulation of health care practitioners and delivery services. This regulation has originated outside the medical profession and has been a measure of self-policing. The new controls are exercised on the community or state level as well as on a federal level.

Some measure of federal control was achieved through Medicare, Medicaid and other health care legislation. Under these laws the government was able to review health care and to regulate these services through cost analysis thereby reducing charges or allowing the government to refuse to pay bills when the services rendered exceeded customary practices.

The government has attempted to regulate further the delivery of health care services through Professional Service Review Organizations. In addition, while seeking to improve the delivery of health care through the funding of Health Maintenance Organizations, the federal government is again likely to achieve some new measures of regulation (although the cost requirements for such comprehensive programs may limit participation).

On the local level, medical societies have attempted self-regulation over the review bills to third-parties (insurance carriers) as well as bills to patients. Hospitals, particularly since the courts have held them liable for the acts of physicians, have established similar committees to review physician's hospital care of patients.

Within the medical profession itself a movement has been growing towards the indirect and direct regulation of physicians by the sponsorship of continuing education programs, by instituting achievement awards, and through the introduction of recertification examinations by medical specialty boards. In several states legislation has been enacted to allow licensing boards to revoke licenses for professional inadequacy, as well as to require the completion of additional educational requirements for the regular renewal of licenses.

The consumer has become an effective voice in the area of regulation. In many localities community organizations have developed an active inter-relationship with hospitals, often taking part in the foundation of hospitals' policy. A few medical societies have included lay members on their various review committees. Both federal and state government agencies have also provided a role for community residents in the new programs for the delivery of health care.

Discussions of these new regulatory thrusts and their effects are represented in the articles selected for this section.

NEW RIGHTS FOR PATIENTS, NEW RISKS FOR YOU

Bart Sheridan

Those big new arrows in the malpractice plaintiff's quiver are his "rights as a human being." At least that's how appellate courts in several states are referring to them, and that was the description on everybody's lips a few weeks ago in Las Vegas, where the country's leading plaintiff's attorneys assembled in the midst of the other high rollers for the midwinter convention of The Association of Trial Lawyers of America. "Human rights" haven't gained the status of established law everywhere, but the trend in judicial thinking, lawyer after lawyer told me, is clear. Any physician who ignores this trend does so at his peril.

Among the most important rights established in recent court rulings are the following:

1. The *right* to know most of the potential risks of any proposed medication or surgery. The physician has the duty to explain those dangers fully in most situations, say the courts, whether the patient asks him to or not. Moreover, the courts are holding, it's the patient, not the doctor, who has the last word on what's to be done to and for his own body.

2. The *right* to have his doctor make sure hospital orders are carried out. No more "write it and forget it" if you don't want to risk suit for the hospital personnel's failure to obey your instructions.

3. The *right* to expect his doctor to call for consultation whenever — and as soon as — necessary, whether or not the patient requests him to get another opinion.

Aren't these the same rights plaintiffs have always had in court? Perhaps. But a new wave of judicial interpretations now invests them with greater practical significance. A violation of any one of those rights makes it likelier than ever that a physician will find himself the loser in a lawsuit — even if the bad result involved isn't caused by any doctor's "negligence" in the accepted clinical sense. So say the able lawyers who have argued for the patient's human rights in court and who will press for them harder in the future.

Here, in detail, is what these men were telling one another and the public about the courts' new love affair with the American patient.

The importance that courts are attaching to a patient's right to understand his problem and participate in decisions was unanimously viewed as the malpractice lawyer's sharpest arrow yet. Indeed, veteran counsel Melvin M. Belli speculated that current judicial thinking about informed consent may give malpractice plaintiffs so great an advantage that the demand for no-fault professional liability insurance would become irresistible. At one of the convention's relaxed evening socials, he went so far as to predict to me that informed consent may eventually become "the new bastion of malpractice litigation."

Few of Belli's fellow lawyers would go that far, but attorney Jim R. Carrigan of Denver held his fellow lawyers spellbound when he laid out the meaning of two informed consent decisions he felt helped make 1972 a "turning-point year" in malpractice liability.

One is the celebrated California case of Cobbs vs. Grant. Surgeon Dudley F.P. Grant had removed an intractable peptic ulcer from the duodenum of his patient, Ralph Cobbs. The surgeon, it was charged, did not beforehand make it clear to Cobbs that complications like a severed artery at the hilum of the spleen occur in approximately 5 per cent of such operations, and thus there was a slight possibility the spleen would have to be removed. Nor did Grant make it clear, according to the suit, that a gastric ulcer was another known risk, and that such ulcers must sometimes be treated by gastrectomy.

The fates were against Cobbs. Surgeon Grant later found himself forced to remove the spleen and, eventually, half his stomach. When the gastrectomy resulted in internal bleeding due to the premature absorption of a suture, Cobbs sued, charging both negligence and lack of informed consent. A jury awarded him $23,800.

The California Supreme Court justice who heard the appeal vindicated Grant on medical grounds and reversed the judgment, agreeing that the evidence did not indicate negligence. The informed consent charge, however, was another matter. Because the lower court's verdict did not indicate whether the jury award was based on negligence or on informed consent, the Supreme Court ordered the case retried on the specific issue of informed consent. Laying down stern guidelines for the lower court to use in instructing jurors and admitting evidence in a new trial, the appellate court took sharp issue with the thesis that medical doctors "are invested with discretion" to withhold information. Unlimited discretion in the physician, the court declared, is "irreconcilable with the basic right of the patient to make the ultimate informed decision."

That meant Grant could be held liable for medical malpractice if he hadn't told Cobbs enough about the risks of removing the ulcer to enable Cobbs to make his own "intelligent" decision on whether he wanted it done. The court did specify, however, that a plaintiff could not use the ruling to claim 20-20 hindsight. To win damages, Cobbs would have to show that he would have decided against the surgery had he known all the risks, and that such a decision was one that might have been made by a "reasonably prudent person."

The second case described by lawyer Carrigan is Spence vs Canterbury, which I found was already being batted around informally by many of the lawyers when I arrived in Las Vegas. It involved paralysis following a laminectomy. Medical negligence was so noticeably absent from the case that a lower court dismissed the action. But a District of Columbia appeals court reviewed the suit on the specific issue of informed consent.(1)

The appeals judge cited an old dictum of Justice Benjamin Cardozo. A concept fundamental in American jurisprudence, Cardozo cautioned, is that "every human being of adult years and sound mind has a right to determine what shall be done with his own body." To escape liability, then, the opinion continued, the physician must meet these criteria:

He must reasonably disclose the full risk of treatment whether or not a patient asks, and whether or not he fears scaring the patient off; and he must follow the spirit of the law, not mere community medical standards, in determining which risks to cover in "reasonable" disclosure.

The clear message to doctors flashed by these two cases: Tell your patients what might go wrong, or else! If you don't and it does, the courts could call it malpractice even if there was no negligence.

"The first thing I look at today is the hospital order sheet," one attorney told me. "Suppose the doctor ordered medication or treatment that somebody forgot to give, and the patient suffered. A few years ago the doctor could have washed his hands of the matter, claiming his responsibility ended when he wrote the orders. Today, I can nail the doctor for malpractice and make it stick."

The reason that's so, he explained, is the courts' increasing concern for the welfare of the individual patient and their reluctance to countenance a physician's abdication of responsibility for that welfare. Herman B. Glaser, an active New York City malpractice attorney, strongly concurred in this view. He told me he's "amazed" at the omissions he finds in checking doctors' order sheets against medication sheets and nurses' records.

Glaser pointed to a recent New York appeals court decision (Toth vs. Community Hospital) as opening the way to malpractice actions against doctors who permit their orders to be disregarded. In that case, consulting physicians had left an order for administration of a certain amount of oxygen. Too large an amount was given, and the patient — an infant — became blind. The appellate court upheld the plaintiff's contention that damages should be assessed not only against the hospital for failing to follow orders but also against the doctors for failing to make sure the hospital had followed through.

"I recently won a case on that very point, against a neurosurgeon and a family practitioner," Glaser told me. "The patient was in very severe straits with a bleeding aneurysm, and the order sheets called for treatment with hypotensive agents, including Naturetin. Well, the Naturetin wasn't given. The patient went through blood pressures of 200-plus for an extended period of time without the doctors or anybody else noticing the oversight. And when that patient died, we got a judgment against both doctors as well as against the hospital."

With medical training and practice increasingly specialized and sub-specialized, physicians are more often finding themselves haled into court for failing to give patients the benefit of colleagues' focalized knowledge. One attorney told me of his pending suit against an internist who, the attorney says, prescribed harmful dosages of prednisone for a patient with a kidney disorder. The treatment resulted in an avascular necrosis, the lawyer contends. The patient claims negligence both in the treatment and in the internist's failure to consult with or refer to a nephrologist.

Plaintiff's attorneys see precedent for this approach in court decisions that emphasize patients must not be deprived of the best appropriate care. One lawyer cited the case of Wilson vs. Gilbert in which a California surgeon was successfully sued for $300,000 by a teen-age boy who lost a leg after the surgeon's unsuccessful attempt to repair a severed femoral artery. It was charged that the surgeon, A.E. Gilbert of St. Helena, had no training in this type of surgery yet he did not call in a vascular surgeon when he was summoned to treat the boy after a hunting accident.

After two grafting procedures failed to restore arterial circulation, Gilbert amputated the boy's leg. An expert witness testified that the first femoral graft had been improperly done, that the restoration of the arterial circulation had been frustrated by presurgical clotting, and that Gilbert had failed to follow applicable standards by not checking for clotting by means of an arteriogram or other appropriate procedure.

Taking the failure-to-consult issue clearly into account, an appellate court declared the evidence sufficient to support the $300,000 verdict against a doctor who, "although he had had no training in vascular surgery, did not call in a vascular surgeon and rather undertook to connect the patient's femoral artery surgically without having an arteriogram performed.(2)

These days not only must physicians consult, they must consult and consult again. Attorney Carrigan told me about Hargess vs. Tatem, which involved a general practitioner who had scrupulously called in a specialist in a difficult orthopedic case. Nevertheless, the G.P. suffered a malpractice judgment because he failed to check a key point with the consultant *after* the patient was returned to his own care. The G.P., William Tatem, who practiced in Bellows Falls, Vt., summoned orthopedist William Chard forthwith when he encountered a comminuted intertrochanteric fracture of the hip in a 77-year-old woman. With Tatem's concurrence and with Tatem assisting, Chard successfully performed an open reduction and internal fixation of the fracture fragments with a Jewett nail. The patient recovered uneventfully under the orthopedist's care, and Tatem resumed full charge.

Chard's daily hospital orders had specified that the patient should not be allowed to put stress on the hip until fully healed. But when Tatem found her able to walk unassisted, he permitted her to walk out of the hospital under her own power and to resume her household duties. The Jewett nail fractured, and a second operation was required to remove the original appliance and insert a new one.

In the resultant lawsuit against Tatem, which was tried without a jury, the lower court ruled: "Dr. Tatem knew of the instructions given by Dr. Chard . . . He made no attempt to advise or consult with Dr. Chard as to the advisability of the full weight bearing which he knew was occurring. In light of his admitted unfamiliarity with the type of device here employed, and his admitted reliance upon Dr. Chard as an expert in the field, we find that permitting the weight bearing and . . . the failure to . . . consult with Dr. Chard was negligence on [Dr. Tatem's] part." The Vermont Supreme Court upheld that finding, terming the "failure of the defendant to inquire" about the weight bearing prior to making a judgment a "gross violation of the due care owed by a physician to a patient."

This new legal arrow being fashioned out of the patient's right to the best possible care was illustrated again in Allen vs. Fort Sanders Hospital, a case described to the trial lawyers' meeting by J.D. Lee of Madisonville, Tenn., president of the organization. According to Lee, a pregnant woman telephoned her doctor to complain of a "paralyzing pain" in the back. Recalling the woman's emotional distress following a previous miscarriage, the physician attributed the paralysis to hysteria and advised the woman to rest. He later hospitalized the woman at her insistence, but hysteria remained his diagnosis. He prescribed codeine and continued rest. Eventually, a neurosurgeon operated and discovered a spontaneous epidural hemorrhage had taken place. But by then the patient was permanently paralyzed.

Attorney Lee claimed malpractice in the physician's failure to verify the hysteria diagnosis with a psychiatrist and to consult a neurosurgeon immediately against the chance that the pain was indeed of organic origin. The case was finally settled out of court, after two trials resulted in hung juries.

Does the new legal climate portend an increase in both the incidence and the success of malpractice suits? Here's how one nationally known attorney sums up the significance of the new climate: "The courts of this country are definitely becoming more liberal. They are placing more obligations on medical people at every level to see that individual patients are not deprived of their right to health. Consequently I am confidently taking cases today that I would have been very uncomfortable with, or maybe have rejected outright, as recently as a year ago."

NOTES

(1) See "Informed Consent: Could You Pass This Court's Test?" MEDICAL ECONOMICS, Sept. 25, 1972.

(2) An indicative sidelight entered this case when it was learned that after having treated the boy, Gilbert took a course on giving arteriograms, and that thereafter he referred similar cases to vascular surgeons.

WHAT THE NEW PEER-REVIEW LAW SAYS
—AND DOESN'T SAY

James A. Reynolds

Now that Congress has approved the idea of the Professional Standards Review Organization — a fancy name for a new kind of physician peer review — you can begin asking how the new program will work. But don't count on getting simple or straightforward answers anytime soon.

That's the conclusion I drew recently after quizzing some of my best Washington sources shortly after the P.S.R.O. legislation became law. The response of one normally well-informed H.E.W. health planner was typical: "You're asking *me* how P.S.R.O.s will work? I was getting ready to ask you the same question!" Another highly placed man at H.E.W. confessed: "Nobody here has the remotest idea how to make this concept fly on a national level."

This is not to say that P.S.R.O.s — pronounced "pisseroes" by Washington wags — will fail to get off the ground. It's just that the enabling legislation seems to raise more questions than it answers. The P.S.R.O. provision, brainchild of Senator Wallace F. Bennett (R., Utah), squeezed through Congress on the final day of the 1972 session as an amendment to a huge Social Security bill. It gives organized groups of physicians — medical societies, presumably, or perhaps some medical foundations — first chance at setting up these new review organizations.

These P.S.R.O.s will take on the task of reviewing services provided under Medicare and Medicaid. In so doing, they must decide whether care is medically necessary and determine whether it measures up to professional standards. They'll also encourage physicians to curb their reliance on costly inpatient care.

The Bennett Amendment originally applied to *all* services, both institutional and ambulatory, provided under Medicare and Medicaid. A last-minute change, however, allows a P.S.R.O. to restrict its review through 1975 to institutional care and services. Only if a P.S.R.O. wants the extra work — and then only if H.E.W. concurs — need it take on the additional task of reviewing ambulatory care. No P.S.R.O. will have any say over physicians' charges, which will continue to be weighed by fiscal intermediaries reporting to H.E.W.

The new legislation provides answers to three basic peer-review questions that have been troubling Congress — and doctors — for some time:

Should peer review be left to physicians — or to physicians plus consumers? The law ensures that P.S.R.O.s will be run by doctors, at least until 1976. Even thereafter, physician-run P.S.R.O.s will get priority. Only if a doctor-sponsored P.S.R.O. won't or can't do the job could H.E.W. turn elsewhere — to a medical school, say, or a local health department, or a health insurer.

The law also says flatly that nobody "who is not a duly licensed doctor of medicine or osteopathy" may make "final determinations" on the conduct of or care provided by a physician. Still, that language may not preclude the use of clerks or computers to sort out cases for scrutiny.

Congress thus rejected the notion that consumers deserve a place in the review process. The lawmakers also refused to create a role for Federal reviewers. A report accompanying the legislation underscored the Senate Finance Committee feeling that physicians alone should be responsible for the success — or the failure — of P.S.R.O.s: "It is preferable . . . that organizations of professionals undertake review of members of their profession. . . . Government should not have to review medical determinations unless the medical profession evidences an unwillingness to properly assume the task."

Should physician peer review simply punish wrongdoing — or seek to prevent it? Says Senator Bennett: "The thrust of P.S.R.O. is informational and educational — not punitive." In areas where P.S.R.O.s function effectively, the Senate Finance Committee states, "the need for sanctions will be minimal."

Those views notwithstanding, the law does have teeth. H.E.W. can recover up to $5,000 in overpayments to anyone who persistently bills Medicare or Medicaid for uneeded, inadequate, or overpriced services. Or the agency can prohibit future reimbursement to such flagrant offenders.

Should peer review take place after the fact — or before it, too? Taking a cue from the Sacramento (Calif.) County Medical Society's plan for preadmission hospital screening, the law empowers a P.S.R.O. to approve in advance any elective hospital admissions or any care that promises to consist of "extended or costly courses of treatment." Such advance approval, the Senate Finance Committee hastens to add, will be "solely for the purpose of determining whether Medicare or Medicaid will pay for the care." All other P.S.R.O. review — and that means most of it — will take place after the fact.

Even though the new peer-review program was tinkered with extensively to meet objections from right and left. I found little enthusiasm for it except among Senator Bennett's brain trusts on Capitol Hill. The A.M.A. and other high-powered health lobbies opposed it, and even H.E.W. gave it lukewarm support. That it was sent to the White House at all attests to the growing

Congressional concern over the soaring costs of Medicare and Medicaid.

All this suggests that Congress sooner or later may be disposed to take another look at the P.S.R.O. concept. Meanwhile, H.E.W. has to tie up a lot of loose ends on questions the new law does *not* answer:

How long will it take to get P.S.R.O.s started? The law tells H.E.W. to establish by Jan. 1, 1974, "appropriate areas" for which P.S.R.O.s may be designated. Each area will include at least 300 practicing physicians and in most cases substantially more. Insiders suggest there will be at least 150 P.S.R.O. areas throughout the U.S. and maybe as many as 250.

Mapping the areas shouldn't take a lot of time, or so one would suppose. "But you know the Government," one bureaucrat sighs. "The areas probably won't be designated until midnight of Dec. 31, 1973."

Of far greater importance than the designation of P.S.R.O. areas will be the regulations that must be drafted before even one of the organizations can begin to function. "No matter whether we spell out every little detail or let the P.S.R.O.s work out refinements for themselves," says one planner, "there'll be a hell of a lot of regulations. You can count on that." H.E.W. will no doubt prepare stacks of position papers, solicit opinions from hither and yon, and maybe even hold public hearings – all before a single regulation goes down on paper. Thus it's not surprising that some insiders think the writing of regulations could drag on for months.

One of H.E.W.'s still-scarce P.S.R.O. experts guesses that no more than a dozen of the new peer-review organizations – out of a projected 150 or more, remember – might be functioning within a year after areas are designated. These early-bird organizations would probably stem from medical foundations, such as the ones in Georgia and in Hennepin County, Minn., that are already undertaking peer-review programs.

Will P.S.R.O.s be hamstrung by feuding among physicians? That remains to be seen. The law says a P.S.R.O. must be open to all physicians in a local area "without requirement of membership in or payment of dues to any organized medical society or association." Those words seem to mean that a medical society itself can't act as a P.S.R.O., unless some of its by-laws are revised. They certainly mean a P.S.R.O. can't discriminate against a physician simply because he isn't a dues-paying member of the A.M.A. or any of its affiliates.

Nor can a P.S.R.O. restrict the right of any doctor to serve as a peer reviewer. The Senate Finance Committee underscores this point: "A P.S.R.O. applicant must provide for the broadest possible involvement, as reviewers on a rotating basis, of physicians engaged in all types of practice . . . such as solo, group, hospital, medical school, and so forth."

Obviously, the intent is to head off any efforts by private practitioners to take over a P.S.R.O. or to discriminate against closed-panel or academic physicians. Dr. C.A. Hoffman, president of the A.M.A., pooh-poohs such possibilities. He declares, "H.M.O.s and academia face many of the same problems that trouble fee-for-service physicians. I foresee a *community of interest* rather than a fight over P.S.R.O. control."

There's little likelihood that private practitioners will be swept into a P.S.R.O. that many of them may oppose. Through 1975, H.E.W. must hold a referendum if 10 per cent of the doctors in an area claim a proposed P.S.R.O. doesn't "substantially represent" the area's practicing physicians. If more than half the doctors responding to the poll turn thumbs down on the organization, H.E.W. can't do business with it.

How will P.S.R.O.s mesh with existing peer-review programs? The law permits a P.S.R.O. to accept the internal review of a hospital or H.M.O. – but "only when and only to the extent and only for such time" as that work meets P.S.R.O. standards. An organization's internal review would be accepted, moreover, only if its physicians share in P.S.R.O. activities.

Congress clearly doubts that many existing internal review programs will measure up. Says Senator Bennett: "Present utilization review activities are just not adequate. In fact, they are characteristically ineffective – fragmented, retrospective, and incomplete."

Though the Bennett Amendment never says so, it implies that conflicts of interest account for such shortcomings. The new law specifies that doctors ordinarily shouldn't be responsible for, although they can participate in, the review of care provided in any hospital in which they have active staff privileges. The law forbids a physician to review services provided to any of his patients, or to review services provided in or by any enterprise in which he or his family has a financial interest.

Senator Bennett warns against "indiscriminate and blanket acceptance" by a P.S.R.O. of hospital or H.M.O. review programs. The Finance Committee goes further: "P.S.R.O. provisions will require full and forthright implementation. Equivocation, hesitance, and half-hearted compliance will negate the intended results" – and, though the committee doesn't say so, invite new legislation.

How will P.S.R.O.s affect health insurance carriers? The law envisions no change in the work of fiscal intermediaries under Medicare and Medicaid, which will continue to review claims for reimbursement as they always have. Some arrangement will be required, however, to let P.S.R.O.s have a crack at the claims forms.

"Maybe an intermediary can program its computer to kick out claims that exceed P.S.R.O. norms," one H.E.W. official suggests. "Or maybe the P.S.R.O. will simply go through all the claims forms after an intermediary finishes with them."

In any event, the law encourages the new peer-review organizations to draw on the know-how and computer technology developed by the California medical foundations and the health insurance industry. But that's not to suggest, the Finance Committee says, that a P.S.R.O. can turn its task over to a health insurer.

What kind of savings will P.S.R.O.s produce? You can hear some rosy projections. The Senate Finance Committee, for instance, says hopefully that P.S.R.O.s "have the potential for moderating the costs of health care by as much as 20 per cent." An H.E.W. planner says his projected savings range between a conservative 10 per cent to a "wildly optimistic" 30 per cent.

To be sure, either figure presupposes a full network of P.S.R.O.s plus their jurisdiction over ambulatory as well as institutional care — a situation that won't exist until 1976 or beyond. The point is, a saving of 30 per cent — or only 10 per cent — will yield big money when you're talking about Medicare and Medicaid outlays of $15 billion a year.

Big savings, of course, would go far toward justifying Congressional faith in the new peer-review program. But nobody knows for sure whether the new organizations will really save money — or even if they'll work at all. When P.S.R.O. watchers are asked to make long-range prognostication, there are three themes that consistently come into view:

1. P.S.R.O.s will never reach full flower as long as they limit themselves to institutional care. Many planners express distress at the Congressional decision to put off peer review of ambulatory care. Many also question the decision to separate claims review and utilization review. As one man puts it: "There's no reason why a P.S.R.O. can't review the cost as well as the quality of care."

2. P.S.R.O.s could become the prime local agency for dealing with Uncle Sam on medical problems, in which case they might ultimately relegate medical societies to much lesser importance. This suggests that medical societies may be eager to rush into P.S.R.O.s, if only to protect themselves. "Don't be too sure," one health planner cautions. "Doctors know that they'll take the rap from Congress if they go big for P.S.R.O.s and P.S.R.O.s fall flat."

3. P.S.R.O.s represent a gearing-up for national health insurance. One official believes that the concept seems compatible with both the Kennedy and Nixon programs. Whether or not national health insurance absorbs P.S.R.O.s, another man suggests, they'll probably be replaced by something else, perhaps a program to measure medical-care quality by assessing outcomes.

Perhaps one H.E.W. man says it best: "I see P.S.R.O.s as an evolutionary process between where we are and where we're going. But where we're going I don't really know."

QUALITY-OF-CARE ASSESSMENT:
CHOOSING A METHOD FOR PEER REVIEW

Robert H. Brook
Francis A. Appel

Increasing public pressure and recent Congressional legislation(1) have focused attention on the need for developing a formal mechanism for using peer review to assess the quality of medical care. The success of this effort, however, depends on the answers to two fundamental questions: whether information describing physician performance (process), or the results of care (outcome), or both, should be collected and analyzed; and how and by whom value judgments should be placed on these data to determine the quality of the care provided.

A review of the literature(2) suggests that answers to these questions are uncertain. Efforts to assess medical-care quality have generally examined physician performance. Few evaluative studies(3-13) have used information about the end results of care, even though the purpose of medical care is to maintain or improve health, and it therefore seems logical to evaluate care in terms of how well this objective is achieved. The question of which kind of data yields the more appropriate evaluation is unresolved.

Assessment of quality of care on the basis of physician performance may be inappropriate because many physicians' activities have not been proved to relate to improved health. However, assessment of quality of care on the basis of the results of care may be similarly inappropriate since the results of care depend not only on the medical care received but also on the demographic, social and economic characteristics of the patient population.

The purpose of this paper is to present the results of a study that attempted to answer these questions by comparing five different peer-review methods of assessing medical-care quality: an implicit judgment of process; an implicit judgment of outcome; an implicit judgment of process and outcome combined (quality-of-care judgment); an explicit judgment of process; and an explicit judgment of outcome (estimation of group outcome).

DEFINITIONS

Process includes what a physician does on behalf of a patient (diagnostic investigations and therapeutic interventions), the sources of medical care, and patient compliance.

Outcome comprises the results of care — i.e., patient response in terms of mortality, symptoms, ability to work or perform daily activities, and physiologic measurements.

Implicit judgments rely on the subjective opinion of the individual judge; no predetermined criteria are used. Explicit judgments rely on predetermined criteria set by group agreement.

STUDY SETTING

The study was conducted at the Baltimore City Hospitals. All members of the senior staff are members of the full-time faculty of Johns Hopkins University School of Medicine. Most members of the medical house staff are United States citizens, and all are fellows in medicine at Johns Hopkins University.

CASE SELECTION

Patients were selected for the study if they had one of three medical conditions, — urinary-tract infection, hypertension, or an ulcerated lesion in the stomach or duodenum (including possible ulcerated gastric carcinoma), — and the quality of their care was evaluated by each of the five methods. Each condition was identified. For urinary-tract infection the bacteriology laboratory's files were used to identify all patients 15 years of age or older who had been in the emergency room from January 1 to May 15, 1971, and who had a clean-catch urine culture indicating a growth of pathogenic bacteria equivalent to 100,000 solonies per milliliter. To identify hypertension, records of all patients seen in the emergency room were reviewed daily from January 1 to April 30, 1971, and a list was compiled of all such patients who had a diastolic blood pressure reading greater than or equal to 115. For ulcerated lesions of the stomach or duodenum, from the x-ray department's records, a list was compiled of all patients examined between January 1 and May 15, 1971, whose x-ray films showed either an ulcerated lesion in the stomach, a duodenal ulcer or chronic changes consistent with peptic-ulcer disease. Although the patients selected either received their initial care in the emergency room or had specific x-ray findings, their subsequent care may have been received in the outpatient department, on the inpatient service, in private physicians' offices or at other hospitals.

METHODS

For the three implicit methods (the implicit judgments of process, of outcome, and of process and outcome combined) the physicians acting as judges read a detailed two-page abstract of each case. Information for the abstract was collected by a review of each patient's record combined with a patient interview, both of which were completed five months after the initial emergency-room visit or x-ray examination. All abstracts were prepared by the principal investigator with use of a structured format developed after a review of the literature and consultation with experts at Johns Hopkins Hospital. The abstract contained all the information in the medical record relevant to a decision concerning the quality of the care received by the patient. The patient interview, performed or supervised by the principal investigator, was conducted to determine patient compliance and condition at the end of the follow-up period (patient outcome) and to verify the use of other medical services.

The abstract differed from the medical record in three ways: it was legible; results of laboratory tests that were performed but not recorded in the medical record were recorded in the abstract; and information was placed in chronologic order. The abstract was used as a basis for forming the implicit judgments instead of the medical record to avoid having these judgments depend more on the legibility and organization of the record than on the content of the record.

The physicians who served as judges were faculty members at the Baltimore City Hospitals for at least one year before the study, had positions equivalent to assistant chief in the Department of Medicine, and were involved in acute patient care. Ten physicians met these qualifications, and all agreed to participate in all five assessment methods.

The first page of the abstract contained both background information, such as demographic data, relevant past history, presenting complaint, physical examination and diagnosis, and medical-care process data for the five-month study period. The second page contained the outcome data also abstracted and summarized. The two pages of the abstract were connected by a seal.

On the basis of the information provided on the first page of the abstract, each of three physicians, who were selected from the 10 by a table of random numbers, decided whether the medical-care process was adequate or inadequate. The judgment was global, and the only instruction the physicians received was that only the processes likely to be of major help in producing an outcome beneficial to the patient should be considered — e.g., treating a hypertensive patient with antihypertensive medication. This decision was the *implicit-process* judgment.

The physician then broke the seal, read the data about the patient's outcome and answered three additional questions. The first was whether the outcome experienced by this patient could have been improved if the medical-care process had been better. This evaluation was the *implicit-outcome* judgment. Secondly, was the quality of the care received by this patient acceptable or unacceptable? This evaluation, based on reading both the process and the outcome data, was the *implicit quality-of-care* judgment. Finally, if the care was acceptable, was this the fault of the patient or of the medical-care system? When the three physicians disagreed, a case was rated adequate if two of the three considered it adequate.

To make explicit process judgments, criteria were first developed. For each of the three medical conditions the 10 physicians were asked to select the criteria that were necessary to provide good care and that were likely to have an important effect on outcome. For this method only, a second group of physicians, in addition to the group previously described, was picked.

The second group, selected from the faculty at Johns Hopkins Hospital, consisted of a subgroup of seven specialists for each of the three conditions studied. Criterial selected by at least five of the seven physicians were applied by the study team to each case to obtain an *explicit-process* judgment.

Estimations of group outcome are a means of developing criteria to make an explicit-outcome judgment. Physicians state what they think various patient outcomes — e.g., blood-pressure control — should be for groups of patients with specific medical conditions within a given time after treatment. The actual level of control experienced by the patients is then compared to what the physicians defined as acceptable. This assessment proceeded as follows: patients with each medical condition were divided into groups based on characteristics likely to affect prognosis (e.g., age for hypertensive patients); and for each of the patient outcomes measured, such as blood-pressure control, the physicians were asked to estimate for each group of patients the number of patients expected to have uncontrolled blood pressure after five months if the entire group of patients received no therapy, received therapy currently being provided at the institution, and received adequate therapy. These estimates were then compared to the patient outcomes, such as blood-pressure level, measured by the study team.

These five methods all involve peer review and have been used as measurements of quality of care. They differ, however, either in the technic or in the data used as a basis to form the peer judgment. (A more detailed description of the methods and lists of the criteria used is given elsewhere.(2))

RESULTS

Initially, 304 patients (112 with a urinary-tract infection, 117 with hypertension, and 75 with an ulcerated lesion in the stomach or duodenum) were included. The medical record was abstracted for 303 (99.7 per cent) of these patients, and a patient interview was completed with 297 patients (97.7 per cent), and only these patients were included in the final study.

The patients had the following demographic characteristics: 42 per cent were white, and 58 per cent were black; 37 per cent were male; 28 per cent were on Medicaid; 35 per cent were between 15 and 34, and 58 per cent between 35 and 64 years of age, and 7 per cent were 65 or older; and most of the women were housewives or worked as domestics or waitresses, whereas the men had blue-collar jobs such as steel workers or mechanics.

Table 1. Distribution of Observed Patient Outcomes after a Five-Month Follow-up Period, According to Condition.

OUTCOME*	CONDITION						
	URINARY-TRACT INFECTION		HYPERTENSION		ULCERATED LE-SION IN STOM-ACH OR DUO-DENUM		TOTALS
	no.	%	no.	%	no.	%	no. %
Total patients	107	100	114	100	75	100	296 100
1. Death	1	0.9	1	0.9	1	1.3	3 1.0
2. Decreased activity	28	26.2	27	23.7	31	41.3	86 29.1
3. Continued symptoms	56	52.3	47	41.2	46	61.3	149 50.3

4. Measurements:

a) For patients with urinary-tract infections (results of clean-catch urine culture at end of study period):

b) For patients with hypertension (control of blood pressure at end of study period)†:

	no.	%
Total patients alive	106	100
1. < 25,000 col/ml	54	50.9
2. >25,000, < 50,000 col/ml	14	13.2
3. >50,000, < 100,000 col/ml	4	3.8
4. >100,000 col/ml	34	32.1

	no.	%
Total patients alive	113	100
1. Blood pressure controlled	63	55.8
2. Blood pressure not con-trolled	50	44.2

*Outcome categories 2, 3 & 4 are not mutually exclusive.

†Blood-pressure control is defined as follows: for patients ≤ 39 yr. of age, end of study period must be ≤ 150/95; for patients 40-50 yr. of age, value must be ≤160/100; & for patients > 59 yr. of age value must be ≤170/105.

At the end of the five-month study period, 50 (44 per cent) of the 113 hypertensive patients who were still alive had uncontrolled blood pressure (see Table 1). Thirty-four patients (30 per cent) did not have a repeat blood-pressure reading taken during the study period to determine whether or not they had sustained dias-diastolic hypertension (Fig.1). Simple tests, such as determinations of potassium and serum urea nitrogen and electrocardiography, were performed for approximately 90 per cent of the 71 patients confirmed as hypertensive, and 60 per cent of these patients had rapid-sequence intravenous pyelography. No case of surgically correctable hypertensive disease was identified. Figure 2 suggests that various problems led to this high rate of uncontrolled hypertension at the end of the study period. These problems were insufficient follow-up care (26 patients), noncompliance with medication (four patients) and inadequate adjustment of the drug dosage by the physician (19 patients). For only one patient was it apparent that the lack of pharmaceutical control was due to the nature of the disease. These data suggest that in this institution emphasis was on discovering underlying causes of hypertension, such as primary aldosteronism or unilateral renal disease, rather than on developing an environment conducive to long-term control.

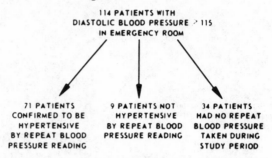

Figure 1. Diagnostic Process for Hypertensive Patients.

Initial antibiotic therapy was appropriate for 94 of the 107 patients with a urinary-tract infection (Fig. 3); however, diagnostic procedures, such as intravenous pyelography, were performed in less than 50 per cent of the cases in which they were indicated. No cases of surgically correctable genitourinary disease were found. For 60 patients (61.2 per cent) the initial urine-culture sensitivities indicated that the bacteria were resistant to the antibiotic originally chosen. In only 11 cases was the patient then questioned to determine progression of the disease, and in only one case was the antibiotic changed. The urine of 10 of the 98 patients who were initially treated with an antibiotic was re-cultured. For only two of the 52 patients who were found by the study team to have a positive or questionably positive culture at the end of the study period were the physicians responsible for their care aware of this continuing infection. Again, initial medical care was appropriate, but follow-up care was deficient.

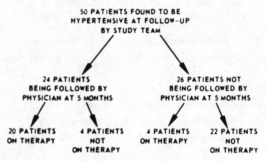

Figure 2. Therapeutic Process for Hypertensive Patients.

In general, acute hospital care for patients with complications of ulcer disease was excellent; however, at the end of the study period, 61 per cent of the patients with an ulcerated lesion were still symptomatic. Twenty-eight of the 75 patients were treated with either antacids four times daily or a six-feeding diet (or both) (Fig. 4), and surgery was performed for two of the five patients with a possible malignant gastric ulcer. Of the 45 patients who were found by the study team to be symptomatic at the end of the study period, 20 had appointments to be seen again, and 19 were taking some type of ulcer medication. Lack of continuing care is again evident.

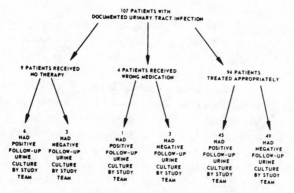

Figure 3. Therapeutic Process and Outcome for Patients with Urinary-Tract Infection.

If the medical-care process is considered adequate when at least two out of the three judges rated it as such, 23.3 per cent of the patients had an adequate medical-care process (Table 2, row 4, columns 1 and 2). The adequacy of the medical-care process varied according to disease, patients with urinary-tract infection being judged as receiving the poorest care (Table 2). At least two judges thought that outcome was unimprovable in 63.2 per cent of the cases (Table 3, row 2, columns 1 and 2). Quality of care was judged acceptable by at least two judges for 27.1 per cent of the cases (Table 3, row 3, columns 1 and 2).

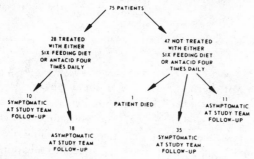

Figure 4. Therapeutic Process and Outcome for Patients with an Ulcerated Lesion in the Stomach or Duodenum.

Tests for the reliability of these judgments were conducted. Since the cases were randomly assigned, inter-physician variability could be tested by examination of the means of all 10 physicians for each judgment. Significant differences were found. When intra-physician variation was tested, the process judgment was changed in 24 of 160 cases (16 per cent). These changes were more likely to occur when there was initial disagreement among three judges than when the judges were in agreement ($p < 0.001$).

The validity of these judgments is difficult to determine. Satisfactory conclusions probably await controlled clinical trials. In lieu of such data, an impression of the validity of the implicit judgments can be obtained by comparison of the process judgment with the actual patient outcomes measured by the study team. It would be expected, if the process judgment had some innate validity, that the cases judged to have inadequate process would suffer a poorer outcome. A significant relation ($p < .05$) was found between the adequacy of medical-care process and the result of follow-up urine culture (i.e., patients with inadequate process were more likely to have a positive follow-up culture). A similar positive relation was observed between the process judgment and the results of the follow-up blood-pressure reading. Positive nonsignificant relations were found in all but one of the other comparisons relating the process judgment to other outcomes, such as activity and symptom levels. These data demonstrate a questionable relation between the process judgment and actual outcome measurement. This relation might have been considerably better if the process judgments had not been so stringent.

CONDITION	PROCESS JUDGMENT				
	ADEQUATE BY ALL 3 JUDGES	ADEQUATE BY 2 JUDGES	INADEQUATE BY 2 JUDGES	INADEQUATE BY ALL 3 JUDGES	TOTALS
	no. %	no. %	no. %	no. %	
Urinary-tract infection	2 1.9	11 10.3	17 15.9	77 72.0	107
Hypertension	19 16.7	12 10.5	29 25.4	54 47.4	114
Ulcerated lesion in stomach or duodenum	8 10.7	17 22.7	12 16.0	38 50.7	75
Totals	29 9.8	40 13.5	58 19.6	169 57.0	296

Table 2. Summary of Process Judgments for All Cases According to Condition.

Four of the 296 cases (1.4 per cent) met all the explicit-process criteria agreed upon by 2/3 of the Baltimore City Hospitals physicians; six cases (2 per cent) met all the criteria similarly agreed upon by the Johns Hopkins Hospital specialty teams (no significant difference). The same number of criteria were not applied to all cases in each condition, since the questionnaires used to elicit these criteria were branched, and patients were classified into subgroups. For patients with a urinary-tract infection a different list of criteria was devised for males versus females, for those with a previous history of urinary-tract infection versus those without evidence of a previous infection, etc. The mean number of criteria applied to the cases of urinary-tract infection was 13.5, to the hypertension cases 18.1, and to the ulcerated-lesion cases 15.2. For each condition the mean percentages of criteria fulfilled were 52, 58 and 35 respectively.

Estimates of group outcomes were obtained for four outcomes for urinary-tract infection, three for hypertension, and three for ulcerated lesion (a total of 10). These outcomes were as follows: mortality and decreased activity for each condition; continued symptoms for patients with a urinary-tract

Implicit Judgment	Result				
	Positive* by 3 Judges	Positive* by 2 Judges	Negative† by 2 Judges	Negative† by 3 Judges	Totals
	no. %	no. %	no. %	no. %	
Process judgment	29 9.8	40 13.5	58 19.6	169 57.0	296
Outcome judgment	135 45.6	52 17.6	33 11.1	76 25.7	296
Quality-of-care judgment	31 10.5	49 16.6	88 29.7	128 43.2	296

*Either adequate process, unimprovable outcome or acceptable quality of care.
†Either inadequate process, improvable outcome or unacceptable quality of care.

Table 3. Summary of Implicit Judgments for All Cases.

infection or an ulcerated lesion; and urine-culture results for patients with a urinary-tract infection or a blood-pressure level for patients with hypertension. All the estimates, except for blood-pressure level and urine-culture results, proved unusable, either because of small numbers (e.g., mortality) or because the observed outcomes were worse than the physicians estimated they would be if the patients received no therapy. For example, the physicians estimated that 45 of the 75 patients with ulcer would still be experiencing symptoms after five months if they received no therapy, and that 25 patients would be experiencing symptoms under present therapy; however, the study team found that 46 patients were still experiencing ulcer symptoms. Analysis of the blood-pressure and urine-culture data permitted an evaluation of quality of care according to the formula: Percentage of patients receiving adequate care equals observed value minus lower limit of the range divided by range times 100. The value of the range for each outcome measure was defined as the difference between the value estimated if the patients received adequate therapy minus the value estimated if they received no therapy. By this formula, 40 per cent of the patients with urinary-tract infections and 44 per cent of those with hypertension had acceptable care. This formula illustrates how group-outcome information can be used, but it is not meant to endow this method with validity or reliability.

DISCUSSION

Previous work in the area of quality assessment has emphasized medical process; however, major differences were found in this study between the methods using process data and those using outcome data. It is apparent that the results of the quality assessment were determined by the method used. The findings ranged from 1.4 to 63.2 per cent of the cases in which care was acceptable (see Table 4). Furthermore, the most widely used method, the explicit process judgment, produced results at the lower end of this range. It seems ironic that at a time when physicians are beginning to appreciate the need to assess quality of care, they should generally choose a method that produces the severest judgments.

Method	Acceptable Quality of Care	
	no.	%
1. Implicit-process judgment	69	23.3
2. Implicit-outcome judgment	187	63.2
3. Implicit-quality-of-care judgment	80	27.1
4. Explicit-process criteria:		
a) Baltimore City Hospitals group	4	1.4
b) Johns Hopkins group (specialists)	6	2.0
5. Estimation of group outcome:		
a) For urinary-tract infections, based on positive urine culture (106 cases)	42	39.6
b) For hypertension, based on uncontrolled blood pressure (113 cases)	50	44.2

Table 4. Summary of the Assessment of Quality of Care as Measured by Each of the Five Methods Studied for All 296 Cases.

From analysis of the implicit approach, three observations can be made. In the first place, the implicit process judgment correlated only weakly with the outcomes measured at follow-up study. These results, combined with conclusions from a review of the literature of efficacy,(2) suggest that the judges were rating medical care in terms of conventional wisdom and not in terms of only the critical processes that would be likely to improve a patient's health. Secondly, all three implicit judgments varied significantly with the condition under study. This was true even though all three conditions were medical conditions requiring follow-up observation and all patients received care at the same institution from the same group of doctors. This variation suggests that a method of assessing quality of care for a limited number of tracer or index conditions, as an indication of the quality rendered for all conditions, may be subject to error. Thirdly, the reliability of the implicit approach was not sufficient to evaluate a group of cases. This means that if this method is to be used in deciding how well a physician performs, a reasonably large number of cases must be examined. Conclusions based on a single case will be faulty owing to the limited reliability of the judgments.

Four of the 296 cases met all the explicit process criteria required by the internists at the Baltimore City Hospitals, and six met all the criteria required by the teams of specialists from the Johns Hopkins Hospital. This occurred in an institution where recording information by young house officers is emphasized. Development of detailed criteria lists may be feasible, and satisfactory agreement can be obtained between generalists and specialists; however, considering mecical-care recording practices and the disagreements of efficacy in the literature, the use of criteria lists, such as those generated in this study, as standards may be likely to decrease efficiency of medical care by dramatically increasing the number of medical-care processes performed without substantially affecting the health of patients. Even if only an average of 15 criteria had been applied to each case, successful compliance with these lists of criteria would have doubled and perhaps tripled the number of physician services and laboratory tests performed. A possible explanation for the strictness of the list of process criteria was that only academic physicians were involved in setting them. However, Payne and Lyons, in work not yet published, examined quality of care on the basis of a list of criteria established by nonacademic physicians and obtained similar results.

Evaluating care through estimations of group outcome proved to be the least satisfactory method in terms of both physician willingness to provide estimates and validity of the estimates. At present this method does not seem to be a practical one for assessing quality of care, even though it is clinically the most logical since it requires a physician to judge care as a function of its results rather than in terms of what the physician does. Its ineffectiveness seems a tacit criticism of both medical education and research.

Development of quality-assessment methods is limited by gaps in information on the natural history of many medical conditions, the relation of the processes of medical care to patient outcomes, and the basic understanding of the principles of quality assessment. Given present knowledge, standard setting based on explicit process criteria, which emphasizes the technical scientific aspect of medicine, may be inappropriate. Even for the medical conditions for which medical care has been shown to be efficacious, a large component of patient outcome is probably dependent on sociologic and psychologic factors. The rapidity with which an ulcer heals could depend more on the way in which the doctor and patient relate than on the duration and level of the antacid dose. The only possible way to account, though indirectly, for these factors is to collect data on the patient's activity and symptom levels, as well as to measure physical findings or perform laboratory tests.

It is ironic that the outcome indicators that are of vital importance to the patient — i.e., his activity and symptom levels — had nonsignificant correlations with either the implicit or explicit process judgments. If routine efforts to assess quality of care are to lead to improved health status at a reasonable cost, three major research objectives must be met. First of all, for the common medical conditions, controlled studies relating processes to outcomes should be conducted. Secondly, experimental studies must be conducted to compare the capability of different methods to assess and assure the quality of medical care. Thirdly, studies that describe the quality of care received by patients who use a given provider of medical care and have been found to have a specific medical condition must be related to studies designed to ascertain percentage of patients, in the population for which the provider or institution (or both) was responsible, needed care for the conditions studied but did not receive any medical services, and also the percentage of patients with one of the specified conditions being seen at the institution but not receiving care for the specified condtion because it had not been properly diagnosed. The present study did not answer either of these two questions. Meeting these objectives will require close co-operation among practicing physicians, physicians from academic medical centers and experts in evaluation design.

This study suggests that the outcome of 73 (70 per cent) of the 104 patients with unacceptable quality of care and improvable outcome could have been improved if the medical-care system had been better. Similarly, 132 (71 per cent) of the 186 patients with inadequate medical-care process and unacceptable quality of care were judged to have received inadequate care as a result of deficiencies in the medical-care system. These data and the description of the care that these patients received (Part 2 of the Results) suggest that a few critical changes in the way care is provided, such as efforts to improve follow-up observation, to teach physicians how to use antihypertensive medications more effectively and to instruct physicians on the importance of obtaining post-therapeutic urine cultures, might improve outcome with little additional expense. Such changes should be encouraged even while definitive results of methodologic research are awaited.

REFERENCES

(1) HR I, 92nd Congress, 2nd Session, Sec 249F, pp 414-453 (in the Senate of the United States October 6, 1972)

(2) Brook RH: A Study of Methodologic Problems Associated With Assessment of Quality of Care (ScD thesis, Johns Hopkins University, 1972). National Center for Health Services Research and Development (in press)

(3) Codman EA: A Study in Hospital Efficiency: As demonstrated by the case report of the first five years of a private hospital: Boston, Thomas Todd Company, 1916

(4) Cabot RC: Diagnostic pitfalls identified during a study of three thousand autopsies. JAMA 59:2295-2298, 1912

(5) Shapiro S, Weiner L, Densen PM: Comparison of prematurity and perinatal mortality in a general population and in the population of a prepaid group practice, medical care plan. Am J Public Health 48:170-187, 1958

(6) Gonnella JS, Goran MJ, Williamson JW, et al: Evaluation of patient care: an approach. JAMA 214:2040-2043, 1970

(7) Thompson JD, Marquis DB, Woodward RL, et al: End-result measurements of the quality of obstetrical care in two U.S. Air Force hospitals. Med Care 6:131-143, 1968

(8) Williamson JW, Alexander M, Miller GE: Continuing education and patient care research. JAMA 201:938-942, 1967

(9) *Idem:* Priorities in patient-care research and continuing medical education. JAMA 204:303-308, 1968

(10) Brook RH, Stevenson RL Jr: Effectiveness of patient care in an emergency room. N Engl J Med 283:904-907, 1970

(11) Brook RH, Appel FA, Avery C, et al: Effectiveness of inpatient follow-up care. N Engl J Med 285:1509-1514, 1971

(12) Fessel WJ, Van Brunt EE: Assessing quality of care from the medical record. N Engl J Med 286:134-138, 1972

(13) Brook RH, Berg MH, Schechter PA: Effectiveness of nonemergency care via an emergency room: a study of 166 patients with gastrointestinal symptoms. Ann Intern Med 78:333-339, 1973

THE CONSEQUENCES OF ACCOUNTABILITY TO THE COMMUNITY

Victor W. Sidel

The message of impending change in national medical care is essentially the same; only our perspectives of the change, and therefore our styles of presentation of the message, are different. I want to try——and I must emphasize my arrogance in trying to do this—to say something from the point of view of the communities we serve.

My viewpoint is a distorted one because it stems from the problems of New York City, which are hardly typical of the country as a whole. What Dr. Ebert has called the "rising dissatisfaction with medical care in the United States" has already risen in New York City. But this viewpoint may, by its very exaggeration of the issues and by its polemical style, give those who have been shielded from it some new insights into the passion with which these issues are felt by at least some of those whom we are supposed to be serving.

A representative of one of these communities might say, in part for its shock value, that we in academic medicine and research are about to be awakened from our elitist dream. For two decades we have lived in a dream world which blissfully lacked—with rare exceptions—appropriate cost accounting to ourselves or to others; lacked lay audit (and for that matter often lacked effective peer review) of our activities; and lacked direct accountability to the community. In some places, money earmarked for research was used for teaching and for patient care; in other places (and in some of the same places) money earmarked for patient care was used for research and teaching; in almost no place was teaching entirely paid for by teaching monies; and in almost all places the decisions on priorities, goals, and methods and the evaluations of their effectiveness were made almost entirely by professionals.

National health insurance of any form——leaving aside tokens such as the AMA Medi-credit proposal or Senator Long's catastrophic health insurance proposal, which cannot in my view qualify for the term national health insurance—will help to wake us from the dream. National health insurance can do so because with the rationalization of methods for paying for medical care should come accounting, audit, and accountability, not only for the practicing physician but also for those of us in academic medicine and research. And with the advent of these three A's should come the demand by our communities that they——not we--set the priorities for the use of their money and for the provision of our services.

Among the things that communities may demand from us, using the leverage provided by national health insurance, are: 1. that the community, rather than the professionals, determine the pattern of recruitment, length of training, and content of medical education; 2. that the community, rather than the professionals, determine the ratio of primary care to specialty care, and therefore the number of primary care physicians and specialists trained; 3. that the community, rather than the professionals, determine the relative wage scales, numbers, and duties of health workers; and 4. that the community, rather than the professionals, determine the areas in which research will be done and the methods which are used.

Not all forms of national health insurance will bring on these changes equally quickly. As we have already noted, some of the current proposals which are called national health insurance will not only fail to produce these changes quickly, but may actually delay them. Other proposals—such as the Kennedy Health Security Bill and even, though to a lesser extent, the Nixon Administration proposals—may at least pave the way for these changes. And some proposals, such as those put forth by the Physicians Forum and by the Medical Committee for Human Rights, while they have not yet reached legislative deliberation because of the power of professional lobbies, would bring these changes very quickly indeed by hastening the end of the entrepreneurial practice of medicine and research, by directing medical education toward areas of urgent need, and by insisting on the right of the consumer to control his own services.

The end of the dream does not mean the end of the world, except for the few of us who are unwilling or unable to adapt to the new rules. For those who can adapt there will be new satisfactions, the most important of which will be the knowledge that we are participating in social change that may help end some of the inequities which have turned the American dream into a nightmare for all too many of our people.

But new forms of satisfaction will be needed, and new people with different attitudes—or fundamental changes in current ones—will be required. Those who gain their satisfaction from being entrepreneurs, from being in a controlling position over others, from being one-up on students, residents, fellows, or patients, from playing abstruse intellectual games, from developing or using complex technical procedures with little thought about their consequences—these individuals may find this new world difficult to live in. But those who feel that the needs are immense and urgent, that the priorities are wrong, that change has been too long in coming, who are willing to lend their expertise to patients and communities in structuring the changes, and to sacrifice their narrow self-interest to the needs of the community—they may find the new world a reasonable and satisfying place in which to work.

I cannot overemphasize the magnitude of the attitudinal change which will be required of professionals if they are to respond successfully—successfully both for themselves and for those they serve—under the new conditions. Everything we have learned about how clever we are, how important we are, how relevant we are, how trusted we are, how self-sacrificing we are, will have to be re-examined. We may be forced to recognize that there are others in the community who are equally clever, equally important, equally relevant, equally trusted, equally self-sacrificing—and whose ideas about how medicine should be taught, researched, and practiced are diametrically opposed to our own. Up to this point we professionals have held almost all the cards; the advent of effective universal national health insurance may turn a few trumps over to nonprofessionals.

One example of this is the list of community demands cited previously. Many of us, in consequence of our training and elite status, may believe deeply that communities composed of laymen have no competence to determine the content of medical education; have no expertise in apportioning primary and specialty care; have no right to determine relative wage scales; and above all have none of the knowledge necessary to influence research priorities and methods. Further, many of us may believe that such community powers would be disastrous to medical education, practice, and research. I would simply point out that such beliefs are attitudes; they are neither self-evident truths nor the conclusions from rational study; and it is these very attitudes, affecting much of what many of us may think we hold most dear, that must change.

I do not wish to waste your time or mine by engaging in dreams—which some may view as nightmares—of my own. I do not mean to suggest that the changes I foresee will occur tomorrow, or next year, or immediately after the passage of a program such as the Kennedy bill, or even immediately after the passage of legislation significantly more powerful which puts all health workers on salary and give significant control over them to lay boards and audit committees. What I do mean to predict is that these changes are coming; that health care as a right rather than as a privilege will change—at whatever speed, and probably in spite of rather than because of the medical profession—from a cliché into a reality; and that that change will have a predictable, and enormous, impact on academic medicine and on research.

We in academic medicine at this juncture have two choices. We can continue what we are doing in our narrow specialties, ignore or even fight against the changes, and while we will probably succeed in delaying them we shall then have precious little to say about the final shape of the national health care system which evolves or the role of academic medicine and research in it. This would be a loss, both for us and for our patients and communities. Or we can embrace the opportunity which the drive for effective national health insurance presents. By working with those who would bring it about we can make certain that the importance to effective medical care of solid grounding in scientific principles is not forgotten; that certain types of research, though apparently more basic or esoteric, are recognized to have greater long-range prospects of success than research more directly related to common or immediate problems; that the satisfaction of the health worker is acknowledged to be an important element in the health services equation which cannot be neglected; that teaching and research funds are clearly separated in budgeting and appropriation from the service funds—as they are in most countries which have universal health care systems—to prevent the demands for services from leaving little or no resources for research or teaching; and that there is a balance between freedom to experiment and teach and responsiveness to society's control which may in the long run serve the country's needs better than total freedom or total control. We shall find, if we but look, that there are many in every community who share our concerns and our hopes for the future, who are eager to learn from us the solutions to the problems of providing effective teaching and research as we perceive them, and who wish to work closely and rationally with us.

If we adopt this course of working with patients and communities to help bring about and shape the changes, we may learn as much if not more than is learned from us. We may learn that the problems and therefore the priorities of many of our communities are very different from our own. We may learn the consequences of *their* dreams having often been repeatedly deferred—drying up, as Langston Hughes has put it, like a raisin in the sun—and we may learn the explosive nature of the consequences of a dream deferred. (1) We may learn that there are other problems to be solved, in the solution of which we can be useful and about which we had not known or had not cared. We may learn that other workers in service, education, or research are equally, or more, competent in their areas than we are in ours, and that we doctors need not always be their leader in all things. We may learn that there are satisfactions which have escaped many of us in work of kinds other than intellectual, and this may bring us closer to those whom we serve and to those with whom we work. Most important, we may learn that academic medicine and research is not the center of the universe, or even of its medical epicycle; that it is a satellite, important but not central; and that it may have to alter radically its size, shape, speed, and direction in order to be most relevant to the community needs at the center.

National health insurance will not by itself make all this happen. Much greater change in the structure of our society and in those who control it will be needed before the current dream vanishes and the new one materializes. But national health insurance can—and I hope will—be used as a lever to bring accounting, audit, and accountability closer.

We academics may rationally fear some of the consequences, as we would anything which may change our comfortable *status quo*. During the long period of our professional dominance, there has been an astonishing concordance between what we said was best for medicine (or education and research) and what was in fact best for medicine's practitioners. It is probably not a coincidence that the era of our professional dominance has produced what much of the public believes—with reason—to be a disastrously unsatisfactory system of medical care.

In a larger sense, therefore, we academics should welcome the impact of effective national health insurance, for the reason that it will help change the system of medical care in the United States and give us opportunities to use in new and effective ways the talent, training, and dedication of which those of us in academic medicine and research have long been proud.

NOTE

(1) Hughes, Langston: Harlem. *In* Selected Poems. New York, Alfred A Knopf, 1959.

HERE'S WHAT H.M.O.
IS ALL ABOUT

John B. Dunne

"Would a rose by any other name smell as sweet?" The poet's question can be used here to ask the question, "Does the renaming of a prepaid group practice to Health Maintenance Organization change the odor or complexion of this once maligned health delivery system?"

I am not prepared to state that its espousal by the present administration has made H.M.O. any more palatable to some physicians and other health professionals. I am inclined to believe that some of these gentlemen (and women) are glad to have someting to distract the health consuming public's attention from the meteoric rise of costs of hospitalization and physicians's fees. Thus, they are willing to cheer for a field goal if they can't have a touchdown. I cannot say whether the traditional foes of this type of "organized" medicine would appear so docile, given other more favorable circumstances. But never has the climate been better for the introduction of many health professionals to what may well be the "wave of the future." Let us pause here to read some of the President's rhetoric, as he introduced the subject to Congress in his health message of Feb. 18, 1971.

In recent years, a new method of delivering health services has achieved growing respect. This new approach has two essential attributes. It brings together a comprehensive range of medical services in a single organization, so that a patient is assured of convenient access to all of them. And it provides needed services for a fixed contract fee, which is paid in advance by all subscribers. Such an organization can have a variety of forms and names and sponsors. One of the strengths of this new concept, in fact, is its great flexibility. The general term which has been applied to all of these units is "H.M.O." Health Maintenance Organization.(1)

Thus did the administration place its advocacy on the type of organization which only ten short years ago was anathema to many physicians and their organizations—not the least of these the Allegheny County Medical Society. Thus, also did the leadership in Washington seek to defuse the rush toward National Health Insurance, as sponsored by the late Walter Reuther and, more recently, by the Woodcock Committee and Senator Edward Kennedy. One must read the bill, which was introduced to start the health ball rolling, to see that prepaid group health organizations, and linkages with them were to be rewarded in this insurance program. Nevertheless, in the months to come, some form of prepaid comprehensive health coverage probably will be recognized as the panacea to many of our health delivery woes and ills. Let us consider more of what President Nixon had to say:

> The H.M.O. also organizes medical resources in a way that is more convenient for patients, and more responsive to their needs. There was a time, when every housewife had to go to a variety of shops and markets and push carts to buy her faimily's groceries. Then, along came the supermarket, making her shopping chores much easier, and also giving her a wider range of choice and lower prices. The H.M.O. provides similar advantages in the medical field. Rather than forcing the consumer to thread his way through a complex maze of separate services and specialists, it makes a full range of resources available through a single organization, often at a single stop, and makes it more likely that the right combination of resources will be utilized.(1)

I am not completely certain that the Kaiser Permamente Medical Program or Health Insurance Program or the Yale Health Care Program consider themselves "supermarkets." I am sure that they look upon themselves as providers of comprehensive one class programs, designed to meet the needs of their members at a reasonable, predictable cost. But a supermarket? No, I don't think so. The implications of a supermarket are that the customer often buys what he sees, rather than what he needs. This is antithetic to the principle of the H.M.O. or prepaid group practice, which attempts to keep the charges for medical services at a reasonable level.

How can we best describe an H.M.O.? It is an organization for the delivery of health care to its members, who have paid a predetermined capitation fee (usually on a monthly basis). This organization can elect to provide all the services by physicians, who are partners or employees, and through owned health facilities, or by contracting for services. It might be stated that a Health Maintenance Organization is based on the following principles:

It is an organized system of health care that accepts the responsiblity to provide, or otherwise assure, the delivery of an agreed upon set of comprehensive services, for a voluntarily enrolled group of persons in a certain area. It is reimbursed through a pre-negotiated and fixed periodic payment made by, or on behalf of, each member or family unit enrolled in the plan.

It should be stated here, and restated often, that a Health Maintenance Organization must be dedicated to maintaining health and preventing disease, as well as providing treatment for disease and trauma, when it occurs. It is only when the members and the physicians and all other health providers fully embrace this concept, that the full effectiveness of an H.M.O. can be realized.

It is, therefore, incumbent upon the organization to provide easy access to outpatient or ambulatory services, periodic health examination, screening services, well baby clinics and, where practical, multi phasic screening.

Also desirable are mental health, alcoholism, drug treatment, diabetes and cardio-vascular support programs.

HISTORICAL BACKGROUND

When we look upon an H.M.O. or prepaid group health program as a recent phenomenon we do a disservice to the pioneers in this movement.

Perhaps we must look back to the time of Lister when a number of surgical titans emerged. Each of these giants developed a new art, and found it desirable to surround himself with a coterie of assistants, diagnosticians and students. This could be characterized as a group practice. Some medical schools began to unify their faculties into something resembling a clinic. An early one was at Johns Hopkins University. Ample funds allowed them to collect an outstanding faculty and group of outstanding practitioners.(2)

In the 1880's, two Mayo brothers journeyed from Minnesota to Baltimore to study the makeup of the Johns Hopkins group, and returned to found the Mayo Clinic in Rochester, Minnesota. Gradually, services beyond surgery were added, and the term "Mayo Clinic" was adopted in 1909. The history of this famous group is medical legend and, based on its success and leadership, others followed and flourished.

The development of a group for the benefit of workers may have had its inception in Colver, Pa., a small coal mine town near Ebensburg in Cambria County. Dr. Frank Martin set up a small hospital and clinic in 1916 to treat the miners of the Colver Mine and their families. The men paid a fixed amount each month from their wages, which was withheld by the company and remitted to Dr. Martin. The hospital was also open 14 hours a day as the emergency room in case of mine disasters. This H.M.O. for Colver miners and families has persisted until today and has 500 members.(3)

In 1929, Dr. Michael A. Shadid in Elk City, Oklahoma, called the farmers in the community together, and offered to build a hospital and provide treatment to them and their families for an annual membership fee. In spite of extreme opposition from county and state medical societies and the A.M.A., the venture was started. The state licensure board tried to deny licenses to physicians who agreed to serve on the staff. The support of Governor Wm. H. Murray and the

Farmers Union helped the project along, in spite of the opposition of doctors and other hospitals.(4)

A $100,000 anti-trust suit against the state and county medical societies finally broke the back of the opposition, and the group in Elk City went on to being an example to the rest of the country in establishment of prepaid group practice.(5)

SETTING UP AN H.M.O.

It is one thing to accept the principle of the Health Maintenance Organization and quite another to set the activity in motion to launch one in a community. In order to do so the following points must be considered: 1. Are there enough physicians, who are committed to the concept of health maintenance through a prepaid group mechanism, to form an adequate staff? 2. Is there a viable organization, with adequate finances to provide health maintenance; medical attention on a continuing basis; complete hospital service; educational and preventive services designed to keep citizens healthy? The answer to this question is probably no—so let's go to the next one. 4. Will the population of the area adequately support an H.M.O.—Maximally? Minimally? 5. Is there sufficient resistance on the part of non-H.M.O. physicians and other health providers to thwart its operation? 6. Will there be harmful competition between groups vying for membership of area citizens? 7. Are there sufficient poverty or marginal cases who need care and are under served? How about title XVIII & XIX Social Security recipients? 8. Can the H.M.O. be expected to expand and eventually contribute to even more adequate care and education of citizens of area?

Answers to these questions should be found before a serious effort is made to initiate an H.M.O. It is not my intention to answer all of these in this brief presentation but comment should be made on some of them.

If there is not a cadre of physicians of sufficient size, which is dedicated to the H.M.O. concept, the chances of success are minimal. Many physicians, who have operated throughout their professional career on a fee-for-service basis, will be inclined to ask many searching questions before acquiescing to a plan that will radically change this pattern. It is only when a physician balances the plus features of a non-predetermined income against the positive aspects of working as a partner in a group, that he will whole heartedly agree to participate, or turn down the opportunity. Several proposed plans have failed to materialize because there was not sufficient commitment on the part of a large enough group of physicians to make the H.M.O. a going concern.

Dr. Cecil C. Cutting, Executive Director of the Permamente Medical Group in Northern California said, in a talk before a symposium held in Oakland, California, March 1971, "Physician responsibility is so inherent to the program that we often overlook it. However, it is the physicians's acceptance of responsibility for providing comprehensive care to the membership, and his responsible role as a partner in administering the program, that are the keys to unlocking the potential of a rational organization of medical care."(6)

The costs of starting such a program are not inconsequential. It is with this in mind that H.E.W. is providing some grants to encourage the launching of some H.M.O.s. I believe that if a group is dependent, to any degree, on such a grant to keep the H.M.O. afloat, until the membership contributions catch up with the disbursements, the project is on very shaky grounds.

The required minimum number of paying members is now thought to be 10,000 to make the group financially sound. At least 70% of this membership should come from unions or associations of employees. If too many single memberships are purchased, or too many persons over 45 are enrolled, there tends to be overutilization of services. This may well skew the experience of the group, and the membership contributions may prove inadequate to keep the organization solvent. The parent organization, therefore, must have resources which will tide the H.M.O. over the lean period it will surely face in the initial stages. In the case of some prepaid group plans, a third party payor, such as Connecticut General Life Insurance Co., has taken over the responsibility of marketing memberships, and has agreed to redress losses of the group for the first few years. Such an arrangement is desirable in many instances, because the health insurors have a marketing organization and also can provide actuarial guidance to the embryonic H.M.O. Sound financial arrangements are a primary consideration in this endeavor.

Prepaid group practice organizations, which have succeeded in the past, have a preponderance of members who work regularly and receive adequate wages. If the population is large enough, but over half of the people are unemployed, or underemployed, the chances are that an H.M.O. could not survive, without a sizable government subsidy. There is no magic formula that can be invoked to make an H.M.O. self sustaining, if there aren't sufficient members who pay the full contribution each month. It is important, therefore, to obtain accurate demographic information, when considering initiating an H.M.O.

Since organized labor has supported several prepaid group health plans in the past, the presence of a fair sized number of union members affiliations is very important.

A certain amount of resistance from physicians and other health professionals can be anticipated. Only if it appears that it will serve as a very divisive force, should it be a deterrent factor. Some groups have started in the face of such resistance, and have become much stronger for having overcome it.

Competition can often be a two-edged sword. It is apparent, as one reads the guidelines set up by H.E.W. covering H.M.O.s, that they consider a certain amount of competition healthy. The thinking probably is that competition will force competing groups to offer better service packages to the members, for their monthly contributions. I agree with this, to some extent, but I think it can also be self defeating. The services offered should be based on what it is economically sound to provide for the members' dollars——not what it will take to beat out the group forming just down the road.

The H.M.O. should clearly define the service area in which it expects to operate, and this will somewhat minimize the chances of harmful competition.

The question of sufficient numbers of the poor has to do specifically with a requirement of H.E.W. if grant money is provided. The H.M.O. must signify a willingness to accept membership from among the indigent, those receiving Title XVIII benefits (Medicare) or Title XIX benefits (Medicaid), Federal Employees, CHAMPUS beneficiaries (armed services dependents) and V.A. benefit recipients. At present there are no specific guidelines to indicate just how many such persons the H.M.O. is obliged to accept for membership.

An experiment was carried out by the Portland Oregon Kaiser Foundation program in 1967. Memberships in the Kaiser group, were provided to 1,200 selected families receiving O.E.O. assistance. It was possible, from this experiment, to study the health care seeking patterns of these persons, under optimal conditions. It was this experience, and that with other groups involving poverty level persons, which stimulated H.E.W.'s interest in involving the poor and medically underserved in the H.M.O.s that it funds. It the statistics are reliable from this experience, and *if* the members from poverty levels are provided memberships at full rates, the emerging H.M.O. should be able to carry a reasonable number of such members, and still be on a sound economic footing. If H.E.W. funds are not sought, the H.M.O. can be as selective as it wishes about its membership—at least until National Health Insurance becomes a reality.(5)

Will the H.M.O. expand? This is a basic question and should be answered with all candor. If the initial thrust to launch the H.M.O. exhausts the funds and the enthusiasm of the incorporators, and there isn't plenty left over for growth and expansion, I, for one, would advise against going into it. It's going to require patience, perseverance, imagination, leadership and energy to start up an H.M O. and keep it going. One can't expect the community to welcome the effort with open arms. There'll have to be a continuing education and public information program to attract members, and keep them, once they've joined. That is why I stressed earlier the need for dedication of physicians. I would like to extend that to include the dedication of everyone connected with the H.M.O.

THE GOVERNMENT AGENCIES INVOLVED

Anyone who is interested in starting an H.M.O., with assistance from H.E.W., must be prepared to deal with several agencies, some of whom will have an input, others of whom will merely review and comment. These are chiefly, but not confined to: comprehensive health planning agencies, on the state, area, and county levels, regional and Central H.E.W. offices, State Hill-Burton Agency, Model Cities Agency (where applicable), and Regional Medical Program.

If this seems like an impregnable bureaucratic wall to the reader, I am not surprised. At this point in time, I am not sure that anyone could tell an applicant who should be approached first. I'd suggest that the area wide Comprehensive Health Planning Agency would be a logical first stop. They've developed expertise in preparation of grant applications for H.M.O.s. Before you approach them, you should have your plans pretty well spelled out in a feasibility report or study. This can be as general or as specific as you wish to make it.

After this disclosure of your intention, you may wish to commence gathering necessary information you will need to flesh out your grant application. You may then wish to seek advice from the *regional* H.E.W Office. They can advise you of pertinent schedule for funding cycles. The Central H.E.W. Office can also be of help at this time.

As you progress you'll want to touch base with the agencies listed above. The format for your grant application is provided by "H.M.O. supplement to Policy Statement, July 1, 1968, Health Services Development Projects Grants, Sec 314 (e) P.H.O. Act," which can be obtained, along with the grant form, from your Comprehensive Health Planning Agency Area Office.

From this point on, you'll have to supply the required information. Be as complete as you can, without padding out your grant request. Clarity and completeness are more important than mere bulk.

UTILIZATION OF PERSONNEL

One of the most important aspects of an H.M.O., is the effective and efficient use of personnel. Merely by drawing a group of doctors together to practice in concert is not going to solve the health manpower shortage, and provide adequate care for the members. A careful reappraisal will have to be made of the roles of those who will deal with the patient. For example, how much are they underutilized at present and how can they assume some of the traditional chores doctors have performed for years?

The unwillingness to share, or even abdicate some of these prerogatives, has in itself contributed mightily to the inability of the physician force to do what it does best—keep people well and treat those who aren't well.

The physicians can decide at early stages if they wish nurses or other designated personnel to take histories, give injections, weigh babies, remove sutures, consult with patients, give certain therapy, do Pap smears and pelvic examination, draw blood, give chemo-therapy etc. etc.

In her testimony before the Senate Committee on Labor and Public Welfare sub-committee on Health on Senate Bill 1182, Doris L. Wagner, Director of Nursing, Harvard Community Health Plan, said:

In the delivery of health care, more recognition should be given to the primary care role of the nurse. Nurses have been engaged in providing preventive services and in promoting good helath practices in communities, schools, industry, the home and in neighborhood health centers, but this role has had less recognition than the role played in crisis related situations in hospitals. Increasingly, they are assuming a primary care role, especially in pediatrics, in maternity care, and in the mental health field. We submit that increased involvement in primary care role of the nurse can result in helping people enter the health care system at a point early enough so medical science can be of help to them.(7)

Other allied health professionals can have salutary effect on freeing up physician hours to see patients. This would include physical therapists, laboratory technicians, medical secretaries, receptionists, multi-phasic screening technicians, etc.

The thrust should be toward delegation of authority to capable persons who make up the H.M.O. team.

In her testimony before the Senate Committee, Miss Wagner emphasized the role of the nurse as coordinator. This role gives her responsibilities for the member, from the time of his introduction to the health delivery system of the H.M.O., right through discharge, and even home health care, if needed. It is such comprehensive care which will make the H.M.O. the service provider of choice over mere indemnity insurance plans. Too much emphasis cannot be given the importance of the nurse to the program, and those other health professionals who will also back up the physician group.

I have previously alluded to certain elements of development and operating a Health Maintenance Organization which had to do with finances. Although service to members and maintaining their health is of primary importance, the H.M.O. operates on money. Therefore no one should attempt to launch an H.M.O. unless the financial aspects are thoroughly understood. Some pertinent things to consider are: 1. Minimum number of members with which a plan can successfully operate. 2. Reimbursement of physicians. 3. Service packages to be offered and their cost to members. 4. What services should be purchased? 5. How can the costs of marketing be amortized? Each of these considerations is important to the fiscal health of the H.M.O. Let's take them in order.

Until very recently, it was thought that a viable membership in an H.M.O. could be as low as 5,000. Presently, however it is considered that 10,000 members is more nearly a feasible figure, and there should be a reservoir of new members to take the place of dropouts. It is better to err on the side of too many members than too few. There is actuarial information available from established groups to assist the new H.M.O. in arriving at optimum figures and the makeup of the membership. Don't be afraid to ask.

The reimbursement of physicians is a most important matter, when establishing a group to function in an H.M.O. No two function the same. Even in the Kaiser Organization, each group has its own reimbursement plan, which is usually worked out by the physicians.

Many groups start physicians recently out of residency at $25,000 plus excellent fringe benefits and pension arrangements. Partners in successful groups are paid between $40,000 and $50,000 plus fringes. All malpractice insurance is paid by group.

However the formula is arrived at, it must be kept in mind that there are rewards (in the forms of bonuses) for keeping members well and for not over utilizing expensive services. Whether the doctors function as salaried employees or as partners in the group, they should be rewarded sufficiently so that they are willing to eschew fee-for-service reimbursement.

The service package which an H.M.O. can offer depend upon what facilities it owns or controls. Also, there is the matter of being competitive with existing health plans which merely indemnify expenditures of the subscriber (such as Blue Cross, Blue Shield). If an H.M.O.'s service packages are not competitive, it will have a difficult time attracting members. It is better to have options that the members can buy or reject, as they desire, rather than one standard package.

To give you an idea of what some plans are charging: Columbia Medical Plan, Columbia, Maryland charges $19.40 for single per month, $38.80 for a couple, and $65.55 for a family of three or more. Group Health Cooperative of Puget Sound charges $15.65 per month for a single, and $47.90 for a family of five to members of the Co-op.

What services can be purchased? Some H.M.O.'s are able to operate without owning their own hospital and clinic facilities. They contract for service for their members. Such an arrangement is less than optimal because the H.M.O. has less control of over-utilization and becomes little more than another health insurance carrier. It is ideal for the H.M.O. to own most of its facilities. In the monograph, "The Relevance of Pre-paid Group Practice to the Effective Delivery of Health Services,"(8) Dr. Saward says, "Data published from the United States Civil Service Commission on Federal Employees show that those under prepaid group practice programs had only 60% as many hospital days as under Indemnity Insurance or Blue Cross plans. The same ratio of hospital savings is indicated by the Medicare figures from our program in Portland: *Our Medicare patients used 1,700 days versus the national average of over 2,700 days.*"

These savings were due, in no small part, to the fact that Kaiser owns its health centers and hospitals. It may be necessary to buy service for patients needing certain specialized care such as kidney transplants etc. These should be the exception instead of the rule, however.

How can the costs of marketing be amortized? If the H.M.O. has a large resource of potential members, such as the membership of a union, or unions or all the municipal employees in a large city, or a similar pool, the costs of marketing memberships will not be great. If, on the other hand, many organizations have to be approached and members recruited from a large area, there can be considerable costs involved in enrollment. If a grant is obtained from H.E.W., an attempt should be made to have these costs covered under the grant. Another method is to seek the assistance of a large health insurance carrier or carriers, and let them do the work of enrollment. In any event, these costs must be considered and dealt with as an expected start up expense.

SUMMARY

This presentation has in no way dealt with all the aspects of organizing and launching an H.M.O. An attempt has been made to view the rewards but at once point out the pitfalls. There is competent help available for those desiring to initiate such a comprehensive health program. Some of the sources have been discussed in this paper. We have excellent examples of successes in the prepaid group health plans which are now operating. There have also been some not so successful. However, in the final analysis, the ideal of providing the type care for our people which puts a premium on keeping them well and not just paying their hospital bills after they are sick, is one which seems worthy of enthusiastic support.

BIBLIOGRAPHY

(1) President Richard M. Nixon's Health Message to Congress, Feb. 18, 1971. U.S. Govt. Printing Office, Washington, D.C.

(2) Richard Feise, Admn. Centerville Clinic, Fredericktown, Pa. Monograph; "H.M.O. and Community Health Center" May 1, 1971.

(3) E.P. Jordany, "The Physician and Group Practice."

(4) Michael A. Shadid, M.D., "Crusading Doctor"; Meador Pub. Co., 1956.

(5) W.A. McColl, M.D., "Group Practice & Prepayment of Medical Care."

(6) Anne R. Somers, "The Kaiser-Permanente Medical Care Program," The Commonwealth Fund, New York. 1971.

(7) Doris L. Wagner, "Statement on S-1182 Health Maintenance Organizations" made before Senate Committee on Labor and Public Welfare Subcommittee on Health. American Nurses' Assoc. Nov. 2, 1971.

(8) Ernest W. Saward, M.D. "The Relevance of Prepaid Group Practice To The Effective Delivery Of Health Services," June 1968. U.S. Dept of Health Education and Welfare Community Health Service, Office Of Group Practice Development.

HEALTH MANPOWER LICENSING AND
EMERGING INSTITUTIONAL RESPONSIBILITY
FOR THE QUALITY OF CARE

Rick J. Carlson

In 1962, Milton Friedman, discussing the growth of occupational licensure, urged its abolition even as to health care practitioners, who are generally considered the most critical subject for licensure. Professor Friedman did not equivocate:

> I am myself persuaded that licensure has reduced both the quantity and quality of medical practice; that it has reduced the opportunities available to people who would like to be physicians, forcing them to pursue occupations they regard as less attractive; that it has forced the public to pay more for less satisfactory medical service, and that it has retarded technological development both in medicine itself and in the organization of medical practice. I conclude that licensure should be eliminated as a requirement for the practice of medicine.(1)

In 1967 the National Advisory Commission on Health Manpower issued a two-volume work which included an extensive discussion of the licensure of health professionals. Its recommendations on this subject were more guarded, to say the least, than Friedman's:

> Careful study, analysis, and consultation among the health professions will be necessary to develop guidelines for legislative resolution of the issue of delegation and other problems in licensure.(2)

Although the problems have been recognized and the challenge made, no effective, comprehensive reforms have yet occurred.

The Friedman argument is not the thesis of this article despite its prescience. His argument is founded in nineteenth century liberalism and laissez-faire dogma. The argument here looks forward and anticipates change in the system for delivering health care, particularly a further increase in government involvement — contra laissez faire — in the restructuring of the system.

The perpetuation of licensure is but one manifestation of the general reluctance of the health care establishment to act affirmatively for change. The purpose of this article is, therefore, to determine the necessity for reform of the licensure system for health professionals and to provide impetus for such reform if the necessity exists. The principal conclusion is that improved provision of health care requires it. In view of this conclusion, a proposal for reform is advanced, with the caution that change in licensure laws will not alone solve the frequently documented crisis in health care nor galvanize the health care establishment to take the measures necessary to solve that crisis. It should, however, be a significant step in the right direction.

CURRENT LICENSURE LAWS

Licensure of health manpower is a function of the state under its police power to legislate for the protection of health, safety, and welfare of its citizens. State medical societies sponsored the enactment of licensure laws[3] in the late nineteenth and early twentieth centuries.[4] Their success was surprising because the flourishing of laissez-faire philosophy had blunted other attempts to secure occupational licensure. The case was stronger, however, for health practitioner licensing: extragovernmental means of control, including efforts by medical societies, had proved ineffective in eliminating rampant incompetence and quackery.[5]

Early laws originated when there were few discernible health manpower categories. These statutes thus dealt only with physicians and authorized those with the specified qualifications to perform all health care functions. As new categories of health professionals developed and gained acceptance, their members were granted more circumscribed licenses enabling them to perform only those functions for which they were qualified by training and experience.[6]

Licensure laws covering health personnel have typically progressed from permissive (merely preventing the use of a given title by the unlicensed) to mandatory (making criminal any action within the scope of a licensed profession by one not licensed in that profession). Functional spheres are defined by statutes and/or by custom, and licensees zealously protect their functional perimeters against encroachment from the outside. As more functions have come within the practical competence of personnel less extensively trained than the physician, and as health care demands have grown, these laws have impeded the allocation of different functions to existing allied health personnel and discouraged the development of new types of paramedical personnel.[7]

To place licensure laws in nationwide perspective, the following listing indicates the extent of licensure in the United States for various types of health care practioners:(8) *Licensed in all states* are dental hygienists, dentists, professional engineers (including those in the health field), optometrists, pharmacists, doctors of medicine, doctors of osteopathy, podiatrists, veterinarians, professional nurses, practical nurses. *Licensed in all but two states* are chiropractors, physical therapists. *Licensed in seventeen to thirty-six states* are midwives, opticians, psychologists, sanitarians. *Licensed in fewer than seventeen states* are clinical laboratory directors, clinical laboratory personnel, naturopaths, social workers. *Licensed in two states* are nursing home administrators, and *licensed in one state* are health department administrators, hospital administrators, x-ray technicians. At present twenty-five health professions and occupations enjoy the benefits of licensure in one or more states, and a single state may require licenses for anywhere from twelve to twenty-one categories of personnel. For example, California licenses twenty-one professions, followed by Florida, Hawaii, and New Jersey, each with twenty.(9) Occupational therapists and dental assistants are not licensed in any state. Neither are such new categories as the physician's assistant or the health aides recently promoted by the Office of Economic Opportunity.(10) However, some new types of personnel have been formally recognized by states in this manner in recent years, as evidenced by a statute passed in 1969 to license the "child health associate" in Colorado.(11)

THE RELATIONSHIP BETWEEN LICENSURE AND MEDICAL MALPRACTICE

Licensure statues affect malpractice law to the extent that in some states violations are admissible as evidence of negligence.(12) The malpractice doctrine most directly related to health professional licensure law is the "standard of care" doctrine.(13) The notion underlying this doctrine is that in order to impose liability on a practitioner for the negligent performance of an act, there must be a discernible standard against which his performance can be measured. The doctrine is, of course, a facet of general negligence theory, which requires a duty with recognizable standards to be identified and imposed before a finding of negligence can be made.

If a person is injured in the course of medical treatment and an unlicensed aide of assistant was involved, and if the assistant was performing an act which only a person possessing a certain license is allowed to perform, the law of some states hosds that the bare fact that a licensure statute was violated may create a presumption of negligence.(14) The performance of extra-statutory acts by a licensed ausiliary may also lead to a presumption of negligence.(15) Such a presumption, although not conslusive, makes it more likely that a finding of negligence on the part of the health assistant will result — because the presumption gives the plaintiff-patient an advantage which must be overcome by the defendant. In such a case, the presumption arises because utilization of the health practitioner in the particular instance did not conform to the legislative allocation of functions and hence presumably departed from the established standard of care. The unlicensed person may have in fact been more capable of performing the act than a licensed person. This, however, would not prevent the presumption of negligence from arising. The result is that providers (physicians and hospitals) may be inhibited 1) from employing and utilizing persons, otherwise capable and trained, for the performance of functions for which they are not licensed, and 2) from optimally utilizing licensed personnel for the performance of health care functions within their practical competence but beyond the scope of their licenses.

A point of great controversy is the extent to which the physician's fear of exposure to malpractice claims leads to distortion of his judgment in ministering to patient needs. The controversy does not wax over *whether* distortion arises but rather over *to what extent* it occurs. The argument may never be completely resolved, as physicians are understandably reluctant to detail unnecessary, defensive, and wasteful practices, and patients usually lack the sophistication to perceive such behavior. The possible consequences of such distortion in terms of the cost of medical care are, however, alarming.(16)

The interaction of malpractice and licensure laws, then, apparently produces two results. First, to the extent that current licensure laws are used as evidentiary tools in malpractice litigation, they unquestionably impede innovation, restrict the potential manpower pool, and frustrate efficient utilization of health manpower. Simply stated, licensure laws tend to lock practitioners into the functional spheres prescribed by statute, which frequently are not commensurate with actual abilities. Potential manpower resources will likely remain untapped due to the inability of many, otherwise desirous of employment, to satisfy statutory requirements for licensing. This is particularly and dismayingly true for the some 30,000 medics discharged annually from the armed services.(17) Second, and closely related to the first, to the extent that licensure laws increase the risk of fear of malpractice litigation, they contribute to the escalation of health care costs.

The problems discussed in this section have not lacked attention. Solutions and remedies have been proffered by both legal commentators and health care researchers. Most of these proposals have, however, been premised on a conception of a static health care industry. This is not surprising since change in the system has been glacial at best. Nonetheless, change is occurring and will inevitably accelerate with sustained pressure on the system. The fact that proposals for change in the law affecting health manpower licensure reflect notions of a static industry tends to reduce their utility and may render ostensible reform efforts either counter-productive or obsolete at inception. In short, we must know something of the substance of the health care industry and the shape it is likely to take in the future before espousing fundamental legal changes. This is necessary if a change in licensure is to have a positive impact on (a) the supply of personnel, (b) the utilization of such personnel, and (c) the way in which the quality of care is regulated. Prior to discussing change, then, we must inquire into what is known about the industry and about supply, utilization, quality of care, and so on.

It is axiomatic that introducing change in one part of a system is unwarranted and premature if the ramifications of that change on other parts of the system have not been anticipated and analyzed. This type of systems analysis is particularly essential with respect to the health care system. Too often changes have been made without careful consideration of their impact — the tarnished examples of Medicare and Medicaid as financing mechanisms will serve to prove the point.(18)

The health care system has been called a "cottage industry."(19) Health care is still provided principally by individual practitioners and diverse free-standing institutions. Few physicians have entered into formal arrangements with hospitals, with most engaging in solo practice and relating legally to such institutions as independent contractors. Occasionally, of course, practitioners and institutions will cluster together, but there has been no powerful centripetal force to facilitate integration of resources. One result is that the "cottage industry" has remained both labor intensive and grossly fragmented in contrast to the mechanization and integration in other industries.(20)

To oversimplify: Before the industrial revolution, commodities and many services were generally in sufficient supply only if the suppliers were physically present to deliver those goods and services. Change was introduced through market exchange mechanisms which both stimulated and followed intensive industrialization, in most instances resulting in a complex network to manage the supply flowing from producers to consumers. The products or services did not necessarily suffer from the increased complexity and may not even have cost more. This "train" of industrialization has swept past the health system — it simply has not been reorganized to achieve integration of the resources for providing health care. It is still controlled by guilds and is particularly feudal in its deployment of labor — specifically, manpower employment, training, and utilization.(21) Entry of new personnel and the utilization of existing personnel are restricted by rigid licensure laws and custom, the features of both deriving from professional sponsorship and activity.

There are some distinct problems associated with the organization of the delivery system for health care which derive in part from its anachronistic character and which interpenetrate manpower considerations. Discussion of these problems is essential to an understanding of the manifold implications of current licensure laws. The problems are discussed under the following headings: the industry's capacity; its structure; financing mechanisms; and the distribution of resources.

CAPACITY OF THE INDUSTRY

The health industry is marked by a shortage of licensed practitioners and an over-all excess of facilities.(22) Although manpower shortages may be exaggerated by the severe maldistribution of personnel, they constitute one of the problems most frequently identified by health care organization experts and politicians alike.

Undeniably such shortages are exacerbated by licensure laws. To be employed in the health field, personnel must fit into licensure categories which vary from state to state but are uniformly restrictive in their application. Legal boundaries around manpower categories have led ineluctably to sub-optimal utilization by precluding the matching of skills with tasks to be performed. Entry barriers created by such laws restrict the supply of new manpower in the health field. State-to-state variations in licensure laws restrain interstate mobility, which possibly would alleviate the shortage caused by maldistribution. At present, millions are unemployed or underemployed in the United States; unemployment rates hover around five to six per cent. Reliable statistics are not available to demonstrate the degree of underemployment, but the phenomenon is presumed to be extensive. Relaxation of entry barriers would facilitate tapping this vast source of manpower.(23)

Despite encroachments of established tradition made by group practice(24) and the large institutional health complex, the progress in this area has been painfully slow. Health manpower recruitment and coordination, which could help solve many of the current delivery problems, continue to be frustrated.

STRUCTURE OF THE INDUSTRY

Optimal utilization of personnel as well as provision of perquisites to attract personnel are in part functions of the size and scope of the organizations that deliver health care services. Large-scale units for delivery of health care are few, scattered, and often inaccessible.(25) Optimal utilization requires more than just freedom from legal constraints which prohibit matching skills with tasks but also embraces the notion that larger organizations provide opportunities for such optimal utilization that smaller units of care do not. The solo practitioner does not have much opportunity to match tasks with demonstrated skills if he has only one nurse.

The archaic structure of the industry has led some to suggest that the alleged manpower shortages are chimerical. It is argued that if the industry were characterized by large health care organizations with the freedom to employ and utilize personnel subject only to responsibility for the "outcomes" of health care services, and if such organizations exerted market pressures upon specialty training institutions and programs to align the supply of specialists with the demand, shortages might disappear.(26) This analysis, while profound and largely supportable, neglects one crucial factor — health care providers themselves are not responsive to market pressures exerted by consumers, because demand levels are not determined by consumers but by physicians (and hospitals and other practitioners to a lesser extent).(27) Health care providers dictate health care needs to a complaisant public. This is a critical point to make but difficult to comprehend despite its apparent simplicity. Health care services differ from almost all other services in that the provider controls the spigot. It is the physician who decides what and how much is needed, when it stops hurting, and how much it costs to make it stop. The argument that manpower shortages would be alleviated if personnel were utilized differently might be tenable, however, if the incentives of the providers were aligned with those of the consumer. The nature of such incentives is determined in large part by the financing mechanisms used for health care services.

The price at which and manner in which something is bought influence the structure and capacity of the industry supplying it. The health care industry offers ample evidence of this proposition. A fee-for-service system focuses upon payment for health services, not maintenance of health. Thus services, the need for which is determined by the providers of those services, are continuously bought by users. This induces inelasticity in demand and leads to increases in cost.

The federal government, principally through the medium of Medicare and Medicaid, now purchases approximately twenty-five per cent of the health care bought in the United States.(28) Under Medicare and Medicaid the fee-for-service system is not only preserved but buttressed, with physicians being allowed to charge the fees that they collectively deem to be reasonable.(29) Since providers have no incentive to reduce them, costs have steeply escalated in recent years.(30)

Efficient use of personnel, utilization of medical hardware to reduce labor costs, and relaxation of entry barriers to paraprofessionals depend upon a competitive market for health care. The current system is monopolistic. The perpetuation of the fee-for-service financing system has precluded market influences which, among other things, would ease manpower shortages and foster innovative utilization practices. Prepayment, as distinguished from fee-for-service payments, such as would be facilitated by the health maintenance organization option proposed under Medicare, alters the incentives by aligning providers and consumers in the pursuit of a common end — maintenance of health.(31) A health maintenance organization would not be paid for a unit of service but rather would be paid a lump sum per patient in advance. This prepayment would cover the costs of all necessary health services, including hospitalization. The health maintenance organization option, therefore, has fundamental implications for the structure of the industry by virtue of its potential for fostering the evolution of large-scale health care organizations which would have incentives to seek economies of scale and comprehensiveness in the array of services and benefits.(32)

Health care resources are poorly distributed.(33) Restrictions on entry of paraprofessionals, together with excessive stringency in the specification and regulation of practice spheres, aggravates this maldistribution. Recognition must be given to the fact that in a system marked by shortages, the supply will be least in areas least attractive to practitioners; rural areas and low-income pockets in large urban areas suffer the most from distribution patterns. The distributional problem is in part circular. Much of the unattractiveness of underserved areas is attributable to the unreasonable workloads created by manpower shortages. The problem can thus be alleviated in two ways: by modification of licensure barriers to allow entry by paraprofessionals and by change in the law to permit more optimal utilization of currently licensed personnel.

Before proceeding to a discussion of proposals for changing current practices, licensure must be viewed in the context of its intended purpose. Licensure is designed to regulate quality of care—but in what way, and how effective is it?

Perhaps the most difficult problem is determining what constitutes "quality" in health care and what measures are essential to ensure this quality, assuming it can be defined. Health care experts find little ground for agreement on what "quality" is;(34) similar uncertainty exists respecting regulatory mechanisms to measure it.

Conceptually, enforceable controls over the quality of care can be categorized as input measures, process or internal measures, and outcome measures. These measures are shown schematically in Figure I. Licensure is an input measure under this schema. As such it is subject to the same infirmities as other input measures—most, at best, are conjectures about what kinds of inputs into a black box will yield good results. When a more direct means of assessing health care outcomes is developed, the utility of their continued use is called into question. Such outcome measures are currently under development.(35)

The confluence of two courses of development forms the basis for a new approach to licensure: first, the growing conviction (and evidence) that input and process measures do not bear a sufficient or defensible relationship to the quality of health care, and second, the imperatives that derive from investing organizations, as opposed to individuals, with the responsibility for providing health care.

To use a homely example, most of us judge a restaurant on the basis of the taste and the quality of the food served. Seldom, except for reasons for epicure, do we inquire as to the chef's lineage and education. Less often do we personally visit the kitchen to inspect the ovens and utensils. The quality of meals and the results of health care are matters of different importance and magnitude, but the analogy is nonetheless instructive. The regulatory measures traditionally employed to control the quality of health care have focused on who renders it, how, and why, more often than on what the results have been.

In defense of input and process measures, it must be acknowledged that assessment of the quality of health services by measuring the outcomes of care is an extraordinarily complex task. Present technology for this purpose is not as sophisticated as the concept. Consequently, reliance upon traditional measures is at least explainable if it is assumed that rational outcome measures have not been available. Even without such alternative measures, however, the question still arises as to whether licensure is defensible without demonstrable evidence of its relationship to the quality of care.

Early licensure laws were the product of concern, if not alarm, on the part of legislatures called to witness egregious quackery.(36) But as licensure laws have evolved, the licensure system has grown cumbersome and outmoded. Its historic course resembles an ecological remedy designed to cure a specific problem only to become one—a species of rodent imported to curb the rapacious behavior of another pest only to succeed to the extent of setting off another imbalance.

Licensure would likely fall of its own weight except for a reverence for professionalism which proves a paraphrase of Veblen's maxim: nothing defends itself more vigorously than a health care profession threatened with the loss of its licensure statute.

Total abrogation of licensure laws may be abstractly possible, but political verities may make a different approach more feasible. Some acceptable substitute to measure quality must be developed to provide the rationale for the elimination or at least the modification of licensure. There are two possible measures, each complementing the other. First, a system of quantitative measurement must be developed to provide indices for measuring actual health care outcomes against scientifically derived standards of outcomes.(37) When results are plotted against such standards, ground would exist for action against the organizations and/or practitioners involved in the provision of the care. A second measure must incorporate the technology of the first. Currently, the findings of medical malpractice litigation serve as outcome measures.(38) They will continue to serve, but a compensation system for medical injuries premised upon outcome technology as an alternative to the current system may be developed. Certainly, given the random magnanimity of the current system and the cost dimensions, some alternative form of compensation system should evolve. There is much ferment regarding compensation arrangements in the context of automobile accidents. The medical injury problem may provide a more manageable and felicitous focus for testing an experimental compensation system.(39)

Development of the mechanisms to test outcomes may take time, and such mechanisms may not of their own force impel the demise of licensure. The emergence of large health care organizations may, however, hasten the deliverance from licensure with or without development of reliable outcomes technology.

THE TREND TOWARDS THE DELIVERY OF CARE BY ORGANIZATIONS

In 1946, 404 groups of physicians practiced medicine in the United States.(40) By 1969 the number had increased to 6,371.(41) The trend is irreversible, especially in view of the increasing complexity of health care services. The projection is for 16,000 groups by 1975.

The proposed 1971 amendments to the Social Security Act would place the government's purchasing power behind large health care organizations referred to in the legislation as health maintenance organizations.(42) Health maintenance organizations were defined in the proposed amendments as a public or private organization which:

1. provides, either directly or through arrangement with others, health services, to enrollees on a per capita prepayment basis;

2. provides with respect to enrollees to whom this section applies (through institutions, entities, and persons meeting the applicable requirements of section 1861) all of the services and benefits covered under parts A and B of this title;

FIGURE I

Health Care System Quality Controls

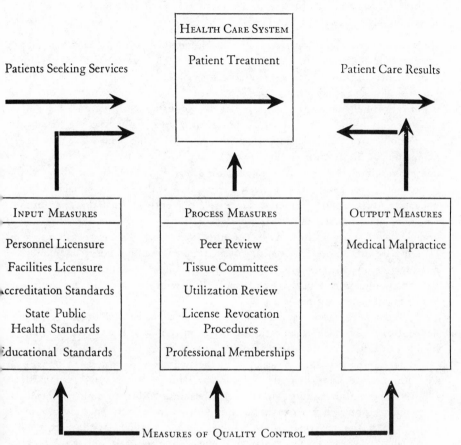

3. provides physicians' services directly through physicians who are either employees or partners of such organizations or under an arrangement with an organized group or groups of physicians which is or are reimbursed for services on the basis of an aggregate fixed sum or on a per capita basis;

4. demonstrates to the satisfaction of the Secretary proof of financial responsibility and proof of capability to provide comprehensive health care services, including institutional services, efficiently, effectively, and economically;

5. has enrolled members at least half of whom consist of individuals under age 65;

6. has arrangements for assuring that the health services required by its members are received promptly and appropriately and that the services that are received measure up to quality standards which it establishes in accordance with regulations; and

7. has an open enrollment period at least once every two years. under which it accepts eligible persons (as defined under subsection (d)) without underwriting restrictions and on a first-come first-accepted basis up to the limit of its capacity (unless to do so would result in failure to meet the requirement of paragraph (5)).(43)

Embraced in the definition are many possible organizational patterns including both nonprofit and for-profit corporations. The emergence of health maintenance organizations to provide health care is expected on a broad scale. How soon, and how many, is problematic, but transformation of the organizational characteristics of the health care industry is certain.(44)

Under established tort principles, organizations generally bear the financial responsibility for the deficient performance of their components. The principal defendant in litigation over injuries to a child hit by a truck is the trucking company. Similarly, health care organizations can assume and bear the responsibility for health care services. Assumption of the obligation need not be under statutory compulsion but can arise from both internal pressures from employee-practitioners and the natural evolution of tort law.(45) Litigation against health care institutions is currently increasing. As illustrated by the *Darling* case in 1965 and the limiting of charitable immunity, hospitals are more and more frequently the targets of successful malpractice claims.(46) The same pattern of litigation is likely with respect to new organizational types such as health maintenance organizations.

If organizations bear the burden of control over the quality of care, the demand to relieve such organizations of the constraints of licensure laws which inhibit utilization practices better calculated to produce high quality health care outcomes can be expected. We can pursue the analogy of the trucking company. The company seeks to limit its exposure to claims by employing responsible drivers and by utilizing those drivers commensurate with their ability; a health care organization will possess the same incentives and should possess the same latitude that the trucking company does, except perhaps with respect to physicians, for whom licensure may continue to be necessary. This suggests the outlines of a proposal for a radical modification of licensure law. Before examining this proposal, however, we should consider some of the other suggestions for change that have been made.

PROPOSALS

Those who believe that legislative change is unnecessary argue that the law now has sufficient flexibility to accomodate the entry of new paramedical personnel and to allow delegation of duties by licensed practitioners to allied health professionals. Many proponents of this view believe that the shortage of health care personnel can be solved by augmenting the numbers of practitioners in existing licensed professions.

Perhaps one advantage to this position is that attention is not called to the deviations from prevailing law in current utilization practices. Of course, there is substance to the argument that the exposure to liability for performance of tasks simply on the basis of a lack of licensure authorization is not extreme. The incidence of claims for malpractice and disciplinary proceedings arising principally from violations of licensure statutes is probably very low given the volume of health care services delivered. But the paucity of claims premised on illegal activity and the failure of disciplinary boards to take cognizance of licensure violations are questionable grounds for satisfaction with the current system. Maintaining the status quo may in reality serve to aggravate the utilization problems which have become apparent. It is true that there is some flexibility in current law by virtue of a general delegatory authority under common law, but the precise nature and extent of this authority, in the absence of statute, is left to be determined by litigation.(47) A more satisfactory resolution of the very real problems of practitioner shortages and permissible utilization practices seems necessary.

If a new health manpower category is identified, a specific licensure statute can be sought to afford recognition to its members. Essentially the same process can be implemented to expand or contract the functions defined by existing licensure laws.(48) There is little doubt that this procedure has some utility. Basically, it is the way in which new categories have been legally recognized since physicians were first licensed in this country.(49) The question to be asked is, Has this procedure been adequate? There are grounds for arguing that it has not. The rationale advanced by those who believe the procedure is deficient can be concisely stated: manpower shortages can be demonstrated, and studies have shown that the duties that can be capably performed by certain health care practitioners are not necessarily those granted by statute and custom.(50) To the extent that its rigidity prevents optimal utilization of personnel, the law prohibits practices which could alleviate the shortages and possibly lead to more economical, comprehensive, and high-quality health care.

Proponents of a certification procedure suggest an expansion of the rule-making power of licensure boards and agencies by vesting in them the authority to certify new paramedical types and to adjust the functional spheres for each group under their jurisdiction. One significant advantage of this proposal is that it may facilitate quicker and more flexible action than is possible through legislation because an administrative board may meet at will whereas a legislature may not. Another advantage may be that boards comprised of health care experts are presumably better able than other authorities to tailor actions to meet specific needs. Finally, because a board's power could be broad, new types of manpower could be rapidly integrated into the industry.

There are various disadvantages to this approach. Boards and agencies are usually composed of professionals from the general category for which licensure authority is granted by statute.(51) For example, nurses are usually responsible for deciding whether an auxiliary category for nursing should be established, and so on. These professional groups may not be willing to create new categories which might pose a threat to the established profession. If each operative board or agency were to be independently granted this additional power, opportunities for intercategory adjustment and shifting of functions would be minimal, at best. For example, even if the board for nurses were given the power to modify the functions to be performed by nurses, its action would be neither binding on nor applicable to other personnel outside the jurisdiction of that board. Finally, certification may actually be nothing more than a form of licensure. Even though it may be a more responsive tool and a more flexible way to deal with emerging paramedical groups, a certification scheme would not necessarily reduce—and might in fact increase—fragmentation in the utilization of health care personnel.(52)

Under decisional law, physicians and (to a lesser extent) other health care practitioners enjoy a general power of delegation, exercisable, however, only if direction and supervision are furnished by the delegating professional.(53) This power is not easily defined, and numerous questions can be raised which may require clarification through litigation. Arizona, Colorado, Kansas, and Oklahoma have attempted to deal with this problem by enacting general delegatory statutes.(54) These statutes have simply codified the right presumed to be available to the physician to delegate health care functions under his direction and supervision. This type of statute is useful because it may vindicate the physician when the delegation of duties results in litigation. Such a statute may also serve to encourage delegation of duties to licensed or unlicensed personnel by explicitly sanctioning the practice.

If a general delegatory statute is not enacted, a specific type of delegatory power may be made available by different means. Thus, rather than a general power of delegation, the physician might be given the express power of delegating to only *one* other type of health care professional, such as a nurse or physician's assistant. Such a statute is necessarily more limited than a general delegatory statute, and its enactment might raise the question of whether specifically authorizing delegation to one type of auxiliary practitioner *implies* that delegation to others is not permissible.(55) Since this approach to the licensure problem is becoming prevalent, it must be subjected to a more cirtical analysis.(56)

Perhaps the best discussion of delegatory statutes is contained in a recent article on health manpower problems.(57) The authors accurately point out some of the limitations in delegation statutes: vague guidelines for delegation; use of swampy terms like "under the supervision and control"; and limitation of delegatees to members of specified professions, either licensed or unlicensed. To remedy these problems the authors suggest that delegations might be allowed only as to persons approved by the appropriate state board of medical examiners pursuant to regulations developed by such board.(58) Control over delegations would therefore be exercised through a two-stage process: first, the board would establish general usage guidelines through regulations; and second, the board would invest the delegating physician with the responsibility for supervision. The physician would therefore be answerable for the negligent conduct of delegatees under accepted principles of vicarious liability.(59) The authors consequently recognize some of the problems inherent in the delegation approach(60) but suggest that "[o]nly time and experience can produce answers ... in jurisdictions adopting this approach."(61)

A variation of the above approach is also presented. This alternative places substantially greater reliance upon the delegating physician.

> Under such a scheme, it would be solely the physician's responsibility to determine that persons to whom he delegates are qualified by formal or informal training and experience to perform the functions delegated. Primary reliance for the public's protection would be placed on: 1. the physician's ethical and professional judgment; 2. the deterrent effect of the malpractice risk attending the use of unqualified personnel; and 3. supervision by physicians' or hospitals' malpractice insurers.(62)

> Generally, there are advantages to these proposals: greater flexibility; protection for the physician; encouragement to the physician to delegate; legal recognition for a common practice; and so forth. There are, however, significant disadvantages. If a delegatory statute is general, authorizing delegation to any other practitioner (licensed or unlicensed), it accomplishes little more than the common law authorization of delegation except to relieve the physician of anxiety and perhaps to encourage delegation to some extent. On the other hand, if the statute is specific as to the delegatee (for example, "to a physician's assistant"), the validity of delegations to persons other than those enumerated is called into question, and this could result in a possible contraction of the common law delegation authority. Definitional problems also arise if delegation is permitted only to a limited group. What is meant by "physician's assistant"? Does this term refer to a generic category of practitioners or to a specific type of practitioner?

The proposals are further deficient in that the authorization is limited to one-half of the delegating equation—the physician. A delegatory statute, while perhaps only codifying general common law delegatory power, does explicitly insulate the physician making the delegation if the controls, both explicit and implicit in the statute, are properly honered. But the legal status of the delegatee is not clarified. This is true both as to licensed personnel—since occasions may arise when the task delegated falls without the scope of practice for the given practitioner—and the unlicensed paraprofessional such as a physician's assistant, since ostensibly no health care services may be performed by unlicensed personnel. This problem may be more apparent than real, however, since ability to accept a delegation can be implied from the law authorizing it.

Another dimension to the problem is that delegation statutes operate only to legitimate delegations to practitioners who are dependent upon the physician. In dependent or semi-independent practitioners such as pediatric nurse practitioners, physical therapists, and, in some instances, emerging types such as the child health associate(63) may require more explicit exemption from medical practice statutes since they do not function exclusively under the physician's supervising shadow.(64)

A final and perhaps most serious difficulty with the approach of sanctioning physician delegation is that no matter how the delegatory statute is phrased, an incentive inevitably arises to clarify the legal status of the delegatee group through the traditional mechanism of licensure. Thus, while the salutary objective of affording the physician some relief from his anxieties about delegation is achieved, the risk is run that a new category or categories of personnel will ultimately be circumscribed by "licensure walls." Naturally, it can properly be argued that a certification mechanism other than licensure could be used to clarify the delegatees' role. While certification would probably be preferable to licensure for reasons already articulated, the practice still falls short of reducing fragmentation since the likely recipient of certification authority is the board of medical examiners. (Certainly this is evident from existing and proposed delegation statutes.) Thus, while another licensure statute may have been headed off, delegatee groups will find themselves in the same camp and wholly subject to the "delegatory imagination" of the physician. This danger is manifestly more clear with the second approach to delegation outlined above which vests substantial supervisory authority in the physician.(65)

To summarize: Delegation is a useful but limited device. It should be utilized only if it is recognized as but a partial remedy and only if it is reasonably certain that its disadvantages can be overcome. This can be done by utilizing the mechanism only in combination with other proposals yet to be discussed.

One proposal is an expansion of the proposal to certify paramedical personnel. It calls for establishing a health manpower committee or board consisting of representatives of all the principal categories of personnel and perhaps lay representatives as well. It overcomes the disadvantages of broadening the power of the various separate licensure boards to certify health care personnel because it would permit more effective intercategory coordination and could thus better facilitate optimal personnel utilization.(66)

There are basically two types of organizations which could be established, a committee or a board. The differences (although not necessarily the terms) are important. A committee might have only advisory authority—that is, it might be empowered only to review proposals for certification of new auxiliary classifications and amendments to present law and make recommendations for action to the various independent boards or agencies possessing certification authority or to the legislature. A board, on the other hand, might be given exclusive certification authority by the legislature. A committee, even without final authority, would be able to deal effectively with gaps and overlaps in functions and might also more objectively judge the necessity for certification of new categories of personnel. A board, however, would possess those advantages as well as the flexibility and responsiveness discussed under the proposal to certify paramedical personnel.

The creation of a committee or board might be effected in several stages. The first stage might be the formation of a coordinating committee with only informal powers. Such a committee could be empowered to make recommendations to licensing boards regarding new categories of personnel and scope of practice changes for licensed personnel. A second stage might couple a freeze on licensure of any new manpower groups with a granting of power to the committee to certify such groups and promulgate regulations concerning utilization in concert with the appropriate licensing boards.

The third and fourth stages might respectively empower the committee (or board) to absorb certain existing licensing board functions and to begin to fuse scope-of-practice boundaries to eliminate gaps. The committee (or board) might ultimately supplant all licensing boards and establish certification procedures for all health care practitioners, except the physician, while affording representation to all cognizable manpower categories. The advantages of this general scheme are apparent (although no more apparent than the likelihood of vigorous politican opposition from entrenched practitioner groups). Further, combining this approach with a general delegatory statute would afford the physician the protection secured by such a statute while cleansing the delegation approach of most of its limitations and dangers.

Aside from engendering controversy, implementation of this scheme is faced with some other problems. First, it will take time. Second, it honors by imitation the notion that licensure and its surrogate forms are vital measures to ensure the quality of care without definitive proof. Third, there is the risk that committees or boards would become calcified and, over time, create fragmentation where flexibility once stood. Fourth, such mechanisms might still be wholly professionally controlled and thus invulnerable to public pressures for changes, except indirectly through the legislative process. Finally, there are grounds for questioning whether boards of this sort would effectively and aggressively develop regulations to guide the performance of practitioners once statutory controls are abrogated.(67)

A theoretical possibility for the future is based on the evidence that the unit for delivery of medical care is increasing in average size.(68) Evidence has been cited that care is being rendered more frequently in institutional settings. Advocates of the ensuing proposal point to these trends and suggest that if present manpower licensure, even if modified, is inherently too rigid and unresponsive to meet the increasing needs for manpower in the provision of health care, a more radical solution should be found. The alternative they propose requires shifting some of the control over practitioners currently exerted by the existing licensure scheme to health care institutions and organizations which would be given the responsibility for hiring and utilizing manpower within guidelines established by the state agency that licenses institutions.(69)

There are, of course, variations on this theme. One such variation contemplates establishing job descriptions for various positions within the institution. Professor Nathan Hershey describes it this way:

> The state hospital licensing agency could establish, with the advice of experts in the health care field, job descriptions for various hospital positions and establish qualifications in terms of education and experience for individuals

who would hold these posts. Administrators certainly recognize the fact that although a professional nurse is licensed, her license does not automatically indicate which positions within the hospital she is qualified to fill. Individuals, because of their personal attainment, are selected to fill specific posts. Educational qualifications, based on both formal and in-service programs, along with prior job experience determine if and how personnel should be employed.(70)

One distinct advantage of this scheme is that it would afford the institutional employer wide latitude in utilizing personnel, subject only to the job descriptions. Presumably, it would allow the flexible use of unlicensed manpower in certain approved jobs.

The proposal is not without difficulties. Some of the questions that can logically be raised are these; (a) How would the scheme affect utilization of institution-based personnel by independent physicians who presumably would bear no responsibility for their employment and utilization? (b) The scheme presents a solution for institutions, but does it offer any solutions to extrainstitutional utilization of personnel, such as physician practices, except perhaps in those instances where a physician group practice may have achieved institutional status? (c) Although purporting to offer a solution to the rigidities of licensure, does not the scheme reintroduce inflexibility at a different level? That is, to the extent that job descriptions become fixed, the functional scope written into the job description becomes limiting and thus may become a constraint to utilization. (d) Is a job description developed in one institution readily transferable to another?

Another variation of this proposal constitutes a rather different and distinct approach which, if adopted, would (a) eliminate present rigidities in licensure; (b) provide the basis for optimal employment and utilization of health manpower; and (c) facilitate the desirable, if not essential, organizational transformation in the health care industry which is resulting in the evolution of large health care organizations.

CONCLUSION: A NEW PROPOSAL

In light of the analysis in this paper, it is proposed that statutory licensure laws be amended to repeal licensure restrictions for all health care practitioners other than the physician when such practitioners are employed by health care organizations registered to do business in the state and licensed to provide health care. All practitioners not employed by health care organizations should be required to obtain certificates of practice from a health manpower board consisting of representatives of health professions, with a majority of nonprofessional representation.

Physician licensure should be retained for all physicians who are not affiliated with health care organizations and even for those physicians who are affiliated with such organizations until such time as geographic mobility would not be impeded by unlicensed status. Physician licensure should then be abolished and replaced by a registry scheme administered by a state health manpower board.

Health care organizations would agree to submit to the process and jurisdiction of the state courts as a condition of licensure and would further agree to participate in a statutory compensation system for medical injuries when such a system is developed. Each constituent element of this proposal is discussed below.

The discussion in this article has revealed that it is not clear that licensure strictures are related to the quality of care; licensure scope-of-practice constraints have precluded optimal utilization of licensed practitioners; entry of new manpower has been blocked by onerous licensure requirements; and professionals have been slow to bring about change, in part due to anticompetitive motivations. If organizations which employ health care personnel demonstrate that they will not substitute the Rube Goldberg for the Dr. DeBakey in open-heart surgery and consent to bear the full responsibility for ensuring that quality care will be rendered on penalty of organizational liability, why keep personnel licensure?

The exception preserving licensure for the physician is bred from a deep-seated fear (and concern that physician political opposition is so easily translatable into action against the advocates of objectionable change). There is no logical reason to keep it, except that the linkage between licensure and quality of performance may be more demonstrable with respect to physicians than with respect to other types of personnel.(71) In addition, because the physician's license authorizes performance of all medical functions, the danger of unreasonable practice restrictions is not present as it is in the case of limited practitioners.

ORGANIZATIONAL LICENSURE

As noted earlier, licensure of organizations(72) is not widespread. Evidence is available, however, that it is spreading. At this writing, Ohio has enacted into law a licensure scheme for health care organizations,(73) and bills are pending in Georgia and Minnesota. The type of mechanism used to enfranchise health care organizations—licensing, chartering, certifying—is not in itself important. Whatever the mechanism, certain requirements can be imposed upon such organizations regarding their employment and utilization of personnel which will serve as surrogates for personnel licensure.

Naturally, if organizations rather than practitioners are to be licensed, such organizations must be accountable to the public. An organization authorized to do business by the state could be required to show, *inter alia*, 1. that its employed personnel (and consulting personnel, if any) a) possess requisite training, b) possess training in specified fields, c) have X amount of experience, and d) possess certification(s) from medical specialty boards, and 2. that capital equipment available for use by the personnel meets certain minimal conditions.(74) Beyond this, of course, the organization could be required to register all employed personnel with a state board and give notice to such board when any employee is terminated or resigns. The reasons for the termination could be certified as well. In this way intrastate and possibly interstate mobility of incompetent personnel could be impeded. The current licensure system possesses no mechanism which either systematically collects data on personnel performance, as reflected in malpractice litigation, or bases disciplinary action on poor performance unless performance data inadvertently comes to the attention of licensing boards.(75)

It must be stressed that any organizational licensure scheme must be more than a mere enfranchising ritual—it must be a regulatory device. In addition to the provisions respecting health personnel, controls over organizational behavior inimical to the public interest must be secured. Since for-profit organizations will enter the field, careful consideration must be given to curbing profiteering and other practices incompatible with the delivery of a vital human service.(76)

This board would possess responsibility for the composition and performance of the health care labor force within a state. In the context of an organizational licensure scheme such a board would have four fundamental mandates: 1. to establish a registry scheme for manpower employed by health care organizations within the state; the registry would collect the data referred to above and possibly publish it as an aid to consumer choice between organizations; 2. to administer a certification system for nonphysician practitioners not employed by organizations and a licensure system for physicians generally; 3. to promulgate regulations regarding delegations by physicians and governing the certification process and related matters; and 4. to conduct a research and development program to improve the operation of the system and to develop new ways to measure the quality of health care services.

A discussion of the means to retread or dismantle the existing medical malpractice system is unnecessarily complicated for this article, even assuming such means exist. The troubles of malpractice are being addressed. A Department of Health, Education, and Welfare secretarial commission to consider this problem has recently been announced; surely a solution is in sight.

Under current law there is nothing to preclude an injured patient from suing an organization and recovering, as is demonstrated by the *Darling* case and its progeny. The individual practitioner remains, nevertheless, the prime target. Large health care organizations like the Mayo Clinic and the Kaiser-Permanente prepaid plans, however, have instituted indemnification arrangements to shield the practitioner from all but the first arrow from the plaintiff and in most cases to spare him the entire cost of defense and recompense. This expedient is certainly workable, although some practitioners may conclude, indemnification notwithstanding, that their exposure to litigation is increased in a group practice setting by the diffusion of management responsibilities for patients. But the cumbersome, random, rancorous nature of the litigation process for medical injuries suggests the need for development of a compensation system for such injuries based not upon fault but upon out-comes technology. While such a system is not at all a condition precedent to organizational development or the scheme proposed for control of health manpower employment and utilization, it is very consistent with the notion of organizational liability for health care services.(77)

There are seven major implications of the implementation of this proposal. Not all will eventuate, but most are highly probable. First, efficient utilization practices by large health care organizations (the best able to institute them) would be sanctioned. Second, entry barriers to the employment of many poor and near poor persons who do not possess gilt-edged credentials but who have or can be trained to have health care skills, will be eliminated. Third, the strangleholds over health care organizations and practice held by organized health care professions will be lessened, leading to increased and continued organizational development and more economical and efficient practice, including increased use of medical hardware. Fourth, an incentive to growth of large health care organizations will be created. Fifth, health care cost escalation should be slowed by economies instituted by health care organizations relieved of unreasonable manpower employment and utilization constraints. Sixth, providers, principally physicians, will be encouraged to make patient care decisions free from some of the restraints posed by the threat of malpractice litigation. And finally, for better or for worse, the seemingly endless and herculean task of dragging the health care system into the twentieth century will be advanced.

NOTES

(1) M. Friedman, Capitalism and Freedom 158 (1962).

(2) Report of the National Advisory Commission on Health Manpower 332 (1967).

(3) A fair amount of literature exists on the subject of health manpower licensure laws. Taken together, the various articles provide a comprehensive analysis which this article will not replicate in full. *See generally* B. Anderson, "Licensure of Paramedical Personnel," paper presented at the 65th Annual Meeting of the Federation of State Medical Boards, 1969; E. Egelston & T. Kinser, Exploratory Investigation of Licensure of Health Personnel (1969); Forgotson & Cook, *Innovations and Experiments in Uses of Health Manpower—The Effect of Licensure Laws*, 32 Law & Contemp. Prob. 731 (1967); Forgotson & R. Roemer, *Government Licensure and Voluntary Standards for Health Personnel and Facilities*, 6 Med. Care 345 (1968); Forgotson, R. Roemer & Newman, *Licensure of Physicians*, 1967 Wash. U.L.Q. 249; Leff, *Medical Devices and Paramedical Personnel: A Preliminary Context for Emerging Problems*, 1967 Wash. U.L.Q. 332; Moore, *The Purpose of Licensing*, 4 J. Law & Econ. 93 (1961); R. Roemer, *Legal System Regulating Health Personnel*, 46 Milbank Memorial Fund Q. 431 (1968).

(4) *See* L. Friedman, *Freedom of Contract and Occupational Licensing 1890-1910: A Legal and Social Study*, 53 Calif. L. Rev. 487 (1965).

(5) *See* Forgotson, Roemer & Newman, *supra* note 3. The authors document the catalytic effect the Flexner report had upon medical practice quackery and medical school "diploma mills." *See* A. Flexner, Medical Education in the United States and Canada (1910). *Cf.* Kessel, *The A.M.A. and the Supply of Physicians*, 35 Law & Contemp. Prob. 267 (1970).

(6) *See* Forgotson & Cook, *supra* note 3, at 735.

(7) There is a discernible pattern to the emergence of health care professional groups. First, an association is formed; second, a trade journal is published; third, informal recognition is sought from other health care professional groups; fourth, demands are made to state legislatures for statutory recognition through licensure laws; and finally, having secured legislation, the group engages in boundary skirmishes with contiguous health care groups on the map of tasks and functions. For a perceptive discussion of this pattern, see Akers, *The Professional Association and the Legal Regulation of Practice*, 2 Law & Soc. Rev.463 (1968).

(8) *See* A. Somers, Hospital Regulation: The Dilemma of Public Policy 79 (1969).

(9) *Id. See also* M. Pennell & P. Stuart, State Licensing of Health Occupations 1-2 (Public Health Service Pub. No. 1758, 1968).

(10) However, physicians' assistants have been the object of other types of legislation, such as certification (California) and general delegation authorizations (Florida).

(11) Colo. Rev. Stat. § 91-10-1 (Permanent Cumulative Supp. 1969).

(12) *See, e.g.*, Monohan V. Devinny, 131 Misc. 248, 225 N.Y.S. 601 (Sup. Ct. 1927); Brown V. Shyne, 242 N.Y. 176, 151 N.E. 197 1926).

(13) *See generally* D. Louisell & H. Williams, Trial of Medical Malpractice Cases ch. 8 (Supp. 1969). For specific treatment of the standard of care doctrine, see McCoid, *The Care Required of Medical Practitioners*, 12 Vand. L. Rev. 549, 558-75 (1959).

(14) Practicing without any license or without a particular type of license is usually considered too remote in the chain of causation to constitute material evidence of negligence—although it may still be a criminal act. *See generally* Annot. 44 A.L.R. 1418 (1926) Annot. 57 A.L.R. 978 (1928). *See also* Willett V. Rowekamp, 134 O. St. 285, 16 N.E.2d 457 (1938); Janssen V. Mulder, 232 Mich. 183, 205 N.W. 159 (1925); Joly V. Mellor, 163 Wash. 48, 299 P. 660 (1931).

(15) *See, e.g.*, Monohan V. Devinny, 131 Misc. 248, 225 N.Y.S. 601 (Sup. Ct. 1927); Barber V. Reinking, 68 Wash. 2d 139, 411 P.2d 861 (1966).

(16) No definitive studies have been made of the actual cost increases which may be attributable to the threat of malpractice. Undoubtedly such a study would be extremely complex. Dr. Michael Halberstam, in a recent article, has asserted that this threat affects physician behavior. While he cites no data to support his assertion, his article presents a perceptive account of such phenomena. *See* Halberstam, *The Doctor's Dilemma–'Will I Be Sued?,'* N.Y. Times, Feb. 14, 1971, Magazine at 8.

(17) Discharged medical corpsmen provide a vast potential supply of paraprofessionals. Many of them have had extensive health care services experience, occasionally in direct provision of care. Among the new training programs established to tap this source are the University of Washington's Medex program and Duke University's Physicians Assistant program. For discussions of various paraprofessional manpower sources, see R. Fein, The Doctor Shortage (1967); Light, *Development and Growth of New Allied Health Fields*, 210 J.A.M.A. 114 (1969).

Another point of critical importance is the impact that removing entry barriers would have on jobs available to the poor—including many blacks who have faced job discrimination which is at least as ubiquitous in health care as elsewhere. Black patients consume health care services proportionate to their percentage of the population and probably will consume a disproportionate amount once the health care system reaches them where they live. Despite these projections the chances of a black patient being seen by a black professional are currently very slight.

(18) While medical expenditures rose from $26 billion in 1960 to $67.2 billion in 1970, 50% of the increase represented higher costs for the same services. Much of the increased cost occurred after 1965, the year Medicare and Medicaid were enacted. Although cost increases were foreseeable in 1965, the dramatic escalations which actually occurred were not; it simply was not expected that physicians and hospitals would exploit these programs to the extent they have. The programs were designed to pay for services, and they have—but in far more units of care than predicted. This cost escalation and a persuasive explanation for it are discussed in Marmor, *Why Medicare Helped Raise Doctors' Fees*, Trans—Action, Sept. 1968, at 14.

(19) *See, e.g.,* Devey, *Towards Automated Health Services,* 57 Proceedings of the Inst. Electrical & Electronic Engineers 1830 (1967); *Our Ailing Medical System,* Jan. 1970, at 79.

(20) Fragmentation, of course, is a conclusionary statement and not necessarily susceptible of empirical demonstration. As used here it has two meanings: first, that the health care is provided by many separate individuals, groups, and institutions, with few large organizations and little integration of practitioners and institutions; and second, that health manpower is classified by rigid licensure laws, resulting in the lack of a rational pattern of manpower availability and utilization.

(21) References to the health care system in terms of industrialization are largely metaphorical. It is recognized that technological development has taken place in this sector; hospitals have employed many new devices, and the science has become very sophisticated in many ways. Consequently, the references to industrialization, guilds, and so forth are directed to the structure and organization of the system, and specifically to patterns of manpower utilization.

(22) Manpower shortages have been variously estimated. Some of the more dependable data reveals that there has been a steady decline in physicians per 100,000 of population. There will also be a projected shortage of 100,000 nurses by 1975. *See* National Center for Health Statistics, Health Resources Statistics (Dep't of Health, Education, and Welfare, 1969). The question of the adequacy of existing facilities depends generally on the nature of the organization of the health care system. If health care is financed by fees paid for services, hospital utilization tends to be as much a function of that financing mechanism as of the exercise of sound medical judgment. Given this arrangement, a determination that facilities are more than sufficient is highly questionable despite statistical sophistication. On the other hand, if health care is financed by prepayment where the providers bear the cost of institutionalization, unnecessary utilization is unlikely, and the sufficiency of facilities determine more by actual utilization practices. Under this latter measure too many institutional spaces are available assuming extrapolation from the data available on prepaid groups which do bear the costs of institutionalization once having entered into a contract to provide services in exchange for consumer prepayment. The entire question of shortages is occasionally paradoxical. Nathan Glazer, in a recent article, *Paradoxes of Health Care,* The Public Interest, Winter 1971, at 62, quotes extensively from Robert Sigmond, a health planner on the question. Excerpts from Sigmond's comments follow:

> During the past year I have been conducting an informal, unscientific, unstructured, confidential survey. I have presented dozens and dozens of practicing physicians with the following hypothetical suppositions and questions:
> Suppose this country faced a national emergency like a long world war that required your region to contribute as many physicians, nurses and other

health workers as possible. Suppose further that you were placed in charge of
the health services in your region and were assured of the complete trust and
cooperation of everyone. Would you be able to contribute any of the region's
physicians, surgeons, nurses and other health workers for national emergency
service, without impairing the quality of the health service provided in your
region?

Every single individual whom I questioned believed that if he could
achieve complete cooperation and commitment, health manpower in the
region could be substantially reduced without impairing quality of care and
without adverse effect on the people's health. The unanimity of response was
striking.

Even more striking were these physicians' responses with respect to the
amount of reduction in health manpower that could be achieved without
reducing the quality or effectiveness of service. When asked to estimate the
proportion of the region's health manpower that could be released for
national emergency service, the answers varied from about 10 to 40 per cent,
with an average of about 20 per cent.

Equally as striking was the conviction of most of these doctors that the
greatest proportion of health manpower could be spared among the most
highly trained health personnel—physicians and nurses, for example, as
contrasted with aides, orderlies, and kitchen workers.

How would manpower reductions be achieved? . . . There was a surprising
consistency of basic themes. 1. grouping physicians (and other practitioners)
in organized settings and centralized locations so that they can make full use
of lesser skilled but specially trained workers in their 'office practices' and
thus provided more service per physician; 2. locating more physicians' offices
at hospitals and removing the distinction between 'office' and 'clinic' to
reduce physician travel time and permit full use of the hospitals' manpower
and technical resources without having to admit patients as bed patients; 3.
redefining many health service tasks so that lesser trained personnel can take
them on . . . ; 4. permitting nurses to make house calls in medically supervised
home health programs; 5. creating closer linkages between related hospitals to
permit grouping of maternity, open heart surgery, and other specialized low
use services at fewer larger hospitals; 6. encouraging all families to develop
more efficient medical care habits by identifying with one nearby physician
group for provision and supervision of all needed health services.

Other ideas were mentioned less frequently: automation and computation,
self-help units in hospitals, intensified health education, multiphasic
screening, etc. No one in the group suggested any lengthening of the work
week. . . . Interesting enough, many of the doctors whom I asked felt that the
process of reorganizing to reduce manpower could produce improved quality
with fewer health personnel. . . .

I . . . asked one last question: suppose the great national crisis was not a
long world war, but the spiralling cost of medical and hospital services and
the many unmet health needs right in your own region, the deaths and
suffering that could be avoided by expanded and improved health
service. . . .Could you deliver? I wish I didn't have to report that most of my
group doubted that it would be possible, under present circumstances, to
achieve the degree of commitment and cooperation that would produce
results. At least, as a number said, 'not in my lifetime.'

Id. at 65-66.
    (23) *See* the discussion in note 17 *supra.*
    (24) Approximately 15% of the physicians practicing in the United States are

now members of medical groups, and the percentage is growing slowly but steadily each year.

(25) For purpose of this article a major distinction is drawn between large health care organizations and group practices. Naturally the line must be drawn somewhat arbitrarily. Examples of large health care organizations include the Mayo Clinic in Rochester, Minnesota, and the Kaiser-Permanente group with facilties in a number of cities.

(26) *See, e.g.,* 1 AMA, Distribution of Physicians, Hospitals, and Hospital Beds in the United States, 1966 (1967); Bureau of Health Manpower, Health Manpower, Perspective 1967 (Public Health Service Pub. No. 1667, 1967).

(27) Of course to say that physicians determine demand is not to say that physicians can set *any* price for their services. While they have great latitude in setting price levels, various constraints do exist. Should prices become prohibitive, patients will defer, if not neglect, health care needs. Furthermore, the Social Security Administration is constantly revising Medicare and Medicaid reimbursement formulae in an attempt to control price escalation. *See, e.g.,* the Health Cost Effectiveness Amendments included in the 1971 Amendments to the Social Security Act now pending before Congress. H.R. I, 92d Cong., Ist Sess. § § 221-43 (as passed by the House, June 22, 1971).

(28) *See* U.S. Dep't of Health, Education, and Welfare, Social Security Admininstration, Size and Shape of the Medical Care Dollar (1969).

(29) *See, e.g.,* Social Security Amendments of 1965, Pub. L. No. 89-97, tit. I, § 102(a), 79 Stat. 322 (enacting 42 U.S.C. § 1395x(v)).

(30) In the past decade consumer medical expenditures have more than doubled, while disposable income has increased only 10%. From 1965 to 1968 medical care prices increased at an annual rate of 5.8% compared with a 3.3% increased for all consumer items. Size and Shape of the Medical Care Dollar, *supra* note 28. *See also* note 18 *supra.*

(31) *See* section 239(a) of the 1971 Amendments to the Social Security Act *supra* note 27. The "health maintenance organization option" provides simply that qualified health maintenance organizations, as defined in the amendments, will be paid by the government for services provided to program eligibles at the rate of 95% of what the government pays fee-for-service providers in the same geographic locale for comparable populations. Health maintenance organizations must operate on a capitation (so much per head) basis. Such organizations tend to emphasize preventive care. Since profitably and stability tend to be functions of organizational size when the price for a commodity or service is fixed (95% of the fee-for-service cost under Medicare), an increase in the size of the units for delivery of health care can be expected when and if health maintenance organizations develop.

(32) Economies of scale are as possible in health care as they are in franchising generally. If each "Holiday Inn" had to purchase building materials and supplies separately, each model unit would undoubtedly cost more. An exhaustive analysis of prepayment of health care services as a means of influencing organizational change in the health care system has been undertaken in Note, *The Role of Prepaid Group Practice in Relieving the Medical Care Crisis,* 84 Harv. L. Re. 887 (1971). A section of that article is devoted to the health maintenance organization development.

(33) For example, only 12% of all physicians and 18% of all nurses practice in rural areas—where 30% of the population is. Specialists are even more scarce in these areas; only 8% of all pediatricians and 4% of all psychiatrists practice outside urban areas.

(34) One of the most informative general articles on the question of quality is Donabedian, *Measurement of Quality in Health Care,* in 2 Nat'l Health Forum, Action Proposals and Discussions 195-236 (1968).

(35) *See, e.g.,* Sanazaro & Williamson, *End Results of Patient Care: A Provisional Classification Based on Reports by Internists,* 6 Med. Care 123 (1968); Department of Medical Care, Johns Hopkins University, Prognostic Epidemiology: Concept, Process and Product (unpublished paper). *See also* Outcomes of Health Care—A Compensation System for Medical Injuries (conference transcript, forthcoming) [hereinafter cited as Outcomes of Health Care].

(36) *See* note 5 *supra.*

(37) *See* note 35 *supra.*

(38) That is, to the extent evidentiary rules permit, a malpractice decision adverse to the health care practitioner and/or institution constitutes a measure of the outcome of litigation. It is an open question how sensitive a measure it is. *See* Outcomes of Health Care, *supra* note 35.

(39) A great deal has been written concerning the substitution of a compensation system for the present tort system of spreading losses caused by automoble accidents. *See, e.g.,* A. Ehrenzweig, Negligence Without Fault (1951); James, *The Columbia Study of Compensation for Automobile Accidents: An Unanswered Challenge,* 59 Colum. L. Rev. 408 (1959); R. Keeton & J. O'Connell, Basic Protection for the Traffic Victim (1965).

(40) *See* Medical Group News, July 1970, at.

(41) *See* note 22 *supra.*

(42) H.R. I, *supra* note 27, § 226.

(43) H.R. I, 92d Cong., Ist Sess. § 239(a) (as originally introduced).

(44) Although it is an encouraging factor in promoting group practice, the health maintenance organization option provided under Medicare is not a sine qua non, since the trend towards organizational development has been apparent in recent years.

(45) Organizational assumption of increased responsibility for tortious conduct is a characteristic of current tort law. There is nothing so unique about health care organizations or practitioners as to justify special treatment of organizational responsibility.

(46) *See* Darling v. Charleston Community Memorial Hospital, 33 Ill. 2d 326, 2II N.E.2d 253 (1965).

(47) *See* Magit v. Board of Medical Examimers, 57 Cal. 2d 74, 366 P.2d 816, 17 Cal. Rptr. 488 (1961). Three persons, trained as physicians but unlicensed in California to practice medicine, were employed by the defendant doctor to administer anesthetics under his direction and supervision. The defendant, however, was found guilty of violating section 2392 of the Business and Professions Code. The court said:

> Under some circumstances, persons not licensed to practice medicine in California may legally perform some medical acts, including the administration of anesthetics. For example, sections 2147-2147.6 of the Business and Professions Code permit certain persons engaged in medical study and teaching at approved hospitals to perform acts which constitute treatment of the sick, but no such exemption is applicable to the activities of Rios, Celori, and Ozbey at the Doctors Hospital, which concededly was not approved for the training of students or interns. Another example is found in Chalmers-Francis V. Nelson (1936) 6 Cal. 2d 402, 57 P.2d 1312, where it was held that a licensed registered nurse should not be restrained from administering general anesthetics in connection with operations under the immediate direction and supervision of the operating surgeon and his assistants.

Id. at 82-83, 366 P.2d at 819, 17 Cal. Rptr. at 491.

In Lesnik and Anderson, Nursing Practice and the Law (2d ed. 1955) pp. 277-279, it is said that nurses perform many functions that are medical acts, and, in the absence of statute, custom and usage generally will control the nature and scope of medical acts performed by them. Among the minimum requirements for a nurse's authority to perform such acts are that she proceed under the order and direction or supervision of a licensed physician and that she comprehend the cause and effect of the order.

Id. at 83 n.5, 366 P.2d at 820 n.5, 17 Cal. Rptr. at 492 n.5.

In the absence of some statutory basis for an exception, such as those with respect to nurses and persons engaged in medical study or teaching, one who is not licensed to practice medicine or surgery cannot legally perform acts which are medical or surgical in character, and supervision does not relieve an unauthorized person from penal liability for the violation of statutes which, like section 2141 of the code, prohibit the unlicensed practice of medicine. (State v. Cornelius, 200 Iowa 309, 204 N.W. 222, 223; State ex rel. Collet v. Scopel (Mo.) 316 S.W.2d 515, 519; State v. Young (Mo. App.) 215 S.W. 499, 501; State v. Paul, 56 Neb. 369, 76 N.W. 861, 862; Gobin v. State, 9 Okl. Cr. 201, 131 P. 546, 547, 44 L.R.A., N.S., 1089).

Id. at 84, 366 P.2d at 820, 17 Cal. Rptr. at 492.

Likewise, a licensed practitioner who aids and abets the performance of medical or surgical acts by an unauthorized person is guilty of unprofessional conduct under section 2392 of the code even though the acts are done under his immediate direction and supervision. (Newhouse v. Board of Osteopathic Examiners, 159 Cal. App. 2d 728, 732, 324 P.2d 687 [license of osteopathic physician and surgeon suspended for 30 days because he directed a chiropractor to insert sutures in the body of a patient under his supervision]; Garfield v. Board of Medical Examiners, 99 Ca. App. 2d 219, 230, 221 P.2d 705 [licensed physician operating a hospital held subject to discipline because he employed physicians licensed in other states but not in California to practice medicine under supervision in the hospital].) It should be noted that in the Garfield case the physicians, while not licensed in California, were graduates of approved medical schools, had served internships in approved hospitals, and were eligible to be licensed in this state on a reciprocity basis. (99 Cal. App. 2d at p. 222, 221 P.2d 707.) The fact that, as is also true in the present case, the unlicensed physicians had training enabling them to practice competently did not exculpate the physician who aided them in practicing. This is the necessary result of our statutory system which, in order to assure the protection of the public, requires that a person's competency be determined by the state and evidenced by a license.

Id. at 84-85, 366 P.2d at 820-21, 17 Cal. Rptr. at 492-93.

The Magit case is still good law in California. *See* O'Reilly v. Board of Medical Examiners, 66 Cal. 2d 381, 426 P.2d 167, 58 Cal. Rptr. 7 (1967). *Cf.* People v. Albert, 358 Mich. 647, 101 N.W.2d 378 (1960). Defendant employed a chiropodist to assist him in performing a mastectomy. The court held that no crime had been committed, because the acts of the assistant were such as could have been performed by an ordinary nurse and the assistant was at all times under the direction and supervision of the defendant.

In addition, the following cases involve suits in which the liability of the doctor was predicated upon the negligence of his assistants or subordinates. However, the cases all seem to involve acts which were within the authority granted to the person performing them by virtue of his license as a nurse or other medical assistant. The doctor's liability was based on theories of *respondeat superior*, but the acts which he directed the other parties to perform in these cases did not seem to be direct delegations of medical practice. *See* Mazer v. Lipshutz, 31 F.R.D. 123 (E.D. Pa. 1962); Natanson V. Kline, 186 Kan. 393, 350 P.2d 1093 (1960); McElroy v. Employers' Liability Assurance Corp., 163 F. Supp. 193 (W.D. Ark. 1958); Thompson v. Lillehei, 164 F. Supp. 716 (D. Minn. 1958); Voss V. Bridwell, 188 Kan. 643, 364 P.2d 955 (1961); McKinney v. Tromly, 386 S.W.2d 564 (Tex. Civ. App. 1964); Minogue v. Rutland Hospital, Inc., 119 Ver. 336, 125 A.2d 796 (1956); Huss v. Vande Hey, 29 Wis. 2d 34, 138, N.W.2d 192 (1965); Honeywell v. Rogers. 251 F. Supp. 841 (W.D. Pa. 1966); Buzan v. Mercy Hospital, Inc., 203 So. 2d II (Florida 1967); Monk v. Doctors Hospital, 403 F.2d 580 (D.C. Cir. 1968); Levett v. Etkind, 158 Conn. 567, 265, A.2d 70 (1969); Stone v. Sisters of Charity, 2 Wash. App. 607, 469 P.2d 229 (1970).

(48) Although the scope of authority for health care practitioner groups can, of course, be changed by amendments, it seldom happens. The type of amendments most commonly enacted simply add a new licensure category to the existing set of statutes. In Minnesota, for example, no certification procedure exists—all health care professionals are licensed pursuant to separate licensing provisions. This development, with years of original enactment for each health care profession, took place as follows: Dentists and dental hygienists, 1885; Pharmacists, 1885; Physicians, surgeons, and osteopaths, 1887; Registered nurses, 1907; Optometrists, 1915; Chiropractors, 1919; Practical nurses, 1947; Physical Therapists, 1951; Psychologists, 1951.

(49) The degree of professional association national activity is related to the spread of licensure. Medicine was the first of the recognized health professions to achieve licensure in all states. It was followed by pharmacy and dentistry and still later by optometry. Chiropractic has never been licensed in all states. The following list indicates the years of enactment and the years of nationalization of association: Medicine—organized nationally, 1847, licensed in all states, 1915; Pharmacy, organized nationally, 1852, licensed in all states, 1935; Dentistry, organized nationally, 1859, licensed in all states, 1935; Optometry, organized nationally, 1897, licensed in all states, 1939; Chiropractic, organized nationally, 1910, licensed in all states, x.

(50) There is of course some degree of deviancy between actual task performance by a licensed health care professional and the task boundaries codified by licensure statutes as modified by custom. The argument that there is some flexibility, however, is two-edged. While it is undoubtedly true that some licensure statutes do not fix the absolute limits of legitimate performance, such statutes leave the placement of boundaries so much in doubt that the performance of tasks beyond those clearly within the legal competence of a practitioner must be assessed on a case-by-case basis. Conversely, where the boundaries are clearly delineated they are so often unrealistically drawn that their breach is the rule and not the exception. The danger is, of course, that the breach can result in litigation. A typical example is Barber V. Reinking, 68 Wash. 2d 139, 411 P.2d 861 (1966), where a practical nurse performed a simple innoculation and upon a complication was, along with the delegating physician, subjected to a malpractice suit. Their defense was that the performance of the task by the nurse was a matter of custom. The licensure statute, however, contained an express prohibition against innoculation by practical nurses.

(51) For a convincing demonstration of the degree to which health care licensing boards are comprised of or controlled by the very professionals under regulation, see Akers, *supra* note 7.

(52) Professor Friedman provides nice definitions of the three terms used

(often too interchangeably) to describe the process of formal legitimation of a health care professional group: registration, certification, and licensure. The terms are generally used in this article as defined by Professor Friedman:

> It is important to distinguish three different levels of control: first, registration; second, certification; third, licensing. By registration, I mean an arrangement under which individuals are required to list their names in some official register if they engage in certain kinds of activities. There is no provision for denying the right to engage in the activity to anyone who is willing to list his name. He may be charged a fee, either as a registration fee or as a scheme of taxation. The second level is certification. The governmental agency may certify that an individual has certain skills but may not prevent, in any way, the practice of any occupation using these skills by people who do not have a certificate. One example is accountancy. In most states, anybody can be an accountant, whether he is a certified public accountant or not, but only those people who have passed a particular test can put the title CPA after their names or can put a sign in their offices saying they are certified public accountants. Certification is frequently only an intermediate stage. In many stages, there has been a tendency to restrict an increasing range of activities to certified public accountants. With respect to such activities there is licensure, not certification. In some states, 'architect' is a title which can be used only by those who have passed a specified examination. This is certification. It does not prevent anyone else from going into the business of advising people for a fee how to build houses. The third stage is licensing proper. This is an arrangement under which one must obtain a license from a recognized authority in order to engage in the occupation. The license is more than a formality. It requires some demonstration of competence . . . and anyone who does not have a license is not authorized to practice and is subject to a fine or a jail sentence if he does engage in practice.

See Friedman, *supra* note 1, at 144-45.

(53) *See* note 47 *supra.*

(54) *See* Ariz. Rev. Stat. Ann. § 32-1421(6) (Supp. 1970); Colo. Rev. Stat. § 91-1(6)(m)(1963); Kan. Stat. Ann. § 65-2872(g) 1964); Okla. Stat. Ann. tit. 59, § 492 (Supp. 1970).

(55) The argument is, of course, a simple one. If the statute specifies only one subprofessional group for a permissible delegation, then, by old dogma, all others are excluded.

(56) State legislatures in North Carolina, West Virginia, Minnesota, Utah, Washington, and Wisconsin have either recently enacted statutes or are considering bills on this subject. Conversation between the author and Dr. Douglas Fenderson, National Center for Health Services Research and Development.

(57) Forgotson, Bradley & Ballenger, *Health Services for the Poor—The Manpower Problems: Innovation and the Law,* 1970 Wisc. L. Rev. 756.

(58) *Id.* at 776-77.

(59) The authors also speculate—with respect to malpractice—that an assistant delegated duties by a physician would be held to the same standard of care as would a physician, since the assistant would be performing service tasks traditionally undertaken by the physician. *Id.* at 779.

(40) A laundry list of other unresolved issues is included in their article:

1. What are some criteria which might be used to evaluate applicants who have not graduated from a formal program? 2. What types of existing office workers and assistants, other than graduates of physician's assistant programs,

should or could seek approval under such a statute? 3. Would such a statute permit foreign trained physicians who failed to qualify for licensure to practice under very attenuated supervision? 4. Is there any given act, task, or function which is not delegable under any circumstances to any assistant, regardless of a physician's direction and supervision, and against which a physician should be forewarned? 5. Should it be possible to approve a physician's assistant if he is to be employed by a hospital? Does this open the door to allowing hospitals to practice medicine? 6. Is there too much specificity in wording such as 'direct supervision and control' and if so, would more general wording such as 'direction and supervision' by the physician be any better? 7. The health field as a license-oriented one, and a certain amount of status accrues with licensure. Is it wise to deprive the new paramedical practitioners of the traditional mode of recognition, especially when this scheme otherwise resembles licensure (*i.e.*, approval, possibility that this approval will be revoked, possibility that it will in fact later be necessary to define a scope of practice, at least insofar as saying what is *not* delegable)?"

Id. at 779.

(61) *Id*.

(62) *Id*. at 780. The scheme is attributed to Professor Clark C. Havighurst of the Duke University School of Law. Professor Havighurst would also accept some administrative oversight of delegation practices, implemented by a power to issue cease and desist orders where unsafe practices were found to exist. *See id*. *See also* Havighurst, *Licensure and Its Alternatives*, in Proceedings of the 3d Annual Duke Conference on Physician's Assistants 121 (1970).

(63) Colo. Rev. Stat. § 91-10-1 (Permanent Cumulative Supp. 1969).

(64) This point is expressly acknowledged in Forgotson, Bradley & Ballenger, *supra* note 57, at 779.

(65) *See* note 62 and accompanying text *supra*.

(66) *See* text accompanying note 51 *supra*.

(67) *See* Forgotson, Bradley & Ballenger, *supra* note 57, at 772.

(68) The phenomenon of increasing size is at best a high-grade surmise. No definitive evidence is available except the documentable trend reflecting an increase in group practice which, to the extent it reduces the numbers of solo practitioners, ineluctably increases the average size of the unit of care.

(69) Unlike personnel licensure, licensing of hospitals is a recent development. At the end of World War II fewer than a dozen states had comprehensive licensing laws, and these in fact were often just "paper" laws. The principal breakthrough came with the Hill-Burton Hospital Survey and Construction Act of 1946. By 1954, thirty-eight states had laws licensing maternity sections of hospitals. This pioneering is still apparent in the strong emphasis on maternity regulations in many state licensing programs.

Although the Hill-Burton law did not explicitly require states to enact licensing laws, it did require them to provide minimum standards of maintenance and operation for hospitals built with the help of Hill-Burton funds. Section 2 of the Hospital Survey and Construction Act provided:

> If any state, prior to July 1, 1948, has not enacted legislation providing that compliance with minimum standards of maintenance and operation shall be required . . . such State shall not be entitled to further allotments. . . .

ch. 958, 60 Stat. 1044 (1946).

Four years later the 1950 amendments to the Social Security Act provided that any state using federal matching funds to pay for care in public or private institutions for welfare recipients must designate an authority "which shall be responsible for establishing and maintaining standards for such institutions." Social Security Act Amendments of 1950, ch. 809, tit. III, § 301(b), 64 Stat. 548. Several states had to adopt or amend hospital licensing laws to qualify for these funds. In time, nearly every state had some sort of hospital licensing program. The literature on hospital licensure is extremely sparse. Some articles available include H. Fry, The Operation of State Hospital Planning and Licensure Programs 4 (American Hospital Association Monograph Series No. 15, 1965); K. Taylor & D. Donald, A Comparative Study of Hospital Licensure Regulations (1957). This latter study compares state licensing provisions with earlier ACS standards. *See also* 2 W. McNerney et al., Hospital and Medical Economics (1962); Somers, *supra* note 8, at 90 n.20.

(70) Hershey, *An Alternative to Mandatory Licensure of Health Professionals*, Hospital Progress, Mar. 1969, at 71, 73.

(71) Physician acceptance of the proposal is not necessarily predictable. Although *any* change in the health care delivery system is generally opposed by organized medicine, there are signs that the AMA knee-jerk phenomenon is abating. For example, the Administration's Health Maintenance Organization development has been tolerated and upon occasion faintly praised, despite medicine's well documented resistance to prepayment and group practice arrangements.

(72) A distinction should be drawn. Licensure of organizations refers strictly to the control of organizations providing for or arranging for provision of health care services. The laws of most states govern the "financing" of health care services by indemnification of costs by commercial health insurance companies and by "service" plans like Blue Cross and Blue Shield. The law referred to here affects organizations providing health care services. The impetus for much of this activity is the Administration's recently announced health program which proposes stimuli to the development for health maintenance organizations. *See* note 43 *supra*. All configurations for such organizations are currently barred in 22 states and their development impeded in nearly all others. *See, e.g.*, Aspen Systems Corporation, Group Practice and the Law (1969); H. Hansen, Legal Rights of Group Health Plans: A Survey of State Laws Through 1963 (1964).

Growing pressure to remove laws inconsistent with the evolution of health maintenance organizations will lead to the enactment of licensing and chartering mechanisms in many states to 1. repeal other inconsistent state law, and 2. fashion regulatory schemes for such organizations.

(73) Ohio Rev. Code Ann. § 1738.01 *et seq.* (1964).

(74) The Ohio law requires, for example, that certain conditions be met by an organization before it may do business. These include:

§ 1738.04 Application for certificate or license.

Before it may issue any contract or certificate to a subscriber, a corporation not for profit desiring to establish, maintain, and operate a health care plan must obtain from the superintendent of insurance a certificate of authority or license to do so. Each application to the superintendent for such a certificate or license shall be verified by an officer of the corporation, and shall set forth, or shall be accompanied by the following:

(A) A copy of the corporation's articles of incorporation, and of any amendments thereto, certified by the secretary of state, which shall define with reasonable certainty the territorial boundaries within which such corporation proposes to operate a nonprofit health care plan, and which shall state the location of the principal office for the transaction of its business;

(B) A list of names and residence addresses of all officers and the trustees of the corporation;

(C) A description of the health care plan which the corporation proposes to operate, together with the forms of all contracts or certificates which it proposes to insure under such plan;

(D) A statement of the assets and liabilities of the corporation.

§ 1738.05 Issuance of certificate or license.

The superintendent of insurance shall issue a certificate of authority or license to any health care corporation filing an application in conformity with section 1738.04 of the Revised Code . . . and upon being satisifed that:

(A) Such corporation proposes to establish and operate a bona fide nonprofit health care plan;

(B) The proposed contracts and the proposed rates therefor between such corporation and the subscribers to the plan are fair and reasonable;

(C) The proposed plan is established upon a sound financial and actuarial basis, in view of the experience of nonprofit health care plans already in existence. If such corporation desires to amend any contract with its subscribers or desires to change any rate charged therefor, a copy of the form of such amendment of any contract or the change of any rate shall be filed with the superintendent of insurance and shall not be effective until the expiration of ninety days after the filing thereof unless he sooner gives to such corporation his written approval thereto. If the superintendent is not satisfied within such ninety day period, that any such change or amendment of either the contract or the rate is lawful, fair, and reasonable, he shall so notify such corporation and it shall thereafter be unlawful for such corporation to make effective any such change or amendment.

§ 1738.08 Annual report.

Every corporation subject to sections 1738.01 to 1738.21, inclusive, of the Revised Code, shall annually, on or before the first day of March, file a report, verified by an officer of the corporation, with the superintendent of insurance, showing its condition on the last day of the preceding calendar year, on forms prescribed by the superintendent, which report shall include:

(A) The financial statement of such corporation, including its balance sheet and its receipts and disbursements for the preceding year;

(B) A list of the names and residence addresses of all its officers and trustees; and the total amount of expense reimbursement to all officers and trustees;

(C) The number of subscribers' contracts or certificates issued by such corporation and outstanding;

(D) The number of physicians and dentists with which such corporation has agreements and the qualifications of the physicians and dentists;

(E) The number and type of services covered under the contract or certificate provided during the year.

Id. §§ 1738.04=.05, 1738.08.

° (75) In 1968, only 66 disciplinary actions involving either suspension or revocation of license were initiated against the more than 300,000 physicians practicing in the United States. *Hearings of the Subcomm. of the Senate Comm. on Governmental Operations* 90th Cong., 1st Sess. (1969). The question of professional policing of the quality of health care is germane, but too complex and of such magnitude as to be beyond the scope of this article. Suffice it to say that it has not worked very well. The scheme proposed offers much greater promise of intervention into the provider system to correct behavior not conducive to quality health care: First, because organizations would be responsible for the quality of care and as such more amenable to "impersonal" and objective penalties should error occur than individual physicians whose penalization must be dished out by their peers; and second, because a new system offers the opportunity to introduce systematic "feedback" of poor performance to a corrective-disciplinary system. For a comprehensive examination of provider self-policing, see R. McCleery et al., One Life—One Physician (1970).

(76) The Medicare amendments dealing with the health maintenance organization option do not prohibit payments to for-profit health maintenance organizations. *See* H.R. 1, *supra* note 27.

(77) *See* note 38 *supra.*

IV

HEALTH SCIENCES IN COURT

IV. HEALTH SCIENCES IN COURT:
FORENSIC MEDICINE

INTRODUCTION

During the last two decades the health care professionals have had an increasing exposure to our legal system and the courts. Federal and state legislatures have enacted innumerable statutes involving health care services. New types of agencies involved with the delivery of health care have been created. All these developments are in addition to the traditional functions of the medical arts practitioners in helping assess claims of medical disability before courts or before administrative agencies.

Personal injury, malpractice, workman's compensation and other medically-related actions have been estimated to account for at least twenty-five percent of judicial activity. A comparable amount of time is spent by attorneys in the pursuit of these activities. A significant amount of physicians' time is similarly engaged.

Despite the great amount of interaction between physicians and lawyers, medical and legal schools tend to overlook the interdisciplinary link. Attorneys and physicians should understand the philosophy, discipline, methodology, approach, practice, aims and requirements of the other. Most lawyers, however do not adequately understand the "grey zones of medicine" and most doctors fail to comprehend the "advocacy system." This lack of understanding accounts, at least in part, for the medical malpractice epidemic, now spilling over into the legal profession as well.

It is inherent in the common law that the court is to remain neutral, and each party, through its attorney, is to seek the evidence most advantageous to it. In order to prove injury, negligency, or breach of the required standard of care, it is usually required that each be established by "expert" testimony. In an adversary system, the court will not usually seek its own independent experts but will rely on the outcome of the warfare between partisan experts. For a variety of reasons, physicians as well as other professionals are reluctant to testify against one another. This reluctance has been termed the "conspiracy of silence."

To overcome the reluctance of experts, courts have for the most part abandoned the "locality rule" requiring an expert to come from the same geographic area. In addition, resort to the principle of *res ipsa loquitur* (being a presumption of negligence when the accident does not ordinarily occur) and a growing emphasis upon the requirement of a patients' "informed consent" to treatment have somewhat lessened the need for experts in the courtroom.

Frequently an experts' impact on the trier of facts, particularly the jury, is not based on knowledge and ability, but rather on personality and demeanor. The use of impartial medical experts, as in the European civil law system, has been recommended. Some experimental projects have been instituted to encourage the appointment of non-partisan experts to the court in lieu of adversary expert witnesses.

Not only the adversary court procedure but also underlying substantive law principles remain troublesome for the medical practitioner. Physicians find it difficult to understand the doctrines of *respondeat superior* and vicarious liability. They resist, therefore, accepting responsibility for the negligent acts of subordinates, affiliates and associates, when they themselves were not negligent and had not made a negligent choice.

In the interfaces of medicine and law, forensic science (which includes pathology, toxicology, serology, chemical analysis, and other specialties) continues to be of focal interest. Autopsies and other forensic science procedures are becoming increasingly critical not only in criminal proceedings but in civil cases as well. It is generally agreed justice has been facilitated with the advancement in these sciences.

EDUCATIONAL OPPORTUNITIES IN LAW AND MEDICINE
IN LAW AND MEDICAL SCHOOLS

Harold L. Hirsh

The legal problems facing the physician and the medical situations confronting the attorney are becoming more frequent, numerous and complex. In some areas they are approaching crisis proportions.

The field of forensic or legal medicine is one of the most rapidly developing and expanding areas in both of the related disciplines—medicine and law. It has been estimated that litigation involving personal injury and malpractice comprise about 25 percent of legal practice. A significant amount of physicians' time must be similarly occupied, particularly when one considers, in addition, the legal aspects of the physician to his relation with third party carriers-private and governmental. Development in forensic science have increased not only the degree of involvement but the importance of the pathologist in criminology and in criminal law. At the same time the increasing importance of forensic science to the law enforcement officer and the criminal lawyer is obvious. Workmen's compensation and ecological or environmental problems are increasingly occupying the time, talent and energy of both physicians and attorney. It is apparent that there is a great need for each profession to have some understanding of the other discipline. As a result a study to ascertain how well our schools are preparing our future physicians and attorneys for the challenges was involved. The primary purpose was to try to determine the medical-legal educational opportunities in both medical and law schools in this country.

A letter of inquiry and a request for a catalog or bulletin was written to all the medical schools and law schools in the country. All of the 148 law schools approved by the Association of American Law Schools and 116 medical schools approved by the American Association of Medical Colleges have replied. The University of Illinois has three separate clinical medical school divisions and each has been considered separately because of the differences in programs. In many situations there is no relationship between the course description in the catalog or bulletin and what is offered. The courses given in the law schools and the medical schools are considered separately for statistical evaluation since there are significant differences in the subject matter or topics covered, the pedalogical approaches, and even in the approach and relationship to the law.

For the purpose of this paper the term *forensic medicine* is used in the broadest sense to include the designations "law and medicine" or legal medicine, "law and psychiatry," legal psychiatry and forensic psychiatry and also forensic pathology, toxicology, serology or laboratory science.

In addition to requesting catalogs or bulletins, specific detailed information was asked for from each of the designated professors regarding the courses offered in legal medicine and forensic psychiatry.

The following is the data abstracted from the information received from the 148 law schools. There were no courses in forensic medicine in 40 schools. One course in "law and medicine" is offered in three schools. Sixteen law schools offer one course in "law and psychiatry" and four schools offer two courses. Thirty-eight schools offer courses both in "law and medicine" and "law and psychiatry." Of these, 22 provide one course each in "law and medicine" and "law and psychiatry." Some offer several courses in "law and medicine" with one course in "law and psychiatry," while in other schools the reverse is true. A few schools provide several courses in both fields. There are a total of 108 courses in "law and medicine" and 79 courses in "law and psychiatry" available at the 148 law schools.

Of the 108 courses in "law and medicine" 75 are lecture courses, 32 are seminar in format and one is a clinical-type course. The apportioned time for the courses was calculated on the basis of the number of credit hours assigned. Sixty courses are allotted two-credit hours, and 43 are assigned three-credit hours. As to the remaining, two are allotted more than three, one is allowed one-and-one half, in another credit is by arrangement, while one is without credit. It is apparent that the greater number of courses in "law and medicine" in law schools are allotted only a minimum amount of credit. About two-thirds of the courses used recognized texts and the remainder use prepared syllabi, mimeographed materials or varied outside reading.

The background of the professors was also analyzed. Of the 108 courses in "law and medicine," 75 are taught by or under the direction of law professors or attorneys. Five courses are taught by lawyers or law professors jointly with physicians from private practice or associated hospitals. Sixteen are taught by men with combined degrees in law and medicine. Two of the courses are presented under the direction or supervision of professors who are neither physicians nor attorneys. Ten of the above courses are presented in an interdisciplinary format with the participation of theologians, psychologists, social workers, sociologists, law enforcement officers, judges and health care administrators. These people come as guest lecturers or as participants at specific seminar sessions.

It was not practical to compare various law school courses in "law and medicine" because of the great variation of content. However, the courses can be generally classified into six types with one of the types being divisible into three sub-categories. The classifications are formulated as to the apparent objective or purpose of the course, and according to their orientation. Forty-four courses are designated as "complete" in presentation covering in general the whole field of forensic medicine. When the purely legal aspects of the courses are emphasized, it is classified as a "survey" course. Twelve of these courses provide a survey of the preclinical and clinical medical sciences plus the pertinent aspects of medical practice. Thirteen courses are sociologically oriented with health care primarily considered. All the aspects of litigation are covered in 17 of the courses. Of these, 11 are essentially concerned with personal injury, one with personal injury and malpractice, one with malpractice exclusively, and four cover the problems of medical-legal litigation generally. Eleven courses are considered moral-ethical in orientation, and five are classified as forensic science. As part of the evaluation, I have graded each course according to the most complete one in its category. Twenty-one courses are considered as excellent in content, 21 good, 40 fair and 26 are minimal.

The analysis of the information reveals that the courses in "law and medicine" and "law and psychiatry" have many facets in common and that there is significant overlap of these two areas of forensic medicine. A total of 79 courses in "law and psychiatry" are offered in the 148 law schools. Forty-two courses are lecture and 34 are seminar in format, while three are presented in a clinic set-up. Forty-five of the courses are allotted two-credit-hours, and 27 are allocated three credit hours. One course allows less than two credits, and six more than three. By far, a minimum of credit is allotted to courses in "law and psychiatry."

The 79 courses in "law and psychiatry" are taught by or are under the supervision of professors with a variety of backgrounds. Thirty-seven courses are taught by law professors or attorneys, 16 jointly by physicians, primarily psychiatrists, and law professors or attorneys, five by psychiatrists with both medical and law degrees, and 16 by psychiatrists. In five of the courses, the faculty varies from year to year. Twelve of the courses are interdisciplinary in format with theologians, sociologists, social workers, penal and law enforcement officers, judges and health care administrators appearing as guest lecturers or as participants in the seminar sessions. Almost all of the courses used recognized texts, while only a small number use prepared syllabi, mimeographed materials or varied outside readings. An analysis of the courses in "law and psychiatry" based on course content indicates that they can generally be categorized into four groups. Thirty-six are considered "broad" in scope as they include an explanation of psychiatric or mental and emotional illness, the various schools of therapy, the relationship of law and psychiatry and the role of the psychiatrist in the field of forensic psychiatry. Thirty-five are primarily concerned with an explanation of mental illness and its legal consequences. Of these, 23 are basically patient-client oriented. They are directed to giving the law student an understanding of the problems of people stigmatized with mental illness and the proper protection of the client in these circumstances. The other 12 are concerned primarily with the role of the psychiatrist in the legal process. Eight courses are essentially concerned with medical-moral-ethical-legal problems in the area of forensic psychiatry.

The courses in each of the groups were compared with each other, and it can be concluded that almost all were excellent or good with few either fair or minimal.

It is of interest to note that there are a number of courses offered in related fields in the 148 law schools. A total of 48 courses are offered in Law and Behavioral Sciences, and 29 in Workmen's Compensation Law in which industrial and occupational medicine is a significant part of the course. Sixteen courses that cover Food and Drug Law are oriented to forensic medicine. Twenty-four courses are in such related areas as Health Care Science and Law. Courses in Law, Technology and Science are offered in 12 schools. Almost two-thirds of the schools now offer courses in Environmental Law.

All of 116 medical schools in this country are included in this study. Seventy offer courses in forensic medicine while 46 do not. Twelve schools offer more than one course. Eight other schools have more than one course but generally they represent two or more courses in forensic pathology that are related one to the other. A total of 91 courses in forensic medicine are offered in the 70 schools. These statistics do not include courses offered to hospital house staff or to physicians on a continuing education basis. The following is a tabulation of the departments responsible for teaching the course in the school curriculum:

Anesthesiology	1
Community Health—Public Health—Preventive Medicine	13
Forensic Medicine (Legal Medicine—Medical Jurisprudence)	4
Humanities	1
Pharmacology	1
Pathology—Medical Examiner's Office	23
Psychiatry	9
Surgery (General Surgery—1; Orthopedic Surgery—1)	2
Interdisciplinary	4
Independent	16

The term "interdisciplinary" indicates that the course is open to the medical students as an elective, and it is under the direction of a School at the University other than the School of Medicine. The term "independent" indicates that the professor is not assigned to or does not answer to any specific school department, but rather that he is a faculty-member-at-large and his responsibility is to the Dean's Office. Twelve of the 46 schools that do not offer a formal course in forensic medicine indicated that the subject of legal medicine is discussed in the various clinical departments—medicine, pediatrics, psychiatry, surgery—particularly on an on-going basis when it is pertinent.

The 91 courses that are offered were tabulated according to the curriculum requirement. Selection of the course is required in 47 courses and is elective in the other 44. The school year in which the student is given the opportunity or required to take the course was tabulated. In 10 schools the course is available in the first year. In four schools the course is offered in parts of both the first and second years. The course is given in the second year in 24 schools and in four schools the course is offered in parts of the second and third years. Eleven schools offer the courses in the third year and five in parts of the third and fourth years. It is in the fourth year that the courses are offered in 21 schools. Twelve of the schools allow the student to take the courses at any time in the medical school curriculum. Most of the courses that overlap school years are in forensic science.

The background of the professors or those responsible for conducting the courses in "law and medicine" was analyzed. Twenty-four are physicians, 26 are attorneys, and ten have combined degrees in both law and medicine. In 12 schools the course is under the joint direction of a physician and attorney. Thirteen of these various courses are conducted by a pathologist who, in many instances, is the medical examiner for the political subdivisions. In 19 schools the course is presented by a group of teachers—"combined group"—including physicians, attorneys, judges, experts in health care, medical practice and insurance matters, theologians, psychiatrists, psychologists, sociologists, social workers, law enforcement and penal experts. It should be noted that the term "physician" and "attorney" includes practitioners and/or professors. In many instances it was difficult to determine whether the teacher was a full-time professor or a practitioner teaching part-time. In general, the physicians or those who had combined M.D.-J.D. degrees are primarily educators. This is true for those in the pathology group as well. The courses taught by attorneys, or by an attorney plus a physician involve primarily practitioners. The "interdisciplinary" courses are all taught on a "combined" teaching basis by professors not on the medical school faculties. The forensic science courses are invariably taught by pathologists and medical examiners. The four courses in "law and psychiatry" are under the direction of professors with combined M.D.-J.D. degrees.

The 91 courses in forensic medicine offered in the medical schools were not uniform in content. They could be classified into four categories based on the material or topics covered or orientation of the courses. Fifty-five were considered to cover the field of "law and medicine" generally, four were considered to cover "law and psychiatry" exclusively, 21 involved forensic science subject-matter, six were moral-ethical in scope and five were directed to health care. Almost all of the courses were considered excellent or good and only a few were thought to be fair or minimal in quality.

CONCLUSIONS

Several conclusions can be made purely from the mechanical aspects of doing the study. As has been indicated, catalogs and bulletins issued by both law and medical schools, particularly the latter, are extremely unreliable. They are frequently out-of-date. Courses are listed that in reality are not being offered. New courses that have been added to the curriculum are not listed. Due to a change in teachers or as a result of the passage of time, the course content in many instances is changed without changing the description in the school publication. Personal correspondence and investigation was necessary in order to receive the information. There was a problem concerning the difficulty in interpreting and analyzing the information and extracting the data. Despite the desire and need to be objective, there is still a degree of personal evaluation involved.

Despite the high incidence of medical-legal problems and the increasing involvement of the physician with the law, programs in forensic medicine are obviously neglected in both law and medical schools' curricula. Courses are not offered in about 27% of the law schools and almost 40% of the medical schools. Part of the problem in both law and medical schools is the unavailability and shortage of either trained or interested teachers of both disciplines. All schools have budgetary problems and many are unwilling to engage part-time specialists to teach forensic medicine. The study revealed that the majority of the courses are limited in scope, and fail to give the student a complete overview of the problems confronting the attorney and the physician in the broad area of forensic medicine. Although some of the courses are classified as excellent, the excellence in many instances is based on the limited orientation of the course and not as a complete course.

Despite the fact that forensic medicine comprises a significant portion of the practice of law, more than one-quarter of the schools do not offer instruction in this field. While 27% of the law schools still do not offer courses in legal medicine, the future on the law school side appears encouraging and promising. Whereas 20 years ago, instruction in legal medicine was very rare, it is now relatively common—73% of the law schools offer courses. Moreover, the trend appears to be toward expansion when one compares the availablity of courses in 1973 as compared recently to 1970. An increasing number of legal educators and law school administrators are becoming increasingly concerned with the area, responsibilities and challenges which it presents. Although the types of courses currently being offered have done only a little to facilitate and assist in improving the interdisciplinary understanding, it is a fact that courses are now being offered where before there was nothing offered in law schools. Every legal medicine course is elective and in most instances only one course is available. Even when there is more than one course, it is extremely rare to find a requirement that the available courses be taken in a particular sequence. It is questionable whether a random exposure to legal medicine, rather than a planned program, is really beneficial, particularly to the interested law student. If the student is particularly interested in legal medicine, should there not be a program which builds upon itself? At the same time it would expose the student to a detailed presentation of the medical model as well as to the ethics of the profession and the mentality of the physician. In this way the student can be better prepared to deal with the medical profession and the different conceptual approaches of physicians particularly in the various specialties. To take one area of medicine out of context and deal with it in some depth, as many law courses in legal medicine now do, without having a grounding in the goals, methods, problems, and aspirations of medicine, as well as the rationales behind them, appears as pointless as telling the medical student about the pitfalls of malpractice without explaining the adversary system so that the student will not feel every attorney is his natural-born enemy.

Almost 40% of the medical schools do not offer any instruction in legal medicine. Considering the tremendous amount of litigation in which physicians must take part and the constant increase in the number of malpractice action being brought against them, the lack of attention to this area is not only shocking and distressing, but it could almost be said to be a dereliction of the duty of the medical schools to both the student and his future patients. This situation is more incongruous when it is realized almost all medical schools are affiliated with universities. Most of the universities include a law school, frequently on the same campus, or the medical schools are in an urban area with at least one law school.

A number of administrators of medical schools not offering courses in forensic medicine have indicated that absence of such courses was due to lack of student interest. In truth, medical school curricula are not evolved solely on the basis of student interest. It appears, rather, that part of the explanation for this selection in medical schools is in the fact that, unfortunately, the teaching of clinical medicine has almost exclusively come under the control of the full-time teacher. Generally the full-time teacher is not faced with the practical problems of medical practice where medicine and law most often interface and confront. Therefore, courses in forensic medicine are not thought to be as important as expansion in areas such as community medicine and other newly-developed aspects of medicine.

In addition to failing to acquaint the student with the importance of legal medicine, the lack of student interest is frequently the result of the failure to present the materials in such a way as to stimulate and maintain the students' interest, especially in an area of such growing importance. The subject is too vital to be ignored. Instead innovation, creative and imaginative methods of instruction should be employed. New techniques of encouraging, rather than policing, attendance should be used to insure the students' exposure to the subject. The material is inherently not only interesting but frequently fascinating. If presented appropriately, the subject matter can readily be exploited to arouse the curiosity, interest and attention of the student. The study revealed that the general failure of the medical schools to innovate and adapt the presentation of legal medicine to the needs and wants of their students seems to reflect an unawareness and conviction on the part of the school administrators and faculty that the subject does not warrant concern or care.

It is true that medical education has reached a stage when deviation from the traditional structure of the past has become imperative and an ever-increasing reality. However, the medical schools seem to be particularly oblivious to or inept at even attempting to educate the students that their patient is simply not a walking medical problem, but is first and foremost a human being with a considerable number of rights and privileges. These must be respected regardless of his illness. The more basic academic problem, however, is how is a medical student to be expected to respect these rights and privileges if the student does not know what they are and/or has no familiarity with the system that created them and is organized and dedicated to protecting them.

In all law schools, because the curriculum beyond the basic course is elective, no significance can be attached to the fact that the courses in legal medicine are not required. On the other hand, where a considerable amount of the medical school curriculum is still required, despite much leeway, more time is spent considering unusual diseases that the physician will either never or rarely see, than on teaching forensic medicine. Yet the legal problems of the physician may be of daily concern and the basis of frequent confrontations. Courses in forensic medicine in medical schools will expose the student to many of the problems that he will be faced with in practice. Many of the courses in the medical schools are offered in the senior year when many of the students are away on elective clerkships or scattered about on service at affiliated hospitals. Therefore, for all intents and purposes the courses are not available to them. In my opinion, it would be better to present the courses in forensic medicine during the preclinical or first or second years, when all the students are still available and when it can be required. As we introduce the medical student into the clerkship, we expose him immediately to the legal problems, hazards and confrontations of the practice of medicine. While experiencing these problems, he can be thinking about them intelligently just as he does about the clinical entities that he must learn. In the meantime, he has had a course which has prepared him for this exposure and learning process. The inadequacies of many programs or courses in forensic medicine in medical schools is glaringly apparent when we examine the content and types of courses offered, the background and expertise of the teachers, and the departments responsible for presenting the course.

Given the ever-increasing interaction between the two disciplines, it is obvious that it is of critical practical importance that each profession educate its prospective members to effectively deal with their co-professionals when they interface or confront. This study was therefore more than of just academic interest. One distressing conclusion is that in many programs, both in the law and medical schools, the courses are designed so that the student is simply instructed how to practice his own profession by utilization, in circumvention, or in spite of the other profession. Despite the fact that many valuable medical-legal problems can be considered and information imparted and absorbed in a variety of different courses in legal medicine comparable to those that are presently being taught, to expose the student to a limited particular aspect of another discipline is certainly inadequate and may be self-defeating any consideration of only a part of another discipline, and applying it to only a particular aspect of one's own discipline is really not to educate the student in legal medicine. For adequate instruction it is necessary to inform the student of the rationales and methodology of the other profession including as well a thorough grounding in its ethics and goals. In addition, there should be an explanation of the conceptual and methodological differences between the professions.

Legal medicine presents many new ideas and methods for dealing with a myriad of problems and issues. As science in general and medicine in particular continue to improve, but at the same time threaten old concepts and procedures and introduce new ones, there is going to be an increasing need for people who are prepared to deal with these new and complex situations. The responsibility for producing these individuals rests with both law and medicine, and both must exercise it. The time to start this education process is during the formal education period. At this time it is something neither discipline is presently doing at a level comparable to the need, particularly at the school level. The point is, however, that progress must be made and the initiative must come from both disciplines, preferably jointly.

It is encouraging to find that there is significant activity among the professional societies of both disciplines to develop an awareness of the problems and need and an effort to find solutions. This is going on within each discipline and on an interdisciplinary basis. The creation by the American Association of Law Schools of a Committee on Law and Medicine is a recognition that legal medicine is a separate and important area within the law. The American Bar Association has also created a Law and Medicine Committee as part of its Section of Insurance, Negligence and Compensation Law. The American Medical Association has joined with the American Bar Association to create a joint Committee which sponsors national meetings every two years devoted to legal medicine. The A.M.A. Journal publishes an article on Law and Medicine in each of its issues. Many other professional and proprietary medical journals publish articles on "law and medicine" regularly. The membership of the American College of Legal Medicine has truly proliferated in the last few years. This is an omen which bodes well for the future of legal medicine.

THE MEDICAL EXPERT
AND THE LAWSUIT

Earl F. Rose

Convincing facts result in favorable verdicts. Expert testimony to establish medical facts is a requirement in the majority of personal injury and compensation cases and in a modest number of criminal trials, particularly those for murder. This is not to denigrate or minimize the importance of legal principles, doctrines or rules as determinants of the outcome of any legal action, but to recognize that although these are important, convincing facts optimally presented are the determining factors in litigation. This was lucidly expressed by a legal scholar who, noting the accommodation of the rules of law to the evidence proffered, stated, "[t]he inevitable accommodation of general legal principles to the 'facts' of specific cases continues to be accomplished by a proliferation of ostensible legal rules, refinements of rules, distinction in the refinements, exceptions to the distinctions in the refinements, and so forth ad infinitum."(1) Hence, the orientation of the "legal realist" is obtaining, understanding, and presenting convincing and cogent medical facts upon which a tribunal can make a determination. That tribunals have their limitations cannot be doubted, but the lawyer pressing his case is best prepared by a developed and refined sense of the limitations and imperfections of both his "facts" and his "experts." To this end this article is addressed.

The initial interview with the client provides the preliminary facts as the client views them, although not infrequently these are at variance with the actual events that transpired. Regrettably, it is not unheard of for a client to relate his story in a manner which he believes would allow his attorney to best represent him—while accurate and detailed information has been freely given to an insurance adjustor in a civil action, or to the police in a criminal case. For his own interests as well as the client's, the lawyer is obligated to amplify and corroborate the medical history as well as other facts. To expand his own knowledge of controverted injury or disease the lawyer must have access to medical publications and skill in the techniques of rapid and comprehensive searching of medical literature. This also serves to prepare the lawyer for the encounter with the physician(s) who are required to prove or disprove the controverted medical issues.

The modern trend in civil and criminal litigation is to remove the element of surprise by giving all parties an opportunity prior to trial to obtain the names of witnesses, physical facts, and even proposed testimony formerly considered secret work product of the attorney. It would appear that the expert's deposition can be taken and even the conclusions of the expert elicited. As a corollary to this, the preliminary investigation which the expert makes would be within the proper scope of inquiry in the deposition. Indeed, some courts require the attorneys to list their witnesses, a summary of the evidence, an estimate of the time required for the witnesses' testimony, and the order in which the witnesses will be called; all in written form to be submitted to the court prior to even the pre-trial conference. The application of the rules covering discovery are left largely to the trial court's discretion, and there are seemingly conflicting decisions in state courts as well as between the states where there is more conflict because of minute variance in laws. These trial court discretionary rulings normally will not be overruled unless there is an abuse of discretion by the trial judge which seriously prejudices the litigants.

When medical facts are the controverted issues, the lawyer prepared for both favorable and adverse medical testimony will be in a position of confidence in dealing with settlement or presentation at trial. He should be amply rewarded for the time spent in preparation, and his ability to present and communicate medicolegal facts in a most convincing manner will win the admiration of the medical profession.

MEDICAL RECORDS:PRELITIGATION ACCESSIBILITY & OWNERSHIP

The records of interest to the lawyer include any ambulance and emergency room reports, hospital charts with nurses' notes, and the physician's records. Files of an employer including pre-employment physical examinations and absentee records may indicate previous injury or prior physical status and should not be overlooked. Not only are all of these medical records important in determining the merits of the case and in providing a factual basis upon which the lawyer makes his own search of the pertinent medical literature, but they form the medical basis for the claim. They also prepare the attorney for his conferences with the medical experts. After litigation between the parties is joined the court decides upon the matter of the availability of these records as a part of the discovery procedures; however, the attorney wishing to inspect his client's medical records prior to filing may have problems. This is particularly true when dealing with the treating physician, for although the lawyer may be armed with the written consent of his client, if he demands to examine or copy the records he may cloud the rapport he wishes to maintain with the treating physician.(2) Most physicians feel compelled to assert the sanctity of the "privileged communication" to the extent of withholding the information from the direct scrutiny of the patient or his counsel. Both physicians and hospitals are sensitized to malpractice suits and do not voluntarily make their records available,(3) particularly if they believe that legal action against them is contemplated.(4) This formidable obstacle can be circumvented by making an appointment with the treating physician in order to examine the records together; however, to peruse a medical record with a physician is time consuming, expensive, and significant aspects of the medical record may be overlooked. If at all possible, a thorough and unhurried examination of all medical records as a preliminary is strongly recommended. The lawyer already familiar with the record or chart can then ask the physician specific and detailed questions regarding particular findings and notations.

The consensus of opinion is that the physician(5) or the hospital(6) owns the physical records themselves; that is, the paper, the ink, and x-ray negatives; but the information contained in the records is the property of the patient to the extent that the physician-patient privileges and confidential relationships extend. The patient then has a proprietary interest and control over the information.(7) This presumably should allow the patient, or his representative, to inspect and obtain a copy of the record.(8) The record holder has a right to charge the patient for a copy of the record.(9) Of course, in the event that a patient dies, the next of kin has a right to information from the record.(10) The fact remains that physicians are reluctant to allow a patient to obtain a copy of his records to examine them directly.(11) However, physicians are conditioned to allow insurance companies, upon proper patient authorization, to inspect or copy medical and hospital records, and it stands to reason that the patient should have the right to get this information himself or to provide this for his attorney during the prelitigation period.(12) The standards established by the Veterans Administration may differ somewhat from those encountered in civilian hospitals.(13) Veterans are limited to information concerning themselves,(14) and a request for a copy of a record from a Veterans Administration Hospital must indicate the purpose for which it is desired,(15) and it may not be released unless it can be shown to serve a useful purpose.(16)

LAWYERS' GUIDE TO MEDICAL LITERATURE

The lawyer able to find current authoritative medical information can effectively evaluate many medico-legal problems which otherwise might be baffling. This may save his time and avoid the expense of consultation with a physician for the purpose of gaining insight into the medical issues. At the very least he will have valuable background information when he has a conference with a physician. Certainly the medical knowledge gained by fruitful reading of pertinent medical literature will be valuable for the examination or cross-examination of the witnesses and in the intelligent framing of hypothetical questions.

The lawyer unfamiliar with a particular medical subject may find textbooks useful as a starting point. There are two publications prepared specifically for the legal profession seeking medical information. These are *The Lawyers' Medical Cyclopedia*,(17) a collection of monographs on nearly all phases of the medico legal field of significance to lawyers engaged in personal injury cases; and *Traumatic Medicine and Surgery for Attorneys*,(18) a multi-volume set with chapters written by leading medical authorities. Medical textbooks are unequaled for lucid explanations of well recognized conditions, syndromes, or diseases. These volumes and textbooks treat a subject in a somewhat superficial manner and may be dated for in rapidly changing areas of medicine, books are considered obsolete by the time they go through the publication process from manuscript to printer. Texts merely provide a background for further investigation of a particular medical topic. The most current developments in medicine, as in other sciences, are to be found in the journals.

Wishing further information on a medical topic, or knowing a set of facts with medical implications, the lawyer proceeds to find in depth and current medical literature by first determining the correct "subject heading." Two sources for subject headings are the "Key Word Index" published by *Excerpta Medica*,(19) and *Current Medical References*.(20) The latter has a detailed subject index and in addition to aiding and locating the correct subject heading will have references which often lead directly to the subject being researched.

Knowing the correct subject heading, the lawyer with a need for a broad and current survey of a limited medical area will find the general surveys of specific medical subjects or review articles with the recent developments very useful. These usually provide a comprehensive discussion and in addition usually include historic details. *Current Medical References*,(21) published biannually, is probably the best for the lawyer in a hurry. This is a selected list of easily available current medical journal articles and books in the English language. *Index Medicus*,(22) published monthly and found in every large medical library, contains a section of review articles with both the author and the subject section.

References to the most recent medical advances and to current research publications are located in the medical library only under the article title, the author, and the journal in which they appear. The title of the publication may give a clue to its usefulness; however, reading and evaluating each published paper on a specific topic is time consuming. *Index Medicus*(23) provides the most complete listing, for it references 2,400 of the most used and best known medical journals published throughout the world. In the exceptional case, a publication in an obscure journal or a foreign language may be useful in litigation.(24) For those desiring rapid access to the titles, authors, and the journals of a majority of published articles in the English language, the National Library of Medicine has published *Abridged Index Medicus*.(25) This monthly issue first appeared in January of 1970, and will be found in practically all hospital libraries.

The lawyer may wish information about a physician—information that can be extremely useful from a tactical standpoint. An adverse medical witness may have written an article, or even a book, which states his views or makes generalizations in terms lending themselves to distinction from the facts at issue. Cross-examination of this witness on relevant material he has published may influence his credibility, and rare is the medical writer who remembers every detail or can defend every statement that he has authored. A physician's publications may be obtained from the author index of the *Cumulative Medical Index*.(26) Information regarding a physician's specialization, age, hospital appointments, background, and education can be rapidly checked in the *Directory of Medical Specialists*,(27) and the American Medical Association also publishes a *Registry of Physicians*(28) which provides a great deal of biographical information.

PRETRIAL PROBLEMS WITH MEDICAL EXPERTS

The legal profession is dependent upon the medical profession for its cooperation in assessing the extent of an injury, rendering an opinion as to the prognosis, explaining and clarifying the plaintiff's medical condition, examining the records of another physician, re-examining the injured plaintiff, or appearing in court as an expert. The lawyer seeking medical consultation from a non-treating physician will, of course, encounter few problems, for the natural selection process eliminates those physicians who are not cooperative. The problem arises when a lawyer seeks to confer with the physician who has cared for the plaintiff regarding available records, amplification of the records, additional information to which the physician is privy, and for the purpose of appearing in court. There is a distinction between the treating physician and the medical expert; however, most lawyers are reluctant to emphasize this distinction to the treating physician. Legal mechanisms to coerce the treating physician into providing additional information are available; nevertheless, the lawyer is hesitant to use these, for the physician confronted with a subpoena is almost invariably antagonistic and uncooperative; and thus creates a climate that is not to the client's advantage. The lawyer sympathetic to the anomalous position of a treating physician may be able to avoid many of the tensions and hostilities; and if the lawyer makes known his own difficulties as well as his objectives in conferring with the physician, he is in a better position to anticipate cooperation.

Most physicians believe that the practice of medicine is limited to the prevention of disease, to the diagnosis and treatment of illness and injury, and that their responsibility does not include the assessment of injury for use by the lawyer. The goal of a treating physician is to return the patient to a condition closely approximating the pre-injury state, and anything less than this suggests that the treatment was less than adequate. A suggestion by the lawyer at the outset that a failure by the physician to cooperate creates a suspicion that he is concealing evidence will do little to insure mutual respect and comity. Physicians are acutely aware of the possibility of malpractice, and if the recovery of the patient is not complete there looms the thought that the treating physician may be joined with the tortfeasor as a joint defendant. There is some foundation to physicians' beliefs that they may be held solely responsible if recovery is not satisfactory.(29) Indeed, if the lawyer finds out that there is a basis for a malpractice suit against the physician his obligations to his client are not entirely clear. Fortunately this is not the thrust of the present article. The lawyer representing an allegedly injured client can reasonably be expected to seek a pessimistic report regarding the extent of injury and the prognosis. This places the physician in a position which might be considered self-derogatory; and statements made, supposedly for the benefit of the injured client of the attorney, place in controversy the physician's diagnosis, treatment, and ultimately his professional competence. The brusque attitude of the physician indicates discomfort when considering the possible exposure to a potentially embarrassing situation, rather than a lack of concern for the patient. Also, not infrequently the physician's bill is unpaid, and when it is explained to him that the financially embarrassed patient cannot pay until there is an award for damages, he may feel that he is being indirectly solicited in terms of a contingency fee. When an opposing attorney also seeks a conference with a treating physician to cover the same records and information, the physician feels imposed on and forced into the posture of taking sides. If later the treating physician realizes that the attorney has employed another physician for the purpose of evaluating the case or for another physical examination, it smacks of lack of trust and appears to be an evaluation of his professional competence and veracity. Although this is rarely the intent of the attorney, it may enhance any existing paranoia.

The pronouncements of august medical and legal organizations do little in the individual situation to promote interprofessional cooperation. Part of the difficulties lawyers encounter with treating physicians might be avoided if 1. the treating physician fully understood the difficulties and expenses the attorney encounters in his investigation and preparation of a case, 2. the treating physician were aware of what is expected of him at the very outset, and 3. the treating physician understood that he is to be reimbursed for time devoted to the case. The treating physician should realize that prior to a conference the lawyer will usually have undertaken an extensive and not infrequently expensive investigation. This will include the procurement of multiple records which may include police reports, accident reports filed by the client and the opposing party, the reports of claims adjusters, and the names of witnesses who frequently are either uncooperative or who have moved. All of this is a necessary preliminary for the attorney to determine if he has a worthy case; and if he does not he will receive no compensation for either his effort or for the expenses that he has incurred.

The lawyer seeking consultation with a physician for discussion of the records or as an expert witness should make the terms of the contract clear to the physician. If the physician is not accustomed to meeting with lawyers he will be reluctant to raise the issue of a fee; and, in turn, it is not unheard of for an attorney to consider it the physician's duty, as part of the patient's care, to provide records and medical evaluation for contemplated litigation, as well as expert testimony. A conference with a lawyer is a time consuming task, and unfortunately, may have the attributes of an educational lecture rather than a service for the benefit of the patient. The physician almost invariably believes that a conference or appearance in court should be chargeable to the attorney, regardless of the ability of the patient to pay for the services he receives directly from the physician.(30) Physicians are not accustomed to time-sheets, and it is unethical for a physician to seek payment for his services based contingently upon the success of the diagnosis or treatment. Payment is based upon the treatment rendered and the patient's ability to pay. For instance, a physician may charge a set amount for an operation, but will make no additional charges for individual hospital or office visits. A recent publication by a physician suggests that compensation be predicated on the time involved either in conference with the attorney or for time out of the office.(31) Courts have also found that a treating physician is entitled to an expert witness fee.(32) If paid on the basis of time the physician will, in most instances, be well organized, concise, and present a clear record. He will know, as will the attorney, that if the conference wanders into the area of speculation the charges will continue. Hourly charges may be assessed according to the earning capacity of the doctor during the same period if he were working in his office. This may be as little as $150.00 for one-half day, or in excess of $500.00 for a full day, depending on the individual doctor's professional circumstances. For the examination of medical records, for the preparation of a report with an opinion, or for a conference, the usual fee varies from $25.00 to $75.00.

THE PRETRIAL MEDICAL REPORT

The report a physician prepares for the attorney is similar in form to a routine medical investigation with records. There are certain noteworthy differences which, if pointed out to the physician, will make the preparation of the attorney's report easier and will enhance its value. The physician's report for the attorney should contain, as a minimum, the following: 1. The circumstances of the physician's first contact with the client. If the physician is an independent consultant who is evaluating the patient the report should make this clear at the very beginning. The report of the treating physician will note the circumstances which are related to the present complaint or injury, and will also have a summary of prior complaints for which the physician has examined the patient. 2. The patient's history which includes his version of the injury or disease with the circumstances leading up to the condition. A physician must have this information in order to make specific examinations and to request diagnostic and confirmatory tests and x-rays. A "check-list" systematically covering the organ systems is valuable and insures that nothing has been overlooked in questioning the patient regarding his medical history. This should include inquiries into the past history of the patient and a history of family diseases. 3. The extent of the physical examination and a report which includes both positive findings indicating pathology, and negative findings. 4. The diagnostic tests and x-rays ordered. The results of these should be included in the report and the significance of deviations from normal explained. The circumstances of the tests and examinations are a part of the record, and these should provide information indicating whether the tests or x-rays were taken by the examining physician or under his immediate supervision, or at his request by another physician such as a radiologist who reads and interprets the films. X-rays, electrocardiograms, and electro encephalograms are frequently interpreted by a physician other than the one ordering the tests. The examining physician should note this, and also indicate if he concurs in the interpretation. 5. The diagnosis (the result of this history, the physical examination, and the tests) forms an important part of the pretrial medical report. This may be reported as an opinion, as an impression, or as a diagnosis. It may be wise to include a differential diagnosis as a part of the report. This is a listing of other conditions which may present in a similar fashion or manifest similar test results. If there is a possibility of another diagnosis or of a different interpretation of the results, the report should discuss the examining physician's reasoning as to why he reached a particular conclusion. It may be of critical importance to the attorney to know if the condition resulted from trauma or was aggravated by or was incidental to trauma; and the results of injury must be differentiated from pre-existing disorders of a congenital, infectious, or degenerative type. 6. The prognosis, a prediction as to the outcome of the injury or disease, with the expected residual disability should be formulated. Ideally this includes an opinion as to the relationship of any disability to the event leading to the litigation. This may include occupational, social, or physical disability.(33) The lines of demarcation between disability and functional impairment are extremely blurred at best. Reasonable minds may differ greatly when an attempt is made to relate either disability or impairment to a specific etiologic cause or an isolated event.

THE MEDICAL EXPERT—QUALIFICATIONS AND EXPERTISE

As litigation deals more and more with areas that are highly technical and sophisticated the need for the expert witness or specialist in a given field increases. "Expert" status gives the witness the privilege of assessing and interpreting data and giving opinions within his expertise, in matters which are generally regarded as beyond the complete understanding of the judge or jury. With increasing demand for expert medical testimony in personal injury, workmen's compensation, and criminal cases, confusion, friction, and dissatisfaction also increase. The requirement of expert testimony has not made the law's function of gathering, sorting, and weighing relevant data easier. Scientific witnesses themselves have contributed to misunderstandings by their contentions that they hold a vested interest in having the fruits of science utilized in the administration of justice. And courts have, on occasion, attempted to shift the burden of responsibility for administering justice to the scientific community—a particularly attractive route in the area of determining criminal responsibility where the psychiatrist can offer an easy avenue of judicial escape.(34) Attempts have also been made to solve complex medico legal problems by the appointment of panels of "impartial" medical experts controlled by elaborate criteria to guide and assist them in their decision-making.(35) Physicians in this expanded role may be seduced by such a heady situation into believing they can resolve judicial and legal issues, for no longer are they in the restricted role of providing information and opinions to aid the trier of fact in reaching a decision, rather they are reaching a decision based upon their own expertise. Few appellate courts are equipped to challenge the collective opinion of experts. Yet, as said by Associate Justice Harlan: "Our scheme of ordered liberty is based, like the common law, on enlightened and uniformly applied legal principles, not on ad hoc notions of what is right or wrong in a particular case."(36) The expert medical witness is qualified to express an opinion as to medical causation, the extent of the injury or disease, the possibility or probability of recovery, and the amount of impairment. The physician-expert is not qualified to consider the issue of responsibility, legal causation, or damages; nor can he assign significance to pieces of evidence challenging the various legal issues raised.(37) It is doubtful whether the field of medical science will ever progress to the point where a man's rights are solely dependent on the findings of a practitioner of medicine or upon current scientific tenets. This is because the history of mankind is replete with illustrations of an undeniable truth, scientifically proved and supported by the best minds of the era, which later becomes the scoffed at, discarded, and scientifically invalidated theory of later times.

The general rule is that every physician is presumed to possess expert knowledge about every aspect of medicine;(38) however, even this sacred presumption shows encouraging signs of death. The precedents eroding the "every physician an expert" doctrine are found in the unlikely area of medical malpractice litigation where the requirement of "a specialist in medicine is required to determine the standard of care of other specialists in medicine."(39) Indeed, common sense dictates that not every physician is qualified to express an expert opinion in a complex or technical area. In fact, there are some areas in medicine traditionally considered the domain of the physician where others who are highly trained, but lacking a medical degree, are allowed to give expert testimony contra to an expert opinion expressed by a physician.(40) The rule suggested by Professor Charles T. McCormick(41) to the effect that any relevant conclusions which are supported by a qualified expert witness should be received unless there are other reasons for exclusion should not be accepted without reservation. However, at the present time in most jurisdictions the possession of the status of physician is the sole prerequisite to giving expert medical testimony. The weight that a judge or jury can give this testimony is, theoretically, dependent upon qualifications such as specialty certification, age, publications, length of experience with the specific condition under controversy and consideration. Widespread restraint will no doubt in time be imposed upon giving expert testimony merely because of the possession of physician status. Until such time the lawyer is constrained to closely examine and cross examine the physician rendering an opinion on a specific issue, on three distinct questions: the validity of the opinion rendered, the possession of the qualifications he alleges to have to render an expert opinion, and his expertise in the field about which he testifies. The expert is also subject to questions on the accuracy of his observations, his credibility, any possible interest or bias he has in the outcome of the trial, and his relationships to the parties at issue.

Stereotypes of the physician's attitude toward trials,(42) and of the type of medical witness sought by lawyers(43) should be discarded in favor of the candid, if not honest, statement acknowledging that lawyers are not really seeking a disinterested physician-scientist, but particularly in the difficult case, need a physician-advocate.(44) A physician or any other scientist appearing as an expert witness is a combination of physician-scientist and physician-advocate, but in varying degrees. A particularly flagrant case of a physician-advocate is noted in the case of *Lardner v. Higgins, Inc.*(45) where the physician for the defendant responded to the question: "Is that your conclusion, that this man is a malingerer?", the defendant's doctor replied, "I wouldn't be testifying if I didn't think so, unless I was on the other side, then it would be a post-traumatic condition."(46) It is a palpable truth that no physician is entirely free of bias or is totally objective, although the situation is not as bad as some had suggested.(47) It is not a matter of the physician's integrity, for the personal physician caring for an injured victim is inclined to give his patient the benefit of every medico-legal doubt. On the other hand, a physician employed by the defendant in cases other than medical malpractice, will be loyal to the one employing his services. It is impossible to be totally independent and uninvolved in the outcome of a case either as a panelist or as an expert witness. However, the physician must avoid any conscious partisanship, for this weakens his presentation. Attorneys are well aware of this and continually caution the physician to maintain the cool of impartiality. Too often it is not realized that reasonable minds can differ over the validity of what, to the lawyer, is ultimate truth, but is in fact an individual opinion. There is no great distinction in kind between medical fact and opinion; the distinction is one of degree. It must be remembered that in the practice of medicine, which is not an exact science, the pursuit of the diagnosis is subject to many imponderables and diagnostic error does occur.(48) Without shifting responsibility from the court to the physician or holding the physician responsible for more than he is professionally capable, the lawyer through examination and cross-examination should be able to provide and present the facts within the scope of the expert in a convincing and lucid manner. The expert should be limited to opinions or inferences which the court finds based on facts or data perceived by, personally known, or made known to the witness within the scope of his special training, skill, and experience to interpret, and which will aid the jury. The making of emphatic or dogmatic statements is alien to the conscientious medical witness and generally, when made by a witness, are due to the fact that the particular witness is expert in nothing so much as in creating the illusion that he is. This type of witness may appear most convincing on superficial examination, but when challenged becomes defensive, overemphatic, argumentative, and will not concede the slightest point. After first examining such a witness about data upon which he bases his opinion or inferences, it will become obvious that he is biased, and the lawyer can usually demonstrate the inadequacy of the witness's examination by collateral attack.(49)

POSSIBILITIES, PROBABILITIES, STATISTICS, AND CERTAINTY

"Certainty generally is illusion," a statement made by Justice Holmes addressed to the legal profession,(50) is generally accepted in medical practice. Therefore, rendering an expert opinion which requires a *degree* of certainty presents a most vexing situation for a physician.(51) It is the function of the expert witness to express an opinion and to indicate the basis on which this opinion is predicated. Medicine is practiced in this manner; however, physicians are unaccustomed to thinking in terms of certainty. The diagnosis of disease is based upon observation, examination, and tests that are performed; and conclusions are based on this data. Expert opinions are derived from the medical conclusions in terms of the physician's own experience, from literature sources, and from information obtained from associates. The interpretation and evaluation of the data are mostly subjective; rare indeed is a medical opinion based on statistical or probability studies, or studies which may approach any degree of mathematical certainty. Reasonable medical certainty or reasonable medical probability(52) mean to the physician that the conclusions which can be drawn from the data would have a high degree of acceptance by other qualified physicians; however, most physicians are unable to quantitate or assign a "degree" to their concept of probability or certainty. The courts have not enjoyed significantly greater success in quantitating certainty. This is witnessed to by the general rule that in a civil trial it is adequate if the plaintiff should make it appear by a fair preponderance of all the evidence that his affirmative proposition of fact is more probably true than not; or stated in another way, if the evidence considered fairly and impartially induces in the trier of fact a reasonable belief.(53) To say that it is more likely than not that the specific act materially contributed to the result obtained is sufficient in a civil suit, even though it does not constitute such a degree of certainty as to preclude reasonable doubt.(54) However, to simply say that an injury "could have" occurred as the result of a specific act does not overcome the presumption that it did not.(55) A mere act, plus the possibility of a particular result, as a matter of law,(56) cannot support a medical determination of the rendering of an opinion as to the probability or certainty of a particular result.(57)

Mathematical probability is the basis of much of the evidence presented in the courtroom although it may not be recognized as such by lawyers and jurors. A number of individual circumstances or observations, although singly of low evidentiary value, might jointly lead statistically to but one conclusion.(58) The significance and importance of statistics and mathematical probability as they relate to problems of medicine are generally recognized, and whenever a physician renders an expert opinion on "probabilities" he is in essence making a statistical evaluation. Unfortunately, there is a serious lack of fundamental data allowing broader application of statistical methods to the formation of a basis upon which to predicate an expert opinion; therefore, when an expert gets into the realm of mathematical probability to establish the existence or nonexistence of a fact, he is departing from the usual standard of "reasonable scientific probability" and is approaching the yardstick of absolute certainty. He is then undertaking an obligation which he need not assume in order to insure the acceptance of his testimony without qualification or reservation. When a witness is certain that he is correct, and where this degree of certainty exists in fact, there is no need for statistical methods. If two opposing and presumably equivalent experts testify, and based upon the same fact information, and using the same kind of subjective evaluations, they disagree, then either one or the other, or both, are wrong to some extent. The obvious remedy is for each to abandon the idea of absolute certainty, so that a fully objective approach to the problem can be made. Subjective opinions, however well based in personal experience, are still subject to several factors, such as inadequate or atypical experience, lack of understanding of fundamentals, or even mental bias of which the possessor may be totally unaware. There is no higher court to which an appeal can be made for objective evaluation of the relative "correctness" of two disagreeing expert opinions—it is solely within the province of the jury to determine which is more nearly correct.

Statistics and the laws of probability may in the future offer a source for objective evaluation of conflicting opinions—at least to the extent of suggesting which opinion is "probably" more correct. Although it is conceivable that statistical information could provide a forum for the resolution of conflicting opinions, the actual use of probability figures in testimony should be approached with caution. Mathematical concepts are generally difficult to grasp even for many of the more intelligent laymen and are often regarded with suspicion. The reason for mistrusting statistical methods stems from misunderstandings as to what statistics are, what their proper function is, and how they may be used to indicate the truth. Statistics can also be made to distort the truth, a fact that has been discussed in various publications, such as one entitled, "How to Lie with Statistics," an amusing but relevant source of healthy skepticism. If only a statistical approach to medico legal problems and conflicts of opinion were employed a great deal of relevant, material, and presently admissible evidence would not meet the test of mathematical certainty. The confusion created by the concepts of statistics is such that if, on cross-examination, an expert would admit that some of the evidence he presented did not meet the test of mathematical certainty, the jury would become confused and might even disregard such evidence. Should an expert in expressing an opinion use mathematical probability in any part of his testimony, he must carefully and lucidly explain why this is significant, and should also explain to the trier of fact that some physical evidence does not fit into such concepts.

The real and practical problem of applying statistical probabilities to medico legal problems and conflicting expert opinions is that there is really very little reference data available for statistical analysis. Most evaluations of statistical significance must rest on the study of a population, which ideally would be the total population involved. This is manifestly impossible in nearly every instance, so that data must be obtained from a much smaller sample. The samples selected for study from a population must be chosen so that they are random with respect to the properties of interest. It is essential to define exactly what is going to be demanded of the analysis, after which method of analysis must be chosen with respect to the type of data which it is possible to gather. The usual calculations of means, variance, independence of variables, and dependence of variables must be considered. A statistician is essential in any study to determine the degree of mathematical certainty, else confusion and error may creep into the study, and conclusions will be misleading. This is particularly true when variables are examined, for not infrequently dependent variables are treated as independent variables—that is, an independent variable being statistically very significant, refers to variables that may be multiplied together to get the combined probability. Again, it is strongly recommended that a statistician be available to evaluate all statistical data, and be consulted before mathematical probabilities are used to buttress expert opinion.

SUBSTITUTES FOR EXPERT MEDICAL TESTIMONY

It is the general rule of law that scientific books and publications, other than those on a topic of exact science, are not admissible in evidence as proof of facts stated therein. The recognized reasons for excluding medical books and treatises as evidence is the lack of opportunity for adequate cross-examination of the author, and the unavailability of any tests by which the accuracy of the statements made in such publications may be gauged. Law recognizes that medicine is a changing art and science with constant improvements in theory and practice. This alone is a valid reason for excluding medical publications. In addition these lack the sanction of the oath. Three jurisdictions make exception to this rule and admit textbooks in lieu of expert testimony if there is a controversy as to proper treatment or management. Alabama, on the basis of case law, recognizes and approves the use of medical books in evidence as proof of the statements therein contained when such facts are relevant to the case on trial.(59) Nevada(60) and Massachusetts(61) have enacted statutes allowing the introduction of medical textbooks as authority if there is an allegation of negligence in a malpractice suit against a physician. This latter statute has been of little value for in the first case tested the judge refused to allow the textbook as evidence unless expert testimony was called to qualify the author of the textbook material.(62) Drug brochures or determinations by the Federal Food and Drug Administration are not admissible at a trial involving medical issues related to them.(63)

It is permissible for physicians giving expert testimony to refer to and to confirm their testimony by scientific publications. However, reading from them by the expert is not well received.(64) Referring to these is not an introduction of them as evidence but is merely corroboration of the expert's own opinion. Most courts decline to allow the reading from scientific works on the cross-examination if the purpose is merely to contradict, test, or discredit the knowledge of the expert witness.(65) If the expert has referred to the scientific publications and has used them as one of the bases for his testimony, it may be so used. But, such use cannot be made of authorities to which he has not referred.(66)

NOTES

(1) L. Loevinger, *Facts, Evidence and Legal Proof*, 9 W. Res. L. Rev. 154, 155 (1958).

(2) D. G. Hagman, *The Non-Litigant Patient's Right to Medical Records: Medicine vs. Law*, 14 J. For. Sci. 352 (1969). The question of making medical records available to the patient was submitted to 100 California and to 100 Minnesota physicians. In response to the question of a patient wishing a copy of his medical record for no particular reason, well over one-half of the physicians answering believed that they would be medically, ethically and legally justified in withholding a copy of the record, although the patient may offer to pay for photocopies.

(3) *Id*. Two-thirds of the 200 physicians responding to the questionnaire did not believe there was a medical obligation to allow a patient to examine his records to determine the identity of a physician who was negligent in treating him.

(4) Mishalow v. Horwald, 231 Cal. App. 2d 517, 41 Cal. Rptr. 895 (1964).

(5) Reeves v. Pennsylvania R.R., 80 F. Suppl. 107 (Del. 1948); McGarry v. J. A. Mercier Co., 272 Mich. 501, 262 N.W. 296 (1935), *noted in* 49 Harv. L. Rev. 489 (1936).

(6) Pyramid Life Ins. Co. v. Masonic Hosp. Ass'n of Payne County, 191 F. Supp. 51 (1961); Wallace v. Univ. Hosp. of Cleveland, 82 Ohio L. Abst. 257, 164 N.E.2d 917 (1959).

(7) Bishop Clarkson Memorial Hosp. v. Reserve-Life Ins. Co., 350 F.2d 1006 (8th Cir. 1965); Abelson's Inc. v. New Jersey State Board of Optometrists, 65 A.2d 41 (N.J. Super. 1949); Pyramid Life Ins. Co. v. Masonic Hosp. Ass'n of Payne County, 191 F. Supp. 51 (W.D. Okla. 1961); McGarry v. J. A. Mercier Co., 272 Mich. 501, 262 N.W. 296 (1935) *noted in* 49 Harv. L. Rev. 489 (1936).

(8) Wallace v. Univ. of Cleveland, 82 Ohio L. Abst. 257, 164 N.F.2d 917 (1959).

(9) *Id.*, *see also* McGarry v. J. A. Mercier Co., 272 Mich. 501, 262 N.W. 296 (1935).

(10) Emmett v. Eastern Dispensary and Cas. Hosp., 396 F.2d 931 (D.C.C. 1967).

(11) The Judicial Council of the American Medical Association is of the opinion that a physician is not required to give a copy of his records to the patient. A.M.A. Judicial Council Opinions and Reports 57-58 (1966). The reason for a physician withholding the medical records from the patient are catalogued in Hayt and Hayt, Legal Aspects of Medical Records (1964), *cited in* Hagman, *The Non-Litigant Patient's Right to Medical Records*, 14 J. For. Sci. 352 (1969). Among the more interesting reasons for withholding the record from the patient is, "furnishing the record could never do any good and might cause harm or upset the patient. For example, an entry of 'patient s.o.b.' might be construed by the patient to mean something else than that he had shortness of breath."

(12) Pyramid Life Ins. Co. v. Masonic Hosp. Ass'n of Payne County, 191 F. Supp. 51 (1961).

(13) 38 C.F.R. § 1.526 (1970); 38 C.F.R. § 17.30(o) (1970).

(14) 38 C.F.R. § 1.525(a)(3) (1970).

(15) 38 C.F.R. § 1.526(a) (1970).

(16) 38 C.F.R. § 1.501(a) (1970).

(17) Lawyers' Medical Cyclopedia, Indianapolis: The Allen Smith Co.: (seven volumes with index and supplementary service).

(18) Traumatic Medicine and Surgery for Attorneys, Washington: Butterworth Pub. Co.; and Brooklyn: Central Book Co.

(19) Excerpta Medica, New York: Excerpta Medica Foundation (1947 to date).

(20) Current Medical References (M. Chatton) Los Altos, Calif.: Lance Medical Publications.

(22) Index Medicus, Bethesda, Md.: National Library of Medicine (1960 to date) (hereinafter cited as Index Medicus).

(23) *Id.*

(24) The court in Sylvania Elec. Products, Inc. v. Barker, 228 F.2d 842 (C.C. 1, 1955) *Cert. denied* 350 U.S. 988, 1956, held that a manufacturer is presumed to have the knowledge if it appears in the scientific literature, for to be exonerated the manufacturer must be "faultlessly ignorant" and scientific literature is admissible as evidence bearing on the extent of the manufacturer's investigation.

(25) Abridged Index Medicus, Bethesda, Md.: National Library of Medicine (1970 to date).

(27) Index Medicus, *supra* note 22.

(27) Directory of Medical Specialists, Chicago: Marquis—Who's Who, Inc. (1970).

(28) Registry of Physicians, Chicago: American Medical Association (25th ed., 1969).

(29) The court in Piedmont Hosp. V. Truitt, 172 S.E. 237 (Ga., 1934) ruled that if the patient in releasing the original tortfeasor expressly reserved in the release his claim against the physician for malpractice, this was a valid reservation. The more liberal interpretation preserving the plaintiff's cause of action against a treating physician is the holding that the release of the original wrongdoer does not, of itself, release the physician and he remains liable for malpractice litigation for injuries arising out of his alleged negligence. Galloway v. Lawrence, 139 S.E.2d 761 (N.C., 1965). *See also* Miller, F.R.: *The Original Tortfeasor Release: A Subsequent Negligent Attending Physician*, 36 Ins. Counsel J. 360 (1969).

(30) Bergen. *Payment of Fees for Services of Medical Witnesses*, 201 J.A.M.A. 309 (1967): Some attorneys who have been unwilling to agree to advance payment of fees for medical witnesses have claimed that it would be unethical to do so. This appears to be a misunderstanding. Canon 42 of the canons of legal ethics of the American Bar Association provides as follows:

> A lawyer may not properly agree with a client that the lawyer shall pay or bear the expenses of litigation; he may in good faith advance expenses as a matter of convenience, but subject to reimbursement.

In an opinion under that Canon, the Standing Committee on Professional Ethics of the American Bar association has indicated approval of a provision in an agreement between a local bar association and a local medical society, as follows:

> It is recognized that when an attorney requests a doctor to examine or to report on the condition of any person, or when an attorney requests a doctor to confer with him, to give his disposition, or to testify in court, the attorney

may in good faith advance the doctor's fees therefor as a matter of convenience, as a part of the expenses of litigation, but subject to a clear understanding that he is to be reimbursed by his client. It is recognized that an attorney may not properly advance or become obligated for items other than expenses of litigation, and that these must be subject at all times to reimbursement from his client. *Id.* at 310.

(31) McNeil, *Compensation for the Medical Witness.* Am. Trial Tech. Q. 93 (1969).

(32) The court in Trosclair v. Higgins, 216 So. 2d 558 (La. C.A. 1968), held that an award by the court of $125.00 to the treating physician for an expert fee was not considered excessive for the physician's testimony was essential for the trial court's determination of the extent of the plaintiff's injuries. A report by another expert that was introduced into evidence did not entitle the physician making the report to be an expert's fee.

(33) Koskoff, *The Neurotic Plaintiff and His Lawyer,* 32 Conn. L. Rev. 223 (1958).

(34) Suaez, *Critique of the Psychiatrist's Role as Expert Witness,* 12 J. For. Sci. 172 (1967).

(35) An example of an appointed panel of specialists to evaluate a particular disorder is that of the "Utah" plan where specialists in internal medicine are available for the evaluation of cardiac disorders. There are strict guide lines for the panelists to follow, the principles can be summarized: 1. the relationship of industrial effort to a heart attack can only be determined by recourse to expert medical opinion. 2. medical opinion must use the most advanced knowledge in the field of cardiology. 3. the medical opinion must be expert. 4. the medical opinion must be unbiased. 5. the medical opinion should be obtained before controversy develops. 6. medical opinion is given to all parties affected by it. 7. medical opinion does not deny due process of law. Q.A. Wiesley, *The Utah Medical Panel System,* in F. Rosenbaum, & E. Beldkna. Work and the Heart: Translation of the First Wisconsin Conference on Work and the Heart (New York: Paul B. Hoeber, Inc., 1959).

(36) *Thoughts at a Dedication: Keeping the Judicial Function in Balance,* 49 A.B.A.J. 943, 944 (1963).

(37) The Wisconsin Supreme Court in Jacobson v. Bryan, 244 Wis. 359, 12 N.W.2d 789 (1944) noted that physicians as expert witnesses are in the position of drawing conclusions as to the extent of the injury and the prognosis, but, if an analogy can be drawn to police officers, they should not be permitted to tell juries as to how an accident happened or who is to blame.

(38) Medical licensure is not a requirement, however, the vulnerability of an unlicensed medical expert to impeachment is amply demonstrated by the cross-examination of Frederick Gibbs, M.D. by Assistant District Attorney Bill Alexander in the trial of Jack Ruby for the alleged murder of Lee Harvey Oswald, as reported in 6 Trauma at 265 (1964).

(39) Because of the complexity of neurosurgical techniques the requirement of expert witnesses to show failure to use care has invariably required the testimony of other neurosurgeons. Gould v. Winokur, 98 N.J. Super, 554, 237 A.2d 916 (1968); Hale v. Heninger, 393 P.2d 718 (Idaho 1964); Hart v. VanZandt, 399 S.W. 2d 791 (Tex. 1965); Gray v. Grunagle, 223 A.2d 663 (Pa. 1966); Clark v. Stowell, 315 P.2d 269 (Okla. 1957); Belshaw v. Feinstein, 65 Cal. Rptr. 788 (1968); Hayward v. Echols, 362 F.2d 791 (5th Cir. 1966).

(40) The Supreme Court of Nevada allowed a toxicologist who was not a physician to testify as to "cause of death," an area traditionally reserved to the realm of a licensed physician. In Miner v. Lamb,–Nev.–464 P.2d 451 (1970) a pathologist as a witness for the State testified that in his opinion death was due

to head injury the result of multiple blunt blows to the head and face with such a heavy object as a fist. A toxicologist testified that the girl died of the synergistic effects of alcohol and barbiturates. The court held that this was equally plausible, and the determination of the weight to be given a conflicting expert was a question for the jury to determine at the time of the trial.

(41) C. McCormick, Handbook of the Law of Evidence, 363 (1954).

(42) Gilbar,*What is an Expert Witness?* 14 The Criminologist 71 (1969).

The average medical practitioner heartily dislikes being called as a witness at all. It wastes his time: and when, after infuriating delays, he does at least reach the stand he sees himself being entrapped into unwary generalizations and made a fool of by cunning cross-examination.

(43) *Id.*, "skillful, impartial with willingness to give evidence in the pursuit of justice. . . ."

(44) Personal hostilities and vendettas have plagued forensic scientists both in the United States and in England. One cannot but wonder if these reputable men have not on occasion been the willing tools of lawyers.

(45) 71 So. 2d 242 (La. 1954).

(46) *Id.* at 244.

(47) Kozol, *The Integrity of the Expert Medical Witness*, 100 Am. J. Psych. 423 (1949). This was a study involving the lawyers in 50 cases where medical experts were used. The plaintiff lawyers estimated that 50% of the defendant's medical experts were unscrupulous and dishonest. The defendant lawyers estimated that 75% of the plaintiff's medical experts were "unfair" in their testimony. Attorneys for each side claimed that 84% of their own medical experts were fair and scrupulous in their testimony.

(48) Gruver & Freis, *Diagnostic Errors: A Study of Clinical and Autopsy Findings*, in W. Curran, Law and Medicine 175 (1960); Lasky, *Significant Diagnostic Errors in Workmen's Compensation Medicine*, 12 J. For. Sci. 387 (1967).

(49) *Demonstrating Bias in a Medical Witness*, 17 Current Med. for Attys, 35 (1970).

(50) Justice Holmes, *The Path of the Law*, 10 Har. Law Rev. 457 (1897).

(51) Conrad, *The Expert and Legal Certainty*, 9 J. For. Sci. 445 (1964). "The procedure of crucifixion reaches its zenith at the time the expert is asked that awful and awesome question, 'Do you have an opinion to a reasonable certainty?' "

(52) The court in Hallum v. Omro, 122 Wis. 337, 99 N.W. 1051 (1904), said that reasonable probability does not differ materially from reasonable certainty. *Id.* at–,99 N.W. at 1051-52.

(53) Shindell, *Medical Evidence in Court*, 194 J.A.M.A. 530 (1965). Reasonable probability is that standards of persuasion that is in quality sufficient to generate the belief that the tendered hypothesis is, in all human likelihood, the fact. Miller & Dobrin Furniture Co. v. Camden Fire Ins. Co. Ass'n, 55 N.J. Super. 205, 150 A.2d 276 (1959).

(54) The court in Housman v. Geiman, 62 S.D. 310, 252 N.W. 857 (1934), expressed itself on the subject of "degree of certainty," in noting that "[a]bsolute certainty is not required of an expert." . . . Obviously, all experts are hesitant to testify to absolute certainty. However, the expert knows that he is required to give testimony which is "something more than conjecture or guess." *Id.* at 314, 252 N.W. at 859.

(55) The court found in Hernke v. Northern Ins. Co., of New York, 20 Wis. 2d 353, 122 N.W.2d 395 (1963): "Although possibilities are not introducible on direct examination, it does not follow that 'mere possibilities' will not be allowed on cross-examination. The opponent to the expert may resist the expert

and is not required to confine himself to 'reasonable medical certainty.' " *Id.* at—, 122 N.W.2d 399.

(56) Housman v. Geiman, 62 S.D. 310, 252 N.W. 857 (1934).

(57) 32 C.J.S. *Evidence*, § 522 (1964): "We find no problem in determining the limits within which an expert may testify. At one end, we say that mere guess or conjecture cannot constitute a proper basis for expert opinion evidence" *Id.*

(58) This has its mathematical basis the law of compound probability for the occurrence of *independent* events. *See* Mode, *Probability and Criminalistics*, 5 Am. Statistical Ass'n. J. 628 (1963).

(59) Watkins v. Potts, 219 Ala. 427, 122 So. 416 (1929); Barfield v. South Highland Infirmary, 191 Ala. 553, 68 So. 30 (1915). The Oregon Supreme Court in Jucke v. State Comp. Dept., 154 Ore. 47, 461 P.2d 269 (1969), held that medical memorandum quoting medical texts, but not based upon an examinination of the claimant was admissible in a workmen's compensation proceedings.

(60) Nev. Rev. Stat. § 51:040 (1963).

(61) Mass. Gen. Laws Ann. ch. 233, § 79c (1956).

(62) Ramsland v. Shaw, 341 Mass. 56, 166 N.E.2d 894 (1960).

(63) Salgo v. Leland Stanford Jr. Univ. Board of Trustees, 154 Cal. App. 2d 560, 317 P.2d 170 (1957).

(64) "The practice of reading from medical treatises in connection with opinions given is condemned." Bixby v. Omaha and C.B.R. & Bridge Co., 105 Iowa 293 75 N.W. 182 (1898); Fisher v. Bernard, 21 Mich. App. 260, 175 N.W.2d 836 (1970).

(65) Swank v. Halivopoulos, 260 A.2d 240 (N.J., 1969); Wilcox v. Crumpton, 129 Iowa 389, 258 N.W. 704 (1935).

(66) Bixby v. Omaha and C.B.R. & Bridge Co., 105 293, 75 N.W. 182 (1898).

MALICIOUS PROSECUTION SUITS AS COUNTERBALANCE TO MEDICAL MALPRACTICE SUITS

Allen P. Adler

A few years ago medical malpractice suits were something of a rarity in the United States.(1) They now appear to be a major national problem.(2) The magnitude of this ever increasing problem can be illustrated by the fact that a Senate subcommittee, chaired by Sen. Abraham Ribicoff, has investigated the increase in malpractice litigation and that President Nixon has ordered the establishment of a Commission on Medical Malpractice, under the Department of Health, Education and Welfare, to research the problem and report a possible solution by March 1, 1972.(3)

There are no accurate figures available on the overall increase in medical malpractice litigation.(4) It is estimated that malpractice claims have increased at the rate of 10% per year for the last five years.(5) The Aetna Life and Casualty Company reports a 43% increase in claims filed against its policy holders between 1964 and 1969.(6) Crawford Morris, a Cleveland attorney, reports a 400% increase in the number of cases in which he has been called upon to defend doctors between 1955 and 1966.(7)

It is estimated that between 6,000 and 9,000 suits are brought against the 250,000 practicing physicians in the United States each year.(8) An investigation by the American Medical Association shows that one doctor in six now practicing in the United States has been sued for malpractice.(9) The A.M.A. also estimates that one doctor in four will be sued before the end of his career.(10)

Along with the increase in the number of malpractice actions, the size of the individual claim has increased. There has been a 200% increase in the claim cost in the last five years.(11) The Nettleship Company of Los Angeles, a medical malpractice insurance carrier, reports an increase in the average closing cost of claims from $2,478.00 in 1957 to $13,325.00 in 1970. These figures include investigation costs, adjustments, defense fees, and settlements.(12)

The above figures go a long way in explaining the rapidly increasing premiums of medical malpractice insurance. Rates increased 110% in California in 1969.(13) The rates in Utah, for the year 1969, were thirteen times what they had been in 1967.(14) Individual premiums as high as $10,000.00 per year have been reported.(15) These premium increases, like any other cost of doing business, are passed on to the general public.(16)

Along with the increase in cost, the increase of malpractice litigation is reflected in the way medicine is practiced. There is marked caution in diagnostic procedure and in the prescription of drugs. This offshoot of the malpractice dilemma does not appear to be all bad.(17)

There have been several suggested cures for the increase in malpractice litigation and the accompanying costs to the medical profession and society as a whole. These cures run from malpractice group insurance and government financed re-insurance pools for doctors who have lost their coverage, to the proposed establishment of local boards of lawyers and doctors to arbitrate malpractice claims.(18) These boards would function much like the one now in existence in Pima County, Arizona. It has also been suggested that patients buy a "no fault" type of insurance that would operate along the lines of workman's compensation or airline trip coverage.(19) The abolition of the private practice of medicine has also been suggested.(20)

It is clear that something must be done by the medical profession or by society as a whole to alleviate the strain of an overabundance of malpractice actions. To completely grasp the situation it is necessary to have some idea of how much of this litigation is well founded. Again, there are no accurate figures and those figures which are available are widely divergent. It is said that only one case out of ten ever reaches the jury.(21) It is also stated that lawyers reject the cases of nine out of ten prospective plaintiffs who seek their advice and that 30% of all malpractice cases have no merit.(22) The reported results of those cases that do come to trial are widely varied. By some estimates the results are half and half, plaintiffs winning 50% of the time.(23) Other sources state that doctors are vindicated in as many as 90% of the cases tried.(24) The most convincing statistics are the results of compulsory arbitration carried out in Pima County, Arizona. Of the sixty-five cases arbitrated there over a twelve year period fifty-seven had no merit.(25)

No matter what source is to be believed, it is obvious that at least some of the thousands of medical malpractice suits brought each year are brought without justifiable cause. This leads to the conclusion that a number of doctors are in fact innocent of the charges of malpractice which have been brought against them. Many doctors feel, and rightfully so, that they are entitled to protection from the harassment of invalid suits.(26)

Working from the premise that the best defense is often a good offense, certain positive steps can be taken to insure that physicians are not set upon by every ex-patient who is dissatisfied with their services.

Doctors, like ordinary people, are protected from defamation. This protection extends to the practice of their profession.(27) It is certain that a practicing member of the medical profession would have a clear cause of action in defamation against anyone who had compared him with a run-of-the-mill meat cutter.

A doctor's reputation clearly suffers when a malpractice action is brought against him. Malpractice is an ill-famed word, nearly synonymous with quack and charlatan.(28) The definition of the term "malpractice" varies from one jurisdiction to another. "In general it means the wreaking of bodily harm by virtue of neglect, abandonment, or the omission or commission of certain actions which fall below the standards of the average medical practitioner."(29) It takes little imagination to realize the harm a charge of medical malpractice might do a practicing physician.

It is conceded that a cause of action for defamation will not lie where the allegations are made in the course of a civil proceeding. The plaintiff in a malpractice suit enjoys immunity to publish false and defamatory material as long as he stays within the scope of the action.(30) However, this privilege does not extend to a suit that is maliciously prosecuted.(31)

The threat of a doctor counterattacking a malpractice suit with a suit for malicious prosecution may cause a disgruntled patient and his lawyer to think twice before bringing a frivolous or poorly founded action. An action for malicious prosecution can be used as an effective weapon to counter the threat of a malpractice suit, but it is necessary to have a general understanding of the elements of malicious prosecution and their adaptability to the facts surrounding a medical malpractice suit. The attorney representing the physician is in a position to watch his case develop as the events making up the facts occur.(32)

Malicious prosecution is an action not favored in the law.(32) The law of malicious prosecution represents an adjustment between the conflicting interests of the parties to a civil suit. The plaintiff is immune from any cause of action arising out of his good faith efforts to secure a legal or equitable determination of his rights. The defendant, at the same time, has a right to be free from unreasonable litigation.(34)

The plaintiff in a suit for malicious prosecution must prove that a suit was instituted against him without probable cause, that it has been terminated in his favor, that there was a malicious motive in instituting it, and that he has sustained damage as a result of the maliciously prosecuted suit.(35)

A majority of the jurisdictions in this country allow suits for malicious prosecution for the institution of a civil action where the other elements are present.(36)

The matter of probable cause will vary from case to case. It is usually a mixed question of law and fact. In a medical malpractice action there is a lack of probable cause when the patient does not honestly believe that the doctor is guilty of the malpractice charged, or where he does believe that the doctor's actions constituted malpractice, that belief is unreasonable.(37)

The second element that must be proved is the termination of the prior suit in the present plaintiff's favor. Generally, any manner of termination, which constitutes a final disposition is sufficient.(38)

The plaintiff must next prove the defendant's malicious intent in instituting the malpractice proceedings. The question of malice is almost exclusively a question of fact.(39) The jury may infer malice from the lack of probable cause.(40) It must be kept in mind that both malice and lack of probable cause are separate elements of the tort of malicious prosecution; they must both be present.(41) Generally, the malice necessary to support an action for malicious prosecution resulting from a civil action is malice in fact. Malice in fact suggests the presence of an evil, wrongful, or improper motive in bringing the action for malpractice.(42)

No damages will be presumed in an action founded upon a civil suit. The plaintiff must prove actual damages.(43) In many jurisdictions, including Ohio, the general rule is that the party maliciously sued must prove injury to or interference with his person or property. This requirement precludes damages for injury to the reputation alone.(44)

It would appear that in jurisdictions where this rule is in effect, a suit for malicious prosecution against a defendant who has brought an unfounded suit for medical malpractice would be barred. There would be no interference with or damage to the doctor's person or property. The only thing that would suffer harm would be the doctor's profession, and in some cases, his private reputation.

There is an exception to this rule where the original civil action is based on lunacy or bankruptcy. These allegations would amount to defamation outside the courtroom.

Almost all jurisdictions allow the plaintiff in a malicious prosecution action to recover for damage done his reputation once actual damages are proved.(45) It also appears that in jurisdictions that do not generally allow damages for injury to the reputation alone, actual damages have been allowed. This is the case in Ohio.(46) It was stated in *Board of Education v. Marting*,(47) "Actions for malicious prosecution are for injuries to an individual's character or reputation."

In a recent law review article the proposition was set forth that injury to the reputation should be a basis for recovery in an action for malicious prosecution.(48) The author of this article dealt with a suit for malicious prosecution brought as a result of damages done to the business reputation of an individual in a wrongfully instituted insolvency action under Oregon law. Oregon is a jurisdiction that allows recovery only where arrest of the person or seizure of property can be proved.(49)

A businessman's reputation and a physician's professional reputation can easily be correlated. Perhaps, the professional reputation of a practicing physician should be given more consideration than the business reputation of a merchant.

An examination of the article and the law used to formulate the author's opinions reveals that the damages allowed for injury to a person's reputation, arising from a maliciously prosecuted bankruptcy action, have their roots in the theory that one who initiates a malicious prosecution is liable for any harm done the defendant from such an action.(50)

One of the first cases to recognize the value of a man's reputation was *Quartz Hill Consolidated Mining Co. v. Eyre.*(51) This case stands for the concept that a businessman's credit is injured by a bankruptcy proceeding before he has a chance to show that the accusation is false.(52)

The author postulated that the defamation theory should be extended to any suit which is based on defamatory matter. He stated:

> If the subject matter of the suit is of itself defamatory, it is submitted that there is sufficient injury to support an action for malicious prosecution; and an allegation of damage to reputation should be adequate to survive a demurrer. The plaintiff must still prove damage to his reputation and must also prove all other elements necessary to his cause of action. For example, a number of cases hold that the institution of lunacy or insanity proceedings is actionable. An action for malicious prosecution likewise should be allowed where the charge is defamatory and where the other elements of this cause of action are satisfied. A cause of action for defamation will not lie when the allegations in a civil action are defamatory, since all parties are accorded a judicial immunity; however, the *Restatement* takes the position that this immunity will not preclude a malicious prosecution suit if the subject matter of the allegation is defamatory.(53)

The author bases his contention, in part, on two cases. *Savile v. Roberts* laid down a three-part test for malicious prosecution: damage to the person, damage to property, and damage to a man's fame.(54) The second case, *Wade v. National Bank of Commerce of Tacoma*(55) holds that the defamatory matter in a complaint is, without interference to person or property, sufficient to sustain an action for malicious prosecution.

In summarizing his view the author states:

> The *Wade* case, cited above, called attention to the fact that the courts should not be used to inflict a wanton injury. This is in accord with public policy. It is not to be expected that every civil action will support malicious prosecution, but it is to be expected that the courts will take care to protect the personal and/or business reputation of those who are maliciously sued. Chief Justice Holt's threefold test for damages to person, property, and reputation is complete and fair. If the pleadings in the original suit are defamatory, they should be actionable without a showing of interference with person or property. This can be reconciled with the majority rule in that these damages to reputation, resulting from a malicious prosecution, are damages that do "not ordinarily result from all suits maintained for like causes." Oregon has rejected the underlying theory of section 678 of the *Restatement of Torts*, but it would seem both logical and desirable to accept and extend the theory of this section to all civil actions where the defendant

has suffered an injury to his reputation. It is submitted that this more liberal rule will tend to discourage those who might otherwise bring groundless suits maliciously.(56)

This more liberal rule of allowing damages in a malicious prosecution proceeding could work as an effective means to counter the increase in medical malpractice actions.

NOTES

(1) U. S. News & World Report, Mar. 7, 1971, at 70; Time, Nov. 2, 1970, at 36; Newsweek, Jan. 19, 1970, at 93.

(2) U. S. News & World Report, *supra* note 1. Even including veterinarians: *see* Oleck, *Veterinarians' Malpractice*, in *The Practicing Veterinarian* (No. 6) 164 (1966).

(3) U. S. News & World Report, *supra* note 1; Time, *supra* note 1.

(4) Brooke, *Medical Malpractice: A Socio-Economic Problem from a Doctor's View*, 6 Willamette, L. J. 225 (1970); Halberstam, *The Doctor's New Dilemma—"Will I Be Sued?"*, The New York Times Magazine, Feb. 14, 1971, at 8.

(5) U. S. News & World Report, *supra* note 1.

(6) Brooke, *supra* note 4, at 227.

(7) *Id*; Newsweek, *supra* note 1.

(8) Newsweek, *supra* note 1.

(9) U. S. News & World Report, *supra* note 1.

(10) Time, *supra* note 1.

(11) Brooke, *supra* note 4, at 227.

(12) *Id*. at 230.

(13) Newsweek, *supra* note 1.

(14) Time, *supra* note 1.

(15) Science News, Dec. 13, 1969, at 552.

(16) Brooke, *supra* note 4, at 232.

(17) *Id*. at 233; Halberstam, *supra* note 4, at 37.

(18) U. S. News & World Report, *supra* note 1.

(19) Newsweek, *supra* note 1.

(20) Science News, *supra* note 15.

(21) U. S. News & World Report, *supra* note 1.

(22) Time, *supra* note 1; Science News, *supra* note 15.

(23) Brooke, *supra* note 4, at 228; U. S. News and World Report, *supra* note 1.

(24) Brooke, *supra* note 4, at 228.

(25) *Id*. at 229.

(26) *Id*. at 226. So do many lawyers: Oleck, *A Cure for Doctor-Lawyer Frictions*, 7 Cleve.-Mar. L. Rev. 473 (1958).

(27) Blende V. Hurst Publications, 93 P.2d 733, (Wash., 1939); *Charging a Physician With Incompetence in a Particular Case*, 73 United States L. Rev. 490 (1939).

(28) Note, *The Malpractice Dilemma*, 9 W. Res. L. Rev. 471 (1958).

(29) Brooke, *supra* note 4, at 225.

(30) Restatement of Torts, § 587 Comment (c) (1938).

(31) *Id*. § 681 (b).

(32) 16 Am Jur. *Trials* § 205 (1969).

(33) 52 Am. Jur. 2d *Malicious Prosecution* § 5 (1970).

(34) Note, *Malicious Prosecution—Essential Elements*, 26 Tenn. L. Rev. 437 (1959).

(35) W. Prosser, Handbook of the Law of Torts 853, 873 (3rd ed. 1964); Note, *supra* note 34; Cassidy, *Malicious Prosecution—Its Scope and Purpose* 22 Geo. L. J. 343 (1934); 52 Am. Jur. 2d *Malicious Prosecution* § 6 (1970).

(36) W. Prosser, *supra* note 34, at 439.

(37) *Id.* at 866; Note, *supra* note 34, at 439.

(38) Babb v. Superior Court of Sonoma County, 92 Cal. Rptr. 179, 479 P. 2nd 379 (1971); *supra* note 34, at 441; 52 Am. Jur. 2d *Malicious Prosecution* § 42 (1970).

(39) W. Prosser, *supra* note 35, at 868; Note, *supra* note 34, at 440.

(40) Restatement of Torts § 669 Comment (a) (1938); Henderson, *supra* note 34, at 440.

(41) Note, *supra* note 34, at 440.

(42) 52 Am. Jur. 2d *Malicious Prosecution* § 48 (1970).

(43) W. Prosser, *supra* note 35 at 875.

(44) Cincinnti Daily Tribune Co. v. Bruck, 61 Ohio St. 482, 56 N.E. 198 (1900).

(45) W. Prosser, *supra* note 35, at 875.

(46) Perry v. Adjustable Awning, Inc., 117 Ohio App. 486 192 N. E. 2d 672 (1962); Edgington V. Glassmeyer, 11 Ohio Op. 2d 439, 168 N. E. 2d 425 (Ohio App. 1959).

(47) 217 N. E. 2d 712 (C. P. Fayette County 1966).

(48) Note, *Malicious Prosecution—Injury to Reputation as a Basis for Recovery*, 6 Willamette L. J. 173 (1970).

(49) *Id.* at 179.

(50) *Id.* at 176

(51) 11 Q. B. D. 674 (1883).

(52) *Supra* note 48, at 177; Restatement of Torts, § 674, Comment (c) (1938).

(53) *Id.* at 177-178.

(54) 91 Eng. Rep. 1147 (1698).

(55) 114 F. 277 (9th Cir. 1902).

(56) *Supra* note 48, at 180-181.

LEGAL RESPONSIBILITY FOR NEGLIGENCE OF ASSISTANTS, SUBSTITUTES, PARTNERS, CONSULTANTS, AND JOINTLY TREATING PHYSICIANS

Elliot Sagall
Barry C. Reed

Mrs. Green had been treated by Dr. Able for over 10 years for chronic congestive heart failure due to rheumatic heart disease. On Monday, Mrs. Green was hospitalized by Dr. Able for treatment of an acute duodenal ulcer. Several days later the doctor left for his scheduled three week vacation, leaving Dr. Baker in charge of Mrs. Green's medical care during his absence. Dr. Able and Dr. Baker were associated in the partnership practice of medicine and Mrs. Green was advised in advance that Dr. Baker would be her substitute attending physician.

Following Dr. Able's departure, Dr. Baker visited Mrs. Green at the hospital daily. She was last examined by Dr. Baker on Thursday morning during his regular hospital rounds when, because of continued symptoms, consultation with a gastroenterologist was suggested and agreed upon. The following morning, Friday, Mrs. Green was examined by Dr. Charles, the Chief of the Gastroenterology Service. Dr. Charles took a detailed history concerning the patient's gastrointestinal symptoms, examined her abdomen, reviewed her hospital records and then wrote a lengthy consultation note outlining his findings and recommendations for treatment of her ulcer. Although his note indicated a complaint of left calf pain, there was no mention of an examination of the legs.

That same day, Dr. Baker suddenly became ill and was unable to attend his patients. A substitute, Dr. Dodge, was secured to handle his practice. Dr. Dodge saw Mrs. Green later that day at the hospital. The nurse who accompanied Dr. Dodge on this visit later testified that Mrs. Green complained to Dr. Dodge of some pain in her left calf but that Dr. Dodge performed no physical examination at that time and wrote no orders for medication.

Sometime that same afternoon Dr. Evans, a dermatologist concomitantly treating Mrs. Green for long-standing psoriasis, came to the hospital to check the progress of her skin condition. Mrs. Green told him about her left calf pain and he looked at her leg, squeezing the calf. Dr. Evans told her husband, who was in the room at the time, that the left leg was slightly puffy and that she "might be developing phlebitis." However, he apparently did nothing further about this, merely writing an order for a new ointment to be applied to her psoriatic lesions.

About 9:00 P.M. that evening Mrs. Green complained to the nurse that her left leg pain was worse. Dr. Dodge was notified by telephone and prescribed a sedative. Three hours later the night nurse heard Mrs. Green suddenly cry out. Rushing into the room, she found the patient cyanotic and pulseless. Resuscitative attempts failed, and Dr. Dodge, arriving about 25 minutes later, pronounced Mrs. Green dead.

Autopsy revealed the cause of death to be a massive pulmonary embolism arising from a left iliofemoral thrombophlebitis. The duodenum showed a recent, healing duodenal ulcer. There was inactive rheumatic heart disease with aortic and mitral valve stenosis and moderate cardiac enlargement.

Mr. Green, understandably upset, blamed his wife's sudden and unexpected death upon negligence of her attending physicians. In a suit for wrongful death due to medical malpractice, he alleged that because of negligent care, the thrombophlebitis of her left leg went undiagnosed and that had this condition been seasonably recognized, prophylactic bilateral femoral vein ligation would have prevented fatal pulmonary embolism, and his wife would still be alive. Joined as defendants in the suit were: Dr. Able, the vacationing attending physician; Dr. Baker, his partner; Dr. Charles, the consulting gastroenterologist; Dr. Dodge, the substitute; and Dr. Evans, the dermatologist treating an unrelated condition.

LEGAL IMPLICATIONS

This case presents a situation not uncommon in clinical medicine in which a patient is examined and treated by several physicians. Dr. Able was the attending physician originally consulted. His partner, Dr. Baker, took over during his vacation absence and then, due to illness, had to call in a substitute, Dr. Dodge. Dr. Charles saw the patient in consultation for treatment of her ulcer. She was also concomitantly treated for an unrelated skin disorder by her dermatologist, Dr. Evans.

The legal ramifications of liability for negligence of one or more of these physicians are several fold, but certain questions are pertinent to the present discussion. What legal responsibility, if any, might accrue to Dr. Able because of harm resulting from professional negligence attributed to any of the other doctors involved in Mrs. Green's illness? And, what liability, if any, might be assessed against each physician for injury due to negligence of one of the other physicians? The fundamental question of negligence will not be taken up at this time since it has been treated in previous clinics. However, it must be remembered that before liability for professional negligence of one physician can be imputed to another, the former has to be judged legally negligent and would be held personally responsible for his own wrongdoing.

Legal precepts affecting responsibility of one physician for negligent actions or inactions of others fall into the area of law that concerns legal relationships between agents and principals (the law of agency). The problems that potentially might arise are multiple, varied, highly complex and often exceedingly difficult to resolve from logical, ethical, and legal viewpoints. To do justice to the intricacies of agency law would require a volume by itself, so that detailed discussion is beyond the scope of this treatise. However, the legal highlights affecting the interrelationship between physicians (other than interns and residents) concomitantly involved in a patient's treatment merit elaboration.

Two dicta generally apply to legal definitions of responsibility of one physician for negligent activity of another. First is the universal rule that each tort-feasor is personally responsible for ill-effects stemming from his own errors of commission or omission, independent of vicarious liability assessed to other physicians. Thus in our illustrative case, each physician, since all were personally involved in Mrs. Green's treatment, could be held responsible for injury attributable to his own negligence (in this case, failure to diagnose her acute thrombophlebitis and to institute potentially life-saving treatment).

Second, and most important, is that failure of a treating physician to detect the wrongful acts or omissions of another physician's treatment, where such detection can be shown to be within the applicable standard of medical care, is included in the legal scope of professional negligence. Also, when negligence in treatment is recognized by a physician, there is a further legal duty to institute action designed to avoid or to remedy injury to the patient. This includes warning the negligent physician of disapproval of his actions and, where applicable, calling the discovery to the patient's attention. Consider, for example, a patient being treated jointly and concomitantly by a psychiatrist and an orthopedic surgeon, the former for a long-standing anxiety tension and the latter for a recent arm fracture. If the psychiatrist notices that the cast has been improperly applied, resulting in circulatory deficiency of the affected hand, he might be held guilty of professional negligency if he neither attempts to correct the situation nor calls it to the attention of the orthopod.

LIABILITY FOR NEGLIGENCE OF PARTNERS

Physicians who practice in partnership are generally held personally liable for tortious acts of their partners, providing such acts are performed during the conduct of partnership business. In the eyes of the law, the partnership practice of medicine is no different than any business partnership, and liability of partners for the malpractice of each other is well specified.

Legally, each partner is an agent of the partnership and the actions of any one partner bind the others. The rule that two physicians employed to treat the same patient and by agreement divide the service as their best judgment dictates are considered as independent agents, each responsible for his own negligence and no more, does not apply where the two physicians are partners. Examples of such decisions are *Telanas v. Simpson* (Mo., 12 S.W. 2d 920 [1928]), *Stephens v. Williams* (Ala., 147 So. 608 [1933]), *Hess v. Lowrey* (Ind., 23 N.E. 156 [1890]) and *Wolfsmith v. Marsh* (Cal., 337 P.2d 70 [1959]). Also, under the doctrine of *respondeat superior* each partner is responsible for negligent acts of any agent or employee of the partnership. To assure himself full protection, a physician in partnership practice should make certain that his professional liability insurance policy specifically covers his liability for negligence of his partner or partners, and their agents.

In our illustrative case, if Dr. Baker is found liable for professional negligence, his liability automatically attaches legally to Dr. Able even though Dr. Able had nothing to do with the course of events and was completely innocent of any act of commission or ommission leading to Mrs. Green's demise.

LIABILITY FOR NEGLIGENCE OF CONSULTANTS

Generally speaking, an attending physician is not legally responsible for the acts of the specialist he calls in to assist him in the management of his patient. The consultant has the status of an independent contractor since he does not ordinarily act under supervision or control of the referring physician. Therefore, legal responsibility for his tortious conduct does not extend to the latter (*Dill v. Scuba*, C.A. 3 Pa., 197 F. Supp. 26 [1960]).

In *Grady v. New York Medical College*, N.Y., 243 N.Y.S. 2d 940 (1963), the court held that referral of a patient by one physician to another competent physician, in the absence of partnership, employment or agency, does not impose liability on the referring physician. The general rule, said the court, is that a physician who is unable or unwilling to assume or continue the treatment of a case and who recommends or sends another physician (not his employee, agent or partner) is not liable for injuries resulting from the latter's want of skill or care unless he did not exercise due care in making the recommendation or substitution. Although the facts in the *Grady* case involved shared office space and arrangements to service each other's patients for a joint fee, and although the court conceded that this arrangement came close to a "joint venture," vicarious liability was not extended to the referring physician since no actual legal control of the treating physician existed.

The degree of participation, however, by a referring physician may determine his liability for a consultant's negligence. In *Arshansky v. Royal Concourse Co.*, N.Y., 283 N.Y.S. 2d 646 (1967), a patient was referred by her physician to a podiatrist, who performed surgery on her feet. The patient later sued both practitioners alleging that the operation was negligently performed. The trial court dismissed the suit. The appellate court held that the patient was entitled to a new trial against the two physicians saying,

A question of fact for the jury was presented as to whether the operation performed on (the patient's) feet was done properly in accordance with standard practice, and whether (such) failure was the cause of her subsequent pain and incapacity. She was the physician's patient, and he referred her to the podiatrist who operated. The referral, in itself, would not render the physician liable . . . He, however, participated in the diagnosis and attended at the operation and assisted therein to a degree sufficient to present a question of fact for the jury as to his liability in connection with the alleged improper operation.

A 1928 Texas case, *Floyd v. Michie*, 11 S.W. 2d 657, involved a family physician who, noting sores on the face and mouth of a child, indicated that he was unwilling to diagnose or treat the case and called in a skin specialist. The dermatologist diagnosed the condition as "chicken pox." A day later he changed the diagnosis to "impetigo" and prescribed ointment. Over the next 10 days, both family physician and specialist visited the child several times. On the eleventh day, the child developed severe vomiting and died before a physician could be called. The court held that the family physician was not liable for the specialist's conduct. Although the family physician did visit the patient, he did not take an active part in either diagnosing or treating the child and merely carried out the prescriptions of the specialist. His freedom from liability was predicated on the fact that diagnosis and treatment were left entirely to the specialist.

An attending physician is always obliged to exercise due care in selecting a consultant. When he is found to be negligent in this regard, he may be held responsible for the latter's acts despite the fact that the consultant acted as an independent contractor.

LIABILITY FOR NEGLIGENCE OF SUBSTITUTES

To prevent charges of abandonment or neglect, a physician, for any reason unable to attend his patients, must recommend or make available a qualified substitute physician. However, except in an emergency, substitution of another physician or surgeon without the consent of the patient is a breach of duty. Ordinarily, when absence from practice is anticipated, the patient should be given reasonable notice to enable him to accept or decline the suggested substitute or to select someone of his own choice.

Usually, a substitute physician is considered to be an independent contractor solely responsible for his own negligence, and the regular attending physician is not liable for the substitute's wrongful acts (*Myers v. Holborn* [N.J. 33 A. 385 (1895)] and *Moore v. Lee* [Tex., 211 S.W. 214 (1919)]). Two situations, however, exist in which a referring physician may acquire such liability. If the original attending physician has not exercised due care in selecting the substitute, he may be deemed negligent and thereby held liable for injury resulting from the substitute's negligence. Secondly, if a substitute acts as the agent of the referring physician, or specifically agrees to carry out a certain course of treatment, or receives payment for his services from the attending physician as with a *locum tenens*, a master-servant relationship may be created. Legally under these circumstances, the doctrine of *respondeat superior* may impute vicarious liability to the referring physician for negligence of the substitute (*Wilson v. Martin Memorial Hospital*, N.C., 61 S.E. 2d 102 [1950]).

LIABILITY FOR NEGLIGENCE OF TWO PHYSICIANS

When two physicians (not partners, substitutes, or consultants) jointly participate in treating a patient, even though their areas of treatment are separate and distinct, negligence of one potentially may create liability in the other. This develops when the latter observes or should reasonably have observed negligence of the first and fails to take appropriate action to remedy the situation or to prevent further injury to the patient. Thus, when an internist and a surgeon tell a patient that they will "work together" in his treatment, a "joint venture" may be established legally, making each liable for negligence of the other, regardless of whether the negligent acts of one physician are observed and acquiesed in by the other or whether they share a common specific medical procedure.

Even in absence of statements creating a joint venture, some courts have recognized that two physicians simultaneously treating a patient share a common duty to him and are mutually liable for the negligence of either. There is, however, one generally recognized exception. Ordinarily, the operating surgeon is not held liable for negligence of an anesthesiologist, provided the latter is a qualified, competent, licensed physician and is not acting under the control and direction of the operating surgeon.

Finally, if a physician recommends another physician whose treatment is negligent, the recommending physician may be jointly liable if he expressly or implicitly approved the treatment given, even though he did not actually participate in such treatment.

LIABILITY FOR EMPLOYEES AND ASSISTANTS

Under the doctrine of *respondeat superior*, a physician is clearly liable for injury resulting from want of proper skill and care by his clinical assistants, nurses, technicians, and other employees, during the course of their employment. Under such circumstances, a master-servant relationship is easily established. The requirement that the negligence must have been committed within the scope of the employment seldom creates any problem since the indictable acts most often are performed within the physician's office or at a patient's home under the physician's order. Such vicarious liability applies even when the physician's employee or agent is another physician.

Liability for negligence of assistants and employees may also accure when the duties assigned have been unlawfully delegated. The scope of authority in administering treatments such as hypodermic injections or intravenous fluid and blood infusion by nurses, for example, and the degree of personal direction and supervision required of the employing physician varies considerably both medically and legally. This is primarily governed by the standards of medical practice generally accepted by the medical profession in the specific community involved.

Certain of the above legal precepts could be applied with jurisdictional variation to the case presented in this paper. Personal liability for negligent failure to diagnose thrombophlebitis and to institute measures aimed at preventing pulmonary embolism could, if substantiated by medical testimony, be legally assessed against Doctors Charles, Dodge, and Evans. Prior to the patient's demise, each of these physicians separately had been apprised by the patient of pain in her left calf, a generally recognized warning symptom of underlying thrombophlebitis. Because of this, each should have examined her legs, presumably then arriving at the correct diagnosis. Dr. Charles and Dr. Dodge failed to examine her leg—a lack of diligence that might well be deemed negligence in view of the circumstances. Dr. Evans did examine her legs, even concluding that she had thrombophlebitis, but failed to impart his findings to either Dr. Baker or Dr. Dodge, the two attending physicians, letting the matter drop after his comment to Mr. Green. This action might well be judged as lacking in due care.

It is unlikely that legal responsibility for Mrs. Green's death could be assessed against either Doctors Able or Baker since neither physician personally attended her during the time that her potentially lethal illness presumably was apparent clinically. Also, while on vacation Dr. Able was covered by his partner, Dr. Baker, and when Dr. Baker became ill, arrangements were made for the patient to be cared for by a substitute, Dr. Dodge. Thus, neither Dr. Able nor Dr. Baker could be charged with abandonment.

Could either Dr. Able or Dr. Baker be held liable for the negligence of Doctors Charles, Dodge, or Evans? Because of the partnership agreement, Dr. Able would be responsible with Dr. Baker for any negligence imputed to as well as performed by the latter. Let us consider each legal situation separately.

Dr. Charles, the consultant, acted as an independent contractor. Ordinarily, he would be expected to send his charge for services rendered directly to the patient and would not receive remuneration from either Dr. Able or Dr. Baker. Thus, his negligence could not be extended under the law of agency to either of the partners.

Dr. Dodge, the substitute, might in the eyes of the law either be an independent contractor or as "servant" of the partners, Able and Baker, depending on the financial arrangements attendant upon his substituting for Baker. If Dr. Dodge was to receive payment directly from Baker or was, without independent judgment, to carry out the plan of treatment prescribed by Dr. Baker, then he might well be considered an agent of the partnership. As an agent, Dr. Dodge's negligence could be extended vicariously under the doctrine of *respondeat superior* to the partnership and, through this, individually to Doctors Able and Baker. Finally, if it could be shown that Dr. Dodge was improperly selected as a substitute by Dr. Baker, the latter could be held negligent for this action, thus saddling Dr. Able, also, with legal responsibility for Dr. Dodge's negligence.

Dr. Evans, a jointly treating physician, would be considered an independent contractor and liability for his negligence would not accrue to either Dr. Able or Dr. Baker. However, if either of the latter became aware or reasonably should have become aware of negligent action or inaction on the part of Dr. Evans, then they, too, would share in his negligence as joint tortfeasors.

From a practical point of view, attending physicians should be constantly aware of their personal potential liability for the medical malpractice of other physicians sharing with them the care of a patient and, most important, should be certain that their professional liability insurance policy covers them for vicarious or imputed liability.

THE MEDICOLEGAL AUTOPSY AND
MEDICOLEGAL INVESTIGATION

William J. Curran

You have heard a great deal about the medical importance of an autopsy in the medicolegal investigation of deaths. For the legal and law-enforcement system, the importance of a complex autopsy can be underscored by noting the opinion of one of the better known modern-day philosophers of the law, Willie Sutton, the bank robber. One day, while Sutton was enjoying one of his frequent interviews with newspaper men, one of the reporters asked, "Willie, you seem to be a very intelligent man. One thing mystifies me, though: Why do you rob banks?"

Willie looked at the reporter as if he must be a very stupid man not to see the obvious. He replied, "Because that's where the *money* is."

To lawyers and to law-enforcement investigators of fatal cases, the autopsy serves the same purpose. That is where the *facts* are. The medicolegal autopsy is the starting point of the investigation and the all-but-indispensable foundation of the prosecutor's case in court.

A NATIONAL SCANDAL

Today in the United States the medicolegal investigation of deaths is poorly handled in well over 60% of American jurisdicitions. Only approximaterly 30% of Americans are protected adequately by competent, well-organized medicolegal investigational departments. This is clearly a national scandal. Seventy per cent of Americans live in serious danger today because of this situation.

Many of the problems have been pointed out by other writers. Their illustrative cases affirm graphically that the fact that it is medically possible and statistically probable that murders go undetected in most parts of this country every year. In terms of numbers the failure to perform adequate medicolegal investigations has its greatest impact in the investigation of accidents. *Thousands of deaths* every year are classified and enter the statistics as due to natural causes or heart disease which are actually due to *preventable accidents*. The results of these errors are widespread in many legal and medical programs. They cause many tragedies in individual families and incalculable financial loss.

REFORM MOVEMENTS

I urge those of you who are lawyers and law-enforcement authorities to work to improve the medicolegal investigation of deaths in your own communities and states. You and your communities have a great deal to gain by such efforts. Do not leave it solely to physicians and medical people to bring about these reforms. If you do, the efforts will fail. Physicians alone cannot succeed in this cause, though they usually support such legislative campaigns enthusiastically. The history of reform in this field in the past 100 years proves this to be the case.

The first medical examiner system adopted in this country was enacted into law in my home state, Massachusetts, in 1877. The leader of the change was a lawyer and later a judge, Theodore H. Tyndale. The next major jurisdiction to reform its coroner system was New York City in 1915, though other New England states followed Massachusetts in changing their law in the late 19th and early 20th centuries. The most important early advocate of reform in New York City was again a lawyer, a most remarkable early leader in medicolegal work and scholarship in this country, Clark Bell, who first proposed a radical reform in a speech in 1881. When the coroner system was finally abolished in 1915, it was the result of the election of a reform mayor and a devastating investigation and report on the coroner system by the city's commissioner of accounts, Leonard M. Wallstein.

In more recent years leadership in the quest for improvement in medicolegal investigation and the advocacy of medical examiner systems has passed to the National Municipal League, the main sponsor of a model state law in the field in 1951, and the National Conference of Commissioners on Uniform State Laws, which published a model law in 1954.

NEW PROBLEMS IN THE 1970'S

New factors and new problems facing American society in the 1970's make even more imperative today the establishment of more effective and more competent systems for independent, scientific investigation of deaths in the United States. These factors are at least four in number: 1. The increase in violent deaths in the United States. 2. The greater difficulty of determining, medically and scientifically, the causes of increasing numbers of deaths due to drug abuse, the therapeutic use of drugs, and other circumstances. 3. The polarization of political activity and the resort to violence in protest movements. 4. The growing distrust and hostility of significant segments of the American people toward the American system of justice and law enforcement.

INCREASE IN VIOLENCE

Over the past 10 years there has been a huge increase in violence and violent crime all over this country. The crime figures of the Federal Bureau of Investigation show this. The general vital statistics of the country show it also. From 1960 to 1969, violent crimes in the United States increased 104%. The rise is particularly sharp since 1963. During this same period the population of the country increased only 11%. Murder rates actually declined from 1960 to 1962, remained stable during 1962, and after that joined the general precipitous increase. The national rate of increase in murder since 1960 is 44%. In many large cities the increase has been even greater in recent years.

I believe we can expect this trend to greater violence to continue. Good medicolegal systems can handle this increased caseload. Actually, they will thrive on it because, in their total caseloads, homicides still will not be very high proportionally. It is the inadequate system which suffers most from an increase in homicides and other violence. Officials are often able to struggle along and to hide their inadequacies when the cases are not obviously criminal in nature. They literally bury their mistakes and fool their communities into thinking that there is no need for more costly and more adequate medicolegal investigation. But when the death rate for violence goes up, when homicide investigations and court trials become necessary, the fragile facade crumbles. Important evidence is lost or never discovered. The necessary reports are delayed repeatedly until they must be presented, when they are found to be incomplete, confused, and largely useless.

DIFFICULTY IN DETERMINING CAUSE OF DEATH

The need for more adequate medicolegal investigation in fatal cases is also greater in the 1970's because of the increased complexity of the problems faced in determining the cause fo death. This is best illustrated by the huge increase in the abuse of dangerous drugs in this country, especially among young people, including teenagers. These persons are not just abusing themselves and becoming addicted; they are killing themselves by a variety of methods: 1. They are overdosing themselves to a lethal degree, intentionally and accidentally. 2. They are administering the drugs improperly and killing themselves accidentally. 3. They are using unclean and contaminated instruments and chemical substances and thus are killing themselves by infection. 4. They are experimenting wildly with all kinds of substances and paraphernalia and are killing themselves in the process. 5. They are dying in all sorts of ways while under the influence of these drugs.

Drug abusers, illegal drug users, are not the only people in this country who are killing themselves with drugs. Many, many deaths every year result from drug use which, in its beginnings at least, is perfectly legal. The deaths in these cases are mainly from overdosage, intentional or accidental, but such cases also run the gamut of the causes listed above.

Medicolegal offices need to be very good these days in order to cope with these new kinds of cases. They require excellent and costly toxicology laboratories and personnel. They require interdisciplinary staffs such as the suicide-investigation team in Los Angeles to conduct "Psychological autopsies" along with standard pathological autopsies.

New techniques are also necessary to investigate other new kinds of accidental death and also deaths related to environmental and industrial hazards.

POLITICAL POLARIZATION AND VIOLENCE

The next factor to be noted is the current political polarization and the resort to violence by radical protest groups.

All who are law enforcement personnel are well aware of this problem. They are trying to cope with it, often without adequate resources, and in the face of what may seem to be sensationalized coverage by news media. If injuries or death should occur to demonstrators or to members of radical groups during such incidents or while such persons are in police custody, the cry of "police brutality" is heard immediately and broadcast instantaneously.

How is public medicolegal investigation involved in this problem? I say it is greatly involved. Public outcry is, of course, greatest if death occurs. There is an immediate demand for a proper investigation. Because police and other law enforcement personnel are involved directly, because they themselves are placed in the incongruous role of possible defendants in murder charges, they are greatly handicapped in their investigations.

Here is where an adequate, professional, *independent* medicolegal investigational office having the confidence of the people can prove its greatest worth to the community. With an exhaustive and well-documented investigation, with a public inquest where authorized in the jurisdiction, this public responsibility can be discharged and the public's need to know the truth can be satisfied.

This is, in its way, a new responsibility for medicolegal programs and even the best of them have much to learn about the most effective methods of carrying it out.

The first example of this type of problem occurred in Los Angeles after the Watts riots of August 1965. A total of 32 inquests were held by the Los Angeles Coroner's Office concerning deaths in that disturbance. In 21 cases the verdict returned was of justifiable homicide by gunshot from police weapons. All of this happened before the major campus uprisings of the later 1960's. Can you imagine the reaction today if another "Watts" occurred and police were charged with shooting and killing *21 people, all black*, in the course of the riot?

The last new factor I point to in the 1970's as significant to the increased need for improved medicolegal investigation is the growing distrust and hostility of many of our people, not only blacks and other minorities, but many of our young people, toward the American system of justice and law enforcement.

The inadequate and sometimes corrupt coroners' offices are a part of that system. To that extent, the charges which antagonists lodge against the system—their distrust and hostility—have a sound basis in fact. We who are interested in preserving the American system as basically sound must correct such abuses within the system if we are to save this land of ours as a nation of free men.

Also, and perhaps more technically, we who are lawyers should support competent, nonpartisan medicolegal investigational systems as an alternative to the current adversary system of presenting expert medical testimony. The adversary system has its place and I defend it strongly, but I believe it is misplaced in the search for scientific and medical truth. This is another area where the hostility and distrust of the legal system is widespread, not merely among racial minorities and radical youth, but among the majority of physicians and scientists of America. It is another place where we who represent law, order, and justice must clean our own house before it is torn down around us.

SOME PRACTICAL SUGGESTIONS

I have been asked to offer some practical suggestions regarding medical testimony involving autopsy protocols and evidence, particularly for law-enforcement personnel and attorneys.

First, as to the autopsy itself: never assume that all autopsies are conducted in the same way. They are not. A *complete autopsy* involves opening all body cavities and all organs of the trunk, chest, and head. Many otherwise complete autopsies will not include opening the head if the cause of death seems adequately explained by examination of the abdomen and chest. This is because: 1. Opening the head may disturb undertakers and the family who may see the head in an open casket. 2. Opening the head is not easy and usually involves the time and expense of assistants. 3. The medicolegal cases in which findings are affected positively as a result of head-and-brain examination are admittedly somewhat uncommon.

Nevertheless, in important medicolegal cases, a full and complete autopsy, including the head, should be done. When a complete autopsy has not been done, the attorney challenging the opinion of the coroner, medical examiner, or other witness should consult a forensic pathologist of his own choosing to ask whether a complete autopsy involving the skull, brain, face, and neck areas might have produced other pathologic findings which could have changed the opinion.

When an autopsy is not complete, never assume that you know what "incomplete" means. The meaning *always* differs. There is no such thing as a uniform meaning to the term "incomplete" medicolegal autopsy. The term is always specific. Ask in detail exactly what was done. To one physician, an incomplete autopsy or postmortem examination means a full trunk and chest exploration, but no head examination. To others, it means merely probing the obvious course of bullet wounds, or taking a sample of heart's blood, or of the stomach contents. *Always ask*. The less complete the examination, the less the examiner knows and the more he is assuming.

The term "postmortem examination" is often used as a simile for "autopsy." Basically, it is not. A postmortem examination means only what it says: that the body was examined after death. It can mean and often does mean that the physician merely looked at the body, fully clothed, or that he "viewed" the body at a funeral home or in a morgue. Do not assume that in either of these places he saw the body undraped. In fact, unless he reports otherwise, assume that it was at least partially draped. Do not even assume he saw it before the undertaker embalmed it or before the hospital did its own autopsy. Always check these things independently in the records of the undertaker and the hospital. You can be embarrassed if your opponent does so and finds a charge made to the family for an embalming or an autopsy that you say was never done.

Next, always remember than in many cases, in perhaps most cases today, the pathologist does not work alone. His examination and his opinion are not alone adequate to support the conclusions in most medicolegal cases. The expert, technical work of other forensic scientists is necessary to produce a full medicolegal opinion. The laboratory work is becoming more complex every year. Be ready to support or to challenge not only the pathological report, but these laboratory work-ups which themselves may be the key element in a particular case. Be ready to call these scientists and technicians as witnesses wherever necessary.

Along the same lines, remember that a forensic pathologist gathers his data not only at the autopsy table and through his laboratory assistants, but through his own personal observation at the scene of the death or the crime and through the evidence supplied him by talking to witnesses, the family, or to police or law enforcement officials. The very best of the forensic pathologists all rely heavily on this sort of evidence. You have heard most perhaps about on-the-scene investigation, which is extremely important. You have perhaps seen photographs taken at the scene of crimes by pathologists and police investigators. But where on-the-scene investigation or photography is not available, pathologists will commonly take into account whatever seemingly reliable stories about the scene or the people involved are made known to them. Many times, perhaps most times, these stories are reliable, but not always, particularly not in homicide cases. Even experienced pathologists fall into the habit of believing the stories they are told in the 90% of their cases which are noncriminal in nature. These habits are still there in the occasional criminal case or other serious matters, especially if they receive and rely on these reports before they are made aware of the importance of the case. Once their opinions are formed, they may be reluctant to go back and to revise them.

In the case of Mary Jo Kopechne, the local medical examiner, who was actually the associate medical examiner who covers for the medical examiner occasionally when he is away, was told that Miss Kopechne was the sole occupant and driver of a car which had gone out of control and had gone off the narrow bridge on Martha's Vineyard island. There were no signs of violence, the vehicle was still in gear, and the girl's body gave every appearance of drowning. On the basis of past practice, he wrote the case off as an automobile accident and drowning and did not order an autopsy. This was consistent with common practice all over Massachusetts at the time. Summer drowning cases were not autopsied medicolegally anywhere in the state. Very few auto accidents were taken under medicolegal jurisdiction. It was not until later in the day that the medical examiner and the district attorney were informed by Senator Edward M. Kennedy that the girl was not the driver and only occupant of the vehicle. The original decision was never changed. There is much controversy over who, if anyone, refused to reverse the earlier decision, the associate medical examiner or the district attorney. It no longer matters. The fact is that official decisions, no matter how lightly arrived at, are diffcult to change. Later, District Attorney Edmund Dinis tried to reverse his position. He tried tragically late after the body had been turned over to the family and buried in another jurisdiction. District Attorney Dinis may well be forgiven his slowness of action, his indecisiveness, and his imprecision in handling the intricacies of the case in Massachusetts and Pennsylvania. Very few public prosecutors or American lawyers have ever handled disinterment cases, which are always difficult and delicate. The precedents for successful reexamination of buried bodies are rare in American case law. Politically, the effort hurt Dinis, who was defeated in the next election.

The lesson should be clear: the mistake lies in the first decision not to autopsy. That decision should be made with the full facts at hand.

Now as to autopsy reports or medicolegal experience in reading and understanding medical reports of all kinds. In addition to the technical language and abbreviation which must be learned, you should have an idea of what a good report is. Recall again the earlier discussion of a complete and an incomplete autopsy. The examiner in an incomplete autopsy may try to disguise this fact. He will report only positive findings. No negative findings will be mentioned. In fact, the weakest type of report—all too common—will have no *findings* at all. It will contain only *opinions* about the pathology of the body without a description of its actual appearance or condition. This is an unreliable report. It should be suspect. It is an opinion without reasons; a scientific report without a scientific foundation. I cannot condemn it severely enough. I admonish all medical educators to train forensic medical specialists *not* to make such reports in medicolegal matters.

In today's modern medicolegal investigations, color-slide photography is as indispensable as the objective findings recorded in a protocol. No medicolegal office should conduct investigations today without a complete photographic record taken serially in each case. These photos are, of course, also an extremely valuable tool in court for the presentation of demonstration evidence. A long line of appellate-court cases have upheld the admission of such pictures against charges of gruesomeness. For those of you who are prosecutors, I strongly suggest that you take full advantage of the use of such photographic evidence.

Finally, may I make some suggestions about methods of handling medicolegal experts, primarily forensic pathologists, on the witness stand. Care should be taken in presenting their qualifications, which are generally formidable. Do not make the mistake of accepting opposing counsel's suggestion that a statement of qualifications be waived. The judge and jury are entitled to hear the qualifications so that they may weigh his opinion intelligently. In presenting evidence, give the expert a good bit of leeway and only some good leading questions before allowing him to be off and running on his own. If photographs are used, get the admissibility questions settled beforehand in chambers so that the presentation is not interrupted.

For those of you who have not been involved in cases where highly qualified forensic pathologists and other forensic scientists have presented evidence I suggest that you are in for a treat: a fine example of medicine, science, and law working together at their best. I commend it to you. Welcome to the field.

THE ROLE OF THE FORENSIC
PATHOLOGIST IN CRIMINAL CASES

Cyril H. Wecht

The presentations of speakers at the Southeastern Trial Lawyers Institute, like Stanley Preiser, Henry Rothblatt, Joseph Cook, Paul Liacos, and others, are very valuable because, with a few exceptions, prosecution attorneys and law enforcement officers are not subjected to enough of the opposite view. It is not only a matter of proselytizing, that is, espousing the defense point of view, and of refreshing your mind about what is contained within the Bill of Rights, but rather it is a matter of your learning more about what is entailed in your job. You have a duty that, as men of good faith, honor, and integrity, you want to fulfill, but this responsibility cannot be properly undertaken with the necessary broad perspective unless you have some understanding of the total panorama of your field of endeavor. Generally, I believe it is a valid observation to state that too many of the people active in this field look at it through a narrow and biased set of glasses.

This is true, as well, of medical people; it is tragically true when applied to pathologists. These men who are called in to help investigate criminal cases, frequently homicides, must take a completely scientific and objective approach. The scientist has to have this objective approach. His role is quite different than that of the homicide detective. This is the reason why the American Academy of Forenic Sciences (the most prestigious organization of its kind, involving professional individuals in the fields of toxicology, psychiatry, jurisprudence, criminalistics, and questioned documents, from all over the country) has repeatedly expressed near-unamimous agreement that, ideally, a medical examiner's office should be kept out of the attorney general's office if it is at the state level, and out of the district attorney's or prosecuting attorney's office if it is at the city or county level. There is nothing of a predetermined prosecutional nature inherent in the medical examiner's office. It cannot be that way. If the examiner starts off as an advocate, then he is going to foul up the case for the D.A., perhaps as often as he will do injustice to the defense.

If the medical examiner begins his scientific investigation with information given to him by people who are supposed eyewitnesses, he will be dealing with answers that have already been accepted by the investigating officers. There is no reason then to do the autopsy. He might as well forget about it. To do a biased study is even more deadly than doing an incomplete autopsy, which is one of the worst things that could possibly happen in an official medical-legal investigation.

I can think of no better example to illustrate and emphasize the danger of starting with answers supplied by other people than the autopsy following the assassination of President John F. Kennedy. Time does not permit discussing the case in full, but the fact that the autopsy was so badly managed illustrates the importance of two points. One, although there were competent hospital pathologists involved, they had little or no experience in forensic pathology. Two, they apparently started off with conclusions having been given to them by television, the newspapers, radio, and law enforcement officers. When they started the autopsy at 8:30 in the evening at Bethesda Naval Hospital on Friday, November 22, 1963, the pathologists "knew" (as did all the world!) that Lee Harvey Oswald was a sole assassin, that from the sixth floor window of the Dallas School Board Book Depository Building he had alone fired all the shots, which came from behind, above and to the right of the President's car. There would then be pressure to make everything fit into these facts, and perhaps even to alter findings that did not fit into these predetermined facts.

While a forensic pathologist wants to have a complete investigative report that begins with an on-scene investigation whenever possible, he should not get into a discussion of who committed the crime. That is really not his business at that point. He wants to learn how, when, and where. These are some of the things that he must determine independently and scientifically. It must be kept in mind that a forensic pathologist's job as coroner or medical examiner is to determine the cause and manner of death, and, when possible, the time and place of death. He is to determine these in a manner that must be scientific and objective. Such information can be very helpful to police in their investigation of homicides. It may give them some idea of what kind of assailant might have committed that particular type of murder: what might have been the psychic makeup, the sex, and the age of the criminal.

Of course, such conclusions cannot be arrived at in a completely unequivocal fashion. I do not want you to think that we can gaze into crystal balls for such answers! However, there are certain kinds of crimes which have repetitive features, and these observations lead one to suspect a specific kind of assailant in a given case. The police can be helped simply by having suggestions given to them that a certain kind of individual might have committed that crime.

Maybe it would be helpful to sweep back through the centuries for a moment to give you an idea of why we have the kind of official medical-legal investigative system that we do in much of this country. I think it is important for you to understand how it all evolved so you can appreciate that what we have in most jurisdictions of the United States is anything but ideal. In eleventh and twelfth century England, the kings wanted to have personal representatives to see that their economic interests were protected. They, therefore, appointed honorable gentlemen, knights of the realm, to positions called "crowners." The name became somewhat bastardized over the centuries, and these officials became known as "coroners." Their job was to see to it that, when personal property and lands were confiscated or otherwise obtained, the king's interest was protected from the clergy and noblemen. The crowners went to the scene, convened a local jury, made on-the-spot medical and legal determinations, and sometimes confiscated property. Through the centuries it ceased being a job done by members of nobility, and it fell into disrepute. Unfortunately, about the time that the colonies came into existence and the English common law was being adopted, the coroner system in England was at its lowest point. So it developed in this country that coroners were elected officials with no prerequisites whatsoever.

Today, there are still only a few jurisdictions, less than a handful, that have an official prerequisite that the coroner be an M.D. Even that requirement is totally meaningless, of course. That is like saying that all physicians who do open heart surgery must be M.D.'s. The next time you go in for open heart surgery, you can be comforted by the fact that the doctor graduated from a medical school. He may not have had a residency in heart surgery, but he does have an M.D. degree! Would this give him some kind of halo that makes him an expert in all fields of medicine? It is the same in forensic pathology. There is nothing extra-special about the field: we are not smarter or better than other medical specialists. But, after a fifth year of training in forensic pathology, over and above the four years of basic pathology, we have acquired experience in dealing with sudden, unexpected, suspicious, violent, and unexplained deaths. That is experience one does not get in hospital pathology.

The ideal would be to remove the medical examiner's office from politics, to make it an appointive rather than an elective office, and to base selection on training, experience, credentials and competitive examination. I have already noted that in most jurisdictions today, certainly in most of the rural communities, you still find elected coroners, who can be, and indeed are, anything. For example, through 1965, the coroner in Allegheny County (Pittsburgh), Pennsylvania, the ninth largest metropolitan community in the country, with a population of nearly two million, was a carpenter by training. In the office there was not a microscope; there was no histology, no toxicology and no chemistry. There was not even an actual autopsy table. A physician campaigned on the medical examiner issue and was elected, but when he took office on January 1, 1966, we had to send out to some of the local hospitals to get jars of formalin, gloves, and cutting instruments to do autopsies.

This is not an isolated example. For instance, it is unbelievable what goes on at the coroner's office in Cook County (Chicago), Illinois. The best, and most recent, illustration that I know about in terms of notoriety is the Black Panther case. They have exhumed Fred Hampton's body two times and have done three autopsies. In the first autopsies they missed bullet holes, did not perform toxicology tests, and so on. Both sides deserved to have objective determinations made, something which is not being done in much of this country today.

A forensic pathologist can—indeed, must—play an important role in criminal investigation. I do not want to pretend that this is our major area of endeavor. As a matter of fact, if one examines on a numerical basis all the cases that the medical examiner or a good coroner's office is confronted with over the course of a year, he will find that the percentage of complex, puzzling, or dramatic homicides is quite low. The incidence has been rising in many communities, but most places are still not the jungles that some of the big cities are, and homicides do not constitute a great percentage of the total cases. Also, most homicides, as you probably know, involve people who are "friends" or relatives. In from fifty to seventy-five percent of the cases, you learn rather quickly, if not immediately, who shot whom and why—jealousy, family arguments, drinking, and so on. These cases do not constitute any big investigative problem. That leaves possibly twenty-five to thirty-five percent of the cases that call for some investigation. Approximately five to ten percent of these really require intensive around the clock investigation. Even that percentage figure may be high, fortunately for all of us! If it were higher, the entire police department would have to be restructured in terms of the number of men working on homicides. The point is, however, that in any one of the cases in which it is necessary to have the benefit of total investigative activity done in a top level manner, you must start at the beginning.

The beginning, so far as a forensic pathologist is concerned, is the on-scene investigation. In most jurisdictions where a good medical examiner system has been in existence for a while, most homicides will have a pathologist present in the initial stages. When the case is reported to the police, they will immediately call the medical examiner's office, and a pathologist will go to the scene. Crime lab people will be there too. This is the way it should be done. One can never restructure, never recapitulate, the on-scene situation as it was initially discovered, intact, with everything *in situ*. Once things are removed, or altered, evidentiary bridges are destroyed that never can be completely rebuilt. Any little bit of lost or altered evidence can destroy, or affect in an erroneous manner, one's valid concept of the case.

The on-scene investigation must be a joint effort. Even though the law makes it quite clear in most jurisdictions that the medical examiner's or coroner's office is in charge of the scene, the rule does not mean to exclude others with a job to do. We are never in any hurry. The crime lab people want to pick up every little fiber and thread, the police want to take photographs, and so on. What the medical examiner must do when he first gets there is to make a determination of rigor mortis and livor mortis, body temperature, and other things of a visual nature, because it may be several hours before the body reaches the coroner's office, depending upon the length and scope of the on-scene investigation. After he has done these things without moving the body any more than he absolutely has to, he should stand back and make his visual inspections, letting the other people do what they have to do.

When the body is removed to the autopsy facility, the scientific investigation continues. The photographer begins to take his shots with all the layers of clothing being removed one by one. Next, the external examination is made. In a medical-legal autopsy the external examination may take a long period of time; it may take hours, depending upon the number of wounds and other external features of note. Every wound should be documented and measured carefully. If there is a cluster of obviously similar to identical wounds, they may be handled descriptively in a categorical sense. If they are asymmetrical, or if they are topographically removed one from the other, it is judicious to see to it that each one is properly identified.

Then the actual autopsy commences. Here, of course, it is a matter of assuring that a complete post-mortem study is done. As I have heard many people say, but perhaps said most eloquently by Dr. Milton Halpern, the Chief Medical Examiner of New York City: "There is something worse than not doing a medical legal autopsy, and that is having it done by somebody who is not trained, or having it done incompletely." Why? Because when you have not done it, you know you have not done it, and you know that you do not know the answer. When you have a one or two-page report, you think you know the answer. Non-medical people would have every right to believe that they know what the answer is.

It is a fascinating thing that in the smallest hospital and in a quite routine case, when a person dies from myocardial infarction, pneumonia, or pulmonary embolism (important only in terms of academic interest; of no medical or legal concern, civilly or criminally; not involving any property, nor the liberty or life of an individual), the hospital pathologist may do a twelve-page autopsy! He tells you the way every coronary artery bends, how wide the lumen is, and so on; everything is there. In a medical-legal autopsy, on the other hand, where a man's life is at stake, you get from the same hospital pathologist, called in by the elected lay coroner, only a page or a page and a half. The organs are not measured; the head is not opened; and everything is lumped together. There is blood in the chest cavity; but how much, and whether clotted or unclotted, the report does not say. It is absolutely fantastic! I testified in a medical malpractice case in New Jersey that involved an autopsy performed on a jockey who had been struck in the chest by a horse and subsequently died. I have seldom seen such an incomplete and sketchy autopsy report. Though it had been done by a "medical examiner," it was less than one page.

For a case in which no autopsy was done in an obvious medical-legal situation, we need go back only a few months to the Mary Jo Kopechne-Ted Kennedy situation. This is another example of where a medical examiner system did not necessarily prevent a poor decision from being made. I state this in order to be perfectly fair to coroners. There is nothing magical about the name "medical examiner"; it is rather what the system implies and, hopefully, what it goes on to implement and practice, as contrasted to the lay, politically-oriented coroner system.

The medical-legal autopsy must be done with great care because the examiner is not going to have another really good chance. Exhumation autopsies sometimes are necessary, but I assure you, having done about twenty-five or thirty of these, they are no pleasure. Forget the aesthetics of it; the point is that an exhumation autopsy can never be as revealing as the fresh case. There are some things that the examiner will never be able to learn again. You are lucky if the specific items that are under investigation are of a nature that can still be found later, for example, a fractured skull and a subdural hematoma. That is a good kind of case because a subdural hematoma. will remain for awhile, and the pathologist will be able to find evidence of it in an exhumation autopsy. Dr. Alan R. Moritz, former Professor of Legal Medicine at Harvard, now at Western Reserve University in Cleveland, had a case in Indiana in which he dug up a woman who had been dead for several years and was able to show that there had been a subdural hematoma. She had been autopsied and signed out as rheumatic heart disease, but no head examination had been done. Subsequently, there was a confession from a man, and indeed, there had been a homicide.

Of course, the number of similar cases is probably legend. If one could go to graveyards and just keep digging up bodies, he would be able to outdo Earle Stanley Gardner or Agatha Christie. What is lying in graveyards is enough to keep twenty-four novelists busy for the rest of their lives!

I should say at this point that in the autopsy room I welcome, of course, the homicide detectives. If somebody wants to come from the district attorney's office, he is also welcome. I would also welcome the defense attorney, if he has been retained at that point, and if he so requests. I do not put out calls to any of these people. The homicide detectives in our jurisdiction are almost always there for a part or all of the autopsy.

I feel that the defense attorney is entitled to information just as is the prosecution attorney. I do not consider our office to be an adjunct of the district attorney's office. I do not feel that what we find is available only to the prosecution; our autopsy report is available to the defense counsel and to the public defender's office for their study and perusal, also. Furthermore, if they want to talk to me about the case and my findings, to get an understanding of what some of the medical terms mean, and to understand the pathophysiological processes involved, I will do that with them, just as I would with the district attorney's office. Why should they have to go out and retain their own coroner, medical examiner, or forensic pathologist, from somewhere else? It is not that I am trying to save them money or be a nice guy. But what can an outside expert do for them that will equal having had an opportunity to speak to the person who did the autopsy?

I say this somewhat with tongue in cheek because there are any number of cases throughout the course of the year where I am involved in the opposite situation, reviewing hospital records where no autopsy was done in civil cases, reviewing autopsy records in civil and criminal cases where there is a question or dispute as to medical opinion, and so on. In these cases I do not have an opportunity to see the body, of course, and am always exposed to this criticism in the courtroom, particularly in the field of pathology. "Doctor, you didn't see the patient; you didn't treat the patient; you are not the attending doctor; and so on." Many attorneys like to be cute, and I have learned to expect this approach. But the stupidity and irony of such a collateral attack never fails to impress me. The guy who is a general practitioner is great because he graduated from medical school. Well, how about the pathologist, who in addition to an M.D. degree has taken from four or five years of residency in pathology, and who teaches these G.P.'s and other medical specialists? All the specialties of medicine and surgery rotate their residents through pathology as part of their training for a period of one to six months.

The autopsy is a matter of understanding what is involved and of having the entire case documented. Do not run the risk of destroying what is a good case by an incomplete and inadequate autopsy. For instance, the pathologist may fail to comment on some things that are seemingly irrelevant to the case, but which can destroy his credibility later on. If credibility is destroyed on three or four seemingly insignificant questions, then when it gets to the real gutty issues of the case, the jury has lost most, if not all, their respect for the examiner in his professional capacity. For instance, "Doctor, what was the appendix like?" The examiner looks at his report, finds no mention of the appendix, and says, "The appendix was o.k.; there was no problem." "Doctor, regarding gastric contents, what kind of food, if any, did you find there?" He sees no notation of gastric contents, so he says, "Well, it was a hundred c.c.'s of food. It looked like a few meat particles, string beans, and so on." "Did you notice if the prostate gland was enlarged?" Since it was a fifty-five-year-old man, an age when enlarged prostates are common, he says, "Yes, it was enlarged, there was some nodular hypertrophy," even though he failed to examine it. "Doctor, were there any stones in the gall bladder?" He looks and finds no mention of gall bladder. "Uh, no, there were no stones in the gall bladder. It was perfectly fine."

"Doctor, could you look at these records and tell me what they seem to be?" The pathologist is handed a bunch of hospital records—1955, 1961, 1967. They show an appendectomy in 1955, cholecystectomy in 1961, prostatectomy in 1967. "Doctor, I don't understand. How many appendixes does a man have? Didn't they really take out his gall bladder and prostate like the records indicate? Five witnesses have told us the victim hadn't eaten for 12 hours—where did the gastric contents come from?"

Medicine, to a significant measure, is still an art. Not everything in pathology is clear-cut, either. I wish that I could shrink each of you to Lilliputian size, put you in my pockets, and take you to a meeting of a national or state pathology society where slides have been sent around previously to pathologists. They have come there to review these slides of interesting cases that various pathologists have accumulated over the preceding several months or so. Frequently they are slides of tumors, regarding which decisions have already been made:

somebody's leg has been amputated, someone else has been getting deep cobalt therapy, a decision has been made not to operate on somebody because the tumor is benign, and so forth. At the meeting then, fifty to seventy-five Board-certified, experienced patholgists are watching a slide on the screen. One of them says, "Fibrosarcoma, amputate the leg." Another says, "It's only a benign nodular fasciitis with some atypical features; I would recommend that the surgeon observe it and do a repeat biopsy in 6 months." Another says something else. Then a vote is taken. There have been eight different diagnoses. Forty pathologists vote for benign; the other forty-five vote for malignant. In the meantime, of course, a decision has already been made, by the original pathologist.

There is nothing wrong with this. We are not gods or geniuses. I do not mean to say that this happens every day. I am saying, however, that in difficult cases it happens with some frequency. In pathology, fortunately, you can take a slide and have it seen and reviewed by various other pathologists in a matter of twenty-four to forty-eight hours. You can have it sent out of town to people who specialize in the field: the Armed Forces Institute of Pathology, and elsewhere. But you cannot do this with a frozen section, when the patient is lying on the table, and a decision has to be made as to whether or not a breast is going to be amputated. In most cases, however, one is able to wait and see.

What often happens in medical-legal autopsies is that the examiners, including those who are trained forensic pathologists, get sucked in by what seems to be the urgency of the situation. I can understand how the situation develops with the police occasionally. "Doc, we have this body. We're holding this guy. What do we do? What's the answer?" Sometimes we have to say, "We don't have the final scientific answer right now to tell you. You'll have to make the decision with the district attorney's office. It's not our business. But don't bring him over here to be arraigned." In Allegheny County, by law and tradition, all homicides-involuntary manslaughter to first degree—are arraigned before the coroner. But, obviously, we are not going to arraign somebody in a case that we have not called homicide. Fortunately, in most of these cases, the suspect is not going to flee to South America or to Europe; he will be around for a while. I do not think this is a big problem.

The much more serious problem is the forensic pathologist who feels that he must jump to a conclusion. For instance, in a hospital autopsy the brain will almost always be saved, and will be examined about seven to ten days later, after proper fixation. (The brain has the consistency of a well-done soft boiled egg. It is hard to get clear delineation of the brain in the fresh state, especially if you are looking for subtle pathology.) In many medical-legal autopsies, however, we frequently will cut the brain immediately. In many cases, it would be ideal to save the brain and study it a week or ten days later. But, since the pathologist may encounter problems with the funeral director, the police, and the family, he will frequently jump the gun. This is dangerous.

Perhaps of greater significance in terms of its statistical involvement is the fact that medical opinions may vary on the same set of pathological findings.

For instance, a man is punched in a barroom brawl; either he does not get up, or he gets up, goes back to drinking or playing pool, or goes home. Later, he collapses and dies. It can be death in a couple of minutes or it can be death a couple of days after an operation. In either case, in an autopsy what do you find? Rupture of an aneurysm, a so-called "berry aneurysm," a little balloon that can range from the size of a half of a tip of a finger to the size of a rather large grape, that has leaked or burst, resulting in subarachnoid bleeding, which leads to death before or after surgery.

Nobody will disagree that the aneurysm is there because it is apparent. It can be shown; there are photos of it. The pathologist may even have saved the brain. "Your opinion, Mr. Pathologist: did the brawl lead to a rupture of the aneurysm?" In some cases there may be evidence of blows to the head, which makes a decision easier; in others, however, there is no evidence from the autopsy of blows to the head or face.

Did the brawl lead to the rupture? It is a tough question. I will not go into this particular entity any further, except to say that every case, as far as I am concerned, must rest upon its own merits and circumstances. I could not make any blanket statement that would have universal application, because the most experienced and competent men will argue very vehemently among themselves in a specific case.

Consider all the big, notorious cases in which forensic pathologists have testified against each other. There are the two Coppolino trials, in New Jersey and Florida respectively. Drs. Joseph Spellman and Richard Ford, medical examiners of Philadelphia and Boston, respectively, testified for the defense; Dr. Milton Halpern testified for the prosecution. In the New Jersey case, the verdict was for the defense. There were other factors involved, but the major one, from the medical standpoint, was whether or not the fracture of the hyoid bone had been caused by ante-mortem strangulation, or whether it was caused by the grave digger's spade going through the collapsed casket, or the casket itself collapsing on the man's neck? No autopsy had been done on the alleged victim in that case, another illustration of what I have mentioned earlier.

In Florida, in the second case, no autopsy had been done on Mrs. Coppolino, a physician in her early 30's; she had been signed out as having some kind of heart disease. The exhumation autopsy, at least as far as Dr. Halpern was concerned, revealed a puncture mark in the buttocks suggestive of a needle track mark. The toxicological examination, done over a period of some six months thereafter by Dr. Joseph Umberger, the chief toxicologist in the New York Medical Examiner's Office, revealed the degradation products of succinyl choline, which is an anesthetic agent pharmacologically similar to curare, the poison used by South American Indians for paralysis of the respiratory muscles. In the Florida trial, there was a whole array of physicians on both sides, outstanding men in pathology, toxicology, clinical pharmacology, and anesthesiology. One could go either way, depending upon whose views he hears.

All of us should be aware, that there are sometimes little feuds going on that could have direct relevance to our cases. You may want to keep it in mind for purposes of determining where you can get an expert witness. I personally welcome a defense attorney in Allegheny County going elsewhere for an opinion. Although the attorneys know that I will testify only as to the facts and try not to have any bias toward either side, there are cases where they want different views.

I recall one case that covers all the things I have talked about: cause and manner of death, time and place of death, and so on. An American G.I. met a German girl in Italy. They became engaged, and he brought her to the United States for their pending marriage. They had some difficulty, however. She lived in his home with his parents and family, and they had arguments quite frequently. One night she left in a huff, walked out at eleven-thirty at night, and was never seen again. Some days later, charred remains of a human body were found on a garbage dump. The part of the dump where the remains were found looked like a funeral pyre made of rubber tires. Was this the same girl? We were able to get determinations of range of age, sex, race and size from the long bones; there were no soft tissues left. Her teeth provided the final bit of identification.

What was the cause of death? How could we find out? There were no fractures. The young fellow who was charged with the murder claimed that he had struck this girl accidentally with an automobile while driving home one night, that he had dragged her to his old, dilapidated, filthy farm house, where he lived alone. He said that he was scared and did not want to report it to the police because he had a criminal record five years before. (This young man at the age of nineteen had attacked his father and mother with a gun and axe, respectively. The parents had survived, and charges were dropped.) He said he tried to revive the girl but failed. When she was obviously dead, he placed her on the dump.

We had photos of the girl lying nude on the floor, which he had taken at his place, and which the police were able to get, fortunately. The question was, could I tell anything from the photos about life or death, about rigor mortis or livor mortis, from facial expression, skin turgor, and so forth?

What about the cause of death? We were able to get some bone marrow from the iliac crest, the only moist marrow remaining, and found that there was a carbon monoxide level of approximately forty percent. We pieced all these findings together, and arrived at the conclusion that this girl had been burned alive. She had been wrapped in a tarpaulin that permitted the smoke to come in; that is why she had inhaled the carbon monoxide fumes before the body was burned.

Because there were unique features in this case, I strongly recommended to the defense attorneys that they go elsewhere, and they did. They went to New York and to Washington, to the Armed Forces Institute of Pathology. They satisfied themselves that the pathological findings were reasonable, and that there would not be any solid way to attack our conclusions. There was a conviction for murder in the first degree.

I truly feel that cases have a right to be reviewed, and that the people involved should not be insulted. Furthermore, you have an obligation and duty in a case of alleged homicide, where there are vital questions to be answered, to see to it that you get other opinions.

Consider for a moment the recent Kavanaugh murder trial in New Jersey. It has to go down as one of the most blatantly insulting cases that the criminal law courts in this country have ever witnessed. If you did not read the article in *Look Magazine* about this trial, I urge you to find it. You will not believe it, but I am not aware of anyone suing *Look Magazine* for libel. In that case, there were two murder trials, and the unbelievable *persecution* of a few people by several individuals who had assumed major roles in law enforcement activities there. You all know what has been going on in New Jersey, I am sure. I do not think that there is any state that ever came closer to being taken over by organized crime, from the top all the way down. In the Kavanaugh case, the attorneys knew enough to go out and get other opinions. Lee Bailey got into trouble during the case because, when he learned what was going on, he called a news conference and blasted the prosecuting attorney and police. One might argue his approach from the standpoint of legal ethics, but I assure you that from the standpoint of substance and validity of his remarks, there is no question about what he said being true.

The Kavanaugh case also contained an interesting, nonmedical, criminal law issue regarding questioned documents. The newspaper publisher who was accused of the crime claimed that he was in Chicago, and that he had signed a hotel register on the night of the murder. The prosecution hired a questioned document expert from New York, one of the outstanding in the country. He checked the hotel register, and said, "Yes, this is his signature." If it was the defendant's signature, then there was no question that he was in Chicago when the murder of the young married woman, Mrs. Kavanaugh, had occurred. Amazingly, the prosecution, in the first murder trial, did not call their own expert, and in fact, failed to tell anybody about his report. Lee Bailey found out about it later, and the expert's testimony was admitted in the second trial. This is the kind of thing that still goes on occasionally in this country. It should never happen, but somehow it does.

After the autopsy and the report have been completed, I feel that there should be a pre-trial conference. In a $1200 whiplash case, the attorneys will get on the phone and arrange everything with the doctor. "Doctor, I've just got to see you. I can't possibly call you into court without a conference. I'll come to your office. I'll see you at midnight tonight when you're through with your patients. I'll see you at eight o'clock on Sunday before you go golfing. But, Doctor, I've just got to see you before the trial." But it is a different matter when you have a murder case and you are the assistant D.A. or the assistant public defender. In a murder case, a man may go to jail for the rest of his life. And yet, in most jurisdictions, the D.A., the public defender, and the private defense attorney are not interested in talking to anybody. They may not even see the autopsy report until the trial commences! The judge has never seen it; the D.A. has never seen it. They are all hearing it from the medical examiner for the first time. They start asking him questions, and then are amazed at some of the answers. The pathologist finds himself being treated almost as if on cross-examination by the district attorney, because the D.A. never bothered to prepare himself.

Pre-trial conferences are very important in these cases, and I am sure that you can have them, along with pre-trial discovery. If we have things in our office that we have saved, tissues, clothing, and so on, the attorneys and their experts are entitled to see them. We do not give out reports that are submitted to us by other offices. I cannot give out a homicide detective report or a crime lab report; that is their decision to make. Things that emanate from our office, however, including our toxicological findings and so on, are available.

Some medical examiners hide behind the statement, "Well, we're not allowed to give out reports without the district attorney's or the court's approval." I have some idea of medical-legal autopsy laws in this country since I was senior author of a book some years ago entitled *Medico-Legal Autopsy Laws of the Fifty States*. I know of very few states, if any, in which the laws prohibit reports being given to anybody but the district attorney. In most cases it is a matter of blindly following what somebody has said in the past, which everyone else has gone to interpret as being the law. I say that an elected coroner makes his own "laws" and regulations to a great extent, as is the case with most medical examiners. In these cases, the rules must be in accordance with proper criminal justice in the year 1970. These are not games we are playing; these are not Perry Mason television shows where a witness is going to appear at the last minute to save the defense.

People want to have an understanding of causal relationship, and the forensic pathologist should be prepared to give it to them. Several cases are illustrative of what I mean. One involves a woman who was found badly mutilated. The breast had been amputated. Marks on the breast proved to be very important later on because we had to determine which of them were teeth marks, if any, and which were wounds from a knife, and what kind of knife. The man who reported finding the body to the police claimed that this woman, who lived as a recluse, had been discovered by him, and that he had seen three men running from the house in the middle of the night but had not paid any attention to them. When he went over in the morning to ask the lady if she wanted anything from the store, he found her. The police interrogated him preliminarily, and he was released. The investigation went on for a couple of weeks. Finally, we were able to be of assistance to the police with certain findings regarding the times at which the different wounds were inflicted and how burns on the body came about. We felt that the burns were from candles, placed there for the very bizarre, macabre amputation of different parts of the body. We also were able to make recommendations to the police about trying to get teeth imprints from the suspect, and some impressions of the different kinds of cutting instruments. Putting all this together, going over things with the suspect again, and then finding the obviously contradictory statements and remarks made by him, they were able to come up with a very strong case indeed. He finally confessed to having murdered the woman. This is the kind of case in which the crime laboratory and the pathology department played important roles, but the police had to do a lot of work themselves. It is often a matter of joint effort.

In another case, a young girl, a nineteen-year-old beautician, was found dead in her apartment early one morning. A plastic garment and part of a slip were present around her neck, along with an electrical cord. There were marks on her neck that we felt were due, in part, to human bites. Protruding from the vagina was the base of a ceramic statue that was removed at autopsy; it was a statue of the Virgin Mary. Here, of course, the usual determinations about the cause and time of death had to be made. Could we do anything in the way of helping the police consider what kind of crime this might have been, the nature of the assailant, and so on? What kind of "message" was being left by the assailant in jamming a statue of the Virgin Mary into the girl's vagina? These are the kinds of cases in which a forensic pathologist can, and should, share his thoughts with the police officers for the purpose of investigation. It helped a great deal in this case in finding out what had happened.

An apparently similar case was that of a twenty-seven-year-old Negro woman found in her apartment on her living room floor in a supine position, legs spread. Again, something was protruding from her vagina. There was some blood on a piece of newspaper, and also on a pillow case which was along one side of her head. It appeared to be a classical case of homicide. The nine-year-old daughter, who lived with her mother, said that there had been a man there; she even had an idea who he was. The police apprehended the man. In the meantime we were doing the autopsy and found spermatozoa in the vagina. There had definitely been recent sexual intercourse.

The man stated that he had been there, that they had had intercourse, but he insisted that when he left she was in good health. Nobody was buying that story, and it certainly seemed that this was a murder. When we finished the autopsy, however, we had not found the cause of death. This woman had not been strangled nor beaten; there was nothing to explain why she had died. We then did what we always do in cases of sudden unexpected death in Negroes, a sickle-cell preparation. We found that, indeed, she had sickle-cell disease. Then the microscopic slides revealed that she had sickle-cell disease. Then the microscopic slides revealed that she also had a viral pneumonitis and viral myocarditis, which can cause sudden death.

The ornamental top of a wine decanter was removed from her vagina, and the vagina showed no injuries. This thing had been deliberately inserted, but there were no injuries to the vagina at all, contrary to the previous case in which something had been shoved forcefully into the girl's vagina.

With additional investigation it all pieced together. This woman was a nymphomaniac. In the words of her boy friend: "She was never satisfied." When he left her, she was very unhappy, because she wanted to have more of the same activity. He had left because he had had enough. When he left, this woman had apparently masturbated with the wine decanter top. She went on to die as a result of natural disease processes. The masturbation and the intercourse had been purely coincidental.

This was an example where thorough on-scene investigation followed by good scientific studies helped solve a very complex case. Had there not been a fully trained forensic pathologist present, this case would have been signed out as strangulation or suffocation. I am positive of it, because they would have gone on the basis of circumstances rather than scientific, objective findings.

I call your attention to the next case because many of you, including experienced law enforcement officers, physicians, attorneys and even pathologists, probably have had no experience with this type of death. It is appropriate in a criminal law discussion simply because it has often been confused with murder. It is involved in the civil law because the question of suicide versus accidental death arises in the context of insurance policy claims and double indemnity clauses.

The deceased was a rather high-ranking executive in one of the large international corporations in Pittsburgh. He did not appear at work one day, so they telephoned for him, but received no answer. His son was the last one to see him; his wife, a registered nurse, had left for work early. The girl and boy, high school students, had left for school while their father was finishing his breakfast. When they came home, they found him in a bathroom in the basement. A black hood was over his head, a rope was around his neck, and a chain was around his waist. There was a mirror on top of the commode, which the man was facing. He had handcuffs on his wrists, and handcuffs around his ankles. The black hood around his face covered his mouth and part of his neck. Certainly it would not have been at all unreasonable for a police officer to conclude that this was a gangland type of slaying. He had obviously been knocked off by someone that knew what he was doing and wanted to make sure that the victim was dead. Ejaculation had occurred during the agonal moments.

This was not murder or suicide. It is a good example of what we call autocrotic accidental death. These people (always men) play all kinds of games. There is almost always some kind of trussing, and something around the neck to make sure no mark is made. Unfortunately, what happens is that they have a vagal reflex, probably because of pressure on the neck; unconsciousness ensues and they die. What they are attempting to do is get increased sexual kicks. They do this by inducing a state of cerebral anoxia (diminished blood flow to the brain). This, in a physiological and psychological sense, apparently increases the libidinal feelings.

We know that neck pressure to induce cerebral anoxia is practiced in various oriental societies; it is common for partners during the act of intercourse to touch each other's throats and to squeeze. We know there are similar games that little Eskimo kids play. They will truss themselves up by the neck and hang; then their friends will come over and release them.

Many of these cases involve transvestism; a lot of them have beautiful feminine attire. We had a case involving the most fantastic set of brand new woman's clothing—beautiful miniskirt, knee-high, black leather boots, panties, bra, and so forth—which were on a male student who was found hanged. It had been written off as a suicide originally. We asked the police to go back to the scene, and they found numerous ropes, belts, and an entire drawer of additional woman's clothing! Subsequent investigation revealed that the student was a loner, who, on the pretext of wanting to study alone, would stay in his apartment and engage in autoerotic activity.

Finally, I should like to discuss a tragic case of a seventeen-year-old high school senior who was found nude except for her boots and socks, lying in a spread-eagle position behind a billboard in a Pennsylvania town. She had gone to a party, and then left, supposedly heading for a boyfriend's house. There were wounds on the fingers recognizable as classical defensive cutting wounds sustained when one tries to protect oneself from a cutting instrument. This was a very important observation in this case.

A small amount of blood was present around the lower pelvis; it was caused by cutting instruments having been placed in the vagina, and having gone through the vaginal wall into the uterine cavity and the peritoneum. Spermatozoa were found in the vagina. The wound which killed her was at the back of the head—a very deep cut with extensive fracturing of the skull. A rock was found at the scene with blood stains on it.

In this case the question of time of death was very important, particularly for the boy whose house she was allegedly going to. As it turned out, this boy could be exonerated on the basis of the scientific findings, as well as on the basis of the police investigation. With some of the material that we were able to give them, plus further evidence that the crime lab was able to supply, the police came up with a fifteen-year-old boy who lived in the area. He had seen the girl walking by herself and decided he was going to steal her purse. Then he decided that he was going to attack her. He claimed that in the struggle she fell, struck her head, and became unconscious. He said that any other wounds on the body were caused by abrasions on the rough terrain.

This is the kind of a case where a forensic pathologist can clearly show that the wounds were caused by a cutting instrument. They were incised wounds. The wounds on the hands were classical defense wounds; the wounds in the vagina could not have come from a penetrating penis, even if the girl had been a virgin. The latter were incised wounds that penetrated deeply up through the vaginal wall. The wounds of the skull did not come from somebody falling backward a couple of feet, but rather from a heavy blow caused by something like a rock. In this case we felt we had the rock in question and proved it by finding microscopic tissue fragments as well as blood on the rock. These are the ways in which a forensic pathologist can help.

In closing, the pathologist's findings sometimes aid the prosecution; other times, they aid the defense. I think that everyone would be satisfied either way, so long as he knows that the medical opinions and conclusions that are being offered to determine innocence or guilt have been arrived at in a scientific and objective fashion, and that nobody is hiding anything or deceiving anyone else.

V

DRUGS
AND
ALCOHOL

V. DRUGS AND ALCOHOL

INTRODUCTION

Drugs and alcohol have been difficult problems of our contemporary society, for the use of these habit-forming and intoxicating substances have had medical, social, economic and legal consequences, involving both the criminal and civil law systems.

Much has been written about the etiology and the recent expansion of the "drug culture." For at least a decade drugs have overshadowed alcohol as a problem in both public and professional awareness. However, during this time alcoholism has become a growing and serious problem. With the development of new tranquilizers, energizers and other stimulants, additional problems have appeared concerning abuse, overuse, habituation, and addiction.

In the public and legal response to drugs one difficulty has been the lack of knowledge and proper differentiation regarding the toxic effects of different substances. As a result—especially in connection with cannabis—a great deal of confusion has arisen on how to handle the problem, legally as well as medically and socially. Originally, the law, by and large, had classified and treated marijuana as a narcotic. When the non-addictive qualities of cannabis were recognized in both the mass media and public debate, the credibility of the old rigid and oppressive laws was much shaken. The movement to abolish all legal regulations gained many adherents. Yet recently, controlled scientific data suggest that cannabis derivatives are not benign compunds. At the very least they may be as harmful and devastating as alcohol. The materials selected for this section are intended to deal with the medical aspects of cannabis and to denote the resultant social problems and legal implications.

The medical management of drug users and alcoholics has suffered from the particular attitude of physicians towards these kinds of "patients." Pervasive throughout the medical response has been a sense of inadequacy and resignation which affects physicians, patients, and their families. A physician is frustrated because he knows very little about the pharmacology, toxicology and treatment of addiction or the less addictive uses of mind-altering substances. Furthermore, a physician usually possesses only a layman's understanding of the socio-psychological forces underlying the resort to artificial euphoria and, more importantly, absolutely lacks control over those forces, whether in a general social setting or in the case of a particular patient.

The criminal law system is in equal disarray in regard to its philosophy, control, and management of the alcoholic and drug addict. Medicine seems unable to provide adequate social controls over drugs and alcohol, and the law seems equally inadequate in terms of either costs or effectiveness.

The articles in this section were selected to give the reader an understanding of man's dependence upon chemical mind-altering materials, and of the medical and legal considerations for the effective social control of such materials.

CANNABIS:
A FORENSIC-MEDICAL REVIEW

John J. Cohrssen
Carl M. Lieberman

No doubt some controls on the sale and possession of dangerous substances are mandatory for the health and safety of the individual and the community. Indeed, for controlling illicit supplies of dangerous substances and for deterring individual abuses, there is no alternative to the criminal law and its sanctions. But the array of substances requiring control is so immense that the task of designating them by law is difficult. In addition, appropriate legal designation is difficult because the health or social danger of any one drug depends not only upon the pharmacodynamics of the particular substance, but also upon who is using it and the circumstances of use. Criminal sanctions for the abusive use of drugs should not be more onerous than the dangers associated with such abuse. Accordingly, an inflexible code of repressive penalties will not yield the optimum control of the illegal use of a particular drug, at a particular time and place, by a certain individual.

Marijuana legislation was enacted in the 1930's(1) because of dangers attributed to its non-medical use.(2) Since then, experience has taught us two lessons. First, we were mistaken in our assessment of the dangers inherent in marijuana use, and secondly, excessive legal penalties are not an effective deterrent to expanding substance abuse. Marijuana is treated by federal law and by most state laws the same as the opiate narcotics,(3) despite the fact that it is not a narcotic. Even though the most satisfactory definition restricts narcotics to opium, its derivatives, and synthetic analogs,(4) narcotics statutes often control a number of drugs (marijuana, cocaine, peyote) dissimilar in structure and pharmacologic action.(5) The abuse of marijuana offers a special challenge because the substance is widely used and control of individual use is most frequently attempted by statutes making simple possession a crime.(6) These statutes are almost unenforceable because complainants or reporting witnesses are invariably lacking. Thus, enforcement officials must rely on informants and surveillance techniques.

An effective control system must provide a punishment commensurate with the crime, a punishment which will deter new crimes, and, most importantly, a device which will encourage the drug users to become socially-productive members of the community. Future legislative controls should carefully avoid the system which we have already found inadequate in the control of marijuana. Harsh and restrictive penalties for possession, sale, and distribution have been ineffective in curbing marijuana experimentation and abuse, and have been even less effective in converting convicted users into useful, achieving members of society.

A MEDICAL DESCRIPTION OF THE EFFECTS OF MARIJUANA

Although Indian hemp, *Cannabis sativa*, was grown in Virginia as early as 1611, the colonists did not indulge in smoking hemp for intoxication.(7) Such indulgence occurred much later, when soldiers, while stationed in the Canal Zone (1916) and in Mexico (1911), were introduced to the inebriating potential of marijuana.(8) The first reports of marijuana use in the United States date to a series of sensational newspaper exposes in the New Orleans press (1926). The articles focused on the use of marijuana by Negroes, its dissemination to young school children by criminal elements, and the commission of several violent crimes by users allegedly deranged by the drug.(9) Today's wave of public concern over illicit marijuana use can be dated to 1963 reports of increased use by university students.(10) Today, the use of marijuana by college and high school students, and even grade school children, has been documented. The hippie subculture has popularized a way of life which, among other aspects, centers on the use of psychoactive drugs. The number of non-narcotic drug abusers, including those dependent upon barbiturates, amphetamines, hallucinogens, and the minor tranquillizers, has never been precisely determined. Survey data suggests that in the United States at least eight to twelve million Americans have experimented with the various preparations of *Cannabis sativa* – mainly the commonly available marijuana, and the more expensive hashish.(11) On a worldwide basis, it is estimated that over 200 million individuals have tried marijuana.(12) Indeed, next to alcohol, it is the second most popular intoxicant in the world.

Cannabis sativa is a hardy weed which can grow to a height of fifteen to eighteen feet. Hashish or "hash" is a golden yellow, sticky resin which is collected from the leaves of cultivated plants. It is five to eight times as potent(13) as marijuana, which consists of the flowering tops, leaves, and stems of unfertilized, non-cultivated plants. Chemical analysis has yielded over thirty cannabinoids, of which delta-8 and delta-9 trans-tetrahydro-cannabinol (known as THC) account for the psychoactive potential of both marijuana and hashish in man.(14) The quantitative content of THC depends upon soil, temperature, and other climatic conditions, with plants grown in sunny, dry zones yielding the highest content of THC.(15) Recently, THC has been prepared synthetically.(16) The procedure, however, is difficult and precludes extensive clandestine efforts at mass production. The illicit THC sold on the streets has been found to consist of mescaline or phencyclidine — both potent hallucinogens.(17)

In this country, the most common form of usage is by smoking, and a deep sustained inhalation is essential for the THC to diffuse across the pulmonary capillaries. The experienced user may become intoxicated with a single puff of a high quality "joint," while inexperienced novices may be unable to "turn on" with large doses of marijuana because of poor smoking technique. Marijuana is less frequently swallowed, but hashish has been a favorite ingredient of many recipes. Case reports of the sequelae of the intravenous injection of marijuana and hashish are rare, and a definitive statement of the effects of such usage cannot be made.(18)

The onset of action after smoking is within ten to twenty minutes, and the effects may persist for three hours.(19) Smokers may maintain the intoxicated state by intermittently inhaling additional material. With repeated administration, tolerance to marijuana does not develop, and cross-tolerance to LSD, mescaline, and other hallucinogens has not been demonstrated.(20) In addition, withdrawal symptoms are not observed.(21) Thus, marijuana and hashish do not have the addictive potential of the opiate narcotics (morphine, heroin, demerol, dilaudid, codeine) in humans.

The psychic effects generally begin with a feeling of relaxation and detachment. Audiovisual sensations are intensified, with color perception often the most affected.(22) Illusions are common, while hallucinations are rare. Time perception is altered, usually manifested by a slowing of subjective time.(23) Emotions are loosened, with euphoria being more common than dysphoria. Some people experience drowsiness and feelings of hunger, while others feel unable to communicate properly. The latter may result from a combination of slowed, halting speech and a defect in the ability to retrieve information from immediate memory banks.(24) The individual is often passive and withdrawn. However, as with all disinhibiting agents, he might behave in an unrestrained emotional manner. While marijuana does not possess aphrodisiac properties,(25) the prolongation of subjective time may alter the perception of an erotic experience.

The most frequent physical effect of marijuana is a conjunctival hyperemia (red eye).(26) This is not due to an irritative smoke effect because it also occurs when THC is swallowed. Pupil size remains unchanged.(27) While an increase in heart rate is regularly noted, blood pressure, respiratory rate, blood sugar, and body temperature do not change significantly.(28) Nausea, a dry mouth from decreased salivation, and a cough from the irritant effects of the smoke are often mentioned.(29) Only some preliminary work on the cytogenetic effects of marijuana has been completed. It is, however, known to cross the placental barrier.(30) No carcinogenic activity has been attributed to marijuana.

The complications of acute marijuana intoxication are infrequent, and usually consist of anxiety or paranoid states.(21) Any individual, especially a novice, may become confused about the changes that he is experiencing. The loss of ego-controls can result in delusional thinking, usually of a suspicious, paranoid nature. Misinterpretation of environmental cues can lead to a partial or complete belief in the paranoid scheme; the patient may panic and injure himself or others. Spontaneous recurrences of the marijuana state ("flashbacks") have also been described.(32)

An absence of controlled research in the United States into the pharmacologic and social consequences of marijuana use has prompted some to extrapolate data obtained in foreign settings to the American scene. A review of the international literature reveals evidence of cannabis psychoses, loss of mental acuity, reduced energy, and social effectiveness.(33) However, the formulation of cross-cultural comparisons may be invalid because of the unsystematic description of the demographic characteristics of the samples, the obvious biases of institutionally selected samples (criminals or mental hospital patients), lack of standardization of mental health diagnoses, and a general lack of research sophistication among the observers. In addition, much of the marijuana used in the United States is of much lower potency than the drug used in these foreign studies. The National Institute of Mental Health is negotiating with certain countries where marijuana use is endemic to evaluate more rigorously the long-term effects of chronic use. Further research is needed to elucidate both the short- and long-term physical and psychic effects of marijuana use. At present, the absence of valid scientific data should not lead to the assumption that long-term indulgence is harmless. As in the case of tobacco and alcohol, it is possible that from chronic use there are serious sequelae which will only become apparent through careful, longitudinal studies.

A question that frequently arises concerns the extent to which marijuana use predisposes use of stronger hallucinogens or heroin. By necessity, the evidence for a progression from marijuana to heroin must rely on retrospective investigations of heroin users. According to the British Advisory Committee on Drug Dependence (1968):

> It can clearly be argued on the world picture that cannabis use does not lead to heroin addiction — a number of isolated studies have been published, none of which demonstrates significant lines of progression (from cannabis to heroin) ... and we have concluded that a risk of progression to heroin from cannabis is not a reason for retaining control of this drug.(34)

Thus far, the American experience indicates that only a small number of regular users of marijuana will try heroin. The fact that a person has tried marijuana on one or more occasions, and then has used more dangerous substances later, does not define a cause-effect relationship.

At the time of the passage of the 1937 Marijuana Tax Act,(35) it was declared that marijuana use leads directly to violence, crime, and insanity.(36) No evidence to counter the crime-insanity hypothesis was offered at that time. Later, the Medical Society of the County of New York flatly stated that there was no evidence that marijuana use is associated with crime or violence in this country.(37) The British Advisory Committee Report of 1968 concluded: "The evidence of a link with violent crime is far stronger with alcohol than with the smoking of cannabis. . . . [I]n the United Kingdom the taking of cannabis has not so far been regarded, even by the severest critics, as a direct cause of serious crime."(38) Perhaps the most unbiased observation is that of the 1967 President's Commission on Law Enforcement and Administration of Justice, which reported that marijuana "might, but certainly will not necessarily or inevitably, lead to aggressive behavior or crime. The response will depend more on the individual than the drug. This hypothesis is consistent with the evidence that marijuana may release but does not alter basic personality structure."(39)

REVIEW OF THE HISTORY OF MARIJUANA LEGISLATION

In January 1929, the same legislation that established two federal narcotics farms included Indian hemp and peyote in its definition of habit-forming or narcotic drugs.(40) "This was the first time that these substances had been included as narcotics under Federal laws dealing with the subject."(41) For reasons unknown, nowhere in the committee hearings or in the *Congressional Record* was there any discussion of the rationale for this categorization, nor are peyote and Indian hemp mentioned in the hearings or the *Record*.(42) Only addiction to opiates is mentioned, and until 1965, peyote was not subject to other federal control.(43)

In 1932, the National Conference of Commissioners on Uniform State Laws proposed the Uniform Narcotic Drug Act, which contained optional provisions extending a state plan of narcotics control to cannabis.(44) Within a few years, many states adopted the Uniform Act,(45) thereby classifying marijuana within the legal definition of a narcotic. A lack of general interest in marijuana at that time is indicated by the fact that passage of the Act went unnoticed by the public — at least there appears to have been no newspaper publicity.(46) Once enforcement of the Act began, the usage of marijuana received extensive popular attention. Enforcement officials occasionally reported seizing large quantities of marijuana.(47) Meanwhile, with its actual intoxicant effects substantially unknown, the alleged effects of marijuana were utilized for the self-serving purposes of users and nonusers alike. According to one reporter, "users painted a bad picture of dependency on cannabis to escape punishment or receive a discharge from the army. In fact, some persons caught . . . committing crimes of violence attempted pleas of insanity due to the influence of marijuana.(48) Nonusing writers or enforcers tended to paint a fearful picture of the habitual user as a violent criminal. It is possible that "[t]he often repeated wildfire spread of reefer smoking in the mid-1930's is . . . an artifact of new state laws. There had been no records of marijuana usage until legislation was passed in the

1930's.(49)

By 1937, it was believed that marijuana presented a health danger so severe that federal controls were necessary to curb its dissemination and use.(50) Thus, the Marijuana Tax Act was enacted.(51) In congressional hearings, it was stated that all forty-eight states already controlled sale, and forty-four controlled possession, but the substance was believed to be so dangerous that state officials clamored for federal control.(52)

The purpose of federal legislation, as stated in both the House and the Senate committee reports, was to discourage the widespread use of a drug thought to be related to a variety of evils:

> Under the influence of this drug, the will is destroyed and all power of directing and controlling thought is lost. Inhibitions are released. As a result of these effects, many violent crimes have been and are being committed by persons under the influence of the drug. Not only is marijuana used by hardened criminals to steel themselves to commit violent crimes, but it is also being placed in the hands of school children in the form of marijuana cigarettes by unscrupulous peddlers. Cases were cited at the hearings of school children who have been driven to crime and insanity through the use of this drug. Its continued use results many times in impotency and insanity.(53)

Almost all of the testimony exposing the toxic effects of the drug was presented by officials from the Federal Bureau of Narcotics. It was reported that use of marijuana could carry effects lasting up to forty-eight hours,(54) could lead to commission of violent crimes,(55) and, in some cases, could cause insanity.(56) "I believe in some cases one [marijuana] cigarette might develop a homocidal mania, probably to kill his brother," was the response to a question on dosage toxicity.(57) It is interesting to note that in contrast to views expressed in the 1950's, the conclusion was strongly stated at these hearings that marijuana use does not lead to the use of narcotics.(58)

> Mr. Dingell: I am just wondering whether the marijuana addict graduates into a heroin, an opium, or a cocaine user.
>
> Mr. Anslinger: No sir; I have not heard of a case of that kind. I think it is an entirely different class. The marijuana addict does not go in that direction.(59)

The only opposition to the bill came from the small industry of hemp fibre growers and birdseed manufacturers who would be adversely affected by it,(60) and from Dr. William C. Woodward, a representative of the American Medical Association. He did not oppose control of marijuana by its inclusion in the Harrison Narcotic Act.(61) Rather, he was concerned that a new control statute would impose an unnecessary burden of additional paper work on physicians, pharmacists, and ancillary personnel.(62) Also opposed was the proscription of marijuana for medical purposes, since the therapeutic potential of the drug had not been completely evaluated.(63)

The Marijuana Tax Act provided maximum penalties of five years imprisonment *or* a fine of not more than $2,000 for illegal transfer or possession. Enacted as a revenue statute, the Act imposed a tax of approximately one dollar per ounce of marijuana on buyers, sellers, importers, growers, physicians, and other persons who dealt in marijuana commercially, prescribed it professionally, or possessed it.(64) However, the Act's enforcement mechanisms made any legal use cumbersome, and thus precluded intensive research by the scientific community.(65)

During the late 1940's, there was growing concern about the spread of narcotic addiction and the abuse of barbiturates. At hearings held in 1951 by Hale Boggs, Chairman of the Subcommittee of the Committee on Ways and Means, drug abuse violators were viewed as chronic recidivists; accordingly, the weaknesses of narcotics-marijuana laws were perceived as stemming from the absence of minimum penalties and some abuse of judicial discretion.(66) Testimony was heard indicating that federal judges were not always giving heavy sentences.(67) The remedy proposed was to amend the Marijuana Tax Act so as to impose long, mandatory sentences after first offenses.(68)

At the 1951 hearings, there was no testimony on health dangers from marijuana use. Rather, the stepping-stone theory was emphasized. In response to Congressman Boggs' observation that "only a small percentage of those marijuana cases was anything more than a temporary degree of exhiliration," Commissioner Anslinger of the Federal Bureau of Narcotics replied, "The danger is this: Over 50 percent of those young [narcotic] addicts started on marijuana smoking. They started there and graduated to heroin; they took the needle when the thrill of marijuana was gone."(69)

On the floor of the House, there was only a limited debate of the amendments imposing mandatory sentencing.(70) Representatives Doughton (North Carolina), Celler (New York), and Simpson (Pennsylvania) opposed the harshness of the new penalties.(71) However, there was no debate in the Senate,(72) and its Committee on Finance reported favorably on the House bill.(73) Although the bill increased the penalties for marijuana offenses, along with those for narcotics offenses, the only mention of marijuana in the Senate Committee report was a statement recommending that penalties take into account the rate of recidivism in marijuana and narcotics violators.(74)

The 1951 Act became known as the Boggs Amendment. It substituted for the old maximum sentence of five years imprisonment or a $2,000 fine the following penalty structure:

First offense: not less than two years nor more than five years.
Second offense: not less than five years nor more than ten years, with probation and suspension excluded.
Subsequent offenses: not less than ten years nor more than twenty years with probation and suspension excluded.(75)

After the passage of the Boggs Amendment, drug trafficking continued to be of great concern to the Congress. Committees in both houses conducted extensive hearings across the country to determine the extent of illicit drug traffic and the need for additional regulatory legislation.(76) It was felt that the Boggs Amendment had stemmed the rising tide of narcotics traffic and narcotic addiction, but that more stringent traffic control was still necessary. Consequently, the Narcotic Control Act of 1956(77) again raised the penalties for marijuana offenses to make them commensurate with those of hard narcotics. Marijuana was so treated mainly because it was believed to be a precursor of hard narcotics usage, and an agent which predisposed the user to commit violent crimes.(78) The dangers perceived were described in the Senate hearings:

> *Senator Daniel.* Now, do I understand it from you that, while we are discussing marijuana, the real danger there is that the use of marijuana leads many people eventually to the use of heroin, and the drugs that do cause them complete addiction; is that true?
>
> *Mr. Anslinger.* That is the great problem and our great concern about the use of marijuana, that eventually if used over a long period, it does lead to heroin addiction. The marijuana habit, it is a habit-forming drug as distinguished from an addiction-forming drug, is relatively easy to break. You can break the marijuana habit probably in a day. But when you get to becoming a heroin user, that is a different story. . . .
>
> *Senator Daniel.* As I understand it from having read your book, an habitual user of marijuana or even a user to a small extent presents a problem to the community, and is a bad thing. Marijuana can cause a person to commit crimes and do many heinous things; is that not correct?
>
> *Mr. Anslinger.* That is correct. It is a dangerous drug, and is so regarded all over the world. . . .
>
> . . . .
>
> *Senator Welker.* Mr. Commissioner, my concluding question with respect to marijuana: Is it or is it not a fact that the marijuana user has been responsible for many of our most sadistic, terrible crimes in this Nation, such as sex slayings, sadistic slayings, and matters of that kind?
>
> *Mr. Anslinger.* There have been instances of that, Senator. We have had some rather tragic occurrences by users of marijuana. It does not follow that all crimes can be traced to marijuana. There have been many brutal crimes traced to marijuana, but I would not say that it is the controlling factor in the commission of crimes.(79)

Dr. G. Halsey Hunt, Assistant Surgeon General, also testified at the hearings. But his comments showed lack of great concern about the danger of marijuana and were not folowed by any questioning.(80) The new penalties under the Narcotic Control Act of 1956 were as follows:

> First possession: Not less than two years nor more than ten years, with probation and parole permitted.
>
> Second possession or first sale: Not less than five years nor more than twenty

years, with no probation, suspension, or parole.

Third possession or second sale and subsequent offenses: Not less than ten years nor more than forty years, with no probation, suspension, or parole.(81)

This basic penalty structure, which carries the possibility of a $20,000 fine, obtains today, but a 1966 amendment permits parole of marijuana offenders after they have served at least one-third of their sentences.(82)

In 1961, the Interdepartmental Committee on Narcotics reported to the President that the more stringent penalties enacted in 1956 were showing a recognizable impact.(83) The Committee made many recommendations for expanded medical treatment of the heroin addict, and for programs to provide education and training. The Committee's only mention of marijuana was a statement that it produces no physical dependence.(84)

The Committee did recommend ratification by the United States of the Single Convention on Narcotic Drugs.(85) The Single Convention sets out in a single instrument an international agreement on narcotic drugs and cannabis. It provides that the substances it controls may be used only for medical and scientific purposes.(86) The Single Convention places no restrictions upon the degree of control to be imposed by signatory nations. The United States had not yet ratified the Convention, but those supporting ratification argued that the existence of a treaty obligation which required the control of marijuana would be useful against the arguments of a vocal few who are advocating its legalization.(87)

SOME CRITICISMS OF EXISTING LAWS

Since 1956, the support for stringent controls of marijuana has very gradually diminished. Harsh controls and the alleged dangers of the drug have begun to receive closer scrutiny.(88) Critics of the current penalty system have cited the increase in drug use and number of arrests as evidence of the failure of harsh penalties to operate as a deterrent.(89) In 1958, James V. Bennett, Director of the United States Bureau of Prisons, stated:

The experience we have had with the severe penalties in the Narcotic Control Act of 1956 indicates that the financial attractiveness for the seller and the psychological needs of the addict tend alike to obscure the seriousness of the penalties.

It must be remembered that the addict released from prison is doubly stigmatized. He must face not only the hostility and the suspicion the community reserves for the ex-con, he is also an untouchable because he uses drugs. . . . In the final analysis the responsibility of the community to provide continuous and long-term care for the addict is not significantly different in my opinion from that which we owe the alcoholic [or] mentally ill. . . .(90)

In addition, an inflexible penalty structure is widely considered unacceptable.

A survey of federal judges, probation officials, and district attorneys has revealed that seventy-three per cent of the judges, eighty-three per cent of the probation officers, ninety-two per cent of the prison wardens, and fifty per cent of the district attorneys opposed the mandatory minimum sentence provisions.(91) The report of the Judicial Conference in 1961 disapproved in principle of those sentencing provisions in proposed legislation requiring the imposition of mandatory minimum sentences.(92) This disapproval was reaffirmed in 1965.(93)

Cost-benefit analyses of the marijuana enforcement structure have also been used to attack the current penalty system. John Kaplan, who has conducted such an analysis,(94) recently commented:

> Even if we were completely convinced about the value of criminalizing marijuana, we might well hesitate before diverting such massive amounts of law enforcement energy from the area of crime against the person and against property. According to the latest statistics from the California Department of Justice Bureau of Criminal Statistics, arrests of juveniles and adults for marijuana violations were running at a yearly rate of 56,000 in 1969. When one considers that the good majority of these arrests were for simple possession of small amounts of marijuana untainted by any commercial dealing, the issue becomes even more stark. Whether or not the importance of shutting off the supply of marijuana justifies a continuing use of scarce law enforcement resources to prevent the trafficking in the drug, it is hard indeed to justify the expenditure of these resources on the huge number of mere possessors.
>
> Moreover, entirely apart from whether the law enforcement energies could better be used elsewhere, there is reason to believe that the application of these resources to marijuana does a good deal of harm. Not only does the very existence of the law tend to bring otherwise non-criminal users into contact with considerably more anti-social drug peddlers, but for the unfortunate few (at least as compared to the total number of marijuana users in our population) who are caught, it is likely that both their criminality and drug use will be increased rather than decreased by the experience.(95)

In the early 1930's the Panama Canal Zone Governor's Committee reported that no deleterious effects could be found among the soldiers who smoked the local marijuana. The study used both observations and experiments to test for residual effects.(96)

In 1944 a report to the mayor of New York City stated: "In most instances, the behavior of the smoker is [that of] a friendly, sociable character. Aggressiveness and belligerency are not commonly seen. . . . The marijuana user does not come from the hardened criminal class and there was no direct relationship between the commission of crime and violence and marijuana. . . . [M]arijuana itself has no specific stimulant effect in regard to sexual desires.(97)

In 1951, the American Bar Association's Commission on Organized Crime expressed its disapproval of the mandatory minimum penalties in the Boggs

Amendment.(98) Continued American Bar Association concern resulted in the Criminal Law Section of the ABA forming a joint committee with the American Medical Association. The committee's final report favored medical rather than penal management of narcotic addiction and stated: "Though drug peddling is acknowledged to be a vicious and predatory crime, a grave question remains whether severe jail and prison sentences are the most rational way of dealing with narcotic addicts."(99) Prior to the release of the committee's final report, its chairman published an appendix in an interim report in which he questioned 1. the value of long sentences in deterring, and 2. whether an effective enforcement campaign which raises drug prices (and profits) can ever dissuade the illicit trafficker.(100)

The Model Penal Code does not deal with the criminalization of simple possession. The official commentary to a draft related that despite agreement that drug abuse is a medical-psychological problem, it is the police who continue to encounter and deal with the vast majority of drug addicts.(101) Section 250.5 of the Model Code, dealing with non-therapeutic drug use, classified public drug intoxication as a fineable offense, but not a crime, thus placing it in the same category as public alcoholic intoxication.(102) An individual committing three violations during a year is charged with a petty misdemeanor with a maximum sentence of one year.(103) The Model Code makes the offender eligible for treatment in lieu of prosecution.(104)

The President's Advisory Commission on Narcotic and Drug Abuse (the Prettyman Commission) reported in November 1963:

> The Commission makes a flat distinction between the two drugs (narcotics and marijuana) and believes that the unlawful sale or possession of marijuana is a less serious offense than the unlawful sale or possession of an opiate.
>
> The Commission believes that the sentencing of the petty marijuana offender should be left entirely to the discretion of the courts. There should be no mandatory minimum sentences for marijuana offenders and no prohibition of probation or parole.
>
> The courts should have the discretion to impose a fixed sentence (with eligibility for parole), to suspend sentence, or to impose an indeterminate sentence. The Commission is opposed to mandatory minimum sentence, even in the case of multiple offenders.(105)

The Advisory Commission did not believe that severe penalties served as a deterrent: "The weakness in the deterrence position is proved every day by the fact that the illicit traffic in narcotics and marijuana continues."(106) Although the Commission recommended that the simple possession of narcotics should be controlled, it did not make any similar recommendation for marijuana.(107)

In 1967, the President's Commission on Law Enforcement and the Administration of Justice issued a report, challenging the relationship between marijuana and crime, violence, and progression to hard narcotics.(108) Although it recognized that research information was incomplete, the Commission stated that "enough information exists to warrant careful study of our present marijuana laws and the propositions on which they are based."(109)

The National Commission on Reform of Federal Criminal Laws will submit its final report to the President and Congress in November 1970. However, the Study Draft of the Commission has recommended a reduction in possession penalties.(110) Drugs are dichotomized into dangerous drugs and abusable drugs, and marijuana is classed in the latter category.(111) First possession of an abusable drug is only a fineable offense, but subsequent offenses are punishable as misdemeanors.(112) A defense to prosecution for possession is proof that the defendant lacks substantial mental capacity to refrain from use.(113) In his comments on the recommendation, the consultant wrote: "More severe punishment for possession should at the least await solid scientific information that marijuana is as harmful as some people believe it is. Deterrence, while of course important, cannot be the sole end of the criminal law. Punishment must also be related to the seriousness of the offense."(114)

The Council on Mental Health, the Committee on Drug Dependence of the American Medical Association, and the Committee on Problems of Drug Dependence of the National Research Council, National Academy of Science, have jointly advocated greater discrimination in penalties imposed upon offenders, and have suggested that "equitable penalties, insofar as they enhance respect for law, can contribute to effective prevention."(115)

A possible change in penalties was suggested in the 1967 congressional hearings on marijuana.(116) A representative of the Food and Drug Administration stated that marijuana was not as dangerous as LSD, and, therefore, its possession penalties should be less severe than those of LSD. Also suggested was that a lack of possession penalties for LSD had not precluded effective control of that substance.(117) Intra-departmental memoranda of the Department of Health, Education, and Welfare were submitted which recommended repeal of the Marijuana Tax Act, placement of marijuana under the Drug Abuse Control Amendments, a felony penalty for sale and distribution, and elimination of a possession penalty for personal use.(118)

In some states there had been legislative reform of marijuana laws. In 1968, California reduced the marijuana possession penalties which had been raised only a few years before.(119) Connecticut removed marijuana from the narcotics definition and classified it as a dangerous drug, thereby reducing the possession penalty to a misdemeanor.(120) And New Mexico amended its Penal Code reducing marijuana possession to a misdemeanor in 1969.(121) Alaska, Washington, Wisconsin, and North Carolina have also followed this trend.(122)

A CONCLUDING OBSERVATION

Given the difficulty of enforcing present laws, a marijuana user may take only a slight risk when using the drug. The magnitude of the risk obviously varies with the setting. For example, in the Haight-Ashbury section of San Francisco, public marijuana smoking is permitted,(123) and it was openly condoned on a large scale at the recent music festival in Woodstock, New York.(124)

Those who do get caught, however, face penalties which, in some instances, may amount to cruel and unusual punishment. *Watson v. United States*(125) held that the mandatory minimum ten-year imprisonment to which a defendant, a convicted narcotic addict, was sentenced, constituted an eighth amendment violation. The District of Columbia court of appeals stated: "The result of this sentencing scheme is that a convicted murderer, kidnaper, arsonist, rapist, traitor, robber, or saboteur may receive a lighter sentence than is mandatorily imposed on an addict who possesses narcotics more than once. And all these dangerous felons may be eligible for release before the hapless addict if they are sentenced to any term less than thirty years."(126) The court expressed its dilemma by indicating its reluctance "to intrude upon the congressional prerogative by dismantling the narcotics sentencing statutes brick by brick until we reach a constitutionally acceptable result."(127)

Leaving to the courts the problems of correcting the severity of penalties mandatorily imposed for violation of the federal drug statutes may be a lengthy process. Legislation pending before the 91st Congress(128) may eliminate the *Watson* court's dilemma, as mandatory minimums and unreasonably long first offense sentences will be abolished. But the question remains whether changing the penalty structure will improve the efficiency of the legal control system and enhance its deterrent effect. Certainly, the health and social consequences imputed to the non-therapeutic use of marijuana demand a concerted scientific research effort. Perhaps of equal importance is the need for a re-evaluation of our Western mores from which proceed our judgments on the various patterns of all non-therapeutic chemical use.

NOTES

(1) Marijuana Tax Act, INT. REV. CODE of 1954, §§ 4741-62.

(2) *See* notes 50-57 *infra*, and accompanying text.

(3) *Compare* Harrison Narcotics Act, INT. REV. CODE of 1954 §§ 4701-26 *with* Marijuana Tax Act, INT. REV. CODE of 1954, §§ 4741-46. *See also* CAL. HEALTH & SAFETY CODE §§ 11001(d) (West 1964); N.Y. PUB. HEALTH LAW § 3301(38) (McKinney Supp. 1969); TEX. PEN. CODE ANN. art. 725b, § 1(14) (1961).

(4) PRESIDENT'S COMM'N ON LAW ENFORCEMENT AND ADMINISTRATION OF JUSTICE, TASK FORCE REPORT: NARCOTICS AND DRUG ABUSE app. A-2, at 40 (1967).

(5) *See* note 3 *supra*.

(6) *E.G.*, INT. REV. CODE of 1954, § 4744(a). Though found constitutionally defective by the Supreme Court in Leary v. United States, 395 U.S. 6 (1969), the Government has interpreted the result as a waivable defect. The statute thus continues in force and the defect can and may be waived by a person facing a more serious charge. Memorandum to All United States Attorneys from Will Wilson, Asisstant Attorney General in Charge of Criminal Division (Memo. No. 630), June 20, 1969). *See also* N.Y. PUB. HEALTH LAW § 3305 (McKinney 1954); TEX. PEN. CODE ANN. art. 725b, § 2 (1961).

(7) 1 R. BROTMAN & A. FREEDMAN, PERSPECTIVES ON MARIJUANA RESEARCH § 1, at 19 (1968).

(8) 1 R. BLUM & ASSOCIATES, SOCIETY AND DRUGS 68-69 (1969).

(9) J. KAPLAN, MARIJUANA – THE NEW PROHIBITION 88 (1970).

(10) 2 R. BROTMAN & A. FREEMAN, *supra* note 7, at 304.

(11) Statement of Dr. Stanley F. Yolles, Director, National Institute of Mental Health at *Hearings Before the Subcomm. to Investigate Juvenile Delinquency of the Senate Comm. on the Judiciary*, 91st Cong., 1st Sess. 267 (1969).

(12) *Id.*

(13) SPECIAL PRESIDENTIAL TASK FORCE RELATING TO NARCOTICS, MARIJUANA, AND DANGEROUS DRUGS, REPORT 8 (1969).

(14) Isbell, Gorodetzsky, Jasinski, Claussen, Spulak & Korte, *Effect of (–)Δ9-Trans-Tetrahydro-cannabinol in Man*, 11 PSYCHOPHARMACOLOGIA 184 (1967).

(15) TASK FORCE REPORT, *supra* note 13, at 7.

(16) Mechoulam & Gaoni, *A Total Synthesis of a 1-Δ Tetrahydrocannabinol, the Active Constituent of Hashish*, 87 J. AM. CHEM. SOC'Y 3273, 3274 (1965).

(17) *Hearings on Marijuana Before the House Comm. on Health & Welfare of the District of Columbia*, 91st Cong., 2d sess. 10 (1970) (statement of Dr. Jesse Steinfeld, Surgeon General, U.S. Public Health Service); S. Cohen, Marijuana: Pharmacology and Physiology 1 (1969) (unpublished report of Director, Division of Narcotic Addiction and Drug Abuse, National Institute of Mental Health, on file with authors).

(18) King & Cowen, *Effect of Intravenous Injection of Marijuana*, 210 J.A.M.A. 724-25 (1969).

(19) Weil, *Cannabis*, 5A SCIENCE JOURNAL, Sept. 1969, at 36, 41.

(20) Grinspoon, *Marijuana*, 221 SCIENTIFIC AMERICAN, DEC. 1969, at 17, 19.

(21) S. COHEN, THE DRUG DILEMMA 53 (1969).

(22) S. Cohen, *supra* note 17, at 2.

(23) Weil, Zinberg, & Nelsen, *Clinical and Psychological Effects of Marijuana in Man*, 162 SCIENCE 1234, 1240 (1968).

(24) Weil, *supra* note 19, at 40.

(25) Jaffe, *Drug Addiction and Drug Abuse*, in THE PHARMACOLOGICAL BASIS OF THERAPEUTICS 300 (3d ed. L. Goodman & A. Gilman eds. 1965).

(26) Grinspoon, *supra* note 20, at 20-21.

(27) Weil, Zinberg, & Nelsen, *supra* note 23, at 1239.

(28) Grinspoon, *supra* note 20, at 20-21.

(29) *Id.*

(30) S. Cohen, *supra* note 17, at 4.

(31) Talbott & Teague, *Marijuana Psychosis*, 210 J.A.M.A. 299 (1969).

(32) Keeler, Reifler, & Liptzin, *Spontaneous Recurrence of Marijuana Effects*, 125 AM. J. PSYCHIATRY 384-86 (1968).

(33) Benabud, *Psychopathological Aspects of the Cannabis Situation in Morocco: Statistical Data for 1956*, 9 BULL ON NARCOTICS 1 (1967).

(34) ADVISORY COMMITTEE ON DRUG DEPENDENCE, REPORT, CANNABIS 13 (H.M.S.O. 1968).

(35) INT. REV. CODE of 1954 §§ 4741-62.

(36) *See text* accompanying note 53 *infra*.

(37) Louria, *The Dangerous Drug Problem*, 22 NEW YORK MEDICINE 241 (1966).

(38) ADVISORY COMMITTEE REPORT, *supra* note 34, at 13-14.

(39) TASK FORCE REPORT, *supra* note 4, at 13.

(40) 42 U.S.C. § 201(j) (1964).

(41) U.S. PUBLIC HEALTH SERVICE, DIVISION OF HYGIENE, PUBLIC

HEALTH REPORTS Supp. No. 97, at 1 (1931), originally published in 44 PUBLIC HEALTH REPORTS 1256-60 (1929).

(42) *Hearings on H.R. 12781 & 13645 Before the House Comm. on the Judiciary*, 70th Cong., 1st Sess. (1928); 69 CONG. REC. 6051, 8241, 8677, 9411-13 (1928), on the establishment of two narcotics farms.

(43) Peyote is classified as a dangerous drug under Drug Abuse Control Amendments of 1965, 21 U.S.C. § 321(v)(3) (Supp. IV, 1969).

(44) Uniform Narcotic Drug Act § 1(14), 9B U.L.A. 415, 417 (1966), approved by the National Conference of Commissioners on Uniform Laws of the American Bar Association in 1932.

(45) Twenty-six states had adopted the proposed Uniform Act by the close of 1935. *Id.* at 409-10.

(46) Survey of newspapers, reported in Mandel, *Problems with Official Drug Statistics*, 21 STAN. L. REV. 991, 1003 (1969).

(47) One author suggests that the reason for the reported large quantities is that the entire hemp plant was seized and weighed at maturity. *Id.* a 998-99.

(48) *Id.* at 1038.

(49) *Id.* at 1003. When a new law is passed, the before and after statistics are misleading because the before statistics are always zero, even if there were significant events which precipitated the legislation.

(50) Lindesmith has indicated that the dangers were made public through a publicity campaign staged by the Federal Bureau of Narcotics. A. LINDESMITH, THE ADDICT AND THE LAW 228 (1965).

(51) INT. REV. CODE of 1954, §§ 4741-62.

(52) *Hearings on H.R. 6906 Before a Subcomm. of the Senate Comm. on Finance*, 75th Cong., 1st Sess. 9-10 (1937).

(53) S. REP. NO. 900, 75th Cong., 1st Sess. 2 (1937); H.R. REP. NO. 792, 75th Cong., 1st Sess. 1 (1937).

(54) *See Hearings on H.R. 6906, supra* note 52, at 12.

(55) *Hearings on H.R. 6385 Before the House Comm. on Ways and Means*, 75th Cong., 1st Sess. 21 (1937).

(56) *See Hearings on H.R. 6906, supra* note 52, at 14.

(57) *Id.* (statement of H.J. Anslinger, Commissioner of Narcotics, Bureau of Narcotics of the Treasury Department).

(58) *Id.* at 14-15.

(59) *See Hearings on H.R. 6385, supra* note 55, at 24.

(60) At one point in the hearings, it was asked whether birds that eat bird seed containing cannabis seeds "sing the same." *See Hearings on H.R. 6906, supra* note 52, at 13-14.

(61) INT. REV. CODE of 1954, §§ 4701-26.

(62) *See Hearings on H.R. 6385, supra* note 55, at 106.

(63) *See* Letter to the Committee, *Hearings on H.R. 6906, supra* note 52, at 33. The absence of testimony by medical and correctional professionals may indicate a significant absence of marijuana usage at this time. If the substance had a popular usage, these people probably would have come forth either to verify or deny the descriptions of marijuana. They would have desired to be heard either "pro," or "con."

(64) INT. REV. CODE of 1954, § 4741.

(65) *See The Marihuana Tax Act*, in THE MARIHUANA PAPERS 424 (D. Solomon ed. 1966). "Obviously, the details of that regulation make it far too risky for anyone to have anything to do with marihuana in any way whatsoever." *Id.* at 425.

(66) *Hearings on H.R. 3490 and H.R. 348 Before a Subcomm. of the House Comm. on Ways and Means*, 82d Cong., 1st Sess. 40-50 (1951).

(67) *Id.* Judges could suspend sentence and place on probation, when it was believed appropriate. "Federal judges are not doing their duty." *Id.* at 48. "In other words the situation is so bad that Federal judges should not be allowed discretion any longer?" *Id.* at 50.

(68) *Id.* at 67. Cunningham: "The dope traffic melts away where people get long sentences." Anslinger: "We find where we have light sentences the traffic is usually heavy, and where heavy sentences are meted out the traffic just disappears." *Id.* at 203. Dr. Paul B. Dunbar, Commissioner of the Food and Drug Administration, also believed in increased penalties. *Id.* at 217-18. A letter from the Department of Justice states, "[T]he principal deterrent to narcotic-marijuana violators is the possible prison sentence. . . . " *Id.* at 80. Also mentioned was the fact that, because stiff penalties had effectively reduced white slave traffic, analogously they would reduce the drug problem. *Id.* at 68.

(69) *Id.* at 206.

(70) 97 CONG. REC. 8195-211 (1951).

(71) *Id.* at 8205-11.

(72) 97 CONG. REC. 13,675-76 (1951).

(73) S. REP. NO. 1051, 82d Cong., 1st Sess. (1951).

(74) *Id.* at 3. Other testimony, quoted from Mr. Harry J. Anslinger, S. REP. NO. 1051, 82d Cong., 1st Sess. 3 (1951), in the Committee report indicated that the proposal was a good solution. "There should be a minimum sentence for the second offense. The commercialized transaction, the peddler, the smuggler, those who traffic in narcotics, on the second offense if there were a minimum sentence of 5 years without probation or parole, I think it would just about dry up the traffic."

(75) Act of Nov. 2, 1951, ch. 666, § 1, 65 Stat. 767, *now* 21 U.S.C. § 174 (1964).

(76) The Subcommittee on Improvement in the Federal Criminal Code of the Committee on the Judiciary of the Senate, 84th Cong., 1st Sess. (1955), operating under S. Res. 67, 84th Cong., 1st Sess. (1955).

(77) 18 U.S.C. §§ 1401-07 (1964); 21 U.S.C. §§ 174, 176, 184 (1964); INT. REV. CODE of 1954, §§ 4744, 4755, 4774, 7237.

(78) H.R. REP. NO. 2388, 84th Cong., 1st Sess. 63 (1956). Apparently, 1952 was the highest point in post-war trafficking arrests. *See id.* at 58, where it was seen that traffic was on the decrease after 1952.

(79) *Hearings on Illicit Narcotics Traffic Before the Subcomm. on Improvements in the Federal Criminal Code of the Senate Comm. on the Judiciary*, 84th Cong., 1st Sess. 16-18 (1955).

(80) *Id.* at 235-36. The testimony went as follows:

Senator Welker. . . . We go now to the proposition of marijuana which, in your field or the medical field, is considered one of the minor narcotics but it causes, if I understand my case correctly, it causes the user to build up a sense of bravery, a sense of well-being that no normal person would ever advocate. He would be a sadist in many cases, a murderer, without any idea that he was, in fact, a murderer. I should not belabor this question with you because I know you know much more about this than I do. I did want your observations, and I hope the staff will furnish Dr. Hunt with a copy of this matter which is generally circulated throughout the Nation. The publicity value alone of that thing, in my opinion, was terrible. Take a young high school kid getting his first shot or chance to take a shot. His parents have told him it was wrong, it was evil, it was going to lead to a bad disruptive life, and yet he reads something like this and he says, 'Heavens above, that is not so bad. Here are a couple of doctors who advocate or argue the question should we legalize narcotics.' Do you see what I mean, Doctor?

Dr. Hunt. I am reminded of the discussions that went on in the late twenties, Senator, with respect to alcohol. The problems have some similarities.

Senator Welker. Thank you very much.

(81) 21 U.S.C. § § 174, 176 (1964); INT. REV. CODE of 1954, § 7237.

(82) These penalties which preclude parole in effect require that an offender serve two-thirds of his term (all prisoners can reduce sentence by one-third on the basis of "good time" behavior), whereas other offenders can be released on parole after one-third is served. 18 U.S.C. § § 4161, 4202 (1964).

(83) INTERDEPARTMENTAL COMMITTEE ON NARCOTICS, REPORT TO THE PRESIDENT OF THE UNITED STATES 1-2 (1961) (on file with the authors).

(84) *Id.* at 4.

(85) *Id.* at 15.

(86) The Single Convention on Narcotic Drugs 1961, *opened for signature* March 30, 1961, [1967] 2 U.S.T. 1408, T.I.A.S. No. 6298, 50 U.N.T.S. 7515. The treaty received the Senate's advice and consent on May 8, 1967, without debate. 113 Cong. Rec. 6442 (daily ed. May 8, 1967). Accession was approved by the President on May 15, 1967; the accession was deposited with the United Nations Secretary-General on May 25, 1967. The treaty entered into force for the United States on June 24, 1967, and was proclaimed by the President on July 12, 1967. [1967] 2 U.S.T. 1407, T.I.A.S. No. 6298, at 1.

(87) Another important reason for becoming a party to the 1961 convention is the marijuana problem. . . . Several groups in the United States are loudly agitating to liberalize controls and, in fact, to legalize its use. . . . If the United States becomes a party to the 1961 convention we will be able to use our treaty obligations to resist legalized use of marijuana. This discussion is going on all over the country, in many universities, and in fringe groups. . . .

SENATE COMM. ON FOREIGN RELATIONS, CONVENTION ON NARCOTIC DRUGS, S. EXEC. REP. NO. 11, 90th Cong., 1st Sess. 20 (1961) (statement of H. Anslinger), *as quoted in* Van Atta, *Effects of the Single Convention of Narcotic Drugs upon the Regulation of Marijuana*, 19 HASTINGS L. REV. 848 (1968).

(88) For example, as recently as 1967 and 1968, the "stepping stone" theory was mentioned at appropriation hearings for Federal Bureau of Narcotics fiscal requests. *Hearings on the Dept. of Appropriations for 1968 Before a Subcomm. of the House Comm. on Appropriations*, 90th Cong., 1st Sess. pt. 3, at 470-71 (1967); *Hearings on Dept. of Treasury and Executive Office of the President Appropriations of 1969 Before a Subcomm. of the House Comm. on Appropriations*, 90th Cong., 2d Sess. pt. 1, at 552-623 (1968). In 1966, when Congress was considering the availability of parole for marijuana offenders, the following was heard:

Mr. Ashmore: You stated, and I have heard before, that marijuana is not a habit-forming drug. Is that correct?

Mr. Katzenbach: That is right. Many marijuana users end up by subsequently leading up to heroin, so it has the effect of leading one into addiction, but it is not addictive in itself.

Mr. Ashmore: How about those who use it? The effect of it is unknown, is it not? It can cause one to commit murder, another sex violence, another something else?

Mr. Katzenbach: That is right.

Mr. Ashmore: In many ways it is as bad as heroin, morphine and what have you?

Mr. Katzenbach: From that point of view it is.

Hearings Before Subcomm. No. 2 of the House Comm. on the Judiciary, 89th

Cong., 1st & 2d Sess. 88 (1966).

At *Hearings on Problems Relating to the Control of Marijuana Before a Subcomm. of the House Comm. on Government Operations*, 90th Cong., 2d Sess. 69 (1967), a "trigger theory" was mentioned in response to whether marijuana was the first step: "Mr. Giordano. Of the 60,697 addicts that are currently heroin addicts, 90 percent of those started on marihuana. I want to be clear on this. It's a steppingstone. Now, this doesn't say that just because somebody smokes a marihuana cigarette he is going on to heroin, but it's a *trigger*." (Emphasis added.)

(89) Burnett, *Crisis in Narcotics – Are Existing Federal Penalties Effective?*, 10 WM. & MARY L. REV. 636 (1969).

(90) Bennett, *A Prison Administrator Views Today's Narcotic Problems*, in SYMPOSIUM ON THE HISTORY OF NARCOTIC DRUG ADDICTION PROBLEMS, BETHESDA, MARYLAND, 1960, at 167-73 (DHEW-PHS No. 1050).

(91) WHITE HOUSE CONFERENCE ON NARCOTICS AND DRUG ABUSE' PROCEEDINGS 230 (1962).

(92) JUDICIAL CONFERENCE OF THE UNITED STATES, ANNUAL REPORTS 98-99 (1961).

(93) *Id.* 20 (1965).

(94) J. Kaplan, *supra* note 9, at 21-51.

(95) Kaplan, *Forward to Marijuana Laws: An Empirical Study of Enforcement and Administration in Los Angeles County*, 15 U.C.L.A.L. REV. 1503 (1968).

(96) *Report of the Panama Canal Zone Governor's Committee, April-December 1925*, MILITARY SURGEON, Nov. 1933, at 274, *reported in* R. BROTMAN & A. FREEDMAN, *supra* note 7, § 2, at 17.

(97) *See* THE MARIHUANA PAPERS, *supra* note 65, at 355.

(98) 76 ABA REP. 387 (1951).

(99) JOINT COMMITTEE OF THE AMERICAN BAR ASSOCIATION AND AMERICAN MEDICAL ASSOCIATION ON NARCOTIC DRUGS, DRUG ADDICTION: CRIME OR DISEASE? 163 (Interim and Final Reports 1961).

(100) Ploscowe, *Some Basic Problems in Drug Addiction and Suggestions for Researach*, in *id.* app. A, at 15-120.

(101) MODEL PENAL CODE § 250.11, Comment (Tent. Draft No. 13, 1961).

(102) *Id.* § 250.5 (Proposed Official Draft 1962).

(103) *Id.* § 250.11 (Tent. Draft No. 13, 1961).

(104) *Id.* § 6.13 (Proposed Official Draft 1962).

(105) PRESIDENT'S ADVISORY COMMISSION ON NARCOTIC AND DRUG ABUSE, FINAL REPORT 42 (1963).

(106) *Id.* at 40.

(107) *Id.*

(108) PRESIDENT'S COMMISSION ON LAW ENFORCEMENT AND ADMINISTRATION OF JUSTICE, THE CHALLENGE OF CRIME IN A FREE SOCIETY 211-37 (1967).

(109) *Id.* at 225.

(110) NATIONAL COMMISSION ON REFORM OF FEDERAL CRIMINAL LAWS, STUDY DRAFT OF A NEW FEDERAL CRIMINAL CODE §§ 1824, 1827 (1970).

(111) *Id.* § 1821.

(112) *Id.* § 1824 (Comment).

(113) *Id.* § 1824(2).

(114) NATIONAL COMMISSION ON REFORM OF FEDERAL CRIMINAL

LAWS, WORKING PAPERS, DOC. NO. 38, at 38 (to be published; on file with authors).

(115) *Marijuana and Society*, 204 J.A.M.A. 1181 (1968).

(116) *Hearings on Problems Relating to the Control of Marijuana Before a Subcomm. of the House Comm. on Government Operations*, 90th Cong., 2d Sess. 56-74 (1967).

(117) *Id.* at 16.

(118) *Id.* at 21-31.

(119) CAL. HEALTH & SAFETY CODE § 11500 (West. 1964).

(120) CONN. GEN. STAT. REV. § 19-481 (1968). "Many jurisists, prosecutors and law enforcement officers appear to regard the present penalties as so oppressive that they utilize various other means to dispose of such charges as an alternative to prosecution for possession." CONNECTICUT DRUG ADVISORY COUNCIL, REPORT OF COMMITTEE TO STUDY MARIJUANA LAWS 21 (1969).

(121) N.M. STAT. ANN. § 54-7-13 (Supp. 1969).

(122) ALASKA STAT. §§ 17.12.010-.150 (Supp. 1969); N.C. GEN. STAT. § 90-111 (Supp. 1969); WASH. REV. CODE § 69.40.070 (1969); ch. 384, § 18, [1969] Wis. Acts 1940.

Canada recently has enacted legislation to reduce possession penalties in response to evidence of widespread recourse to marijuana and to insufficient substantiation of toxicity to justify the earlier, harsher penalty structure. Possession is now punishable as a "summary conviction," which is comparable to a misdemeanor and carries a maximum imprisonment of six months. CAN. REV. STAT. c. 41 (1969); Speech by Hon. J. Munro, Minister of National Health and Welfare, Montreal, May 22, 1969.

(123) Mandel, *supra* note 46, at 1029.

(124) At least 90 percent of those present at the festival were smoking marijuana. In addition, narcotics of any and all description, from hash to acid to speed to horse, were freely available. Perhaps out of fear of rousing the crowd to hostility, police made fewer than 100 arrests on narcotics charges. By and large, the U.S. has accepted the oversimplification that all narcotics are dangerous and thus should be outlawed. The all but universal acceptance of marijuana, at least among the young, raises the question of how long the nation's present laws against its use can remain in force without seeming as absurd and hypocritical as Prohibition. TIME, Aug. 29, 1969, at 32.

(125) No. 21,186 (D.C. Cir., Dec. 13, 1968).

(126) *Id.* at 19.

(127) *Id.* at 20.

(128) S. 3426, 91st Cong., 2d Sess. (1970).

CIVIL REDRESS:
NEW WEAPON IN THE
WAR ON NARCOTICS

Sidney H. Willig

The term "criminal" negligence is variously defined. Some equate it with negligence arising out of or occurring concomitantly with criminal conduct. That is obviously inaccurate. What the term more correctly signifies is a form of negligence which by its grossness, its show of callous disregard for the individual harmed, betrays an indifference to the rights of society as a whole. It is, therefore, a form of negligence that if supported by a satisfactory preponderance of evidence, will give rise to punitive damages, rather than merely compensatory damages for the out-of-pocket costs to the individual harmed. Punitive damages are used then as a deterrent, much as fines or imprisonment might be used to give society a remedy against one whose criminal guilt has been proven.

It is, therefore, possible for law abiding persons not now or previously charged with commission of a crime to be sued for their negligence which is alleged to be "criminal" or "gross" in degree.

PROFESSIONAL STANDARDS AND CRITERIA

This is especially true where there already exist certain patterns of conduct for criteria, or where professional standards are required to be met and maintained in line with statutory guidance in the form of professional practice acts or public protection laws of other types.

One rather broad area which is seeing a metamorphosis in the approach taken by plaintiff's attorneys is that of drugs and narcotics. Despite the vast spectrum of available laws, the number of enforcement personnel and the organized efforts of professional groups in our society, this continues to be an area rife with illegality and the meanest fruits of injudicious and illicit conduct.

As society has defended itself, unlawful trafficking in drugs has brought stiff penalties to those apprehended, while professional licensure has been refused, suspended or revoked for many health care professionals for abuse of their "legal" prerogatives as to compounding, prescribing, administering and handling such drugs.

CIVIL REDRESS

There seems little need to talk in terms of common law negligence to purveyors of drugs in illicit trafficking. Anyone who manufactures drugs in violation of drug and narcotics laws that limit the "who," "what" and "how" of such activities is a criminal in the eyes of the law, simply and certainly. In fact these laws are effective against persons (in personam) and against the articles (res). Lest it be bypassed however in terms of culpability described by misdemeanors, felonies, fines, terms of punishment, there are concomitant liabilities for those involved in such criminal activities in the form of financial judgments that may be handed down separately with criminal negligence as a cause of action.

It may seem therefore both superfluous and trivial by comparison with the criminal justice sought by society, yet the man who manufactures or imports or exports drugs and narcotics in violation of the law is liable to the affected person, that person's dependents, parents or guardian as well as to the general public. The same is true for the one who sells or gives away the substances in violation.(1) This is of course no different than the civil redress that has developed in accompaniment of criminal violations involving alcohol.

ALCOHOLIC BEVERAGE CONTROLS

Many states historically have enforced statutes, as has the federal government, designed to prevent illegal manufacture and distribution of alcohol. The states, by police power prerogatives, if we omit reference to the ill-fated Volstead Amendment, have most especially busied themselves with distribution and sale of intoxicating beverages through a system of qualifying those who may sell and those who may purchase.

The "dram shop acts" which developed from the English Common Law approach further sought to safeguard the public by investing the proprietor of the tavern or liquor store with the need to monitor his customers both as to age, condition of sobriety, and size of purchase.(2)

The analogy to parmaceuticals is not too farfetched,(3) except that in the latter set of controls, the state besides its own authority, grants special authority to certain classes of professionals such as physicians, osteopaths, dentists and pharmacists, and therefore qualifies receipt by need rather than age.

NEGLIGENCE PRINCIPLES

The principles of common law negligence very clearly attached to failures to observe the necessary guidelines and where such laws were clearly flaunted, often the court, if not willing to accept a premise of statutory negligence, was at least willing to accept a reasonable presumption of proprietor negligence and permit a shifting of the burden of proof.

The potentialities of employer responsibility where employees are drug and alcohol and narcotics abusers are so great and ramified that they are the subject of a recent text by the author.(4)

In seeking legislation which finally culminated in the Controlled Substances Act of 1970, the Bureau of Narcotics and Dangerous Drugs pointed out that a major source of the illicit drugs and narcotic traffic supplies came from initially legally manufactured and distributed materials. Thefts from drug manufacturers' stocks, robbery and burglary of pharmacies are not uncommon, in fact, the frequency of the latter has rendered some premises uninsurable, and record keeping by pharmacists and law enforcement officials impossible. Coincidentally, law enforcement officials note that suspect proprietorships are often the victims of such incidents and in many cases this simply compounds their suspicion. Let us look to the rare renegade pharmacist and our concept of civil damages.

As a perfect example of how this might occur where a pharmacist or other presumed legitimate purveyor of drugs or narcotics, rather than a "pusher" or supplier with no color of legal authority is involved, let us examine a few recent cases. Again we may make it even more practical examining it in the light of some ill advised sales pharmacists are making of quantities of legally obtained exempt narcotic cough mixtures to minors and adults. We are using a hypothetical case patterned closely after several law suits.(5)

Jones, the employee of a drive-in theatre is injured when struck by a motor vehicle driven by a youth under the influence, or "high" through abuse of an exempt narcotic cough preparation. Jones, hurt badly and facing a lifetime of the need for care brought suit against the pharmacist(s) who had sold the drugs to the youth. This was aside from criminal charges lodged against the youth by the police. There was evidence that the pharmacist had sold the youth 24 four ounce bottles of cough medicine under circumstances which should have indicated to the pharmacist that the minor was either going to abuse it himself or share it with others for that purpose. The youth's subsequent use and intoxication was the cause of the accident and injury to Jones. The court could easily conceive that there was sufficient evidence to support a jury finding of causal relationship between the circumstances of the pharmacist's injudicious and/or illegal sale, the resulting impairment of the user's mental and driving ability and the final injury of Jones. Kvanli, 139 N.W. 275, a Minnesota case, and Hughson v. O'Reilly, a Michigan case, 151 N.W.2nd 888, 1967 are very much on point here.(6)

Carrying the analogy to the court's reaction in alcohol cases even further, a landmark decision in New Jersey some years ago (Rappaport vs. Nichols, 156 A.2nd 1, 1959) set down precedents that have been accepted for their perspicacity in many other jurisdictions. In essence that court in viewing the horrible accident report totals that involved drunken driving, held that no law was necessary to punish for the sale of intoxicants to those who seemed foreseeably capable of wreaking damage upon others. In short, whether or not the pharmacist in the prior example was breaking a law in selling to a minor, or in selling in excess of four ounces, or in selling without recording, or in selling with illegal frequency — was not really essential to Jones' legal rights against him.

RESPONSIBILITY OF VENDOR

A vendor of drugs, narcotics, "exempts" etc., even though he be registered, licensed, franchised by the state to do so, retains the common law responsibility for prudence and reasonable care. He may therefore be liable for the injurious results of his negligent selling, as well as for the harmful results of his illegal sales, both to the intoxicated purchasers and to third persons harmed by the dimmed capacities of those users. The courts in Indiana (Elder vs. Fisher, 217 N.E.2nd 847, 1966), New York (Berkely vs. Park, 262 N.Y.S.2nd 290, 1965), as well as in Massachusetts, Iowa, Minnesota have quickly followed this line of reasoning with alcoholic intoxication. There is no reason why they would not be receptive to it in any chemical intoxication and in fact as early as 50 years ago the New York courts did exactly that in Tidd vs. Skinner, 225 N.Y. 422, 1919.

The foregoing foreshadows the fashioning of a fresh approach to the problem of offering civil redress for criminal wrongdoing in the illicit trafficking of drugs and narcotics of any degree of potency in a nation with a per capita road death ratio of horrendous and still growing proportions. The public has already taken note of accidental injury and death caused by negligent advice as to the use of drugs legitimately manufactured, prescribed, dispensed or otherwise merchandised and sold. The courts have unhesitatingly held liable manufacturers whose labeling in its inaccuracy or inadequacy constituted a misbranding. It has held responsible manufacturers whose products caused unsafety through their adulterated quality.(7) It has held liable pharmacists who have issued misbranded drugs whether by prescription or contrary to prescription.(8) And, it has even held the physician to the task of describing to his patient the dangers associated with using the drug while driving.(9) There is ground to believe that if evidence and expert testimony disclosed to a court's satisfaction that careless prescribing or dispensing (or over prescribing or over dispensing), of drugs or narcotics had created either dependence or a psychic or mental state resulting in harm to the patient or others, that a civil remedy might be in order against the negligent prescribing or dispensing practitioner.

It might well have been anticipated that the future will see this same liability to the person harmed, as well as to harmed bystanders, exercised in instances where the medicinal substances or narcotic was in some manner an illegal transfer, whether by "amateurs" or "professionals."

DAMAGES

Civil redress on grounds of criminal negligence offers more than the substantial compensatory damages that may be the natural consequences of the act. If Jones is unable to work the rest of his life, if he is to need medical and nursing care, the judgment could exceed a million dollars, depending on the surrounding circumstances such as his age, likely pay, cost of care, etc. That would be "compensatory" damages. However, the courts have maintained that in the case of gross neゞigence or criminal negligence, where the defendant in the civil case has shown a callous disregard for the safety of humans, they will consider the imposition of punitive damages as well. These may be in many instances far in excess of the compensatory damages.(10) (Toole vs. Richardson Merrell; Roginsky vs. Richardson Merrell).(11) They are meant not only to punish the wrongdoer for a heinous offense against the one harmed, but to deter other similar offenses against the public at large.

In "DRUG ABUSE IN INDUSTRY: Legal Considerations,"(12) it was pointed out that Workmen's Compensation Boards are passing the financial burden caused by drug abuse back to what they find the causative mechanism, rather than penalize the employee drug abuser and his family.(13) Where, as a result of employment-associated pain or derivative stress, the employee abuses drugs supplied directly by the employer's physician, or the employee's personal physician through prescription, the Workmen's Compensation Board will strain to treat the effects as "job-connected" injuries compensable through the employer's fund. They have paid survivors of fatal drug abuse "accidents" on the same premises and have ruled these non-suicidal to make such payments. Employers may also be affected in terms of Product Liability.

In all, it may be anticipated that plaintiff's attorneys will look beyond the prosecution of criminal charges, toward financial redress where the client has been harmed through illicit traffic in drugs and narcotics.

NOTES

(1) People v. Brac. 167 P2nd 535 (Cal. 1946).

In commenting on the Brac case, the Journal of the American Medical Association points out to their physician readers that this case "Illustrates the caution that should characterize . . . the danger in the unlawful, unprescribed dispensing, of same . . . a prime example of factually preventive law." Jama Sept 11, 1967, Vol 201, No. 11, Pg. 339.

(2) The Dram Shop Act, 5 Baylor L. Rev. 385 (1953).

(3) The Federal Food, Drug and Cosmetic Act. 21 U.S.C. 301 et seq.

The Pennsylvania Drug, Device 2d Cosmetic Act (P.L. 693).

The Pennsylvania Pharmacy Act (P.L. 699).

(4) "Drug Abuse in Industry: Legal Considerations" published by Halos & Associates, Miami, Florida 33156.

(5) People v. Brac. 167 P2nd 535.

(6) See also so-called "bystander cases" such as Darryl v. Ford Motor Co., 440 S.W.2nd 630 (Texas, 1969). "Recovery under the strict liability doctrine is not limited to users and consumers."

(7) Escola v. Coca Cola, 150 P2nd 436.

(8) Scott v. Greenville Pharmacy, 48 S.E.2nd 324.

(9) Kaiser v. Suburban Trans., and Dr. Faghin, 398 P2nd 14 (1965).

(10) Toole v. Richardson Merrell, 60 Cal. Rptr. 398.

(11) Roginsky v. Richardson Merrell, 254 F. Supp. 430, 378 F2d 832.

(12) Supra.

(13) Kislowski v. Empire Boarding Stable (168 N.Y.S.2nd 793-796).

ATTITUDES OF PSYCHIATRISTS
AND PSYCHOLOGISTS
TOWARD ALCOHOLISM

Wilma J. Knox

The legal profession is making efforts to prevent jailing and punishment of alcoholics for public drunkenness. Legal definition of alcoholism as a disease could lead to the use of hospitals to the exclusion of jails for people labeled as alcoholics. In this event, a large and generally demanding group would be competing for mental health services that are acknowledged to be in short supply. Because the course of law is extremely difficult to change once it has been codified, I examined the attitudes of a group of psychologists and psychiatrists toward a shift from jail to hospital treatment in order to determine their consistency and to assess the manpower theoretically available for hospital treatment.

A survey of psychiatrists and psychologists working in Veterans Administration hospitals was selected, since this group was available to me and since its members come in contact with a patient population that contains many diagnosed as alcoholics(1). VA psychologists listed in the 1966 directory of the American Psychological Association were surveyed first, and the 480 responses from that survey have been reported on elsewhere(2). The procedure for collecting data from psychiatrists was identical, except that the psychiatrists' names were obtained from a comprehensive list supplied by the VA's Central Office. Only those who were listed as full-time psychiatrists were included; residents, associates, and consultants were omitted. A letter and questionnaire were sent to VA psychiatrists, noting a recent court decision that an alcoholic should be immune from being jailed for public drunkenness. The question was raised as to whether alcoholism should be handled primarily within a treatment setting. The accompanying questionnaire was mimeographed on two and a half pages.

There were 580 questionnaires sent out. If no reply was received, a second letter and questionnaire were sent, identical to the first with the exception of the word "Please!" handwritten across the letter. Forty-one questionnaires were unclaimed and returned. Four replies were received from psychiatrists no longer employed by the VA. Eighteen physicians representing other specialties submitted answers; their answers were not used in this analysis. A sample of 517 remained. A total of 345 (66.7 percent) answers were received from these VA psychiatrists. Nine (1.7 percent) returned their questionnaires but declined to answer; 163 (31.5 percent) did not reply. Answers were entered on IBM cards and tabulated by a computer.

The first section of the questionnaire was composed of six items to be completed by checking *all* of the answers with which the respondent agreed. After making checks, the respondent was asked to rank the answers checked in order of preference. The multiple choices offered to define alcoholism and its cause were derived from a survey of theoretical considerations(3). The second section was composed of ten items to be completed by checking the one answer that best expressed the respondent's opinion. Additional space was provided for comments or for descriptions of a treatment method that the respondent thought might be effective.

RESULTS

Table 1 presents a summary of the answers to questions permitting multiple responses. The percentage of respondents selecting each answer is shown for both psychiatrists and psychologists along with the rank of that answer. The Spearman rank correlation coefficient (r_s) between psychiatrists and psychologists is given for each question. In every ranking except those for behavior typical of alcoholism and financial benefits the correlation is significant at the .01 level of confidence. In some instances the distribution is obviously different. For example, in defining alcoholism psychiatrists had no marked preference among calling alcoholism a behavior problem, a symptom complex, or an escape mechanism, while psychologists selected "behavior problem" first by a wide margin.

Drinking daily to excess, drinking upon awakening, many current arrests for drinking, memory blackouts, periodic drinking, and drinking until out of money were all accepted to some degree as behavior typical of an alcoholic. Alcoholics Anonymous and group therapy were clearly the preferred treatments, but individual therapy, milieu therapy, tranquilizers, and disulfiram were also selected. As pointed out above, financial benefits were a source of dissimilarity between psychologists' and psychiatrists' opinions. About half of the psychologists and 40 percent of the psychiatrists felt that an alcoholic is entitled to sick leave. Psychiatrists selected no financial benefits about a third of the time, while psychologists selected Social Security pensions, veterans pensions,

TABLE 1

Summary of Responses to Multiple-Choice Questions

RESPONSES	PSYCHIATRISTS		PSYCHOLOGISTS	
	PERCENT	RANK	PERCENT	RANK
Definition (r_s = .94)*				
Behavior problem	57.4	1	81.3	1
Symptom complex	54.5	2	64.8	3
Escape mechanism	53.4	3	71.5	2
Habit	42.1	4	54.8	4
Disease	35.4	5	33.8	5
Causes (r_s = .96)*				
Low tension tolerance	62.7	1	72.9	1
Conflict over dependency	52.5	2	70.6	2
Excessive dependency	49 3	3	58.1	3
Poorly restrained impulses	46.4	4	51.9	5
Conditioning	43.2	5	55.2	4
Behavior (r_s = .60)				
Drinks daily to excess	68.2	1	75.4	1
Drinks upon awakening	42.7	2	50.4	2
Successful treatment criteria (r_s = 1.00)*				
Abstinence	77.2	1	70.6	1
Decreased problems reported by family	42.9	2	55.8	2
Increased time between drinking bouts	40.3	3	53.5	3
Preferred treatment (r_s = .94)*				
Alcoholics Anonymous	70.8	1	76 5	1
Group therapy	56 3	2	58.3	2
Financial benefits (r_s = .56)				
Sick leave	42 7	1	51.3	1
None of these	35.7	2	27.5	5

$p < .01$.

and disability retirement 30 to 40 percent of the time.

Both psychiatrists and psychologists rarely selected "disease" as a definition of alcoholism; it was left blank approximately two-thirds of the time. Over 60 percent of both samples did *not* select as causes of alcoholism: physiological predisposition, marital problems, childhood threats to security, mood swings, unrealistically high goals, and economic problems. Simply drinking daily was not considered typical of alcoholic behavior. Jail terms and court probation were rejected as offering treatment potential for the alcoholic.

In responding to questions limited to one answer, most psychiatrists and psychologists felt that the known alcoholic, drunk and staggering on the street, should be taken to a hospital; this was closely followed by selection of "taken home." There were less agreement on and fewer selections of "left alone," "taken to jail," and "taken to jail only if he starts to commit a crime" (r_s = .70, $p > .05$). The agency selected as the one equipped to handle most of the problems related to alcoholism was primarily a neuropsychiatric hospital for psychiatrists and Alcoholics Anonymous for psychologists. Each selected the other's first choice as second. Courts and the general medical and surgical hospital drew few selections in either group as the appropriate agency ($r_s = .75$, $p > .05$).

Although courts were rejected and hospitals were accepted by large numbers of both groups, the help to be gained by hospital care was generally considered minimal. Table 2 divides the respondents of both groups into "agree" categories (made up of "strongly agree," "agree," and "mildly agree") and "disagree" categories (made up of "mildly disagree," "disagree," and "strongly disagree"). Note that when the subcategories were so totaled opinion fell clearly into the "agree" or "disagree" column. Correlations between psychiatrists and psychologists are shown for the rank order of the number selecting the six categories; in every instance psychologists and psychiatrists were in agreement at a statistically significant level.

TABLE 2

Tabulation of Responses to One-Choice Questions*

QUESTIONS	AGREE CATEGORIES (PERCENT)		DISAGREE CATEGORIES (PERCENT)		Correlation For All Categories
	Psychiatrists	Psychologists	Psychiatrists	Psychologists	
Alcoholics stop drinking after hospital treatment.	27.2	23.1	69.9	74.6	$r_s = 1.00$**
Alcoholics temporarily stop drinking after hospital treatment.	80.9	82.1	15.7	15.6	$r_s = .89$***
Alcoholics cannot drink socially without creating further problems.	90.4	82.7	8.7	15.4	$r_s = .94$**
High motivation to stop is important to success of hospital treatment.	90.4	92.5	8.4	6.9	$r_s = .94$**
Verbal promise to stop drinking is successful.	12.5	8.1	84.6	90.4	$r_s = .94$**
Prognosis for remaining sober is poor.	80.0	86.7	17.1	11.5	$r_s = .89$***

*Responses for the questions do not total 100 percent because some respondents did not answer all questions.
**$p < .01$.
***$p < .05$.

Hospital treatment was recommended despite the poor prognosis for alcoholics, but both psychiatrists and clinical psychologists were largely unwilling to devote much of their own time and effort to the treatment of alcoholics. When given a choice of selecting one of six figures ranging from 100 percent to none as the maximum amount of professional time the respondent was willing to devote to the treatment of alcoholism, psychiatrists and psychologists were in complete agreement ($r_s + 1.00$, p. 01) in selecting ten percent most of the time, followed by 25 percent, 50 percent, and none. Categories representing 25 percent or less of their time were selected by 70.7 percent of the psychiatrists and 74.8 percent of the psychologists. Further, reaction to this hypothetical situation was assessed: If you received definitive notification that your present position was to be primarily devoted to the treatment of alcoholism, you would: leave (ranked third), grudgingly comply (second), neutral reaction (first), be somewhat pleased (fourth), be enthusiastic (fifth). Again psychiatrists and psychologists were in complete agreement on the rank order of the number selecting each answer ($r_s = 1.00$). Of the psychologists, 41.9 percent rate themselves unwilling to undertake full-time work with alcoholics and 18.8 percent welcome it; of the psychiatrists, 38.0 percent are unwilling to undertake full-time work with alcoholics and 20.9 percent welcome it.

DISCUSSION

The marked agreement between psychiatrists and psychologists in this survey of their attitudes toward alcoholism may surprise some readers. Each group is highly qualified to comment on alcoholism, and the majority of each group rejects the highly publicized disease concept. Psychiatrists and psychologists have many opinions in common and share a marked inconsistency in their attitudes toward alcoholism.

To me, this shared inconsistency is only one of many ironies apparent in considering alcoholism. The disease concept that has been pushed so vigorously for many years has been actively promoted by Alcoholics Anonymous, a group of laymen who are prepared to try to work with the alcoholic and whose helping efforts meet with some favor in the groups surveyed here. While medicine has ties with science and objectivity, Jellinik(4), a leading professional proponent of the disease concept specifically states that propaganda is necessary to promote the idea that alcoholism is a disease. Other writers have called for new conceptualizations in preference to the disease concept: "The unworkableness of this approach may be seen in the mutual dislike alcoholics and mental health workers have for each other" (5, p. 585).

The Supreme Court recently upheld conviction of chronic drinkers, but the five-to-four decision led some observers to feel that the problem would be considered again. Leaders in the field of alcoholism propose to gather "stronger medical and legal evidence" that will support the disease concept of alcoholism(6). Groups supporting the disease concept include the American Bar Association, American Medical Association, National Council on Alcoholism, and the Surgeon General of the U.S. Public Health Service.

One may argue that Veterans Administration psychiatrists and psychologists are atypical clinicians, but they do demonstrate some areas of agreement with other professional groups that have been surveyed. In a survey of 46 psychiatrists and 35 residents(7), all but one acknowledged negative feelings when working with alcoholics. Three-quarters of a group of professional and nonprofessional personnel in community clinics working with alcoholics were committed to the importance of motivation, and three-fifths of them considered alcoholics unmotivated(8). Seventy-three percent of state hospital administrators consider alcoholics poorly motivated(9). A survey of psychiatrists in private practice in Massachusetts revealed that 23 percent of the respondents would not accept any alcoholics for treatment(10).

A survey team for the Joint Information Service of the American Psychiatric Association and the National Association for Mental Health(11) sent questionnaires to 260 psychiatrists in private practice. When given a choice of only two answers, 71 percent defined alcoholism as a symptom of personality disorder, 15 percent as a disease, and 13 percent as both a symptom and a disease. This group also considered a high level of motivation for treatment important, but differed from the VA respondents in that 99 percent stated that they used individual psychotherapy either in most cases or in some cases. Bellak(12) has mournfully noted: "I often feel that it is wishful thinking to expect that addictions and major asocial and antisocial forms of acting out will respond to our current psychiatric therapeutic armamentarium. . . . "

It is interesting that in some respects alcoholic veteran patients agree with VA psychiatrists and psychologists(13). After orientation by an ex-alcoholic, 200 patients having problems related to their heavy drinking were asked what types of common alcoholic treatment had helped each of them, and which types they thought might help. The six top choices on what had helped were: talking to other alcoholic patients, talking to an ex-alcoholic counselor, group therapy, Alcoholics Anonymous, and movies on alcoholism. When asked what they thought would help, they suggested one-to-one interaction with a staff psychiatrist or psychologist, lectures, or question-and-answer sessions with staff members. It has recently been questioned whether the individual attention fantasied by this group and many other groups is actually a benefit to hospitalized alcoholics(14). This fantasy overlooks the fact that treating known alcoholics on a one-to-one basis could utilize the full time of every physician and fill every hospital bed in this country(15).

Professionals working in industry have reported sketchily but have made some provocative statements. One program sponsored by a private employer has been reported to show a net savings of more than $600,000 just in reduced use of sick leave. Others claim rehabilitated employees, a reduced employee turnover rate, and increased productivity. One company reported that employees whose job security was threatened had a 90 percent rate of seeking treatment. Of the group whose job security was not threatened, only ten percent sought treatment. Over the past ten years this company calculated that savings on disability and pension costs amounted to twice as much as was invested in the alcoholic consultation center.

In this study of professional experts in alcoholism, the typical psychologist and typical psychiatrist were not committed to the disease concept. Yet they were in favor of removing the alcoholic from jail and placing treatment responsibility in hospitals, although they considered treatment benefits limited at best and did not wish to be associated with it personally to any degree. If these experts are to make cogent comments to courts or legislators on the problem, this study suggests that the individual expert should examine the inconsistencies in his own attitudes in relation to the gross disparities among the magnitude of the problem, the results of therapy, and the facilities for treatment(16). He should also be aware of the contrast between the experts' lack of support for the disease concept.

This survey suggests agreement that hospital treatment is not a panacea for pathological drinking behavior and that psychiatrists and psychologists have only limited interest in treating hospitalized alcoholics. In reacting to society's current concern about alcoholism, an appropriate position might be to favor: 1) sparing the already overloaded general medical and surgical hospital facilities the addition of alcoholics, and 2) having additional experimental clinical work on the problem take place within mental hospitals as current bed capacities permit. Experimental work also appears appropriate for alcoholic treatment programs allied with public or private industry. Psychologists and psychiatrists might consider making their contributions as consultants to the jail system, trying to effect therapeutic changes and treatment within that system. Just as "snake pits" have largely been remade into mental hospitals, so jail could conceivably become protective custody.

NOTES

(1) Harrington LG, Price AC: Alcoholism in a geriatric setting, I: disciplinary problems, marital status and income level. J Amer Geriat Soc 10:197–200, 1962

(2) Knox WJ: Attitudes of psychologists toward alcoholism. J Clin Psychol 25:446–450, 1969

(3) Zwerling I, Rosenbaum M: Alcoholic addiction and personality (nonpsychotic conditions), in American Handbook of Psychiatry. Edited by Arieti S. New York, Basic Books, 1959, pp 623–644

(4) Jellinek EM: Disease Concept of Alcoholism. New Haven, Conn, Hillhouse Press, 1960

(5) Drucker MB: The bottle? The man? Review of books on alcoholism. Contemporary Psychology 13:585–588, 1968

(6) High court not convinced of alcoholism as disease; cites shortage of facilities. Recovery 2(2):1–3, 1968

(7) Robinson L, Podnos B: Resistance of psychiatrists in treatment of alcoholism. J Nerv Ment Dis 143:220–225, 1966

(8) Sterne MW, Pittman DJ: The concept of motivation: a source of institutional and professional blockage in the treatment of alcoholics. Quart J Stud Alcohol 26:41–57, 1965

(9) Moore RA, Buchanan TK: State hospitals and alcoholism: a nationwide survey of treatment techniques and results. Quart J Stud Alcohol 27:459–468, 1966

(10) Schulberg HC: Private practice and community mental health. Hosp Community Psychiat 17:363–366, 1966

(11) Glasscote RM, Plaut TF, Hammersley DW, et al: The Treatment of Alcoholism. Washington, DC, Joint Information Service of the American Psychiatric Association and the National Association for Mental Health, 1967

(12) Bellak L: The concept of acting out: theoretical considerations, in Acting Out. Edited by Abt LE, Weisman SL. New York, Grune & Stratton, 1965, pp 3–19

(13) Gordon HL, Hooker CA: Opinions of alcoholics concerning effectiveness of various treatment methods. Newsletter for Research in Psychology 11:24–26, Feb 1969

(14) Tomsovic M: A follow-up study of discharged alcoholics. Hosp Community Psychiat 21:38–41, 1970

(15) Ross S: Manpower and psychology. Amer Psychol 23:307, 1968

(16) Blum RH, Funkhouser ML: Legislators' views on alcoholism: some dimensions relevant to making new laws. Quart J Stud Alcohol 26:666–669, 1965

PSYCHIATRY
AND THE UTILITY
OF THE TRADITIONAL CRIMINAL LAW APPROACH
TO DRUNKENNESS OFFENSES

L. S. Tao

The notion that chronic alcoholism is a "disease" carries with it two implications: that it is a medical problem; and that it is primarily the medical profession's responsibility to determine who is suffering from such a disease and what are its symptoms. That a disease is not a crime and a sick person cannot be punished as a criminal is axiomatic, particularly in view of the landmark case of *Robinson v. California*.(1) One is tempted to conclude, therefore, that when an accused is designated by a medical expert as suffering from the disease of chronic alcoholism, it is absurd for the lawyer to question that observation.

Were it true that the label of "disease" in the case of addictive alcoholism carried with it an intelligible and definite meaning and that medical experts had reached agreement as to the nature of alcoholic addiction, it would be justifiable for a court to place heavy reliance on the premise that alcoholism is a disease or even to substitute such a principle, where applicable, for existing rules of criminal responsibility. An adequate inquiry, however, reveals that the "disease concept" of alcoholism and the medical knowledge about the addictive condition are far from indisputable. Moreover, the traditional rules of criminal law are not entirely obsolete in the effort to define the criminal responsibility of the public drunkenness offender.

It is the purpose of this article to examine the basic issues involved in the offense of public drunkenness, explore the reasons for the confusion in applying the law, and determine the relevance of medical knowledge to the court's disposition. Hopefully, this analysis should identify and clarify the fundamental issues and the applicable criminal law rules, and reveal the conflict of perspectives between law and psychiatry. Finally, a principle is suggested for ascertaining the criminal responsibility of the public drunkenness offender. My contention is a three-fold one: (a) the offense of public drunkenness is based upon strict liability, and thus it is not a "general intent offense"(2); (b) it is *actus reus*, and not *mens rea*, that is relevant in the strict liability offenses; and (c) medical evidence as to an offender's alcoholism is relevant only in proving voluntariness or involuntariness of the act of drinking and public display of drunkenness, thereby providing a basis on which the court can decide the existence of *actus reus* in a given case. Treatment, as a result, is best carried out within the confines of traditional concepts of responsibility.

THE CASE LAW

Much of the present confusion concerning the criminal responsibility of the chronic alcoholic stems from the Supreme Court's decision in *Robinson v. California*. Reversing a conviction for narcotics addiction, the Court asserted that addiction was a disease, and that it could not, consistent with the eighth amendment, be subjected to criminal sanctions. The California law making the status of addiction a crime was found unconstitutional because it punished a defendant solely for having a disease, and thus inflicted "cruel and unusual punishment in violation of the Fourteenth Amendment."(3)

Mindful of the Supreme Court's pronouncement, and the subsequent acceptance by several medical groups of alcoholism as a disease,(4) many courts became hesitant to enforce statutes which seemed to impose criminal sanctions on chronic alcoholics. In *Driver v. Hinnant*,(5) the Fourth Circuit Court of Appeals, reversing a drunkenness conviction under a North Carolina statute,(6) maintained that "no crime [had] been perpetrated because the conduct was neither actuated by an evil intent nor accompanied with a consciousness of wrongdoing. . . . "(7) Similarly, in *Easter v. District of Columbia*,(8) the D.C. Circuit Court of Appeals held that "one who is a chronic alcoholic cannot have the *mens rea* necessary to be held responsible criminally for being drunk in public."(9)

In *Seattle v. Hill*,(10) however, the Washington Supreme Court interpreted a local ordinance(11) as requiring only a showing of volitional conduct. The court addressed itself to the fundamental distinction between *mens rea* and *actus reus*, and found that the former was not a necessary component of the offense. Guilt was established once it was determined that the offender "possessed the capability of avoiding public drunkenness" for the "*actus reus*, the volitional conduct, was thus present."(12)

Most recently, the U.S. Supreme Court in *Powell v. Texas*(13) reexamined the alcoholism defense, stating that "[t]he entire thrust of Robinson's interpretation of the Cruel and Unusual Punishment Clause is that criminal penalties may be inflicted only if the accused has committed some act [*i.e.*] some *actus reus*."(14) The Court held that Powell's constitutional rights were not violated by his conviction for public intoxication. *Robinson* was found inapplicable because Powell was convicted "not for being a chronic alcoholic, but for being in public while drunk on a particular occasion."(15) Rather than punishing for mere status – chronic alcoholism – the Court imposed a criminal sanction on specific behavior, *i.e.*, intoxication in a public place.

Although *Powell* may have the effect of frustrating the recent trend toward the therapeutic treatment and rehabilitation of chronic drunkenness offenders,(16) it is reconcilable with the previous cases. Moreover, by precisely delineating the limits of *Robinson*, and thus defining the boundaries of criminal responsibility for drunkenness, the decision helps to bring order to this area of the law. By emphasizing the fact that public intoxication is a strict liability offense,(17) we can eliminate the spurious consideration of *mens rea* and its equally spurious psychiatric proof, and concentrate on the true relevance of medical testimony.

THE MENTAL ELEMENT IN DRUNKENNESS OFFENSES

There is, in criminal theory, a fundamental difference between the voluntariness of an act and the *mens rea* of the actor. The former is an element of *actus reus*, and the latter is a description of the actor's subjective mental state at the time of, or in relation to the commission of the act in issue.(18) For example, in criminal negligence cases an inadvertent act apparently is committed by the person in absence of *mens rea*, yet it is voluntary in the sense that the actor is aware of his own physical conduct.(19) On the other hand, if a person under the compulsion of a certain disease, *e.g.*, schizophrenia, commits an act, he is not only without *mens rea*, but also in a condition of involuntariness. This distinction is of vital importance, since involuntariness or lack of *actus reus* will free an individual from all criminal liability, including strict liability imposed by statute, while lack of *mens rea* does not exculpate one from responsibility for the violation of a statute which punishes certain conduct without requiring any *mens rea*. A person in an involuntary state will never be capable of exhibiting the requisite *actus reus*; thus involuntariness can never be the basis for criminal liability.

Although the material elements of drinking offenses vary with the statutes, it is commonly prescribed that drunkenness in public is an essential condition for conviction.(20) Invariably, however, no *mens rea* is required. A typical statutory approach is that followed by Texas: "Whoever shall get drunk or be found in a state of intoxication in any public place, or at any private house except his own, shall be fined not exceeding one hundred dollars."(21) The exclusion from the statute of "knowingly" or "willfully," coupled with the provision for only a small fine, indicate that the public intoxication law is predicated upon strict liability.(22)

But even in strict liability offenses, some mental element must be established as part of the *actus reus*. The criminal law does not punish all prohibited acts, but only those that are attributable to a particular defendant. Thus, intoxication is not an offense unless committed in a public place. Being in a public place is the *actus reus*; it implies a minimum degree of consciousness of one's bodily movements and voluntariness associated with the act. This level of mental participation is part of the *actus reus* — without it the law would be punishing spasms, sleepwalking, and cataleptic acts.

In light of these distinctions between *mens rea, actus reus,* and their requisite mental elements, *Driver, Easter, Hill,* and *Powell* appear to be reconcilable. In *Easter* and *Driver* the prosecution did not establish beyond a reasonable doubt that the defendant's act was voluntary.(23) Conversely, drunkenness convictions were sustained in *Hill* and *Powell* because the defendant was unable to present sufficient evidence to show that his acts were uncontrollable, *i.e.*, lacking the voluntariness necessary to establish the *actus reus* of the offense.(24)

PSYCHIATRIC TESTIMONY AND CRIMINAL RESPONSIBILITY

It is commonly recognized that two or three drinks do not generally produce uncontrollable actions. Some inhibitions disappear but others remain, and judgment and perception are not seriously impaired to important degrees. Of course, sensibilities may be affected to a considerable extent, but except in extreme cases, a drunken person is still aware of his behavior and actions. Thus, in this situation, if *actus reus* is proved, conviction is justified.

There are, however, great differences between the effects of insanity and those of intoxication. Ordinarily, there is some choice in whether or not to drink. Any choice carries with it responsibility; in particular, the choice to drink alcohol increases the risk of public drunkenness or even doing harm to others.(25) Although mental disease may in some cases be the result of a great many unwise decisions over a period of time, one obviously cannot choose tomorrow's insanity in the same way he can elect tomorrow's drunkenness. This is precisely the ground upon which judicial decisions as to criminal responsibility rely.(26) But there is an exception: with the diseased, compulsive drinker, our judgment, moral or legal, should be different. For if drinking alcohol is compelled by a disease, then there is no free choice just as there is none in the case of mental disease. Voluntariness cannot exist where there is no free choice.(27) In the absence of voluntariness there is no *actus reus*; the offender is not responsible for his public drunkenness, even though he knows through prior experience that his consumption of alcohol may result in public intoxication. This is perhaps a proper description of the problem of most chronic alcoholics.(28) Apparently, for such individuals the question is whether the consumption of alcohol is voluntary in the first place.

Leaving the extreme cases, there is a class of people who are not under the compulsion of a disease nor coerced to drink. With this group the question of prior experience will become important. Distinction can be made between the normal offenders who have no previous experience with intoxication which caused them to lose self-control over their public conduct, and those with such experience.(29) The inexperienced drunkenness offender is not responsible for public intoxication even though he voluntarily consumes alcohol. This conclusion, of course, assumes that he has lost that minimum degree of consciousness of his bodily movements and that this loss resulted in a public display of drunkenness.(30) Drinking alcohol and publicly displaying drunkenness can be seen conceptually as two distinct matters; furthermore, because the public intoxication is involuntary,(31) the offender is not criminally liable by reason of lack of *actus reus*.

The experienced normal inebriate, on the other hand, presents a completely different problem. He has been intoxicated and has experienced loss of perception and control on at least one occasion prior to the behavior in question. He knows that once intoxicated, he may wander out and be found in a stuporous condition in public. Although he is in a state of unconsciousness when apprehended by the police, he has, or should have, anticipated that consequence, and he has voluntarily increased the likelihood of his resultant condition by drinking. In this situation, drinking and public intoxication are in natural sequence not only in terms of his behavior, but in terms of his knowledge and awareness of the probable consequence. This public display of drunkenness is voluntary, and for that reason, there is the necessary *actus reus*.(32)

Once the nature of the offense of drunkenness is understood we can assess the proper role of medical and psychiatric testimony in the prosecution of each of the types of offenders mentioned in the preceding classification.

The preceding analysis gives rise to several principles. First, the degree of intoxication and the extent of sense impairment must always be examined. Save in extreme cases, all normal offenders are criminally responsible if they retain an awareness of their behavior. Second, where intoxication exists to such a degree that perception is totally lost, experienced drinkers should be differentiated from their inexperienced counterparts. Normal drinkers who have experienced intoxication are criminally liable for public drunkenness if, having been intoxicated, they display drunkenness in public as proscribed by the law. Third, normal drinkers who have had no previous experience of intoxication, and who have no reason to anticipate loss of self-control, are not responsible if they become intoxicated and display drunkenness in public. Finally, chronic alcoholics are not responsible for public drunkenness, provided it can be established that their consumption of alcohol is compelled by the disease and is done without free choice. The test of criminal responsibility is based upon the general doctrine of *actus reus*. In the first and second cases there is *actus reus*, while in the other situations there is none.

In all these cases, psychiatric testimony is relevant to the extent that it can show whether consumption of alcohol is symptomatic of the disease of alcoholism; it can demonstrate that the person has no free choice and is compelled to drink. It can also show degrees of intoxication and the extent to which perception or awareness is impaired, *i.e.*, whether the offender is slightly intoxicated with no loss of awareness, or grossly drunk and not conscious of his own behavior. Medical testimony in this regard can aid a court in determining the existence of "drunkenness" and voluntariness, a determination required by the law.(33)

Psychiatric testimony should be limited to the question of voluntariness. The justification for assigning to medical science this circumscribed role lies in the difference in perspective between the legal and medical professions, and the unsettled state of medicine regarding the definitions and nature of alcoholism and disease.

DIFFERENCE IN PERSPECTIVES

Every branch of science rests upon certain axioms or postulates which are accepted by experts in the particular field. Basically, psychiatry is preoccupied with the origin, growth, development, and ultimate expression of certain deep human drives. Sex and aggression are conceived of as innate biological forces which undergo an incredibly varied series of transformations before they manifest themselves in their adult forms. Detrimental influences affect the development of these biological forces. If these harmful influences are not overcome, psychopathology results. The symptoms of the resultant psychopathological states are explainable as consequences of the dynamic interaction of the pathological drives and the defenses of the ego.(34) Though this description is somewhat over simplified, psychiatry does in fact view human nature in terms of drives and dispositions which operate in accordance with universal laws of causation. In particular, the alcoholic's mind is believed subject to casual emotional experiences, especially early sexual experiences, which give it certain characteristics so that at the moment of action they completely determine the person's choice.(35)

The law, on the other hand, is concerned not with diagnosis or prognosis, but with evaluating and passing judgment on human conduct in particular factual situations. Its view of human nature asserts the reality of free choice and rejects the thesis that the conduct of the normal adult is a mere expression of imperious psychological necessity.(36) Indeed, recognition of a certain degree of free will or autonomy is a necessary postulate of any criminal law. The concept of responsibility is derived from that postulate.

The differences in perspective — between free will and psychological necessity — also determine the attitudes toward punishment. Thus sociologists conceive of punishment as group vengeance, while psychiatrists view it as a measure subserving the emotional needs of the public.(37) But from the perspective of the law, punishment signifies accountability of the person who voluntarily chooses to do an act proscribed by the law. To a great extent, this may reflect a moral judgment that a normal person who voluntarily engages in socially harmful conduct is culpable.(38) According to this view, punishment serves the public good by giving concrete effect and publicity to the community's standards of right and wrong by incapacitating the convicted harmdoer from further harmdoing, and by facilitating a certain amount of rehabilitation within the legal framework.(39) Punishment is therefore a corollary of responsibility based upon the concept of man as capable, within limits, of making free moral choices. Consequently, if human beings are in any sense free moral agents, treatment cannot be wholly substituted for punishment. It would not be justified, even on humanitarian grounds, to treat all criminals as sick persons.(10)

ALCOHOLISM AS A DISEASE

Shortly after *Robinson*, the American Medical Association and the American Psychiatric Association adopted position statements to the effect that alcoholism is an illness and is entitled to treatment by whatever means are at our disposal.(41) These statements, coupled with a similar announcement of the World Health Organization, have been regarded as authoritative by some courts. The court in *Driver*, for example, following the *Robinson* dictum that disease cannot be made criminal, relied heavily upon the premise that alcoholism is a disease.(42) Consequently, it becomes important to know, when the medical profession designates alcoholism as a disease, what are the implications of this designation. The relevance of the disease concept of alcoholism to law depends largely upon such an inquiry.

In the majority of cases, persons who seem ill and report themselves as feeling sick are persons whose so-called component parts are not in equilibrium; one or several parts are working in such a way as to be beyond the limits of their natural functions. This is perhaps the common view of physical illness,(43) which is in turn based upon the finding of some underlying tissue pathology, or biochemical or neurophysiological aberration. Such malfunctioning clearly exists in the human body when malnutrition, cirrhosis, polyneuritis, or gastrobleeding result from excessive drinking.(44)

The physiological definition of disease,(45) however, is obviously not what was meant by the World Health Organization when it announced that: "Alcoholics are those excessive drinkers whose dependence upon alcohol has attained such a degree that it shows a noticeable mental disturbance or an interference with their bodily and mental health, their interpersonal relations, and their smooth social and economic functioning, or who show the prodromal signs of such developments."(46) Disease is used in this context to refer to the uncontrolled, apparently compulsive and self-harming characteristics of the alcoholic's drinking patterns.

As the effort to find chemicals in specific beverages which might be responsible for alcohol addiction has not been successful, most observers tend to explain the phenomenon of alcoholism in psychiatric terms. The Freudians have attributed alcoholism to one of three unconscious tendencies: self-destructive urges, oral fixation, and latent homosexuality.(47) The Adlerians have explained alcoholism as a striving for power, a reaction to a pervasive feeling of inferiority.(48) The interpersonal psychologists believe that alcoholism may be a response to a number of different motives, but most commonly to a suppressed conflict between dependent drives and aggressive urges.(49) Many psychiatrists claim that they frequently find in alcoholics certain personality characteristics, such as emotional dependency, immaturity, low tolerance for anxiety, and frustration.(50) But it must be noted that most individuals with these latter traits who consult psychiatrists are not alcoholics. While a few people may be predestined to become alcoholics, psychological predisposition is not an adequate explanation for most alcoholism.

Psychiatrists generally consider alcoholism a form of mental disease.(51) Some authorities believe that an alcoholic's drinking is a compulsion just like the stealing of a kleptomaniac. Others attempt to define alcoholism in terms of mental disturbance, interference with interpersonal relations, or impairment of health.(52) The practical difficulties encountered by the experts in attempting to define alcoholism are similar to those met in attempting a clear-cut definition of "mental illness."(53)

The lack of consensus regarding alcoholism is further illustrated by the fact that certain medical authorities believe it is an habituation.(54) To say that addiction is "habituation to some practice"(55) has important legal implications. A habit is not necessarily a disease, and bad habit will not excuse one from criminal responsibility.(56)

Sociologists, on the other hand, have considered alcoholism to relate to a variety of social correlates. Some of them tend to view such compulsive diseases as neurosis and alcoholism in terms of differential association and role theory.(57) The premise is that the behavior is learned and the compulsive act is "motivated" through social interactions. Since disease cannot be learned, the sociological interpretation is not quite consistent with the commonly accepted view of disease.

Moreover, psychiatrists themselves have occasion to see only a small number of the estimated six million alcoholics.(58) Normally, they draw their evidence from an analysis of post hoc samples — alcoholics who have already been committed to a mental hospital or who have already approached a clinic for psychotherapy. Because most alcoholics conceal their drinking problems, few are ever observed by the clinic psychiatrists. As a result, there seems no sufficiently sound basis on which to decide whether certain personality traits are the cause or result of excessive drinking.

In psychiatry, laboratory evidence is not very useful in demonstrating specific pathological signs objectively. Thus, both the initial diagnosis and the estimate of the degree of illness become a function of the skill, experience, and theoretical orientation of the diagnostician.(59) Diagnoses made on the basis of clinical judgment are inevitably variable; because of this variation, few experts have offered clear-cut criteria for defining alcoholism other than the usually stated relationship with the norms set by the social environment.(60) In reality, however, to say that alcoholism is a form of mental and physiological disturbance which interferes with the individual's "smooth social and economic functioning" is to say that it brings about socially undesirable results. This is a proposition that does not seem to convey much definite meaning. Nor is the attempt to include alcoholism in the category of mental illness very useful. Psychiatrists have not reached a consensus on the criteria upon which to define who is mentally ill.(61) The fact that psychiatry cannot demonstrate by pathology that a given person has been under such compulsion as to be unable to control his behavior makes it very difficult for a court to view him as being sick and to accept the proposition that he does not have the power to avoid public drunkenness.

The designation of alcoholism as a disease then is primarily a question of social policy.(62) Such a labelling may have the desirable effect of making problem drinking a topic for systematic study rather than a moral issue. It may provide a common ground upon which law and medicine may work together for the solution to the problem of how to deal with alcoholics. It is, of course, pointless to deny the advantages to be derived from the effort to label alcoholism as a disease. But in the absence of a consensus among psychiatrists and other experts on the pathology, mental condition, and symptoms of alcoholism, the designation of alcoholism as an illness does not provide an authoritative basis upon which courts might conclude that it is a disease.

Terming alcoholism a disease, or characterizing a public drunkenness offender as a sick person, implies that the medical profession should assume primary responsibility for the ultimate solution to the problem. It does not, however, constitute a sufficient *legal* basis for exculpating the person from criminal liability. The fundamental issue is whether the behavior in question is voluntary in the sense that the offender was aware of his own conduct and the material facts of his offense. If the offender did not have the degree of voluntariness required by the criminal law, no criminal sanction should be imposed on him.

POST-RESPONSIBILITY DETERMINATIONS AND PSYCHIATRY

Undoubtedly medical science, particularly psychiatry, has much to offer in the improvement of the law and its administration.(63) The problem is to establish a sound theoretical basis to enable medicine and law to work harmoniously together. This is a difficult problem: but difficult as it may seem, it can nevertheless be achieved by the cooperative efforts of the professions and disciplines concerned. The principal barrier at present seems to be a lack of understanding of the grounds on which psychiatry and law can meet to establish a positive method of dealing with the offense of public drunkenness.

The law dealing with public drunkenness is punitive in nature and not remedial. The wisdom of the laws punishing public drunkenness has not been under attack in this paper, although their validity is open to serious question.(64) It is conceivable, however, that even through the administration of the punitive aspects of the law, remedial help may be afforded chronic alcoholic offenders. Pragmatically, the law may work in remedial ways although it is not institutionally designed for this purpose. The first question to be determined, however, is who shall be subjected to the control of the State.(65) Once it is decided that a person is criminally responsible and thus liable for his acts, the second question will then be: What kind of control shall be exercised by the State? This inquiry goes to the social interpretation of punishment and asks whether punishment or treatment is a more desirable way of dealing with the drunkenness offender. One of the basic assumptions here as elsewhere in other studies is that there are important differences between hospitals and prisons.(66)

THE EXPERT IN THE ADMINISTRATION OF THE LAW

I have attempted to show what the role of the medical expert should be in the administration of the antidrinking laws and to justify my belief that his participation at the responsibility stage must, at least presently, remain limited. Once responsibility has been fixed, however, the expert should assume a more important role by advising the court in determining the proper disposition. In this role the expert can be of great assistance to the court in determining the appropriate sentence to be imposed on a LeRoy Powell or a Joe Driver.

Within the existing legal framework which provides definite standards for determining responsibility, there can and should be a substantial measure of individualization. It is important to note that a clear understanding of the function of the law makes apparent the conclusion that much can be done to individualize the treatment of criminals without weakening the legal safeguards accorded each individual.(67) One serious difficulty with the drunkenness offender is the short duration of time within which the State can exercise compulsory measures of treatment or rehabilitation upon him. This time limitation not only limits the deterrent effect, but may also preclude the possibility of treatment, even after a finding that treatment is desirable.(68) The problem of the cost of establishing appropriate medical facilities for the treatment of alcoholics and staffing them with trained personnel is also not an easy one to solve. Most penal institutions lack the resources necessary to provide adequate medical and psychiatric services. Rather than engaging in futile disputes as to what is alcoholism and the relevance of the disease idea to the determination of the offender's criminal responsibility, medical experts and lawyers might better join in a common effort to have more resources allocated to provide such services.

Medical knowledge concerning "alcoholism," while capable of contributing to the understanding of the problems faced by the individual, must be carefully scrutinized and fit into the legal framework in a useful manner. Although "alcoholism" is a proper concern of psychiatry, present psychiatric knowledge regarding the concept is far from having reached the point of unimpeachable scientific certainty.(69) Until a thoroughgoing definition of "alcoholism" is provided, it would be undesirable, and indeed entirely unjustified, to abandon the traditional criminal law approach which at least offers some definite standards upon which a court may decide the responsibility of a drunkenness offender. The abandonment of legal standards would result in arbitrary proceedings in which the chance that an individual would be subjected to abuse is as great as the chance that he would be given humanitarian treatment. The principal consequence of such an abandonment would be the hospitalization of many offenders who should be imprisoned, or an extension of their hospitalization for a period much longer than their potential prison sentence.(70) No doubt this would tend to undermine the value of the law.

CONCLUSION

Medical knowledge about the pathological, psychiatric, and physiological aspects of alcoholism has much to offer the law. This medical knowledge, however, is presently very limited. Lack of consensus as to what constitutes "alcoholism," for example, defers wholesale modifications in the legal rules concerning criminal responsibility of the public drunkenness offender. Moreover, because the criminal law embodies and safeguards important values, its abandonment is not justified even by cumulating the results of all the medical studies on alcoholism. While the medical profession has much to contribute to the law, especially to the administration of the law and its examination and adoption of post-conviction policies, it has not reached the stage to supplant the legal determination whether the offender should, or should not, be responsible for his act. Consequently, with reference to the question of criminal responsibility, the most promising contribution that the medical expert can offer is to assist the court in deciding whether a given act or conduct is voluntarily committed by the accused.

NOTES

(1) 370 U.S. 660 (1962).
(2) See Kirbens, *Chronic Alcohol Addiction and Criminal Responsibility,* 54 A.B.A.J. 877, 879-80 (1968).
(3) 370 U.S. at 667.
(4) See COOPERATIVE COMM'N ON THE STUDY OF ALCOHOLISM, ALCOHOL PROBLEMS: A REPORT TO THE NATION 27-28 & apps. A & C (T. Plaut ed. 1968).
(5) 356 F.2d 761 (4th Cir. 1966).
(6) "If any person shall be found drunk or intoxicated on the public highway, or at any public place or meeting . . . he shall be guilty of a misdemeanor, and upon conviction shall be punished . . . by a fine . . . or imprisonment." N.C. GEN. STAT. § 14-335 (1953).
(7) 356 F.2d at 764.
(8) 124 U.S. App. D.C. 33, 361 F.2d 50 (1966).
(9) *Id.* at 36, 361 F.2d at 53.
(10) 435 P.2d 692 (Wash. 1967).
(11) "It shall be unlawful for any person to be guilty of . . . drunkenness . . . or of any conduct tending to disturb the public peace, or . . . tending to debauch the public morals." SEATTLE, WASH., CITY CODE 12.11.020, § 1.
(12) 435 P.2d at 698.
(13) 392 U.S. 514 (1968).
(14) *Id.* at 533.
(15) *Id.* at 532.
(16) See Pittman, *Public Intoxication and the Alcoholic Offender in American Society,* in PRESIDENT'S COMM'N ON LAW ENFORCEMENT AND ADMINISTRATION OF JUSTICE, TASK FORCE REPORT: DRUNKENNESS 7-28 (1967); MacCormick, *Correctional Views on Alcohol, Alcoholism and Crimes,* 9 CRIME & DELINQUENCY 15(1963); Murtagh, *Status Offenses and*

Due Process of Law, 36 FORDHAM L. REV. 51 (1967); Smith, *Nonpenal Rehabilitation for the Chronic Alcoholic Offender*, 32 FED. PROBATION, Sept. 1968, at 46.

(17) *See* J. HALL, GENERAL PRINCIPLES OF CRIMINAL LAW 146-58 (2d ed. 1960) [hereinafter cited as HALL]; Binavince, *The Ethical Foundation of Criminal Liability*, 33 FORDHAM L. REV. 1, 27-34 (1964); Sayre, *Public Welfare Offenses*, 33 COLUM. L. REV. 55, 67-70 (1933).

(18) "The true translation to my mind of *mens rea* is . . . 'the intention to do the act which is made penal by the statute, or by common law.' " Stallybrass, *A Comparison of the General Principles of Criminal Law in England with the "Progetto Definitivo Di Un Nuovo Codice Penale" of Alfredo Rocco*, in THE MODERN APPROACH TO CRIMINAL LAW 406 (L. Radzinowitz & J. Turner eds. 1945), *citing* Allard v. Selfridge, [1925] 1 K.B. 129. *See also* Sayre, *The Present Significance of Mens Rea in the Criminal Law*, in HARVARD LEGAL ESSAYS 411 n.33 (R. Pound ed. 1934). Another commentator has defined *mens rea* in terms of two elements: "It [*mens rea*] consists first of all of the intent to do an act, and of a knowledge of the circumstances that makes that act a criminal offense." Devlin, *Statutory Offenses*, 4 J. SOC'Y PUB. TEACHERS OF L. 213 (1956).

For discussions of the meaning and function of *actus reus*, see Kilbride, *The Actus Reus of an Offense*, 1 N.Z.U.L. REV. 139 (1963); Sim, *The Involuntary Actus Reus*, 25 MOD. L. REV. 741 (1962).

(19) *See, e.g.*, People v. Lynn, 385 Ill. 165, 52 N.E.2d 166 (1943); People v. Robinson, 253 Mich. 507, 235 N.W. 236 (1931); People v. Orr, 243 Mich. 300, 220 N.W. 777 (1928).

One commentator believes that intention and recklessness should be subjected to criminal liability, while negligence, in the sense that it denotes the actor's inadvertance, should be excluded from criminal liability: "Negligence implies inadvertance, *i.e.*, that the defendant was completely unaware of the dangerousness of his behavior although actually it was unreasonably increasing the risk of the occurrence of an injury." HALL. *supra* note 17, at 114; Hall, *Negligent Behavior Should Be Excluded from Penal Liability*, 63 COLUM. L. REV. 632 (1963).

(20) *See* 28 C.J.S. *Drunkards* § 14(b) (1941). The requirement, adopted in many statutes, that the offense must have been committed in a public place, implies that some act in addition to the mere state of drunkenness justifies the intervention of the State into the individual's private life. *Cf.* J. BENTHAM, THE PRINCIPLES OF MORALS AND LEGISLATION 204-08 (Hafner ed. 1948); J.S. MILL, ON LIBERTY 9-32 (Liberal Arts ed. 1956).

(21) TEX. PEN. CODE ANN. art. 477 (Vernon 1952). The statutory wording "found" may bar the defense of involuntarily being in a public place. It is important to note that even a statute of strict liability does not punish one who is taken to a public place by physical compulsion; he did not go there voluntarily, hence there was no act. But if one is guilty for simply being "found" in a public place, the plea of involuntariness is not a good defense. This distinction illustrates the need for great care in considering statutory language. The expression of being "found in the state of intoxication in a public place" shows that punishment is directed against a state of being, rather than an act.

(22) The statutory strict liability offenses depend on the particular wording of the statutes by which they are created, and the elements of each offense must obviously be ascertained by construing the statute. For a discussion of the rules governing the interpretation of statutes imposing strict liability, see Jackson, *Absolute Prohibition in Statutory Offenses*, 6 CAMB. L.J. 83, 84-85 (1938).

(23) In *Driver*, the defendant was found to have no control over his behavior.

The court compared his actions "to the movements of an imbecile or a person in a delirium of a fever." 356 F.2d at 764. This inability to control his behavior applies not to the determination of *mens rea* but rather to the more fundamental determination of *actus reus*.

(24) The *Powell* Court was unable to conclude that the defendant was under such compulsion that he was unable to control his behavior. 392 U.S. at 535. Because Powell was both able to control his actions and capable of refraining from being in public after he became drunk, the requisite *actus reus* was present. Since the criminal sanction was based solely on voluntary conduct, the presence or absence of *mens rea* was immaterial.

(25) *See, e.g.*, Myerson, *Institute on Modern Trends in Handling the Chronic Alcoholic Offender*, 19 S.C.L. REV. 303, 348 (1967).

(26) *See* People v. Decina, 2 N.Y.2d 133, 138 N.E.2d 799, 157 N.Y.S.2d 558 (1956). *See also* HALL, *supra* note 17, at 530.

(27) R. PERKINS, CRIMINAL LAW 652-55 (1957); *see* Gunn v. State, 37 Ga. App. 333, 140 S.E. 524 (1927).

(28) Powell v. Texas, 392 U.S. 514, 518 (1968); *cf.* S. WALLACE, SKID ROW AS A WAY OF LIFE (1965).

(29) These distinctions, however, are meaningful only in the situation where the person's public drunkenness is committed involuntarily. Criminal liability for one whose public act is with self-awareness is not open to question.

(30) If the offender has not lost his awareness, criminal responsibility should follow. *Cf.* Paris & Great N.R.R. v. Robinson, 104 Tex. 482, 486, 140 S.W. 434, 436 (1911).

(31) Involuntariness in this context refers to an individual's being grossly intoxicated and not aware of his behavior.

(32) *See, e.g.*, State v. Sevier, 20 N.E. 245 (Ind. 1889).

(33) The determination of "drunkenness" is an especially difficult problem. *See* Holley v. State, 25 Ala. App. 260, 144 So. 535 (1932); People v. Rewland, 335 Ill. 432, 167 N.E. 10 (1929); Clark v. State, 63 Tex. Crim. 529, 111 S.W. 659, 660 (1908). Even an arresting officer's observation is not always taken at face value. *See* Wise v. State, 38 Ga. App. 195, 143 S.E. 574 (1928).

(34) *See, e.g.*, Diamond, *The Simulation of Sanity*, 2 J. SOCIAL THERAPY 158 (1956).

(35) *See generally* THE INDIVIDUAL PSYCHOLOGY OF ALFRED ADLER 423 (H. & R. Ansbacher eds. 1956). The deterministic view of human conduct can be seen in Belby, *Psychoanalysis and Crime*, 4 J. CRIM. PSYCHOPATHOLOGY 639, 647-49 (1943); Brill, *Determinism in Psychiatry and Psychoanalysis*, 95 AM. J. PSYCHIATRY 597 (1938). *But see* Lewis, *The Humanitarian Theory of Punishment*, 6 RES JUDICATAI 224 (1953).

(36) *See* Cressey, *The Differential Association Theory and Compulsive Crimes*, in CRIME AND INSANITY 49, 52-53 (R. Nice ed. 1958). *See generally* Mueller, *The Public Law of Wrongs: Its Concepts in the World of Reality*, 10 J. PUB. L. 203, 236-38 (1961).

(37) *See generally* White, *The Need for Cooperation Between the Legal Profession and the Psychiatrist in Dealing with the Crime Problem*, 7 AM. J. PSYCHIATRY 493, 502 (1927) (the criminal law represents "vengeance" which functions under "the disguise of deterrence").

(38) *See* HALL, *supra* note 17, at 70-104.

(39) *See generally* L. SUTHERLAND & D. CRESSEY, PRINCIPLES OF CRIMINOLOGY 335-64 (7th ed. 1966).

(40) *See* Davidson, *Irresistible Impulse and Criminal Responsibility*, in CRIME AND INSANITY 29, 45 (R. Nice ed. 1958). Calling alcoholism a disease seems a logical concomitant of the psychiatric theories that all crime is a

pathological phenomenon. One psychiatrist has even said that "the time will come when stealing or murder will be thought of as a symptom, indicating the presence of a disease." *See* Menninger, *Medicolegal Proposals of the American Psychiatric Association*, 19 J. CRIM. L.C. & P.S. 367, 373 (1928). *See also* White, *supra* note 37, at 503.

(41) *See* COOPERATIVE COMM'N ON THE STUDY OF ALCOHOLISM, *supra* note 4.

(42) 356 F.2d at 763-64.

(43) "Disease" is defined in part as "[t]he failure of the adaptive mechanisms of an organism to counteract adequately the stimuli or stresses to which it is subject, resulting in a disturbance in function or structure of any part, organ or system of the body." BLAKISTON'S NEW GOULD MEDICAL DICTIONARY 354 (2d ed. 1956); *see* M. JAHODA, CURRENT CONCEPTS OF POSITIVE MENTAL HEALTH 113 (1958); *cf. Symposium – Work, Health and Satisfaction*, 18 J. SOCIAL ISSUES, July 1962.

(44) *See* ALCOHOLISM: BASIC ASPECTS AND TREATMENT (H. Himwich ed. 1957).

(45) *See* note 43 *supra*.

(46) WORLD HEALTH ORGANIZATION, EXPERT COMM. ON MENTAL HEALTH, ALCOHOLISM SUBCOMM. SECOND REPORT 16 (WHO Technical Rep. Ser. No. 48, 1952).

(47) M. CHAFETZ & H. DEMONE, ALCOHOLISM AND SOCIETY 39-42 (1962); K. MENNINGER, MAN AGAINST HIMSELF 149 (1938).

(48) *See e.g.*, THE INDIVIDUAL PSYCHOLOGY OF ALFRED ADLER 423 (H. & R. Ansbacher eds. 1956).

(49) *E.g.*, WHITE, THE ABNORMAL PERSONALITY 417 (1948).

(50) Selber, *Psychodynamic Therapy*, in SELECTED PAPERS DELIVERED AT THE SIXTEENTH ANNUAL MEETING OF THE NORTH AMERICAN ASS'N OF ALCOHOLISM PROGRAMS (1965).

(51) *See* Diethelm, *Current Research on Problems of Alcoholism*, 16 Q.J. STUDIES OF ALCOHOLISM 565 (1955).

(52) *E.g.*, Keller, *Definition of Alcoholism*, 21 Q.J. STUDIES OF ALCOHOLISM 125, 132-33 (1960).

(53) *See* Redlich, *The Concept of Normality*, 6 AM. J. PSYCHOTHERAPY 551 (1952). "[I]f psychiatry seems not a little vague about what mental health and disease are, scientific medicine does not actually fare much better." Zilboorg, *The Struggle For and Against the Individual in Psychotherapy*, 104 AM. J. PSYCHIATRY 524 (1948); *cf.* Waelder, *Psychiatry and the Problem of Criminal Responsibility*, 101 U. PA. L. REV. 378, 384 (1952).

(54) *E.g.*, Reinert, *The Concept of Alcoholism as a Bad Habit*, BULL. MENNINGER CLINIC 35 (1968); Reinert, *Alcoholism: Disease or Habit?*, 32 FED. PROBATION, Mar. 1968, at 12.

(55) STEDMAN'S MEDICAL DICTIONARY 26 (21st ed. 1966).

(56) In *Seattle v. Hill*, the Washington Supreme Court upheld a finding of criminal liability despite the fact that the defendant "acknowledged that drinking 'is kind of a pastime and a habit.' " 435 P.2d 692, 698 (Wash. 1967).

(57) *See* Cressey, *supra* note 36; Ullman, *Sociocultural Backgrounds of Alcoholism*, 315 ANNALS 48, 50 (1958). For the theory of differential association, see E. SUTHERLAND & D. CRESSEY, *supra* note 39, at 81-82. For a general discussion of the role theory, see G. MEAD, MIND, SELF & SOCIETY (1934) and Foote, *Identification as the Basis for a Theory of Motivation*, 16 AM. SOC. REV. 14 (1951).

(58) This is the estimate of the National Council on Alcoholism. AMERICAN PSYCHIATRIC ASS'N, THE TREATMENT OF ALCOHOLISM 11 (1967).

(59) *See* A. HOLLINGSHEAD & F. REDLICH, SOCIAL CLASS AND MENTAL ILLNESS 155-57 (1958); Knight, *A Critique of the Present Status of Psychotherapies*, 23 BULL. N.Y. ACAD. MED. 100 (1949).

(60) *See* MILBANK MEM. FUND. INTERELATIONS BETWEEN THE SOCIAL ENVIRONMENT AND PSYCHIATRIC DISORDERS (1953). *See also* Lewis, *Health as a Social Concept*, 4 BRIT. J. SOC. 109 (1953).

(61) *See* Lapouse, *Who is Sick?*, 35 AM. J. ORTHOPSYCHIATRY 138, 141 (1965); Redlich, *supra* note 53.

(62) "[A] disease is what the medical profession recognizes as such." F. JHLINFK, THE DISEASE CONCEPT OF ALCOHOLISM 12 (1960); *see* Seeley, *Alcoholism is a Disease: The Implications for Social Policy*, in SOCIETY, CULTURE AND DRINKING PATTERNS 586 (D. Pittman & C. Snyder eds. 1962).

(63) *See* materials cited note 16 *supra*.

(64) Justice Marshall noted in *Powell* that "[t]he fact that [many] conceal their drinking problems, is indicative that some powerful deterrent operates to inhibit the public revelation. . . . " He implicitly pointed out, however, that the conclusion that this was the result of antidrunkenness laws was assumed, and that it was not supported by relevant known facts. Moreover, he attributed this deterrence at least partially to the moral sanction imposed by society rather than the punitive sanction imposed by the law. 392 U.S. at 530-31.

However, any deterrent which may exist, whether legally or morally imposed, has not effectively operated in relation to known alcoholics or recidivist public intoxication offenders. There seems little doubt, therefore, that punishment of mere presence in public is a futile gesture so far as unscrupulous and, particularly, homeless drunks are concerned. Thus, if the nature of the offense precludes a presumption or requirement of *mens rea* on the part of the offender, and no sound justification can be found for the law, either in terms of traditional distinctions or in terms of its practical effect, serious doubts will be raised as to the desirability of such legislation. *Cf.* PRESIDENT'S COMM'N ON LAW ENFORCEMENT AND ADMINISTRATION OF JUSTICE, REPORT: THE CHALLENGE OF CRIME IN A FREE SOCIETY 234-36 (1967).

(65) *See* J. BENTHAM, *supra* note 20, at 205-08. *See also* J.S. MILL, *supra* note 20, at 13.

(66) *See* S. RUBIN, PSYCHIATRY AND CRIMINAL LAW 23-51 (1965).

(67) *See* HALL, *supra* note 17, at 56-57.

(68) *See* MacCormick, *supra* note 16.

(69) *See* Waelder, *supra* note 53; *cf.* Zilboorg, *supra* note 53.

(70) If "cure" is the objective, the person might well be confined indefinitely in a hospital since alcoholism is considered an incurable disease by some experts. *See* Logan, *Alcoholism: A Legal Problem?*, 36 DICTA 449 (1959).

ATTITUDINAL BARRIERS
TO PHYSICIAN INVOLVEMENT
WITH DRUG ABUSERS

John N. Chappel

The statement, "Once an addict always an addict," typifies the hopeless and the negative attitudes that interfere with the treatment of drug dependence. Myths and stereotypes permeate the attitudes of both patients and physicians. These attitudes interfere with physician-patient involvement on at least three levels. First, patients with drug-abuse problems are reluctant to seek medical help. When they do, there is very little revelation of the full details of their drug abuse. Bakewell and Ewing have commented on the number of physicians' wives whose undiagnosed illnesses led to psychiatric referral and the discovery of drug dependence.(1) Second, physicians, including psychiatrists, are reluctant to participate personally in the treatment of drug dependence.(2) Physicians report that management of alcoholics is difficult, time consuming, and unrewarding, and that drug-dependent patients are unwilling to participate in treatment or to follow advice.(3) Finally, hospitals often refuse to admit or treat recognized cases of drug dependence. We have had former heroin addicts currently receiving methadone hydrochloride turned away from hospitals with the statement, "We don't treat junkies."

In spite of these barriers, the pressure on physicians, hospitals, and medical societies for involvement with drug-abuse patients is likely to increase. There is no sign that the problems are diminishing. It is probable that 5% to 10% of our population is involved with extensive nonmedical drug use, including alcohol, stimulant, and barbiturate addiction.

Whether the physician treats drug dependence or not, he is almost certain to manage patients with drug-dependence problems. Adequate diagnosis and treatment of any medical condition requires both communication and cooperation in the context of a physician-patient relationship. This article explores the nature of the barriers obstructing development of a physician-drug-abuse patient relationship.

Physicians have had a prominent role in the history of interactions between men and drugs. The dangers of unsupervised and ignorant drug use have led to the development of physicians as "gatekeepers" for many drugs.(4) The widespread use of opium and morphine following the Civil War led to passage of the Harrison Act in 1914. Originally designed to control the distribution and sale of opiates, this law was later used to close medical treatment facilities and to prosecute and imprison physicians who attempted to treat narcotics addicts with opiates. The large prison-hospitals at Lexington and Fort Worth were built, and the treatment of narcotics addiction was removed as a responsibility of physicians in practice.

In the meantime, medical societies advised physicians not to attempt to treat narcotics addicts. The use of narcotics in medical schools was often taught in a way that encouraged a phobic response in the young physician. The failure of prohibition to control human drug use did not deter the development of medical views that abstinence was the treatment of choice for drug dependence. Freedman has described the early leaders in psychiatry as "fervent prohibitionists."(5) Unfortunately, this attitude often led to the prohibition of the drug-dependent individual as a medical patient when he failed to achieve and maintain an abstinent state.

Drug-dependent individuals frequently exhibit a strong resistance to treatment. Denial of the problem is an almost reflexive response to even the most gentle confrontation. Projection of problems onto various aspects of the environment enables the drug abuser to further avoid the need for treatment. When these defenses fail, the simplistic stance that drugs are the total problem may be taken. "All I need to do is stop taking this stuff and everything will be OK," is a frequently heard refrain. Procrastination is easy, and there is a strong tendency to postpone seeking help. Supporting the delay is a strong wish for magical solutions. If taking a drug can mentally relieve tension, discomfort, and pain, then surely somewhere there is something that will magically relieve the need to compulsively repeat the drug experience.

These comments on the psychodynamics associated with drug dependence should not be taken as a description of the addictive personality.(5,6) Beneath the behavior patterns associated with drug use, the drug-dependent individual is very much like other troubled persons with various social or psychiatric maladaptations.(7)

The behavior of the drug abuser poses major problems for a physician-patient relationship. Compulsive drug seeking may lead to lying, stealing, forging prescriptions, demanding, manipulating, smuggling, and various other types of behavior designed to obtain drugs. There often appears to be intense underlying anxiety and depression for which the drug-dependent person seeks to obtain relief by chemical rather than by interpersonal means. Help is viewed as some form of drug replacement, rather than as treatment that starts with a cessation of drug use.

Relationships formed with physicians or other treaters often have a transient, hit-and-run quality. The drug abuser makes contact, becomes quickly disappointed or frustrated, withdraws, and looks elsewhere for help. Some patients seem frightened by the possibility of success and drop out of therapy entirely. The self-destructive aspects of this behavior can be a source of despair for physicians.

Sources of help may be rejected, alienated, and provoked by the drug-abusing patient. Cohen et al, in a study of the interpersonal patterns of young drug abusers, have described dominating, critical behavior which makes any helper feel competitive and resentful.(8) Cohen et al view this nonconforming behavior as an attempt to establish a negative identity that serves to avoid facing the anxiety-provoking questions of who the person is, and what he means to others.

The values of many drug abusers add another barrier to involvement with physicians. Traditional values may be rejected as well as authority figures. There is a tendency to form subcultures that provide a sense of identity and pseudointimacy with others using the same drugs. Some drug abusers specifically reject the value of hard work, restraint, and discipline.(9) The value of money, education, and job security, on the other hand, is accepted. The disparity between the values inherent in these choices presents the problem of accepting an end, but rejecting the means by which that end is attained. These conflicting attitudes could lead to simultaneous dislike and envy of the physician.

Many physicians are unprepared and uneducated in the management of drug dependence. The subject is all too often avoided in medical schools. Phobic concern over narcotic use contrasts with an almost blase indifference to the dependence-producing aspects of stimulants, sedative hypnotics, and minor tranquilizers. Drug-dependent patients, especially alcoholics and narcotics addicts, rarely find their way into teaching hospitals. When they do, the negative attitudes of medical school faculty are quickly picked up by the students.

The experience of physicians with drug-dependent patients has often been bad. In addition to behaviors described here, the patient may leave the hospital against medical advice, refuse to cooperate with treatment recommendations, and, worst of all, fail to get better, and, occasionally, even die. The physician is left disappointed, depressed, and bitter. He may become very pessimistic and conclude that effective treatment is impossible. Containment in specific hospitals or wards is viewed as the treatment of choice, even though the benefits are recognized as being extremely limited.(10)

Direct conflict with cherished values may lead to a moralistic view of the drug-dependent person as an undesirable patient. The physician has worked hard, disciplined himself, and exercised restraint in most areas of life. Much of his time and energy is spent in the acquisition of skills and in the pursuit of excellence. The drug abuser rejects these values verbally and behaviorally. It thus becomes easy for the physician himself to become moralistic and rejecting. He may even impose his own values on the patient by insisting on a rapid achievement of abstinence. Withdrawal is viewed as the treatment of choice for all forms of drug dependence even though there is mounting evidence that it may be the least effective initial therapy.

The physician's own anxiety may make involvement with drug-abusing patients difficult. We are particularly vulnerable to the development of drug-dependence problems ourselves. Avoidance or rejection of the drug abuser as a patient may, in some cases, be a reaction formation protecting the physician from his own impulses.

Physician authority is challenged by the drug-dependent patient. The medical model is based on a patient voluntarily seeking help and cooperating with the physician in his treatment. The drug abuser rarely fits this model. He is compliant rather than cooperative, and the overt or covert challenge he presents may place him in the category of undesirable patient.

The dilemma faced by the physician attempting to treat drug dependence can be uncomfortable and disconcerting. Steiner describes the alcoholic game where the unwary physician is put first in the role of the "rescuer."(11) This role is readily assumed since the physician may also see himself as a rescuer. When the rescue attempt fails, the physician becomes the "patsy," and, with the provision of repeated medication, often the "connection." Attempts to apply structure or discipline in a situation where he feels out of control, turn the physician into a "persecutor." Cohen et al pose the pertinent question, "How does one move unflinchingly into an arena where he is made to feel unwanted, incompetent, and even malevolent?"

SOLUTIONS

The attitudinal barriers encountered in relationship between the physician and the drug-abusing patient are formidable and may even appear to be insurmountable. Problems encountered within the drug abuser are not likely to change. Physicians will continue to be challenged to find ways to effectively help these troubled individuals in spite of their problems. We must start with ourselves in replacing negative, subjective reactions, which may blind us into seeing only objectionable stereotypes.

The medical society can play an important role in influencing, educating, and shaping the attitudes of its members. The support of organized medicine can help in the development and evaluation of adequate drug-dependence treatment programs within the existing health care system. Medical schools will need encouragement to develop effective teaching programs on the management of drug dependence, including alcoholism, at both undergraduate and postgraduate levels. Useful guidelines for this purpose have been developed by the American Medical Association's Council on Mental Health and the Committee on Alcoholism and Drug Dependence.

Three new developments have taken place in the last decade that have greatly increased the effectiveness of treatment of drug dependence.

1. Development of Effective Chemotherapeutic Supports — The transition

from drug dependence to human interdependence seldom occurs abruptly. If legal drugs can be safely substituted under medical supervision, the process of treatment is facilitated. The most effective substitutes are cross-dependent with the drug of dependence. Methadone as a substitute for heroin and other opiates is the prototype of chemotherapeutic support that makes psychological treatment possible. It is safe; it can be given orally without the psychological and health hazards of parenteral administration; and it is long-acting, requiring only one dose every 24 hours to suppress withdrawal symptoms and quell drug hunger.

Substitutes like methadone act as a kind of "treatment glue." They keep the drug-dependent individual exposed to the clinic staff and to the interpersonal aspects of treatment aimed at long-term behavioral change. Physicians are essential if chemotherapeutic supports are to be used in flexible, intelligent, and responsible ways.

2. Development of Drug-Detection Technology — The treatment of drug dependence in an outpatient requires rapid, efficient, objective means of detecting illicit or excessive drug use. In clinical practice the assessment of levels of blood alcohol by breath-testing devices and the use of thin-layer chromatography for determining the presence of drugs in urine have provided "chemical consciences" for monitoring drug use. These tools help both clinician and patient examine the evidence and conduct an exploration that can lead to better understanding and self-control.

3. Development of Former Drug Users as Paraprofessional Mental Health Workers — The value of peer-group pressure in treating compulsive drug use was first demonstrated by Alcoholics Anonymous. Similar results with narcotics addicts have been obtained by Synanon in California, Daytop Village in New York, Gateway Houses in Chicago, and many others. These ex-addict-run therapeutic communities have tended to be antichemotherapy and antiprofessional, but they have demonstrated greater effectiveness than traditional forms of treatment run by professionals.

In the Illinois Drug Abuse Program we have found ex-addict counselors extremely valuable. They have become the "firing-line therapists" in all of our clinics. The counselor, in addition to other things, performs three valuable functions that either require inordinate time and energy or cannot be done at all by professionals. The ex-addict paraprofessionals provide sources of 1. identification and hope for the addict who considers himself hopeless and beyond help, 2. communication without the need to cross socioeconomic, racial, cultural, and other attitudinal barriers (frequently the counselor may act as interpreter or liaison between physician and patient), and 3. behavioral control. Counselors are far more effective than professionals in stopping self-destructive acting out and in introducing the drug-dependent person to a treatment relationship.

Effective drug-dependence treatment programs put these features together in multimodality, community-based operations, providing inpatient, outpatient, chemotherapeutic, and abstinence-based forms of therapy. It is now possible to meet the varying needs of the drug-dependent individual during different phases of his problems. Supportive or intensive treatment can be appropriately continued while he develops roles as family member, friend, worker, and productive participant in the social life of his community.

These drug-dependence treatment units function best, in our experience, when physician, nurse, and counselor can work together as a treatment team. Like most relationships, constant effort is required to maintain communication and cooperation. Each member must respect, and be willing to learn from, the other members of the team.

The physician is a key member of the treatment team, either on a full-time basis or as a consultant to a clinic. He is obviously needed to provide the chemotherapeutic aspects of treatment. Of particular value is the physician's clinical judgment when the team makes decisions that may involve some element of risk for the clinic member. In addition, the physician provides important support and education for both the nurses and counselors who are often under great stress from clinic members.

Relatively few physicians will choose to become directly involved in the treatment of drug dependence. An equally important role remains for the physician in practice. He may have the first opportunity to make an early diagnosis and refer the drug-dependent person for management. Preparation of the patient, communication of hope, and the provision of emotional and chemotherapeutic support may be critical in getting the patient into a treatment program. Physicians will continue to be called on to manage drug overdoses, severe drug withdrawal, and drug-related emergencies. Drug-dependent individuals will continue to get pregnant, have accidents, and suffer from any of man's illnesses. The attitudinal barriers described may mean that early access to medical care is not available. The physician holds the key to obtaining ready access for the drug abuser to the benefits of our health care system.

Changes in attitude are necessary at both physician and institutional levels if drug dependence is to be adequately treated. Such a change in attitude is possible. The history of mental illness shows a gradual shift from medieval rejection and punishment to increasingly effective treatment which is more and more being incorporated into the mainstream of medical care.

REFERENCES

(1) Bakewell WE, Ewing JA: Therapy of non-narcotic psychoactive drug dependence. *Curr Psychiatr Ther* 9:136-143, 1969.

(2) Knox WJ: Attitudes of psychiatrists and psychologists toward alcoholism. *Am J Psychiatr* 127:1675-1679, 1971.

(3) Gray RM, et al: Physician authoritarianism and the treatment of alcoholics. *Q J Stud Alcohol* 30:981-983, 1969.

(4) Medical school education on abuse of alcohol and other psychoactive drugs, AMA COUNCIL ON MENTAL HEALTH. *JAMA* 219:1746-1749, 1972.

(5) Freedman DX: Implications for research. *JAMA* 206:1280-1284, 1968.

(6) Rosen AC: Some differences in self-perceptions between alcoholics and non-alcoholics. *Percept Mot Skills* 23:1279-1286, 1966.

(7) Ottenberg DJ, Rosen A: Merging the treatment of drug addicts into an existing program for alcoholics. *Q J Stud Alcohol* 32:94-103, 1971.

(8) Cohen CP, White EH, Schcolor JC: Interpersonal patterns of personality for drug-abusing patients and their therapeutic implications. *Arch Gen Psychiatry* 24:353-358, 1971.

(9) Cohen M, Klein DF: Social values and drug use among psychiatric patients. *Am J Psychiatry* 128:1017-1019, 1972.

(10) Knox WJ: Attitudes of psychiatrists and psychologists toward alcoholism. *Am J Psychiatry* 127:1675-1679, 1971.

(11) Steiner C: *Games Alcoholics Play*. New York, Grove Press Inc, 1971.

VI
MENTAL
HEALTH

VI. MENTAL HEALTH

INTRODUCTION

The scientific origins of psychiatry are new. As a recognized discipline it is only half a century old and has undergone vast development, change and expansion. Particularly in the last twenty years, it has achieved almost universal professional and public acceptance as a medical discipline.

Increasingly, psychiatry has become a vital ingredient in our legal system. Its practitioners are relied upon to differentiate between the sane and the insane offender, to identify and detain those individuals requiring mental treatment, to release those who are cured, and generally to aid the law in many issues of mental competence and health. As a result a complete subspecialty has evolved of legal or forensic psychiatry.

The full blossoming of psychiatry could not take place until the abandonment — in both professional and public conscience — of the primitive belief that mental illness was a manifestation of evil, or at the very least the product of some personal guilt. The recognition that the mentally ill had community and legal rights which had to be protected evolved next. These developments have led to our considering the mentally ill person not as a near-criminal but as a patient. Similarly, psychotherapy and psychiatrists have been recognized and accepted like any other medical discipline and its specialists. Mental health, indeed is not limited to mental institutions; its relevance in understanding delinquency, deviance, criminal conduct, mass violence, family instability, anxiety, and alienation is well established.

The emphasis upon mental health or psychiatry has in fact come into competition with the traditional penal or correctional response to crime.

Defining the offender as being more ill than evil, the mental health approach stresses therapy over punishment. The "therapeutic state" has thus been advanced as a more suitable and humane alternative to the "criminal system", claiming to offer more effective responses to such growing problems as crime, juvenile delinquency, alcoholism, and drug addiction.

The growing role of psychiatry has been made possible by a shift from the strict and time-consuming Freudian methods of diagnosis and treatment. Several newly accepted modes of therapy — the dynamic, organic and group approaches — are available to larger segments of the population. In addition, chemotherapy and psychosurgery have been increasingly employed in selected situations.

The functions of psychiatry and mental health are not limited to the service and reformation of the criminal law. They play a significant role in several areas of the civil law. Traumatic neurosis has been given growing recognition in tort cases, competency remains a major issue in wills, and family counseling is playing an increasing role in family law.

Legal psychiatry is a specialty which ought to be part of every medical school curriculum. Law and mental health should similarly be given a regular place in legal education. Yet this need for inter-professional insights and education is not usually met. The selections in this section should help reveal the potential interactions of law and psychiatry.

THE SCOPE OF LEGAL PSYCHIATRY

J.M. Suarez
Jan Hunt

Law and psychiatry as distinct disciplines overlap inevitably in many ways. There are many areas in which the two potentially or actually have concerns in common, and these seem to be expanding all the time. These areas are rather heterogeneous, and range from the understanding and treatment of the criminal offender to social issues such as abortion or gun control, and all the way to highly philosophical problems such as confidentiality or the involuntary detention of the dangerous. In actuality, however, the degree and type of interaction between the two disciplines has been remarkably narrow and constricted as this article will demonstrate in depth.

It is the purpose of this article to suggest and promote a much broader scope of interaction between law and psychiatry. More important perhaps, it will attempt a critique of the nature of such interaction, since such is offered as the core problem in the existing difficulties. The article will begin with a review of the traditional collaboration between the disciplines; it will then examine different speculations or explanations that have been offered as to the sources of failure and friction; and finally, it will consider ways in which the interaction can be improved in the future.

TRADITIONAL ACTIVITIES OF THE LEGAL PSYCHIATRIST

Traditionally, the legal psychiatrist has been identified in one of two ways: as the expert witness who provides either a personal appearance in court or some report or communication which he has prepared; and as the therapist of offenders usually functioning in the context of an impatient penal or correctional setting. To date, both of these roles have created an amazing amount of friction, misunderstanding, and widespread dissatisfaction amoung members of both disciplines. Legalists typically complain that they are dissatisfied with psychiatry, that they have no faith in its contributions, that they feel it is basically wasteful, and that therefore they have little if any use for it as they know, define, and understand it. Likewise, it is no secret that most of the members of the psychiatric profession have a strong aversion to becoming involved with anything that has legal implications. As a result, the task has been left to a small band of "professional" experts who carry the bulk of all activities in connection with interacting with the legal process. In Los Angeles, for example, over ninety percent of all the evaluations and testimonies needed in various criminal, commitment, and domestic relations matters are provided by a group of psychiatrists that could be listed in approximately a dozen names, and whose activities are almost exclusively devoted to legal consultations. The rest of the several hundred psychiatrists in the area rarely, if ever, become involved with anything that could be called legal. Thus, to most legalists, the entire profession is identified and represented by the small group with which they have frequent dealings.

THE EXPERT WITNESS

This is the one traditional area of direct interaction and exhange between the psychiatric and legal professions. It has done little to bridge the gaps between the disciplines, to promote reciprocal education, or to avoid a mounting frustration on both sides of the fence. Legalists view psychiatric expert witnesses as confusing the issues rather than resolving them. Psychiatric experts feel that their contributions are repeatedly misunderstood and ignored, and that the activity results in predictable embarrassment and frustration. Certainly, in a series of recent celebrated cases behavioral scientists—by their performances (with Ruby, Sirhan, etc), inadvertently did a great deal to interfere with the public image of psychiatry.

It is not within the scope of this paper to attempt a review of the problems with the expert witness. Suarez has already published a probing analysis of this dilemma (1). Suffice it to say that the problem is viewed as one of failure of *role* definition. That is, the legalists expect certain contributions which the psychiatrist is not able to provide, and psychiatrists have typically failed to inquire critically as to the appropriateness and value of the task expected of them or as to possible alternate contributions that they might be able to offer.

With regard to the treatment of offenders, one again encounters a very interesting phenomenon because penologists, judges, and others will categorically state that psychiatry has proved to be a dismal failure in terms of rehabilitating and correcting offenders, and in preventing them from repeating. However, a more objective analysis would evidence the fact that the entire question of the therapy of offenders has never really been attempted to date.

There have been very few psychiatrists who have been connected with the penal system. Their contributions have been almost exclusively within the context of either individual or group therapy to the offenders, regardless of orientation; and thus it has been limited to direct service to the inmates. Given what we know of the impact of institutions on their patients or inmates, it is not at all surprising that even the best staffed of institutions providing "adequate" therapy to its population would not be able to tip the balance and overcome the many anti-therapeutic aspects of the institution itself.

A position in a correctional institution is, of course, not a very appealing prospect to the psychiatrist. Typically, it pays a small salary, and cannot hope to compete with private practice. It exists in out of the way locations, which are not culturally or intellectually appealing to a professional. It exposes the professional to unending red tape, and to frustrations above and beyond the failures of his therapeutic attempts. He usually ends up performing a great deal of administrative work, attending meetings, doing evaluations, and writing reports. It is not surprising that, with some known exceptions, the type of individual that is attracted to this job is someone who tends to be rather schizoid, with a fairly high propensity for alcohol, and who functions in an apathetic and unimaginative way. Thus, for a number of reasons psychiatrists have not answered the challenge appropriately, and instead of providing large numbers of the most qualified within their ranks, they have provided very few and many of questionable ability.

SOURCES OF INTERDISCIPLINARY CONFLICT

Many explanations have been offered to account for the obvious interdisciplinary failures. These will be reviewed in order of increasing substance and sophistication, as follows: semantics and terminology; philosophy and orientation; mutual ignorance; and most important the *roles* of psychiatrists in the legal system.

The most obvious problem, and unfortunately the most commonly overrated as the main source of conflict, is that of semantics. The semantics issue does, of course, produce its share of misunderstanding by blocking effective interdisciplinary communication. A semantics problem exists even within the psychiatric profession, for it employs terms that are vague, poorly defined, highly conceptual, and rather imprecise, thus resulting in their being used in radically different ways. Attempts to adopt a universal psychiatric nomenclature(2) have helped more with the completing of insurance forms than they have with the meaningful and consistent communication within the profession.

Legal terminology is no better, and where law and psychiatry overlap, the legal profession has unfortunately adopted terms that are medical and psychiatric sounding, such as "insanity," "incompetency," and "mentally disordered sex offender." The latter term, for example, masquerades very strongly as a diagnostic label and is often mistaken as such by psychiatrists who should know better, and who persist in labeling patients they evaluate as such, losing sight of and confusing the fact that this is really a legal judgment, just as insanity is a legal judgment, and not a diagnostic assessment.

The word "insanity" itself, which is no longer used in psychiatric communications, is used in the legal system in countless ways, such as in the context of criminal responsibility, involuntary commitment, and different types of competency. It is unfortunate that this word is used so extensively in legal contests to denote so many different things, and that the legal profession somehow assumes that it has a very definite and applicable definition in the psychiatric context as well.

Even so, if the issue of semantics were the only gulf dividing the disciplines, it would have been overcome quite easily by now. But as will be seen below, semantics is not the sole problem, nor is it anywhere near the most critical one.

In analyzing the two disciplines from the viewpoint of philosophy and orientation, it is easy to see why the two do not accommodate each other more harmoniously. It is all too clear that the external demands made on psychiatry are very dissimilar and divergent from those made on the legal system. As a result, law tends to see the world in terms of black and white, while psychiatry sees it in gradations. Robitscher(3) has pointed out that law is all logic and reason, or at least it sets out to be; but, for a legal system to function, it must be more than merely logical and reasonable. It must be definite, relying on precedent and rules. So, in the course of time, all functioning legal systems become legalistic, and in the process some of the logic and reason gets left behind.

By contrast, contemporary psychiatry, highly influenced by the psychodynamic approach, deals with the illogical and the unreasonable. Freud's central idea was that human actions have their sources both in the conscious, which may be governed by reason, and the unconscious, which is not governed by reason, intellect, or logic, and which, in fact, is by definition unreasonable. Psychiatry as a science has the capacity to examine itself and change according to the demands of new knowledge and new needs. By contrast, law as a process seems extremely rigid to the scientist because of its reliance on precedence and authority, and its reluctance to roll with the punches or to adjust to new situations. In all interactions, psychiatry when consulted by the law has been asked to provide narrow and precise observations in keeping with the legal structure. The time has come when we can begin to wonder if perhaps we could expect the legal process to make certain alterations and adjustments in order to abandon its absolutistic approach, its dealing with issues as if they were black and white, and the drawing of sharp lines in the context of cases where then the situation must be simplistically placed on one side or the other of that line.

Another source of potential conflict is the mutual ignorance of how each discipline functions. This is exemplified by the attitudes and actions of the legal profession toward psychiatry, which evidence little knowledge and many misconceptions about psychiatric orientation, theory, practice, and ultimate aims. This phenomenon is well illustrated by a consideration of the notion and definition of "mental illness."

In the 19th Century, when psychiatry was very much linked to neurology, it was fashionable to seek an organic explanation for every condition, and short of that, to develop a nosology of very precise symptom complexes and classifications that led to a rigid scheme of diagnostic labels. At this stage, the classical medical model for illness was employed in the psychiatric context. As the psychiatric scope has broadened, and we have become more sophisticated in understanding the causes and manifestations of psychopathology, we have found it of little use to continue to employ the classical medical model. Mental illness or psychopathology is now viewed as the interaction of complex forces which defy categorization along the criteria demanded by the narrow use of the medical model.

At the forefront of the attack on the medical model are the writings of Thomas Szasz, who in *Law, Liberty and Psychiatry*,(6) states that there is not such a thing as "mental illness," but that the term exists "only in the same sort of way as do other theoretical concepts." Szasz adds that "mental illness has outlived whatever usefulness it may have had and that it now functions as a convenient myth. As such, it is a true heir to religious myths in general, and to the belief in witchcraft in particular." Szasz concludes:(7)

> When I assert that mental illness is a myth, I am not saying that personal unhappiness and socially deviant behavior does not exist; but I am saying that we categorize them as diseases at our own peril.

> The expression "mental illness" is a metaphor which we have now come to mistake for a fact. We call people physically ill when their body functioning violates certain anatomical and physiological norms; similarly, we call people mentally ill when their personal conduct violates certain ethical, political, and social norms. This explains why many historical figures, from Jesus to Castro, and from Job to Hitler, have been diagnosed as suffering from this or that psychiatric malady.

The changes within the psychiatric approach to the concept of mental illness have not been felt or acknowledged at all within the legal context. A good illustration of this is how the term is used in delineating the law on insanity or criminal responsibility. Regardless of the test of criminal responsibility, which varies from one jurisdiction to another, it is always found that "mental illness" or "disease" is a premise that must be satisfied before one goes on to prescribe the specific criteria to be used in ascertaining the presence or absence of criminal responsibility. Since the statutes or the courts never define mental illness in this context, it is evident that legalists assume this to be a clear and viable concept which can be ascertained in every given case, and which can be readily identified and answered by the behavioral scientist before considering the presence of the stricter "legal" criteria for the test of insanity. There is very little in any statute or decision that reflects the fact that the behavioral sciences are beginning to look at psychopathology as being synonymous with the lifestyle and actions of the individual himself, rather than as the result of some discrete "illness," such as appendicitis or tuberculosis, from which stem all the actions which are found to be unacceptable.

It should also be recognized that psychiatrists tend to be very ignorant and demeaning of the legal process. It is imperative that any behavioral scientist who hopes to make some contribution to and possibly some change within the legal process must gain some understanding of that process and thus must have a fair degree of awareness of the setting in which he is working. That does not mean that he must embrace, agree with, or limit himself to the philosophy and orientation of the system, but without some degree of such awareness and sophisitcation in the area, he is likely not only to be lost, but to be mocked and dismissed as naive.

Beyond the problems of semantics, philosophy and orientation, and mutual ignorance, is yet another and probably the most important problem in the interaction between law and psychiatry, namely the definition and delineation of the roles that are to be played by the psychiatrist in the context of the legal process. We shall analyze this contention in the context of several major legal areas where psychiatrists have traditionally been called upon to lend their expertise. In all major areas of interaction between the disciplines, the consultation has been sought by the legal process; and the ground rules for the psychiatrist's activity have been strictly set by legalists. As will be illustrated below, this state of affairs, and the failure of any challenge against it by the psychiatric profession, has led not only to the perpetuation of the system as it was found, but worse yet, to the severe obstruction and failure of the potential and meaningful contributions that could have been made by the psychiatric consultant.

For a long period in history, even before the formal birth of psychiatry and the existence of psychiatrists, the mentally ill were handled in such a way that they were often not only committed and put away, but at times were even punished for their illness. Thus the concept of using various guises—such as the categorization of the mentally ill as demons or witches—to segregate and eliminate them has existed for quite some time. In fact, Pinel made a name for himself in history by removing the chains from the "prisoners;" that is, those patients who had been placed in institutions because they were sick and weird, rather than because they had committed any criminal offense. Although Pinel's contribution called for a more humane and meaningful treatment of the mentally ill, it was not very long before psychiatrists were involved directly and actively in the process of involuntary commitment. In all jurisdictions the mentally ill are still involuntarily committed; and worse still, they are often placed in institutions where they receive very little care, and which sometimes offer very little more than did the institutions of centuries ago. The basic difference, of course, is that the psychiatrist's evaluation in the form of a report or testimony has now become a key item in the commitment procedure, with apparently very little concern or challenge on the part of psychiatrists as to the fact that they may be relegating patients to lengthy periods of institutionalization, a decision that is likely to prove anti-therapeutic in most cases.

The dilemma of involuntary commitment should raise a number of vital questions with regard to psychiatric participation. Should the term "mental illness, be used as a means of institutionalizing socially disabled persons? If so, by what criteria are behavioral scientists to define such mental illness and thus utilize it in the determinations? How can a line be drawn between the individual who is put away and one who is not? What kind of care will the individual receive in the particular institution to which he is committed? Should he not have a moral and constitutional right to receive at least adequate treatment? Should not psychiatrists insist upon designating the place and maximum length of commitment? Do psychiatrists always consider practical alternatives to commitment in each case, such as the availability of outpatient therapy and other essential care?

There is very little debate about these questions, and most of the psychiatrists who participate in involuntary commitments do little more than evaluate each case, present the needed testimony, and serve as rubber stampers for the process. In short, psychiatrists are now failing in both their social and professional roles by accepting and carrying out the narrow and potentially dangerous role given them by the legal process without bothering to explore in any depth the consequences of such a role or more meaningful and desirable alternative methods of interaction.

Incompetency to stand trial, a much overused concept provides another good example of the problems with role definition. The concept of incompetency to stand trial was originally developed as an aid to the defendant. It was felt that it would be unfair to try individuals who were so disoriented or removed from the reality that they could not properly participate and aid in a meaningful defense. It was decided that it would be more just in such instances to postpone the trial until such a time as the defendant was in a more satisfactory mental condition. From this humane and altruistic beginning, however, incompetency to stand trial has, especially in this country, degenerated ironically into yet another form of putting away undesirables for indefinite periods of time, all without having to be very much concerned about some of the due process issues that are present in the criminal law. Most of the psychiatrists who have participated in such hearings would undoubtedly be shocked and disturbed to learn that data available from studies, such as in Massachusetts and Pennsylvania, reveal that almost all of the individuals who are found to be incompetent to stand trial end up spending fantastically long periods of time, often an entire lifetime, in institutions where they are tragically forgotten and receive little or no care. Just because that is the result of the existing legal system and its process, however, is no justification for psychiatric participation. Both out of concern for the patient involved, and more specifically because psychiatrists are so directly involved, it is essential that they confront themselves as well as the legal process with the issue of whether to continue to participate in an activity which has proven by a wide margin to be actually harmful to those people it is purporting to help. And yet, despite the available data, most psychiatrists, in most jurisdictions, day in and day out, continue to provide testimony as to incompetency which represents the critical data necessary for court decisions to institutionalize such individuals.

Several centuries back, the courts and legislators decided that there were some criminal offenders who were so deranged that on moral grounds they should be treated differently from the "run of the mill" offender who committed similar antisocial acts. This always relatively small group was to be classified as "insane" or "irresponsible" and awarded a different, supposedly better, fate. At one time in history, this was reasonable and appealing, because offenders were generally treated so ruthlessly and inhumanely that the prospect of an alternative handling of such individuals was appealing to crusaders who wanted to undo some degree of the existing injustice. Such a concept probably also served to soothe the guilt felt by all for the manner in which most offenders were treated. It was not long before psychiatrists were involved as important agents in these determinations.

The continued participation in this particular determination can and should be challenged on both theoretical and practical grounds. In theory the notion hinges on the premise that there are two types of offenders, the "bad" and the "sick." Legal criteria for differentiation, or at least for those who are to be put in the "sick" category are spelled out, and the psychiatrist is then expected, using both his general expertise and the application of those criteria, to isolate the rare case that meets the criteria. In fact, given the evolution of the concept of mental illness and given all that is understood about its different sources, today it is not theoretically sound or defensible to speak of two distinct categories of the "sick" and the "bad." These determinations are now more a matter of moral or social judgments, and have no justification or basis in scientific fact. Studies of inmate populations in different penal institutions reveal that inmates tend to run the entire gamut of personality types and psychiatric disorders, not too dissimilarly from the population at large.

In practice, the defense of insanity has proven to be so unwieldy and undesirable to the defendant who succeeds with it, that it is rarely used, except in cases where there is a threat of capital punishment, and only then as a last resource. The available data shows that individuals who have succeeded in the plea of "not guilty by reason of insanity" usually serve very long periods of time in institutions that are for all practical purposes no different from correctional ones. Thus the appeal for the defense has markedly dwindled. Fortunately, with the recent U.S. Supreme Court holding as to the unconstitutionality of capital punishment, it is likely that the insanity defense will be used far less frequently in the future.

The serious challenge remains, however, as to whether the psychiatric profession can continue to participate in any sort of psychiatric defense as it now exists, and which seems to be indefensible on both theoretical and practical grounds. Instead, it seems that psychiatrists should press for the more critical issue, namely the enlightened handling of the offender with a focus toward rehabilitation, and away from retribution or mere custody. By participating in the exercise of a psychiatric defense, psychiatrists are clearly perpetuating not only the concept, but also its current utilization; and they are simultaneously failing to direct their attention to the potential contributions that the psychiatric discipline can offer in terms of the offender's post-verdict and pre-sentence handling and his ultimate therapy and rehabilitation.

The history of the social and legal attitudes toward sex that have culminated in specific statutes is fascinating and has been reviewed extensively and critically. Suffice it to say that whereas a dual reason is usually offered as to the rationale for such legislation, namely the protection of society and the rehabilitation of the offender, in practice only the former is seriously considered, at least to the extent that such unfortunate individuals spend lengthy periods in institutions, thus apparently protecting society. Psychiatrists tend to become involved primarily in the context of "sexual psychopath" statutes, in which they evaluate the alleged offender by law, and submit a report which becomes a critical document in the determination of whether the individual is to be found a "sexual psychopath" or not, and possibly sent away to an institution for a period of from "one day to life."

Psychiatric participation in laws dealing with sexual behavior perpetuates the existence of legal practices which are extremely severe and unbelievably outdated. By concentrating their sole efforts in the direction of examining selected candidates and submitting reports, psychiatrists are failing to carry out tasks which include the education of lawyers, judges, legislators, and the public; and they are also not placing increased emphasis on the issue of rehabilitation instead of mere isolation and removal from society.

Unlike the previous examples where the use of a psychiatrist raises grave questions of appropriateness and social validity, in the area of domestic relations his utilization to date is much less controversial. Given the laws on divorce and the custody of children, it is appropriate for courts and lawyers alike to turn to the behavioral sciences for help in some of the determinations. Although psychiatrists are failing to act as educators and legislative consultants to any marked degree, nevertheless, the data and opinions that they can contribute, if done properly and in a professional way, are helpful to both the individual litigants and society as a whole. However, as with previous situations, psychiatrists have accepted the tasks all too readily, and have not generally bothered to inquire as to how else they might be effective. In this context specifically, they have fallen into the trap of conceding to the magical thinking displayed by the legal system and assuming that all of the problems of divorce and custody are disposed of by a judicial determination, no matter how unwise or poorly founded.

As a matter of fact, the post divorce period often represents an even more traumatic and difficult phase for the people involved in family disruption. As behavioral scientists, psychiatrists have failed to emphasize this period and have failed to persuade or acquaint the judiciary with the need for further jurisdiction and involvement in the post-divorce period. In other words, in reviewing the different legal steps involved in divorce and custody problems, it is not difficult to see that all of the effort, both diagnostic and therapeutic, is channeled into the pre-divorce period that is culminated by the judicial decision, and very little, if any, attention is paid to the subsequent fate of the litigants. Psychiatrists know that there are problems because they are seen as isolated cases in therapy, and because the litigants often return to the courts over and over again to settle the most minute of disputes which are, of course, nothing more than illustrations of the failure of proper adjustment by the parties concerned.

CONCLUSION

Through the use of a number of examples of contemporary interaction between law and psychiatry, this article has promulgated the thesis that the basic problem between law and psychiatry today is the fact that psychiatric involvement has always been called for and regulated by the legal system. This had resulted in both the perpetuation of the laws of the system as they exist, but even more important, in the failure of the psychiatric participants to be challenged and stimulated to identify and formulate other and often more meaningful contributions than those that they were being asked to provide.

Legal psychiatry should perhaps be the purest example and epitome of social psychiatry. A consultant is or should be someone who does more than accept the task given to him and merely carry it out. Instead, he should rephrase the questions posed to him, redefine and re-identify the problems from his perspective; and then ultimately modify and remold the task for which he is called. For the most part, psychiatrists have failed to do that in their interactions with the legal system. As a result, not only have they disappointed those who call them in as consultants, but they have done very little to bring about a significant contribution on behalf of the psychiatric profession, the greatest of which would be the bringing about of changes within the legal system that would allow it to operate more meaningfully and successfully.

Frazer(4), in *The Golden Bough*, writes that "The movement of highest thought has been from magic through religion to science." Law is, or should be, a behavioral science. There is not much problem in supporting such a proposition. Law is concerned with the way things should be. It tries to maintain and protect the desired order. It identifies, in a systematic way, the disruptive elements. And finally, it is committed to preventing or correcting the existing deviations. Perhaps the greatest contribution would be to help it become more scientific and less magical and religious.

Roche(5), in the first chapter of his book, *The Criminal Mind*, attempts to clarify the concepts of "science" and "scientific." He points out that we often fail to regard science as a method of thinking, of viewpoints and attitudes that lead to a successful solution of social problems. The legal system is not basically scientific, and in fact it often behaves in a very unscientific way. Psychiatrists cannot afford this, either as professionals or as citizens. Becoming scientific does not involve any change in its goals or ideals. It does imply a greater concern with methodology. If the psychiatric profession can succeed in enabling the legal system to assess itself and its functioning, then a great task shall have been accomplished; for as it exists now, the system is not at all geared to be introspective or self-challenging, nor does it function with any degree or attempt at global coordination. Psychiatric interactions, as defined and arranged by the legal system are unimaginative and feed the self-perpetuation. If psychiatrists begin by examining and challenging their roles in the legal process, then in time, they may be able to offer it something new and useful.

REFERENCES AND NOTES

(1) Suarez, J. M., "A Critique of the Psychiatrist's Role as Expert Witness," *Journal of Forensic Sciences*, Vol. 12, No. 2, 1967.

(2) *Diagnostic and Statistical Manual—Mental Disorders, Diagnostic and Statistical Manual of Mental Disorders*, 2nd ed., American Psychiatric Association, 1968.

(3) Robitscher, J. B., *Pursuit of Agreement—Psychiatry and the Law*, J. B. Lippincott Co., 1966.

(4) Frazer, J. G., *The Golden Bough*, Macmillan, New York, 1953.

(5) Roche, P. Q., *The Criminal Mind*, Grove Press, New York, 1958.

(6) Szasz, T. S., *Law, Liberty, and Psychiatry*, Macmillan, New York, 1963, pp. 11-12.

(7) Ibid., pp. 16-17.

THE NEW FACE OF LEGAL PSYCHIATRY

Jonas Robitscher

The 19th-Century psychiatrist occupied an important but circumscribed position in society; his influence did not extend far. He was primarily the custodian, the hospital superintendent. He dealt with the mentally ill and did not concern himself with social reform except as it applied to patients in his custody.

One of the few times he assumed a more prominent role was when he appeared as a forensic psychiatrist, taking the witness stand as an expert in order to testify that a defendant did or did not have criminal responsibility or that a deceased testator had or did not have testamentary capacity.

When Freud's medical psychology promulgated a theory of the cause and cure of neuroses, the psychiatrist expanded his role and became an office practitioner who now dealt with outpatients as well as inpatients. Although his views began to influence child raising, education, the structure of social and family life, and arts and letters, the psychiatrist remained essentially a private individual, once-removed from the legislative and the administrative process. Psychiatrists continued to have a "low visibility profile."

One reason for the privatism of psychiatrists was the Freudian ideal of anonymity; another was the medical tradition that prohibited self-advertising and self-aggrandizement; and still another was the low level of public concern with many phases of the psychiatrist's activities, such as his work with state hospital patients, in a prison setting, and with juvenile delinquents.

Our modern changing and complicated society has thrust psychiatrists into a more public role at the same time that it has stimulated the profession to reexamine concepts of health and disease. The forensic psychiatrist is the main emissary of psychiatry to society; he is the psychiatrist who appears in court, works in corrections, advises on legislation, teaches lawyers.

The courtroom, and the criminal trial in particular, continues to be the place where forensic psychiatrists receive the most exposure; the testimony of Manfred Guttmacher in the Jack Ruby case, which emphasized Ruby's weak ego structure and its disruption under the impact of the Kennedy assassination, and the testimony of Bernard Diamond in the Sirhan Sirhan case, where Diamond proposed a theory of the reactivation of a self-hypnotic state as a cause of the second Kennedy assassination, led to great public exposure for the testifying psychiatrists. The Leopold and Loeb and Alger Hiss cases are other examples of the psychiatrist in the public eye. New legal rules of criminal responsibility and new psychiatric theories relating social factors to psychopathology lead to testimony that assumes increased importance in the trial process(1).

But the forensic psychiatrist has widened his role to include much more than the courtroom appearance. He uses his psychiatric background and his familiarity with law and the legislative process to deal with juvenile delinquency, aggression, violence, drugs, sexual standards, and a host of other problems that have psychiatric, legal, social, and even political and economic components.

In this atmosphere forensic psychiatry finds itself forced to become more truly interdisciplinary. In place of the old psychiatrist-law professor dialogue, which often bogged down in philosophical discussions of free will and determinism, the conversation has broadened into a colloquium in which law, psychiatry, sociology, psychology, social work, and other behavioral science disciplines all share. As one illustration of the merging of disciplines and the merging of legal and social psychiatry, let me cite the program I headed until recently at the University of Pennsylvania. After searching for a name to fit the National Institute of Mental Health sponsored program, which emphasized teaching at the medical school and residency levels and the preparation of teaching materials, the older titles such as "Legal Psychiatry" or "Forensic Psychiatry" seemed too narrow, so the title eventually emerged as "Social-Legal Uses of Forensic Psychiatry" (2). The term "social-legal psychiatry" seems to describe better than the older ones the multidisciplinary quality of the patient-society interaction(3).

GROWING INTEREST IN FORENSIC PSYCHIATRY

Two developments indicate the growing interest in forensic psychiatry. First, a number of interdisciplinary courses and institutes have been developed to foster research and to sponsor advanced training. Boston University, Harvard, Yale, the Menninger Foundation, George Washington University, Emory University, Temple, Tulane, the University of Pittsburgh, the University of Maryland, the University of Southern California, and the University of California, Los Angeles, are some of the pioneers in these programs.

Second, in late 1969 the American Academy of Psychiatry and the Law

(AAPL) was formed. This formal group was the outgrowth of an informal group of about 15, mainly directors of forensic psychiatry fellowship training programs, who had met in connection with the American Psychiatric Association meeting in Boston in 1968. This new group now has about 250 members, all interested in some phase of legal psychiatry; it has published 11 issues of a quarterly newsletter, which is more truly a small journal, and it has held two annual meetings (4). The by-laws of AAPL list six aims: to exchange ideas and experience among forensic psychiatrists in North America; to elevate the standards of study and practice in this field; to develop training programs for psychiatrists desirous of acquiring skills in forensic psychiatry; to take leadership in initiating and monitoring research in the field; to improve relationships between psychiatrists on the one hand and attorneys, legislators, jurists, and penologists on the other; and to take leadership in informing the public of the needs of those involved with the law and the contributions available from psychiatry(5).

An indication of the broadened application of forensic psychiatry is the definition found in the by-laws:

> . . . The phrase "forensic psychiatry" will include all aspects of psychiatry which remain in close and significant contact with the law, legislation or jurisprudence, including, but not limited to, problems in the psychiatric aspects of testamentary capacity, criminal responsibility, guardianship, evidence, competency, marriage, divorce, annulment, custody of children, commitment procedures, personal injury evaluation, malpractice litigation, preservation of the civil rights of the mentally ill, addiction to alcohol and drugs, psychiatric testimony in courts and before other tribunals or legislative bodies, management and treatment of all offenders, and confidentiality of records(5).

Legal psychiatry can be defined simply enough as the area where law and psychiatry meet or as the body of law and customs that accords special treatment (sometimes specially favorable and sometimes specially unfavorable) to individuals whose mental or emotional status entitles them to be treated differently. But as the field extends, these simple definitions are seen to encompass a host of not-so-simple relationships to other disciplines.

The relationship of forensic psychiatry to law requires an understanding of the historical development of this specialized branch of law. Also, since law deals with analogies and precedents that originate in one field of law but are then applied to another, the forensic psychiatrist soon finds himself a victim of "cultural spread"; he has to become aware of other branches of law, other aspects of society.

For example, the law dealing with psychiatric patients is very similar to the law dealing with minors or the law dealing with seamen—both groups need special protection because of their diminished capacity to deal effectively with authorities—and very similar to superseded law dealing with the inferior position of women (especially married women), blacks, and indentured servants. The protection of the rights of the mentally disabled requires a knowledge of the legal problems of other minorities. Legal psychiatry and race relations become intertwined in decisions like *Brown v. Board of Education* (6), in which the basis for overturning the concept of school segregation is the psychological harm caused by the segregation; they are related more generally in that both fields are concerned with the enforcement of the legal rights of those at a legal disadvantage.

The treatment of juveniles in juvenile courts, the treatment of mental or "moral" defectives under defective delinquency laws, and the treatment of sexual deviates under sexual psychopath laws are topics that carry the forensic psychiatrist away from the narrow definition of legal psychiatry and involve him in a broader world of criminology, sociology, and rehabilitation by nonpsychiatric means. The question of whether an involuntarily committed patient should be entitled to a lawyer at the time of his commitment cannot be studied without getting into such related areas as the question of whether a prisoner who has violated the conditions of his parole should be entitled to a lawyer when the parole board considers returning him to jail, or the question of whether an indigent who cannot afford a lawyer because of poverty is entitled to legal help.

Law deals with analogies and precedents, and the logic that develops in one area is applied to another. This forces the legal psychiatrist to consider not only the problems of the mentally disabled under the law but to delve into other legal areas; it forces him to understand the problems of those suffering from nonpsychiatric disability (nonadults, racial minorities, the indigent, the imprisoned) and to find out how the law has developed in those areas.

Besides being forced into other legal fields, the forensic psychiatrist is forced to extend himself into nonpsychiatric areas of medicine, the nonmedical therapies, and other helping professions. For example, confidentiality is a major concern of legal psychiatry—especially during this period of developing community mental health centers—but although there are special concerns that make confidentiality more important in psychiatric therapy than in other therapies, confidentiality is of concern to doctors generally (7, 8).

Informed consent is of special concern to psychiatrists. How can we be sure that a patient who is psychotic, mentally retarded, and (just to make the example as difficult as possible) is also a minor, has her rights protected in a decision for eugenic sterilization (9)? But informed consent is also of concern to doctors generally; the use of patients as subjects for scientific experiments and for testing the efficacy of drugs has medical implications that are of interest to internists as well as psychiatrists.

Psychiatric malpractice is a specialized topic because psychiatric practice is difficult to define and includes treatment methods unknown to medicine generally; nevertheless, psychiatric and medical malpractice are topics that are closely related.

The forensic psychiatrist can no longer define his field narrowly. Since many of the topics that have special meaning for forensic psychiatry have meaning for

other branches of medicine as well, some forensic psychiatrists have suggested
that the home for their specialty is not the department of psychiatry—although
this is where it is usually found—but as an independent medical school
department of medical jurisprudence.

THE PRESENT STATE OF LEGAL PSYCHIATRY

The present state of legal psychiatry represents a reaching out, although still
somewhat amorphous and ill-defined, into other branches of medicine and other
disciplines. These areas are of concern primarily to five disciplines—psychiatry,
law, psychology, sociology, and social work—although other disciplines as varied
as anthropology, education and special education, and hospital administration
can also be involved(3). It would not be difficult to give a list of 50 or 100
topics, all of which involve other disciplines, that interest a forensic psychiatrist.
They might range from abortion and addiction at one end of the alphabet to
violence and victims at the other, in contrast to the three traditional aspects that
previously attracted attention from forensic psychiatrists and lawyers—criminal
responsibility, commitment processes, and testamentary capacity. Although
criminal responsibility remains interesting and although it represents
complicated moral and philosophical questions that underlie all phases of
social-legal psychiatry, it has not deserved the 90 percent of the attention that it
has received.

In descriptions of the history of forensic psychiatry in America, the names
that appear are all identified with legal psychiatry mainly because of their
contributions to the law of criminal responsibility—Isaac Ray; Bernard Glueck,
who studied Sing Sing prisoners; Vernon Briggs, author of the Massachusetts
"Briggs Law," which provides for the psychiatric examination of certain classes
of defendants by impartial psychiatrists; Manfred Guttmacher, long connected
with the Baltimore court system and author and co-author with Professor Henry
Weihofen of books and articles on criminal responsibility; Winfred Overholser;
Franz Alexander; Gregory Zilboorg; and Benjamin Karpman. Starting in 1952,
APA has presented the Isaac Ray Award (annually if a suitable candidate is
available) to a specialist particularly distinguished in the field of psychiatry and
law; the award includes the obligation for a lecture series, which usually appears
in book form. With only four exceptions the award winners have used their
lectureships to make further contributions to the field of criminal responsibility
and correctional psychiatry—Gregory Zilboorg(10); Judge John Biggs, Jr.(11);
Professor Henry Weihofen(12); Philip Roche(13); Manfred Guttmacher(14);
Alastair MacLeod(15); Judge David Bazelon (16); Sheldon Glueck(17); Karl
Menninger(18); George Sturup(19); and Bernard Diamond(20).

The award has been presented only four additional times. The 1959 winner,
Maxwell Jones, contributed a volume(21) that was undoubtedly important but,
with the exception of a brief chapter on prison psychiatry, dealt with social
psychiatry rather than legal or social-legal psychiatry. The 1963 award winner,
Judge Morris Ploscowe, delivered a lecture series at Vanderbilt University on sex

and law, the theme of a book he had published 12 years previously(22); the lecture series has never been published.

It thus appears that only two of 15 winners produced books that dealt with the widened scope of legal psychiatry. In 1952 the first award winner, Winfred Overholser, in "The Psychiatrist and the Law"(23) sought a closer relationship between law and psychiatry, considered the lot of the committed mental patient, and discussed the role of the psychiatrist as witness. In 1964 Judge Justine Wise Polier dealt with such noncriminal aspects of legal psychiatry as adoption, custody, and the availability of psychiatric services for noncriminals; the series, published as *The Rule of Law and the Role of Psychiatry*(24), stimulated an important discussion by Tapp of the relationship of law and the behavioral sciences, especially social psychology(25).

But although the Isaac Ray Award Committee has stressed the criminal functions of forensic psychiatry, a flood of major texts and monographs in the last decade has emphasized the widened scope of social-legal psychiatry. An important event in 1960 was the appearance of the comprehensive, carefully researched study by the American Bar Foundation, *The Mentally Disabled and the Law*(26). This book brought together and tabulated the laws of all jurisdictions on a comprehensive range of legal psychiatric topics and has been the chief research source of many subsequent studies.

CURRENT LITERATURE

We have had a number of other meaningful books: the huge Katz, Goldstein, and Dershowitz text *Psychoanalysis, Psychiatry and Law*(27); the less comprehensive but still very helpful and much less overpowering text of Allen, Ferster, and Rubin, *Readings in Law and Psychiatry*(28); a new edition of Davidson's *Forensic Psychiatry*(29); and my own *Pursuit of Agreement: Psychiatry and the Law*(9). There have also been specialized works on criminal responsibility such as Yale Law School Dean Abraham Goldstein's(30) and in England, F. A. Whitlock's(31); on mental incompetency, including Allen, Ferster, and Weihofen's *Mental Impairment and Legal Incompetency*(32); on confidentiality in psychiatry, such as Slovenko and Usdin's *Psychotherapy, Confidentiality and Privileged Communication*(33); compilations such as *Psychopathic Disorders and Their Assessment*(34), *The Mentally Abnormal Offender*(35), and *Sexual Behavior and the Law*(36); specialized studies on commitment such as *Mental Illness and Due Process*(37) and *Hospitalization and Discharge of the Mentally Ill*(38). Within the past decade social-legal psychiatry has developed its own literature. Instead of the earlier subject matter, emphasizing psychic determinism and free will and the old debate about criminal responsibility, this is a varied literature emphasizing many practical problems of a host of people.

Much work is now going on. A. Louis McGarry, Director of the Division of Legal Medicine for the Massachusetts Department of Mental Health; Donald Hayes Russell, Director, Massachusetts Court Clinics Program; William Curran,

Professor of Legal Medicine, Harvard Medical School; Alan A. Stone, Lecturer in Law, Harvard Law School, and Associate Professor of Psychiatry, Harvard Medical School; Jay Katz, Adjunct Professor of Law and Psychiatry, Yale Law School; the George Washington University Institute of Law, Psychiatry and Criminology, headed by Richard Allen (who has collaborated with Elyce Zenoff Ferster and Professor Henry Weihofen of the University of New Mexico School of Law); John Suarez, Director of the Psychiatry and Law Program at UCLA; Seymour Pollack, Director of the Institute of Psychiatry and Law at the University of Southern California School of Medicine; John Macdonald, Director of Forensic Psychiatry at the University of Colorado Medical Center; Jonas Rappeport, Clinical Professor of Psychiatry, the Psychiatric Institute. University of Maryland School of Medicine; Ames Robey, Director, State of Michigan Center for Forensic Psychiatry, Ann Arbor; Andrew Watson, Professor of Law and Professor of Psychiatry, University of Michigan; Seymour Halleck, Wisconsin Division of Correction and the University of Wisconsin Medical School; Melvin Heller, Co-Director, and Robert Sadoff, Training Supervisor in Forensic Psychiatry, Unit in Law and Psychiatry, Temple University Schools of Law and Medicine; Irwin Perr, Clinical Professor of Legal Medicine, Case Western Reserve Law School; Herbert Thomas, University of Pittsburgh's Schools of Law and Medicine—these are representative of a growing list of psychiatrists and lawyers, many of whom have published only in the last ten years, who are developing an imposing body of books and studies on varied aspects of legal psychiatry.

There is also a growing literature in antipsychiatric thought by such people as Michael Hakeem(39); Thomas Szasz(40, 41) and Ronald Leifer(42), respectively Professor of Psychiatry and Associate Professor of Psychiatry, State University of New York in Syracuse; and Alan Dershowitz(43), Professor, Harvard University Law School; as well as the legal and sociological works of Edwin Schur(44, 45), Professor and Chairman of the Department of Sociology, Tufts University, and Herbert Packer(46), Professor of Law, Stanford University, which if not overtly antipsychiatric would like us to redefine many of those we view as patients as merely socially different. These works make many psychiatrists uncomfortable, but they also force psychiatrists to redefine our fields and our roles.

In another category, not antipsychiatric but critical of our failure to define our role and to provide meaningful help, are papers by Saleem Shah, Chief of the Center for Studies of Crime and Delinquency, National Institute of Mental Health, who has written about our incapacity to precisely define what is social deviancy and the harm to the individual that may result(47), and by Bertram Brown, Director of the National Institute of Mental Health, and Thomas Courtless, Director of Criminological Studies, the George Washington University Institute of Law, Psychiatry, and Criminology. Brown and Courtless(48, 49) have called our attention to the plight of the mentally retarded offender caught up in the correctional process and of the mentally abnormal offender; these offenders are not provided with meaningful help by either mental health or correctional systems. "The Right To Be Different" by Nicholas Kittrie(50),

Professor of Criminal and Comparative Law at American University, is an important recent addition to this category.

Besides the growing literature there is a growing list of important court decisions: the Robinson(51), Driver(52), and Easter(53) cases, and *Powell v. Texas*(54), all of which deal with addiction and alcoholism as medical problems; *Carter v. General Motors*(55), which upheld the finding of a Workmen's Compensation Board that schizophrenia had been caused by work stress; *Marable v. Alabama*(56), the case that did for the segregated state hospital system what *Brown v. Board of Education* did for the school system; and *Wyatt v. Stickney*(57), which said that state hospital patients have a constitutional right to treatment that meets standards approved by the court. A host of other recent cases attempt to define the law's position on abortion, commitment, confidentiality, psychiatric disability, and homosexuality. We also have an accumulating library of legal psychiatric teaching materials—compilations of cases and records on family law, marriage, divorce, custody, and adoption, which are not yet published but are available for teaching purposes. So we can see that forensic psychiatry in the last decade has developed a body of literature to be taught.

CONCLUSIONS

Forensic psychiatry—or, more appropriately, social-legal psychiatry—has burst its boundaries. It has found itself a broadened subject matter, it has extended out to cooperate with other disciplines, it has established in the AAPL its own "trade association," and it has developed its own literature and teaching materials.

Most important, it has involved itself in the body politic and the life of society. It has become the connection between psychiatry and a host of institutions—the courts, the prisons, administrative bodies, social agencies, and legislatures. It is now a focus for students who want to find ways to use psychiatric knowledge in the larger context of society.

REFERENCES

(1) Robitscher, J.: Medical limits of criminality. Ann Intern Med 73:849-851, 1970.
(2) Robitscher, J.: Three forensic psychiatry programs in the greater Philadelphia area. Newsletter of the AAPL 2(1):1-9, 1970.
(3) Robitscher J.: Social legal psychiatry. Read at the 12th International Conference on Legal Medicine, American College of Legal Medicine, Miami Beach, Fla., May 12-13, 1972.
(4) Rappeport, J.: The American Academy of Psychiatry and the Law: a history. Newsletter of the AAPL 2(3):23-32, 1971.
(5) By-laws of the American Academy of Psychiatry and the Law. Newsletter of the AAPL 1(1), 1969.
(6) Brown v Board of Education 349 US 310(1955).
(7) Robitscher, J.: Doctor's privileged communications, public life, and history's rights. Cleveland-Marshall Law Review 17:199-212, 1968.

(8) Robitscher, J.: Public life and private information. JAMA 202:398-400, 1967.

(9) Robitscher, J.: Pursuit of Agreement: Psychiatry and the Law. Philadelphia, J.B. Lippincott Co. 1966, pp. 68-92.

(10) Zilboorg, G.: The Psychology of the Criminal Act and Punishment. New York, Harcourt, Brace & Co., 1954.

(11) Biggs, J.: The Guilty Mind: Psychiatry and the Law of Homicide. New York, Harcourt, Brace & Co., 1955.

(12) Weihofen, H.: The Urge to Punish. New York, Farrar, Straus and Cudahy, 1956.

(13) Roche, P.: The Criminal Mind. New York, Farrar, Straus and Cudahy, 1958.

(14) Guttmacher, M.S.: The Mind of the Murderer. New York, Farrar, Straus and Cudahy, 1960.

(15) MacLeod, A.W.: Recidivism—A Deficiency Disease. Philadelphia, University of Pennsylvania Press, 1965.

(16) Bazelon, D. L.: Equal Justice for the Unequal. Washington, D.C., American Psychiatric Association, 1961 (processed).

(17) Glueck, S.: Law and Psychiatry: Cold War or Entente Cordiale? Baltimore, Johns Hopkins Press, 1962.

(18) Menninger, K.: The Crime of Punishment. New York, Viking Press, 1968.

(19) Sturup, G. K.: Treating the "Untreatable": Chronic Criminals at Herstedvester. Baltimore, Johns Hopkins Press, 1968.

(20) Diamond, B.: Criminal Responsibility of the Mentally Ill. Baltimore, Johns Hopkins Press (to be published).

(21) Jones M.: Social Psychiatry. Springfield, Ill., Charles C. Thomas, 1963.

(22) Ploscowe, M.: Sex and the Law. Englewood Cliffs, N.J., Prentice-Hall, 1951.

(23) Overholser, W.: The Psychiatrist and the Law. New York, Harcourt, Brace & Co. 1953.

(24) Polier, J. W.: The Rule of Law and the Role of Psychiatry. Baltimore, Johns Hopkins Press, 1968.

(25) Tapp, J.: What rule? What role? Reacting to Polier's *Rule of Law and Role of Psychiatry*. UCLA Law Review 17:1333-1344, 1970.

(26) Brakel, S. J., Rock R. S. (eds): The Mentally Disabled and the Law, Report of the American Bar Foundation, rev. ed. Chicago, University of Chicago Press, 1971.

(27) Katz, J., Goldstein, J., Dershowitz, A. M.: Psychoanalysis, Psychiatry, and Law. New York, Free Press, 1962.

(28) Allen, R. C., Ferster, E. Z., Rubin, J. G.: Readings in Law and Psychiatry. Baltimore, Johns Hopkins Press, 1968.

(29) Davidson, H. A.: Forensic Psychiatry, 2nd ed. New York, Ronald Press Co. 1965.

(30) Goldstein, A. S.: The Insanity Defense. New Haven, Yale University Press, 1967.

(31) Whitlock, F. A.: Criminal Responsibility and Mental Illness. London, Butterworths. 1963.

(32) Allen, R. C., Ferster, E. Z., Weihofen, H.: Mental Impairment and Legal Incompetency. Englewood Cliffs, N.J., Prentice-Hall, 1968.

(33) Slovenko, R., Usdin, G. L.: Psychotherapy, Confidentiality and Privileged Communication. Springfield, Ill. Charles C. Thomas, 1966.

(34) Craft, M. (ed): Psychopathic Disorders and Their Assessment. Oxford, Pergamon Press, 1966.

(35) De Reuck, A. V. S., Porter, R. (eds.): The Mentally Abnormal Offender. Boston, Little, Brown and Co., 1968.

(36) Slovenko, R. (ed.): Sexual Behavior and the Law. Springfield, Ill., Charles C. Thomas, 1965.

(37) Special Committee to Study Commitment Procedures, Association of the Bar of the City of New York: Report and Recommendations on Admission to Mental Hospitals Under New York Law: Mental Illness and Due Process. Ithaca, N.Y., Cornell University Press, 1962.

(38) Rock, R. R.: Hospitalization and Discharge of the Mentally Ill. Chicago, University of Chicago Press, 1968.

(39) Hakeem, M.: Critique of the psychiatric approach to crime and correction. Law and Contemporary Problems 23:650-682, 1958.

(40) Szasz, T. S.: Psychiatric Justice. New York, Macmillan Co., 1965.

(41) Szasz, T. S.: The Myth of Mental Illness. New York, Dell Publishing Co., 1967.

(42) Leifer, R.: In the Name of Mental Health: The Social Functions of Psychiatry. New York, Science House, 1969.

(43) Dershowitz, A.M.: The psychiatrist's power in civil commitment: a knife that cuts both ways. Psychology Today 2(9): 42-47, 1969.

(44) Schur, E. M.: Law and Society. New York, Random House, 1968.

(45) Schur, E. M.: Our Criminal Society: The Social and Legal Sources of Crime in America. Englewood Cliffs, N.J., Prentice-Hall, 1969.

(46) Packer, H. L.: The Limits of the Criminal Sanction. Stanford, Calif., Stanford University Press, 1968.

(47) Shah, S.: Crime and mental illness: some problems in defining and labeling deviant behavior. Ment. Hyg. 53:21-33, 1969.

(48) Brown, B. S., Courtless, T. F.: The mentally retarded in penal and correctional institutions. Amer J. Psychiatry 124:1164-1169, 1968.

(49) Brown, B. S., Courtless, T. F.: The Mentally Retarded Offender, Department of Health, Education, and Welfare Publication No (HSM) 72-9039. Washington, D.C., U.S. Government Printing Office, 1971.

(50) Kittrie, N. N.: The Right To Be Different: Deviance and Enforced Therapy. Baltimore, Johns Hopkins Press, 1972.

(51) Robinson v California, 370 US 660 (1962).

(52) Driver v Hinnant 356 F 2d 761 (4th Cir 1966)

(53) Easter v District of Columbia 361 F 2d 50 (DC Cir 1966)

(54) Powell v Texas, 392 US 514 (1968).

(55) Carter v General Motors, 361 Mich 577, 106 NW 2d 105 (1960).

(56) Marable v Alabama 297 F Supp 291 (MD Ala 1969)

(57) Wyatt v Stickney 325 F Supp 781 (MD Ala 1971).

PSYCHIATRIC TESTIMONY, WITH SPECIAL REFERENCE TO CASES OF POST-TRAUMATIC NEUROSIS

S. A. Strauss

Psychiatric evidence has in this century become of increasing importance in the administration of justice. In criminal law the psychiatrist is now playing a major role in assisting courts to assess the criminal liability of accused persons suspected of mental disorder, especially in cases of homicide and attempted homicide and other crimes involving violence. In civil and administrative law the aid of psychiatry is invoked in a wide range of judicial issues, including reception orders, the validity of wills, contracts and other documents, the assessment of delictual liability, and the *quantum* of damages due in terms of the law of delict or of social legislation.

Despite the ever-increasing involvement of psychiatry in the forensic arena, it must be observed—regretfully—that the dialogue between the law and psychiatry has not always been constructive. It has not at all times been on the same "wavelength," to use a popular expression of our time. At times the dialogue assumed the form of a "parallel monologue" in which premises, objectives and terminology differed substantially(1). This is especially true of the criminal law(2). Glueck(3) tersely summed it up thus: "Lawyers tend to look upon psychiatrists as fuzzy apologists for criminals, while psychiatrists tend to regard lawyers as devious and cunning phrasemongers."

Courts have at times shown a certain amount of scepticism towards expert psychiatric evidence and the science of psychiatry generally(4). One of the most eminent judges ever to adorn the South African Appellate Division, Mr. Justice F. P. van den Heever, in a 1953 case(5) on the basis of the expert evidence before the court, referred to psychiatry(6) as "an empirical and speculative science with rather elastic notation and terminology, which is usually wise after the event." In South Africa, psychiatric evidence supporting a defense of irresistible impulse has traditionally been approached by the courts with out-and-out scepticism(7), although the defense itself has been accorded unequivocal recognition as part and parcel of our criminal law since 1899(8). Jurists in turn have been accused by psychiatrists of oversimplification of the criteria which they have evolved in defining criminal liability(9), and of being unscientific in demanding the sole prerogative of defining these criteria which, it is asserted, relate to a purely medical or psychiatric issue(10).

Although this difference in outlook is not the main subject of this article, I hope that I will be permitted to make one or two comments on it in passing, in view of its relevance to psychiatric evidence generally. The truth, in my opinion, lies somewhere between these two extreme views. In order to obtain the maximum benefit from psychiatric expert testimony, jurists must be prepared to concede the limitations of law as a normative science, which can and may set up minimum standards to which human conduct will be required to conform, but which in the formulation of such standards, and especially in the interpretation of an accused's conduct in a specific case, must of necessity be guided by the views of the expert in human behavior, the psychiatrist. This will require some understanding on the part of the lawyer that psychiatry is in essence a therapeutic science with a "long term" view of the patient whilst the objective of the law is "short term" in the sense that it wants to arrive at a definite conclusion on the legal responsibility of the accused here and now. The psychiatrist, on the other hand, must be prepared to concede that although mental disease, its causes, its classification and its cure, are medical matters, criminal responsibility is a concept which belongs primarily to the field of normative science, *i.e.* the law. The law deals with the element of the *sollen*, what ought to be, and it is for the law to decide whether specific conduct conforms to the accepted norms of society. In the words of Guttmacher(11), responsibility is "a social judgment." But the psychiatrist is fully entitled to demand that his science be accorded proper recognition in both the formulation of minimum standards of conduct and the assessment of liability in a specific case. To disregard modern scientific knowledge in the reform and practice of law would be altogether short-sighted and unjustifiable. If this is done, the law would run the risk of degenerating into some kind of intellectual game unrelated to the realities of life. We should endeavor to strike a balance in the administration of justice between law and psychiatry. Have we succeeded in attaining such a balance? Have we succeeded in giving adequate recognition to the science of psychiatry in our courts?

Confining my remarks to the field of criminal law and to the country with which I am best familiar, South Africa, it is my conviction that we have not achieved this satisfactorily so far. I say this with due deference to our judges and our magistrates. It is not their fault. Under our precedent system, courts are bound by previous decisions of our Supreme Court, in particular of the Appellate Division. For many years now our courts have had to operate with legal formulae which are obsolete in the light of modern scientific knowledge. We are obviously in need of law reform. This, again, must be preceded by education of the general public. There is also a need for the closest cooperation between lawyer and psychiatrist, so that we can endeavor to understand better and appreciate each other's language, methods and objectives. The work of the Rumpff Commission(12) was a breakthrough in this regard in South Africa in the area of criminal law, and its excellent report will serve as a basis for communication between lawyer and psychiatrist for many years to come.

THE PSYCHIATRIC WITNESS IN CIVIL COURTS

Coming to the field of private law, it may be stated that the judicial attitude to psychiatric evidence is undoubtedly far more positive than in criminal law. In the former branch of law social defense is not involved and the points in issue are usually confined to private interests. However, it may be observed that some of the scepticism which is to be found amongst criminal law practitioners has spilled over to civil courts as well. There is still some evidence of the naive belief that a condition which is mental is not "real" but "phoney."(13) Moreover, one hears that rather smug complaint from time to time that psychiatric expert witnesses seem to differ diametrically in their views on one and the same case, depending frequently upon the schools of thought to which they belong. Lawyers do not always realize that there are few subjects in the whole field of medicolegal work which are more complex, and therefore more fraught with disagreements between experts, than the determination of post-traumatic neurosis(14, 15), which does not in itself involve visible injury(16) and which may be simulated(17).

Nevertheless, on account of these differences of opinion, courts find themselves in the dilemma that they have to make a choice between the opposing views of expert witnesses(18). In our age of specialization it does sometimes seem strange that laymen in the field of science are called upon to act as arbiters between scientific specialists, and judges have frequently commented on it. This becomes even more paradoxical in those jurisdictions where the factual issues are decided by juries consisting of laymen who are untrained in both the scientific discipline involved and the law. But this must be seen as an inherent feature of the system of "general" courts rated so highly in democratic societies(19). Although in our century there has been a growth in the number of specialized tribunals in most Western societies, e.g. in the areas of taxation, licensing, workmen's compensation, industrial conciliation, there is still powerful resistance against the introduction of such tribunals in the general sphere of the law of obligation (i.e. law of delict or tort, and law of contract). Not only the legal profession but the general public seems to favor the adjudication of disputes of this nature by the regular civil courts.

The problem of a "lay" court being called upon to make a choice between conflicting expert opinions might perhaps be solved by the introduction of a system whereby specialized issues are referred to experts *by the court* on its own initiative, instead of relying exclusively or at all upon evidence adduced by the respective parties. Whatever the advantages may be of such a system, variations of which are in fact well-known on the Continent(20), it would clearly find little favor in countries where the Anglo-American adversary system applies. Lawyers steeped in the traditions of the latter system are often apprehensive of any suggestions whereby the court would assume a less passive role than it does under present rules of procedure. There is, in particular, the fear that the evidence given by a court-appointed expert would be accorded an exaggerated importance(21). Yet, in the United States, sheer desperation in coping with the volume of litigation has induced courts and lawyers in recent years in a number of jurisdictions to make increasing use of court-appointed medical expert witnesses in personal injury cases resulting from automobile accidents(22, 23), and this trend has evoked praise from both lawyers and psychiatrists(23).

In regard to the judicial dilemma of having to make a choice between opposing expert views, there is one redeeming feature which must be mentioned. This is that conflicting expert opinions will sometimes be based on different factual hypotheses. In such a situation the court's choice will depend on an antecedent finding on the facts, and in deciding simple factual issues the judge will usually be in a better position than any of the experts witnesses. The case of *Botha v. Minister of Transport*(24) may serve as an example. In this case the plaintiff alleged that he suffered from mental disability as a result of brain damage caused by an accident. This allegation was supported by an expert psychiatric witness. On behalf of the defendant, however, it was testified that certain factors indicated a picture that was more consistent with the bulk of the plaintiff's brain condition having an origin in disease such as arteriosclerosis. In preferring the evidence of the former expert as being more sound on the balance of probabilities, the judge was guided by a finding that the plaintiff's personality changes had only come about immediately following the accident.

Apart from a judge making a finding on the facts which will determine his preference for a particular medical view of a case, there is another possibility for a judge to escape the dilemma of choosing between equally convincing expert opinions which are in conflict: by application of the rule that the *onus* is on the plaintiff to prove his case on a preponderance of probabilities, the judge may rule in such a situation that the plaintiff has failed to discharge the *onus*(25).

THE EXPERT AS AN OBJECTIVE WITNESS

There is another aspect of expert evidence which stems from the adversary system and which is deserving of some comment in the present discussion. I am referring to the problem of "partisan" evidence, which may be relevant to criminal as well as to civil proceedings, although it is perhaps of greater importance in the latter.

From a theoretical point of view the expert witness is not there to support "at all costs" the views of the party calling him. He is there as an independent witness whose reservoir of knowledge and expertise is at the disposal of both parties as well as the court. In practice, however, it is not always possible to maintain this independence, and, I wish to emphasize, this is of course not necessarily so on account of any dishonesty or corruption on the part of the witness whatsoever. The truth of the matter is that in the normal course of events the expert witness would not have found himself in the witness box had he not scientifically supported the factual views of the party which called him as a witness. His briefing by counsel on the issues in question might have been incomplete on account of counsel's limited or one-sided insight into these issues. His own preparatory work might have been somewhat superficial or one-sided. Moreover, once he steps into the witness box, he enters a hostile atmosphere, where he becomes subject to questioning by a skilled cross examiner whose objectives will range from an aggressive investigation into the validity of his scientific views, to shaking his integrity as a witness and ridiculing his expertise.

It is a common phenomenon that an expert witness may in these circumstances tend to become unduly sympathetic towards the side which has called him as a witness, thereby clouding his own vision and judgment(26). Quite apart from this, the expert witness may find that the side that has called him will sometimes be inclined to emphasize only those parts of his opinion which are most favorable to that party's cause, expecting the witness to keep all other material in the background. Such an attitude, which is only natural from the lawyer's point of view(27), may seriously inhibit the expert in presenting an objective scientific view to the court. As Guttmacher(11) observes, retaining one's objectivity in this situation "is as difficult as remaining neutral at a college football game while seated in a student cheering section."

The expert witness should guard against these dangers. and should always strive to maintain his independence as an expert whose sole duty is to present to the court the "whole" scientific truth(27). If the witness feels that his objectivity is being hampered by too narrow a line of questioning, he should never hesitate to assert his independence by proferring to the presiding officer such other information as he (the expert) deems proper(28).

PSYCHIATRIC ASPECTS AND THE QUANTUM OF DAMAGES

It is a well-known fact that even relatively minor injuries to the head—and the vertebral column, it may be added—can lead to accident neurosis; frequently, in fact, the psychological effects are more serious than the physiological results(29, 30).

It is a generally recognized tenet of Western legal systems that an injured party may recover damages also for mental disability caused by the defendant's unlawful conduct. Damages for post-traumatic neurosis are in fact claimed almost invariably in delictual actions involving head injuries.

I want to come now specifically to psychiatric aspects which are juridically relevant in the assessment of the *quantum* of general damages in these cases. I am speaking as a lawyer, of course, and my observations will relate mainly and selectively to South African law. (It may be pointed out, however, that the same fundamental considerations will be found in Anglo-American systems(31, 32), which in fact have left a noticeable imprint upon the South African law of delict.)

Mental disabilities which have been recognized by the courts in awarding damages take a variety of forms, ranging from total impairment of mental capacity to anxiety neurosis, and including personality changes, insomnia, epilepsy, compensation neurosis, diminution of intellectual capacity, hysterical blindness or paralysis, impairment or loss of memory and a disturbance of the plaintiff's emotional balance(33).

The courts have repeatedly emphasized that it is impossible to assess general damages with mathematical accuracy. The best a court can do is to endeavor to place some realistic financial value upon a disability which is proved by the plaintiff. As is to be expected, especially in view of the endless variety of circumstances, the amounts of individual awards differ widely.

As far as the medicolegal implications of a post-traumatic neurosis are concerned, the main problem facing the psychiatric witness will be to diagnose the neurosis. Once this has been done, the following facts *inter alia* will need to be determined: Was the neurosis partly or wholly precipitated by the accident? What is the nature of the neurosis? Is it permanent or is it transitory? What medical treatment is likely to be required, and how long is the period of treatment likely to continue? What is the effect of the present litigation upon the neurosis? Has there been any disablement from work, whether manual or intellectual? Has the neurosis handicapped the individual socially?(34)

I shall next deal with a number of the main practical issues as they have manifested themselves in case law. It is not intended to go in detail into all the different categories of mental disability which formed the subject of awards by the courts: This will be impossible in a paper of this scope.(35)

The *onus* of proving damage rests upon the injured party. This means that he must prove among other things a causal *nexus* between the defendant's wrongful conduct and his damage. As regards mental disability, it is sufficient if it is established that such a condition was caused by the defendant's wrongful act. It does not matter whether the mental condition flowed directly from the wrongful act itself(36, 37) or from the bodily injuries caused by the wrongful act(33, 38, 39). The defendant is liable even where the mental condition is only partly caused by the wrongful act, however much it may also be due to some physical condition of the plaintiff which has no connection with the wrongful act(33, 40). Thus in *Creydt-Ridgeway v. Hoppert*(41) (a case of dog bite) the plaintiff was held to be entitled to damages although her nervous condition was due to both the injury and the fact that she was going through a change of life.

In *Wilson v. Birt (Pty) Ltd*(42) the plaintiff claimed damages in consequence of a head injury caused by a pole falling on his head. Afterwards he suffered epileptic fits. Some three or four years prior to the accident he had sustained a stab wound in his forehead. After both these injuries, the court found, there was obvious damage to the brain which would in all probability have produced scarring of the brain which is the most usual cause of traumatic epilepsy. Although the stab wound had contributed to this condition, the defendant was nevertheless held liable. The court confirmed the legal principle that "a negligent defendant must take his victim as he finds him." (With this case may be compared the British case of *Dupey v. T. F. Maltby*(43) in which the plaintiff, a lorry driver, sustained a blow on the head from the swinging chains of a crane, which rendered him incapable of doing heavy work. His incapacity, it was found, was due to a). pre-existing heart trouble, b). neurosis. The neurosis itself was due 70% to the heart trouble and 30% to the accident. It was held that the defendants must take the plaintiff as they find him, that is, with his already vulnerable personality. It was further held that if the 30% of the neurosis due to the accident made the difference between working and not working then the defendants would have to recompense the plaintiff for all the special damage arising from the 100% neurosis.)

It is clear that as far as liability is concerned, it does not matter that a physical disability has a purely psychological basis, provided that the psychological condition is attributable to the wrongful act(44, 45). Thus in *Morris and Another v. S.A.R. and H.*(46) the plaintiff had suffered *inter alia* a disability of the right hand and wrist ever since the accident. There was some difference in opinion between the medical witnesses as to whether this disability was permanent in character or whether this as well as other pains and discomforts which she suffered were not psychological in character. The court held that this was irrelevant, because in either event the disability was attributable to the accident. Another case in point here is the Rhodesian case of *Moehlen v. National Employers*(47) where it was held that dizziness caused by an anxiety neurosis was not too remote to be the subject of an award of damages. However, in *Koch v. Ocean Accident and Guarantee Corporation Ltd*(48) the court, upon appeal, ruled that it was not persuaded that an attack of thrombosis which the plaintiff suffered had been contributed to by nervous tension and worry caused by the accident. The medical evidence on this point was directly contradictory.

Naturally, as Corbett and Buchanan(49) point out, if the mental condition is one which arose independently of the wrongful act, or as a result of a *novus actus interveniens*, then it must be disregarded.

The courts recognize the fact that mental and physical disabilities may be closely interrelated and may together contribute to an impairment of the plaintiff's health(50). This is illustrated by *Abelson v. Guardian Assurance Co. Ltd.*(51) although this was not a case of head injuries. The plaintiff, who had suffered from asthma for many years, had received a severe blow on the chest causing a lump and a bruise which had continued to be very painful. The mental stress caused by the pain increased the attacks of asthma which intensified the pain and aggravated the attacks. The court took all these factors into account in computing the plaintiff's damages.

In *Dielman v. Liquidators of Parity Insurance Co. Ltd.*(52) the plaintiff suffered amongst other things from paralysis of her right leg, limitation of neck movement, neck pain and headaches, as a result of a whip-lash injury to her neck. While it was common cause that these disabilities were due in part to organic and in part to psychogenic causes, the degree to which they were attributable to psychogenic factors was hotly disputed. Those expert witnesses who attributed these disabilities largely to a psychogenic overlay, believed that they would in time clear up almost completely. Viewing the medical evidence as a whole, the court was unable to find that the plaintiff had discharged the *onus* of proving that her disabilities were largely organic in origin, and therefore that they were permanent.

The approach in regard to mental disability is essentially a subjective one(44). Thus in *Marshall v. Southern Insurance Association Ltd.*(53) it was shown that the plaintiff had not faced the results of the accident in which she was injured with the fortitude and courage which could have been expected from a normal healthy young woman but had surrendered to her troubles and had allowed her "nerves" to get the better of her. The problem was whether this fact should cause her to be compensated on a reduced scale for the diminished suffering she would have undergone if she had faced her troubles with reasonable fortitude and courage. The court ruled against this proposition, expressing itself in the following terms: "Assuming equality of disturbance of the nervous system of two persons, one of them may be able to control his nerves more easily and will recover more quickly than the other. An insurance company (under the Motor Vehicle Insurance Act) covers both risks and . . . it is liable to pay more compensation in the second case than in the first."

The subjective approach is also apparent from the rule that if the plaintiff's neurosis and consequent pain and disability are brought on by his doing certain things, it is no answer for the defendant simply to say that the plaintiff must desist from doing these things.(50). This was held in the English case of *Liffen v. Watson*(54) which will undoubtedly be followed in South Africa. In this case it was held as follows in regard to an alleged neurotic pain: "If the plaintiff can avoid the pain by not doing certain normal things, then she has been damaged, because she cannot do them."

It is a general principle of delictual law, however, that there is a duty upon the plaintiff to mitigate his loss. Although in regard to disability this does not mean that the plaintiff must desist from performing normal activities in order to escape pain, it does mean that the plaintiff should submit to an operation or other medical treatment which will have the effect of diminishing his disability(55).

The main difficulties in cases of neurosis are to determine *a.* whether the plaintiff's condition is genuine or not, and if so, *b.* how long it will probably last(44, 56). In deciding these two questions the courts will be largely guided by psychiatric evidence, but a great deal will depend upon the impression made by the plaintiff himself(44). In several South African decisions courts have recorded their observations of a plaintiff's demeanor in court during the trial, usually to support a finding that the plaintiff's neurosis is genuine. Courts and counsel are aware of the possibility of malingering(57) and psychiatric witnesses should be prepared to make and substantiate their findings on this.

In this connection the phenomenon of "compensation (or settlement) neurosis" becomes relevant, *i.e.* the plaintiff's condition may be attributable to the litigation brought by him and a desire for compensation—a neurosis, therefore, which will appear once the claim is settled(44). Compensation neurosis has been recognized by South African courts as a factor in the computation of damages. If it is shown to be present in a case the court will not award anything for future disability caused by such neurosis, but on the other hand, the plaintiff will probably be entitled to damages for loss suffered by reason of his neurosis prior to trial(44).

In *Moehlen v. National Employer's Mutual*(47) the plaintiff's main complaint was dizziness associated with headaches. The defense theory was that this feeling of dizziness ought to have disappeared after a few days or a few weeks, but that a "compensation neurosis" had caused that feeling to continue, although there was now no physical basis for it. The court held on the facts of the case that if anxiety neurosis was the sole cause of her present condition, the litigation and the plaintiff's desire for compensation were not its only causes, though they may have intensified it. Her neurosis was basically caused by a fear that on account of the dizzy spells she would not be able to earn her living through easy, congenial employment offered to her. This was consequential damage for which the defendant was liable.

In *Cesler v. Caledonian Insurance Co. Ltd.*(58) the court seems to have taken judicial notice of the possibility of "compensation neurosis" in the following words: "(A)lthough the opinion was expressed that improvement would now halt, it is a common experience that after the anxiety of a pending action is over there is a very definite change for the better."

A problem peculiar to compensation neurosis as a factor in the assessment of an award was stated tersely in the English case of *Tuckey v. Green and Silley Weir Ltd*(59), thus: "The real trouble in assessing damages in this case . . . is this: it is very easy to be wrong either way. If one gives a very large sum, the man may recover in a very short time and go back to full work. On the other hand, if one gives a very small sum, the man may not recover and will lose a great deal of future wages, and suffer a great deal of pain and suffering, and the sum may be much too small."

In *Richter v. Capital Assurance Co. Ltd.*(60) it was held that in assessing damages, some allowance must be made for the fact that the plaintiff's disability could be diminished if he underwent psychiatric treatment, in other words that the plaintiff can "learn to live with his disabilities." In *casu* psychiatric evidence was also given to the effect that the plaintiff would respond better to such treatment once the action had been disposed of and the strain was therefore less.

In recent years pain and suffering, which include other accompanying woes such as mental pain, anxiety, embarrassment and humiliation, have become of increasing importance in the computation of damages(61). This item represents one of the most intangible elements in an action for damages, and various attempts have been made, especially by jurists, to evolve more concrete criteria to enable courts to compute awards(62). Psychiatric witnesses may expect to be closely questioned on these. I do not intend to comment on this factor in general. I shall confine my remarks to only one aspect which is of significance to psychiatric witnesses and has been the subject of judicial consideration also in South Africa, *viz.* whether an injured person may recover damages for pain suffered during a stage of mental disorder and unconsciousness.

In *Botha v. Minister of Transport*(24) it was argued on behalf of the defendant in mitigation of general damages for pain suffered, that in regard to much of the early pain he now has no recollection because of amnesia which supervened. The judge rejected this reasoning in the following words: "I am not at all sure that the body and the mind are not affected by pain that is suffered at a time when the mind is in a state of disorder. I certainly find it difficult to accept that a person is not entitled to compensation for pain suffered while the mind was disordered which pain on a restoration of the mind is not remembered." In *Sigournay v. Gillbanks*(63) the Appellate Division (per Schreiner J.A.(64)) pointed out that it was important to keep clear the distinction between pain actually experienced, though possibly subsequently forgotten, and what would have been pain but for anaesthesia. The learned Judge added: "Whether that anaesthesia is induced intentionally by drugs as when an operation is performed, or is the chance result of a head injury, can make no difference." It is quite clear that a plaintiff can recover damages only for pain "actually," *i.e.* consciously, suffered(65). In *Gillbanks'* case there was evidence of symptoms of excruciating suffering—sounds of moaning or wailing—but the court held on the medical evidence that part of this was during a stage of unawareness of pain. The learned Judge observed: "The fact is that most of what might have been excruciating pain was not pain for the plaintiff and compensation under this heading (pain and suffering) is given for pain, not for the seriousness of the injuries or the risk to plaintiff's life. Injuries may leave after effects and may cause mental anxiety, but they are not themselves pain."(66)

In this connection reference should also be made to *N.O. Gerke v. Parity Insurance Co. Ltd.*(67); where the court had to decide upon an award of damages for loss of amenities and shortened expectation of life in favor of a plaintiff who had been unconscious since he received the injury. Having sought guidance from English precedents, Ludorf J. ruled as follows: In making an award of damages the test *a.* is objective in that something falls to be awarded for "loss of happiness" even in a case where the victim has been reduced to a state in which he has and will never realize that he has suffered the loss; *b.* is, however, subjective, in the sense that the Court, in fixing *quantum*, will have regard to any relevant data about the individual characteristics and circumstances of the plaintiff which tend to show the extent and degree of deprivation; *c.* is subjective also in the sense that any realization which the plaintiff has, or did have or will have, of what he has lost, is most material and important. This is the true compensable suffering (as distinct from pain) which will carry far heavier damages than the somewhat artificial and notional award referred to in *a.* above. This suffering will continue only for the expected duration of his life. The learned Judge observed that there is no reason why separate awards should not be made for each of the items pain, suffering, loss of amenities, and loss of the expectancy of life, in the appropriate case. One can conceive of cases in which there has been no pain but there is suffering because of the loss of an amenity, or vice versa. (It must be pointed out that *in casu* the parties had agreed upon an amount as damages for pain and suffering.)

The fact that a plaintiff, although for the time being facing his physical disability with fortitude, may suffer a mental breakdown at a later stage when the full extent of his disability is brought home to him, is also considered a consideration in the assessment of damages. But in *Gillbanks'* case(63) this was ruled to constitute only a "small factor."

THE PRESENTATION IN COURT OF EXPERT EVIDENCE

This brief paper would not be complete without some reference to the attitude and demeanor of an expert witness in presenting his evidence in court. Much has been said and written on this subject, but it would be hard to improve upon the views expressed by East(68) as long ago as 1927 in his book on forensic psychiatry. What follows is a restatement of his suggestions, paraphrased slightly to conform to modern South African (non-jury) forensic procedure.

When in the witness box the medical officer should remember to speak clearly so that the judge and counsel can hear him distinctly. If a question is not understood an explanation should be asked before a reply is made. It is well to watch the judge writing, and adjust the rate at which one gives evidence to the movements of his pen. Any suggestion of an attempt to appear profound should be avoided lest the judge in mischievous mood decide to lay bare the ignorance of the witness. And it is a good plan to go over one's evidence critically the first leisured moment after leaving the box, and see where it might have been improved upon. It is important never to lose one's temper, not to argue, but not to allow oneself to be put in a false position; and to bear in mind that medical evidence is given to assist the court on technicalities, and that the personal achievement of a witness is measured by his ability to do this, and should not necessarily be estimated by the acceptance or rejection of his view by the court. The witness should remember not to take sides; the more he can show the court that his attitude is unbiased the more weight is his evidence likely to carry, and if hard pressed by opposing counsel he may appear prejudiced unless cautious in supporting his opinion. He should accept with equanimity some petulance and disapprobation at the hands of opposing counsel, remembering that the legal advisers of the contestants may have an exceedingly responsible and perhaps harassing task before them.

The medical witness should always, but does not invariably, remember that it is necessary for his evidence to be understood by those who may be ignorant of scientific terminology. If the expert uses simple words he may be understood by all and he will be appreciated by those whose constant professional attendance in court renders them justly suspicious that unfamiliar polysyllables disguise ignorance. The initiated will recognize the skill whereby a witness explains in simple language not only the mental condition of the party concerned, but his reasons for arriving at his conclusion. A resourceful use of ordinary language should be cultivated, at times no easy matter.

Finally East reminds the medical officer that it is only by the intensive study of cases, of modern literature, and of modern conceptions, that he can hope to withstand frequent examinations in the witness box with success.

To East's practical suggestions may be added the following: The expert witness should prepare himself thoroughly in a specific case. Here he should obtain assistance from counsel in knowing beforehand what the conflicting claims are or may be in the litigation and what medical issues may arise(69). In cases involving issues such as the plaintiff's response to psychiatric treatment or alleged changes of personality, it is of the utmost importance for the expert witness to assess what the plaintiff's personality was before the accident and to acquaint himself with treatment given by other medical practitioners(70). In giving evidence in court the expert must stick to his expertise and should never allow himself to be induced to comment upon aspects falling outside his specialty(71). His assessment of a case should be on scientific grounds only, irrespective of the law. It is for the court to make a finding on the legal consequences flowing from the expert's testimony(72).

NOTES

(1) *Cf.* S. A. Strauss, Legal aspects of mental disorder, *Tijdskr. Hedendaagse Rom.–Holl. Reg.* 33 (1970) 1, p. 3 *et seq.*

(2) *Cf.* South African *Report of the Commission of Inquiry into the Responsibility of Mentally Deranged Persons and Related Matters*, RP. 69/1967 (known, and hereinafter cited as the *Rumpff Report*), par.1, p. 13 *et seq.*

(3) S. Glueck, *Law and Psychiatry*, Hopkins, Baltimore, 1962, pp. 4-5.

(4) *Cf.* M.S. Guttmacher, *The Role of Psychiatry in Law*, C. C. Thomas, Springfield, Ill., 1968, p. 5.

(5) *R. v. von Zell*, 1953 (3) S.A. 301 (A), p. 311.

(6) *Cf.* the remarks quoted by an American jurist, E. J. Bellen, The forensic medical man in criminal courts, in *Jus Medicum*, Centrum voor Medisch Recht, Ghent, 1969, p. 361, at pp. 361 and 368.

(7) S. A. Strauss, *Tijdskr. Hedendaagse Rom.–Holl. Reg.* 33 (1970) 1, at p. 10.

(8) *R. v. Hay*, (1899) 16 S.C. 290.

(9) *Rumpff Report*, par. 5.3, 5.4, 5.16, 5.27.

(10) *Rumpff Report*, par. 5.10, 5.20.

(11) M.S. Guttmacher, *The Role of Psychiatry in Law*, p. 77.

(12) See ref. 2, *Rumpff Report*.

(13) *Cf.* A. Larson, Mental and nervous injury in workmen's compensation, *Vanderbili Law Rev.*, 23 (1970) 1243.

(14) A. Mann, *The Medical Assessment of Injuries for Legal Purposes*, Butterworths, London, 1967, p. 52.

(15) D. M. Palmer, Mental reactions following injuries, *J. Forens. Med.*, 1 (1954) 222.

(16) J. Munkman, *Damages for Personal Injuries and Death*, 4th ed., Butterworths, London, 1970, p. 111.

(17) *Cf.* H. Merskey, Psychiatric sequelae of head injuries, *Med. Sci. Law*, 8 (1968) 193, at p. 196.

(18) *Cf.*, M.M. Belli, Medical evidence in social legislation, in Civil, Administrative and Penal Law, in *Jus Medicum*, 1969, p. 347, at p. 353. See also the remarks made by the judge in *Goldie v. City Council of Johannesburg*, 1948 (2) S.A. 913 (W), at pp. 916-917.

(19) *Cf.* S. A. Strauss, The physician's liability for malpractice: A fair solution to the problem of proof? *S. Afr. Law J.*, 84 (1967) 419, at p. 426.

(20) *Ibid.*, p. 426 n. 39.

(21) *Cf.* E. J. Bellen's observations on German practice in *Jus Medicum*, pp. 367 *et seq.* For American attitudes, see Guttmacher, *The Role of Psychiatry in Law*, p. 80.

(22) M. M. Belli, *Jus Medicum*, p. 354.

(23) M. S. Guttmacher, *The Role of Psychiatry in Law*, pp. 78-80 and pp. 87 *et seq.*

(24) *Botha v. Minister of Transport*, 1956 (4) S. A. 375 (W).

(25) *Cf.* the reasoning of the judge in *Dielman v. Liquidators of Parity Insurance Co. Ltd.*, 1966 C.P.D., reported by M. M. Corbett and J. L. Buchanan, *The Quantum of Damages in Bodily and Fatal Injury Cases* (as supplemented annually), Juta, Cape Town, 1966, p. 720.

(26) *Cf.* M. M. Belli, *Jus Medicum*, p. 353.

(27) *Cf.* E. J. Bellen, *Jus Medicum*, p. 366.

(28) *Cf.* the eloquent remarks made by I. Gordon, reported in *Jus Medicum*, pp. 372-374.

(29) *Cf.* E.A.D.E. Carp, *Gerechtelijke Psychiatrie*, Scheltema and Holkeman, Amsterdam, 1956, pp. 293-294.

(30) D. Blair, *Med. Sci. Law*, 8(1968) 198, at p. 199.

(31) *Cf.* J. Munkman, *Damages for Personal Injuries and Death*, pp. 111-113 on English Law.

(32) *Cf.* A. Larson, *Vanderbilt Law Rev.*, 23 (1970), on American law in regard to workmen's compensation cases.

(33) *Cf.* M. M. Corbett and J. L. Buchanan, *The Quantum of Damages in Bodily and Fatal Injury Cases*, p. 32.

(34) *Cf.* A. Mann, *The Medical Assessment of Injuries for Legal Purposes*, pp. 52-53.

(35) See generally M. M. Corbett and J. L. Buchanan, *The Quantum of Damages in Bodily and Fatal Injury Cases*, Chap. 1. For English cases see D.A.M. Kemp, M. S. Kemp and R. O. Havery, *The Quantum of Damages, Personal Injury Claims*, Vol. 1, Chap. 14, (hereinafter cited as Kemp and Kemp), Sweet and Maxwell, London, 1961.

(36) See, for example, *Bradfield v. British Railways Board*, 1965, cited by Kemp and Kemp, p. 651.

(37) *Cf.* A. Larson, *Vanderbilt Law Rev.*, 23 (1970) 1251.

(38) *Goldie v. City Council of Johannesburg*, at p. 917.

(39) *Cf.* A. Larson, *Vanderbilt Law Rev.*, 23 (1970) 1249.

(40) *Cf.* the English case of *Shepherd and Another v. Ellis and Another*, 1961 Q.B.D., cited by Kemp and Kemp, at p. 267.

(41) *Creydt-Ridgeway v. Hoppert*, 1930 T.P.D. 664.

(42) *Wilson v. Birt (Pty) Ltd.*, 1963 (2) S. A. 508 (D). Also reported in M. M. Corbett and J. L. Buchanan, *The Quantum of Damages in Bodily and Fatal Injury Cases*, p. 177.

MEDICINE, LAW AND PUBLIC POLICY 343

(43) *Dupey v. T. F.Maltby*, (1955) 2 Lloyd's Rep. 645.

(44) M. M. Corbett and J. L. Buchanan, *The Quantum of Damages in Bodily and Fatal Injury Cases*, p. 33.

(45) A. Larson, *Vanderbilt Law Rev.*, 23 (1970) 1244.

(46) *Morris and Another v. S.A.R. and H.*, 1961 E.C.D., reported by Corbett and Buchanan, p. 296.

(47) *Moehlen v. National Employers*, 1959 (2) S.A. 317 (R).

(48) *Koch v. Ocean Accident and Guarantee Corporation Ltd.*, 1962 E.C.D., reported by Corbett and Buchanan, p. 316.

(49) M. M. Corbett and J. L. Buchanan, *The Quantum of Damages in Bodily and fatal Injury Cases*, p. 32-33.

(50) M. M. Corbett and J. L. Buchanan, *The Quantum of Damages in Bodily and Fatal Injury Cases*, p. 34.

(51) *Abelson v. Guardian Assurance Co. Ltd.*, 1953 O.P.D., reported by Corbett and Buchanan, p. 208.

(52) *Dielman v. Liquidators of Parity Insurance Co. Ltd.*, 1966 C.P.D., reported by Corbett and Buchanan, p. 720.

(53) *Marshall v. Southern Insurance Association Ltd.*, 1950 (2) P.H. J6 (D), quoted by Corbett and Buchanan, p. 33.

(54) *Liffen v. Watson*, (1940) 1 K.B. 556; (1940) 2 All E.R. 213.

(55) M. M. Corbett and J. L. Buchanan, *The Quantum of Damages in Bodily and Fatal Injury Cases*, p. 34, and authority cited there.

(56) Kemp and Kemp, p. 42.

(57) *Cf.* A. Larson, *Vanderbilt Law Rev.*, 23 (1970) 1256.

(58) *Cesler v. Caledonian Insurance Co. Ltd.*, 1959 E. C., reported by Corbett and Buchanan, p. 339.

(59) *Tuckey v. Green and Silley Weir Ltd.*, (1955) 2 Lloyd's Rep. 619, p. 630.

(60) *Richter v. Capital Assurance Co. Ltd.*, 1963 (4) S.A. 910 (E.C.), reported in full by Corbett and Buchanan, pp. 101 *et seq.*

(61) M.M. Belli, *Modern Damages*, Vol. 2, Bobbs Merrill, Indianapolis, 1960, p. 837.

(62) H. Kornblitt, Evaluating pain and suffering in personal injury suits, in S. Polsky (Ed.), *Medico-Legal Reader*, Oceana, Philadelphia, 1956, pp. 156 *et seq.*

(63) *Sigournay v. Gillbanks*, 1960 (2) S.A. 552 (A).

(64) Schreiner, J. A., who delivered the majority judgment.

(65) *Contra*: Van Wyk A.J.A., at p. 589G of the judgment.

(66) *Cf. Dorfling v. Bazeley*, 1961 E.C., reported by Corbett and Buchanan, at p. 134.

(67) *N. O. Gerke v. Parity Insurance Co. Ltd.*, 1966 (3) S.A. 484 (W).

(68) W. N. East, *An Introduction to Forensic Psychiatry in the Criminal Courts*, Churchill, London, 1927, pp. 41-42.

(69) R. P. Bergen, Medical Testimony without Bias, in *The Best of Law and Medicine*, Am. Med. Assoc., Chicago, 1966-1968, p. 161.

(70) D. Blair, *Med. Sci. Law*, 8 (1968) 189.

(71) *Cf.* S. A. Strauss and M. J. Strydom, *Die Suid-Afrikaanse Geneeskundige Reg.*, Van Sehaik, Pretoria, 1967, p. 569.

(72) *Cf.* A. Langelüddeke, *Gerichtliche Psychiatrie*, De Gruyter, Berlin, 1959, p. 242.

CIVIL COMMITMENT IN PERSPECTIVE

Ralph Slovenko

Since 1954, approximately half of the states of the United States have appointed special committees to study various phases of the law on the commitment of mentally disordered persons. In 1950 the Council of State Governments and the Federal Security Agency prepared a Draft Act Governing Hospitalization of the Mentally Ill, which was transmitted to all state governments as a working model.(1) With one recent exception (California), the state committees have generally followed the recommendations embodied in the Draft Act, resulting in a body of law even more elaborate than the preexisting law.

While this development has taken place, others question the morality of any involuntary commitment, and instead of revision, urge outright repeal. The American Association for the Abolition of Involuntary Mental Hospitalization (AAAIMH), recently organized, seeks members to "oppose currently accepted psychiatric and psychological practices resting on the use of state-supported force and fraud." Thomas Szasz, professor of psychiatry at the State University of New York and a fellow of the American Psychiatric Association, has provided the groundwork and leadership for AAAIMH. Some practices that Szasz regards as deceptive and coercive, he says, are so well accepted as proper forms of psychiatric practice that they may not offer grounds for suits for malpractice or tort. Among these he includes the idea that "mental illness is like any other illness," a theory put forth by the American Psychiatric Association and other national medical organizations, and the practice of involuntary mental hospitalization, "a type of indefinite imprisonment justified as psychiatric treatment."(2)

The merit of either of the above approaches, elaborate revision or total repeal, is open to serious question. The first is a face-saving and wordy formulation; the second is an outright denial of reality. It is the contention of this article that involuntary or nonprotested commitment is justified, but only in exceptional circumstances, which may be governed by one or two statutory provisions.

The mental health laws, which were originally enacted about a century ago, provide in great detail various procedures for admission to and discharge from mental hospitals. Some of the laws provide a "bill of rights" for the person while in the hospital. Since special legislation does not exist in the case of physical illness, we might question why mental health laws and the commitment of the so-called mentally ill ever came to pass.(3)

Historical studies indicate that during the Middle Ages "insanity" was in many respects considered a part of everyday life. Fools and madmen, as they were called, walked the streets in much the same way as they appear in Shakespeare's King Lear and Cervantes' Don Quixote. There was a high tolerance for odd or unusual behavior.

Following the Middle Ages, such tolerance waned. During the Renaissance, many of the so-called mad were put on ships and entrusted to mariners. It was believed that folly and water had an affinity for each other (the Greeks and Romans earlier regarded water as a universal remedy). Water is soothing, and nothing is more soothing than the undisturbed blue of the ocean. "Ships of Fools," as they were known, crisscrossed the seas with their comic and pathetic cargo of passengers. Like a cruise today, the voyage was often therapeutic. It provided a change of scenery; it removed stresses of the old environment; and it sometimes offered the opportunity to start a new life in a new place.(4)

Originally the Colonies were viewed as a place to send the undesirable, the idle, the worthless person. A high incidence of persons sent from England to America had been so damaged by squalor, forced drifting, or some other social trauma as to be chronic bad risks. Given another chance under stimulating new conditions, many of these people did straighten up (at best into a settler and builder, at worst into a robber baron). After the Revolution, when America was no longer available, England developed Australia as a new depository.

During the seventeenth and eighteenth centuries, the construction of enormous houses of confinement took place. To some extent, confinement replaced embarkation. Within a century after the era of the mad ships, there appeared the "Hospital of Madmen," the "madhouse." The Hospital General, which was founded in 1656 in Paris, was not based on a medical concept; it was rather a sort of semi-judicial structure, an administrative entity. The term "Hospital" meant a place of reception or hospitality.(5)

Confinement, a massive phenomenon, was found all across eighteenth century Europe. There was an effort or attempt to put a wall between the so-called insane and the rest of humanity. In America, the commitment of the mentally ill (the "distracted") in its modern sense was unknown until the early part of the nineteenth century;(6) the eighteenth century was known as the era of moral treatment. Institutions were small; care was provided; the atmosphere was idyllic; results were remarkable.(7) The original commitment procedures were extremely informal. Thereafter, however, as the population increased with the influx of immigrants, the number of commitments to large impersonal facilities and the absence of controls and supervision resulted in abuses. People were isolated and abandoned in crowded wards.(8) As a consequence, elaborate and detailed commitment procedures, which form the basis of modern commitment statutes, were adopted.(9)

The most famous crusader for the enactment of these commitment laws was Mrs. E.P.W. Packard. She had differed publicly with her husband, a preacher, on religious issues. He apparently won the argument by having her committed under the Illinois statute, a law which preceded the emancipation of women, that provided that a married woman can be committed on the petition of her husband "without the evidence of insanity or distraction required in other cases."(10) Upon her release, in 1890, following three years of confinement, she began a crusade to stir up public concern about the "railroading" of people into lunatic asylums. Her campaign resulted in the introduction of many of the strict procedural and substantive safeguards in this field, including the right to a hearing and a jury trial.(11)

Mental hospitals are still regarded as fearful places. A recent survey reports that one out of four persons sees state mental hospitals as prisons. The survey also reports that four out of five persons feel that state mental hospitals are necessary to protect the community (not the patient).(12) At the same time, the public wants the law to make sure that only the truly "crazy" are committed, and that they are committed legally. If for no other reason than, "There but for the grace of God go I."

Over a hundred years ago, Alexis de Tocqueville observed that America tends to transform its political or social problems into legal problems. However, according to Thomas Szasz, America now tends to transform its legal problems into mental health problems. In a number of repetitive but provocative writings, Szasz has argued that much of the phenomena now called and treated as mental illness is not illness at all, but rather an expression of behavior in response to problems or crises that arise in the course of living. The disease or illness concept with its implication of deviation from a healthy norm, a concept which is so crucial to medicine, has been applied inappropriately to the psycho-social area. Undoubtedly, a diseased brain will influence behavior, but the physical illness concept has been extended to include the psycho-social area as well. As a result, Szasz says, America is well on its way to becoming a Therapeutic State.(13)

According to Szasz in the perennial conflict that is life, control of the weak by the strong has been justified by rhetoric appropriate to the prevailing ideology. In the twentieth century the credo is Mental Health, and in its name those who deviate from accepted social norms are often victimized and dehumanized. During the Middle Ages there arose a concept of the witch as the enemy of society. In order to protect the faith and even to save the soul of the witch, authority came to regard the elimination of witches as its sacred duty. The lowliest baron had the power to arrest, try, and convict a witch; today, the psychiatrist has replaced the baron. The myth of mental illness has replaced the concept of witchcraft, and Institutional Psychiatry has replaced the Inquisitors in ferreting out the deviant. The procedure is again justified because it protects society and is also for the patient's own welfare, but in reality, Szasz says, the patient is again persecuted by denial of his legal rights, involuntary hospitalization, and forced treatment.

Szasz claims that psychiatrists and other "mental health workers" are the greatest dangers to American society.(14) He says that the idea of mental illness is popular in our day because psychiatrists and other mental health workers achieve a sense of importance as they proceed to "treat" their "patients."(15) One's conception of self depends in some measure upon one's conception of the other. Master needs slave and vice-versa, said Hegel. The "new frontier" of the "Therapeutic State," says Szasz, gives life-meaning to the therapists by robbing "patients" of their life-meaning. In a bit of one-upmanship, mental health workers relegate some people in effect to second-class citizenship by labeling them "mentally ill."(16)

Robert Coles, another psychiatrist questioning the humanity and compassion of psychiatric dogma, tells us that the ruling circles in America would not be quite so taken with psychiatry if more psychiatrists emphasized that men are psychologically enslaved not only by unconscious drives but by social and economic conditions.(17) He tells us that much of the psychiatric talk is pap that diverts the nation from social concerns. Similarly, Professor Howard Zinn in *Politics of History* says:

> Psychological explanations are comforting to those of us who don't want our little world upset, because they emphasize the irrationality of the protester rather than the irrationality of that which produces protest. It seems much easier for us to believe that Abolitionists were vehement because they were up-ward striving than that they grasped in some small way the horror of slavery. It is easier to believe that students have "intense, unresolved Oedipal feelings, a tremendous attachment to their mothers, and a violent hostility to their fathers" rather than that they are outraged at a society which (speaking precisely) will not let them live.(18)

Critical of David Donald's psychological history of the abolitionists(19) and Lewis Feuer's treatment of the student radicals,(20) Zinn says that those who suggest the agitator comes into being because of a psychological failing on his part ignore the possibility that the agitator appears because "there is evil in the world."(21) While many writers have emphasized the allegedly "sick" quality of radicals, Zinn feels that those who function in a society that is both corrupt and cruel and remain other than radical are more likely to be "sick."(22)

Undoubtedly, the mental health worker, like any one else, feels an enhanced self-esteem when he considers himself superior or helpful. And labels or categories do tend to channelize and determine destinies. A person tends to live up to the implications of the role ascribed to him. But man is a labeling animal and needs to categorize or generalize in order to cope with the world. To varying degrees, labels or categories sacrifice validity for convenience, but it becomes a matter of concern only when the validity of the label or category is lost in the convenience of its use.(23)

The fact which cannot be denied is that so many individuals in today's society feel alienated and isolated. Psychiatry, however, did not make them that way, by labeling or otherwise. While it may engage in name calling, psychiatry at least tries to be a helping profession. At the same time that life is becoming more stressful, the isolation of people from kinship groups that once offered support to troubled people means that in increasing numbers they must look elsewhere for support. Szasz says, though, that psychiatry, instead of helping, is depriving people of their liberty and dignity. But, in reality, of what is psychiatry depriving them? Is it their "right" to a nervous breakdown? to hallucinate? to commit suicide? to harm others? The real question is whether we are providing help appropriate to their needs. We must be genuinely more concerned, not less, over the needs of others.(24) Camus in his book *The Fall* presents a poignant account of the downfall of a prominent citizen whose initial steps to degeneration are dated from the moment he refused to respond to a stranger's cry for help.

To be sure, psychiatric concepts and jargon are now part of everyday language. The question, however, is whether the blame ought to fall on psychiatry. Why the emergence of the so-called therapeutic state? For one thing, America is an innovative country, relatively unbound by tradition, open to new ideas. For another, psychiatry apparently is being used to fill a cultural gap. We are creating a psychological culture in the sense that other countries have created a literary or artistic culture, says playwright Arthur Miller, because the deep and steady use of literature is so sparse in this country.(25) The salons of Europe were literary affairs; on the other hand, at the contemporary cocktail party, bellyaches and activities of the day fill the air. The United States could be called "hypochondriacal USA," for frequent subjects of conversation at social gatherings are cholesterol levels, gall bladder operations, and other tales of woe.

The reality of madness is not denied by its classification as "illness" or as anything else. A rose by any other name is still a rose. Moreover, the use of the word "health" or its opposite "illness" or"sickness"when referring to the mental functioning of the individual is not without justification. The word "health" comes from an old word, "hal," and means "wholeness."(26) The words, "healthy," "holy," and "whole" have this common etymological derivation. When a body is healthy, all the parts work together as a whole. When the body is sick, it is not functioning as a whole. To his credit, though, Szasz questions the assimilation of "madness" to medicine; that is, the medicalization of the nonmedical. Seeking to avoid the medical framework, the Metropolitan Hospital in Detroit and the Bradley Center in Columbus, Georgia, among others, announce that they deal with "the problems of living."

Undoubtedly, it can be granted that the concept of mental illness is inadequate, but there is little evidence to show that there have been serious abuses of the commitment process or that psychiatry has aligned itself with authority against nonconformists. The commitment process suffers from lack of psychiatric involvement, rather than from overinvolvement. As far as judicial authority is concerned, judges seem to accept a psychiatric opinion only when it suits them.

The American Bar Foundation, which recently conducted a field investigation of mental hospitals of six states, concluded that "railroading" is a myth.(27) A few years earlier, the Subcommittee on Constitutional Rights of the Committee on the Judiciary of the United States Senate conducted hearings and it too came up with no evidence of railroading.(28) In short, the Szaszian position is based on some kind of fantasy about railroading and not on any real knowledge. Szasz, a psychiatrist, writes like a person who has never visited a psychiatric institution.

The remedy for quarrelsome marriages, which provoked Mrs. Packard's commitment has moved from flogging, imprisonment, or commitment to our current "enlightened" situation. Separation or divorce under the law without commitment is now readily available. Who then are committed? Before attempting to answer this question, it might be illuminating to note some of the persons who despite socially deviate or bizarre conduct are not committed.

People dress and act in culturally inappropriate ways. Young men dressed in orange robes like the Swamis wear in India stand on street corners fingering beads and chanting "Hare Krishna, Hare Krishna." They are not committed.

A man in San Francisco dressed in shorts and tennis shoes and wearing boxing gloves shadow boxes as he goes down a main thoroughfare of the city, but he is not committed.A man in New Orleans walks around hotel lobbies; he says he sees lions and bears; he draws attention, but he is not committed.

A woman on New York's Park Avenue has six dogs on a leash, all dressed in expensive apparel. As they go down the street, the dogs bark and fight, and she scolds them. Her whole life is devoted to the dogs, to the exclusion of men and children. She is not committed.

At a coffee shop near the Fisher Building ("the cathedral of business") in Detroit, there is a regular patron who will tell you that he is hearing voices, from all that junk orbiting in space. He says the Russians have only water to live on, so they want to conquer the world. He always has with him a copy of *The New Mathematics Dictionary and Handbook*, which he says contains all the solutions to the world's problems. He is not committed.

New York is said to have more philosophers than ancient Athens. One of them is Moondog, who stands guard at the corner of 53rd Street and Sixth Avenue, dressed as a viking, with long beard, helmet, and spear. He is not committed. Finally considered a human interest story, he was interviewed on television in a program called *Success May Spoil Moondog*.(29) He is obsessed with the idea that the military-industrial complex is primarily responsible for the calamity of the country. Who *is* crazy? Concerning the manufacture and sale of arms, Karl Menninger says, "This whole wicked, hypocritical dumb show is more irrational and more self-destructive than anything *any* psychiatric patients do."(30)

Pathology in leadership has never been checked by mental health laws. Governor Earl Long of Louisiana dismissed the Superintendent of Hospitals when he was put in a mental hospital. Hubert Humphrey, when no longer Vice-President, said, "I had a President who was absolutely paranoid about the war," but at the time he said or did nothing about it.(31) Institutional checks and balances were inadequate to contain Hitler or Stalin (Khrushchev says in his memoirs that Stalin was "not quite right in the head").(32) If power tends to corrupt and absolute power corrupts absolutely, as Lord Acton said in a widely accepted maxim,(33) then the need for control is more crucial now than ever. A match can now cause a big explosion: people in power have access to nuclear triggers that can touch off a world holocaust. Opportunistic Ralph Ginzburg was sued for having published a nation-wide survey of psychiatric opinion on the mental competency of Barry Goldwater, then a presidential candidate (Julius Fast may read the "body language" of politicians but psychiatrists may not "read their minds").(34)

Unlike churches, schools, and restaurants, gunshops have never been segregated in the United States. They are open to one and all—black or white, moron or psychotic. The National Commission on the Causes and Prevention of Violence estimates ninety million firearms in private possession in the United States;(35) other authorities put the figure as high as 200 million;(36) perhaps a third to a fifth of these are handguns, mostly concealable. More persons are murdered annually in the City of Baltimore than in the entire United Kingdom. Physicians are required to report epileptics to the motor vehicle department, but in contrast they are to do nothing about the significant numbers of persons they encounter who possess guns despite serious and obvious psychopathology. Gun control would likely reduce violent killings, but the "right to bear arms" remains essentially unrestricted.

People enclose themselves in little containers propelled by internal combustion engines polluting the air and doing permanent damage to their nervous system. The body count is over 56,000 a year. No one is committed on that account. George Wald, Harvard biologist, compares man in the automobile to the dinosaur—a small brain in a big body, and he reminds us that the dinosaur is now extinct.(37) A. Q. Mowbray in his book, *Road to Ruin*, which discusses the destruction of America by its cars and freeways, says, "It is becoming quite clear that the free passage of automobiles throughout the land is antisocial behavior. Further, the attempt to pave the land so as to encourage such free passage is antisocial. Both activities must be curtailed. But the forces working to encourage them are strong, and hope for salvation is dim."(38)

Whether or not a person is considered mad depends on the degree to which his personality or behavior is disturbed or egodystonic, and the attitudes of the members of his social group towards him. In this sense, mental disorder is perhaps more dependent on social factors than is physical illness. Thus, there may be found greater tolerance of, or greater apathy toward, the mentally ill in one society than in another.(39) The cases listed above go unnoticed or unattended, perhaps because nothing feasible can be done, perhaps because of vested interests, or perhaps because no one cares. Perhaps human life may not be considered worth very much. The cruelty of the twentieth century has especially hardened people.

The attempt to provide adequate criteria for commitment is a difficult if not impossible task. The Draft Act(40) makes compulsory hospitalization possible when the person is 1. mentally ill, and 2. dangerous to himself or others or 3. in need of care and lacking in the capacity to make a rational choice about his need.

The terms in the Draft Act—"mentally ill" and "dangerousness"—are essentially undefined and undefinable. It is one thing to see and feel mental disorders, another to deal with them abstractly. To delineate these matters, it would be better to paint a picture or make a film than to define by category or label. A painter or photographer can tell it with a clarity that words alone could not. In some matters, Goethe said that if you can't feel it, you can't grasp it. Philosophers have difficulty defining the color "yellow."

The concept "mental illness" is defined in the Draft Act as a "psychiatric or other disease which substantially impairs (a person's) mental health."(41) A precise behavioral content or operational meaning of "mental illness" or "insanity" cannot be defined in a way that would be helpful to the law. The manual of mental disorders of the American Psychiatric Association could cover almost anyone within its diagnostic categories. Pragmatically, from a psychiatric point of view, the concept of mental illness may be broken down into two components: a biological condition or behavioral condition. Mental illness may be attributed to a physical disease or injury (neurosyphilis, toxic psychosis); or it may be attributed to a psychological disorder or stress (functional psychosis).

As the concept "mental illness" is elusive, it is made a necessary but not sufficient reason for commitment. In addition to the requirement of "mental illness," some jurisdictions say that the person must be "dangerous to self or others" or "in need of care or treatment."(42) In other jurisdictions, the requirement is "need for care of treatment."(43) In a few states, the requirement is "for his own welfare" or "for the welfare of others."(44)

It takes little imagination to include nonconformity or antisocial criminal behavior within the purview of civil commitment statutes. In Samuel Butler's *Erewhon* (nowhere), persons who are usually considered as "sick" are deemed "bad," and those who are usually considered as "bad" are deemed "sick," and disposition is made accordingly. Alcohol and drug addiction are notable examples today where many people feel that education and treatment are preferable to penal punishment, and so the addict is at times labeled "sick" instead of "bad."(45)

While criminal statutes are numerous, covering nearly every conceivable type of behavior, they are specific in the type of behavior that is prohibited, and the disposition is limited. Civil commitment provisions on the other hand are vague or elastic as to persons covered, and they are indeterminant as to disposition. As a result, according to Szasz and others, injustice results. Moreover, the fact of considering behavior as "sick" has led authorities to be lax in taking effective or forceful action.

To be sure, sickness has been used as an excuse for crime. But the reason for this is that the criminal process has proven ineffective in dealing with antisocial behavior. No one has a good word to say on behalf of the penal system. For example, Ramsey Clark, former Attorney General of the United States, says in his book *Crime in America* that the American system of criminal justice fails miserably in prevention, conviction, and correction. In March 1971 three major periodicals (*Life, Look* and *Newsweek*) carried lead articles on the shortcomings of the criminal law process.

However, it is an erroneous assumption to assume that the civil commitment process has been very much used as a rescue adjunct to the penal system. Moreover, the erroneous assumption has also been made that because a person is "sick" he is by that fact "treatable" and should receive treatment. While "sickness" may indeed explain some antisocial behavior, it has not proven to be a useful concept in determining what disposition to make of "sick" offenders. The report of the President's Commission on Law Enforcement and Administration of Justice, *The Challenge of Crime in a Free Society*, stated that procedures are needed to identify mentally disordered or deficient persons and to help officers who administer criminal justice to deal with them by means other than the ordinary criminal processes. The report concluded:

> The Commission believes that, if an individual is to be given special therapeutic treatment, he should be diverted as soon as possible from the criminal process. It believes further that screening procedures capable of identifying mentally disordered or deficient offenders as early in the process as possible can be improved by training law enforcement and court officers to be more sensitive to signs of mental abnormality by making specialized diagnostic referral services more readily available to the police and the court.(46)

In the case of some criminal behavior, usually bizarre in nature, the incompetency-to-stand-trial plea has been used to detain for a considerable period of time those individuals who if prosecuted might have escaped detention altogether by acquittal or might have been confined for only a short period of time. While the competency-to-stand-trial tactic is subject to abuse and criticism, it is not a matter of civil commitment. These individuals are sent to special units for the so-called criminally insane. When and if the criminal charge is dropped, and civil commitment is sought, hospital personnel invariably are aroused. They are opposed to the use of the civil hospital to care for persons who have been involved in criminal behavior. They find it upsetting and stigmatising, and they discharge the person at the first opportunity.(47) In his book *Psychiatric Justice*, Szasz sets out four illustrations of psychiatric injustice—but all of them involve cases of criminal behavior: three deal with the issue of fitness to stand trial, and the fourth deals with the plea of not guilty by reason of insanity. While "hospitalization" in a colony for the so-called criminally insane is not hospitalization but imprisonment, the real issue involved is the right to treatment and the operation of the criminal law, not the process of civil commitment.

At times, the incompetency-to-stand-trial technique has been used in response to political pressures. From the United States to the Soviet Union, political dissenters are sometimes labeled paranoid or schizophrenic and are detained in mental institutions. A number of political dissidents in the Soviet Union have recently been hospitalized as mentally ill and incompetent to stand trial.(48) It has been surmised that political considerations played an important part in the commitment of Ezra Pound (charged with treason) as incompetent to stand trial, or if the original commitment was proper, that its duration was attributable to political rather than psychiatric considerations.(49) Another notable American case with political overtones was the unsuccessful attempt to commit General Edwin Walker, as incompetent to stand trial. In such cases, the issue is the tolerance of political dissent, not the process of commitment. If the hospital process were not used, some other process (such as the tax laws) would be employed. The corridors of history echo with the cries of men put away by irrational or arbitrary procedures, but as Justice Douglas asks, does the answer to that problem involved defining the procedure for conducting political trials or does it involve the designing of constitutional methods for putting an end to them?(50) Observers of trials of persons accused under the Smith Act(51) in the United States, of alleged communists in Greece, of "social disorganizers" in Mexico, of "counter-revolutionaries" in the Soviet Union, cannot really advocate one procedure over another. While the cases are not *ejusdem generis,* the real issue is whether there should be political trials at all.

As far as the civil commitment process is concerned, it is hardly a secure method of detention, for the hospital as well as the judiciary has control over discharge. Although a person may have been committed by the court, the hospital has power to discharge without court approval.(52) Moreover, in the usual case, when a person seeks discharge, the hospital is more than pleased to let him go. In the event of hospital refusal to discharge, the individual has resort to the court by writ of habeas corpus. The writ may be used to challenge not only the original admission procedure but also the propriety of continued detention.(53) Invariably, rather than get involved in litigation, the hospital will discharge although it may not be in the best interest of the individual.

The real problem is that the hospitalized person is unwanted and has no place else to go. A large percentage of the long-term persons in state mental hospitals are the elderly. The work in these institutions is not peculiarly psychiatric. The shame is not that few psychiatrists are interested in working there; the shame is not the concept of civil commitment; the shame rather is that so many people have no where else to pass their last years. In the United States today, family units are small, the generations live apart, and the aged are isolated and largely unemployed. The aged are regarded as the "unwanted generation"(novelist Saul Bellow says the aged are treated with "a kind of totalitarian cruelty, like Hitler's attitude toward the Jews").(54) Nearly a million old people, approximately 5 percent of the over sixty-five population, now live in nursing homes or convalescent facilities provided by Medicare.(55) Nursing homes are badly needed, and many that are available are atrocious. The large, isolated mental hospital—the insane asylum—has evolved into a sort of asylum (without the term insane) for the elderly. They do not leave, because they have no place else to go. On occasion, some may stray into the fields and die, not missed for years.(56)

The railroading myth regarding civil commitment might have been born out of feelings of guilt about not caring for aged or helpless members of a family, or out of feelings of fear of aged or helpless family members that they will be abandoned. But is it railroading when relatives of a disorganized, troublesome, or helpless family member desperately look for assistance? They often genuinely need respite from a burdensome situation; further, the disturbed person himself is often relieved by separation from a pathogenic situation. Szasz' claim that "mental illness" is the prevailing ideology by which the strong control the weak hardly squares with reality. The mentally disordered person surely cannot be called "weak," mentally or physically. He can tear up an entire family (Hitler shook the world). Physically, even a small body may seem possessed of some frenzied, superhuman strength. It takes the combined efforts of a number of men to restrain even a little old lady who is delusional.

The real problem is not getting out of a hospital, but rather it is obtaining emergency psychiatric care, getting into a decent hospital, and staying there without too much expense. (When a person is sick in America, says one immigrant, dollars fly like feathers in a pogrom.) Consider the following pleas for help:

"Is there anywhere in New Orleans a person can go for psychiatric help which is free of charge or for a very nominal fee?"(57)

"Our son was released in August from Northville State Hospital. He's still not well. He's violent, and tries to set the house on fire. The police won't help and I don't have the money to get an ambulance or doctor. What can we do?"

"My husband has a wild look in his eye. He physically abuses me. I am afraid. Where can I get treatment for him? The police won't help."

"Our son is involved with drugs. Where can we get help? We don't want him in jail."

"Please help me with my parents—they are irrational—shouts, fights, complete ignoring of reality."

"My husband stays at home all day. He weeps and bangs his head against the wall. He sits in the sofa in a prenatal position. What can I do?"

"My wife became extra violent after passing a sleepless night. When the sitter came in the morning, she attacked and scratched her, and called me all sorts of names. I had to call the police to subdue her and strap her to a cot. What now?"

"May I ask your help?" a law student pleaded anxiously, just as I was working on this manuscript. "My grandmother is beserk. She is going out into the street at night, shouting and disturbing the neighbors. She lives alone. What can we do?"

During the last year, while approximately four million Americans received treatment for "mental illness" in state hospitals, general hospitals, out-patient clinics, and in the offices of private practitioners, another two million were turned away because of the lack of treatment personnel to handle them. As far as emergency care is concerned, the situation in most United States cities is chaotic—if a call for help is successfully placed, the police "paddy wagon" rather than an ambulance is dispatched.

Among the criticisms of psychiatry, it is said that psychiatrists are rather inaccurate forecasters, particularly likely to overstate the potential for antisocial behavior. (Everyone wants to play it safe.) "Among every group of inmates presently confined on the basis of psychiatric predictions of violence," one study says, "there are only a few who would, and many more who would not, actually engage in such conduct if released."(59) Prediction studies, however, are rather misleading on several scores. They tend to focus on the quantity or number of acts rather than on the quality of the act. When a person is out of control, he is *really* dangerous—like an airplane crash, it statistically rarely occurs, but when it does, it is devastating. Prediction studies tend to detract from the fact that, in reality, civil commitment primarily is not a measure to control odd or deviant behavior, or to protect the safety of others, but rather it is a type of assistance for a person unable to care for himself, and whose problems have exhausted the resources of his family and friends. Moreover, it is not so much a matter of predicting behavior—whether the person will at some future time be dangerous, or whether the psychiatrist or psychologist or someone else can most ably make the forecast—as it is a matter of evaluation of current status or situation.

Before one's very eyes, in these cases, there is a person who has grossly inadequate control over his body or mind, a person who is significantly out of contact with reality. To use an analogy, suggested by Harry Golden: when a baby cries, the mother does not dwell on the distant future or the past, but rather she attends to the situation at hand—the first worry is the formula, next the spoon and cup. In short, what is called for is not an elaborate strategy, but a sound application of common sense to the specific situation at hand. The function of mental concepts or evaluation is not so much to predict, but rather to ascribe or assert a characteristic or condition. The primacy of the assertive function, while it does not deny prediction, alters instead its logical place.

The usual case of involuntary commitment actually ought not to be called "involuntary" or "contested." The commitment is not so much involuntary as it is nonprotested. The individual who is withdrawn like a vegetable or who is wild-eyed and agitated is not even able to say "yes" or "no." The individual who is either so regressed in behavior that he approaches a vegetable state, or who is so floridly psychotic that he is out of contact with the world, often does not mean what he says. In these cases, it is not a matter of overriding the individual's will. His ego is overwhelmed or shattered. He is delusional, incoherent, or irrational. Consider the case of one person who said that he could not consent to admission to the hospital because "dead men cannot consent." Believing himself dead, he responded when confronted with bleeding, "Dead men bleed." The contractual relationship that calls for a "meeting of the minds" is the model of the psychoanalytic situation, but not for these kinds of cases.(60) Contract calls for competency of the parties.

In other cases of so-called involuntary commitment, where there is not such a break with reality, the individual may initially object to going to a mental hospital. Who is not ashamed to admit that he is "crazy"? Who is not ashamed to admit that he needs help (it is a kind of confession of weakness)? Who is not ashamed to admit he is not needed or wanted at home? Moreover, to go to a new place, of whatever kind, tends to arouse fear and anxiety. Invariably, however, after a brief period, when a relationship has developed in the hospital, the individual is quite willing and often eager to stay there for an extended period of time if necessary.

Empirical observations show that persons who initially object to admission later have a different view. Invariably individuals who violently and vociferously protest their hospitalization during the first day or two of hospitalization, after a brief period, become grateful and appreciate the fact that they were not allowed to leave. By far the majority of persons who protest their hospitalization during an acute phase of their condition concede at some point later that their own judgment had been incorrect when they resisted hospitalization. The law often emphasizes the protest of an individual in an acute condition and yet seldom recognizes that within a period as short as forty-eight to sixty-four hours he will have completely reversed his attitude about the necessity of treatment.(61)

Under the new California civil commitment law, effective July of 1969, a person may be detained for seventy-two hours on the written statement of a police officer or professional person designated by the county.(62) The psychiatric staff may then certify the person for further observation for fourteen days without any prior judicial review. If he is deemed suicidal, he may be certified for an additional fourteen day period following the first fourteen day certification. The person after being certified may request a hearing, which is not automatic, through the writ of habeas corpus. A suicidal person may be detained for thirty-three days without judicial review if he does not seek a habeas corpus.(63)

To what extent should the law be governed only by the "immediate present"? The important issue in the enactment of civil commitment laws is whether a time period (such as fifteen, thirty, forty-five, or sixty days) of hospitalization should be provided notwithstanding the individual's lack of expressed consent. The typical commitment case today involves hospitalization in a regional mental hospital for about two months. The law's problem is how far to liberalize involuntary commitment procedures to provide for the earlier admission (leading to earlier discharge), long before persons gravely decompensate or become dangerous. When Humpty Dumpty fell off the deep end, all the king's horses and all the king's men could not put him back together again. It was too late.

Sometimes when people object they actually wish to say something else. A person, for example, who attempts suicide may not wish to die but may wish instead to indicate a need for attention. A professional person who simply accepts at face value the literal meaning of a depressed person's suicidal communication is naive. Mutually contradictory desires to live or die or to be rescued or abandoned are part of suicide. Therefore one can never assume that a statement, "I want to die," accurately expresses a person's state of mind. Clinical experience shows that in most cases these words may actually be communicating a need for help or feelings of desperation.

What a person does not say is often more important that what he does say, and what he does say often conceals his thoughts. As Stendahl put it, speech is given to mankind not only to express thoughts but also to conceal them.(64) Is the dignity of a person enhanced by attempting words at face value (whatever that might be) or is it better served by really making an effort at hearing what is being said? People are grateful when someone is "tuned" in on their "wave length."

Civil commitment ultimately involves the question whether a person has the right to destroy his life and whether that decision may be irrationally made. Does a person have the right to kill himself? The United States was the creation of men who believed that each man has the right to do what he wants with his own life as long as he does not interfere with his neighbor's pursuit of happiness. Some consider the right to kill oneself a cornerstone of liberty. In an article on legalizing marijuana, Gore Vidal says, "Every man has the power—and should have the right—to kill himself if he chooses."(65) Szasz contends that an individual has "an unqualified consitutional right to be dangerous to himself—whether it be to take up smoking, have an abortion or commit suicide."(66) And he says,

> Certainly he should be discouraged, just as a friend should be discouraged from buying a bad stock or marrying the wrong woman, but I object strenuously to the term "rational" because it involves the judgment of one person by another. It is obvious that an intelligent person might conclude that another person's behavior with respect to marriage, divorce, economics, suicide, etc. is stupid. That does not give him the right of coercion or the psychiatrist the right to call the police or to commit him to an institution.(67)

Albert Camus begins his book *The Myth of Sisyphus* with the statement that there is but one truly serious philosophical problem—namely, the problem of suicide. To decide whether a question is important, one must take into consideration the consequences entailed. Determining whether or not life is worth living, Camus says, amounts to answering the most fundamental question of philosophy. All other questions—whether the mind employs ten or twelve categories, or whether the world has three dimensions—come afterward.

Civil commitment law is based on the social value judgment that human life can be and ought to be made worth living. The attitude "let everyone do as he pleases," is appealing, but it is an infantile fantasy, and actually is destructive. That attitude absolves us from social responsibilities. There must be more genuine concern—not less—for the needs of others.(68) Moreover, apart from the question of whether or not a person has the right to destroy his life, cases involving civil commitment invariably involve individuals who are so disorganized that it would be fanciful to say that they are capable of making a reasonable decision. In the case of a person who refuses a lifesaving blood transfusion or refuses to wear a helmet while riding on a motorcycle, it may be said that the decision is rational; he is not out of contact with reality and he is clearly distinguishable from a person who is at a low level of organization or regression.

Attempted suicide or suicide is generally considered only *per se*, without regard to effects it has on others. However, in one novel case, the infliction of emotional distress on others was urged as the basis of a cause of action at law. In this case, the decedent, a guest in the plaintiff's home after his wife had left him, decided while the plaintiff was absent to commit suicide by cutting his throat in her kitchen. When she returned she found his corpse, and blood all over the premises. She suffered a nervous shock. The decedent's estate was held liable to her on the basis that the act was committed in deliberate disregard of the consequences.(69)

Civil commitment statutes provide, as noted, that a person needing care and treatment may be committed when he is of danger to himself, and some statutes say when he is also dangerous to others. Is the dichotomy between danger to self and others viable? Studies show that suicide and homicide—to take the extreme situations of self-destruction and destruction of others—are two sides of the same coin. It is a mere fortuity that a person directs his rage inwardly rather than outwardly or in both directions.(70) A person who would hurt or kill himself may just as likely hurt or kill someone else. Freud's paper, *Mourning and Melancholia*, which describes the dynamics of depression as essentially the turning of an individual's hate against himself, also provides the basis for the psychoanalytic theory of suicide. In Freud's words, "No neurotic harbours thoughts of suicide which are not murderous impulses against others re-directed upon himself."(71)

Moreover, the person who seriously considers taking his own life places a tremendous burden on others. Agnes in Edward Albee's play *A Delicate Balance* shouts, "What I cannot stand is the selfishness! Those of you who want to die and take your whole life doing it." There are many instances where a child is asked to watch over a potentially suicidal parent, "Call daddy right away at the office if mamma seems real upset." Or, "Make sure you watch and go with her if she goes down to the basement." This enormous burden transforms to equally intense guilt when the child fails to give a warning or to stop the suicide.(72)

The late Eric Berne in his book *Games People Play* illustrates that "mental illness" may be a strategy to gain that which might otherwise be refused. For one thing, a suicide attempt is used to obtain care and attention. The attempted suicide may say or think, "Can't you see how I hurt? I'm bleeding. Take care of me." In *Cactus Flower*, Toni's attempted suicide makes her boyfriend Julian feel like a "bastard," as he put it, and to make things up to her, he asked her to marry him. For another, a suicide attempt is an act of revenge. A suicide, direct or even indirect, often implies, "I'll die and then they will be sorry."

Literature provides pertinent illustrations of suicide as a way of punishing the depriving, frustrating figure by induction of guilt. Mark Twain's Tom Sawyer was frustrated by his aunt, and he was comforted by the thought of committing suicide by drowning himself in the Mississippi. He thought to himself how sad his aunt would be when his pale, limp body would be brought into her presence. He imagined her saying, "Oh, if I had only loved him more. How differently I would have treated him if I had only known." Leo Tolstoy's Anna Karenina, before throwing herself beneath the wheels of a passing train, contemplated the guilt the suicide would induce in her husband Vronsky, "To die! And he will feel remorse; will love me; he will suffer on my account." In *Oklahoma,* Jud stands over his supposedly dead self and sings of how he is going to be missed, and how other people are going to be hurt by his death:

Pore Jud is daid . . .
And folks are feelin' sad
Cuz they useter treat him bad,
And now they know their friend has gone fer good.

After a suicidal attempt, a person may say to members of the family, "Now, are *you* satisfied?" making them feel extremely guilty. Attempted suicide, as a means of negotiation, is a manipulation in interpersonal relations which is unfair and one-sided. And a "successful" suicide ends in nothing. Joshua, the Heavenly Friend, says in *Carousel* to Billy Bigelow, "As long as there is one person who remembers you, it's not over."(73)

Suicide, then, is not an act that is isolated in effect. To say that a person may do with his life as he wishes is to ignore the reality that what he does with it mightily affects others. The tenet "man is made in the image of God" means that man should be good to himself and to others. As John Donne put it, "No man is an Island, intire of it selfe."(74) To be sure, the law imposes no duty to aid another unless a special relationship exists such as parent-child or a relationship is undertaken such as patient-physician.(75) Generally speaking, the law imposes liability for misfeasance, not nonfeasance. Society as a whole has the responsibility to render aid to a person unable to care for himself.

Naturally, deprivation of an individual's liberties should occur only when absolutely necessary. As a general principle, it may be stated that a physician cannot force the benefit of his skills upon a protesting individual. As one court put it, "The doctor-patient relationship cannot be imposed upon a competent patient without his consent."(76) It is to be noted that the court qualifies the statement by the term "competent." Moreover, some social policy has dictated that individuals be subjected to compulsory sterilization, compulsory smallpox vaccination, and flouridation.

Commitment in some cases is justified, but assuredly this is a complex problem that cannot be resolved by simple rules. Often commitment may not be in a person's best interest since his problems may be complicated by his having to face the additional trauma of the stigma that is attached to the label "mentally ill." He might lose his job and his friends because he is "mentally ill." Given the opportunity, he may be able to work out his difficulties in the context in which they arise.

The terms in the statute on civil commitment—"mental illness," "need of treatment," "danger to self," or "danger to others"—cannot be defined with any realistic precision that would make them applicable in a general fashion. In the case of physical illness, a physician cannot formulate a general rule stating when a person should be admitted to a hospital. Likewise, in the case of emotional disorder, the decision has to be on a case-by-case basis, after consideration of the degree and kind of disability and the effect the individual will have on the people around him.

Focus on commitment laws may draw attention to the plight of people in distress and to the condition of institutions, but lest the tail wag the dog, it is to be remembered that the quality of institutions determines public attitudes, the commitment laws, and their interpretation. Further development of pharmocological drugs, community-based programs and involvement of a larger segment of the public will cause civil commitment laws to be regarded as an archaic vestige of a bygone era. In this day of open wards, the kind of fears prompting legalistic provisions are becoming increasingly out of place. The repute of legal commitment procedures is universally proportional to the degree of public confidence in the treatment programs. For example, at Veterans Administration hospitals, unlike many state mental hospitals, waiting lists of people beg for admission.

In a way, the heritage of Mrs. Packard has led us astray. The rights of hospital patients became a matter of controversy in the latter part of the nineteenth century with the emergence of the "madhouse," a large, far-removed custodial institution. As the result of that experience, civil commitment laws in most states now are so complicated that they make criminal and tax laws appear simple in comparison. A law-library study of the statutes on civil commitment of the various states, however, affords little or no indication of the actual operation of the laws in that particular state or of the differences between the states. Observation reveals that these statutes are ignored, for essentially two reasons: they are so complicated that they are beyond the understanding of persons working in the field who are responsible for their operation; and they are for the most part unnecessary. However, a lengthy code, while most of its provisions are ignored, usually contains the one or two needed provisions.

Unlike most other areas of law, the laws on civil commitment are not administered or supervised by practitioners of the laws. Even though the civil commitment laws provide for judicial supervision, there has been little or perfunctory involvement of the legal profession, even during Mrs. Pachard's time when conditions were atrocrous. As a practical matter, commitment laws are administered by hospital administrators, physicians, nurses, and aides, who have little or no familiarity with the laws on commitment, although they are supposedly governed by them. When they do attempt to read the law, they find it unintelligible or unworkable.

Since the commitment laws are administered by lawmen in the law, they need to be simple. For the admission procedure, all that is needed is a provision providing for involuntary institutionalization of the incompetent person in need of care and treatment for a brief period. For the provision on discharge, the ancient writ of habeas corpus meets the needs of the institutionalized person. The special provisions now in the Draft Act and some state codes providing a bill of rights for a person while in the institution are unnecessary. By the approach I recommend, when a person has a problem—be it for physical reasons or mental reasons—he will be regarded by the law in essentially the same manner. The movement in psychiatry toward more community-based treatment facilities in comprehensive community mental health centers will likely encourage this development.

The special provisions in the Draft Act and the mental health codes of some states, providing a bill of rights for a hospitalized mental patient, set forth the right to "humane care and treatment," the right to the highest standards of medical care possible with the facilities and personnel available, the right to the writ of habeas corpus, the right to communicate by mail, to receive visitors, to be employed at a useful occupation depending upon the patient's condition and the available facilities, and to exercise civil rights, including the right to dispose of property, to make contracts, and to vote, except insofar as one may have been expressly declared incompetent to exercise such rights.(77) These provisions add nothing to the law. Commitment to a hospital does not of itself constitute a determination of incompetency or a deprivation of civil or political rights, hence the status of a mental patient is or should be the same as any other individual. He would have all of the rights listed in the mental patient's "bill of rights" without their enumeration. Indeed, by a special bill of rights, the implication is that the mental patient has only these rights while in the hospital and proscribes loss of certain civil rights which under previous legislation were forfeited by the patient adjudged mentally incompetent.(78)

As a matter of fact, the "bill of rights" and other provisions enacted in the wake of Mrs. Packard were hardly applied even immediately following their enactment. Jury trial on commitment has been so rare as to be almost nonexistent. The patient in the large state hospital has "humane care and treatment" only in the sense that he is provided a place to live out his days. The patient has the right to communicate by mail provided he has the money to buy postage and stationery. The patient is not in a position to dispose of his property, if he has any, or to make contracts because he is away from the scene and his capacity to contract is in doubt (so a guardian would be appointed in these cases). The patient lacks political effectiveness, for while he is not legally disenfrancised as a convicted felon, he in effect is deprived of the right to vote since he does not vote absentee, and even though he may be a lifetime resident at the hospital, he does not vote in that area either (the hospital vote could control the election of local public officials). The patient is generally not engaged in useful occupation at the hospital (and not remunerated for it when he is) because work is usually unprovided for or unavailable. The patient is unaware of the availability of the writ of habeas corpus, even though a constitutional right, or he is unaware as to how to petition for it.

Laws are not self-executing. Laws on the books may be a salve to the public conscience, or may defuse public outrage, but unless carried out, they may have little other consequence. Attorneys are no more interested in rendering service to persons in mental hospitals than they are to persons in prisons, for there is little or no remuneration. A number of law schools have developed programs in recent years, initiated in 1965 by Professor Paul Wilson of the University of Kansas, under which students provide legal services in jails and prisons. The results indicate that for the law student the legal service needs of the prisoner provide an opportunity for the exercise of legal training and skills and a profound intellectual and emotional challenge, as well as a service to the inmates.(79) A good case can be made to the effect that law students should also be exposed to the hospital system.

There are real problems that need attention—Szasz though gives us imagined problems. The lawyer in the hospital setting would find that patients need assistance in regard to insurance, social security, their last will and testament, and sundry contractual matters. The lawyer may find that the patient is ready to leave the hospital, which may be effectuated, if necessary, by the writ of habeas corpus. He may find that he can bring some pressure on the State to improve the level of care in the hospital.(80) Perhaps he may even come across a case of railroading, about which he might advise Szasz.

For the admission process, a coroner or other health officer serves a useful function. A public aware of his services could look to him in the case of emergency. Physicians too, find his office helpful. Reluctant to leave their office or to get involved in the commitment process, physicians prefer to turn to him for assistance in the commitment of a patient. Even the large state mental hospitals have barriers, set up by hospital administrators and physicians, which make it difficult for patients to volunteer for treatment, and the coroner may act as a lever to break through these barriers.

The new Maryland law on commitment permits the involuntary commitment of persons for an indefinite period on the certificate of two physicians without a prior judicial or administrative hearing, or a mandatory subsequent judicial or administrative hearing. Procedural due process, however, requires that a hearing if requested be held at some reasonable point in time. A demand or request for release may be treated as a petition for a writ of habeas corpus.(81)

Szasz has urged lawyers to begin a major legal attack against institutional psychiatry by bringing lawsuits for false imprisonment against anyone who participates in the commitment process. He calls for a major legal attack on commitment practices, which he says, "would at least be effective in raising malpractice premiums for psychiatrists who lock up people."(82) If nothing else, Szasz adds unnecessary stigma to the hospital system. Actually, apart from the stigma, the mental hospital is not such a horrendous place in view of the alternatives available to people in trouble. The fear of losing one's mind is one of man's greatest fears, and any place where supposedly "mind tampering" goes on is frightening. The stigma surrounding psychoanalysis and psychotherapy, however, is now disappearing. In fact, people now speak publicly about their psychiatric sessions. Not so long ago, they were either ashamed or afraid even to admit that they had seen a psychiatrist. The change in the climate of the times is indicated by people who write openly of their experiences in psychotherapy.(83) Some day the mental hospital too will lose its stigma, but no thanks to Szasz.

Hospitalization may be a blow to one's self-esteem, but while it is nothing to be proud of, it is nothing to be ashamed of either. There is nothing criminal about the need for hospitalization, whether recognized by the patient or by his family or friends. There is nothing harmful about short-term hospitalization, except the stigma. On the other hand, there are many social institutions which carry no stigma but more or less are crippling. The school system is said with good reason by many educators to be a police state—everyone in it is in lock step.(84) Even the criminally insane colony—much more the civil hospital—seems civilized when compared to many high schools. The military system calls upon people to kill or be killed. The work system for so many people is dehumanizing. In contrast, the mental hospital sometimes seems a paradise. It is one the the few places where a person can simply be and forget about twisting himself by social role playing. Indeed, the honesty, openness, and lack of pretense found among the hospital population is refreshing; it prompted James S. Gordon, psychiatrist at Albert Einstein College of Medicine, to write' "Perhaps mental hospitals, reversing history, can become ships of sanity."(85)

With messianic zeal, Szasz urges the abolition of all involuntary commitment, whereas a century ago Mrs. Packard, who recognized the need of commitment in some cases, urged the enactment of safeguards. Amidst all of his writings, Szasz himself hedges on his thesis, albeit inconspicuously. In one place, a single page near the end of his 255-page book, *Law, Liberty, and Psychiatry*, he makes, perhaps in an unguarded moment, two exceptions which turn out to be very broad—the passive, stuporous, uncommunicative person and the aggressive, paranoid person who threatens violence.(86)

These cases cannot go unattended. Total repeal of the statutes on civil commitment would simply have to rely on the case law of the pre-Packard era, which in effect has always remained the law though in different form. The statutes on civil commitment are an outgrowth of the unwritten common law rule that any person has a right to detain one who is mentally ill and dangerous to himself or others.

NOTES

(1) United States Public Health Service, Publication No. 51 (rev. ed. 1952) (hereinafter referred to as the Draft Act). A summary of the act, by one of its authors, appears in Felix, *Hospitalization of the Mentally Ill.*, 107 Am J. Psychiatry, 712(1951).

(2) American Association for the Abolition of Involuntary Mental Hospitalization, Platform Statement, September 1, 1970. The certificate of incorporation of AAAIMH states its purposes as:

> To create and promote an understanding of the dehumanizing effects of involuntary psychiatric interventions, especially involuntary mental hospitalization; to foster a desire for the abolition of involuntary psychiatric interventions, especially involuntary mental hospitalization; to promote the movement to obtain legislative and judicial action making such involuntary psychiatric interventions, especially involuntary hospitalization, unlawful; to aid individuals who seek assistance in avoiding involuntary psychiatric interventions, especially involuntary mental hospitalization, by all lawful means; to establish centers for the members in order to coordinate efforts at abolition, exchange information and provide opportunities for further study and dissemination of information concerning involuntary psychiatric interventions, especially involuntary mental hospitalization; and to do such other lawful things as the members shall approve to further the end of such abolition.

The directors of AAAIMH are George J. Alexander, Dean and Law Professor; Erving Goffman, sociologist; and Thomas S. Szasz, psychoanalyst.

(3) Provisions on intake include voluntary admission, judicial commitment, coroner's commitment, and emergency commitment. Provisions on discharge include a provision on release and the writ of habeas corpus. *See, e.g.*, Iowa Code Ann. § 229.37 (1969). The laws which have a section on "rights of the patient" list his medical and legal rights. Ross, *Commitment of the Mentally Ill: Problems of Law and Policy*. 57 Mich. L. Rev. 945 (1959); Slovenko & Super, *The Mentally Disabled, the Law, and the Report of the American Bar Foundation*, 47 Va. L. Rev. 1366 (1961); Slovenko & Super, *Commitment Procedure in Louisiana*, 35 Tul. L. Rev. 705 (1961); Projects, *Civil Commitment of the Mentally Ill*. 14 U.C.L.A. L. Rev. 822 (1967).

(4) Barchilon, *Introduction* to Foucault, Madness and Civilization (1965). It may be noted that California today sends out on "trains of fools" immigrants who are in need of mental treatment, but they are returned to their state of residence. There is a "kick the habit" cruise sailing from New York to Caribbean ports, organized by the "Institute for New Motivations," which is designed "to turn the desire to stop smoking into a pleasureable experience." Detroit Free Press, Oct. 11, 1970. § B at 15.

(5) M. Foucault, Madness and Civilization. 40 (1965). The oldest hospital in Western Europe, the Hotel Dieu (Hospital of God), was founded at Lyons in 542 A.D. It was a charitable institution which embraced every form of aid for the poor, including an inn, workhouse, asylum, and infirmary. There is a hospital named Hotel Dieu in New Orleans.

(6) A. Deutsch, The Mentally Ill in America (2d ed. 1949). Likewise, the system of imprisonment of criminal offenders is relatively recent. Originally,

prisons were built to detain offenders temporarily until they were executed, maimed, pilloried, or banished. The offender was held in prison not *as* punishment, but *for* punishment. Detention was an intermediate step to await the execution of the formal punishment. Subsequently, imprisonment itself was regarded as punishment. More recently the idea developed of "correction" in prison.

(7) *See generally* J. Bockoven, Moral Treatment in American Psychiatry (1963).

(8) *See generally* G. Grob. The State and the Mentally Ill (1966).

(9) Kittrie, *Compulsory Mental Treatment and the Requirements of "Due Process,"* 21 Ohio St. L. J. 28 (1960).

(10) Ross, *supra* note 3. The 1851 Illinois commitment statute used to commit Mrs. Packard provided that "married women and infants, who in the judgment of the medical superintendent are evidently insane or distracted, may be received and detained in the hospital on the request of the husband, or the woman or parent or guardian of the infants, without the evidence of insanity or distraction required in other cases. Ill. Laws. 1851, at 9.

(11) Albert Deutsch, raising the issue of Mrs. Packard's credibility, points to her childhood institutionalization at the Worcester State Hospital, and the psychiatric history that showed at one time she claimed to be the Mother of Christ and the Third Person of the Blessed Trinity. A Deutsch, *supra* note 6, at 424. Guttmacher and Weihofen say that Mrs. Packard was "a women of forceful personality, although probably a 'borderline' case." M. Guttmacher & H. Weihofen, Psychiatry and the Law, 300 (1952).

(12) Am J. of Pub. Health, Sept. 1966.

(13) T. Szasz, Law, Liberty and Psychiatry 40 (1962). Throughout this book Szasz capitalizes "Therapeutic State." The initials "T.S.," curiously enough, also stand for the author's name. And, it may be noted, Szasz has apparently never urged that his Department of Psychiatry separate from the medical school. He invariably lists "M.D." after his name. Although medical training is mostly irrelevant to the practice of psychotherapy, Szasz like all psychiatrists takes advantage of the esteem and magic given to the medical profession. On the other hand, lawyers who studied engineering do not identify themselves as engineers for it is irrelevant to their work.

(14) *Id.* at vii-vii, 248 (*semble*).

(15) T. Szasz, The Manufacture of Madness 207-210, 241 (1970).

(16) Szasz puts it thus:

As I see it, there are tremendously powerful ideological and economic interests in Western society—especially in American society—which demand that ever-greater numbers of people in the population be mentally disabled, or that they be regarded as treated as mentally disabled. This has to do in part with the fact that in the industrially advanced nations people are becoming increasingly superfluous and unnecessary as producers. So they must be consumers of goods and services, and what better service to consume than "mental health care"? When people consume that, they elevate the dignity and self-esteem of those who are doing the "servicing." How people love to volunteer nowadays for "mental health work"! In this way, people are slowly being transformed into a produce on whom other people can work. We thus live in an age characterized by a tremendous need for vast numbers of "madmen" upon whom, as products or things, a large part of the rest of the population can work, and which the non-made part can proudly support. The result is what I call "The Therapeutic State"—a state whose aim is not to provide favorable conditions for the pursuit of life, liberty, and happiness, but to repair the defective mental health of its citizens. The officials of such a state parody the role of physician and psychotherapist. It's a neat arrangement: it gives life-meaning to the therapists by robbing the "patients" of their life-meaning. Truly, this is the new frontier. We can persecute millions of people, all the while telling ourselves that we are great healers, curing them of mental illness. We have managed to repackage the Inquisition and are selling it as a new scientific cure-all.

Szasz, *A Psychiatrist Views Mental Health Legislation*, 18 New Physician 453 (1969), reprinted in 9 Washburn L. Rev. 224, 242 (1970).

(17) Coles, *The Measure of Man, New Yorker*, Nov. 7, 1970, at 51. In another place Coles says, "We try to help our patients 'live within the world they're a part of.' I heard that phrase over and over again when I was in training. I wonder why we weren't encouraged at least to discuss other possibilities—to consider whether both we and our patients didn't have more of a responsibility to be skeptical, uncompliant, and rebellious." D. Berrigan & R. Coles, *Dialogue Underground: II,* N.Y. Review of Books, Mar. 25, 1971, at 24.

(18) H. Zinn, The Politics of History 165 (1970).

(19) D. Donald, The Psychological History of Abolitionists (1970).

(20) L. Feuer, Student Radicals (1970).

(21) H. Zinn, *supra* note 18.

(22) *Id.*

(23) Toch, *The Care and Feeding of Typologies and Libels*, 34 Fed. Probation 15 (1970).

(24) Slovenko, *The Psychiatric Patient, Liberty and the Law*, 13 Kan. L. Rev. 59 (1964).

(25) R. Evans, Psychology and Arthur Miller 102 (1969).

(26) Webster's New International Dictionary 1043 (3rd ed. 1966).

(27) R. Rock, M. Jacobson & R. Janopaul. Hospitalization and Discharge of the Mentally Ill (1968).

(28) *Hearings Before the Subcommittee on Constitutional Rights of the Senate Committee on the Judiciary*, 87th Cong., 1st Sess. (1961).

(29) October 3, 1969.

(30) *See generally* K. Menninger, The Crime of Punishment (1968) The Renaissance scholar Erasmus put it thus: "If you might look down from the moon, as Menippus did of old, upon the numberless agitators among mortal men, you would think you were seeing a swarm of flies or gnats, quarreling among themselves, wagering wars, setting snares for each other, robbing, sporting, wantoning, being born, growing old, and dying. And one can scarce believe what commotions and what tragedies this animalcule little as he is and so soon to perish, sets agoing." D. Erasmus, *In Priase of Folly* 70 (1964 ed.).

(31) N.Y. Times, Oct. 11, 1970. § 6 (Magazine), at 26.

(32) N. Khrushchev, Khrushchev Remembers (1970).

(33) J. Acton, Essays on Freedom and Power, 364 (G. Hinmefart ed. 1948).

(34) J. Fast, Body Language (1970).

(35) G. Newten & F. Zernring. Firearms and Violence in American Life: A Staff Report Submitted to the National Commission on the Causes and Prevention of Violence 3, 17 (1968).

(36) *Id.* at 3.

(37) Address at Annual Meeting, Association of American Law Schools, Chicago, Ill., Dec. 28, 1970.

(38) A. Mowbray, Road to Ruin (1970).

(39) The joking exchange between Hamlet and the Clown (Hamlet, act V, scene 1) provides an illustration, *Hamlet:* Ay, marry, why was he sent into

England? *First Clown:* Why, because a' was made; a' shall recover his wits there; or, if a' do not, 'tis no great matter there. *Hamlet:* Why? *First Clown:* 'Till not be seen in him there; there the men are as mad as he.

The word madness was used loosely by the ancients, as "crazy" or "mentally ill" is today, to characterize widely varying phenomena. George Rosen in his historical sociology of mental illness, *Madness in Society*, writes: "When a Greek or a Roman spoke of madness, at one extreme the term might be applied to nothing more than queer or unreasonable behavior, at the other it might well designate undoubted neuroses and psychoses. As in English, a strange or unexpected act might lead a Greek or a Roman to exclaim 'He's mad!' without necessarily implying the existence of mental derangement in a strict sense. Certain words might at times be used to express such rhetorical exaggeration and denote little more than great folly and unreasonableness, but they might also be employed with strong connotations of mental aberration." G. Rosen, Madness in Society 90 (1968).

(40) Draft Act, *supra* note 1.

(41) *Id.* § 1.

(42) *See, e.g.,* Wash. Rev. Code Ann. § 72.23.010 (1962). *See also* Minn. Stat. Ann. 245.51 (1971).

(43) 34A N.Y. Consol. Laws § 2 (McKinney 1951).

(44) N.Y. Mental Hygiene Law § 2 (McKinney 1951).

(45) A Connecticut statute, Conn. Gen. Stat. Ann. § 19-484 (1969), for example, provides specifically for an alternative to a jail sentence, as follows: "If a prosecutor or judge of any court before whom a criminal charge is pending has reason to believe that a person accused of a violation of this act is a drug-dependent person, such prosecutor may apply to the court for appointment of, or the court in its own motion may appoint, one or more physicians to examine the accused person to determine if he is drug dependent. If the accused person is reported to be drug dependent by such physician or physicians, upon agreement between the prosecutor and the accused person, the court may enter an order suspending prosecution for the crime for a period not to exceed one year for a misdemeanor, and two years for a felony and release the accused person to the custody of the commission of adult probation for treatment by the commissioner of mental health..... The statute of limitations shall be tolled during the period of suspension." *See also* Federal Narcotic Addict Rehabilitation Act of 1966. 28 U.S.C. § § 2901-04 (Supp. V., 1969).

(46) The President's Commission on Law Enforcement and Administration of Justice, The Challenge of Crime in a Free Society 14 (1967).

(47) Hilles, *Problems in the Hospital Treatment of a Disturbed Person*, 30 Bull. of the Menninger Clinic 141 (1966).

(48) *See* Newsweek, Aug. 10, 1970, at 43.

(49) J. Cornell, The Trial of Ezra Pound (1966).

(50) Illinois v. Allen, 397 U.S. 337, 356 (1970).

(51) 18 U.S.C. § § 2385-87 (1964).

(52) R. Braceland, Testimony, Constitutional Rights of the Mentally Ill 64-65 (1970).

(53) Williams v. Robinson, Civil No. 23, 763 (D.C. Cir., June 19, 1970) (habeas corpus used to question legality of patient's transfer from a medium security division to maximum security division of hospital); Covington v. Harris, 419 F.2d 617 (D.C. Cir. 1969) (habeas corpus used to require hospital to justify not only the need for continued detention on the hospital but in a particular part of the hospital); Rouse v. Cameron, 373 F.2d 451 (D.C. Cir. 1966) (an institutionalized person has the right to test in a habeas corpus proceeding the adequacy or appropriateness of treatment); Geddes v. Daughters of Charity of

St. Vincent De Paul, 348 F.2d 144 (5th Cir. 1965); Billingsley v. Birzgalis, 20 Mich. App. 279, 174 N.W. 2d 17 (1969) (function of writ of habeas corpus is to test legality of detention of any person restrained of his liberty); G. Farmer, The Rights of the Mentally Ill 42 (1967); R. Sokol, Federal Habeas Corpus 95 (2d ed. 1969); Note, 80 Harv. L. Rev. 898 (1967). In some states that provide review procedures, the courts hold that habeas corpus may be used only to test the legality of the original admission and not to inquire into the condition of the petitioner at the time the writ is requested. Douglas v. Hall, 229 S.C. 550, 93 S.E. 2d 891 (1956); Ross, *supra* note 3, at 978.

(54) Time, Aug. 3, 1970, at 49.

(55) Time, Aug. 3, 1970, at 50.

(56) Detroit Free Press, Oct. 11, 1970, at 3, col. 1. Sometimes, it has been witnessed, the body is devoured by vultures, so long has the person gone unnoticed.

(57) *Ask the States-Item*, New Orleans States-Item. Aug. 28, 1969, at 20, col. 3. "I know that the state has very little money," pleads a 14-year-old girl, "but it could spend more money for the emotional disturbed [sic] cause damn it I know what's like to be sick and in a dump like Mandeville and it's hell." The girl was transferred from Mandeville's Southeast Louisiana State Hospital to an institution in Texas because there are so few facilities in Louisiana. New Orleans Times-Picayune, Nov. 27, 1970, at 5.

(58) *Action Line*, Detroit Free Press, Oct. 3, 1970, at 1, col. 1.

(59) Dershowitz, *Psychiatry in the Legal Process: A Knife That Cuts Both Ways*, 4 Trial 29 (1968).

(60) The contractual model for psychoanalysis is discussed in T. Szasz, The Ethics of Psychoanalysis (1965).

(61) Knight, *Social and Medical Aspects of the Psychiatric Emergency*, in Crime, Law and Corrections 494 (R. Slovenko ed. 1966).

(62) Cal. Ann. Welf. & Inst. Code § § 5000-401 (West 1970).

(63) Cal. Ann. Welf. & Inst. Code § § 5151, 5250, 5260, 5275 (West 1970).

The Subcommittee Report . . . notes that a review of recent legislative actions throughout the nation with respect to mental health services "illustrates the tendency to make the process either more medical, as in New York, or to increase legal protections, as in the District of Columbia. This had tended to place state legislatures in the uncomfortable position of having to choose between the medical objectives of treating sick people without legal delays and the equally valid legal aim of insuring that persons are not deprived of their liberties without due process of law." . . . Although the [California] act authorizes a procedure somewhat more medical than the former civil commitment procedures which it repealed, nevertheless the provisions of the act requiring notice of the 14-day certification for involuntary intensive treatment to be given to the superior court, and to various attorneys, among others (§ 5253), and the express specification of the rights of a patient who requests release to have counsel appointed and to seek habeas corpus (§ § 5275, 4276), demonstrate the concern of the Legislature that the patient's rights receive full protection at all times.

Thorn v. Superior Court of San Diego, 83 Cal. Rptr. 600, 605, 464, P.2d 56, 61 (1970).

(64) A CIA textbook says: "To understand a statement by any official spokesman—whether British, Soviet, Egyptian or Israeli—remember that it was made not merely to inform but to achieve a purpose. Don't ask yourslf what it means; ask why it was made. Look for motive, not meaning." *Life*, Oct. 9, 1970, at 36. Theodor Reik tells us to listen with a third ear; Marshall McLuhan tells us

that the medium is the message; Julius Fast tells us about "body language." According to scholars of kinesics, words express at most only 35% of what people wish to convey.

(65) N.Y. Times, September 26, 1970, at 29C, col. 1.

(66) Address at International Conference on Suicide Prevention in London, Chicago Daily News, Sept. 27-28, 1969, at 22, col. 6.

(67) Id.

(68) Slovenko, *supra* note 24.

(69) Blakeley v. Shortal's Estate, 236 Iowa 787, 20 N.W. 2d 28 (1945).

(70) O. Locicero, Murder in the Synagogue (1970); D. West, Murder Followed by Suicide (1966).

(71) S. Freud, *Mourning and Melancholia*, in 4 Collected Papers 162 (1953).

(72) Cain & Fast, *Children's Disturbed Reactions to Parent Suicide*, 36 Am. J. Orthopsych. 873 (1966).

(73) Usdin, *Broader Aspects of Dangerousness*, in The Clinical Evaluation of the Dangerousness of the Mentally Ill 43 (J. Rappeport ed. 1967).

(74) J. Donne, Devotions XVII (1623).

(75) A physician who fails to take appropriate suicide precautions when there is a patient-physician relationship may be held liable in negligence. *See* Note, 29 La. L. Rev. 558 (1969) (hospital's duty to protect mental patient from suicide). *See also* Comment, *Liability of Mental Hospitals for Acts of Their Patients Under the Open Door Policy*, 57 Va. L. Rev. 156 (1971).

(76) Stowers v. Ardmore Acres Hospital, 172 N.W. 2d 497 (Mich. 1969).

(77) Draft Act, at Part IV, §§ 19-26; La. Rev. Stat. 28:171 (1969); 50 Penn. State. Ann. 4423 (1969); Tex. Civ. Stat. Ann. art. 5547-86 (1957). Louisiana in 1888 enacted legislation giving a mental patient the right to write to one person in the outside world. In 1946 it adopted a mental health law providing patients' rights. La. Act. 303 of 1946, *now* La. Rev. Stat. 28:1 (1969).

(78) Ca. Ann. Welf. & Inst. Code. § 5325 (West 1970). On the other hand, a person convicted of a felony was considered civilly and politically dead. In Roman law the diminution of the personality of an individual for conviction of a crime was known as *capitis deminutio*. R. Slovenko, Handbook of Criminal Procedure and Forms 1084 (1967). But deprivation of civil and political rights has never theoretically been a part of the civil commitment process, and even in the criminal process it is no longer the result of a conviction. In 1943 the Sixth Circuit Court of Appeals declared: "A prisoner retains all the rights of an ordinary citizen except those expressly or by necessary implication taken from him by the law." Coffin v. Reichard, 143 F. 2d 443, 445 (6th Cir. 1944).

(79) Jacob & Sharman, *Justice After Trial: Prisoners' Need for Legal Services in the Criminal-Correctional Process*, 8 Kan. L. Rev. 493 (1970).

(80) The Mentally Ill and the Right to Treatment (G. Morris ed. 1970); Sansweet, *Patients' Rights*, Wall Street Journal, Nov. 3, 1970, at 1, col. 1. The Hill-Burton Act requires that as a condition to receiving funds a hospital provide serves, presumably outpatient as well as inpatient care, for some persons "unable to pay."

Recently a patient guardian in Alabama sued the state mental health board to protest the hospital's deficiencies. United States district court Judge Frank Johnson gave the state six months to submit evidence that it had established appropriate treatment programs, and if the state failed to take such steps, Judge Johnson said that he would appoint a panel of mental health experts to show Alabama how to improve its programs. Time, April 5, 1971, p. 36.

(81) Solomon, 315 F. Supp. 1192 (D. Md. 1970).

(82) Address at annual convention of American Trial Lawyers Association, Aug. 4, 1970, reported in Psychiatric News, Sept. 16, 1970, at 1.

(83) *See, e.g.*, L. Freeman, Celebrities on the Couch—Personal Adventures of Famous People in Psychoanalysis (1970).

(84) Ladd, *Allegedly Disruptive Student Behavior and The Legal Authority of School Officials*, 19 J. Pub. L. 209 (1970).

(85) Gordon, *Who is Mad? Who is Sane?*, The Atlantic, Jan. 1971, at 50.

(86) T. Szasz, *supra* note 13, at 226. Usually, though, Szasz says he opposes involuntary mental hospitalization under any circumstances and makes no exceptions. *See e.g.*, Szasz, *supra* note 17, 9 Washburn L. Rev. at 234.

PRIVILEGED COMMUNICATIONS BETWEEN PARTICIPANTS
IN GROUP PSYCHOTHERAPY

Wayne Cross

In group psychotherapy the Hippocratic Oath is extended to all patients and binds each with equal strength not to reveal to outsiders the confidences of other patients entrusted to them. . . . Every patient is expected to divulge freely whatever he thinks, perceives or feels, to every other in the course of the treatment sessions. He should know that he is protected by the "pledge" and that no disadvantage will occur to him because of his honest revelations of crimes committed, of psychological deviations from sexual or social norms, secret plans and activities.(1)

It seems to me that, while certainly a patient is entitled to the security that the privacy of his communications will be kept in trust, no reliable guarantees against the danger of betrayal is assured by subjecting the therapeutic group membership to a "pledge" of secrecy.(2)

The two passages quoted above express the authors' common concern for the preservation of confidentiality within the group therapeutic setting. At the same time, however, they emphasize a fundamental disagreement regarding the appropriate means of protecting group communications. In the first quoted passage, Dr. Jacob L. Moreno, a founder and principal pioneer of group therapy,(3) suggests that group silence would be assured by the simple administration of a group oath(4) before commencing therapy. On the other hand, Dr. Alexander Wolf's skepticism regarding the efficacy of this approach highlights the need for a reexamination and an expansion of the law of privilege in this area. The precise problem is whether evidence of group communications should be excluded from a trier of fact because of some special quality inherent in the group relationship.

The doubts expressed by Dr. Wolf are perhaps too critical of the ethics and reliability of the group membership with regard to private disclosures, but it can hardly be argued that a mere "pledge" would suffice to silence an individual member when confronted by a judicial order to speak. It would be both unreasonable and unrealistic to expect a patient to brave contempt proceedings in order to obey some vague ethical imperative of collective silence. Any effective protection in legal proceedings of the confidences disclosed in group psychotherapy must come, therefore, from the law rather than from psychology.

THE DEVELOPMENT OF GROUP PSYCHOTHERAPY

Group therapy was introduced near the turn of the century in Europe and was subsequently refined and developed in this country by Dr. Moreno during the 1930's.(5) The technique did not attain prominence however until immediately after World War II when it proved useful in treating victims of combat fatigue (shell shock). Its growth in the last two decades has been mercurial and shows no indication of slowing in the foreseeable future.(6)

The scarcity of qualified therapists and the high cost of individual therapy are among the most immediate and pragmatic reasons for the growth of group practice. There are at present fewer than 30,000 qualified psychiatrists and clinical psychologists in this country. This dearth of practitioners, in light of the inestimable number of disturbed Americans, makes the use of group therapy vital to the welfare of thousands.(7) Moreover, with prices ranging from 25 dollars to 100 dollars per session, individual analysis is virtually the exclusive prerogative of the rich. By contrast, a typical group session costs each patient between 5 and 25 dollars.(8) The relative ease with which group therapy may be obtained has recently elevated it to a position of prominence from which it is beginning to threaten the hegemony of more orthodox individual therapy.(9) In light of this prolific expansion, one must consider, and ultimately balance, the interests of group therapy and those of the law—the requirement of silence against the need for disclosure.

PRIVILEGED COMMUNICATIONS

The court's need to receive all relevant, nonrepetitive information, is fundamental in the law of evidence. Any claim of privileged exclusion necessarily seeks to deny the court access to pertinent material, thereby inhibiting its ability to make an informed decision. Thus, any proposed privilege must be rigorously scrutinized in order to determine its overall social utility. Professor Wigmore states the general rule succinctly:

For more than three centuries it has been recognized as a fundamental maxim that the public (in the words sanctioned by Lord Hardwicke) has a right to every man's evidence. When we come to examine the various claims of exemption, we start with the primary assumption that there is a general duty to give what testimony one is capable of giving, and that any exemptions which may exist are distinctly exceptional. being so many derogations from a positive general rule. . . .(10)

Privileged communications statutes, being derogations of both the common law and the general rule requiring full disclosure, are generally very strictly construed by the courts.(11) This strict approach necessarily limits the possibilities for expansion of privilege statutes. Thus, an advocate who seeks to find protection for a patient in group therapy in one of the traditional statutes is likely to meet almost isurmountable obstacles. The traditional privilege statues involve relationships in which the professional effectiveness of one party depends upon a cloak of strick confidentiality (attorney-client, physician-patient, and priest-penitent). Most of these statutes are little more than a codification of professional ethical standards.

The intrusion of a third person into the confidential relationship usually materially changes the nature of the privilege enjoyed by the parties. In many jurisdictions the existence of third party auditors completely destroys the privilege on the theory that any communication made in the presence of such third parties could not have been intended to be confidential.(12) The rule in other states is that the privilege remains in effect between the principal parties, but that the third party is free to testify because he was not essential to the purposes of the consultation and therefore the communication was not confidential with regard to him.(13) This latter rule has been relaxed in instances in which the third party was an agent of the doctor or attorney and whose presence was essential to the purposes of the consultation.(14)

The propriety of any evidentiary exclusion is, in the last analysis, a balancing process. Thus, the benefit that society will derive from the effective treatment of those in need of psychotherapy must outweigh the detriment to the efficient administration of justice that will invariably result. Professor Wigmore has reduced the many factors that must be weighed in deciding on the merits of a proposed privileged relationship to four conditions precedent to granting a privilege: 1. The communications must originate in a *confidence* that they will not be disclosed; 2. This element of *confidentiality must be essential* to the full and satisfactory maintenance of the relation between the parties; 3. The *relation* must be one which in the opinion of the community ought to be sedulously fostered; and 4. The *injury* that would inure to the relation by the disclosure of the communications must be *greater than the benefit* thereby gained for the correct disposal of litigation.(15) It should be noted at this point that it is generally understood that those communications protected by privilege statutes are not limited to verbal conduct, but may include other forms of expression.(16) Thus, forms of expression found in psychodrama (a form of group psychotherapy) that are strictly verbal would be protected by any privilege statute covering group communications.

Although psychiatry has become a familiar and accepted discipline in our society, group therapy is relatively unknown and misunderstood. Psychiatry deals with mental illness by analyzing and subsequently treating the individual's psyche.(17) Individual therapy traces the patient's emotional problems back to the traumas of childhood and tends to ignore the impact of more recent environmental and social influences.(18) Because of its emphasis on introspection, psychiatry necessarily involves only the therapist and patient in a classic dyadic relationship. The relationship corresponds perfectly to the lawyer-client prototype on which most privilege statutes are modeled. Therefore, commentators generally agree that Wigmore's four tests of legitimate privilege are met in the case of individual psychotherapy.(19) Many states have, in fact, granted such a privilege either under the coverage of a traditional physician-patient privilege or by legislation aimed explicitly at psychiatry.(20)

Group psychotherapy differs from psychiatry both in theory and in practice. The most obvious distinction, of course, is that group therapy involves a group of individuals, only one of whom is a trained therapist. More importantly, perhaps, group techniques seek to treat the diseases of interrelated individuals and interrelated groups.(21) The group setting provides insights into problems of social interaction that frequently are unavailable in individual therapy. In short, group therapy is not exclusively egocentric but instead examines many facets of the patient's existence.

There are two fundamentally different theoretical approaches to the group. One approach is concerned with the individuals within the group, and the other focuses on the group as an independent entity.(22) Within each category, however, there is considerable variation in theory and technique.

The individual-oriented therapists view the group essentially as a medium in which they can more effectively deal with each patient individually. Some groups formalize this outlook by employing a procedure known as the "hot seat." Each group member must eventually occupy the "hot seat" during which time he is the exclusive subject of group discussion. The seats next to the "hot seat" are always empty. The occupant is thus simultaneously isolated and scrutinized, simulating his situation in the real world. By placing the patient in a setting that is very much like the real world but is free from the normal societal inhibitions, the group allows him to express his thoughts, fears, and fantasies with relative impunity. The only pressure the group applies is that which requires honesty. The other members criticize and cajole the subject until he abandons evasion and faces himself in front of the group.(23)

By contrast, the other individual-oriented groups are conducted as more or less free wheeling discussions that examine individual problems only as they become apparent in the course of the conversation. In these sessions, the therapist intervenes only to provide guidance whenever the group ignores or flounders on a particular problem.(24) Except for these infrequent interuptions the group functions basically as a self-analytic entity. Its emphasis is, however, always on the problems of individual members.

Still a third approach to the individual-oriented group envisions it as a re-creation of the basic family unit. The therapist becomes, in effect, a parental figure while the participants assume sibling roles. In the course of the sessions transference relationships develop that are analogous to those developed in the usual family situation. Theoretically, this structure will eventually reactivate old neurotic patterns and ultimately eradicate them.(25)

Conversely, therapists who conceive of the group as an independent organic entity treat it as though it were, in fact, a patient. Such a therapist might remark that the group "feels hurt" or that it "is angry" on a particular day. This kind of remark generally elicits responses from individuals within the group. They seek to relieve the group symptoms by analyzing their own feelings in terms of the tensions they create within the group. Thus, a functioning social unit is formed in which individuals shed their feelings of isolation and fear and work together to solve the group's problems. They simultaneously achieve a better understanding of themselves.(26)

Regardless of which approach is adopted by the therapist, the chief characteristic of group therapy that distinguishes it from individual analysis is that each patient becomes the therapeutic agent of the others. This distinction is central to the privilege analysis.

> In individual methods the patient is a patient always. The only therapist is the therapist. . . .In group psychotherapy the patients can function as auxiliary therapists for each other. . . .The social interaction taking place between the individuals forming the group can be used as guides towards their therapeusis. It is the relationship among individuals of the group, the principle of therapeutic interaction, in which the autonomy of the participating individual is not lost.(27)

The group, not the therapist, becomes the focus of therapy. Effective social interaction within the group is therefore a crucial prerequisite to group therapy. The type of interaction required can only be achieved, however, when group members respond to each other spontaneously, both in their speech and their actions. In short, the key to successful therapy lies in the total, unhindered participation of the group's individual members.(28) Each group participant must freely test his impulses and images against group norms. Although the group's reaction to these probes are frequently quite brutal,(29) it is this unyieldingly honest attitude that forces the member to examine his responses and illusions with the care required to achieve therapeutic results.

Because "[i]nteraction analysis emphasizes, not only what happens within an individual's psyche, but also what happens between him and his surroundings, individuals and objects,"(30) an honest, intimate relationship with the other group members is essential. This reliance on third parties, which is the central feature of group therapy, acquires obvious significance when one attempts an evaluation of the propriety of granting a privilege to group communications.

RATIONALE FOR THE PRIVILEGE

In each of these—attorney-client, priest-penitent, and physician-patient—a privilege is conferred upon the person coming to the professional relationship, because it is assumed that the function performed by the professional would be seriously impaired if the cloak of confidentiality were removed.(31)

Thus the propriety of excluding evidence of communications made between patients in group therapy depends upon two vital considerations—the importance of confidentiality to group therapy, and a comparison of the damage to the group relationship that would result from disclosure with the benefit such disclosure would provide to the administration of justice. Wigmore's four conditions offer a useful framework in which to make these evaluations.(32)

1. Do group communications originate in a confidence that they will not be disclosed by other members of the group? Dr. J. L. Moreno expresses the pervasive assumption of confidentiality that is central to group therapy: "In group psychotherapy the Hippocratic Oath is extended to all patients and binds each with equal strength not to reveal to outsiders the confidences of other patients entrusted to them,"(33) The therapeutic virtue of groups lies in their potential for uninhibited expression. Group members are free to respond in socially unacceptable ways. They must frequently confide conduct and impulses that transcend societal norms. In fact, their treatment is inexorably linked to completely frank self-disclosure in an environment that accepts their confidences without qualification and holds them inviolate to outsiders.(34) It would seem that a mutual trust is inherent in the sort of multilateral soul-bearing that occurs in group sessions. No group participant would make himself vulnerable to community scorn and loss of spouse, job, or freedom by placing his most secret thoughts before the group, unless he could be assured of confidentiality.(35)

Since meaningful group communications can occur only if they originate in a confidence that they will not be disclosed, one of the first tasks frequently confronting a group is the resolution of innate fears of betrayal. When the therapist senses that fear of disclosure is inhibiting the group, he broaches the subject openly, and the process of establishing mutual confidence becomes a topic for group action. If this trust cannot be established many patients will discontinue therapy and others will be unable to make worthwhile contributions to the group.(36)

2. Is the element of confidentiality essential to the maintenance of a proper therapeutic relationship between group members? Emotionally disturbed individuals who seek therapy are generally filled with a sense of isolation and betrayal.(37) Often predisposed to inordinate suspicion and insecurity, they are frequently reticent to confide in others. In individual therapy, the patient enters a familiar setting of trust with a professional whom he knows is dedicated to helping him. In that reassuring context, confidentiality is assumed, and inhibitions to speech surmounted with relative ease. By contrast, the group therapy patient who enters therapy with the same anxieties is confronted by several total strangers, not one of whom is initially dedicated to anything more than his own therapy. The primary task of the group therapist is to overcome this natural suspicion and hesitancy in order to create a cohesive unit from this disparate mass.(38) This job would be insuperably complex if group members were aware of the possibility of forced disclosure at some later time.

Professor Ralph Slovenko has concluded that the exposure of a psychiatrist as a traitor who violated the confidences of his patient would prove fatal to that therapeutic relationship. Furthermore, he suggests that even the knowledge that a psychiatrist might be subpoenaed to testify would probably inhibit the patient, and thus destroy the effectiveness of the relationship.(39) It would seem that the group relationship, which is under great initial strain,(40) would be even more susceptible to inhibition if it were known that the privacy of the relationship could be violated in some later litigation. Thus, absolute confidentiality has even greater significance in the therapeutic group than it does in individual therapy.

Viewed from still another perspective, confidentiality is of paramount concern to the success of group therapy. As discussed above,(41) spontaneity is a crucial factor in the group—the individual must react to group stimuli immediately with complete candor in order to have his responses effectively weighed by the group.(42) If he feels compelled to consider the possible implications of his statements for his personal welfare, he is once more subject to normal societal inhibitions. The purpose of the group is thereby defeated.(43) It is clear, then, that the confidential nature of group communication must be maintained in order to preserve the effectiveness of the group as a therapeutic instrument.

3. Is the group relationship one that in the opinion of the community ought to be sedulously fostered? It is practically beyond dispute that society should encourage the treatment of its emotionally disturbed and mentally ill. State psychiatric facilities and public clinics abound for these purposes and millions of public dollars are devoted annually to the study of mental disease. More explicitly, several states have granted an express privilege to psychiatrists, thereby excluding evidence of communications between the patient and the therapist.(44) Still other states have granted a similar privilege under their physician-patient statutes.(45) Implicit in these privileges is the judgment that the community should foster the confidential relationships involved in mental therapy.

It has already been established that group therapy is necessary to the treatment of countless individuals for both its intrinsic and pragmatic reasons. In view of the current shortage of psychotherapists, some authorities even predict a time in the near future when patients will be treated primarily in group situations.(46) If it is initially assumed that the community wishes to provide therapy for its mentally ill, then it seems both obvious and inevitable that it should wish to foster the maintenance and development of effective group relationships.

Aside from pragmatic considerations, societal approval of group psychotherapy would seem to flow from the inherent virtues of the method. Group techniques deal with an individual's problems in relating to his environment.(47) A society that seeks to promote the treatment of individual problems that affect it only indirectly should certainly foster the correction of those syndromes that directly affect its ability to function. From the viewpoint of society it might even be appropriate for this kind of therapy to take precedence over individual methods. Because group therapy explores the participant's social relationships, it can frequently isolate and treat problems in advance of any conduct that is detrimental to such relationships. Since the highest goal of any corrective process is prevention, society should certainly foster a relationship that has an important prophylactic effect and thus shields both society and the patient from the consequences of antisocial behavior.

4. Is the injury that would inure to the group relationship by disclosure of the communications greater than the benefit gained thereby for the correct disposal of litigation? The relationship that exists between the participants in group therapy is unique. More traditional privileged relationships (attorney-client, physician-patient, husband-wife, and priest-penitent) all involve situations in which a breach of confidence will not totally destroy interaction between the parties. The effectiveness with which the relationships function and the solutions they achieve may indeed be limited by disclosure of confidential communication, but in most instances the relationship continues. Thus in this context, weighing competing social values as required by Wigmore's fourth condition becomes a complex task of evaluating intangible losses and gains on both sides of the balance.

The group relationship, however, is not simply limited in its effectiveness if members hesitate to confide or withhold their responses—it is destroyed. The therapeutic process depends upon the total spontaneity and unhindered participation of group members.(48) If this candor is inhibited by fears of betrayal the relationship is rendered useless. Thus, the intellectual problem of analyzing Wigmore's fourth condition is somewhat less complex because it demands a consideration of intangibles on only one side of the question.

The loss to litigation may indeed be substantial in some cases in which actual criminal conduct is disclosed. More frequently however, the patient is simply encouraged to reveal his private personality. "Incongruous attitudes emerge which are completely at variance with the patient's everyday functioning personality."(49) The major function of group therapy is to allow patients to express themselves unshackled by normal societal inhibitions.(50) The material revealed may be mere fantasy, but if disclosed in court it could be devastating to a person's reputation and life.(51) Furthermore, if one participant is subpoenaed and forced to testify, it could prevent countless others from seeking therapy.(52) It would seem, therefore, that although there may be occasional losses to the criminal justice system, such sporadic occurances are overshadowed by the potential destruction of the therapeutic relationship.

THE EXISTING LAW

Many states have physician-patient privilege statutes. Most of these acts are however, narrowly drawn(53) and typically receive strict construction.(54) Consequently, they cannot be relied upon to exclude evidence from group communications. Indeed, there appear to be no cases on record that have held that a privilege exists for this type of communication. Professor Slovenko, in one of the few written commentaries on privilege for group communications, concludes that the physician-patient privilege cannot be extended to include group members within its penumbra.

> Patients in group therapy develop transferences between themselves, but legally, and strictly speaking, patients *inter se* do not constitute a physician-patient relationship. Hence, it would seem that the medical privilege does not protect against disclosure in court by a member of the group.(55)

He later notes that the courts have traditionally found that privileged communications exist only in the classic dyadic relationship of a professional to his patient (client). Hence, it would appear that if an existing privilege is to be found, it must be in a statute directed specifically to psychotherapeutic relationships. Selected state statutes will be examined to determine their impact upon the availability of group psychotherapy privilege.

The one remotely possible exception to the rule stated above is New York, which allows liberal construction of its physician-patient privilege in order to provide maximum protection for the relationship.(56) The New York statutory provisions, although narrowly drawn, could include group communications. Three separate sections are involved in this analysis: section 4504, referring to physicians;(57) and section 4507, which indicates that psychologists shall be treated the same as attorneys under section 4503 of the Civil Practice Laws and Rules.(58)

Both the attorney-client (psychologist-client) and the physician-patient privileges are very narrowly drawn. The presence of third persons would normally destroy the confidentiality of the relationships and consequently the privilege. The New York Court of Appeals has declared, however, that the existence of a privilege in these circumstances will depend upon "whether in the light of all the surrounding circumstances, and particularly the occasion for the presence of the third person, the communication was intended to be confidential."(59) Thus, the presence of group members is not enough, by itself, to destroy the privilege.

Neither of these statutes, however, directly *excludes* testimony by the third persons who are present, although the attorney-client (psychologist-client) privilege prevents disclosure by those persons who obtain evidence of the communications without the knowledge of the client. Inasmuch as the draftsmen of section 4503 restricted that provision by excluding only the testimony of those third persons who were not present, it must be assumed that any third person who is present would be allowed to testify. Similarly, section 4504 only prevents disclosure by the physician.

These conclusions are consistent with the rule established in *People v. Decina.*(60) The court in *Decina* held that a privileged relationship existed between an accident victim and an attending physician, and that the privilege was not destroyed by the presence of a police officer who overheard their conversation. The doctor was, accordingly, not permitted to testify in litigation resulting from the accident. The court did indicate, however, that it was merely preserving the privilege existing between the physician and patient. The court cited an Appellate Division case, that stands for the proposition that a third person who was present might be permitted to testify, although the doctor's testimony is excluded.(51) Despite the liberal standards of *People v. Decina*, therefore, evidence of group communications is not presently excluded by these provisions. Since New York appears to be the only state that permits liberal construction of privilege statutes, it must be concluded that Professor Slovenko is correct in his finding that no standard physician-patient privilege will be sufficient to protect group communications.

The Kansas statute, unlike New York's Act, is a very broadly drawn physician-patient privilege that defines a physician as "a person licensed or reasonably believed by the patient to be licensed to practice medicine or one of the healing arts, as defined in [*Kan. Stat. Ann.*] § 65-2802 . . . in the state or jurisdiction in which the consultation or examination takes place."(62) The healing arts as defined in section 65-2802 include practically any kind of therapy.(63) Consequently, it would seem that both psychiatrists and clinical psychologists are included in the privilege. This is an essential element of any effective privilege for group communications because so much group therapy is performed by psychologists.

The Act further defines "confidential communications" in a way that specifically provides for the presence of those third persons who are "reasonably necessary for the transmission of the information or the accomplishment of the purpose for which it is transmitted."(54) Since the other group members are admittedly essential to the patient's therapy, group communications are confidential despite the presence of third party auditors within the group session.

Section 60-427 is also very comprehensive with regard to who may be prevented from testifying. The chief limitation found in the New York statute, for instance, was that only the physician, by the words of the Act, was prohibited from speaking. Kansas provides that the holder of the privilege may "refuse to disclose, and to prevent a witness from disclosing."(65) Therefore, any third person who is present during the transmission of a confidential communication, as defined above, may be prevented from testifying. Obviously, this statute would exclude testimony of group members.

Confidential communications, however, must be "between physician and patient"(66) in order to be excluded under the Act. This requirement places severe limitations on the application of the privilege to groups. The precise interpretive problem is whether communications transmitted from one patient to another are nonetheless *between* a patient and physician.

An advocate might argue that because of the nature of group therapy any communication that the physician receives from a patient is between them, even though the patient addresses the statement to another patient. Although this construction is perfectly consistent with the kind of communication that does occur within the group, it requires that one read the language very permissively. Since liberal interpretations of privilege statutes are not generally acceptable, it must be concluded that the Kansas Act, absent any positive indications to the contrary, cannot be interpreted to include group communications within its protection.

In Georgia, two provisions provide a privilege for both the psychiatrist-patient and psychologist-client relationships. Section 84-3118(67) simply places the psychologist-client relationship on the same basis as the attorney-client under section 38-418.(68) Consequently, both psychiatrists and psychologists are similarly protected.

Despite their explicit exclusion of some communications in the psychiatric field, these statutes offer no protection for the group relationship. They neither have provisions for the presence of third parties to the communication, nor do they exclude the testimony of such third persons. Considering the limitations of strict construction that are placed on privilege statutes, these statutes are hardly broad enough to protect communications between group members.

The Illinois(69) and Connecticut(70) statutes are identical for purposes of the present analysis. Both statutes read in pertinent part:

> [I]n civil and criminal cases, in proceedings preliminary thereto, and in legislative and administrative proceedings, a patient, or his authorized representative, (and a psychiatrist or his authorized representative) has a privilege to refuse to disclose, and to prevent a witness from disclosing, communications relating to diagnosis or treatment of the patient's mental condition between patient and psychiatrist, or between member of the patient's family and, the psychiatrist, or *between any of the foregoing and such persons [who participate], under the supervision of the psychiatrist, in the accomplishment of the objectives of diagnosis and treatment.* (emphasis added)(71)

The italicized portion of this statute perfectly describes the relationship existing between the members of a therapeutic group. Dr. Moreno describes each member of the group as the therapeutic agent of each of the others.(72) Each individual remains under the supervision of the psychotherapist, but participates freely in the therapy of other members. Any group member may, by the operation of this provision, prevent a witness from disclosing communication between himself and any other member. This exclusion, therefore, explicitly grants complete protection from disclosure to all communications made within a group therapy session conducted under the supervision of a psychiatrist.

The term "psychiatrist," however, is limited by the statutes to mean a "person licensed to practice medicine." Clinical psychologists are thereby excluded from its coverage and any effectiveness that the statute may have in protecting group thereapy from judicial exposure is correspondingly limited. Despite this deficiency, these two statutes by their specificity provide a great measure of protection for the group sessions that are included within its terms.

The California legislature, realizing the inadequacies of traditional physician-patient privilege, in 1965 enacted sections 1010-1026 in an attempt to provide comprehensive protection of psychotherapeutic relationships.(73) They clearly intended to establish a very broad privilege for the intimate and necessarily confidential communications that are essential to therapy. Both the psychiatrist-patient and psychologist-client relationships fall within the penumbra of these sections.(74) This pervasive quality effectively corrects the chief deficiency of the Connecticut and Illinois statutes.

The only real obstacle to finding a protection for groups in the California statutes lies in the definition of "confidential communication between patient and psychotherapist" in section 1012. This phrase is defined as:

> . . . information . . . transmitted between a patient and his psychotherapist . . . by a means which, so far as the patient is aware, discloses the information to no third persons other than those who are present to further the interest of the patient in the consultation or examination. . . .(75)

Because of these requirements of group therapy, a communication to one patient is simultaneously a communication to every other member, including the psychotherapist. More significantly, group participants know that this multilateral communication network is functioning. Implicit in this knowlege is the fact that any group communication is "between a patient and his psychotherapist."

Although this interpretation of "between" was earlier rejected in connection with the discussion of the Kansas statute and is also contrary to the conclusions of the other principal article written on the subject,(77) it seems that it would probably prevail in a California court. The Kansas statute was found deficient on the ground that the interpretation of "between," in the absence of any positive indication to the contrary, was simply stretching the word too far. The California Law Revision Commission, however, clearly recommended that group therapy be included within the California statute. It recommended that section 1012 be amended to read, in pertinent part: "discloses the information to no third persons other than those who are present to further the interest of the patient in the consultation, *including other patients present at joint therapy.*"(78) In its comments on the recommended amendment, the Commission indicates that the change is made "in order to foreclose the possibility that the section would be construed not to embrace marriage counseling, family counseling, and other forms of group therapy."(79) Although this amendment does not go directly to the heart of the ambiguity that lies in the word "between," it does give a clear indication that section 1012 should be read to include group therapy.

In light of the statements of the Commission, the suggested interpretation of "between a patient and his psychotherapist" does not place excessive strain on the legislative language. Group communications are confidential within the statutory language and may be excluded by section 1014.(30)

The draftsmen of the Proposed Federal Rules have created a very comprehensive "psychotherapist-patient privilege" that undoubtedly prevents disclosure of group communications. Rule 5-04 resolves the ambiguity found in the California statute and, at the same time, provides much broader coverage for groups than that granted by the Connecticut and Illinois Acts.(82)

"Psychotherapist," as defined by the rule, encompasses both psychiatrists and licensed psychologists. Practically any therapeutic group would seemingly be covered by this definition. This portion of the rule is apparently strongly influenced by section 1010 of the California Evidence Code.(83) It is therefore instructive that the California Law Revision Commission has recently recommended that section 1010 be broadened to include school psychologists, clinical social workers, and marriage, family, or child counselors. This expansion of the privilege's scope seems particularly significant in the group therapy context because many of these counselors are involved daily in group sessions. Thus, while the regular therapy group is already covered by proposed rule 5-04, its expansion to include these counselors would undoubtedly provide valuable and necessary protection for those groups on the periphery of group psychotherapy.

The proposed rules define confidential communications in such a way that information transmitted between participants in group therapy is excluded in two different ways:

> A communication is "confidential" if not intended to be disclosed to third persons *other than those present to further the interest of the patient in the consultation, examination, or interview,* or persons reasonably necessary for the transmission of the communication, *or persons who are participating in the diagnosis and treatment under the direction of the psychotherapist,* including members of the patient's family.(84) (emphasis added)

It is patent from the previous discussion that the other members of the group are "present to further the interest of the patient." Group therapy is, indeed, predicated upon the belief that a benefit will be derived from third parties who work with the therapist in the treatment of the individual patient.

Dr. J. L. Moreno refers to each group member as the therapeutic agent of every other member.(85) Each patient remains under the direction of the psychotherapist, but by his comments and responses he is instrumental in the diagnosis and treatment of his fellow patients. It is therefore apparent that group communications are confidential because they are intended to be disclosed only to those third persons "who are participating in the diagnosis and treatment" of the patient.

Furthermore, the advisory committee's notes indicate that the standard of confidentiality established by proposed rule 5-04(a) (3) is intended to be essentially the same as that promulgated for the lawyer-client relationship in rule 5-03(a)(5),(86) the notes to which plainly indicate that confidentiality "is defined in terms of intent. . . . The intent is inferable from the circumstances. Unless intent to disclose [to the public] is apparent, the attorney-client communication is confidential."(87) It is manifest that no intention to disclose group communication to the public can be inferred from the circumstances of group therapy.(88)

While it is undoubtedly true that group communications are confidential within the definition established by the advisory committee in proposed rule 5-04(a) (3), in order to eliminate any remaining confusion or doubt concerning this confidentiality, the draft should be amended to read: "including members of the patient's family *and other patients participating in group therapy with the patient.*"

The language that distinguishes the proposed rule from similar statutes and that provides the clearest indication that the rule protects the confidentiality of group communications appears in subdivision b:

> A patient has a privilege to refuse to disclose and to prevent any other person from disclosing confidential communitions *among himself*, his psychotherapist, *or persons who are participating in the diagnosis or treatment under the direction of the psychotherapist*, including members of the patient's family.(89) (emphasis added)

The principal interpretive problem encountered in the Kansas and the California statutes was the ambiguity created by the use of the word "between." The only communications that are deemed privileged by those statutes are those "between" the therapist and his patient. This usage raises serious questions concerning the status of communications transmitted by one patient to another. The proposed rule eliminates this ambiguity by substituting "among" for "between." Because other group members are understood to be essential to his therapy, the disclosures made by a patient in the course of a group session are necessarily "communications *among* himself, his psychotherapist, or persons who are participating in the diagnosis or treatment under the direction of the psychotherapist." This provision is given full effect by the patient's right to prevent "any person" from revealing such communications. Although it is clear that protection of group communications is contemplated by rule 5-04(b), that protection could, as suggested above with rule 5-04(a) (3), be made more explicit by likewise amending it to read: "including members of the patient's family *and other patients participating in group therapy with the patient.*"

Rule 5-04, as drafted, provides a pervasive protection for the confidentiality of communications transmitted between patients participating in group therapy. It eliminates the ambiguity discovered in some privilege statues and expands the coverage of still others. Although amendments have been suggested in the course of this discussion, they are proposed only to preclude the possibility that the protection that is inherent in the proposed rule might be emasculated by the application of strict construction standards.

NONPROFESSIONAL GROUPS

Most of the discussion in this article has centered on the problems of preventing disclosure of communications originating in the psychotherapeutic group. There are in addition, however, a large number of groups conducted by nonprofessional personnel that, although not strictly psychotherapeutic in nature, nonetheless warrant consideration and possibly protection. These groups are primarily concerned with the rehabilitation of former narcotic addicts and alcoholics. It must be observed at the outset that none of the statutory provisions discussed above offer the slightest hope of protection for these groups. Even the very liberal California statute and the proposed federal rule limit their definitions of psychotherapist to licensed or certified personnel. The groups in question are generally conducted by former addicts or alcoholics who, with rare exceptions, hold no licenses or certificates that would qualify them.

These nonprofessional groups draw on the techniques of group therapy inasmuch as they emphasize spontaneity and honesty. Their primary virtue is the opportunity that they provide for a member to discuss in complete candor, without rationalization or deception, the unique problems that contributed to his addiction. They eliminate feelings of isolation and shame and force the individual to face himself honestly. The group leader brings to the group a sensitivity to the realities of addiction. At the same time he will not tolerate evasion and self-delusion by the other participants. He has simply heard it all before and has lived most of it himself. In this context, the leadership of a nonprofessional is indispensible to successful rehabilitation.

It would seem, at least on summary analysis, that this type of relationship meets Wigmore's four conditions.(90) It would verge on the absurd to argue that disclosures by an ex-addict do not originate in a confidence that they would not be revealed by other members of the group. The facts of an addict's existence create an innate fear and suspicion of his surroundings. Maintaining a drug habit necessarily involves criminal conduct in every jurisdiction, admissions of which could result in imprisonment. It must be assumed that no person who is already predisposed to suspicion would entrust information of this nature except in a strictly confidential relationship. Similarly, this confidentiality is essential to the effective maintenance of the group relationship. Any breach of trust would, of course, silence the group.

The Supreme Court has suggested that narcotic addiction is in the nature of an illness and should be treated as such rather than punished.(91) Implicit in this judgment is the decision that society should sedulously foster the maintenance of the rehabilitative group relationship. Furthermore, society should foster rehabilitation simply because of the manifest suffering caused by addiction, both for those addicted and for those who fall victim to their need for funds to support the habit.

Finally, since *Robinson v. California* said that a state may not punish drug addicts for their addiction,(92) admissions of prior addiction made in group sessions have no relevance in court. The only possible relevance group communications could have to legal action would be information concerning the prior criminal conduct of the group members for their sources of drugs. Because the theoretical goal of criminal justice is the prevention of future crime, the rehabilitation of addicts serves the ends of justice better than convictions for their past conduct. Therefore, evidence of prior illegal activity should be subordinated to the requirements of confidentiality. Furthermore, it would seem that the transient nature of drug sources would render evidence of the suppliers of ex-addicts largely useless to police officials. Consequently, the rehabilitation of these addicts clearly outweighs the rather questionable loss to law enforcement occasioned by granting a privilege to these groups.

Viewed from an analytic standpoint, a privilege for these specialized nonprofessional groups appears to be imminently appropriate. These groups could be incorporated with relative ease into the penumbra of either the California statute or the proposed federal rule. The problem facing the draftsman in this area, of course, is the difficulty of defining the qualifications of the group leader with sufficient specificity to include these groups but, at the same time, exclude groups of more questionable desireability. Despite the difficulty of this task, it is incumbent upon the law to reevaluate the scope of the privilege statutes in this crucial area and to attempt the expansion.

NOTES

(1) J. Moreno, Code of Ethics for Group Psychotherapy and Psychodrama: Relationship to the Hippocratic Oath 5 (Psychodrama and Group Psychotherapy Monographs No. 31, 1962) [hereinafter cited as Moreno, Code of Ethics].

(2) *Id.* at 8 (comment by Alexander Wolf, M.D.).

(3) Jacob L. Moreno is widely viewed as the founder and foremost pioneer of group psychotherapy. He is credited with suggesting the method in a report entitled "The Application of the Group Method to the classification of Prisoners." J. Meiers. Origins and Development of Group Psychotherapy: A Historical Survey, 1930-1945 (Psychodrama Monographs No. 17, 1946). Another writer has concluded that the intervention of Moreno in the embryonic field was necessary to ignite the spark that led to the development of the science. P. Renouvier. The Group Psychotherapy Movement: J. L. Moreno, Its Pioneer and Founder (Psychodrama and Group Psychotherapy Monograps No. 33, 1958).

(4) Moreno, Code of Ethics 3:

This is the group oath to therapeutic science and its disciples.

Just as we trust the physician in individual treatment, we should trust each other. Whatever happens in the course of a session of group therapy and psychodrama, we should not keep anything secret. We should divulge freely whatever we think, perceive or feel for each other; we should act out the fears and hopes we have in common and purge ourselves of them.

But like the physician who is bound by the Hippocratic Oath, we are bound as participants in this group, not to reveal to outsiders the confidences of other patients.

Like the physicians, each of us is entrusted to protect the welfare of every other patient in the group.

(5) J. Meiers, *supra* note 3.

(6) *Psychiatry, Strength in Numbers*, Time, Feb. 8, 1963, at 38.

(7) Adler, *A Reporter at Large—The Thursday Group*, New Yorker, Apr. 15, 1967, at 55, 58.

(8) *Id.*

(9) R. Slovenko, Psychotherapy, Confidentiality, and Privileged Communications 119 (1966) [hereinafter cited as Slovenko].

(10) 8 J. Wigmore, Evidence § 2192 (3rd ed. 1940) [hereinafter cited as Wigmore].

(11) Cepeda v. Cohane, 233 F. Supp. 465 (D.C.N.Y. 1964) (journalist privilege); Sacramento Newspaper Guild v. Sacramento Country Bd. of Supervisors, 263 Cal. App. 2d 41, 69 Cal. Rptr. 480 (1968) (lawyer-client privilege); Lindsay v. Lipson, 367 Mich. 1, 116 N.W.2d 60 (1962) (physician-patient privilege). Slovenko 119; Slovenko, *Psychiatry and A Second Look at the Medical Privilege*, 6 Wayne L. Rev. 175, 181 (1960); Note, *Group Therapy and Privileged Communication*, 43 Ind. L.J. 93, 99 (1967).

(12) Leathers v. United States, 250 F.2d 159 (9th Cir. 1957); State v. Tornquist, 254 Iowa 1135, 120 N.W.2d 483 (1963); State v. Cofer, 187 Kan. 82, 353 P.2d 795 (1960).

(13) Goddard v. Gardner, 28 Conn. 172 (1859); Hobbs v. Hullman, 183 App. Div. 743, 171 N.Y.S. 390 (1918).

(14) United States v. Kovel, 296 F.2d 918 (2d Cir. 1961); In re Bretto, 231 F. Supp. 529 (D. Minn. 1964); D.I. Chadbourne, Inc. v. Superior Court, 60 Cal. 2d 723, 388 P.2d 700, 36 Cal. Rptr. 468 (1964); People ex rel Dep't of Pub. Works v. Donovan, 57 Cal. 2d 346, 369 P.2d 1, 19 Cal. Rptr. 473 (1962).

(15) 8 Wigmore § 2285.

(16) City & County of San Francisco v. Superior Court, 37 Cal. 2d 227, 231, P.2d 26 (1951); Grand Lake Drive In, Inc. v. Superior Court, 179 Cal App. 2d 122, 3 Cal. Rptr. 621 (1960).

(17) J. Moreno, Open Letter to Group Psychotherapists 11 (Psychodrama Monographs No. 23, 1947) [hereinafter cited as Moreno, Open Letter].

(18) *Psychoanalysis: In Search of its Soul*, Time, Mar. 7, 1969, at 68.

(19) Slovenko 39.

(20) Cal. Evid. Code §§ 1010–1026 (West 1966); Conn. Gen. Stat. Rev. § 52-146d (Supp. 1970); Ga. Code Ann. § 84-3118 (1955); Ill. Ann. Stat., ch. 51, § 5.2 (1966); Kan. Gen. Stat. Ann. § 60-427 (1964); N.Y. Civ. Prac. Law & Rules § 4504 (McKinney 1963).

(21) Moreno, Open Letter 11.

(22) There are also several other forms of group-type therapy sessions that are not discussed here because their foundations do not lie within the scope of traditional psychotherapy, such as nude therapy, marathon sessions, Synanon groups, and Alcoholics Anonymous.

(23) Interview with Professor David Singer, Department of Clinical Psychology at Teacher's College, Columbia University, In New York City, Apr. 7, 1969 [hereinafter cited as Singer Interview].

(24) Id.

(25) Adler, supra note 7, at 58.

(26) Id.

(27) J. Moreno, The First Book on Group Psychotherapy xii (1957) [hereinafter cited as Moreno, First Book].

(28) Id. at xv. "It is what I have called the principle of spontaneity."

(29) The following excerpt is part of a dialogue held between a group of former drug addicts in a group session:

"And you Paul," Micky said to the second boy, "how come you're always wearing your shades on visitor's day? Think you're a movie star?" "Naw, man. They're prescription," Paul said. Micky said nothing. "Look, Micky," Paul said, "my old man and my mother both wore—"

"Spare us your mother, will you, man?" another older member said. "Micky don't want to hear Freud. He asked you a question." "O.K.," Paul said, cracking his knuckles and staring down at a tattoo on his arm. "I guess I'm ashamed on visiting day. Being a junkie. Being here." Adler, supra note 7, at 72.

(30) Moreno, First Book xiv.

(31) Goldstein & Katz, *Psychiatrist-Patient Privilege: The GAP Proposal and the Connecticut Statute*, 36 Conn. B.J. 175, 176 (1962).

(32) 8 Wignore§ 2285, *See* text accompanying note 15 *supra*.

(33) Moreno, Code of Ethics 5.

(34) Note, *Group Therapy and Privileged Communication*, *supra* note 11, at 96-97.

(35) Adler, *supra* note 7, at 60.

(36) Singer Interview.

(37) Slovenko 41.

(38) Moreno, Open Letter 27.

(39) Slovenko 41.

(40) Note, *Group Therapy and Privileged Communication*, *supra* note 11, at 97.

(41) *See* discussion of group psychotherapy above.

(42) Moreno, First Book xv.

(43) Singer Interview.

(44) Cal. Evid. Code §§ 1010-1026 (West 1966); Conn. Gen. Stat. Rev. § 52-146d (Supp. 1970); Ga. Code Ann. § 84-3118 (1955); Ill. Ann. Stat., ch. 51, § 5.2 (1966).

(45) *See, e.g.,* Kan. Gen. Stat. Ann. § 60-427 (1964); N.Y. Civ. Prac. Laws & Rules § 4504 (McKinney 1963).

(46) Slovenko 119.

(47) Moreno, First Book xiv.

(48) *Id* at xv.

(49) Slovenko 47.

(50) Adler, *supra* note 7, at 60.

(51) Slovenko 47.

(52) Singer Interview.

(53) *See, e.g.,* Ariz. Rev. Stat. Ann. § 12-2235 (1956); Idaho Code Ann. § 9-203 (1969); Mich. Comp. Laws Ann. § 600.2157 (1968).

(54) *See* note 11 *supra*.

(55) Slovenko 119.

(56) People v. Decina, 2 N.Y.2d 133, 138 N.E. 2d 799, 157 N.Y.S.2d 558 (1956).

(57) PHYSICIAN, DENTIST AND NURSE. a. Confidential information privileged. Unless the patient waives the privilege, a person authorized to practice medicine . . . shall not be allowed to disclose any information which he acquired in attending a patient in a professional capacity, and which was necessary to enable him to act in that capacity. N.Y. Civ. Prac. Laws & Rules § 4505 (McKinney 1963).

(58) ATTORNEY. a. Confidential communication privileged; non-judicial proceedings. Unless the client waives the privilege, an attorney or his employee, or any person who obtains without the knowledge of the client evidence of a confidential communication made between the attorney or his employee and the client in the course of professional employment, shall not disclose . . . such communication. . . . *Id.* at § 4503.

(59) People v. Decina, 2 N.Y.2d 133, 138 N.E.2d 799, 157 N.Y.S.2d 558 (1956).

(60) *Id.*

(61) Hobbs v. Hullman, 183 App. Div. 743, 171 N.Y.S. 390 (1918).

(62) Kan. Stat. Ann. § 60-427(a) (2) (1964).

(63) DEFINITIONS. For the purposes of this act the following definitions shall apply: a. The healing arts include any system, treatment, operation,

diagnosis, prescription, or practice for the ascertainment, cure, relief, palliation, adjustment, or correction of any human disease, ailment, deformity, or injury, and includes specifically but not by way of limitation the practice of medicine and surgery; the practice of osteopathy; and the practice of chiropractic. *Id.* at § 65-2802.

(64) "[C]onfidential communication between physician and patient" means information transmitted between physician and patient, including information obtained by an examination of the patient, as is transmitted in confidence and by a means which, so far as the patient is aware, discloses the information to no third persons other than those reasonably necessary for the transmission of the information or the accomplishment of the purpose for which it is transmitted. *Id.* at § 60-427(a)(4).

(65) *See* Kan. Stat. Ann. § 60-427(b)(1964).

(66) *Id.*

(67) Ga. Code Ann. § 84-3118 (1955): Communications between psychologist and client as privileged. For the purpose of this Chapter, the confidential relations and communications between licensed applied psychologist and client are placed upon the same basis as those provided by law between attorney and client, and nothing in this Chapter shall be construed to require any such privileged communications to be disclosed.

(68) Ga. Code Ann. § 38-418 (Supp. 1965): CONFIDENTIAL COMMUNICATIONS, ETC. There are certain admissions and communications excluded from consideration of public policy. Among these are: 1. Communications between husband and wife. 2. Between attorney and client. 3. Among grand jurors. 4. Secrets of state. 5. Psychiatrist and patient.

(69) Ill. Ann. Stat., ch. 51, § 5.2 (1966).

(70) Conn. Gen. Stat. Rev. § 52-146d (Supp. 1970).

(71) Illinois grants the privilege to the psychiatrist as well as the patient, although Connecticut grants it only to the patient.

(72) Moreno, First Book xii.

(73) Cal. Evid. Code §§ 1010-1026 (West 1966).

(74) *Id.* at § 1010.

(75) Cal. Evid. Code § 1012 (West 1966): § 1012. "Confidential communication between patient and psychotherapist." As used in this article, "confidential communication between patient and psychotherapist" means information, including information obtained by an examination of the patient, transmitted between a patient and his psychotherapist in the course of that relationship and in confidence by a means which, so far as the patient is aware, discloses the information to no third persons other than those who are present to further the interest of the patient in the consultation or examination. . . .

(76) R. Blake, Group Training vs. Group Therapy 35 (Sociometry Monographs No. 35, 1958).

(77) Note, *Group Therapy and Privileged Communication, supra* note 11, at 101.

(78) California Law Revision Commission, Recommendation relating to The Evidence Code 513 (Nov. 1968).

(79) *Id.*

(80) Ca. Evid. Code § 1014 (West 1966).

(81) Committee on Rules of Practice and Procedure, Preliminary Draft of Proposed Rules of Evidence for the United States District Courts and Magistrates (Mar. 1969) [hereinafter cited as Fed. R. Evid. (Prelim. Draft 1969)]. *Rule 5-04. Psychotherapist-Patient Privilege.* a. DEFINITIONS: 1. A "patient" is a person who consults or is examined or interviewed by a psychotherapist for purposes of diagnosis or treatment of his mental or emotional condition. 2. A

"Psychotherapist" is (i) a person authorized to practice medicine in any state or nation, who devotes a substantial portion of his time to the practice of psychiatry, or is reasonably believed by the patient so to be, or (ii) a person licensed or certified as a psychologist under the laws of any state or nation, who devotes a substantial portion of his time to the practice of clinical psychology. 3. A communication is "confidential" if not intended to be disclosed to third persons other than those present to further the interest of the patient in the consultation, examination, or interview, or persons reasonably necessary for the transmission of the communication, or persons who are participating in the diagnosis and treatment under the direction of the psychotherapist, including members of the patient's family. b. GENERAL RULE OF PRIVILEGE. A patient has a privilege to refuse to disclose and to prevent any other person from disclosing confidential communications among himself, his psychotherapist, or persons who are participating in the diagnosis or treatment under the direction of the psychotherapist, including members of the patient's family.

(82) *See* section The Existing Law above.

(83) *See* Fed. R. Evid. 5-04, Advisory Committee's Note at 89 (Prelim. Draft 1969).

(84) Fed. R. Evid. 5-04(a)(3)(Prelim. Draft 1969).

(85) Moreno, First Book xii.

(86) Fed. R. Evid. 5-04, Advisory Committee's Note at 89 (Prelim. Draft 1969).

(87) Fed. R. Evid. 5-03, Advisory Committee's Note at 82 (Prelim. Draft 1969).

(88) *See* Rationale for Privilege above section IV (1) *supra*

(89) Fed. R. Evid. 5-04(b)(Prelim. Draft 1969).

(90) *See* Privileged Communications above.

(91) *See* Robinson v. California, 370 U.S. 660, 666 (1962).

(92) *Id.*

INSURANCE COVERAGE FOR MENTAL ILLNESS:
PRESENT STATUS AND FUTURE PROSPECTS

Evelyn S. Myers

During the past three decades the extension of private health insurance protection to the U.S. population has been impressive. At the end of 1968, between 77 percent and 87 percent of the civilian population under 65 (depending on the source of data) had some health insurance coverage of hospital expense. Between 74 and 80 percent also had some coverage of surgical expense.(1,2) For hospital expense, if we use the higher estimate, this is about 13 times as many people as were covered in 1940 and for surgical expense it is about 28 times.(2)

The coverage for out-of-hospital care, while it has also increased substantially, is still much less than for hospital care; at the end of 1968, 43 percent of the population had some coverage for physician services in the office and home.(1) As Helen Avnet points out, "The history of mass purchase of voluntary medical insurance in this country has reflected a preoccupation with the dramatic expenses associated with hospitalization and far less concern with the problems of keeping the patient vertical."(3)

One other set of statistics is relevant here. Voluntary health insurance met only 36 percent of all consumer medical care expenses in 1967. It met 74 percent of hospital care expense, 38 percent of expenditures for physician services, and only 4 percent of expenditures for other types of care;(1) also, about 24 million Americans, mainly in the lower income groups, are without private health insurance of any kind.(4)

During the period when health insurance coverage was growing dramatically, there were equally dramatic changes in the care of the mentally ill. The psychoactive drugs, introduced in the mid-50s, proved of value not only in the treatment of hospitalized patients but in keeping many other mentally ill people out of the hospital. A trend toward community care began. The number of admissions of psychiatric patients to general hospitals rose. While the number of admissions to public mental hospitals also continued to rise, there were shorter stays and higher discharge rates even of long-term patients, so that the number of patients resident in these hospitals began to decline. In fact, the number of patients in public mental hospitals decreased by 24 percent between 1955 (the peak year) and 1967.(5) A host of new treatment modalities were introduced and soon proved their usefulness: partial hospitalization, group therapy, family and conjoint marital therapy, to name a few. Short-term treatment and especially crisis intervention began to be considered respectable. The federal government participated in the trend toward community treatment by passing the Community Mental Health Centers Act of 1963, providing a federal subsidy for part of the construction costs; funds for initial staffing of the centers were authorized later.

All of these developments were reflected in a changed attitude toward mental illness—shared, if not by all of the public, at least by a substantial part of it. People no longer generally view "psychiatric care" as a synonym for "custodial care." Psychiatric illness is now seen as potentially curable or at least controllable in much the same way as high blood pressure or diabetes.

With mental illness more effectively treatable, such treatment also became more readily insurable. It is difficult to estimate with any degree of precision how many people are now covered for psychiatric care under some kind of health insurance, both because of the multiplicity of health insurance carriers and the swift pace of developments. One study was reported by the Health Insurance Association of America, which includes the major commercial health insurance carriers. It showed that of the persons covered under a sample of new group health insurance policies issued in 1968, 80 percent had some form of major medical coverage; 97 percent of those covered by either supplementary or comprehensive major medical were covered for nervous and mental disorders if they were hospitalized, and 88 percent were also covered for out-of-hospital treatment.(2)

Another approach toward getting some meaningful estimates was made by the Joint Information Service of the American Psychiatric Association and the National Association for Mental Health in a 1968 survey.(6) Instead of relying on data from the insurers, they went to providers of care—ten hospitals and a sample of psychiatrists in private practice. An analysis of insurance coverage of 1,000 psychiatric admissions to ten hospitals (five voluntary general hospitals, two private psychiatric hospitals, and three public general hospitals) showed that 74 percent of the patients in the voluntary general hospitals had health insurance coverage for a portion of their bill (an average of 71 percent of the bill paid by insurance); in the private psychiatric hospitals 69 percent of the patients had insurance coverage and an average of 58 percent of the bill was paid; and in public general hospitals 35 percent of the patients were insured and an average of 70 percent of the bill was paid.

Coverage for outpatient care was much less: only 26 percent of 12,917 patients seeing psychiatrists in private practice had insurance coverage for some part of the bill. Forty-four percent of the patients on whom information was available about the extent of their coverage had approximately 50 percent of the bill paid, another 36 percent had about 80 percent paid, and the remaining 20 percent, less than 50 percent. If these percentages seem low, they should be compared to the situation ten years ago, when coverage for out-of-hospital care was minuscule.

As already indicated, the improvements in psychiatric care coverage owe much to the expansion of health insurance for all illness and to the more effective treatment of the mentally ill. In addition, in the past ten years there have been a number of developments that have served as a spur to further progress or have given an indication of the increasing feasibility of improved coverage. These are listed briefly, roughly in chronological order, with two caveats: they are illustrative, rather than all-inclusive, and to a certain extent they also reflect my own biases as a former employee of the National Institute of Mental Health and a member of its Task Force, and a current staff member of the American Psychiatric Association. I will confine myself to voluntary health insurance and will not consider such important programs as Medicare and Medicaid or the Civilian Health and Medical Program for the Uniformed Services (CHAMPUS).

GROUP HEALTH INSURANCE PROJECT

The first major experiment in providing large-scale outpatient care occurred in 1969 when Group Health Insurance, Inc., of New York City undertook a project, financed by the National Institute of Mental Health, to demonstrate the insurability of mental illness by offering short-term psychiatric treatment to 76,000 members. During a two-year period 923 patients, or 1 out of 76 enrollees, sought psychiatric service; the utilization rate was 7 per 1,000 the first year and 5 per 1,000 the second. Conclusion: "In the present stage of acceptance of psychiatry, there appears to be little danger that the costs of insuring the extent of coverage offered by the project would be prohibitive if spread over an average cross-section of the 1960 population."(7)

INDUSTRIAL PLANS

Many large employers have substantial psychiatric coverage in their health care plans; some of these go back at least ten years. For example, International Business Machines Corporation covers 135,000 employees for psychiatric illness. This plan, which makes no distinction between mental and other illness, covers 365 days of hospitalization and 75 percent of the cost of out-of-hospital care after a deductible of $200 is satisfied.(6) The Eastman Kodak Company's major medical expense plan also makes no distinction between mental and other illness. After a deductible is satisfied (the amount varies with the salary bracket of the employee) the plan pays 80 percent of the cost of inpatient and outpatient care. (Most employees also have basic hospital and surgical coverage in addition.)

SOUTHERN CALIFORNIA PERMANENTE PROGRAM

In 1961 the Kaiser-Permanente pre-paid group practice health plans in Southern California simultaneously established a department of psychiatry and agreed to offer outpatient psychiatric services to a contracting union, Retail Clerks Local 770. That union later set up its own independent clinic; the program at Kaiser-Permanente now serves a number of contracting groups including 85,000 federal employees, a lesser number of state employees, United Auto Workers members, and others. The federal employees may have 20 individual office visits for psychiatric care without charge; beginning with the 21st visit there is a $5 fee.(8)

NIMH GUIDELINES

President John F. Kennedy, in his historic mental health message to Congress, directed the Secretary of Health, Education, and Welfare "to explore steps for encouraging and stimulating the expansion of private voluntary health insurance to include mental health care." In response to this directive a Task Force on Insurance was established within the National Institute of Mental Health in 1963. It developed some suggested principles for improving coverage that included emphasis on early referral and short-term intensive therapy, with low deductibles and low co-payment by the patient; expanded in-hospital benefits and coverage of partial hospitalization; increased recognition to "all the professional skills essential to treatment and rehabilitation," and coverage of prescribed drugs for ambulatory as well as hospitalized patients.(9)

UAW CONTRACT

A psychiatric care program of great significance in its own right and also for its "ripple effect" on other programs is the one negotiated in 1964 between the United Auto Workers and a number of major automobile and agricultural implement firms, to become effective in 1966. Covering nearly three million workers and dependents, it provides hospitalization up to 45 days per confinement and out-of-hospital treatment up to $400 per year, plus psychological testing up to $45. One of its major innovations is that it reverses the usual insurance co-payment approach. The insured pays no deductible; for out-of-hospital therapy with a private practicing physician the first five visits are fully covered; the patient pays 15 percent of the cost of the next five visits and 30 percent of the cost of the next five. For all visits after the 15th, he pays 45 percent of the charge up to the $400 limit. In addition, to encourage the development of organized programs employing the mental health team approach, there are no patient payments in most such programs; in a few there is co-payment beginning with the 11th visit.(10)

AMERICAN PSYCHIATRIC ASSOCIATION GUIDELINES

In 1965 the APA organized a small conference of psychiatrists "to hammer out definitions, principles, and standards which could serve as guidelines to psychiatrists and other physicians working with insurance carriers to improve coverage." This action was in response to complaints by insurers that there was need for better definition of mental disorders and of acceptable treatment modalities, as well as machinery for controlling claims abuse. The result was the first edition of *APA Guidelines for Psychiatric Services Covered Under Health Insurance* in 1966.(11) A second conference, this time attended not only by psychiatrists but by representatives of insurers and the federal government, led to a second edition of the guidelines, which was published in March, 1969.(12)

FEDERAL EMPLOYEES HEALTH BENEFITS PROGRAM

While this program began in 1960, the most significant developments in regard to mental health benefits did not occur until 1967 and 1968.(12,p.28) The program, which now covers eight million persons, consists of 36 different plans. The two largest, Blue Cross/Blue Shield and Aetna, cover nearly 80 percent of participating employees. Before 1967 there was a requirement of 50 percent co-payment by the patient for outpatient psychiatric care under Blue Cross/Blue Shield. This type of care is now covered at 80 percent of the charge (after a once-yearly $100 deductible) under the high option, 75 percent (with a $150 deductible) under the low option. The plan now also includes 365 days of hospitalization under its high option and 30 days under the low option (the same as for other illnesses). The plan covers day and night hospital care, group therapy, family therapy, and services of members of the mental health team besides the physician.

The Aetna Indemnity Benefit Plan pays all of the first $1,000 room and board charges in a hospital, 80 percent of other charges (75 percent under the low option), and 80 percent of all expenses after the first $1,000. Initially this plan made the same provision for out-of-hospital treatment of mental illness as for other illness, but in late 1961 this was cut back to a limit of $250 a year and 50-50 co-payment by the patient. In 1967 the plan added coverage for day and night hospital care, group therapy, family therapy, and services of a psychologist or psychiatric nurse when authorized by a psychiatrist. Effective in 1968, the benefit was raised to 80 percent and the $250 per year limit was removed.

Of the remaining 34 federal employee plans, 31 provided in-hospital and out-of-hospital care for psychiatric illness as of January, 1969, although such benefits are often more limited than those for other illnesses; two others provide in-hospital care only, which one provides out-of-hospital care but excludes hospitalization for mental illness.

STEELWORKERS   CONTRACT

The United Steelworkers introduced psychiatric benefits in three contracts negotiated in 1968 with the can, basic steel, and aluminum industries, to go into effect in 1970. This was the second major nationwide program of negotiated mental illness benefits. The can industry contract includes out-of-hospital coverage similar to the UAW plan. The basic steel contract uses the major medical approach, with the plan paying 80 percent of the cost of outpatient care up to a $1,000 maximum per individual per year. There is a deductible of $50 per individual and $100 per family. The aluminum industry contract has benefits similar to those in the basic steel industry. Including dependents, the United Steelworkers psychiatric benefits will be available to about two million persons.(12,p.29)

MASSACHUSETTS BLUE CROSS

In 1968 this plan announced a new type of psychiatric benefit available under a special rider to master medical groups of 75 or more members. There is no deductible or co-insurance; "usual and customary" fees will be paid to psychiatrists for out-of-hospital care costing up to $700 in a 24-month period, with another $700 allowed for psychological testing and services of mental health professionals other than physicians. The monthly premium for the rider is 90 cents for an individual and $1.40 for a family. It is expected that eventually the plan will be extended to about three million persons; at present it is available to about one million.(13)

Blue Cross of Massachusetts has made a financial commitment to support the Harvard Medical School Community Health Plan, which is already in operation in Boston and includes psychiatric benefits. The Connecticut General Life Insurance Company is underwriting the Columbia Hospital and Clinic Foundation, which is staffed by faculty members of Johns Hopkins Hospital and Medical School in Baltimore, Maryland. Services of this prepaid group practice plan are being provided to residents of the new city of Columbia, Maryland, and psychiatric care is covered; the total premium is $43.50 a month per family. In both these plans teaching and research are included as well as health services.

SOME TRENDS

A number of trends are discernible from this admittedly incomplete list of "milestones." The first is the influence of the nationally negotiated health programs covering large numbers of employed persons. By 1969 negotiated plans accounted for almost half the employees covered by health benefit plans in private industry. In regard to psychiatric benefits, the United Auto Workers of course did the pioneering work; the United Steelworkers have followed the lead, and the United Rubber Workers are now in the process of negotiating psychiatric benefits. Other unions are expressing interest. Spurred by the negotiated plans, or in some cases acting independently, industry has also shown a substantial interest in improving health benefits. Comments by both labor and management representatives support the view that industry plans are stressing two major lines of improvement: broadening the scope of benefits to cover more kinds of health care, and increasing the efficiency of expenditures to get more service of higher quality for the money spent.

The second trend concerns the role of the federal government. The NIMH guidelines, with their emphasis on short-term care and coverage of all mental health professionals, have undoubtedly had an important effect. As a purchaser of care through the Federal Employees Health Benefits Program the federal government has influenced developments significantly: all 36 federal health insurance plans now have some mental illness coverage. The government, through NIMH, has also sponsored significant research in this area. The Group Health Insurance project already described was of major importance, and research related to the UAW program is being funded by NIMH.

The increasing interest by insurers has been another encouraging recent trend. Although it is too early to predict the impact, the National Association of Blue Shield Plans announced in 1968 that participating plans should have available after April, 1969—to all groups willing to buy it—a fully paid benefit for outpatient psychiatric treatment. And among the benefits the Blue Cross Association is promoting among its 75 member plans is treatment of nervous and mental disorders, along with out-of-hospital prescription drugs and vision and dental care. Significantly, Blue Cross has eliminated its categorical exclusion of benefits for treatment of alcoholism, drug addiction, and mental disorders in its basic national benefit certificates.

The commercial health insurance carriers, as represented by the Health Insurance Association of America, are also broadening the scope of benefits available under their coverages. Late in 1969 HIAA urged its 313 member companies to consider a number of recommendations including: 1. placing emphasis on ambulatory care, including prepaid group practice, community ambulatory care centers, and other facilities that are less costly than hospitals; 2. relating their coverages to preventive services; and 3. restructuring co-insurance and deductibles that the individual must pay to make them less burdensome.(14) Within the broader scope of benefits now being contemplated, psychiatric coverage seems to be assuming an important role; there are those who think that it may well be the major health insurance development of the 1970s.

Also, there has been increasing interest and activity on the part of the mental health professionals. The American Psychiatric Association Guidelines have already been mentioned. Other professional groups have also become active: for example, the American Psychological Association has issued a pamphlet called *The Psychologist and Voluntary Health Insurance.*(15)

Finally, the major citizens' association in the field, the National Association for Mental Health, has devoted an increasing amount of attention to the subject. Sessions at national and divisional meetings have been devoted to improving

mental health insurance coverage, and a recent pamphlet offers practical
suggestions to NAMH components.(16)

All of this adds up to the conclusion that extended coverage for psychiatric
care under health insurance is bringing this kind of care to a much broader
segment of society than formerly was able to afford it. Perhaps as many as 15
million persons have been covered by new or expanded psychiatric benefits in
the last ten years—for the most part people formerly not able to manage the
out-of-pocket expense yet earning too much to be eligible for publicly supported
services.

"SOCIAL" VERSUS "BUSINESS" APPROACH

From this review of developments, it is evident that no one pattern of
benefits has prevailed. Helen Avnet makes a distinction between the two
differing paths outpatient coverage has taken that is useful in assessing where we
are and what the future might hold. These paths, she notes, are based on
opposing philosophies of the purpose of insurance. "The hard-headed business
approach . . . has been modified by many insurers over the years, at least for
groups of enrollees, its application to coverage of preexisting conditions and
elective procedures; but it is still far from the point of encouraging people with
not-obviously-disabling emotional or environmental problems to seek help at
company   expense . . . [It]   has   resulted   in   ambulatory   coverage   that
characteristically   provides   financial   deterrents   both   to   initiation   and
continuation of treatment." On the other hand, the social approach "works on
the hypothesis that today's emotional or social problems may be tomorrow's
major mental illness; therefore mental insurance must provide easy access to
early help for problems that interfere with the individual's ability to function
optimally."(3)

The NIMH guidelines clearly take the social approach in their
recommendations for short-term intensive therapy, for low co-payment by the
patient to encourage early referral; and a sliding scale of co-insurance, with the
first five visits to be provided at no cost to the patient. While the APA guidelines
do not take a position in favor of short-term therapy, they state that "financial
arrangements for psychiatric coverage should be structured in such a way as to
encourage prevention, early diagnosis, and early treatment, and to eliminate or
minimize financial barriers to service."

In stating the case for a social approach, one must keep in mind that in
addition to the financial deterrents under the "business approach," there is
another deterrent facing any person seeking psychiatric help. This is the stigma
attached to mental illness that still lingers in our society. To overcome this
barrier, education is needed both as to the availability of help and its appropriate
utilization. Some of the prepaid group practice plans and unions are beginning to
undertake efforts in this direction. Greater cooperation between family
physicians and mental health resources is also needed. An NIMH-sponsored pilot
project at the Jamaica Medical Group of the Health Insurance Plan of Greater

New York indicated that family doctors in the medical group altered their referral practices following two years of contact with the mental health service. The change was particularly noticeable in the case of family physicians who initially had made few referrals of patients.(17)

Another argument in favor of the social approach is that while those plans with no initial financial deterrent to services usually have a fairly low limit on the amount of service available, this amount has usually proved sufficient for most users of the service. For example Glasser, reporting on the first year's experience under the UAW psychiatric benefit program among members in Michigan, notes that the average number of outpatient services received by patients was 8.5 and that "it appears that the $400 benefit for out-of-hospital services was adequate for well over 90 percent of the patients."(10)

Before mental illness insurance was as widespread as it is now, insurers raised a number of objections to broader coverage. Some of them related to definitions of mental illness and lack of knowledge about treatment modalities. Many of these have been dispelled; among those that persist is the "real illness" problem. Auster calls attention to the question raised by insurers of making sure "that benefits be paid only for treatment of 'real illness' and not for the ordinary strains of living." This same question, he notes, "is *not* asked when we urge people to see their physician for a complaint that may be an early symptom of a treatable, progressive condition but more often is probably a reflection of those very same strains of living." Many insurance carriers will provide coverage for extensive x-ray and laboratory testing that may be required for evaluation of such complaints but balk at providing coverage for evaluation of psychiatric symptoms on the grounds that they do not constitute a "real illness."(18)

Another question has to do with the chronic nature of mental illness. While acknowledging that many mental disorders are in fact chronic, Auster observes that, as is true with many chronic medical conditions, "treatment may be needed for only brief periods and only infrequently—to keep the condition under control."

Still another question has to do with the ability of the insurance mechanism to finance such services as consultation to community agents. This has rarely been financed through insurance except in a few cases involving prepaid group practice plans. The matter came up for extensive debate during the conferences leading to the second edition of the APA *Guidelines for Psychiatric Services Covered Under Health Insurance Plans*. The language finally agreed upon was as follows: "It is recognized that the effectiveness of psychiatric therapy and of efforts to prevent mental disorders is related to the community milieu in which the insured individual or groups of individuals live and function. It follows that there should be provision for professional counseling to appropriate community agencies—e.g., parents, schools, labor unions, family service agencies—when a therapeutic gain for a group of insurees may be anticipated."

Perhaps an even stickier problem is that posed by the availability of public money to pay for psychiatric care services and the consequent reluctance of insurance carriers to make insurance benefits available for such care, for example, in the state hospital. The entrance upon the scene of the federally supported community mental health center has raised other questions related to payment for services rendered in contracting or affiliated components of a center, particularly when these are not medical facilities. Much more experience in the operation of centers will have to accumulate before a clear indication of the importance of health insurance in their financing can be discerned.

Thus far this paper has raised a good many questions and has suggested very few answers. Perhaps in this final section a few general comments on recent developments may give some clues as to what we can expect in the future both in regard to psychiatric benefits and health insurance in general.

There are strong indications that psychiatric benefits have proved their usefulness, are here to stay, and will probably increase in the future. For example, as already noted, the two largest plans participating in the Federal Employees Health Benefits Program now have generous benefits for psychiatric care. Changes have been made in both plans since the present benefit levels became effective—three times in the case of Blue Cross/Blue Shield and twice in the case of Aetna—but the higher mental illness benefits have been maintained.

A number of experts in this field think that a logical next step will be the development of a paid-in-full outpatient benefit for mental illness treatment. This would mean that there would be no deductible and no co-payment by the patient for a benefit that would be limited to a certain dollar amount or a certain number of visits. This approach, presently in effect in the UAW program and many prepaid group practice plans, is also undergoing experimentation by Blue Cross/Blue Shield and commercial insurance carriers, where it is not limited to psychiatric care but extends to other health services.

However, this kind of prediction does not make much sense when we consider the kind of ferment going on in regard to the financing and delivery of *all* health services. Inevitably the future coverage of mental illness depends on the resolution of this larger issue.

There has been widespread speculation that by the mid-70s, we are going to have a universal health insurance scheme in the United States. The Nixon administration has appointed a task force headed by Blue Cross President Walter McNerney to look into problems of financing health care. While some feel that the task force recommendations will stress the private sector of the economy, McNerney himself has made some forthright statements emphasizing the need for a coordinated approach between the public and private sectors. Addressing the Group Health Institute in New York City on June 5, 1969, he said:" . . . it has become apparent that with the absence of both true competition and genuine consumer choice . . . self-regulation is significantly lacking, and the assumption that well-meaning professionals can carry the day doesn't hold. Solutions to large-scale problems of productivity and allocation require more basic pressure than personal or professional idealism can muster alone. . . . The challenge facing us is to construct a flexible and publicly accountable organizational type model which exploits the assets of both the public and private sectors. . . ."(19)

Other indications of support for changes in the health care system came at the September 2, 1969 meeting of the National Governors' Conference, which endorsed a plan that would require employers and employees to buy health insurance from private carriers; the self-employed would buy their own and the federal government would purchase insurance for the poor. Less than a week later the American Hospital Association announced the formation of a committee to review its thinking on the financing and delivery of health services.

By mid-1970 a half-dozen proposals for some form of national health insurance had either been introduced in Congress or were being readied for introduction. The approaches vary widely. The American Medical Association's "Medicredit" proposed would grant an income tax credit ranging from 10 percent to 100 percent of the premium cost of a health insurance policy; taxpayers in the lowest income group would receive a certificate good for the full cost of the premium. Tax credit bills introduced by Representative Richard H. Fulton and Senator Paul J. Fannin use a similar approach. At the other end of the spectrum is the proposal of the Committee for National Health Insurance, chaired by United Auto Workers President Leonard Woodcock; in addition to providing practically universal coverage and a comprehensive scope of health care benefits, including hospital, medical, and dental, it would affect the delivery system by offering incentives favoring a more rational organization of services. The AFL-CIO has espoused a similar approach, and a bill that includes many of the features emphasized at the October, 1969, AFL-CIO convention was introduced in February, 1970, by Representative Martha W. Griffiths, a member of the House Ways and Means Committee.

Other groups and individual Congressmen will undoubtedly bring forth their plans. Only time will tell which will win out. In the meantime, it is hard to quarrel with Mike Gorman's comment: "Any discussion of models of delivery of mental health services in the coming decade is unrealistic until we devise a *universal* mechanism for payment of these services. If we do not go about the business of developing a national plan, we will witness . . . an even greater multiplicity of competing kinds of payment that will only further confuse the mental patient."(20)

One can hope that a rational system for financing and delivering health services will evolve. One can also hope that such a system will include a broad, comprehensive scope of mental health benefits.

REFERENCES

(1) Reed, Louis S. Private Health Insurance, 1968: Enrollment, Coverage, and Financial Experience. Social Security Bull. 32:12, 3-19 (Dec.), 1969.

(2) 1969 Source Book of Health Insurance Data. New York: Health Insurance Institute, 1969.

(3) Avnet, Helen H. Psychiatric Insurance—Ten Years Later. Am. J. Psychiat. 126.5: 667-674 (Nov.), 1969.

(4) Facts of Life: Health and Health Insurance. Washington, D.C.: Committee for National Health Insurance, 1969.

(5) National Institute of Mental Health. Patients in State and County Mental Hospitals, 1967. PHS Publ. No. 1921. Washington, D.C.: Gov. Ptg. Office, 1969.

(6) Scheidemandel, Patricia; Kanno, Charles; and Glasscote, Raymond. Health Insurance for Mental Illness. Washington, D.C.: Joint Information Service, 1968.

(7) Avnet, Helen H. Psychiatric Insurance. New York: Group Health Insurance, Inc., 1962.

(8) Green, Edward L., Psychiatric Services in a California Group Health Plan. Am. J. Psychiat. 126.5:681-688 (Nov.), 1969.

(9) National Institute of Mental Health. Improving Mental Health Insurance Coverage. PHS Publ. No. 1253. Washington: Gov. Ptg. Office, 1965.

(10) Glasser, Melvin A., and Duggan, Thomas. Prepaid Psychiatric Care Experience with UAW Members. Am. J. Psychiat. 126.5: 675-681 (Nov.), 1969.

(11) American Psychiatric Association. APA Guidelines for Psychiatric Services Covered Under Health Insurance Plans (1st ed.). Washington, D.C.: American Psychiatric Association, 1966.

(12) American Psychiatric Association. APA Guidelines for Psychiatric Services Covered Under Health Insurance Plans (2nd ed.). Washington: American Psychiatric Association, 1969.

(13) Myers, Evelyn S. Psychiatric News, American Psychiatric Association, December 1968, p. 3.

(14) HIAA Recommendations Aimed at Medical Care Improvement. Pension and Welfare News 6, 4:10-12 (Jan.), 1970.

(15) American Psychological Association. The Psychologist and Voluntary Health Insurance (revised). Washington, D.C.: American Psychological Association, August 1968.

(16) Action Guidelines, Health Insurance Coverage on Mental Illness. New York: National Association for Mental Health, Inc., 1969.

(17) Goldensohn, Sidney S.; Fink, Raymond; and Shapiro, Sam. Referral, Utilization, and Staffing Patterns of a Mental Health Service in a Prepaid Group Practice Program in New York. Am. J. Psychiat. 126.5: 689-698 (Nov.), 1969.

(18) Auster, Simon L. Insurance Coverage for "Mental and Nervous Conditions": Developments and Problems. Ibid. 126.5:698-705 (Nov.), 1969.

(19) McNerney, Walter J. Needed! A New Coordinated Approach to the Effective Delivery of Comprehensive Health Care. Speech delivered at the 19th Annual Group Health Institute, New York, June 5, 1969.

(20) Gorman, Mike. National Health Insurance: An Idea Whose Time Has Come. Am. J. Psychiat. 126.5:698-705 (Nov.), 1969.

VOLUNTARY MENTAL HOSPITALIZATION:
AN UNACKNOWLEDGED PRACTICE OF MEDICAL FRAUD

Thomas S. Szasz

There are, so our language and laws tell us, two types of mental hospitalization: voluntary and involuntary.(1) This terminology would lead us to believe that voluntary mental hospitalization occurs when a person defines himself as a mental patient and seeks admission to a mental hospital, which he is free to leave when he wishes, and that involuntary mental hospitalization occurs when someone is defined as a mental patient by others and is confined in a mental hospital against his will until such time as those in charge of him release him.

Actually, only half of the foregoing statement is correct: involuntary mental hospitalization is just that—hospitalization in opposition to the will of the so-called patient. The other half is incorrect: voluntary mental hospitalization is often actually a type of involuntary psychiatric confinement.

CONSTRAINTS ON VOLUNTARY MENTAL PATIENTS

In their comprehensive review of "The Rights of the Mentally Ill," Lindman and McIntyre devote a chapter to "Voluntary Admission."(2) The semantics is, again, important: Chapter 2 of their book is entitled "Involuntary Hospitalization," and Chapter 3 "Voluntary Admission." There is no chapter entitled "Voluntary Hospitalization." Perhaps this is because there is no such thing.

Moreover, not even the "voluntary admissions" considered by these authors are truly voluntary. "As used in this Report," they write, "the term 'voluntary admission' refers to procedures for admission to a mental hospital which are commenced originally by the affirmative action of the patient himself or of someone empowered by law to act in the patient's behalf."(3)

The extent to which voluntary patients are constrained in their relations to the mental-hospital system is revealed by the abridgments of their liberty to leave the hospital that they have ostensibly entered of their own free choice.

In the majority of the states (in 44 out of 50, according to Lindman and McIntyre), a voluntary mental patient may, despite his desire to leave and his written request for it, be held in the institution for periods ranging from 48 hours to 30 days. This period is intended to provide sufficient time for those interested in committing the patient to make appropriate judicial arrangements for hospitalizing him involuntarily.

Furthermore, "Four states and the Draft Act [write Lindman and McIntyre] specify that hospitalization proceedings cannot be initiated against a voluntary patient unless he has requested his release."(4) Although this provision is a clear admission that voluntary mental patients are actually, or at least potentially, prisoners—their incarceration remaining tacit so long as they do not challenge it—Lindman and McIntyre interpret this arrangement as follows:

> The implicit intent of this provision is probably to prevent patients from concerning themselves with the threat of involuntary hospitalization. One wonders, however, if the same provision may not have the effect of making some patients afraid to request release. The states which do not have such a provision presumably can initiate at any time involuntary hospitalization procedures against voluntary patients who exhibit the characteristics bringing them within the purview of involuntary hospitalization laws.(5)

This brief review of the laws governing voluntary psychiatric hospitalization makes it unmistakably clear that what is called "voluntary mental hospitalization" is often actually a type of involuntary mental hospitalization. Typically, this is the case when a person is forced to sign himself in as a voluntary patient under the threat of commitment, and when, having been admitted to the hospital as an ostensibly voluntary patient, he is not unqualifiedly free to leave when he wishes.

A recent court decision offers further support for the foregoing critical interpretation of the true nature of voluntary mental hospitalization.

COURT INTERPRETATION

A woman who admitted herself as a voluntary patient in the Utah State Hospital died. Her heirs sued the hospital for her "wrongful death." The hospital claimed immunity under the Governmental Immunity Act and was upheld by the Supreme Court of Utah.(6) The Court's decision was based on what it regarded as the fundamental similarities between jail and mental hospital:

> We are of the opinion that in reading the whole section [of the Utah Governmental Immunity Act], the words "other place of confinement"

obviously referred to something other than a "jail" or "state prison," including a hospital where one cannot be released without some kind of permission. . . . There was no request here for a release, but even so, counsel's urgence that there was or is no involuntary confinement or restraint under the act cannot stand the test of the statute cited. . . .

It is true that a patient may demand his release forthwith—*except* that he cannot obtain it if the superintendent, within 48 hours of such a demand or request, goes to court to prevent it, which action, if pursued successfully may result in no release at all, and may result in "confinement" or "incarceration" for the patient's lifetime. Hence, it is obvious that the patient is "confined" against his will for whatever period of time he has been at the hospital, up to the time he demands his release, and even then he is confined for another 48 hours waiting for the superintendent to act. . . . We think the legislature had no intention of waiving sovereign immunity in the case where a hospital attendant or guard is involved any more than it did where a nurse in a prison or a jailer is involved, and in logic and sense it seems that to treat the two differently would reflect a departure from legislative intent, simply by playing upon the adjectives "voluntary" and "involuntary," when it is obvious that there was a "confinement" at the time of the injury. . . .

We might suggest that a voluntary patient at the hospital is as much "confined" and has as little freedom as a mentally alert trusty in a jail or prison.(7)

In short, there is no such thing as voluntary mental hospitalization, nor can there be so long as there is involuntary mental hospitalization.

IMPLICATIONS FOR VOLUNTARY PATIENTS

Although this decision of the Supreme Court of Utah leaves no doubt about the actual status of the so-called voluntary mental patient, its implications—especially for law and psychiatry—invite two comments.

In the first place, if it is generally true that voluntary mental patients are in effect prisoners (the Court compared them to "trusties" in jail), present legal and psychiatric practices regarding voluntary mental hospitalization are nothing but strategies of entrapment: to avoid the inconvenience of involuntary hospitalization, increasing numbers of Americans are seduced or coerced into assuming the status of involuntary mental patient "voluntarily."

Secondly, if mental-hospital patients—even voluntary mental patients—"have as little freedom as a mentally alert trusty in a jail," it follows that psychiatrists who confine such persons in mental hospitals behave like jailers, not like doctors. This confronts university administrators and medical and psychiatric educators with a moral dilemma: Are medical schools and psychiatric residency programs the appropriate institutions in our society for the training of jailers and wardens?

For a long time, medical schools and their affiliated hospitals have trained physicians to deprive patients, under the guise of mental illness and treatment, of their liberty. Neither medical schools nor any other institutions of learning have trained professionals to help mental-hospital patients regain their liberty. This is as if law schools trained their students only to serve as prosecutors, and as if there were no academic or professional recognition of a legitimate need for defense lawyers—district attorneys being defined and socially accredited as the protectors of the "best interests" of the accused.

I believe that we can evade the moral and political character of mental hospitalization no longer. The Supreme Court of one of the states has now ruled that even a voluntary mental patient is "confined and has as little freedom as a mentally alert trusty in jail or prison." The time has come for university administrators, and for medical and legal educators to re-examine their responsibility for supporting the present principles and practices of psychiatric hospitalization.

NOTES

(1)Webster's defines "voluntary" and "involuntary" as follows: "Voluntary: 1. Proceeding from the will or from one's own choice or consent. 2. Unconstrained by interference: self-determining . . . 5. Having power of free choice . . . Involentary: 1. Done contrary to or without choice. 2. Compulsory. 3. Not subject to control of the will . . . "

(2)The Mentally Disabled and the Law: The Report of the American Bar Foundation on the rights of the mentally ill. Edited by Ft Lindman, DM McIntyre Jr. Chicago, University of Chicago Press, 1961, pp 107-115.

(3)*Idem*: pp 108-109

(4)*Idem*: p 113

(5)*Idem*: p 113-114

(6)Emery vs State, 483 P 2d. 1296 (1971)

(7)*Idem*: pp 1297-1298

CONDITIONAL VOLUNTARY
MENTAL-HOSPITAL ADMISSION

A. Louis McGarry
Milton Greenblatt

No more troubling responsibility exists for judges and physicians than their involvement in the involuntary commitment of the mentally ill. The desirability of voluntary admission as an alternative even under conditional circumstances (such as notice in writing in advance of intention to leave) has therefore been little questioned. Authorities in the field have accordingly given support to the practice of so-called "conditional voluntary" admission to mental hospitals.(1,2)

Although Dr. Szasz(3) challenges the practice of conditional voluntary mental-hospital admission, his main attack is on the social policy that authorizes involuntary mental-hospital admission, and he favors its total abolition. Many people of goodwill and good intentions are being misled by this simplistic approach to public policy.

A major flaw in the abolitionist position concerning involuntary mental-hospital commitment is that it is dated. This idea had much more relevance 20 years ago than today. Not taken into account are the extraordinary improvements in the care and management of the mentally ill in recent decades. In the last 10 years, the doors of most mental hospitals have been opened. If a mental patient, whether on voluntary or involuntary status, wants to go home, for the most part, he has only to put one foot before the other. Thus, at Boston State Hospital in fiscal 1971, 2492 patients who received residential care and treatment on 1367 occasions left the hospital on their own decision. In only 165 cases did the hospital designate the departure as an "escape"—i.e., seriously dangerous to the patient or others; hardly the characteristics of a jail or of jailors. It would be a curious jail, indeed, that permitted unilateral withdrawal by its prisoners many hundreds of times a year.

A second fact is that there has been great progress in recent years in public mental hospitals in terms of shorter hospital stays and accelerated rates of discharge. Although more patients are being treated in such institutions each year, the census has dropped successively for the past 15 years. Thus, in 1956 the census of public mental hospitals in America was 559,000. By 1970 the figure had dropped to 339,000—and it is still falling.(1) Much of this phenomenon can be ascribed to psychotropic medication, but much also is attributable to the community focus of new programs throughout the country.

If civil commitment of the mentally ill were to be abolished altogether, what would be the consequences? Since mental-health facilities must assume responsibility for suicidal, homicidal and gravely disabled mental patients, occasions do arise when the uncontrolled exercise of freedom would result in disaster. Although, as we have indicated, the doors to facilities are for the most part open today, psychiatrists do have to manage patients who are assaultive or actively suicidal. Is it wrong to try to prevent the personal, social, and familial tragedies of unbridled assaultive and self-destructive behavior?

Dr. Szasz has written elsewhere that it is his conviction that people have a right to kill themselves.(5) Not everyone would agree. Patients who have recovered from severe depression during which they were actively suicidal would not agree. Regarding psychotic antisocial conduct dangerous to others, Dr. Szasz here, too, appears to eschew preventive measures (beyond attempts at verbal dissuasion or persuasion)(6); he advocates instead that such behavior should be subject to criminal prosecution, after the antisocial act is committed. Then, such a patient would be committed to what Dr. Szasz calls "Prison Hospitals."(6)

In the context of the ethical responsibilities of a physician dealing with a suicidal patient, Dr. Szasz has taken the position that a physician ought not to go beyond attempts at persuasion or dissuasion.(6) Presumably, if Dr. Szasz's reasoning were followed, it would be proper for the physician to confront a suicidal patient with the destructive impact that his suicide would have on those close to him. Does this begin to be something more than "persuasion" and perhaps approach "seduction" or "coercion"? When a surgeon recommends to a reluctant patient that the elective removal of a gallbladder full of stones will improve his chances of survival, as opposed to waiting until an acute cholecystitis has developed, does this represent "coercion" or "seduction"? We suggest that persuading a mentally ill person, who needs treatment, to consent to a conditional voluntary admission, with its increased measure of autonomy and dignity, is comparable to the two other examples of "persuasion" above, both of which would presumably be acceptable to Dr. Szasz.

It is essential to consider all the consequences in human terms of the abolition of involuntary mental hospitalization. Many who need treatment would not get it. This would be particularly tragic in an era, again unlike 20 years ago, when successful treatment modalities for large classes of mental illness are available, especially in the form of psychotropic medication. The human cost to such people, their families and their communities, if treatment were denied, would be incalculable.

Another predictable consequence of the abolition of civil commitment would be the sharp increase of the number of mentally ill persons who would be processed by the criminal-justice system. In California, with the recent adoption of very strict and rigid criteria for involuntary civil commitment, there has been a sharp increase in the use of criminal commitment procedures for the mentally ill.(7) In effect this criminalizes the management of many mentally ill persons. We have seen how destructive and antitherapeutic such management can be.(8)

Dr. Szasz's contention is largely correct that voluntary mental-hospital procedures in this country do have involuntary provisions that may be petitioned for by hospital authorities. However, his contention that voluntary admission ". . . . does not exist" is not accurate. Dr. Szasz cites the 1961 edition of The Mentally Disabled and the Law, but the second edition, published in 1971, lists eight states that provide by statute for unconditional voluntary, or "informal," admission as it is also called. Under "informal" admission procedures the patient is totally free to leave the hospital at any time. The book cited calls this "a new development." No statistics are given to indicate how frequently these procedures are used, however. Massachusetts "de facto" has had informal admission since 1959, when Dr. Walter Barton established it at Boston State Hospital.(9)

As officials in a state department of mental health, we can report that the greatest pressures on us come from family members and the community to admit and retain the mentally ill and retarded. Our sharpest and angriest critics among practicing legal and medical professionals and the citizenry are those who are convinced that we deny admission too frequently, that we discharge patients too soon and that we do not pursue patients who leave our hospitals without authorization.

The Rules and Regulations of the Massachusetts Department of Mental Health, by the authority of statute, have established two types of voluntary admission. One is called "voluntary" and is a true total, or "unconditional" voluntary. The second is the "conditional voluntary" admission in which the patient agrees to be retained for three days after he has given written notice of his intention to leave, and he may be subject to judicial commitment if the superintendent of the hospital so petitions a court. If hospital authorities decide that the patient must be retained, the burden is on them to prove to the satisfaction of a district-court judge that there "is substantial likelihood of serious physical harm" if the patient is discharged. If indigent, the patient is provided with an attorney to represent him at the hearing. The court, too, may appoint an independent psychiatrist to offer his opinion about the need for commitment.

We believe that "conditional voluntary" mental-hospital admission is a highly desirable alternative to involuntary commitment. It avoids the necessity of a court-mediated process with criminal overtones. Conditional voluntary status gives a much greater degree of dignity and autonomy to a patient than could possibly exist in a state that admits only on an involuntary basis.(10) The conditional voluntary admission (rather than being a fraud) has proved in practice to be a reasonable contractual compromise in the best interest of both patients and the community. It has helped to destigmatize mental-hospital admission. It is hoped that informal or totally voluntary admission will be used increasingly, but there will probably continue to be a few mentally ill citizens who will require conditional voluntary admission and a few who will require involuntary admission.

Massachusetts was the first state to adopt the practice of voluntary admission to mental-health facilities in 1881.(10) Recently, great progress has been made under our new mental-health code.(11) During the first three months of its operation (November, 1971, to January, 1972) 77.2 percent of our admissions were conditional voluntary, as compared to 28.8 percent for the corresponding period of the year before.

The abolition of involuntary mental hospitalization would have destructive and regressive consequences. Its practical effect would bring about a situation in which misdemeanor charges such as "disturbing the peace" or "disorderly conduct" would increasingly be leveled against the mentally ill for disturbed behavior, and commitment would be accomplished under criminal procedures. Abolition would be a large step backward on the long road that we have traversed since the mentally ill and the criminal were lumped together and their isolation from society enforced by high walls, locked doors and neglect.

NOTES

(1) Laws Governing Hospitalization of the Mentally Ill. Group Adv. Psychiatry [Rep] 618, 1966.
(2) The Mentally Disabled and the Law. Revised edition. Edited by SJ Brakel, RS Rock. Chicago, University of Chicago Press, 1971. pp 464-465 (Appendix A. A Draft Act).
(3) Szasz TS: Voluntary mental hospitalization: an unacknowledged practice of medical fraud. N Engl J. Med. 287:277-278, 1972.
(4) Kanno CK: Eleven Indices. Washington, DC, The Joint Information Service of the American Psychiatric Association and the National Association for Mental Health, 1971, p. 9.
(5) Szasz TS: Law, Liberty and Psychiatry: An inquiry into the social uses of mental health practices. New York, The MacMillan Company, 1963, p 229.
(6) *Idem*: p 227.
(7) Abramson MF: The criminalization of mentally disordered behavior: possible side-effect of a new mental health law. Hosp Community Psychiatry 23:101-105, 1972.
(8) McGarry, AL, Bendt, RH: Criminal vs civil commitment of psychotic offenders: a seven-year follow-up. Am J Psychiatry 125:1387-1394, 1970.
(9) McGarry, AL: From coercion to consent. N Engl J Med 274:39, 1966.
(10) The Mentally Disabled and the Law, p 18.
(11) Chapter 888, Acts of 1970, Commonwealth of Massachusetts, as amended by Chapter 470, Acts, 1971.

VII

MEDICINE
AND THE
CRIMINAL

VII. MEDICINE AND THE CRIMINAL

INTRODUCTION

Concomitant with the development of medicine and psychiatry is the recognition of the medical and psychiatric aspects of crime. Classical criminology borrowed much from medicine and relied heavily upon genetic and hereditary factors for the understanding of crime. The subsequent growth of psychiatry gave a new emphasis upon the psychopathological vision of criminal behavior, which later gave way to sociological theories. Most recently, however, new claims are again being made for the genetic and neuro-psychiatric explanations of criminal conduct.

Since World War II, extensive studies of the psychiatric implications of criminal behavior have been made. As a result, the psychiatric aspects of criminality have become fairly well understood. Unfortunately, few comparable studies of other medical aspects of criminal behavior have been made, but from some studies undertaken, it is obvious that organic disease often plays a role in criminality.

The involvement of psychiatry in criminal law has had many desirable consequences. Because of its emphasis upon treatment, psychiatry has tended to humanize the correctional system. Psychiatry has also helped to produce a better understanding of the offender and his psychological inadequacies. Yet in the struggle between traditional penology and modern treatment, psychiatry is often a helpless pawn pulled in all directions by expert adversaries.

Medical or psychiatric professionals have consequently, and too frequently, found themselves not in their traditional role of therapist, but in a debate with their own professional colleagues as well as with skeptical legal opponents. Consequently, the role of medicine in the criminal law system has become obscure to (or even misunderstood by) the public, unwelcome to the physician, and a holiday for combative lawyers.

The articles that have been included deal not only with traditional issues of medicine and crime, but report the ongoing debate regarding the use of behavior control techniques in the penal system, particularly in the treatment of recidivists.

CRIMINAL RESPONSIBILITY AND COMPETENCY AS INFLUENCED BY ORGANIC DISEASE

Earl F. Rose

It is customary to classify diseases as either organic or functional. Organic diseases are those with demonstrable pathology, that is, with gross microscopic or biochemical abnormalities. These are associated with morphologic changes, disorders of energy utilization and metabolism, and interference with the organs' supply of oxygen and nutrients. In functional diseases there are no demonstrable anatomical, biochemical, or physiological abnormalities. It is the functional mental illnesses such as the neurosis, schizophrenia, and manic depressive psychosis that have been emphasized in the law and literature of criminal responsibility and competency, almost to the exclusion of the organic disease syndromes.(1)

Organic disease as a cause of altered conduct is not a recent medical observation. As early as 1912, Karl Bonhoeffer(2) described reversible psychoses that he called "exogenous reactions" brought about by organic disease or exposure to toxic substances. Today, there are a number of such diseases which suggest that an affected person is more likely to react with criminal behavior when placed in a particular situation. Probes into these areas are evidenced by the recent medical literature and occasional judicial rulings concerning genetic defects in criminals. Genetic abnormalities and other organic disease conditions lend themselves to clinical evaluation, laboratory quantification, and scientific diagnosis to a greater degree than do the functional psychoses that psychiatrists are concerned with. However, this does not imply that functional psychoses are less real than organic disease. The finding of an organic disease that is capable of affecting conduct could be of significance both in predicting the individual's potential for criminal behavior and, when considered from purely the legal standpoint, in determining criminal intent or competency and in assessing sanctions.

It is the purpose of this article to survey legally significant organic diseases that may be contributing factors in criminal conduct or lead to criminal incompetency. An exhaustive cataloging of diseases is not intended, but rather the goal is to create an awareness in the practicing attorney, who finds himself defending an individual of questionable mental stability, of the possible medical theories that may be argued in defending his client. It is hoped that the material presented herein will alert the attorney to the necessity of seeking an expert medical opinion whenever the attorney suspects that his client is suffering from some mental abnormality.

The organic diseases to be considered are: metabolic and endocrine disturbances; infections; neoplasia (cancer); senility; genetic abnormalities; alcohol, delirium tremens, and drugs; and organic brain lesions, rage reactions, and seizures. Before discussing the individual organic disease syndromes associated with altered mental function and aberrant behavior, it may be useful to briefly review: 1. the concepts of criminal competency and criminal responsibility; 2. the applicable principles of criminal psychiatry; 3. the legal tests for competency and responsibility; and 4. the level of medical certainty necessary to establish organic disease and to demonstrate a causal-connection between the disease and the criminal act.

There is a clear legal distinction between criminal responsibility (insanity) and criminal competency. Criminal competency is related to the time period beginning after the act has been committed and ending with sentencing. The criteria of criminal incompetency are inability of the accused to understand the nature and purpose of the proceedings against him, inability to assist counsel in defense, and inability to understand the nature and purpose of a sentence upon conviction. Incompetence of the accused tolls the criminal proceedings, but it does not affect his ultimate criminal liability if he was sane at the time of his acts. If there is a question as to the accused's mental competence, a hearing(3) will be ordered at the urging of either the defense counsel or prosecutor, or upon the court's own motion.(4) This, however, does not preclude the offering of additional evidence of incompetency or lack of responsibility at the time of trial.

In the United States the issue of mental disorder in criminal law has conventionally been associated with the defense of insanity. Lack of responsibility—the active doctrine of *mens rea* (guilty mind or criminal intent)—at the time of the commission of the act is a complete defense. This concept is based on the assumption that a person has a capacity to control his behavior and to choose between alternative courses of conduct. The plea of not guilty by reason of insanity, whether based on a functional psychosis or organic disease, puts in issue the existence of a particular mental condition essential to the commission of a crime.(5) Although the precise test of insanity varies with the jurisdiction, two general requirements are evidence of mental disease or defect and evidence of a causal relationship between the mental disease or defect and the criminal act. It should be pointed out that the evidence necessary to establish either of the above requirements may not be sufficient to warrant commitment to a mental institution for treatment.

The oldest of the commonly used legal tests for criminal responsibility is the "right-wrong" test or *M'Naghten* rule.(6) Under this rule if, at the time of the criminal act, the accused was either laboring under such a defect of reason from disease of the mind that he did not know the nature and quality of his act, or if he did know the nature and quality of this act he did not know right from wrong, he is legally insane.

In some American jurisdictions the *M'Naghten* rule has been supplemented by the "irresistible impulse" doctrine. This doctrine holds that even though one accused of a crime knows the nature and quality of his act and knows it is wrong, if he is compelled to do the act by an impulse which he is unable to control because of a disease of the mind, he is to be found not guilty.(7) Some members of the medical community have cast doubt on the "irresistible impulse" doctrine by maintaining that if there is a mental disease which would cause an irresistible impulse, there would also be sufficient impairment to provide the accused with an adequate defense under the *M'Naghten* rule. (It is well documented that organic disease can and does on occasion precipitate rage reactions that are uncontrollable even though the individual is conscious at the time.)

The *Durham* rule,(8) adopted by the Court of Appeals of the District of Columbia, proceeds on the assumption that there is no adequate legal test for insanity. Rather it is best handled as a question of fact as to whether the criminal act was the result or *product* of the mental condition. Under this rule the question of whether the accused was insane at the time of his acts and whether his insanity caused the wrongful acts are left to the jury.

Finally, the *Freeman* rule, which is found in the Model Penal Code of the American Law Institute, provides as follows:

> A person is not responsible for criminal conduct if at the time of such conduct as a result of mental disease or defect he lacked substantial capacity either to appreciate the wrongfulness of his conduct or to conform his conduct to the requirements of the law.(9)

This rule represents a softening of the stringent requirements of the *M'Naghten* rule by recognizing that total incapacity from mental disease or defect should not be a required minimum, but instead, substantial mental impairment is enough.

For the accused to escape accountability for his acts because of incompetency or insanity there must be specific medical testimony establishing lack of responsibility for the act, the defendant's inability to comprehend the nature of the charges against him, or his inability to effectively cooperate with counsel in his defense.(10) These requirements must be met for organic diseases as well as for functional mental disturbances. However, as noted above, organic diseases more readily lend themselves to clinical evaluation, diagnostic procedures, and laboratory testing. Juries tend to accept laboratory results because of their ease of application, objectivity, and relatively high reliability. But the mere fact that there is an abnormal laboratory result, or that the accused suffers from an organic disease does not establish lack of responsibility or criminal incompetency. To testify as to criminal competency or responsibility, the physician need only be able to form the type of clinical opinion that he is accustomed to relying upon in the practice of his profession.(11) It need not consist of mathematically demonstrable certainties.

When it is claimed that there is an organic disease underlying criminal conduct or incompetency, there are two issues to be proven. First, it must be demonstrated by medical evidence that the accused suffers from an organic disease. As noted above, this is a relatively easy task. Second, a causal connection between the disease and the conduct at either the time of the alleged act or the mental condition at the time of the hearing must be shown. The mere fact that the client may have engaged in conduct that was offensive, repulsive, or objectionable is not a sufficient justification for ruling him incompetent or not responsible.(12) When the question of intent or mental competency is in issue, it must be determined whether the objectives in the mind of the accused were the same as the act performed. The role of the disease in either attenuating control of action or influencing conduct must be critically evaluated and presented in the most favorable light, for the law assumes that the act bespeaks the mind. The fact that organic diseases frequently progress and are often easier to demonstrate than are functional disturbances may lighten the burden of the defense counsel to some extent. However, it should be remembered that the mere fact that an individual has a mental disturbance which is precipitated by an organic disease does not mean that he is incapable of functioning normally in society. For example, diabetes is considered to be an incurable disease but it can be controlled so that the patient can live a normal life. The same can be said for a variety of conduct-influencing organic diseases that can be linked with aggressive or criminal behavior.

METABOLIC AND ENDOCRINE DISTURBANCES

It is hardly an exaggeration to say that every disturbance of metabolism, whether it is a disease of the liver, intestinal tract, kidney, or lung, is reflected to some extent in the functioning of the brain. And it is true that a metabolic disorder with cerebral manifestations may be severe enough to cause either coma or death. Examples include diabetes and uremia which are both disorders of metabolism. Nevertheless, there are few legally significant metabolic disorders, for as a group they are seldom characterized by aggressive or hostile behavior or psychotic reactions. Frequently, when aggressive behavior does occur, it is in a hospital setting and consequently there is no prosecution for injury-producing conduct. The individual may become unable to cooperate with counsel or understand the nature of the legal proceedings as the disease becomes clinically apparent weeks, months, or even years following the prohibited conduct.

Disabling neurologic disorders frequently develop in patients with advanced liver disease. These disorders are characterized by recurrent disturbances of consciousness, impaired intellectual function, neuromuscular abnormalities, and a slowing of the electroencephalogram. Behavioral disturbances include irrational behavior, drowsiness, delirium, convulsions, slowing of thinking, and frank psychosis.(13) In primary liver disease the cause of mental aberrations has not been established, but evidence suggests that they are due to abnormal concentrations of metabolites, particularly nitrogenous substances, accumulating in the body and affecting the nervous system. The brain is very susceptible to toxic substances and, in addition, when there is chronic liver damage, the cerebral metabolism is impaired. This explains the exquisite sensitivity of patients with severe liver disease to opiates, sedatives, lack of oxygen, and electrolyte imbalances. In some instances cerebral and hepatic damage are independent effects of the same agent. Dietary deficiencies such as beriberi and pallegra, or metabolic disorders such as Wilson's disease, may injure both the brain and the liver.(14) Anatomic changes of the central nervous system may on occasion occur in liver disease and are a manifestation of irreversible lesions.

Either a deficiency or excess of functioning insulin constitute metabolic disorders of the type predisposing to aberrant behavior. Diabetes mellitus, a genetically determined error of carbohydrate metabolism, is characterized by an insufficient amount of functioning insulin resulting from a disproportion between the requirements of the body for insulin and the ability of the islets of the pancreas to meet the demand. When the need for functioning insulin is not met, fats and proteins are used instead of the normally metabolized sugars, and toxic substances and metabolic acids accumulate in the body. Behavioral changes frequently accompany the accumulation of these acids, a phenomenon that was claimed to have caused criminal incompetence in the case of *Featherston v. Clark*.(15) In this case the defendant in an income tax evasion prosecution claimed that he had blackouts lasting from 48 to 72 hours. During these blackouts he would transact business and behave normally, but would not be fully aware of what he was doing. Later, he could not remember what transpired during the blackouts. These periods would come and go with no outward warning, and they could not be detected without chemical tests even by a physician. The court found that the accused should be committed to a governmental facility for an examination as to his mental competence, and that when the case came to retrial, it might be necessary to take a blood test of the accused every morning and to keep him under the constant supervision of a physician.

An excess of insulin, hyperinsulinism or insulin shock may result from an overdose of insulin used in treating diabetes, from benign or from malignant tumors of the pancreas, or from insulin-like material that on occasion is liberated from tumors in other parts of the body. The excess insulin causes the level of the blood sugars to fall, resulting in hypoglycemia with symptoms of faintness, incoherent speech, irritability, hostility, and the outstanding characteristic of hypoglycemia (aggressiveness).(16) Complete and prompt relief of the hypoglycemic attack can be obtained by the administration of sugars, but if the cause of the hyperinsulinism is not treated the attacks will recur.

The porphyrias are a group of metabolic disorders characterized by episodic abdominal pain, sensitivity to sunlight, and intermittent bouts of behavioral disturbances similar to toxic psychosis with symptoms varying from irritability and a demanding attitude calculated to arouse hostility in others to aggressiveness, delirium, and hallucinations. Porphyrias result from an error of metabolism in which heme (blood) synthesis regulation is disturbed and there is an overproduction, accumulation, and excretion of the porphyrin and porphyrin precursors. The disease occurring in adolescents and young adults is usually genetically determined although acute intermittent porphyria can skip generations and some genetic carriers show no abnormality in porphyrin excretion.(17) Symptoms of abdominal pain, drowsiness, hysteria-like behavior, and depression may manifest early in life with more severe character changes developing in later adulthood. The various psychotic symptoms occur in over 50 percent of individuals with the overt disease.(18)

In a series of cases involving individuals with acute intermittent porphyria the legal dispositions included institutionalizing 20 percent for mental illness.(19) The same author that reported the above cases noted a frequent preoccupation with suicidal thoughts and cited one verified attempt to commit suicide. Degenerative changes throughout the nervous system may render the individual permanently damaged. Unfortunately, the porphyrias are difficult to diagnose and, in addition, acute attacks producing personality changes, agitation, and mood disorders may be precipitated or aggravated by drugs or other illnesses. Barbiturates, sulfa drugs, estrogens, anticonvulsants, pregnancy, acute infections, and the ingestion of alcohol present particular dangers to people with porphyrias. The true incidence of porphyrias in the mental hospital population has not been determined because the excretion of the abnormal substances evidencing the disease are also found during remissions.

Hormones, substances produced by the endocrine glands, are important in influencing behavior and modifying brain function. Although the interaction between the endocrines and the nervous system is complex and poorly understood,(20) behavioral disturbances due to endrocrinopathies are probably due to influences upon brain metabolism. The basis for this view is best illustrated by hyperfunction of the thyroid gland, a condition called hyperthydroidism or Graves' disease. People with hyperthyroidism tend to overreact to external stimuli by developing anxiety, apprehension, irritability, and manic excitement. Hallucinations and a paranoid state with systematized delusions may also exist. However, there is relatively little basic scientific information to explain why this may on occasion lead to aggressive, antisocial, or criminal behavior. It has been suggested that although these are somatic psychoses, they are also psychogenic in an individual with a pre-existing mental disturbance.

Postpartum psychosis and postpartum depression may also be explained by rapid hormonal fluctuations. Despite the gratification a woman usually experiences after the birth of a healthy infant, there is statistically a four to five-fold increase of transient psychosis immediately following the birth of a child(21) which may be attributable to hormonal fluctuations. English law has recognized that the mother of an infant is vulnerable to killing the infant (infanticide) by treating a woman with leniency if she kills her child prior to its attaining the age of one year.(22) This would seem to lend legal credence to the concept of altered responsibility resulting from metabolic disturbances. However, because of the medical uncertainties involved, one cannot form an opinion as to the competency of a woman committing infanticide that would be admissible in a court of law.

INFECTIONS

Mental aberrations and behavioral disorders can result from either a direct invasion of the brain or meninges by infectious organism or from an infection located elsewhere in the body accompanied by fever or a toxic-infectious type of reaction. The infectious diseases most frequently affecting cerebral function include influenza, typhus fever, meningitis, encephalitis, rabies, infestations, and neurosyphilis. The affected cerebral function during the acute phase of the disease is referred to as a febrile delirium. Occasionally the delirium may develop during the prodromal period before there has been a rise in temperature. The spectrum of mental changes ranges from irritability and agitation to a full-blown psychosis including hallucinations, delirium, and delusions. There may be periods of lucidity and calmness alternating with rapid shifts to fear and terror accompanied by retrograde amnesia.(23) During a terror period a patient may do great harm to another or himself, but obviously, a person with this type of reaction is incapable of forming the intent to purposefully harm another or commit suicide.

It is in this context that the physician or hospital may be found negligent in failing to provide adequate protection for the patient. In the recent case of *Lord v. United States*(24), involving a suit brought under the Federal Tort Claims Act, a judgment against the hospital was settled for $75,000. In this case a patient hospitalized for an infectious asthmatic condition took his own life by jumping from a ninth-floor hospital window. The suit alleged the hospital was negligent in leaving the patient unattended when it was known or should have been known that there was a significant risk of self-injury. Malpractice liability may also arise where an alcoholic or drug user arrives at a hospital suffering with a toxic bacterial psychosis and no tests are conducted to discover this condition.(25)

Psychosis is not uncommon with the various forms of viral encephalitis, a disease that may occur sporadically or in epidemic proportions. Rabies encephalitis is associated with lesions primarily of Ammon's horn and is characterized by marked aggressive behavior which often begins as a hallucinatory experience or delusional distortion of the environment.(26) However, because rabies is uniformly fatal, the issue of criminal responsibility for aggressive behavior does not arise. Other encephalitides may not be fatal and the mental symptoms may be either acute during the infectious stage of the disease or chronic due to residual injury to the brain. During the acute phase of the encephalitis, there is often depression of cortical function with lethargy, stupor, slowness of intellectual function and coma. Symptoms include irritability with restlessness, excitability, and delirium. Behavioral changes following the disease are attributable to cortical pathway injury rendering the cerebral cortex unable to exert an inhibitory effect on aggressive drives. Fortunately, the disturbances following these diseases are usually confined to motor function.

The effect of syphilis on the nervous system is too well recognized to warrant an extended discussion. Suffice to say that this disease has not been conquered and that the progressive degeneration of the brain becomes manifest many years after the primary disease. Early symptoms of central nervous system syphilis consist largely of exaggerations of previous personality traits. An individual whose previous life was exemplary may on occasion cease to conform to social norms. He may be unkempt, inconsiderate, lacking in social amenities, and quarrelsome. There may also be a breakdown of higher ethical and cultural sentiments and standards. The moderate user of alcohol may become dissipated and his sexual activities may become excessive. Later, delusions of grandiose nature develop which either may reach the height of absurdity or become persecutory or depressive. Progressive dementia ultimately follows.

NEOPLASIA

Neoplasma (new growths or cancers) of organs other than the brain may lead to disorders of the nervous system with resulting behavioral aberations—symptoms not due to the presence of metastasis or pressure from the neoplasm. It is only within the past twenty years that these types of neurological disorders have been clearly defined and classified.(27) Their incidence has been estimated from slightly over one percent to five percent of those persons with a cancer.(28) The highest incidence of altered behavior is associated with carcinoma of the lung.(29) Neurological syndromes associated with tumors may take several forms and involve any level of the nervous system.(30)

When these syndromes occur, the patient may show dementia of varying severity, progressive deterioration of the intellectual function and memory, or severe disorders of mood with agitated depression and anxiety. The reason for these symptoms is puzzling for in most instances no pathologic or morphologic changes can be demonstrated to account for the altered behavior and mental symptoms. The tumor appears to intoxicate the host in a subtle way and the existence of a number of *neoplasticae noxae*, toxins arising in the neoplasm, have been postulated. Although the presence of such a single "cerebral toxic agent" has not been established this is the simplest explanation. The nervous system is very sensitive to abnormalities of hormonal secretion and hormones or substances with a wide spectrum of hormonal activity have been isolated from primary tumors of practically every organ in the body.(31) These tumor-hormone-secretions can produce a wide range of metabolic abnormalities. An example of this is the production of insulin-like material with activity leading to a hypoglycemic (low blood sugar) state evidenced by abnormal electroencephalography.(32) This is more than an academic medical exercise since some of these tumors grow slowly thereby permitting surgical resection which can produce long-term remissions and occasionally a cure.

SENILITY AND CEREBRAL ARTERIOSCLEROSIS

Senility consists of progressive mental deterioration with brain atrophy and loss of memory. In many instances arteriosclerosis is a causal part of senile dementia. Senility begins gradually and is progressive in character. In its gradual advance to incompetency it embraces a wide range of infirmities.

The occurrence of a criminal act by one over sixty years old, particularly a first offense, should bring to mind the possibility of an organic degenerative mental disease, for aggressive criminal behavior in those past sixty is unusual.(33) Aggressive behavior, loss of emotional control, and failure to grasp concepts are patterns to be noted during the earlier phases of the cerebral aging process. As the degenerative process progresses, there is a decline in awareness of the surroundings and aggressive tendencies subside resulting in affectlessness and ultimately in a state of apathy.(34) Although there may be fluctuations on a daily basis, the course is usually progressive. Sexual offenses by the elderly can frequently be attributed to senile degeneration of the brain or to an arteriosclerotic insufficiency of the cerebral vessels. These conditions may deprive the patient of control of sexual desire, while not infrequently, increasing the desire itself. This results in a breach of decorum and sometimes attempts at crime, especially upon children because they are physically weaker than the assailant. Mental impairment may be slight at this state of the disease. More violent acts in aged men, such as attempts to kill a spouse or other relatives, often arise in a setting of mental disorder and may be perpetrated in a most brutal manner. But what may seem to be a crime directed against a person or property or an accident, often on closer inspection may prove to be a suicide attempt.

The excitement surrounding an investigation of criminal activity may further confuse the individual who has the early manifestations of senility. Although there may be no loss of intellect with the criminal behavior, the offender may become incompetent to stand trial because of a deterioration of his mental competency between the time the act was committed and trial. This deterioration itself is evidence that degenerative cerebral disease was a factor in the original act. In these subjects life expectancy is reduced and frank dementia, with overt pathological changes of the brain, is usually manifest within a short time after the prohibited act.

GENETIC ABNORMALITIES

Inherited constitution has an important role not only in predisposing man to disease but in producing disease. The role genetically determined diseases play in personality and conduct, particularly in provoking anti-social or criminal activity, is not yet understood. That these conditions may be of legal significance is demonstrated by recent legal and medical publications which have implicated inherited diseases with chromosomal abnormalities as being a causal factor in criminal conduct.(35) In order to anticipate current and future developments the attorney needs some familiarity with the basic principles of genetics.

Basic to all of the living world and the science of genetics is the concept of heredity information carried by genes. Many thousands of these genes are arranged in linear order along the lengths of the chromosomes. Normally there are 46 chromosomes in the cell of each human, one-half of this number, or 23, are inherited from each parent. Some of the genes are responsible for the synthesis of a particular enzyme or protein, others regulate the control of protein production, while still others determine the chemical and physical attributes by which the individual is known.

Of immediate medical-legal significance are the sex chromosomes. The sex chromosomes of the human female, a pair of equal size, are called X chromosomes (XX). In the human male there is one X chromosome which is paired with a smaller Y chromosome (XY). During the division of the chromosomes from either parent, the sex chromosome may fail to divide causing either the ova or the sperm, as the case may be, to contain an abnormal chromosome pattern. These chromosomal abnormalities are not limited to the sex chromosomes, but may also affect the somatic tissue. A common example of somatic chromosome defect is the so-called Down's syndrome, the trisomy 21, or Mongolism.

Criminals and mentally defective men with an XYY chromosomal pattern (karyotype) have provoked a great deal of current medical-legal interest. This abnormality was first reported in 1961,(36) followed in 1965 by the discovery of a high prevalence of XYY among men with criminal records in a maximum security hospital.(37) This finding has been confirmed by studies done in prisons, mental hospitals, and male juvenile delinquency centers.(38) The incidence of this condition in criminal offenders is approximately eight times that of a comparable group of mentally deficient males and approximately 89 times the incidence in the general population.(39) There is an association of the XYY phenotype with aggressive or antisocial behavior and, on occasion, mental impairment. The incidence of the syndrome approaches that of mongolism, which occurs once in every 600 births.

Why the extra Y chromosome affects conduct is yet unknown; however, experimental work with certain fish has shown that it is possible to breed male fish with two Y chromosomes and no X chromosome.(40) These fish demonstrate physical superiority, undue belligerence, and unusual sexual prowess. It has been postulated that the Y chromosome acts as a mediator for the production of testosterone and the presence of an excess of this male hormone in the circulation primes the developing central nervous system to its greater aggressive tendencies. The presence of an extra Y chromosome can thus precipitate the chain of events leading to the development of excessively aggressive individuals. An elevated level of testosterone has been demonstrated in some, but not all persons with an extra Y chromosome.

Obviously, it cannot at this time be conclusively shown that the XYY syndrome causes criminal behavior. The limited data does not permit an unqualified assertion that the XYY chromosomal defect, although found many times more frequently in a criminal population, is the cause of antisocial behavior. Given our present level of medical knowledge all that can be said is that an extra Y chromosome (karyotype) may have an effect on the susceptibility to abnormal behavior which becomes apparent only on exposure to adverse environmental circumstances. The legal question is whether individuals with these abnormal sex-chromosome complements can be held to suffer from *diminished* or lack of responsibility. At trial the evidence dealing with the chromosomal defect would be admissible only if medical experts could establish with a reasonable degree of medical certainty that there was a causal link between the abnormality and the individual's conduct. However, even if lack of responsibility cannot be proved, the showing that the XYY defect makes it difficult for a person to restrain his aggressiveness may be of value in mitigating punishment.(41) It can be said that research in medical genetics must progress a great deal before this information can be used in the courts to show lack of criminal responsibility.

INTOXICATION, DELIRIUM TREMENS, AND DRUGS

Instances of the deliberate or unwitting use and abuse of alcohol, chemicals, and drugs are probably far more prevalent than is commonly recognized. Industrial or other environmental exposure to toxic substances is also possible. Hydrocarbons and halogenated hydrocarbons such as are found in glue, gasoline, or cleaning fluids are usually sniffed with the deliberate intent of inducing a "high". Inhalation of these toxic substances, particularly gasoline, leads to aberrant behavior during intoxication, and if used repeatedly mental deterioration may result. Fainting, stupor, dream-like states, twilight-states, and depersonalization are results of drug usage; and toxic psychosis that first appears as simple intoxication may progress to delirium, schizophrenic and paranoid reactions, or hallucinotoxic psychosis. In some instances the psychotic state may persist for long periods of time independent of etiology. Although it might be said that all depressive and hallucinatory drugs are poisons of consciousness causing intoxication, the courts have not been particularly sympathetic to the plea of criminal incompetency or lack of responsibility due to the influence of chemicals, drugs, or alcohol.

For intoxication to constitute a defense to the commission of a crime there must be proof that the accused was so intoxicated as to be unable to form the specific intent required.(42) Where intoxication is so extreme and permanent as to amount to delirium tremens, it may be treated as a form of insanity.(43) On proper showing that there is a question of criminal responsibility, the court should order a hearing if significant evidence has come to its attention which indicates that the accused is currently using drugs or narcotics.(44)

Controversy presently exists as to the legal status of the chronic alcoholic. Some consider chronic alcoholism as a disease while others, equally authoritative, believe it to be a behavioral aberration with an addiction overlay. The issue of punishment of an alcoholic for public intoxication is not to be confused with the issue of criminal responsibility for conduct while under the influence of alcohol.(45) In the case of *Vick v. Alaska*(46) the court in dictum points out that to permit chronic alcoholism as a defense to the crime of public drunkenness, thus holding a person unaccountable for his acts, would logically require extending the defense to other crimes such as murder, rape, assault, and battery whenever the defendant could show that he was a chronic alcoholic. However in disallowing this defense, the court noted that among members of the medical profession, there is disagreement as to whether alcoholism is a disease. In summary, it may be said that chronic alcoholism as a defense for criminal responsibility is too tenuous to be granted legal recognition, and therefore the chronic alcoholic is not to be relieved of accountability for his acts because of his drinking habits.

Delirium tremens, one of the forms of alcoholic psychosis, has fared somewhat better in the courts as a defense for prohibited conduct than has the claim of chronic alcoholism. Delirium tremens is an acute mental disturbance marked by delirium with great excitement, anxiety, and mental distress. An episode of delirium tremens may occasionally occur spontaneously in the chronic alcoholic or it may be precipitated by withholding alcohol from the individual. It is clearly accepted by physicians that this syndrome obliterates comprehension, and therefore, a person suffering from delirium tremens is not responsible for the consequences of his conduct. Physicians traditionally have considered delirium tremens to be more serious in its effects than has the law. The medical viewpoint is summarized in a statement by Doctor Henry Davidson. "In delirium tremens . . . the patient is clearly in no condition to plan, deliberate, weigh consequences, evaluate the wrongfulness of the act, or understand its quality."(47) On the other hand, the law holds that delirium tremens *may* obliterate comprehension of conduct and the likely consequences of particular conduct. This position is typified by the case of *Horn v. Kentucky*,(48) where the court stated:

> If the temporary insanity produced by delirium tremens is not to the degree or extent of temporarily depriving the accused of knowledge of right or wrong, or the ability to comprehend the effects of his act in committing the crime, then his condition would not furnish a total defense.

The extent of adverse reactions and toxic psychosis due to sedatives, tranquilizers, and depressants in the total prevalence of abnormal conduct and mental illness is unknown.(49) These drugs are not only obtained by prescription or through illicit sources, but in addition, they are proprietary medications obtainable without a physician's prescription. The use of these drugs alters the state of consciousness and, on occasion, may lead to psychosis. Bromide provides the classic example of a medication which is rarely administered by the medical profession but which is capable of causing rapid deterioration and frank psychosis when taken excessively as self-medication. As for the legal implications of sedatives, tranquilizers, and depressants in regard to criminal competency and responsibility, there is judicial acknowledgement that these drugs are capable of producing an unnatural impact on the mental, physical, and emotional structure, and may cause deterioration.(50) The competency of an accused may be compromised by tranquilizers, for they may affect his attitude, appearance, and demeanor(51) and similarly a plea entered under medication by tranquilizers is subject to being set aside or withdrawn if it can be shown that the plea was improvident.(52)

Of particular note are amphetamines which are used in large amounts for weight reduction, by truck drivers and night-shift workers to stay awake on their jobs, and by many students and executives to meet every day stresses. Psychological sequelae among abusers are frequently misdiagnosed as transient de nova psychosis.(53) Although disorientation is noted at times, there is usually no clouding of the sensorium unless drugs, particularly barbiturates or alcohol, are taken concomitantly.

Amphetamine psychosis usually appears as an acute paranoid phase in a setting of clear consciousness. Auditory and visual hallucinations are often present. Most patients show distractibility, flight of ideas, pressured speech, and hyper-alert sensitivity to environmental clues.(54) After withdrawal of the drug there is a period of lassitude, sleepiness, and depression which usually clears within five to ten days but may take longer. Chronic use of amphetamine derivatives may lead to demonstrable brain lesions that will clinically be present as a form of dementia.(55)

Considering the widespread usage of Cannabis derivatives, there is a relative paucity of reported adverse reactions to smoking marihuana.(56) Adverse reactions to marihuana are varied but the experiences are said to be generally unpleasant, threatening with anxiety, fear, depression, suspicion, depersonalization, disorientation, confusion, paranoid ideation, delusions, and auditory hallucinations. There is impaired cognitive function including impairment of orientation, memory, intellectual functions and judgment. Because of its ubiquity, marihuana smoking should be considered as a casual or precipitating agent whenever a young person presents an acute psychosis having paranoid features.(57)

Lysergic acid diethylamide (LSD) is one of several hallucinogens which have lately become prominent as psychedelic drugs. LSD is similar in its effect on the individual to drugs such as mescaline found in peyote cactus, harmine found in vines, bufotehine found in mushrooms, and the more recently developed synthetics such as spylocybin and dimethyltryptamine. LSD is the most popular and easily obtainable of the hallucinogens. In a review of the pertinent medical literature, Smart and Bateman(58) listed the main features of the adverse reactions to LSD, which include along with 142 reported cases of prolonged psychotic reactions, eleven spontaneous recurrences of delusions, nineteen attempted suicides, four attempted homicides, eleven successful suicides, and one successful homicide. The self-destructive impulse occurring shortly after taking LSD is illustrated by one case report of a 20-year-old student, who had frequently taken LSD with friends, suddenly disrobing and jumping from a window.(59)

For unknown reasons, frightening delusions of hallucinations have reappeared weeks or months after the last LSD ingestion and after an interval of apparent normality. One such spontaneous recurrence of a frightening experience took place four weeks after the hallucinogen was taken and resulted in self-destruction.(60)

It appears that the LSD releases psychopatic personality trends and makes social, self-destructive, sociopathic, or criminal behavior possible in some individuals. There is one reported instance of a homicide occurring after the accused had ingested LSD—that of a 25-year-old woman who murdered her boy friend several days after taking the hallucinogen.(61) The homicide was not committed during the time the accused was experiencing the acute effects of the LSD and because she was also a chronic alcoholic with a prior diagnosis of psychopathic personality, the causual connection between the LSD and the criminal acts is uncertain. (The judicial disposition of this case is not available).

ORGANIC BRAIN DISEASE AND SEIZURES

Any organic disease of the brain, particularly lesions of the temporal lobe, frequently forms an organic basis for violence with the host being predisposed to antisocial conduct or criminal behavior. The conduct may vary from the so-called "dyscontrol syndrome" with irrational temper fits, mainfesting themselves in a variety of ways from wife and child beating, to multiple auto accidents, frank psychosis, and criminal episodes. Profound social and psychological influences also exist between temporal lobe dysfunction and criminal sexual activities ranging from exhibitionism to extreme perverse behavior.(62) The underlying causes of the organic brain lesions may vary from encephalitis, involving the limbic system of the temporal lobes, to tumors which may be primary in the brain or metastatic from other organs. On occasion, lesions of parts of the brain other than the temporal lobes are associated with aggressive behavior, dementia, or hallucinations.(63)

Pathologic rage due to organic brain disease is characterized by excitement and indiscriminate attacks against anyone who happens to be present. The rage has excessive proportions, its course is aimless, and it cannot be interrupted. Patients describe their condition as "a feeling as if the rage builds up in spite of themselves until it has conquered their thoughts and left them no choice but to let it freely run its course."(64) The mere appearance of a person, a gesture, noise, or tactile stimuli may elicit the massive outburst of rage. Cases have been reported where patients would grasp objects that happened to be near and hurl them blindly to the ground or against people in the vicinity. Serious attacks against nursing personnel and visiting relatives have been described.(65)

The possibility of a brain tumor as a cause of homicide should be considered in the case of Charles Joseph Whitman, the sniper who in August, 1966, shot 44 persons and killed 14.(66) A highly malignant tumor found in Whitman's brain may have contributed to the shooting of these 58 people. A task force appointed by Texas Governor John Connally to investigate this possibility reported:

> The relationship between the brain tumor and Charles J. Whitman's actions on the last day of his life cannot be established with clarity. However, the highly malignant brain tumor conceivably could have contributed to his inability to control his emotions and actions. Without a recent psychiatric evaluation of Charles J. Whitman, the task force finds it impossible to make a formal psychiatric diagnosis.(67)

Seizures, along with automatism and somnambulism are usually classified as disorders of consciousness with or without uncontrollable motor activity. Some authorities classify these three disorders under the common title of epileptic or epileptiform attacks; epilepsy being defined either as a condition not in itself a disease entity, but rather a symptom of disordered cerebral function with persistent liability to occasional seizures or as a symptom complex characterized by episodic variations in the state of consciousness, with or without convulsive movements, somatic sensory symptoms, visceral motor or sensory symptoms, and abnormal speech or behavior.(68) In approximately one-third of the individuals experiencing seizures there are definable antecedent causes including head trauma, brain tumors, malformations, chronic meningitis or encephalitis, and cerebrovascular lesions;(69) however, in the majority of instances the cause of the symptom complex remains unknown.

Four main categories of seizures are based on their clinical manifestations. The first category is the *grand mal* or major motor seizure. This seizure is characterized by a warning or aura, involuntary cry, loss of consciousness, a tonic phase and a clonic phase, followed by a period of unconsciousness with urinary or rectal incontinence or seminal emission. The second major category is the Jacksonian seizure which is a focal seizure, usually with motor (occasionally only sensory) or with both motor and sensory components. The seizure begins in one part of the body such as the thumb, foot, or angle of the mouth, and may spread to involve the entire extremity or face and other parts of the body. The third major category is the *petit mal* seizures or absences. These seizures, which almost always begin in childhood, last for less than a minute and are characterized either by the cessation of all activity accompanied by staring (absence), by a single or few involuntary jerking movements, or by a short period of unconsciousness and falling. The fourth major category is the psychomotor seizure and/or automatism which is characterized by psychic or motor activity, or both, continuing for longer than a minute, none of which the patient remembers. These four main categories of seizures contain only a few subvarieties or variants such as hallucinatory seizures (uncinate fits), status epilepticus, tonic or cerebellar attacks, and seizures evoked by sensory stimuli like music or running water.

The courts have been reluctant to accept the defense of inability to form criminal intent or of the presence of an irresistible impulse to excuse sudden misbehavior based upon seizure episodes(70) even in the presence of abnormal electroencephalograms.(71) Although there is demonstrable organic brain damage and uncontrollable rage reactions, the defendant has the burden of showing that the mental defect affected him *on the day of the crime* and that he lacked the capacity to form the intent to commit the crime.(72) It appears that the law regards this type of misbehavior as psychogenic and not based upon primary brain pathology over which the individual can exert little or no control.

Automatism, a variant of seizures, is the performance of nonreflex acts without conscious volition. Individuals can carry out complex automatistic activity while in this state of impaired consciousness. Automatism may be classified as normal (hypnosis), organic (temporal lobe epilepsy), psychogenic (dissociation fugue), or feigned. Extensive and painstaking investigation is necessary to clarify the diagnosis.(73) Jurists have rarely accepted automatism as a defense except to help substantiate a plea of insanity.(74)

Homicide committed in a somnambulistic trance (sleep-walking) is uncommon and is rarely used as a defense. Although a number of foreign cases indicate that such a condition will remove the necessary element of mens rea from the homicide,(75) the somnambulistic homicide defense has not fared as well in the United States. As can be attested to by August Schwartz who was convicted of murder and sentenced to life imprisonment, lack of proper intent and the defense of somnambulism do not always provide an adequate defense.(76) However, in one Kentucky case involving a sixteen-year-old girl who was said to have dreamed that robbers were in the house attacking her family, and then killed her father, her six-year-old brother and injured her mother with two guns, the defendant offered evidence that she has suffered previous nightmares and was a confirmed somnambulist. This evidence plus the prosecutor's inability to establish the proper intent resulted in the girl's acquittal.

A CASE IN POINT—JACK RUBY

The author of this Article performed the autopsy on Jack Ruby, assassin of Lee Harvey Oswald. The assassination of Oswald took place on November 24, 1963, three years, one month and ten days prior to Jack Ruby's death on January 3, 1967. The trial of Jack Ruby for homicide took place in February and March of 1964, two and one-half years before the development of symptoms heralding a lung cancer that led to his death. With the benefit of the knowledge of his disease gained through the autopsy and with the prior discussion in mind, conjecture as to the effect of organic disease on Jack Ruby's criminal competency and responsibility can be discussed.

In brief, the autopsy findings included carcinoma of the lung with local spread and metastasis to bone, lymph nodes, and brain. In addition, there was an occult primary carcinoma of the prostate gland totally distinct from the tumor of the lung; this was noted only microscopically and was not significant in his death. The terminal event was a blood clot arising in a leg vein and embolizing to the lung, a not uncommon event in people who have cancer or are confined to bed. Death was due to "pulmonary emboli secondary to carcinoma of the lung," the lung tumor being the direct cause of Jack Ruby's death.

Bundles of newsprint, articles and books have been written about the defendant, the defense strategy, and the trial.(77) The issue upon which the defense based its case was lack of consciousness at the time of the killing and the inability of Ruby, whom the defense claimed had a type of seizure, epilepsy, or epileptic variant (psychomotor epilepsy), to form the proper intent.

The biological behavior of tumors, particularly Ruby's lung tumor, represents a partial affirmative answer to the question, of "could the primary lung tumor have been present at the time of the assassination?" Although X-rays of the lungs taken in 1964 failed to reveal the presence of the tumor, it is doubtful that the diagnosis would have been made with even the most sophisticated diagnostic procedures available, for in order to be demonstrable by X-rays tumors must be quite well developed in their growth. Nevertheless, from our knowledge of the biological behavior of tumors, it must be concluded that the tumor antedated both the trial and the criminal act.(78) Similarly this tumor could well have been the source of *neoplasticae noxae*, toxins arising in tumors.

Cancers of the lung are those most often associated with systemic effects, including aberrant behavior, not attributable to tumor metastases or pressure on the brain. Tumor metastases to the brain of Ruby were demonstrated at the time of the autopsy. This is significant because electroencephalographic (EEG) abnormalities, a subject of controversy among batteries of experts, were confined to the side of the brain opposite the tumor metastasis which makes it most unlikely that the EEG abnormalities were attributable to tumor spread. Suffice it to say, the localization of the EEG abnormalities, if they did indeed exist, were not at a site of demonstrable tumor metastasis or gross abnormality. Thus, based upon the author's knowledge of medicine in general and pathology in particular, it is impossible to express a categorical scientific opinion as to the causal relationship between the lung neoplasms, the tumor spread, tumor hormones, constitutional background, and/or EEG abnormalities and the murder of Lee Harvey Oswald by Jack Ruby.

It is difficult to correlate organic disease to criminal behavior, for the causal relationship may be quite subtle. Proof might be possible if a particular type of action were relieved by the removal of a tumor or the curing of the organic disease, but this type of scientific investigation is not available to the trial court. At the time of Ruby's trial there was no suspicion of an organic disease, aside from the belabored EEG's. Indeed, this issue could not have been raised at the time of the trial, for it was not until his terminal illness that an autopsy was performed and the presence of the organic disease was discovered.

A question still unanswered is why organic disease causes aberrant behavior in one person and not in another? There are disturbances that are sufficiently characteristic to permit the diagnosis of an affective or cognitive disorder of organic etiology. This leads to the concept of what has been called "vulnerable individuals" who are especially susceptible to pathological influences. From a brief sketch of Ruby's background one can conclude that he was a "vulnerable individual."(79) He grew up in a Chicago ghetto; he was known for his aggressive posture and flare ups that earned him the nickname of "Sparky"; he was emotion-ridden, violent, and had a personality beset by impulsive outbursts. Emotional tensions and limited control characterized his tenure as a nightclub proprietor. It is known that in a person of such background, who also suffers from an organic disease, there is a predisposition to inhibit or even eliminate emotional controls and to discharge behavior at a primitive level without regard for normal considerations. Such organically determined outbursts are characterized by inability to establish controls, an absence or clouding of memory of the act, inability to change the direction of the outburst until it is completed, and lack of any demonstrable feeling afterward. Ruby did exhibit these symptoms. By reason of the organic defect, it is possible for the sufferer to commit an aggressive or criminal deed of which he might not be capable in his normal state.

CONCLUSION

There is very limited medical insight into those aspects of human existence which are essentially correlated with consciousness such as perception, learning and memory (knowledge), and the forming of intent. Yet, the basic premise of the law is that without knowledge there can be no intent and without intent there can be no crime. We tend to regard the problems of consciousness as those of behaviorism, and the rules of knowledge and intent about which we know so little form the basic rules for determining criminal culpability.

The factors which interest the medical man are not necessarily the same factors which concern the trier in disposing of the controversy before him. However, it is the duty of law as well as of medicine to continue to seek answers for the fair handling of criminal conduct; lawyers must present new theories to the courts even in our present imperfect state of knowledge. It is far more reprehensible for society to punish the organically diseased individual for conduct over which he can exert no control than is any crime which he could commit. For indeed, he is punished for our ignorance of his disease, and will continue to be punished until the disease is fully understood and translated into legal practices.

NOTES

(1) The terms "disease," "insanity," and "mental illness" are difficult to define medically in a legal context, for in any given case they may mean whatever the expert witness says they mean. To quote Dr. Roche in the *Symposium on Criminal Responsibility and Mental Disease*, 26 Tenn. L. Rev. 221, 240 (1959):

I will say there is neither such a thing as "insanity" nor such a thing as "mental disease." These terms do not identify entities having separate existence in themselves. . . . "Mental illness," a medical term, borrowed from the mechanistic concepts of classical physical disease, refers to an altered internal status of the individual vis-a-vis his external world as interpreted by others. In a way the term is a misnomer, since the "mental illness" is not actually something limited to a place called the "mind," but rather is a changed interrelationship of the individual with his fellow creatures.

(2) Bonhoeffer, *Die Symptomatischen Psychosen in Gefolge von akuten Infektionen und inneren Erkrankugen*, in Hankbuch Von Aschaffenburg, spez. Teil. Leipzig, Franz Deuticke (1912).

(3) The proceeding is termed a hearing because it is conducted separately to determine the issue of criminal incompetency in addition to the trial to determine the issue of guilt. Unless waived by the defendant, a special jury is mandatory for criminal incompetency hearings in Alabama, Georgia, Idaho, Kentucky, Louisiana, Missouri, Montana, New Mexico, Illinois, Oklahoma, and South Dakota. Morse, *The Criminal Mental Incompetent*, 200 J.A.M.A. 233 (1967).

(4) Pate v. Robinson, 383 U.S. 375 (1966), established the requirement of a hearing to determine the mental competence of the accused to stand trial. The defendant does not waive his right to a competency hearing by failing to request it, for he is not competent to waive a hearing if he is not competent to stand trial. The court is required to order a competency hearing on its own motion if there is sufficient doubt as to the ability of the accused to be tried. *See also* Rhay v. White, 385 F.2d 883 (9th Cir. 1967) and United States v. Anderson, 280 F.Supp. 565 (D.Del. 1967).

(5) Diamond, *Criminal Responsibility of the Mentally Ill*, 14 Stan. L. Rev. 59 (1961).

(6) M'Naghten's Case, 8 Eng. Rep. 718 (1843).

(7) Commonwealth v. Chester, 337 Mass. 702, 150 N.E.2d 914 (1958).

(8) Durham v. United States, 214 F.2d 862 (D.C. Cir. 1954).

(9) Section 4.01 of the ALI Model Penal Code is often referred to as the "Freeman Rule." The name of the rule stems from the case of United States v. Freeman, 357 F.2d 606 (2d Cir. 1966), where the court gave strong endorsement to this rule and effectively swept away the *M'Naghten* rule within its jurisdiction.

(10) Illinois v. Brown, 31 Ill. 2d 415, 201 N.E.2d 409 (1961).

(11) Wright v. United States, 250 F.2d 4 (D.C. Cir. 1957).

(12) *In re* Sealy, 218 So. 2d 765 (Fla. App. 1969).

(13) Adams & Fowly, *The Neurological Disorders Associated with Liver Disease*, 32 A. Res. Nerv. and Ment. Dis. Proc. 198 (1953).

(14) Victor, Adams & Cole, *The Acquired (Non-Wilsonian) Type of Chronic Hepatocerebral Degeneration*, 44 Medicine 345 (1965).

(15) 293 F. Supp. 508 (W.D. Tex. 1968).

(16) Podolsky, *The Chemical Brew of Criminal Behavior*, 45 J. Crim. L.C. & P.S. 675 (1955).

(17) Chisolm, *Porphyria in the Adolescent: Diagnosis and Treatment*, 62 So. Med. J. 713 (1969).

(18) Peters, *Porphyric Psychosis and Chelation Therapy*, 4 Res. Adv. Biol. Psychiat. 204 (1962).

(19) A. Goldberg & C. Rimington, Diseases of Porphyrin Metabolism (1962).

(20) R. Michael, Endocrinology and Human Behavior (1969).

(21) Pugh, *Rates of Mental Disease Related to Childbearing*, 268 New Eng. J. Med. 1224 (1963).

(22) *Infanticide Act of 1938*, cited and discussed in Simpson, *Infanticide Criminal Aspects*, in 2 Taylor's Principles and Practice of Medical Jurisprudence, c. 12 (12th ed. 1965).

(23) Gooddy, *Disorders of Time Sense*, in 3 Disorders of Higher Nervous System c. 13 (P. Vinken & G. Bruyn ed. 1969).

(24) Dist. Ct. N.J., Docket No. 966-66 (D.C., N.J. 1970).

(25) Teitelbaum, *Misdiagnosis of Drug Abuse*, 210 J.A.M.A. 2092 (1969).

(26) Geataut & Mileto, *Interpretation Physiopathogenique des symptomes de la rage furiese*, 92 Rev. Neurol 5 (1965).

(27) Brain, *The Neurological Complications of Neoplasms*, 1 Lancet 179 (1963).

(28) Henson, *et al. Carcinomatous Neuropathy and Myopathy: A Clinical and Pathological Study*, 77 Brain 82 (1954).

(29) Charatan & Brierley, *Mental Disorders Associated With Primary Lung Carcinoma*, 1 Brit. Med. J. 765 (1956).

(30) Brain & Henson, *Neurological Syndromes Associated With Carcinoma*, 2 Lancet 971 (1958).

(31) Greenberg, *et al., A Review of Unusual Systemic Manifestations Associated With Carcinoma*, 36 Am. J. Med. 106 (1964); *See also* Lipsett, *Hormone Syndromes Associated With Neoplasia*, in 3 Advances in Metabolic Disorders 112 (R. Levine & R. Luff ed. 1969).

(32) Lebovitz, *Endocrine-metabolic Syndromes Associated With Neoplasms*, in The Remote Effects of Cancer on the Nervous System, c. 11 (L. Brain & F. Norris ed. 1965).

(33) Roth, *Cerebral Disease and Mental Disorders of Old Age As Causes of Antisocial Behavior*, in The Mentally Abnormal Offender 35 (A. deReuck & R. Porter ed. 1968); *See also* Moberg, *Old Age and Crime*, 43 J. Crim. L.C. & P.S. 764 (1953).

(34) Larsson, *et al., Senile Dementia: A Clinical, Sociomedical and Genetic Study*, 39 Acta. Psych. Scand. Supp. 167 (1963).

(35) Comment, *The XYY Chromosomal Defense*, 57 Geo. L.J. 892 (1969).

(36) Sandberg, *et al., An XYY Human Male*, 2 Lancet 488 (1961).

(37) Jacobs, *et al., Aggressive Behavior, Mental Subnormality and The XYY Male*, 208 Nature 1351 (1965).

(38) Marinello, *et al., A Study of the XYY Syndrome in Tall Men and Juvenile Delinquents*, 208 J.A.M.A. 321 (1969).

(39) Melnyk, *et al., XYY Survey in Institution for Sex Offenders and Mentally Ill*, 224 Nature 369 (1969). *See also* Sergovich, *et al., Chromosome Aberrations in 2159 Consecutive Newborn Babies*, 280 New Eng. J. Med. 851 (1969).

(40) Abdullah, *et al., The Extra Y Chromosome and Its Psychiatric Implications*, 21 Arch. Gen. Psych. 497 (1969).

(41) Comment, *The XYY Chromosome Defense*, 57 Geo. L.J. 892 (1969).

(42) People v. Conley, 64 Cal. 2d 310, 411 P.2d 911, 49 Cal. Rptr. 815 (1966). Such a defense is not available in the states of Missouri and Vermont.

(43) Horn v. Kentucky, 292 Ky. 587, 167 S.W.2d 58 (1942).

(44) Grennett v. United States, 403 F.2d 928 (D.C. Cir. 1968).

(45) Powell v. Texas, 392 U.S. 514 (1968). In Watson, *Chronic Alcoholic Court Offenders: An Alternative To The Drunk Tank*, Geo. L. Rev. 54 (1968) there is a discussion of legislation for replacing the present criminal method of handling "chronic alcoholic court offenders" with a treatment oriented program.

(46) 453 P.2d 342 (1969).

(47) H. Davidson, Forensic Psychiatry 17 (2d ed. 1965).

(48) 292 Ky. 587, 167 S.W.2d 58 (1942).

(49) Hollister, *Psychopharmacological Drugs*, 196 J.A.M.A. 125 (1966).

(50) Schulz v. Feigal, 273 Minn. 470 142 N.W.2d 84 (1966).

(51) Murphy v. Washington, 56 Wash. 2d 761, 355 P.2d 323 (1960).

(52) Goldman v. California, 51 Cal. Rptr. 835 (Cal. App. 1966).

(53) Breitner, *Appetite Suppressing Drugs as an Etiologic Factor in Mental Illness*, 5 Psychosomatics 327 (1963).

(54) Beamish & Kiloh, *Psychosis Due to Amphetamine Consumption*, 106 J. Mental Sci. 337 (1960); Bell & Threthowan, *Amphetamine Addiction*, 133 J. Nerve. Ment. Dis. 489 (1961); Bell, *Comparison of Amphetamine Psychosis and Schizophrenia*, 111 Brit. J. Psych. 701 (1965).

(55) Lemere, *The Danger of Amphetamine Dependency*, 123 Am. J. Psych. 569 (1966).

(56) Talbott & Teague, *Marihuana Psychosis*, 210 J.A.M.A. 299 (1969).

(57) Milman, *The Role of Marihuana in Patterns of Drug Abuse in Adolescents*, 74 J. Pediat. 283 (1969).

(58) Smart & Bateman, *Unfavorable Reactions to LSD: A Review and Analysis of the Available Case Reports*, 97 Can. Med. Assoc. J. 1215 (1967).

(59) Keeler & Reifler, *Suicide During an LSD Reaction* 123 Am. J. Psych. 884 (1967).

(60) Cohen, *Suicide Following Morning Glory Ingestion*, 120 Am. J. Psych. 1024 (1964).

(61) Knudsen, 40 Acta. Psych. Scand. Supp. 389 (1964).

(62) Hooshmand & Brawley, *Temporal Lobe Seizures and Exhibitionism*, 19 Neurology 1119 (1969): Taylor, *Sexual Behavior and Temporal Lobe Epilepsy*, 12 Arch. Neurol. 510 (1969).

(63) Zeman & King, *Tumors of the Septum Pellucidum and Adjacent Structures with Abnormal Affective Behavior; An Anterior Midline Structure Syndrome*, 127 J. Nerv. Ment. Dis. 490 (1958); Bingley, *Mental Symptoms in Temporal Lobe Epilepsy and Temporal Lobe Gliomas*, 33 Acta. Psych. Scand. Supp. 120 (1958).

(64) Lechner, *Der Lobus limicus und seine funktionellen Beziehungen zur Affektivitat*, 16 Wien. Z. Nervenheilk 281 (1959).

(65) Poeck, *Pathophysiology of Emotional Disorders Associated with Brain Damage*, in 3 Disorders of Higher Nervous System 343 P. Vinken & G. Bruyn ed. 1969).

(66) *Governor's Committee Recommends Health, Safety Measures for the University of Texas Campus*, 62 Tex. Med. 120 (1966).

(67) *Id.* at 123.

(68) Ajmone-Marsan & Abraham, *Epilepsy* in Progress in Neurology & Psychiatry (E. Spiegel ed. 1963).

(69) Freytag & Lindenberg, 294 *Medicolegal Autopsies on Epileptics: Cerebral Findings*, 78 Arch. Path. 274 (1964).

(70) Taylor v. United States, 7 App. D.C. 27 (1895); Smith v. Kentucky, 268 S.W.2d 937 (Ky. App. 1945).

(71) Armstead v. Maryland, 227 Md. Rep. 73, 175 A.2d 24 (1961).

(72) Coogler v. California, 77 Cal. Rptr. 790, 454 P.2d 686 (1969).

(73) McCaldron, *Automatism*, 91 Can. Med. Assoc. J. 914 (1964).

(74) Williams, *Automatism*, in Essays in Criminal Science 12 (G. Mueller ed. 1961).

(75) In the Scottish case, H.M. Advocate v. Fraser, 4 Couper 70 (1878), a man was acquitted of the killing of his son during a dream in which he believed himself to be struggling with a wild goose. An Australian case, The King v. Cogdon, Supreme Court of Victoria 1950 (unreported), from Morris, *Somnambulistic Homicide: Ghosts, Spiders, and North Koreans*, 5 Res. Judicta

29 (1951), involved the successful use of the somnambulistic homicide defense where a mother killed her 19-year-old daughter with an axe alleging she dreamed that soldiers were in her daughter's room attacking the daughter. The story was supported by her physician, psychiatrist, and psychologist. In R. v. Bolshears, an unreported English case, from Simpson, *Mental Disorder and Responsibility*, in 1 Taylor's Principles and Practice of Medical Jurisprudence 486 (12the ed. 1965), the jury accepted a defence plea that homicide was committed during sleep.

(76) Schwartz v. North Dakota, (unreported) from Polodsky, note 16 *supra*.

(77) An unabridged transcript of the medical, psychological and psychiatric testimony given at Ruby's trial entitled *State v. Jack Ruby* is found in 6 Trauma 5 (1964). A quotation from the introduction is germane to this discussion. "The psychiatric and psychological testimony in the Ruby transcript fails to disclose the slightest thread which will support a valid finding that Ruby was criminally insane either at the time of trial or at the time he shot Lee Harvey Oswald."*Id.* at 6.

(78) S. Robbins, Pathology 99 (3rd ed. 1967).

(79) G. Wills & O. Demaris: Jack Ruby c.1 (1967).

SENTENCING–AS SEEN
BY A PSYCHIATRIST

John Gunn

It surprises and flatters me that magistrates should want to hear what a psychiatrist has to say about sentencing. I am sure that doctors would close their ears to any advice from magistrates about medical matters. However, the invitation being issued, it would take a stronger man than me to resist such a tantalizing temptation.

As this century has advanced so courts and lawyers have, wherever questions of mental instability have arisen, become more and more concerned with constructive sentencing and less concerned with questions of mental responsibility. This is a welcome trend because it shifts the area of debate from philosophy to practicality.

REMANDS

We are all acutely aware of the prison overcrowding problem and yet sometimes we forget just how important is the remanded prisoner. In 1968, 110,813 male receptions were made by the prison department, 56,360 (51 percent) of these were remand receptions, 38,455 (35 percent) being untried prisoners. Many of the latter men had social and medical inquiries made and it is clear that medical reports for courts throw a very considerable burden upon the prison medical department. Furthermore, the remand in custody for medical reports is frequently very damaging to the lives and families of some defendants. Although, technically, it is supposed to be quite different from a sentence of imprisonment, many of its effects are identical—loss of accommodation, loss of job, loss of reputation, and possibly family break-up. This would not be so important if all the men remanded in custody were eventually going to be imprisoned, but this is by no means the case. For of the 38,000 untried prisoners, some will be found not guilty and many will be sentenced to non-institutional punishments such as fines and probation. Each year some men who are ineligible for imprisonment—even if convicted—are remanded in custody. A number of prisoners are convinced that the remand in custody process is used as a punishment—as a mini-prison sentence in fact.

Is there any evidence for such a viewpoint? If we turn to juveniles, there is. As part of the evidence to be submitted to the ill-fated Royal Commission on the Penal System, the Institute of Psychiatry carried out a survey in 1962 by asking the magistrates at one of the metropolitan juvenile courts to state their reasons for each remand in custody. It appeared that warnings, and policy decisions of the "teach them a lesson" kind, constituted about one-third of the reasons for custodial remand.

Is this, then, an argument against remands for psychiatric reports? Not in the least. The psychiatrist often has something important to contribute to the court situation, even if it is only what medical treatment *cannot* do. Perhaps then no medical remands should be carried out in custody? Not exactly. There is clearly a place for some defendants to be remanded in custody but surely this should only be done for carefully evaluated reasons, and as a last resort.

Some magistrates believe that psychiatric reports can only be reliably obtained from prison medical officers working in the custodial setting. This is not quite accurate, especially now that since 1967 examining doctors working for the Health Service can be paid a fee for a court report. It is certainly difficult for a busy NHS consultant to provide an interview of 1-1½ hours during a busy out-patient clinic but most doctors are willing to see offenders at other times. The main difficulty seems to be in getting courts and doctors to establish the necessary referral machinery.

If it is possible, a psychiatric report on bail is preferable for if any health service treatment is to be recommended or arranged then the reporting psychiatrist is much better placed than his prison colleague to undertake this. A second advantage is that the patient can be seen in his own social context; relatives, friends, employers and other significant actors in the patient's drama can all be interviewed if needs be—a task very difficult to undertake in the prison setting. Thirdly, if in-patient or out-patient treatment is to be the court's decision, then as little damage as possible will have been done to the patient's social situation and the maximum therapeutic potential preserved. Finally from the purely punitive point of view it is, to say the least, debatable as to whether more constructive anxiety is generated within a prison where bitterness, resentment, anger and self-sorrow are often the dominant features, or within the patient's normal environment.

A recent, as yet unpublished, paper by Dell and Gibbens reports that, by using the fairly strict bailability criteria of the American Vera system one-third of the women remanded in custody in Holloway prison in 1967 could have been given bail without much risk to the community, and one-quarter had actually proved this by a successful period on bail before they were remanded in custody. To be bailed under the Vera system, the offender must have an address where he can be reached and a minimum number of points scored from five social categories: the number of previous convictions, the strength of family ties, the length of time in his present employment, the length of time in his present residence, and the length of time in the area. In other words, it is trying to weed out for custodial remand the rootless, wandering, unattached offender. The Dell and Gibbens figures seem to suggest that currently Holloway prison is being used as a kind of secure clinic where medical reports and opinions are readily obtainable.

Returning to the survey conducted by the Institute of Psychiatry at the London remand home for boys, several positive and noteworthy reasons for custodial remand were given: drug abuse; an adolescent in revolt against his home and in the process of running away; repeated absconding or breaking bail; repeated taking and driving away; a persistent and quick succession of offenses such that a bail opportunity might actually lengthen the offender's record; an integrated gang member; a serious offense such as arson or grievous bodily harm; no suitable home to return to—perhaps because of disturbed parents; and finally an offender deemed vulnerable to reprisals from others.

Combining the Vera system of bailability with the positive suggestions which came out of the Institute of Psychiatry study and always remembering that a lot depends upon the relationship which is established between the court and local psychiatrists we have then what seems to me a practical and constructive approach to obtaining as much medical advice as possible with a minimum use of custody.

SENTENCING

The Streatfeild Committee (1961) reported that originally court sentences were purely punitive and based on a tariff system. The primary object was to fix a sentence proportionate to the offender's culpability. A second hidden element of deterrence was also present in this system. This second element has been stressed more and more in recent years but the biggest change has been the introduction of a reforming or a correctional element. This sometimes produces conflicts in the sentencing situation for a sentence which is appropriate for punishment may be inappropriate for deterrence or for correction and vice versa.

Psychiatrists, also, have been caught up in these shifts of emphasis. Originally the doctor's job was to decide only between sanity and insanity and leave it at that. The insane could escape punishment, the sane could not. As psychiatry and psychology have grown, however, three trends have taken place. First, we have gained in our understanding of the determinants behind all sorts of human thought processes and behavior including anti-social behavior. Secondly, treatment methods are being tried and sometimes are effective for behavior disorders, which in turn have brought increasing pressure from the public for doctors to take on more and more areas of human deviancy and human unhappiness as medical problems, sometimes thereby shifting the doctor uneasily into a priestly role. Thirdly, there has been a parallel trend for some psychiatrists to oversell the efficiency of psychiatry and present it as a kind of modern panacea.

The doctor in court is under pressure to be as constructive as possible in his recommendation but is aware that psychiatric treatment is relatively ineffective with many anti-social behavior disorders, and even if he finds a client with rather more therapeutic potential than usual he may well not be able to find a hospital or clinic placement for him simply because the appropriate services are not available. Paradoxically, the prisons themselves and the prison medical department may provide the best available assistance. This poses an obvious ethical dilemma.

Faced with these difficult issues many forensic psychiatrists take the view that they are still only competent to decide ill or not ill and that giving further advice is going beyond their area of competence and gives misleading impressions about psychiatry.

This view would be wholly justified if any alternative viewpoint was tantamount to a kind of judicial system run by doctors. However, the arguments put forward by Lady Wootton (1959) and others suggest that we should increasingly regard the sentence and the sentencing process itself as a kind of correctional, rehabilitative, or even therapeutic framework. Such a viewpoint clearly fits with the best aims of society for, in the long run, it protects both the offender and any potential victims. Within a judicial system which has a heavy emphasis on rehabilitation and reform the psychiatrist will always be called upon to play a small part because his day-to-day activities are concerned with setting out programs for behavior modification. Furthermore, medicine has considerable experience—not all of it rewarding—with the therapeutic role. Let us therefore look at the broader aspect of the sentence as a correctional instrument bearing in mind some of the lessons learned from medicine. To simplify this task let us take the three functions of sentencing separately and begin with punishment.

PUNISHMENT

Clearly in its more unadulterated form punishment has little resemblance to anything that medical science might undertake. Even so it is important for all of us to remember that for a very long time man has worked on a punishment/reward system in his social structure and under certain circumstances we expect, even need, a punitive consequence to our actions. The growing child, for example, requires the limits of his behavior to be set by such a system of reward and punishment. We have all heard the child who comes from a disturbed environment pleading for rules and sanctions.

One of the functions of punishment in normal individuals is to assuage any feelings of guilt they may have following an anti-social act. Given a normal personality structure punishment can be seen in this context as constructive and in no way opposed to reform and rehabilitation. A case history will illustrate: a man, many years ago, remonstrated with his wife's lover, the inevitable fight ensued and the interloper was killed. The man was subsequently convicted of manslaughter. At the time he suffered unbearable guilt and prayed for a stiff punishment. The court took a more lenient view of his behavior and gave him a conditional discharge. He was amazed and appalled. He felt that he had been deprived of a chance to redeem himself and ran away from home and drowned his sorrows in drink. Since that time he has been a severe and persistent alcoholic and is convinced that if he had had a reasonable punishment—two or three years in prison—he would not have deteriorated. It is difficult to know how far to accept this man's version of his difficulties—many would regard him as a vulnerable personality initially and the degree of guilt and his response to it as pathological. However, he does raise an interesting point for discussion.

Punishment is of course not entirely alien to psychiatry and here I am not referring to some of the mental hospital brutalities of the past but to aversion treatment in which pleasurable but undesirable behavior, such as a sexual perversion, is coupled with an unpleasant sensation like an electric shock, in the hope that the unwanted behavior will diminish and eventually die out. Three important aspects of this treatment may provide lessons for penology—first, it is only successful in a small proportion of carefully selected cases; secondly, it is applied voluntarily to a willing patient; and thirdly careful research and follow-up is an essential component of applying the treatment effectively.

Social punishments for criminal behavior are almost never applied in this way. Punishment is often regarded as a nostrum. To some ears careful selection of cases is almost heretical, and research is very rudimentary. We are beginning to learn that fines are perhaps more effective than other forms of punishment but we have insufficient data to know how to apply them optimally and we certainly have not yet broken down our punishment methods into the various components to see which, if any, are effective.

In aversive treatment it is being increasingly found that punishment alone is insufficient to produce lasting change. It is also necessary to reward the replacement behavior which is desired—in the case of the sexual deviation, the normal sexual behavior is rewarded by praise and an increase of status in the eyes of family and physician. Surely there is a pointer here for constructive penal work. Too much of what we do in court seems to the offender to be purely negative—often he feels that all his efforts are forgotten and only his mistakes remembered, and this perhaps in a man who has never received normal and adequate reward for any of his activities.

The motorist is an obvious choice for an experiment in reward. Insurance companies have for some time applied a reward/punishment system to accident behavior—why not a more extensive state-sponsored version of this plan—good conduct certificates, tax concessions for a long conviction-free period, a graduated series of speed limits which have to be earned by good behavior and so on?

Nevertheless an important point must not be missed. No matter how severe the punishments, how enticing the rewards, one cannot control everybody's behavior by this system alone. Even if public flogging were to be introduced for parking offenses, someone would always be sure to park on the double yellow line. Some people are incapable of conforming to the laws and social mores in the same way that some people are incapable of learning to read and write.

As always, the psychiatrist has a name for this group of people. He calls them psychopaths or men with a severe personality disorder. Diagnosed in a more positive fashion these are people who have disorganization of several important areas of their bio-social functions. The men who can never get or keep jobs; the men with grossly disturbed sexual behavior; the men who just do not know how to give or take love, who cannot therefore form satisfying relationships with other people; the men who are impulsive and never seem to progress because they fail to learn from previous experience. Needless to say, these men are the persistent offenders and they form a large proportion of the prison population.

It does not require a psychiatrist to point out, after this description, that these people are unlikely to respond to the normal punishment and reward system. Indeed they have almost been defined by observing their failure to respond to the normal social sanctions and regulations. What alternative systems of management are available? Well, let it be admitted at once that services for the psychopath are rudimentary, and treatment prospects disappointing. Efforts are being made in a few isolated centers to cope with the psychopath and skills are developing which may eventually be of considerable importance, but the management and treatment of behavior disorders is still an infantile science. Interestingly, some of the most strenuous efforts are being made within the prisons. Here then we are confronted with the ethical dilemma mentioned above. Right throughout our correctional system is a tension between punishment and treatment, between retribution and rehabilitation. Nowhere is this more clearly illustrated than in deciding on a suitable disposal for a criminal psychopath. All the experts may agree about the diagnosis and yet there is rarely suitable medical treatments available except in prison and so the medical recommendation is a period of imprisonment. Furthermore, the period of imprisonment which would be awarded on punitive grounds alone using the tariff system can frequently be less than the period of secure management thought necessary on medical grounds. It is then possible for a doctor to find himself recommending longer sentences than retribution would require. No wonder some defendants are wary of psychiatric evidence on their behalf!

Very few patients are ever forced to have treatment in the health service, or in the prison service either for that matter although at the time of sentencing it sometimes sounds as if treatment is being prescribed irrespective of the patient's wishes. One of the cardinal features of successful treatment in medicine is that the patient wants treatment, understands its purpose and consents to it. It may sound a bit like heresy but it has always seemed to me that for both punishment and rehabilitation it would be useful for the sentencer in a court to discuss openly the pros and cons of the past behavior and of the future disposal. In this way it would be possible for the judge to ascertain clearly what the offender thinks might punish, deter, or rehabilitate him and sometimes to obtain his agreement about the prescribed course of action. I think this would enable a court to fit sentences to the offender much more precisely, and hence more effectively. To carry the medical analogy a bit further—another cardinal feature of medical treatment is that as few irreversible decisions as possible are taken and that progress is constantly reviewed. Why not apply the same to the court situation? Certainly probation officers constantly do this with their clients, every long-term prisoner is constantly assessed by the Prison Department, and the Parole Board is a further step in this direction, but why should not a good measure of control be retained by the court so that assessment interviews and reports would be an integral part of any prolonged disposal and so that variations, within limits defined by law, could be made to the sentence in the light of progress. I do not believe it is intelligent or just to make irrevocable decisions at one moment in time which can affect for good or ill not only the distant future of an individual but equally his dependants and the society in which he lives.

DETERRENCE

Usually this is thought to be part and parcel of punishment, for seeing others punished for an offense is thought to dissuade would-be offenders committing the same offense. Two points seem fairly obvious here. First, this does not apply to the psychopath or persistent offender for, as already explained, he does not learn by experience of this sort. Secondly, we have no information on which to base our assumptions.

Let me make a plea which I cannot emphasize too strongly and which applies to the whole of penal practice. We need research, we need data, we need information. Scientific inquiries should not be regarded as an optional extra—they are no more luxuries than are the headlights of a car—both illuminate the way ahead. Neither are they an infringement of public freedom or civil rights. They are a civilized essential to the making of correct decisions.

Nowhere is research more neglected than in this issue of deterrence, but research should also apply to the whole of the court process. If sentencers were regularly informed of an offender's progress after the initial day of sentencing in the way already suggested then it would not be difficult, indeed it would be essential, to store information about that man and to plot his progress. This type of information would be invaluable for determining who does well with what sort of sentence, what are the subsequent effects of a change in sentencing policy and so on.

REHABILITATION

Paradoxically some aspects of this have already been covered under the heading of punishment but, as has been made clear, it is sometimes difficult to separate the two completely. When deterrence has failed and an offender is caught then successful rehabilitation will not only be good for him but also good for society because he will offend less often in the future. Rehabilitation is in fact an essential component of the war on crime—it is prevention of further crime. Punishment may be effective rehabilitation. However, what do we do with the persistent offender who fails to respond to punishment? We can try prevention—removing a driving license from the persistent motoring offender or giving an extended sentence to the persistent bicycle thief. However, there comes a time in a civilized society when we try again and (except in the case of the severely dangerous criminal, who usually goes to hospital anyway) we return the offender to ordinary society. Our sentencing procedure has been a pretty futile exercise if at this point he is just as likely, or perhaps even more likely, to offend again. Here let me introduce you to another fairly simple and obvious medical axiom which could well be carried over to penal work. *If you cannot make someone better, whatever you do, do not make them worse.*

Lombroso (1899) called prisons the universities of crime and maintained that "the state does not think of the morrow. It shuts the prisoner up and when he has served the term of his sentence it sets him at liberty again, thus increasing the danger for society, for the criminal always becomes more depraved in the promiscuity of the prison, and goes out more irritated and better armed against society."

It is an amazing fact that, even in the second half of the twentieth century, we spend vast sums of money collecting together juvenile delinquents, young offenders and other vulnerable personalities into large, outdated, overcrowded institutions where information, skill and expertise about criminal methods is handed from one inmate to another so that the mildly delinquent or potentially criminal youngster becomes in a year or so a skilled safe-blower with a host of new-found criminal friends. Whenever Joe Soap, an inadequate twenty-year-old who has an appalling social background; whose only solace is heavy drinking; and who cannot keep his hands to himself, is sentenced to borstal or imprisonment, he is just about to start his serious criminal apprenticeship. This is not to say that a number of important and constructive changes are not taking place within the prison system itself and for selected individuals there seems no argument that a period of institutional care is required. The difficulties arise because too many individuals are fed into an overburdened system which is isolated from the community it should serve.

Prisons have become twentieth-century asylums for alcoholics, drug addicts, compulsive gamblers, sexual deviants, persistent car thieves, homeless inadequates, and so on. In short, asylums for persons with personality disorders. Now asylums have been found wanting for the treatment of the mentally ill. As they are currently constructed, are they any better for those with psychopathic personality disorders? Almost certainly not. Usually the psychopath is impulsive, has few social skills, finds work impossible, not because he is not trained as a bricklayer, or motor mechanic, but because he just does not have the basic work skills of persistence, application, discretion; he has a disordered sexual life, and, above all, is unable to understand and feel for his fellow men. In prison he is constantly reminded of his inadequacies, given no responsibility, given few opportunities to make lasting relationships with normal individuals, given no opportunity for genuine heterosexual contact, has to work in a grossly abnormal work situation which he frequently finds loathsome, is given little or no discretion and is even deprived of decision-making about when he will have a bath or go to the lavatory. At the end of this kind of management he is rapidly ejected into the real world with no fall-back arrangements and few supports.

For the mentally ill the asylum system is gradually being replaced by a complex framework of community care. The essence of good community care is a variety of services which are staged, and in which an individual can move from stage to stage according to his needs. The complex may contain an intensive care hospital ward, a day hospital, an outpatient clinic, home visits by a familiar social worker, night hostels, rehabilitation workshops, domiciliary visits by doctors. How far can this model be transferred to the penal system? We already have some of the services operating, prisons themselves, some with treatment units, probation officers, aftercare hostels, social clubs for ex-prisoners, employment agencies, and so forth. The essential missing ingredients are a close working relationship to a correctional unit (a term I would prefer to prison) with its surrounding community; good staff communication between one aspect of the complex and another about a particular case; flexibility of disposal arrangements after a court decision has been made, and training of all personnel involved (including the prison officers) in the skills of management.

In essence, to get more effective and economic rehabilitation we need to restructure our services and to tailor each decision regarding an offender to that particular individual's needs, and most important, we need continuous review and reassessment of progress as time passes. Returning to an earlier point, it seems that courts should be an integral part of the system outlined above, should take all decisions whether stern or lenient, in close consultation with the offender and, if possible, the victim, and should review those decisions regularly in light of experience. Most important of all the agencies involved, courts, probation officers, prisons, etc., should *all* be equipped with a research facility, a data-collecting process, to evaluate the system, to test new ideas—to supply the facts.

Well, this is all very nice for the possible future but what about the present? I make no apologies for stressing the need for new systems, for political change in fact, because unless all of us at every opportunity examine the inadequacies of our present system, and press for changes, we shall continue to shore up the crumbling edifice with an ever increasing lack of success. However, what I have said implies a much freer use of non-institutional sentences than we are currently accustomed to.

The Wootton sub-committee in 1970 made several suggestions for non-institutional alternatives to imprisonment. Until these proposals are implemented the only ones we are left with are: discharges, being bound over, fines and probation. Notice that the suspended prison sentence was omitted from this list. The suspended prison sentence is exactly what it says—a prison sentence. Unless the court is dealing with a well-balanced, well-integrated personality whose anti-social habits are going to be *deterred* by prison, then the suspended sentence is an institutional sentence. The man who has been in and out of prison several times and who is a persistent offender is exceedingly unlikely to be deterred by a suspended sentence. His imprisonment may be postponed a month or two but he will probably serve longer when he does get there. It may be that we can explain at least part of the recent explosion in the prison population by an inadequate understanding of this issue on the part of some sentencers.

It is also worth remembering that for some people a fine is also a prison sentence in effect, for they are unwilling, or more often, unable to pay the fine. Thinking in terms of our persistent offender however the probation order seems to be one of the most valuable tools at the court's disposal. Not if it is applied blindly of course, or without reference to the particular officer's personal skills and work load.

Returning to the doctor's point of view, the probation order under section 4 of the Criminal Justice Act with a condition of medical treatment provides a particularly useful opportunity for pressure to be brought to bear, on a suitable offender, at least to consider seriously the possibility of medical treatment, without forcing him into a hostile corner where treatment becomes quite impossible. The involvement of the probation officer can be minimal and the whole accent of the order is on persuasion, remaining in the community, a dialogue between doctor, social worker and offender, and an opportunity to adapt the therapeutic structure to all sorts of changing needs. Perhaps this type of disposal is not used frequently enough, perhaps doctors are reluctant to accept such cases, and perhaps courts sometimes feel that only very minor cases can be handled in this way, but my limited experience suggests that minor offenses are not dealt with successfully by this process—neither offender nor doctor takes it seriously—a sexual assault, however, or some other more serious offense, often generates enough anxiety in everybody concerned to be of therapeutic advantage.

Before leaving probation, an important American finding should be mentioned. In the Community Treatment Project in California it has been found that one of the most important determinants of success has been matching of client to therapist (see Warren, 1970). It is no use sending the next case to the next probation officer on the list—each has to find the other acceptable, and the therapist has to be skilled and adept in his training and personality structure at handling the particular type of cases he is asked to take on. This of course suggests a program of very careful research (we are back to the indispensable component) and selection on the part of the probation departments. It also suggests that if probation has failed or is failing, a change of officer is the first remedy that should be tried.

Brief mention must also be made of the hospital order, or section 60 of the Mental Health Act. It has a definite place in the management of the psychotic, or mentally ill offender, although authorities such as Dr. Henry Rollin have their doubts even about that, but to send a psychopath under such an order to a mental hospital which is not equipped to treat him can do both the patient and society a disservice. If he runs away, as so many do, he is not having any correctional management at all; if he is locked in he becomes bored and resentful, regards the hospital as a kind of prison, and is in danger of institutionalization. If in-patient treatment has a place then it must be in a center which is specially equipped—but not necessarily exclusively equipped—to deal with him. In many ways he would be better off with a probation order under section 4 of the Criminal Justice Act.

SEX OFFENDERS

A final word should deal with the sex offender who presents an interesting problem and an increasingly psychiatric problem. Lawyers and courts are saying more and more that this type of offender has an uncontrollable urge and that it is for the psychiatrist to treat him for the condition. This view is reinforced by the fact that there is an increasing amount of evidence that suggests that the doctor may be able to do something. The main standby at present is hormonal treatment—giving the man concerned a largish dose of female hormones which will balance out his body's production of male hormone. This reduces or obliterates his sex drive—it does nothing to change its direction from perverse to normal—and it is reversible so that if he stops the treatment his sex drive returns. The treatment is best given either by surgically implanting a small pellet of hormone under the skin every few months, or by injecting the chemical into a muscle every few weeks. It is least satisfactory when given in tablet form because these have to be swallowed once or twice a day and hence the treatment is at the mercy of the patient's fluctuating motivation. As with all treatments a large degree of motivation and cooperation is required on the part of the patient. He cannot be forced to have it and he has to put up with unpleasant side-effects such as breast enlargement. The other treatment which is being tried for the sexual deviant is behavior therapy. This is the treatment mentioned above with its complicated system of punishments and rewards aimed at redirecting the deviant sexual desire to more acceptable goals. But for both of these methods of treatment the more disturbed the basic personality, the less likely is the treatment to succeed. Furthermore, they do not modify other forms of deviant behavior such as stealing.

Most of the sexual cases currently receiving treatment are receiving hormones and they have begun their course in prison. This is reasonable enough when prison is unavoidable for some reason, but the treatment is designed for a real-life situation where sexual temptation exists and it can only effectively be tested outside of prison. Some individuals who begin with a circumscribed deviancy are damaged by imprisonment—they become resentful and refuse treatment or have institutional inadequacies added to their problems, or sometimes learn additional criminal habits from their erstwhile friends. Some of these offenders are eminently suitable for out-patient treatment whilst on probation, always provided that an interested psychiatrist can be found, and a recent Appeal Court decision (*R. v. Farmborough*, March 13, 1970) made a new type of binding-over order with conditions of medical treatment which last longer than the twelve months from the day of conviction allowed with a probation order.

CONCLUSION

I have tried to suggest that without radical changes in the law it is possible to accelerate the current trend in sentencing towards rehabilitation. Furthermore this acceleration is urgently required, for it will form a central feature of any *effective* war on crime. First, remands in custody need to be kept to a bare minimum and more opportunity taken of any facilities which will provide the necessary social and medical inquiries whilst the defendant is on bail.

Punishment and rehabilitation need not be seen as polar opposites provided each is tailored to meet the exact requirements of each case. Research and fact finding about the efficacy of any particular type of court disposal should be regarded as obligatory. The psychopathic or persistent offender should be tackled by establishing a new series of inexpensive community services which can to some extent contain his behavior. Added to this the court itself should become much more closely integrated with its local community, sentencers should have closer and more informal contact with both offender and victim and should have a continuing responsibility for any offender whilst he remains within the correctional systems.

REFERENCES

Dell and Gibbens (1971). *Medicine, Science and the Law,* July, 1971.

Home Office (1970). *Report on the Work of the Prison Department 1968—Statistical Tables.* Cmnd. 4266. H.M.S.O.

Kittrie, N. N. (1969). "Can the Right to Treatment Remedy the Ills of the Juvenile Process" in *The Right to Treatment.* Ed. by D. S. Burris. New York: Springer.

Lombroso. C. (1899). *Crime: Its Causes and Remedies.* Paris: Schleicher. (Translated by H. P. Horton. London: Heinemann. 1911.)

Rollin, H. (1968). "The Conventional Mental Hospital and the English Penal System" in *The Mentally Abnormal Offender.* Ed. by A. V. S. De Rueck and R. Porter. London: Churchill.

Royal Commission on the Penal System in England and Wales. *Written Evidence from Government Depts. Miscellaneous Bodies and Individual Witnesses— Volume II Miscellaneous Bodies.* H.M.S.O.

Streatfeild Committee (1961). *Report of the Interdepartmental Committee on the Business of Criminal Courts.* Cmnd. 1289. H.M.S.O.

Warren, M. (1970). *Correctional Treatment in Community Settings. A Report of Current Research.* Prepared for the VIth International Congress on Criminology, Madrid.

Wootton, B. (1959). *Social Science and Social Pathology.* London: Allen & Unwin.

THE POWER OF THE
PSYCHIATRIC EXCUSE

Seymour Halleck

The power of the psychiatrist to affect the status quo is not confined to his work with patients or to his public pronouncements on abnormality. Sometimes he directly helps society make critical decisions affecting its stability as well as the privileges and freedom of some of its citizens, and one of the most significant ways in which he does this is to excuse selected individuals from meeting ordinary social obligations.

In a civilized society few expectations are placed on those who are severely ill. A man with a high fever will not be required to go to work; and a boy with a crippling orthopedic condition will not have to serve in the armed forces. Because our society looks upon some forms of emotional suffering as illness, we often excuse the emotionally disturbed from fulfilling some of their obligations. Sometimes the psychiatrist has the official power to sanction such an excuse; at other times he only recommends an excuse, and a judicial agency has the ultimate power. Although psychiatric excuse-giving seems to be a human practice, I am convinced that it contributes to our social ills, usually because it strengthens an oppressive status quo.

Psychiatric excuse-giving has three major characteristics. The first is selectivity: only certain individuals have the opportunity to obtain a psychiatric excuse, and it is seldom even considered unless the patient complains vehemently about his suffering or behaves in a bizarre or unreasonable manner. The person who suffers quietly or the person who harbors bizarre thoughts but keeps them to himself will probably not be considered eligible for a psychiatric excuse. The very act of requesting preferential treatment requires a certain degree of aggressiveness of the part of the patient or perhaps on the part of his attorney. Those who know the laws and are aware that an excuse is available are most likely to request and to receive one. A prestigious social position and lots of money help. Psychiatric excuses are rarely given to members of lower socioeconomic groups.

A second characteristic of psychiatric excuse-giving is that it usually compels the psychiatrist to be dishonest in interpreting his opinions to legal agencies or the public. Most psychiatrists identify with their patient and want to help him avoid what both parties consider to be an overwhelming or unjust obligation, but strong partisanship destroys the psychiatrist's objectivity. Sometimes, it is true, the psychiatrist can persuade himself that his patient is too sick to assume an obligation. At other times, however, he is not certain that his patient is terribly ill but is tempted to recommend a medical excuse simply because it seems to offer a rational and humane solution to the patient's problems. Even when the psychiatrist is convinced his patient is ill, he has no objective means to determine whether the illness is severe enough to impair the patient's conduct or capacities so that he deserves to be treated in a privileged manner.

The third characteristic of psychiatric excuse-giving is that it tends to strengthen existing social systems. The person who is given an excuse may be one who would otherwise have confronted the system. If he is compelled to fulfill his obligation, his plight may arouse considerable public sentiment and concern. However, once a person is declared too sick to meet his obligation, society assumes that the issue has been justly settled. The excused person loses much of his motivation to confront the stressful system, and there is no pressure on society to examine the oppressive nature of the obligations it imposes on people or to change the system.

When release is sought from a social mandate such as carrying a child to term, being punished for a crime, or serving in the armed forces, the emotions engendered are usually so intense that they obscure any rational examination of the issue. The consequences of excuse-giving are best clarified by examining the problem from a more-or-less neutral standpoint. I will try to describe the impact of excuse-giving on a relatively trivial social system—an impact that was not profound, either for the system or for the individual.

EXCUSE-GIVING IN A SMALL SOCIAL SYSTEM

Students at the University of Wisconsin who want to live in a dormitory are required to sign a contract, obliging them to pay for room and board for a full academic year. The contract is made either with the university itself or with private owners of dormitories who have been licensed by the university to provide student housing. During the course of an academic year certain students become dissatisfied with their living arrangements: sometimes they do not like the dormitory itself; sometimes they cannot get along with their roommate or with other individuals on their floor; or sometimes they make new friends of the same or opposite sex with whom they prefer to live. However, the student can change his residence only if he pays off his contract, sells it to another student, or obtains a medical excuse.

If a student becomes severly ill and has to leave school, he is usually excused from his housing contract simply upon request. If his illness is not severe, however, he cannot be excused so easily. Sometimes a student will develop a severe allergy or a condition like diabetes and will need special living arrangements or special food; in those cases excuses are obtained painlessly. But, in general, young people do not develop many medical conditions that justify breaking a housing contract. What often happens, however, is that the student who desperately wants to change his housing arrangements is tempted to argue that he is emotionally disturbed and that being forced to live in a particular dormitory is contributing to his disturbance.

When I first began to work as Director of Student Psychiatry at the University of Wisconsin, I found that it was the practice of the University Housing Bureau to honor any letter from a psychiatrist recommending that a student be excused from his dormitory contract obligations. A student who wanted to change his residence had only to find a psychiatrist who would write a note to the housing authorities stating that the student was mentally ill and that he would become more disturbed if he continued to live in his present dormitory. The Wisconsin situation was not unique; many other universities have honored psychiatric excuses in a similar manner and some of them still do.

A number of students request excuses directly from the University Psychiatry Clinic rather than from private practitioners. In reviewing their cases I began to realize that the possibility of any student obtaining an excuse depended upon the social and moral biases of the particular university-employed psychiatrist whom he saw. I also came to appreciate that psychiatrists at the University Clinic were more likely to turn down a request for an excuse than those in private practice. In effect, students who could afford to see a private practitioner had little trouble breaking their contracts. Some letters recommending excuses were written by physicians who had never even seen the student. In order to minimize inequities in the excuse-giving process, I convinced the administration that all students requesting excuses should be examined by one psychiatrist; I persuaded them that I should be the only person who could sanction an excuse. By making this seemingly wise and fair decision I let myself in for some bitter experiences.

When I began to review the cases I soon learned that those students who came to beg my indulgence were a special group: they had taken the time to learn about the housing system and were extremely aggressive in pursuing their own goals; they also seemed to be accustomed to getting their own way. Their determination to be relieved of the obligation to fulfill their housing contract by any possible means (other than simply paying for it, as specified in the contract) could be described as relentless or grim. Other students who requested excuses, however, seemed to be seriously disturbed. Some had been in psychotherapy and some had even been hospitalized for mental disorders. These students aroused my sympathy, but so did those who did not appear to be too disturbed. They seemed to be so unhappy in their surroundings and argued so convincingly that they would be happier elsewhere that I was almost always tempted to accede to their requests.

At the beginning of my tenure I was quite liberal in writing excuses; I wrote them for students who were experiencing mild depressions or anxiety attacks. Because their symptoms seemed to be relieved following a change of environment, I felt justified in having told the authorities that these students were sick. Unfortunately, as more and more students requested and received excuses, the housing administrators became irritated with me. Every time a student was excused from a contract, somebody lost money: the university was able to incur the loss without too much pain, but the private owners of dormitories were quite incensed.

Eventually I was forced to sharpen my criteria for offering excuses; I decided I would recommend them only if the patient were suffering from a severe emotional disorder that seemed to be generated or aggravated by his housing situation. But I found it was very difficult to adhere to such criteria; I could not easily decide who was terribly sick and who was not. Some students exaggerated the degree of their suffering more than others. Some could present excellent social and humanitarian reasons for being released from an oppressive situation, but these students often seemed to have relatively stable personalities. I never made a decision to excuse one person and not another without feeling that it was rather arbitrary. As I reflect upon my practices at that time, I realize that my recommendations were probably based as often on the patient's charm or aggressiveness, or how I was feeling a particular day, as on any psychiatric insight. In short, my recommendations were dishonest. At different times I tried to lighten my burden by having others participate in the excuse-giving process so that a committee would make the final decision. These efforts neither simplified my task nor relieved my conscience; the other participants eventually came to feel as perplexed and dishonest as I.

In the course of listening to students and administrators I began to realize that a number of questionable practices were going on in the dormitories. Some landlords had established highly arbitrary and oppressive rules and were oblivious to the emotional needs of students. Others failed to give the students what they promised them. I also began to wonder if it made sense to force a seventeen- or eighteen-year-old youth, who perhaps had never seen a particular dormitory, to sign a contract obliging him to remain there for a year. Because of these considerations and the obvious frustrations of trying to decide which students should be excused, I radically altered the policy of the University Psychiatry Service: I simply ruled that there would be no further psychiatric excuses for this purpose unless the student was so disturbed that he had to leave school. I agreed to providing the housing authorities with a psychiatric evaluation of any student who requested an excuse, but I insisted that excuse-giving was not a medical function and worded my reports accordingly.

Before taking this step, I discussed the problem with the university housing administrators; I told them of my frustrations and of my feelings that difficult ethical problems were merely being passed on to the psychiatrist. They were sympathetic but unmoved. When I finally decided not to issue any more excuses, some housing administrators vehemently opposed me. They argued that my own actions were arbitrary and disruptive, that they could never decide which students should be excused without the benefit of a medical judgment. For a time they even considered returning to the policy of honoring excuses from private psychiatrists or from other counseling services on campus. The only way I could prevent further involvement in writing excuses was to maintain an attitude of unrelenting stubbornness.

I believe that my initial willingness to give excuses to selected students prevented them from expressing their dissatisfaction with dormitory life to the university administrators. This, in turn, prevented the administrators from looking at the conditions that were creating dissatisfaction. When I stopped providing psychiatric excuses, many changes in the management of the dormitories began to take place. The housing administrators became more aware of some of the problems in the dormitories, and students began to demand more changes in their dormitories. I realize, of course, that some of these things happened because of the concurrent rising militancy of the students, but I am also convinced that if I had continued to serve as a source for relieving pressure in the student housing system, these changes would have come about more slowly. By performing what had seemed to be a humanitarian function and by helping to disguise a social problem as a medical problem, I had helped the dormitory system resist reform; I had served as an agent of the status quo.

THERAPEUTIC ABORTION

In our country a woman who finds herself with an unwanted pregnancy has several alternatives. She can carry the baby to term and make the best of it; she can seek out a criminal abortionist who, for a price, will terminate her pregnancy; or she can go to another country (or to a state such as New York) where she can obtain a safe abortion. She can also try to obtain a legal abortion in most states in this country by finding a doctor who will recommend it, but this usually means that she must convince a doctor that she is sick enough to have her pregnancy terminated on medical grounds.

Although the situation is rapidly changing, therapeutic abortion is still, for the most part, granted in this country only when a doctor makes a formal statement that carrying a child to term will seriously threaten the mother's life. As of this writing, only a few states will sanction a therapeutic abortion in situations where the mother's health rather than her very existence is threatened. In most states doctors cannot legally recommend a therapeutic abortion even if they are nearly positive that the child will be born defective, nor can the abortion be sanctioned if the pregnancy results from incest or rape. In practice, doctors are usually willing to recommend therapeutic abortion when a woman has such a severe heart, respiratory or urinary disease that there would be a substantial risk of her dying if she had to carry the child to term. It is much more difficult to know if abortions are granted when there is reasonable certainty that carrying a child to term would aggravate the mother's health but would not result in her death. It is quite possible that many doctors recommend abortion in those cases, but they usually do so quietly and illegally.

Conceivably, a woman might be so emotionally disturbed that there would be a strong likelihood that she might kill herself if she were forced to carry her child to term; in those cases recommendations for therapeutic abortion are made by a psychiatrist. If he believes abortion is justified, he is only required to submit a written report stating that the patient's life would be gravely threatened by the continuation of her pregnancy. In many hospitals this report will probably not be seriously challenged by other psychiatrists, the obstetrician who does the abortion, or any type of review board. At the present time it is very hard to know what criteria are actually being utilized in granting therapeutic abortions on psychiatric grounds. Policies differ from state to state and from hospital to hospital: some doctors will recommend therapeutic abortion only when they are absolutely convinced that the patient is gravely ill and suicidal; others will recommend it when there are fewer ominous signs of psychological disturbance. From my own experience and from what I have learned from colleagues, it seems clear that women who are granted therapeutic abortions are a special group: they are often among the community elite; not surprisingly, many are relatives of physicians. It requires a certain knowledge of the law and familiarity with psychiatrists even to know how to go about asking for a therapeutic abortion on psychiatric grounds. Therefore, this type of abortion is largely a privilege granted to upper-middle-class whites; it is rarely available to the poor, the uneducated, and the black.

When the psychiatrist writes an official report stating that a given woman will endanger her life by carrying a child to term, he is on shaky intellectual grounds. Many women who have serious emotional disturbances and are reluctant to have a baby would never contemplate suicide; their lives are in no danger at all. Other emotionally disturbed women who find themselves with an unwanted pregnancy will threaten suicide, but it is quite difficult to evaluate the seriousness of their threats. The psychiatrist generally knows that even the woman who is sincerely threatening suicide can be treated by more traditional means without having to resort to abortion; he is also aware that the suicidal patient, once she knows there are no other alternatives, would probably respond well to psychotherapy, drug therapy, or hospitalization.

A woman who knows the laws of her state and is looking for an abortion on psychiatric grounds quickly learns that she must talk suicide if she is to get her way. It is very easy for a woman with an unwanted pregnancy who knows that illness is a way out to convince herself that she is ill; it makes little difference whether she does this consciously or unconsciously. To the extent that a woman's personal suffering enables her to avoid carrying a child to term, she will probably feel more depressed and more suicidal. The psychiatrist can accelerate this process by directly or indirectly letting the patient know that she must present grave signs of illness before he can recommend abortion.

Many psychiatrists will recommend therapeutic abortion for humanitarian reasons even when they are not convinced that the patient will destroy herself; to do this, however, they must state that the patient is suicidal. To salve their professional consciences, these psychiatrists subtly teach the patient (and usually she is an apt pupil) to be as sick as possible and to say the right words ("I'll kill myself if I'm forced to have this baby") before they will write a psychiatric excuse. After the patient has gone through a convincing display of her "illness" she can have her abortion. A few doctors who are more honest about their dishonesty will be less scrupulous in documenting the need for an abortion; they will simply say that a woman is suicidal even though they know she is not.

There are many reasons why a woman might not want to have her baby. Children can be an economic or psychological burden: sometimes the birth of an additional child within a family or the birth of a child out of wedlock can make a previously adequate life seem intolerable. Many mothers bring unwanted children into the world; many of these mothers, if they had been sufficiently aware and determined, could probably have convinced psychiatrists that they were too sick to carry their children to term. For every woman who receives an abortion on psychiatric grounds, there are probably a dozen others whose plight is more tragic and whose emotional handicaps are more serious. No psychiatrist, if he is honest with himself, will claim to be able to distinguish among women's possible selfish, practical, idealistic, and irrational motivations. Nor can he describe any scientific criteria that would enable him to know which unhappy woman should have pregnancy terminated and which should not. When he recommends an abortion, he usually lies. It is a kind lie, a dishonesty intended to make the world a little better, but still a lie. Consider the following case:

A twenty-four-year-old woman came to see me requesting a therapeutic abortion. She was in her third month of pregnancy. The possibility of receiving a therapeutic abortion was brought to her attention by her psychiatrist, who had been treating her in conventional psychotherapy for about six months.

She was one of six children raised in a poverty-stricken, unhappy home. She remembered that, as a child, she was shy and frightened most of the time. Her father drank heavily and at times beat the children. Her mother was an intensely religious woman who repeatedly harangued the children with the virtues of piety and chastity. When the patient was thirteen years old, her father left home. At this time she came to be even more strongly dominated by the mother's puritanical influence.

Surprisingly, the patient did well as a student and was the only member of her family to finish high school. She worked as a secretary for two years, saved her money, and entered a teachers' college. By continuing to work nights and by saving every penny, she eventually managed to obtain a teaching certificate and secured a position as an elementary school teacher in a rural district. By this time the other children had left home and the patient provided the sole support for her mother. After a year of teaching she began to feel depressed. She had few friends and rarely had the opportunity to go out with members of the opposite sex. When she began to experience crying spells she consulted a psychiatrist.

During the course of her therapy she began to feel more confident, overcame some of her shyness, and started to date a few men. One of these dates was an aggressive man who managed to get her intoxicated and forced her to have intercourse. This was the patient's first and only sexual experience and she became pregnant.

The patient knew that if she carried the baby to term she would lose her job, and there was no other means of financial support. She also feared that because of the moralistic attitude of her community, it would be extremely difficult for her to obtain another teaching job. She had no idea of what she would do with the baby. It seemed unlikely that her mother would help her; in fact, she feared that her mother would totally reject her.

When I interviewed the patient I was very much aware that she was experiencing profound emotional anguish. At the same time, however, I was impressed with her character and her psychological strength. At no time did she threaten suicide. She was only mildly demanding and certainly not histrionic. There was little or no doubt in my mind that she could carry her baby to term without endangering her life, but I was also deeply moved by the tragedy of her situation.

The position I found myself in was not too different from what a psychiatrist usually encounters when he evaluates patients for therapeutic abortion. The most humane and decent thing I could do was to recommend abortion, yet it would have to be a lie. I had the choice of lying outright by saying that the patient was suicidal or by training her to talk about suicide in order to bribe my conscience a little. Whatever I did in this situation would be morally questionable.

The psychiatrist who recommends a therapeutic abortion should be aware of how his recommendation affects the patient. Many of those who request therapeutic abortion do not have the personality strength of the patient I have described. Granting excuses to emotionally disturbed individuals may, in the long run, harm them. Although there is probably no great danger of depression following a therapeutic abortion, what is learned in the process of securing a psychiatric excuse from meeting an obligation may be quite damaging. The excused patient may learn to use her "illness" as a means of avoiding other obligations; she may also learn to view herself as a person who should not be held responsible for her actions.

Even though the psychiatrist who helps a woman obtain a therapeutic abortion may believe that he is performing a humane act, the over-all impact of such excuse-giving upon the social order does not promote humanistic goals. Helping a few women find an easy solution to their problems does nothing whatsoever for the millions of women who risk their lives in going to criminal abortionists or who bring unwanted children into the world. Furthermore, granting therapeutic abortions to a select few acts as a safety valve or mechanism to neutralize some of the forces that would otherwise press for needed social change. If society had to witness the tragedy of highly disturbed women bringing unwanted children into the world, it might examine the whole issue of any woman bringing an unwanted child into the world. If women of position, sophistication, and power could not easily rid themselves of unwanted pregnancies, they would be more inclined to do something to change existing abortion laws. If physicians could not occasionally salve their consciences by legally aborting some of their patients and friends, they, too, would be more willing to try to change the abortion laws. The very presence and use of therapeutic abortion serves as a kind of social opiate; excuse-giving masks the pain but does little to cure a social problem.

Many psychiatrists, social scientists, and attorneys have argued that the United States should liberalize its abortion laws; they believe that if abortion were granted when pregnancy represented a threat to the mother's health or resulted from incest or rape, the whole problem could be handled in a convenient and humane manner. Yet, the experience of Colorado with its liberal law has not been salutary.(1,2) In Colorado, therapeutic abortion for psychiatric reasons is still available only to a limited segment of the population. Permission for abortion depends on the liberalism and benevolence of the particular examining physician, and sometimes the decision is based only on the number of cases that a local hospital can handle comfortably. Psychiatrists must still be less than honest in speculating on what effects childbearing will have on their patients' mental health; some are completely disillusioned with Colorado's liberalized system because they feel it obscures the social problem even more than the former, more restrictive system.

Many physicians, attorneys, and legislators have reached an obvious conclusion.(3,4) They believe that every woman should have the right to have an unwanted pregnancy terminated. They insist that rules governing abortion should not be part of the criminal law but that the decision should simply be made by the patient and a qualified doctor. They recommend legislation (already passed by a few states) permitting abortion upon request provided that a doctor believes it will help and not harm the patient; this recommendation seems to be an indirect but effective means of legalizing abortion. We need such legislation as well as sufficient facilities to accommodate all abortion patients. Unfortunately, even those states that have effectively legalized abortion have not appropriated the funds to make quick, inexpensive abortions available to all citizens. No woman should have to undergo a criminal abortion, bring an unwanted child into the world, or falsely label herself mentally ill and irresponsible.

CRIMINAL RESPONSIBILITY

In order for someone to be found guilty of a crime, there must be proof that he intended to commit the crime. Our society has always been guided by the principle that it will not punish unless it can impose blame. Without evil intent or *mens rea* an offender cannot be designated a criminal; but, of course, illegal acts can be committed without criminal intent. A crime may be committed accidentally, under duress, or in self-defense; and a child under seven is usually not considered mature enough to have developed a criminal intent.

Since the seventeenth century it has been held in Britain and then America that some individuals who break the law are so incapacitated or deranged by mental illness that their criminal behavior cannot be viewed as intentional. An effort has been made to excuse these people from responsibility for their criminal actions. In most jurisdictions the rule by which a person is adjudged mentally responsible or nonresponsible is derived from the nineteenth-century English law. As enunciated in the McNaughten case over a hundred years ago, the rule states that, "To establish a defense on the grounds of insanity, it must be clearly proved that at the time of committing the act the party accused was laboring under such a defect from disease of the mind as not to know the nature and quality of the act he was doing or, if he did know it, that he did not know he was doing what was wrong."

Various alternatives to the McNaughten rule have been proposed, the most notable of which was enunciated in 1954 by David L. Bazelon, chief judge of the United States Court of Appeals for the District of Columbia, in the case of Monte Durham: "The rule we now hold is simply that an accused is not criminally responsible if his unlawful act was the product of mental disease or mental defect. We use 'disease' in the sense of a condition which is considered capable of improving or deteriorating. We use 'defect' in the sense of a condition which is not considered capable of either improving or deteriorating and which may be congenital or the result of injury or the residual effect of a physical or mental disease." This rule, although initially hailed as a progressive step by psychiatrists, has never had much popularity in this country. The McNaughten rule, or the so-called right or wrong test, is still widely used.

Psychiatric excuse-giving for criminal responsibility has received a great deal of public attention because the psychiatrist must appear in court and carry out his work in public. He can expect to be cross-examined by hostile attorneys. Psychiatrists will often take opposing positions, one arguing that an offender should be excused and another arguing that he should not. Any disagreement between psychiatrists is likely to receive considerable publicity.

The public spectacle of an insanity trial, while providing superb emotional and intellectual diversion for the public, exposes the psychiatrist at his worst possible moment; he often looks like a fool or a charlatan. Psychiatrists regularly find themselves obliged to take theoretical positions that contradict the conceptual basis of their practice outside the courtroom. Other participants in the proceedings are equally frustrated: lawyers and judges find psychiatric pronouncements confusing and sometimes unintelligible, and the disturbed offender rarely receives the kind of treatment that would enable him to return to society as a free and useful citizen. No matter what the outcome an insanity trial seldom accomplishes anything of a humanistic nature.

Perhaps our legal system would be more tolerable if all men—regardless of race, social position, or economic status—had the opportunity to obtain a psychiatric excuse for a criminal act. Unfortunately, most disturbed offenders seldom ever have the chance to plead that they are not guilty by reason of insanity unless there has been a spectacular and unusually violent crime (which might entail a long sentence); even when the potential consequences of a conviction are grim, this plea will not always be raised. The decision to use this plea will sometimes have nothing to do with the personality disturbance of the offender; it will often depend upon the availability of forensic psychiatrists, the laws of the state, the attitudes of the community, and the offender's social or economic class. In many jurisdictions, for example, an uneducated black would probably not plead insanity nor be found not guilty by reason of insanity.

As in the case of therapeutic abortion, the psychiatrist has no scientific guidelines to help him decide who should be excused and who should not. In an insanity trial the psychiatrist must judge an offender's responsibility for a particular act. Assigning personal responsibility depends more upon philosophical or moral rather than scientific considerations. Everyone has an opinion on this issue, and a psychiatrist's training and experience probably do not provide him with any special expertise. In some ways he has more difficulty in making decisions about personal responsibility than the ordinary citizen. As a scientist the psychiatrist may be a strict determinist, but in his day-to-day practice he knows that if he is ever going to help people cope with their difficulties, he must constantly implore them to assume responsibility for their actions. The psychiatrist tries to teach his patients to be totally accountable for their thoughts, actions, and dreams; he does this even when the patient is considered to be mentally ill and his behavior is believed to be unconsciously determined. When the psychiatrist enters the courtroom, however, he is often asked questions that tempt him to forget his own teaching.

What seems to happen in a criminal insanity trial when psychiatrists with different values examine the same patient is that they agree about scientific questions but disagree about moral questions. Psychiatrists generally agree about the nature of the offender's disturbance and about the kind of treatment that might lead to his rehabilitation. When asked to comment upon the offender's responsibility for his behavior, however, psychiatrists answer in terms of their own belief systems. The psychiatrist who is more politically liberal, psychoanalytically oriented, and deeply committed to the cause of social justice will be more likely to find a given offender nonresponsible than the one who is more politically conservative, biologically oriented, and committed to the cause of individual rights and privileges.

To excuse a criminal offender the psychiatrist must somehow relate a highly arbitrary concept of mental illness to the philosophical concept of responsibility. The legal rules that are supposed to guide the psychiatrist in determining this relationship are based on the presumption that mental illness can be clearly defined. I and many other psychiatrists have repeatedly emphasized that this is not so.(5) Even if there were more objective criteria for defining mental illness, we would still have no means of deciding whether those whom we call mentally ill either regularly or even occasionally fail to recognize the moral implications of their behavior. The McNaughten and Durham rules are based on totally erroneous notions of the nature of human suffering. Actually, a strong case could probably be made that social factors such as poverty and race, whose effects are easier to study and measure, should be given more weight in mitigating responsibility than the weight currently given to psychological factors.

When a psychiatrist testifies in a criminal insanity proceeding he must deceive either himself or others. Probably the majority of forensic psychiatrists deceive themselves; they believe that mental illness is an affliction and that their expertise in human behavior enables them to know precisely when one is ill enough to be nonresponsible. Other psychiatrists know better, but they participate in insanity proceedings only to pursue humanistic goals. Sometimes they agree to testify in order to help the offender avoid a death sentence. Usually the psychiatrist who testifies for the defendant wants to temper the harshness of punishment in general.

As in the case of excuses for pregnancy, the psychiatric excuse for criminal behavior helps to preserve the status quo. Finding selected offenders nonresponsible represents a shabby compromise, allowing society to mitigate a harsh punishment for only a few mentally disturbed offenders while ignoring the plight of others. By investing an incredible amount of energy in trying to help a small group of offenders, psychiatrists have done little more than lend our correctional system a deceptive facade of decency. When a psychiatrist helps an insane offender escape punishment, he actually strengthens the present system of correctional justice. The public, which is spared the agony of watching the punishment of a mentally ill offender, is more willing to tolerate the merciless and irrational treatment of ordinary offenders.

An enormous amount of psychiatric zeal and energy has been invested in the issue of criminal responsibility, which unfortunately has drained the profession's attention away from more critical issues—reforming our current system of correctional justice and treating offenders. Psychiatrists have actually done very little to help reform our correctional system. So much energy has been invested, so much emotion spent, and so much talent wasted in dealing with the issue of criminal responsibility that one observer (Dr. H. G. Whittington) has referred to it as psychiatry's "Vietnam." The solution of this problem may be the same as what seems to be the most expeditious solution to the war in Vietnam: withdrawal.

If psychiatrists simply refused to help determine criminal responsibility, neither they, the law, nor most offenders would suffer.(6,7,8) Psychiatrists could then turn their attention to more important matters—trying to create a more humane correctional system and treating offenders. Administrators of our correctional system (including attorneys) would then have to deal with the real issues of crime in our society. A few offenders might suffer if they could not find a psychiatrist to testify that they were insane; this might be a critical factor in cases where a criminal conviction could result in capital punishment. But it should be noted that the death penalty has not been carried out in the United States for a long time, and any disturbed offenders who might receive prison sentences probably would not be worse off than they were before. Many offenders who are found insane spend almost as much time in custodial institutions as those convicted of crime. Furthermore, if our correctional system were reformed no offender would ever have to spend an inordinate amount of time in any dehumanizing environment, whether a hospital or a prison.

Refusal to participate in criminal insanity trials would not deprive the psychiatrist of an important role in the correctional process. If society really wanted to rehabilitate all offenders who could be helped and to control all those who were dangerous, the psychiatrist could advise the judge or jury on the matter of disposition. If punishment were not the major issue, all offenders, including those believed to be emotionally disturbed, could be tried in court for the sole purpose of determining if they had actually committed an illegal act. Mental illness would not mitigate criminal intent. All persons found to have committed a crime (except where *mens rea* does not exist for reasons other than mental illness) would be considered fully responsible. Psychiatrists and other behavioral scientists would then have the responsibility to treat offenders and assist society in deciding what to do with the offender.

PSYCHIATRY AND THE DRAFT

Decisions to excuse certain individuals from the obligation to serve in the armed forces are generally made by government-employed physicians. They are quite likely, however, to by influenced by what they learn from other physicians. If a doctor, for example, sends a letter to the induction center stating that his own patient has a serious heart ailment, the draft board physician will probably respect that advice and examine the patient carefully. The same thing holds true for psychiatric excuses. If a young man appears for a selective service physical examination with a letter stating that he has a mental illness that would seriously affect his military service, he will receive special medical attention. His chances of being excused from military duty will be far greater than that of the average draftee.

In the armed forces there have probably always been questionable uses of medical and psychiatric excuses. The issues raised by such practices, however, seem more agonizing with respect to the unpopular war in Vietnam. In the past five years I have had no male patient eligible for the draft who did not ask me to help him stay out of the armed forces.(9) Every day someone comes to our clinic requesting our assistance in avoiding military obligations. As in other situations, excuses from military duty are most likely to be granted to the sophisticated, the aggressive, and the wealthy. To receive such an excuse, one must know something about how draft boards operate, be willing to approach a psychiatrist, be willing to define some of his everyday problems as an illness, and be able to afford to stay in therapy long enough to convince the psychiatrist that he is disturbed. One of my patients who returned from his physical examination where he was found unsuited for military service (at least partly because of the letter I had written for him) summarized the situation as follows: "It was awful. There were about twenty of us who asked to talk to the psychiatrist to try and convince him we were unfit. And some of those guys really looked pretty sick and messed up. But it was only the three of us who had letters who got out. The ones who didn't have a letter from a psychiatrist never had a chance."

It is hard to understand why a draft board accepts one candidate and rejects another; it is also difficult to understand how they evaluate letters from psychiatrists. Some psychiatrists will write letters stating plainly that their patients are too sick to serve in the armed forces. Others, like myself, will merely say that a patient is in therapy and that it might be useful to have him examined by a psychiatrist. From my own experience, it seems that almost any kind of letter from a reputable psychiatrist significantly helps the young person avoid his military obligation.

The whole matter of providing excuses from military service has agonized and corrupted the psychiatric profession. Many psychiatrists strongly oppose the war and will do whatever they can to keep their patients from risking their lives in what both parties believe is an immoral conflict. Some psychiatrists may have lied in order to help their patients escape the draft. If he is not biased, the psychiatrist undoubtedly finds it difficult to say honestly that a given individual is too emotionally disturbed to serve in the military. Of course, a patient's emotional disturbance itself is often brought about by his fear of military service. The best a psychiatrist can usually do is to write a very neutral letter suggesting that the draft board physicians themselves decide whether a candidate is suitable. In the words of our youth, however, this is a "cop-out"; it does not absolve the psychiatrist's guilt. He is still excusing selected individuals who happen to have been born in more fortunate circumstances than others.

By providing such excuses, the psychiatrist may feel that he is striking a blow against the war and furthering radical reform, but his efforts actually help the selective service system function with greater stability and smoothness. The young men who are deferred for psychiatric reasons are probably those who would have confronted the system because of their radical viewpoints. When they are deferred the selective service administrators are able to comfort themselves that they have kept out those who are unfit for service; they may also reassure themselves that it is the radical students who often seem unfit. Even without the radicals, there are still enough young men who can be drafted to fight an unpopular war. By excusing a select few, psychiatrists have helped to hinder useful confrontation and dissent. Perhaps we have not really helped our patients at all: they might have been better off entering the service, going to a foreign country, or fighting for their cause and going to jail.

A CONCLUDING NOTE ON PSYCHIATRIC EXCUSES

I have taken a relatively firm position on the issue of psychiatric excuses. Whenever I discuss this with my students, they usually remind me that with fewer excuses some individuals would suffer needlessly; furthermore, psychiatrists can simultaneously grant excuses and work to reform the social system. Some students argue that social change might be facilitated if psychiatrists committed themselves to such a dual role, but unfortunately, there is no evidence to substantiate this. What a psychiatrist does to initiate change will depend upon his ethical convictions and his previous experiences. My own experience has led me to believe that less excuse-giving will allow the psychiatrist to retain his professional integrity as well as hasten the process of reform. In the short run giving fewer excuses may hurt a few individuals, but in the long run it may help many.

I have also noted an insidious tendency on the part of psychiatrists who grant excuses to feel that when they have excused a few, they have won an important battle. Many of them do nothing directly to try to change malignant social institutions. While I appreciate their humanitarian motives in trying to help individuals who need urgent care, I would also urge them to take an active part in trying to change the institutions that oppress so many who are not fortunate enough to be their patients.

NOTES

(1) Heller, A., and Whittington, H.G. "The Colorado Story: Denver General Hospital Experience with the Change in the Law for Therapeutic Abortion." *American Journal of Psychiatry* 125 (1968): 809-816.

(2) Whittington, H.G. "Evaluation of Therapeutic Abortion as an Element of Preventive Psychiatry." *American Journal of Psychiatry* 126 (1970): 1224-1229.

(3) "The Right to Abortion: A Psychiatric View." Committee on Psychiatry and Law, Group for the Advancement of Psychiatry, 1969.

(4) Shainess, N. "Abortion is No Man's Business." *Psychology Today*, May, 1970.

(5) Halleck, S.L. "The Psychiatrist and the Legal Process." *Psychology Today*, February, 1969.

(6) Halleck, S.L. *Psychiatry and the Dilemma of Crime.* New York: Harper & Row, 1967.

(7) Roche, P.Q. *The Criminal Mind.* New York: Farrar, Straus and Cudahy, 1958.

(8) Menninger, K.A. *The Crime of Punishment.* New York: Viking Press, 1968.

(9) Halleck, S.L. "Students and the Draft." *The Progressive*, September, 1968.

EVERYTHING YOU WANTED TO HAVE
IN SEX LAWS

Ralph Slovenko

There are many laws on sex—to name a few: rape, crime against nature, exhibitionism, voyeurism, indecent behavior with minors, sexual psychopath legislation, prostitution, pornography, divorce, and abortion. To what extent are these laws necessary?

Law is designed to control behavior. It is designed to limit one's own impulses and the impulses of others. In the best personality development, external controls turn into self-control. When self-control is a fact, security imposed from the outside may be an insult. However, the needs of individuals vary, and in some measure, we are all relieved to know that there are external controls.

What should be the nature of control in the area of sexual behavior? Laws governing sexual behavior are justified, it seems, when the behavior is public or when it is aggressive, whether public or private. In either case, the aim of the law would be better served by non-sex laws.

So-called sex crimes are expressions of aggression usually representing a considerable degree of personality disorganization. Non-sex laws dealing with aggression are ample enough to cover the waterfront. The nontraumatizing or nonviolent type of behavior, which too can be covered by non-sex laws, may be considered solely from the point of view of indecency.

As is often recommended, the emphasis of the law ought to be the deterrence of untoward aggressive activity, gross public indecency, and the seduction of juveniles and children. The law ought not to be concerned with activity performed in private and between consenting adults, be it heterosexual or homosexual. In all of these cases, the issue is really not sex but rather protection of the helpless from indecent behavior or attack.

RAPE

Women are primarily interested in the prevention of rape, not in the apprehension of an offender. They fear the violence and transgression of their integrity. Whatever the concern of others, the particular woman who has actually been raped usually wants to fade out of the picture as quickly and quietly as possible. Apprehension of the offender seems to her like closing the stable after the horse is out. Especially, she is not interested in assisting law enforcement officials in prosecuting the offender when the proceedings would tend to humiliate her. She wants nothing to add to her distress. Moreover, in rape cases, the prosecutor must establish beyond a reasonable doubt that she "resisted to the utmost," which is very difficult to prove. An acquittal, which is more probable than not, leaves the public with the impression that she voluntarily had sexual intercourse with a vagrant. Her reputation is stained. Often, the woman who does shout rape is regarded simply as vindictive and the reality of her complaint is doubted. As a result, the law on rape goes largely unenforced. Only a small percentage of rapes are reported and fewer are prosecuted.

The criminal law postulates that the apprehension of an offender serves to deter others from crime, but the present law is self-defeating. A rape victim would be more likely to assist law enforcement officials if the proceeding were less humiliating. The crime of "kidnapping," "indecent assault" or "assault and battery," with adjustment in penalty, could replace the rape charge. Penetration or chastity of the victim is irrelevant in a kidnapping or battery case. No distinction, moreover, need be made between heterosexuality and homosexuality. The sex is irrelevant. The homosexual rape can be as devastating as the heterosexual rape; Lawrence of Arabia is the classic illustration of a mental breakdown that resulted from a homosexual attack. Originally rape referred to a carrying off or seizure of the person, not necessarily a female.

CRIMES AGAINST NATURE

The typical case of "crime against nature" nowadays involves a person who shows lack of discretion by committing homosexual acts in a public restroom. This type of conduct is as offensive and against public decency as would be the performance of a heterosexual act in public.

Forms of human behavior rooted in biology are relegated to the private arena, at least in the civilized world as we know it. Perhaps we want to hide those activities we do in common with animals or at least do them in dignity. As Chekhov put it, man should strive to be beautiful—in character, dress, and behavior. To do certain things in public would not be considered in the best of taste. Hence, to eat in a public cafeteria is a relatively styleless activity—it almost resembles the pig's stall. Eating is surely not the same as dining. To be invited to a person's home to dine is an honor, but to carry on sexual activity in public is the greatest affront to good taste, as well as utterly demeaning to the parties involved. It is poor taste even to talk publicly about it.

Homosexual or other abnormal sexual activity is to be prescribed like heterosexual activity to the private sphere, not because it is evil as some moralists might put it, but because there is a proper time and place. Law-enforcement practices reveal, actually, that homosexual behavior is generally punished only when it occurs in public. The important question is: What should be considered "in public"? Suppose it is done secretively but in a public place (for example, behind a partition wall in a theater restroom). As regards homosexual behavior, we know that those who "neck" in public (daytime or nighttime), even on lover's lane, are sometimes charged with "disturbing the peace" or at least told to move along.

The community has a need to control as well as to express its feeling about gross violations of established social amenities but it can do so without sex laws. If the criminal law is to be applied, individuals who display their privates in public places can be charged with "public disorder," "disturbing the peace," or "assault and battery." These crimes protect the public and at the same time carry less stigma than "crime against nature" or "sodomy," which could then be removed from the statute books. Embarrassed by a sex charge, even if unfounded, the already miserable offender generally pleads guilty. He wants to get out of the process as quickly as possible and the sex charge, in effect, deprives him of a fair hearing.

NUISANCE BEHAVIOR

What was once generally assumed about sex offenders is not to be assumed any longer. The image of the sex offender has been one sexually very potent. In actual fact, he is often impotent. He needs all the cooperation that a woman can possibly muster before he can come close to her. He is an emotionally immature person who has deep feelings of inadequacy.

Unable to relate to others, an individual may instead simply show himself or look. He is as though a spectator to the human race. The exhibitionist and the voyeur (peeping tom), however, make nuisances of themselves when the showing takes place on a public street or the looking takes place through a bedroom window. Fear is understandable: how can a person distinguish the harmful from the harmless? Again, however, sex laws are not necessary; there are other laws to prohibit these activities.

Frightened by adults, an individual may turn to a minor. An exhibitionist may be unable even to get physically close enough to a woman to exhibit himself, so instead, finding it less threatening, he may exhibit himself to a child. Confinement, if that is in order, should be in a hospital (not a special sex-offender hospital) rather than a prison. In prison, they not only receive no treatment but are the subject of every brutality; usually they are prey to vicious, homosexual attacks.

Criminal assaults on young girls are sometimes committed by aging men who have the task of adjusting themselves to a decline in physical strength and sexual power. Another characteristic of aging may be a shift from genitality to pre-genitality. There may be increasing interest and engagement in scatalogical activities. Pornographic books and pictures are in great demand and peeping-tom tendencies may occur in old age as well as in adolescence. A great deal of the sexual behavior of old people is not basically genital in origin but results from their emotional isolation. One of the different problems facing the aged person is how to employ his remaining love and energy. Contemporary society is remiss in not providing activities for and encouraging relationships among the aged.

Then there are the various perversions. Some people must go through bizarre, unusual, or extremely specific rituals before they can have sexual stimulation or intercourse. A man may have to dress in women's clothing or have his hair pulled or twisted before intercourse or an orgastic discharge can occur. Some men may have to "play rape"—break down a door or break through a window—and the woman must play that she is being attacked; only then may her partner feel like a man. Breaking a door or window is permissible at home ("a man's home is his castle"), but it may be disturbing to neighbors.

The law can cope with such situations through non-sex laws. But how has the law met these problems? The law has responded by emphasizing sex, by enacting special legislation and providing special institutions. Since sex organs are involved, it has been natural for legislators to think in terms of sex. Almost half of the states have responded with the enactment of legislation providing for indeterminate confinement of the "sexual psychopath." All the statutes do not agree on a definition but usually such a person is defined as one lacking the power to control his sexual impulses or having criminal propensities toward committing sex offenses.

Special institutions such as the one in Atascadero, California have been created in a few states to implement these statutes. To put it mildly, they have not worked out; in blunt opinion, they are a fraud and a hoax. A special institution is theoretically justified when there is a homogeneity within the group and a particular institution can offer some special service for that group. For the so-called sexual psychopath neither criterion is met. One might assume that sexual deviates are people with much in common, a class apart. However, such homogeneity assuredly does not exist. Among the deviates are neurotics, schizophrenics, schizoid personalities, alcoholics, persons with chronic brain damage, mental defectives—the entire gamut of mental disorders. All that they share is a single trait, one that psychiatrists must consider a symptom.

The special sexual psychopath proceeding was adopted in an effort to detain the dangerous, aggressive offender; but the type of person usually confined has been the mental defective or impoverished farm boy who is bewildered by city life. Moreover, the proceeding was designed to offer treatment, but, whatever that is supposed to constitute, it is assuredly not available. Instead, the proceeding serves only to stigmatize the inmate. He is labelled a "sexual psychopath." In the institution he himself puts around his neck a sign that reads,

"I am a masturbator," "I am a peeping tom," etc. His self-esteem was low before; now it is utterly devastated. His troubles with the opposite sex are multiplied. Imagine, if you will, his problem later when seeking the companionship of a girl. Surely, no parents would want their daughter to go out with a "sexual psychopath." Surely, no employer is likely to hire him. The sorry experience of states that have enacted sexual psychopath legislation and have established special institutions furnishes ample evidence that their approach is not to be followed.

PROSTITUTION

Prostitution, an age-old activity, is the only institution that has survived all revolutions. In one form or another, it is likely to remain with us. The Wolfenden Report, which dealt with prostitution as well as homosexuality, did not recommend that prostitution should be made illegal as that is an impractical objective. It did recommend that legislation should be passed "to drive it off the streets" on the ground that public solicitation is a nuisance. The problem was expressed as being one of "high-visibility," thus supporting, at least functionally, the position taken by Mrs. Patrick Campbell in correspondence with George Bernard Shaw that she did not particularly care what people did as long as they did not do it in the streets and frighten the horses.

Following a series of complaints from businessmen, tourists, and area residents in midtown New York, that city's police department recently cracked down and made a "cleanup." Checking on the backgrounds of the 1,250 female and 52 male prostitutes it arrested during a three-month period, the department discovered that about 40 percent of those arrested had been previously arrested for other crimes—drugs, possession, burglaries, robberies, larcenies—and half of the 40 percent had a history of violent crime, including, in some cases, homicide. Offenses usually do not occur singularly or in isolation, and laws covering these non-sex crimes were amply available to loop these individuals into the criminal law process.

In addition to these criminal laws, municipalities usually have an ordinance providing, "no soliciting or peddling without permit." Designed to control salesmen, its scope also covers the prostitute. Using this approach, the enforcement problems in the law on prostitution, such as a policeman's affair with the prostitute, are avoided.

PORNOGRAPHY

Considering today's society, the figleaf is like the patch that an adolescent puts over a pimple on his face, thinking that it is his only problem or that it will cure all of his worries. (One poster asks: Remember when the air was clean and sex was dirty?)

Obscenity is more than the display of one's private parts. Obscenity includes the exploitation of man's sexuality for nonsexual ends. Sex is used as a lure.

Consider, for example, the banality of commercial advertising, which exploits the emotional life of man, his joy and pain, in every conceivable way in order to sell any marketable object. Emotions appropriate for a moonlight ride are evoked over a deodorant or other product and utterly debase man's emotional life: "Super Bright toothpaste gives you sex appeal."

Legal restrictions on the private use of pornography or obscenity are objectionable not because the term is difficult to define but because censorship is a restriction on the mind. Does this mean that nothing can or should be done about the display of pornographic or obscene materials in public places? In this connection, the issue needs to be focused differently. It is the commercial exploitation of pornography or obscenity that gives it a character different from private use. At common law, a public nuisance was always crime and punishable as such, as well as giving rise to liability in tort. The public nuisance concept is based on an interference with the interests of the community or the comfort or convenience of the general public. The concept is also applied where a hogpen or the keeping of a malarial pond interferes with the public health.

Where the displays of bookstore windows and entrances to motion picture theatres of explicit sexual materials sully the surroundings, the public can be protected by public nuisance principles. Ownership or rental of property abutting public thoroughfares does not create a constitutional right to present any matter for public view, even matter that may not be legally obscene and may be constitutionally protected when sold indoors to a voluntary audience of adults. The public has the right to regulate the public display of materials that offend the sensibilities.

The highways and byways are strewn with signs which are no less obscene or ugly than the four-letter word. Surely they must go. Physicians and lawyers are restricted by their associations to the size and type of shingle they may display. Liquor stores in many states may not have signs larger than four by six inches, bearing only the words, "liquor store." Why should not this principle apply generally to all advertising?

The issue is really not one of free speech but one of aesthetics. People can talk "junk" under the First Amendment, but should they be allowed to breed and foist their junk upon the unwilling? This is an issue independent of sex.

DIVORCE

How helpful is the law to persons who are going through a divorce—a grievous time of life? Divorces are easily obtained (the approaching rate of nearly one out of two marriages attest to that) yet the parties are obliged to go through a legal procedure that is degrading and widens the gap already existing between them.

Divorce other than the property settlement aspects ought to be taken out of the courts. Courts are congested (the average lawsuit being tried today in Chicago was filed six years ago), a principal reason for the congestion being that courts handle many matters that are more administrative than judicial. Divorce is one of those matters that may be better handled out of the courts.

The common evaluation among judges and lawyers is that divorce and custody matters are "trash" cases. This is due to the modest fee and the demeaning procedure. In New York, where, until recently, adultery was the only grounds for divorce, one judge regularly began his docket by declaring, "Let the perjury begin." An allegation of cruelty is the most common ground for divorce, and the petition usually reads something like this:

> Your petitioner avers that the defendant has beat her severely on numerous occasions, and during these periods of intemperate conduct he has, in addition to causing physical injury to the petitioner, made her highly nervous and apprehensive for the safety not only of herself but of the children as well.
>
> Your petitioner notwithstanding has at all times during the existence of said marriage to defendant been a dutiful and faithful spouse and mother to their minor children, providing the defendant the respect and devotion of a loving wife.

The petition alleging cruelty, as is true with the other grounds, stigmatizes the defendant as a malevolent and sadistic person. The divorce law, like the criminal law, has long been based on an offense theory. Today, with the exception of a few states where it is sufficient simply to allege "breakdown of the marriage," a matrimonial offense, such as adultery or cruelty, must be alleged.

Divorce at the request of one party after one or two years' separation is a growing procedure in many states. To establish separation, however, the petitioner must bring in a neighbor or two to testify that no reconciliation took place during that time. The husband during this period of time may have come, perhaps weekly, to see the children and the neighbors surely know not a whit about what has occurred between the parties. The proceeding thus calls for fraud from the neighbors as well as from the parties. In law a single act of intercourse constitutes a reconciliation. It is irrelevant that the wife may have consented in order to attempt a reconciliation or to avoid an argument in the belief that peace and quiet would be in the best interest of the children.

Since a divorce can now be obtained as easily as candy at Christmas, why not handle it in a more proper setting? Courts are set up to decide issues, and there is really no issue in a divorce case. Present procedure, which rigs up an issue, is demeaning and degrading. Divorce is really now an administrative matter and should be handled accordingly.

ABORTION

The prevailing law in most states allows abortion only when the life of the mother is endangered. Such action may be justified, without positive sanction of law, however, as self-defense. The Spanish rabbi Maimonides long ago (1168) reasoned that the fetus might be destroyed if a woman's life is endangered by pregnancy, just as in self-defense an attacker could be justifiably killed.

Thirteen states have recently revised their law to allow abortion when the birth would cause serious mental harm to the mother, when the pregnancy is the result of forcible or statutory rape or incest, or when it is likely that the child would be born with a grave physical or mental defect. These changes were recommended by the American Law Institute (A.L.I.).

To obtain an abortion under these laws, however, a woman must allege that she has been raped, or that she will commit suicide, or that she is crazy or will go crazy if she must bear a child. She must get the attestation of one or two physicians or psychiatrists, to whom she must pay a relatively handsome fee, for nothing more than a signature. What doctor will refuse to approve an abortion for a woman who says she will kill herself or go crazy? He will perfunctorily assent but the woman is degraded in the process. In one way or another, members of her family and friends will learn that she obtained an abortion because she is "crazy," and she will be bothered by the label. Having German measles is the only nondegrading ground for abortion.

In discussions on abortion, two historical considerations are rarely noted. First, abortion as a crime was not, historically, designed for the protection of the woman; it was designed for the protection of the unborn child. Abortion was prohibited because the technical methods were so poor that injury was often done to the fetus but it was not aborted. To protect against an unsuccessful abortion resulting in a deformed birth (and a public charge) no abortion was permitted. Today, an abortion, properly performed, is not technically hazardous. Secondly, if bearing a child posed any risk to the woman, abortion was allowed the healthy woman but not the deranged, on the theory that there was nothing to lose for one already deranged. Judge Macnaghten of the House of Lords, in the classic case of *The King v. Bourne*, said that an abortion may not be performed on a girl who is "feeble-minded" or has what he called a "prostitute mind." As a healthy woman by definition would not be threatened by childbirth, apart from physical reasons (that is, a small pelvis), the net result was that no one was entitled to abortion except, as Judge Macnaghten put it, "a normal, decent girl brought up in a normal, decent way" who had been raped.

"Therapeutic abortion" is the basic concept of the A.L.I.-style abortion law. Under it, the disturbed woman—not the healthy woman—is allowed an abortion. But what is a "therapeutic abortion"? The mechanical procedure of abortion lies within the province of the obstetrician, but the decision to terminate the pregnancy should not. The decision is neither medical nor theological. The real question is whether the woman herself may decide whether or not to bear a child. To confuse the operation with the decision to undergo it is to convert a nonmedical decision into a medical one, and the medical books do not provide the answer.

When would it be "therapeutic" to terminate a pregnancy? Statistics reveal that few pregnant women commit suicide. Postpartum depression sometimes follows the birth of a child—separation is psychologically difficult for some women—but the condition is one that can be remedied easily enough. The concept "therapeutic abortion" is but a method to obtain enactment of more "liberal" law—in short, a gimmick, but in the process it denigrates the woman (and her husband). The fundamental question is: Does a woman own her body? The issue, too, is whether the law can stand the fraud of "therapeutic abortion."

The Reverend Robert Drinan, former Dean of the Boston College School of Law and now Congressman, says that having no abortion laws at all is more compatible with Catholic teaching than is the present "liberalized" abortion law recommended by the A.L.I. He states: "Abortion on request—or an absence of law with respect to abortion—has at least the merit of not involving the law and society in the business of selecting those persons whose lives may be legally terminated. A system of permitting abortion on request has the undeniable virtue of neutralizing the law so that, while the law does not forbid the abortion, it does not on the other hand sanction it."

The prevailing anti-abortion law, Drinan realizes, can not be preserved, and he observes: "Public authorities today are generally unable or unwilling to carry out the enforcement of existing anti-abortion laws. When the common conviction or the consensus that originally supported a law of a penal nature have eroded, it is sometimes wise for the law to withdraw its sanctions rather than have the majesty of the law brought into disrepute by open disobedience and unpunished defiance." Four states to date have repealed entirely their laws on abortion, making it completely legal.

CONCLUSION

Aristotle once observed that if man kept his actions slow, his voice low, and his words controlled, he would command respect. This, too, ought to be the way for the law, especially in matters that are as sensitive and delicate as sex. Oliver Wendell Holmes, writing about the criminal law, once asked, "What have we better than a blind guess to show that the criminal law in its present form does more good than harm?" As far as sex laws are concerned the answer is clear. Not only are sex laws unnecessary, the harm they do exceeds any good that they may possibly do. The legitimate goals of present-day sex laws can be better accomplished by non-sex laws.

PRISONS OR BEHAVIOR CONTROL:
–LEGAL AND SOCIO-POLITICAL CONSIDERATIONS

Nicholas N. Kittrie

Our prisons are undergoing convulsive reassessment. And even such "strict constructionists" as Attorney General John Mitchell and Chief Justice Warren Burger call for the overhaul of the existing system. Concurrently, an intensive search for new tools of social control is underway.

What was science fiction only yesterday, might be reality now. Testifying before a Congressional committee, Professor D. N. Michael described new potentials for electronic and computer control of deviants. He painted a picture of prison gates being opened to release hosts of inmates into the community. These "parolees will check in and be monitored by transmitters embedded in their flesh, reporting their whereabouts in code and automatically as they pass receiving stations (perhaps like fireboxes) systematically deployed over the country as part of one computer-monitored network." Looking into the future, he could foresee the day where emotionally ill people would be allowed the freedom of the streets, providing they are effectively "defused" through chemical agents implanted in their bodies. "The task, then, for the computer-linked sensors would be to telemeter, not their emotional state, but simply the sufficiency of concentration of the chemical agent to insure an acceptable emotional state."

Recently, Harvard researcher Ralph K. Schwitzgebel proposed a similar electronic surveillance and rehabilitation program as a new alternative to the incarceration of chronic offenders. The system would permit not only the monitoring of the locations of recidivists but also the regulation of specific offending behaviors in the community. A parole officer could easily send a signal to the deviant asking him to call in. Signals could also be used to reward or warn a deviant regarding certain types of behavior. Thus, for example, if a parolee who had previously been very inconsistent in his work patterns was at work on time he might be sent a signal from the parole officer that meant, "You're doing well," or that he would receive a bonus. On the other hand, if it appeared that the parolee was in a high crime-rate area at two o'clock in the morning, he might be sent a signal reminding him to return home.

For nearly two hundred years, the most widely used tool of society in controlling those it feared most—the criminals and the insane—has been through commitment to "total institutions." These prisons and asylums (in which the inmates were to live, pray, work and learn) had been designed to furnish security for the public. Hopefully, they were also to afford an opportunity of reformation to the offender. And for a long time institutional confinement, introduced in this country for the first time by reform-minded Quakers in 1776 continued to be viewed as a great progressive advance.

This it no doubt was, when compared with its predecessors: public executions, maiming, and transportation to devil islands.

But the promise once thought to be contained in prisons is quickly fading. The benefits of solitude, religious reawakening, education, vocational training and psychological counseling (the practitioners of which have each taken turns in promising the ultimate cure) have not been able to ban recidivism. Inadequate facilities and staffs resulted in greater attention to institutional security than to rehabilitation. Isolation from the community, as well as the system's total unaccountability to those it was set up to reform, have been advanced as the major causes of failure. Most critical are the recent conclusions that even an unblemished institutional adjustment offers little preparation for coping in the everyday milieu to which the offender must return.

Given an increasing disaffection with institutional isolation, recent experiments have been towards community based corrections. We have seen greater reliance on probation—including new diversion projects where an offender may choose voluntary therapy over traditional sentencing. There has been growing utilization of halfway houses in which soon-to-be released inmates can gradually readjust to their return to a normal environment. But totally new methods for controlling deviant behavior, derived from recent scientific discoveries in neurosurgery, pharmacology and psychology, are increasingly being pointed to as the wave of the future.

A Reuters dispatch from Shrewsbury, England, carried the proposal of a British psychiatrist that compulsive speeders be "cured" not by fines or jail but by electric shock treatment. According to Dr. John Barker of the Shelton Hospital, treatment would start with a film of a driver exceeding 70 miles per hour past speed limit signs. In the consulting room, the patient would receive shock up to 70 volts through a strap attached to his wrists. It simply boils down to associating excessive speed with discomfort and pain, Dr. Barker is reported to have said.

Yet another cure was prescribed for a 21-year-old English ice cream salesman,

Eric Edward Wills, charged with larceny and obtaining property under false pretenses. Sent to a Lancashire mental hospital for observation, Wills was diagnosed as a compulsive gambler, the medical report recommended brain surgery, in the hope that the leucotomy operation would cure him of his compulsion. The magistrate, heeding the medical report, ordered that he be hospitalized and operated upon.

Science will soon offer many additional alternatives to the old-fashioned and ineffective tools for reforming behavior. Some will attempt to redo the adult offender, others will seek to prevent his very creation. Hormone injections have been demonstrated to alter the intensity of sexual drives and modify the response to sexual stimuli. Drugs that act on the brain and central nervous system to modulate moods and alter states of consciousness are already in use in many mental institutions. Psychosurgical techniques have advanced in recent years beyond the early lobotomies. Brain stimulation by electronic impulses through implanted electrodes has proved capable of modifying human behavior.

In their formulation, these new therapeutic solutions for social control could have great public appeal. In the first place, they will affect only a selected, troublesome segment of the population. They can be related to the humanistic desire for therapy and improvement, and they offer social controls and improvements without dreary institutions and with ostensible freedom. No chains—only change.

Yet to many the prospect of the new technologies is a source of grave concerns. Responding to the magistrate's decision that the young gambling ice cream salesman required brain surgery, London's *Sunday Times* questioned: "Is the drastic measure of operating on a man's brain an appropriate remedy for what respected pundits have called a national psychosis?" Going a step further, one soon awakens to the realization that the remedy offered to Eric Edward Wills might be equally justified for all gambling Englishmen. And if gambling is a sufficiently serious national malady, in England or America, what other undesired behaviors would support similar reforming campaigns?

THE NEW REVOLUTION

It is not merely an overzealous magistrate and a few over-reaching scientists that we must prepare to meet. There is, in fact, a human modification revolution upon us, which in its magnitude is not unlike the industrial revolution of nearly two hundred years ago. But while the industrial revolution was directed toward the physical world and the production of its goods—and affected in the first place man's environment rather than man himself—the new revolution focuses upon man as the central actor in our universe and aims at his direct control and reform.

One out of every four Americans has been prescribed or has taken some mood or mind-changing drug within the past year, according to the National Institute of Health.

Hearings before the House Privacy Subcommittee in September of 1970, disclosed that 300,000 American children are being given stimulants or tranquilizing drugs in order to calm their hyperactive and often disruptive class behavior. And this is only the beginning, according to experts. Most of the subjects so far are elementary school children of average or above average intelligence, alleged to suffer from minimal brain dysfunction (MBD) which is said to hinder them from achieving their full educational potential. Some four to six million underprivileged school children, almost one third of the ghetto juvenile population, might be the next recipients of the new therapy. Such treatment is encouraged by the *Journal of Learning Disabilities* conclusion that: "Disadvantaged children function similarly to advantaged children with learning disabilities."

A recent report in the National Education Association's journal, *Today's Education*, projected the future educational trend: "Biochemical and psychological mediation of learning is likely to increase. New drama will play on the education stage as drugs are introduced experimentally to improve in the learner such qualities as personality, concentration, and memory."

Pharmaceutical manufacturers already market a drug, proved successful in laboratory experiments with rats, which is used as a memory-improving aid for humans. And what we develop some drugs to do, others are designed to undo. Working with goldfish, University of Michigan researchers have developed antibiotics that can effectively "erase" the memories of recently acquired experiences.

Testifying before a Senate subcommittee, the former Director of the National Institute of Mental Health predicted that the next five to ten years will see a hundred fold increase in the number and types of drugs capable of affecting the mind. Awareness of the initial successes of behavior modifying drugs in the educational arena is likely to have a spillover effect. A special panel of the prestigious American Association for the Advancement of Science meeting in December of 1971, carefully explored the utilization of new behavior control and modification techniques as alternatives to such traditional penal methods as prisons and probation.

The possible application of behavior modification techniques in the political arena is obvious and was recently advocated in Dr. Kenneth Clark's presidential address to the American Psychological Association. Dr. Clark called for new drugs that would routinely be given to political leaders the world over in order to subdue hostility and aggression. Reporting that we are on the threshold of electrical and chemical discoveries that could "stabilize and make dominant the moral and ethical propensities of man and subordinate, if not eliminate, his negative and primitive behavior tendencies," Dr. Clark predicted that new psycho-technological controls could be implemented within a few years, "and with a fraction of the cost required to produce the atom bomb."

But the newly developed tools of behavior control, which promise more effective procedures for the management of unruly and deviant people, also post difficult questions of public policy and ethics: Is the use of drugs for hyperactive school children justified if the function of the drugs is to make children more "teachable?" And what of drug use merely to permit calm to be restored for both tired parent and overburdened teacher? Should a mentally ill or mentally retarded patient be administered medications or be psychologically conditioned to allow understaffed hospitals better management over their wards? Should a chronic alcoholic be required to undergo brain manipulations to cure him of his disease? Should an adult homosexual be made to go through behavior modification? And what about all the other non-conformists, rebels, deviates, and never-do-wells?

Only a few nineteenth century romanticists were alarmed by the prospects of the Industrial Revolution when it first came on the scene. Many more people of diverse philosophical persuasions are now concerned with its manifestations as they have become apparent over the years: the unequal distribution of its benefits, and its effects on the family, on employment, on natural resources, on the environment, and on the quality of life generally.

Can we forecast and guard against the hazards of the new revolution? Five years ago, Dr. David Krech, a highly respected professor of psychology at the University of California, called attention to the urgency of the moral and social questions raised by the new scientific discoveries which permit the manipulation of man's mind and behavior. Of particular concern to Dr. Krech was the prospect of chemical brain control agents that can be used unobtrusively and without the cooperation or even knowledge of those affected. Most other forms of behavior control require that you first "catch the man" you seek to manipulate. But "chemicals placed in water supplies, in food, or in the air we breathe, can perform their work on a mass basis and without the victim's knowledge."

Lately the concern with behavior research and control has transcended the scientists' laboratories and has found a resounding echo in the political arena. Lashing out against the use of psychodrama and psychological drugs in the schools, Vice President Spiro Agnew strongly condemned the new scientists and "futuristic planners" who no longer wish to rely on religion, moral philosophy, law, and education as tools for improving mankind, but instead want to tinker with man himself.

While the awareness of the new and drastic potentials for behavior control is growing, it is essential that the implicit questions posed by the new sciences be recognized and debated as valid public issues: who is to control science—and especially the human modification sciences—and how can we make certain that science is made to serve rather than abuse us?

One cannot allow these questions to become crank or partisan issues, to be taken up alternatively by radical elements on either the left or the right. For what is in issue is the nature of the society that we seek to create for ourselves and our children. And what we may be asked is to choose between a well-planned and controlled uni-culture, on the one hand, or the pursuit of a pluralistic society in which conflicting ideologies, religions, races, and life styles can be accommodated, and tolerated, on the other.

Since writer-scientist Jean Rostand (the son of the author Cyrano de

Bergerac) asked *Can Man Be Modified?* in his 1956 book, the state of the man-modifying sciences has undergone drastic growth. Chemical birth control agents have been developed to change the fertility cycle, and organ transplants are routinely changing the physical composition of humans. As present means for diagnosing and correcting abnormalities in a person's genetic code are becoming more sophisticated, geneticists propose to manipulate the human embryo or ovum in order to improve the offspring or at least preselect it to better fit social demands.

While chemists and pharmaceutical houses are concocting and promoting their medications designed to mold behavior to predetermined standards—a host of other behavior modification experts labor feverishly in their laboratories. Several concentrate on electricity as an instrument for both the monitoring and modification of behavior. Electronic devices have been fashioned which not only permit the long distance monitoring of a person's location and movements, but also of such psychological activity as blood pressure and penile erection, as possible predictors of forthcoming behavior. A bellboy paging system has been used experimentally to permit communication and crisis intervention with persons engaging or about to engage in undesirable behavior.

More potent means of intervention and control have been provided by electrophysiology. By implanting tiny electrodes in the brain of animals, experimenters can send electrical impulses in order to create specific behavioral responses—"now making them cringe, now sending them into furious attack, now making them drink, now making them sexually hyperactive." The mass media has widely reported the successful experiments of Dr. Jose Delgado of Yale's School of Medicine, who has managed through remote controls to stop and reverse his "brave bulls" in the middle of their bull ring charge. Current research, concludes Dr. Delgado, supports "the distasteful conclusion that motion, emotion behavior can be directed by electrical forces and that humans can be controlled like Robots by push buttons."

Other behavioral scientists find it unnecessary to rely upon surgical, chemical or electric agents, which must directly operate on the human physiology, to achieve behavior modification. The classical work of Ivan Pavlov in conditioning his dogs to salivate everytime the dinner bell was struck, whether food was served or not, has in recent years given way in the United States to sophisticated systems of conditioning, where a series of reinforcers (popularly called "rewards") are used to encourage the emission of "correct" behavior responses. "A reinforcer such as food, money, or time out from a task is known to be a reinforcer when it increases the rate, or changes the form of the behavior it follows." If the correct response is not emitted by the individual, no reinforcer is given. Generally, it is the goal of the process to so condition the individual that he continues to "voluntarily" cooperate in order to receive his reinforcement.

Describing the techniques of one of the better known of these systems (operant conditioning), Dr. Perry London concluded in his book *Behavior Control*: "Operating entirely with incentives given as the individual acts in ways which approach the controller's goals for him, virtually any skill of muscle or attitude of mind can be taught, if only it can be applied with sufficient ingenuity."

By far one of the most ingenious users of the psychological conditioning techniques is Harvard's Dr. B. F. Skinner. Through his fictional hero in *Walden Two* (1948), Skinner asserts what might be the motto of the behavior controller: "I've had only one idea in my life—a true idee fixe. To put it as bluntly as possible—the idea of having my own way. 'Control' expresses it. The control of human behavior. In my early experimental days . . . I remember the rage I used to feel when a prediction went awry. I could have shouted at the subjects of my experiments. 'Behave, Damn you! Behave as you ought!' "

But what are to be the societal goals of the modification of human behavior? To the tired school administrator, modification may be desirable to achieve conformity with educational standards as they now exist; to the reformer modification may mean more stimulated students. To the overburdened mental hospital administrator it may mean patients who make no trouble, and possibly no demands; to the ambitious innovator it may stand for institutional overhaul. To some behavior modification means adjustment to things as they are; and to others it may mean compliance not with the world as it is but the world as they perceive it should be.

Some of the contradictions inherent in behavior control came to light in response to Dr. Clark's suggestion for a drug therapy program for political leaders. Critics warned that using chemical and behavioral controls to reduce abuses of power would reduce positive exercise of power as well, and could turn people into "jellyfish." Moreover, a system aiming to humanize and reduce the aggressiveness of political leaders would not work unless the total populace was treated likewise, or else the humanized leaders would be left to the mercy of the more aggressive and primitive members of their constituencies.

Like all scientific knowledge, the tools of behavior modification can serve many and opposing masters. They can maintain the status quo or can work against it. They can serve the dreamers of eternal justice and peace, or just as easily and effectively strengthen the reactionary forces of bigotry and hatred. They can eliminate both majorities and minorities and even dictate the final parameters of good and evil. Will it then become only a question of who dares and who can afford to pick up these tools and use them?

AND WHERE DOES MAN FIT IN?

The new sciences of behavior modification have developed and relied upon a concept of man which is at clear variance with past religions and philosophies. Grounded in animal experiments, they view man as a member of the animal world with few differentiating attributes. Frequently, these sciences describe man as a mere biological container or machine, "rejecting the myth that each individual is born with a mental homunculus, and accepting the fact that we are merely a product of genes plus sensory inputs," according to Dr. Delgado. It is upon this neutral mechanism, say the behaviorists, that environment acts and leaves its accumulated impressions. Thus, it is the environmental input—through man's sensory capacity—which is superimposed upon the genetic machine and determines what man is. So viewed, man is not admitted to possess any spiritual qualities and becomes stripped of conscience, free will or any other inner values. Indeed, the very existence of inner-man is now denied.

The behaviorist's view of how the human machine operates is primarily hedonistic. Man is a mechanism which favors pleasure and abhors pain. According to Skinner, one characteristic of the human organism "is the avoidance of or escape from so-called 'aversive' features of the environment." Consequently, by offering rewards for desired behavior and following undesirable behavior with averse reinforcement, a skillful behaviorist, much like a machine operator, could ellicit from his subject any behavior to suit his operational goals.

For man so naked of values, of spirit and of natural rights, what kind of world is being proposed by the behavioral scientists? In the first place the present social order is condemned by both Dr. Skinner and Dr. Delgado as beyond repair. Both agree we must design a new culture in which many would be allowed to develop a new and better style of life.

Having perfected conditioning technologies, Skinner is anxious to use them for the building of the world of the future. What is that world to be, however? To answer this question, Dr. Skinner is required to go beyond his role of experimental scientist and must assume the mantle of the philosopher or cultural designer. Viewing the history of Western culture, he suggests in his 1971 book, *Beyond Freedom and Dignity*, that man has been conditioned to abuse his powers. It is not difficult, Skinner asserts, "to demonstrate a connection between the unlimited right of the individual to pursue happiness and the catastrophes threatened by unchecked breeding, the unrestrained affluence which exhausts resources and pollutes the environment, and the imminence of nuclear war." We must, therefore, abolish "autonomous man . . . the man defended by the literatures of freedom and dignity, who is the cause of most social evil." Like George Orwell in his *1984*, Dr. Skinner pronounces that "Freedom is Slavery," and concludes that a new type of man, who is to be free of the urge for freedom, need be produced.

Dr. Skinner proposes "a world in which people live together without quarreling, maintain themselves by producing the food, shelter, and clothing they need, enjoy themselves and contribute to the enjoyment of others in art, music, literature, and games, consume only a reasonable part of the resources of the world and add as little as possible to its pollution, and bear no more children than can be raised decently. . . ." What is proposed is an escape from poverty, from war, from overpopulation, from ignorance, and from most other ills which have plagued civilized man. That being so, why have the brave new world images of Dr. Skinner engendered so much recent controversy?

In the first place opposition is voiced to the very idea that one could presume to design a total and comprehensive culture or society. Precisely what kind of society is to be sought by those who wield the new powers of control? It is now that one suddenly discovers the uncertain present day goals of the Western, Christian or American society. Is competition or socialistic cooperation to be preferred? Is simple monastic life to be given preference over urban plenty with a chicken in every pot and two cars in every garage? Is the work-ethic to be preserved or is leisure to be encouraged? Are sex, sensuality and other traditional vices to be discredited as socially wasteful or are they to be promoted? Is a Lincoln, Emerson or a Walt Whitman the American dream—or is it Hugh Hefner, Abbie Hoffman and William Kunstler, individual, or all put together?

The behaviorists' talk of a new culture contains in it undercurrents of messianic zeal. Such culture implies a hierarchy of values, well ordered and maintained, which may stifle and suppress unorthodox cultural goals. Cultural authorizationism thus becomes a specter.

A planned culture suggests also that in lieu of conflicting social organizations—such as families, different religious faiths, political parties, schools, and economic classes—each advocating and trying to advance its own version of the cultural goals, and thus producing a constant reformulation of these goals, there may be created a new single, uniform, and inflexible conditioning machinery for the achievement of one preprogrammed culture. Totalitarianism and the stifling of social evolution thus loom as a second objectionable ramification of the new revolution.

Thirdly, in their proposals for the design of the new culture, Dr. Skinner and others seem most concerned with the survival of "the culture"—which they do not always particularize yet somehow endow with the unquestionable right to life. At the same time, the view of man advanced by them is devoid of any inner meaning or rights. What could be at stake, therefore, is the de-emphasis of man and his "natural rights" (as previously conceived in the literatures of freedom and dignity) vis-a-vis the "community" or "fasces" and the needs of its efficiency and prosperity. Since behaviorists deny inner man, there is the constant apprehension that they will be callous to the invasion of the domains of man's personality and inner values by behavior controls. In the pursuit of a "sane" and "tranquil" culture, the individual may thus be perceived as the rim in the societal wheel, rather than its nave.

The behavior modifiers forthly seem to exhibit little faith in the ability of individuals to share in the design of the needed culture, through some form of participatory process. Proposing to design a new world, Dr. Skinner pointedly notes that the aim is to create "a world which will be liked not by people as they now are but those who [will] live in it." Urgently calling for the braver new world, Skinner believes that "a world that would be likely by contemporary people would perpetuate the status quo." But if today's collective man, due to his faulty past conditioning is not able to conceive and plan his future world, are we willing to turn over the undertaking to Dr. Skinner, or to some other outstanding and benevolent scientist? And what precisely makes Dr. Skinner (unless he is the only one to have escaped faulty conditioning) free of the near-sighted vision of his fellow contemporaries?

Finally, the very tools of new behavior control are viewed with alarm by some as being overly massive for the precarious balance of man and society. There is nothing newly drastic in the behavior modification techniques, Dr. Skinner and others assure us. We have always been the product of our environment, our schools, our parents, and our friends. Why not accept behavior modification as a more beneficient, rational and advanced influence upon our lives?

After all, it is a major function of all societies to mold behavior to pre-determined standards. The Ten Commandments were proclaimed in order to control behavior. And in primitive societies, the manipulations of witch doctors were usually intended to affect human changes.

But these and other early approaches, one soon recognizes suffered from two major defects as social control agents, and it is these limitations which made them acceptable: they either were only one influence among many other factors, or else they relied exclusively on the questionable power of punishment to affect control.

Even the most repressive penology has thus had only limited power over the individual, for he usually possessed the option to choose punishment over conformity. It is the promised effectiveness of the new scientific techniques and the relative helplessness of those to be affected by them which raise many of the new objections. For these tools may be so effective that they no longer preserve individual options. And once instituted at early stages of individual life, those affected might even be conditioned to like the lack of options.

None of these questions have been satisfactorily answered by the behavior modification leaders. Responding to the warning that a planned culture necessarily means uniformity, regimentation and restraints on evolution, Dr. Skinner in his recent book advances the need for "planned diversification." This apparently means again that somebody, somehow, will determine how much deviance from norms can be tolerated: how many musicians, artists, rebels, red-heads, anarchists, democrats and so on should be created or cultivated through careful diversification.

No meaningful answer has been advanced by the new technologies regarding the ethical issues involved in behavior modification work with involuntary subjects—criminals, juveniles, the mentally ill and the retarded, alcoholics and other deviants. Are all these fair game for behavior modification in the name of social good?

One additional critical question remains: even if we grant the total benevolence of our leaders of science, how are we to protect the new behavior techniques against abuse, commercial exploitation, power seekers, over-zealousness and selfishness? It required the atomic scientists twenty-five years to develop an urgent sense of their special social responsibility. Can we allow the behavior modifiers to continue with their research endeavors, lending their tools to all kinds of social experiments, and defer the question of their science's social accountability?

Despite all the fears, hesitations, and uncertainties, it is evident that many new behavior modiciation technologies are with us, and many more are to come. The mounting demands for social order, as well as increasing hopes for a better world, will produce both popular and scientific calls for more experimentation and greater use of these techniques. Are we, however, to be overrun by the new revolution as we have been by the industrial one, or is there a system of safeguards and scrutiny which will help assure that the new techniques be so utilized and absorbed into the social fiber as to help improve the human condition rather than debase it?

In 19th century England, there were those who set out to block the coming of the industrial state and attempted to destroy or sabotage its machinery. Only their name, not accomplishments, remains with us—the Luddites. They were not successful. Neither is it realistically possible now to engender sufficient public consensus in order to turn the clock back to a pre-human modification age. But we must make certain that the lessons of the industrial revolution do not go unnoticed. The best intended of revolutions require planning in order to prevent anarchy and to make certain that the revolution's adverse side effects do not become more undesirable than the ills it sets out to cure.

For the industrial revolution, the entrepreneur was the focus of decision-making; he decided what to produce and sell. In more complex industrial states, the entrepreneur was joined by both the capital supplier and by professional management. Consideration for the employee came much later, and direct input from the eventual consumer and from the community at large did not fully materialize to this day. To justify this questionable and unbalanced exercise of controls, the industrial revolution supported and relied heavily upon the philosophy of free enterprise which pleaded that the total social good was being served by leaving the entrepreneur to his own devices. We obviously do not ascribe to this conviction any longer, or else we would not have created a National Labor Relations Board, minimum hourly wages, prohibitions of child labor, and the latest wage and price controls.

Our experience with the entrepreneurs of the industrial revolution and their latter day brethren warns us against turning similar unrestrained power to the new entrepreneurs: the behavior modification technicians, their capital suppliers and their sales forces. If the man-modifying revolution has potentials for both good and evil, and its progress can no longer be turned back, vital questions must be answered: How are we to monitor the revolution? How are we to direct it? Can it indeed be controlled? And for what purposes? What should be the function of government? Of the scientific community? Of the people?

Justice Brandeis warned us some forty-five years ago that "the greatest dangers to liberty lurk in insidious encroachment by men of zeal, well-meaning, but without understanding." We know from experience that justice and benevolence-seeking prophets much too often end up carrying out their prophesies through bloodshed and inquisitions. Behavior modification could readily "snowball" out of control simply because it has the potential for becoming big business. One cannot accept on face value the assurances of the behavior modifier that the purpose of his ministrations is totally beneficient. Reforms which have long been claimed by our juvenile court agencies as benefiting children have often been nothing more than so much additional social control for bureaucratic convenience and conformity. Half of our mental hospital populations, allegedly there for a cure, find themselves locked up not for their own benefit but for the public's convenience and peace of mind.

WHO WILL CONTROL THE CONTROLLERS?

Our protection against possible zeal, arbitrariness and antihumanistic exploitations of the new scientific technologies lies in the definition and curtailment of the power of those who control them. In structuring a system of control over the new revolution, we must carefully consider separately the needs of the persons who are proposed to be modified, their immediate families, their children, their parents, their teachers, their pupils, their employers, their employees, the representatives of the community and the spokesmen of official government. It is faulty to assume that the interests of pupils and teachers, parents and children, or of individuals and society always or frequently coincide.

We must advance and enforce the public's right to know the facts about behavior control plans and practices. Should not the state, the medical profession, the teaching profession, therapists and others be prevented from administering new behavior modification techniques unbeknown to the major parties concerned. Are parents not to be consulted regarding the school's prescription of pills to their child? At the same time should a parent or teacher be free to authorize such techniques without the benefit of any other scrutiny? These are important public issues, which cannot be left within the sole domain of the scientific and medical community.

We must determine when and under what circumstances decisions regarding behavior modification are to be designated as private, subject to the individual discretion of the person affected, or his therapist, and in what cases they are to be viewed as public questions, requiring an open inquiry where more than mere personal preference might be considered. To be decided is whether any involuntary administration of these techniques is to be permitted, and if so, upon whose authority and subject to what scrutiny. Finally, certain modification practices, such as lobotomies, may be so objectionable as to be totally outlawed through legislative enactment.

It is significant that the whole body of American law and jurisprudence, founded as it is on Age of Enlightenment's assumptions regarding the benevolence of man in the state of nature (derived from Jean Jacques Rousseau and John Locke), sought to protect the individual from the excesses of "evil" government. Our constitutional safeguards have thus been framed not to grant positive rights but to assure against the government's encroachment upon the individual's own pursuit of life, liberty and property. The constitutional protections against unreasonable "search and seizure," or against "cruel and unusual punishment" are proper examples. But the scientific advances of recent years pose new types of ethical and jurisprudential issues in the relationship of man to the state.

Increasingly we are presented with instances where governments, as well as lesser units of social organization, are offering programs of action and intervention for the asserted purpose of improving the individual's lot rather than restricting it. Yet in doing something *for* people, government also does something to them. Often, these programs are sought to be extended to non-voluntary recipients—with the assertion, however, that they are intended not as punishment but as therapy and self-improvement. But while experienced in combat against "evil" government, American jurisprudence has never advanced or studied the necessary norms for the control and supervision of the new programs or scientific techniques which are offered by an allegedly beneficient state.

The professed change in motive and in the degree of effectiveness of the new techniques for behavior and human modification clearly require a new look at existing schemes of ethical and legal control. Just as American society once was able to rely upon the prohibition of littering as a sufficient protection of our environment, yet finds this restriction inadequate to meet the hazards of present day pollution, so previous legal protections may be insufficient in light of the new realities. Reassessment is required not only of the workings of official government, but also of the decision-making or sanctioning processes of public and quasi-public institutions, such as hospitals, professional organizations, and therapeutic practitioners.

In the past when we became concerned with the distribution, control or modification of natural assets or natural resources, we usually created regulatory agencies to help protect the public interest. This is what the Federal Communications Commission, the Federal Power Commission and the Tennessee Valley Authority were set up to do. These agencies have not always been vigorous enough in the pursuit of the common good—but we are probably better off with them than without them. Now that the human resources of this country are becoming subject to concentration research, manipulation and control, there is the need to determine and set policies which many encourage or discourage the new practices.

But the need is not merely for the open discussion and formulation of public policies and regulations which could affect public funding for behavior modifications, as well as determine the adequacy of professional self-policing. There must also be created a central exchange for information, and a procedure designed for the effective monitoring of new developments and the assessment of their effect upon the public interest. There is a need for a public forum, administrative or juricial, where affected or other interested parties might be heard and assisted. There is a need for a new therapeutic bill of rights to help guarantee man's right to be and remain as different as is compatible with social survival. (I have spelled out the details of such a bill of rights in my new book, *The Right To Be Different.*)

Man created an industrial revolution and it has taken him two hundred years to realize that it must be controlled before it chokes him to death. Civilization evolved an atomic bomb without controls and is now frantically seeking restraints under the shadow of annihilation. Humanity is today on the threshold of a world "beyond 1984" where behavior modifiers offer drastic new tools not only to change man but also to redesign society. If indeed our major cultural goal is to preserve and promote a society where pluralism—individual, religious, artistic, economic, and political—takes precedence over the desire for tranquil uniformity; if our commitment is to continue social experimentation and a constant readjustment of the power balance between man and society, we must protect our future options and our right to be different now, while we still have the will and power to do so.

PSYCHIATRIC MORBIDITY AND
TREATMENT OF PRISON INMATES

Emanuel Tanay

The failure to provide adequate treatment for persons committed to mental institutions has recently received considerable attention. The doctrine of "the right to treatment" has been judicially expressed in the now famous Rouse v. Cameron decision (373 F 2d 451), (D.C. Cir., 1966). Rouse was sent to St. Elizabeth Hospital in the District of Columbia after he was found not guilty of a crime by reason of insanity. Three years later he sought release stating that he was not receiving adequate treatment to which he was entitled. The District of Columbia Court of Appeals stated that the possibility of "indefinite commitment without treatment of one who has been found not criminally responsible may be so inhuman as to be cruel and unusual punishment." A great deal of legal literature has been devoted to this issue.

It is my effort to call attention to a subject which is but another aspect of the "right to treatment" doctrine, namely, the right to treatment of individuals confined to county jails. I restrict myself to county jails which are primarily holding institutions for individuals pending the outcome of a trial or transfer to a correctional institution. Only a small proportion of the inmates of county jails are serving actual prison terms while in confinement. In other words, we are dealing here with individuals who, in a great many instances, are legally and at times factually innocent of crime. The jail setting constitutes an ideal design for inducement of psychopathology and psychiatric morbidity among the prisoners. The majority of the county jails throughout the country fail to provide psychiatric care and treatment for individuals who suffer from psychiatric illness. This neglect is the result not only of limited capabilities and resources but is the consequence of a failure to make a distinction between legal insanity and psychiatric illness.

This paper is not the result of survey research, but is based upon clinical impressions of the author gained on occasional visits to various county jails in the midwest.

THE JAIL AS PSYCHIC STRESS

I do not know of systematic studies of the psychological stress imposed by the jail environment and the reactions that follow the exposure to this particular stress. It is my impression that a person placed into the jail setting undergoes an ecological shock. The degree of recovery from this trauma depends upon the personality strength, the length of confinement, and many other factors. I am unable to provide an exhaustive listing of all the stresses which impinge upon an inmate of a county jail. I will concentrate upon the more apparent ones.

The mere deprivation of liberty and the attendant helplessness are a powerful psychological stress. Minimal needs essential for the adequate functioning of a human being are not sufficiently met within the jail setting. I am referring to such items as opportunity for sleep, clothing, food, the need for privacy, stimulation, communication with other people, and frustration of such instinctual needs as aggression and sexuality.

Furthermore, the newly admitted inmate has either been through the ordeal of a trial or faces it in the near future. He is exposed to actual danger of aggressive and homosexual assault. He is confronted with the diversities of racial and cultural backgrounds of his fellow inmates. It has been well established that during times of stress and danger there is increased dependence upon love objects and membership in a primary group. The inmate is separated from such protective figures and experiences intense separation anxiety. The affiliative needs are not only frustrated, but the prisoner undergoes a massive desocialization. He loses his "street personality." In short, he undergoes a process of dehumanization.

What I call "ecological shock" is described vividly by J. V. Bennett, Director, U.S. Bureau of Prisons, in an address before the American Law Institute, Washington, D.C., on May 20, 1954:

> When the iron gate ominously clangs behind the prisoner he is in a state of shock if he is a normal human being. He is depressed, worried about his family, despairing, fearful and suspicious of all about him. But probably also if he stood trial he is bitter . . . and not little of his cynicism and anomosities stem from the inexcusable deplorable conditions of the jails and lockups, where he was held when on trial.

In the prison most individuals experience a devastating sense of social isolation. A prisoner writes (1): "Gradually the loneliness closed in. Later on I was to experience situations which amounted almost to physical torture, but even that seemed preferable to absolute isolation." Experimental studies and autobiographical reports of such people as religious hermits, explorers, and prisoners establish isolation as an extreme psychological stress.

Goffman states that one of the characteristics of total institutions is the mortification process which he describes as a stripping of the self. Personal identity equipment is removed, indignities imposed, no room for autonomous decisions, channels of communications are closed, etc., etc. (2) The sexual frustration is well described by a prison inmate, addressed to the Connecticut Prison Study Committee, October 17, 1956(3):

> Have you ever tried going without Sex for year in and year out, can you imagine what this alone does to a person, much less all the other items he has to do without. Well take it from me, you have to have a very, very strong mind to keep from being somewhat unstable from this. And I don't care who the person is, if he doesn't miss Sex and don't care for it or don't want any, well then, he just isn't normal. . . . Well I have had no Sex since incarcerated here and it has just about drove me out of my mind—But what can you do—All you can do is just suffer and suffer until you crack up—that is if you don't have a very strong mind. . . .

We know that the regimented life of such relatively benign institutions as the Army or the Navy lead to acute psychiatric decompensation. It should be kept in mind that those inducted into the military service undergo a selection process designed to eliminate people with potential for psychiatric illness. No such selection takes place for admission to the prison setting. "Misfits of every description are squeezed into a single facility. Most men who commit crimes are beset with deep emotional problems. They are 'out of whack' with society."(4)

I wish to emphasize that the inmates of prisons are not necessarily hardened criminals.

Professor Teeters, the noted crominologist, has estimated that fifty percent of a prison's population at any given time is unconvicted. Sixty-two percent of this untried group are eventually discharged without conviction. These citizens will have served prison terms ranging from a few weeks to six months, two years, and even more. Thus, our democratic society tacitly condones a practice which results in vast numbers of legally innocent persons spending long periods in unmerited confinement.(5)

PSYCHIATRIC ILLNESS AMONG PRISON INMATES

Based upon the description of the stresses and the assumption about the personalities of those incarcerated, one can theoretically postulate a high expectancy rate for the incidence of psychiatric illness among inmates of county jails. When I speak of psychiatric illness, I am not referring to character disorders which might be related to the crime for which the individual is confined; but I have in mind the presence of a severe neurotic or psychotic illness which would necessitate psychiatric intervention if the individual would be free to seek such help. In other words, I am not speaking of psychiatric treatment as a method of dealing with crime. My concern is related to the incidence and prevalence of definite acute psychiatric illness in the prison setting. I know of no studies which address themselves to this particular issue.

At Sing-Sing Prison in the fifties, a study was conducted of individuals convicted of sexual felony. In this study the object was to determine the incidence of psychiatric illness in the sexual offenders as compared to the rest of the prison population. Seventy-nine percent of the homosexual pedophiles were diagnosed as suffering from psychotic illness. Fifty-six percent of the control group were so diagnosed.(6) On repeated occasions, when visiting the county jails, I would encounter individuals suffering from acute psychiatric illness who would not be receiving appropriate treatment. The following case illustrates the situation rather well.

Mrs. Jones, a 26-year-old, married, white female, mother of four children, has been examined at the Wayne County Jail in Detroit on the request of her attorney. Mrs. Jones was charged with the slaying of her five-year-old daughter. The cause of death of the child was given by the Medical Examiner as "severe trauma to head, with cerebral hemorrhage and other injuries." The autopsy report of the child also revealed injuries of the vagina and lacerations of the hymen.

Here are excerpts from my report to the attorney: "Mrs. Jones is being held on the 6th floor of the jail, which is an area reserved for women prisoners. Upon my entering this section, I was impressed with the fact that a number of women prisoners were in a state of acute psychotic disturbance. For example, one 34-year-old woman, Cathy B, was continuously screaming incoherent remarks and was obviously hallucinating. According to the personnel, she did not have a 'stick of clothing on her body in two weeks and was screaming in this fashion day and night.' Thirteen other women were identified by myself to be acutely psychotic. I call this to your attention since an adequate examination of your client was impossible under such conditions. Furthermore, the impact of this setting upon your client has also to be taken into consideration.

Mrs. Jones is a 26-year-old, white female, moderately obese, who appeared to be a rather attractive woman. She was acutely depressed, tremulous, fearful. Her eyes were red and it was apparent that she had done considerable crying. She spoke in a hesitant and halting manner. In response to questions she broke down and cried profusely, but made efforts to control the crying. When I asked about her obvious depression she stated: 'I hate myself, I am no good, I never was any good. I shouldn't live.' The patient has made overt suicidal gestures and expressed suicidal wishes."

My report concluded with the following statements: "Mrs. Jones is a severely depressed person who is not able to obtain adequate help or even an adequate evaluation under the conditions of her present confinement. May I call to your attention that the prison physician did recognize the fact that Mrs. Jones is psychiatrically ill, inasmuch, as he has prescribed for her 50 mg. Thorazine three times a day. In view of the medical situation in which Mrs. Jones finds herself, it is urgently recommended that arrangements be made for her transfer to a medical facility. It was not possible to accomplish this task on medical grounds. However, with the cooperation of various officials, the patient was declared incompetent to stand trial and was transferred in January 1968 to the Michigan Center for Forensic Psychiatry. The official report, in fact, read that the patient was found incompetent to stand trial "because of the acute suicidal risk she represented at the time." The patient remained in the hospital for the maximum legally permissable time for such an examination, namely, six months. She was discharged with the diagnosis of psycho-neurotic depressive reaction, acute, severe, presently in apparent remission."

During her confinement to the Forensic Center, the patient had been brought to my office on five separate occasions for psychotherapeutic sessions. Subsequent to her discharge from the Forensic Center the patient was placed on bond awaiting trial. She resumed living with her husband, secured employment at a department store as a saleslady, and visited her psychiatrist at weekly intervals. She continued to be depressed, but was no longer suicidal, was able to function in her work situation. In November 1968, after the usual plea bargaining, the charge against Mrs. Jones was reduced from Second Degree Murder to Manslaughter, to which she pleaded guilty. The judge was given a five page report prepared by myself. He sentenced Mrs. Jones to an 8-15 year term on the charge of manslaughter. Subsequent to this sentence, upon the request of the parents and husband, I wrote a letter to the judge from which the following excerpt is taken:

> It is my opinion that without appropriate psychiatric treatment Mrs. Jones will most likely develop a psychotic illness and possibly commit suicide. During her short-lived period while out on bond, Mrs. Jones was able to work and seek treatment, which provided a good possibility for rehabilitation of this young woman. This work could have been continued without endangering anyone, since there is no evidence to suggest that Mrs. Jones has any criminal or antisocial propensities from which the society would have to be protected. . . . May I once again indicate that I take the liberty of writing to you, Judge Burdick, based upon the firm conviction that in spite of the enormous wrongfulness of her act, Mrs. Jones, in my opinion, would have been a suitable candidate for probation. Furthermore, I am deeply troubled by the fact that I can foresee another human life being ruined through illness. . . . The need for psychiatric therapy for Mrs. Jones is established rather firmly in the record of this case; therefore, availability of treatment becomes an important consideration. There are no means of treatment available at the Detroit House of Correction.

My letter was not answered. The patient was confined to the Detroit House of Correction, where her family found her to be depressed and making frequent references to suicide. I have been requested by the family to send medication prescriptions to the jail and to make a visit to see the patient for therapeutic purposes. Throughout 1969 I have made repeated efforts to make a professional visit; this was denied on repeated occasions. On one specific occasion the warden denied this privilege because "Mrs. Jones was giving us trouble." Ultimately, my visiting Mrs. Jones was approved, providing that the prison physician was present during my interview with the patient. On the day in August 1969 when I was to visit Mrs. Jones, she was transferred to the Michigan Institution for the Criminally Insane in Ionia. Prior to her transfer she was examined in the Detroit General Hospital Emergency Room, which provides the medical care for the inmates of the Detroit House of Correction. Without official permission, but with the cooperation of the Emergency Room physicians, it was possible for me to interview Mrs. Jones on August 20, 1969. The clinical picture she presented was that of severe depression. She was tearful, lost a great deal of weight, and appeared to be highly anxious. She stated that she was unable to sleep, she cries constantly, and is preoccupied with "my horrible crime." She emphasized that she still did not remember what actually happened even though she made numerous efforts to do so. "Why was I born and why do I live?" She stated that she was not worth all the attention from her family, that she brought disgrace and suffering upon them. She went on to say: "I can't go on living with all I have done." She described the fact that in the Detroit House of Correction she is in constant danger of being homosexually attacked. "I am afraid to death of it." Later on she stated: "I will never be good to anybody if I stay in that place anymore. Nobody can hate me more than I hate myself." She stated that the inmates are being very harsh on her, calling her "baby killer, nuts, crazy," etc. My opinion was that Mrs. Jones was in desperate need of psychiatric attention. There was, however, no possibility for effecting a transfer to a psychiatric institution.

A similar case is that of Jack Ruby, whom I had examined for the first time in June 1964, at which time I found him to be suffering from one of the most malignant diseases known to mankind, namely, paranoid schizophrenia. He was not in a hospital. He was not receiving treatment. He was held in the Dallas County Jail. In April 1964 he was diagnosed by Louis J. West, Professor of Psychiatry and Chairman of the Department of Psychiatry at the University of Oklahoma, to be overtly psychotic and in need of treatment. In his report he stated:

> Mr. Ruby's prolonged confinement in a jail while suffering from this illness, when modern psychiatric hospital treatment could be made available, is cruel and inhuman, even of a condemned prisoner. Once again, I urge all concerned to take the steps necessary to provide Jack Ruby with the benefits of proper medical care until such time as he regains a sufficient degree of mental health to cooperate in his own defense.

Subsequent to this, he was examined by Dr. Verner Teuteur who also found him mentally ill.

In spite of the unanimity of all psychiatrists who have examined Mr. Ruby after the trial, he did not receive psychiatric treatment to the time of his death. It is significant to note that at the moment when he developed physical symptoms he was immediately transferred to a hospital setting and received appropriate treatment.

LEGAL CONSIDERATIONS

Subsequent to my visit to the Wayne County Jail in Detroit, to which I have referred above, I had written a letter to Circuit Court Judge Victor J. Baum, who was chairman of a committee appointed to evaluate conditions in the jail. Judge Baum and the Presiding Judge, Joseph Sullivan, initiated a very active movement among the responsible officials to provide "adequate facilities for the proper care and retention of mentally disturbed prisoners in the Wayne County Jail." Many meetings were held. A special committee of the Board of Supervisors of the County of Wayne was appointed, and opinions were received and studied. The end result is, however, that two years later no adequate treatment is provided for the prisoners of the Wayne County Jail. Some of the difficulties in providing such adequate treatment related to the notion that the prisoners have to be cared for within the County Jail itself. No such requirement is imposed upon the treatment of medical conditions.

In practice, therefore, the mentally ill prisoner has to establish his legal insanity in order that he may receive treatment for psychiatric illness. In criminal cases, this occurs either via the statute declaring the person unable to stand trial or upon the finding of Not Guilty by Virtue of Insanity.

For centuries medical treatment has been a matter for medical judgment and has been made available to all who are in need of it. Even those condemned to death are not excluded from this privilege or right. There is no legal provision, to my knowledge, requiring that psychiatric illness be treated in a different fashion. Nevertheless, this is not the case. In many instances throughout the country, psychiatrically ill prisoners are not given appropriate treatment, pending resolution of legal issues. It goes without saying that psychiatric illness as it pertains to criminal responsibility is a matter for the courts to decide, a procedure which frequently requires extensive litigation. However, psychiatric illness as it relates to the administration of treatment in a medical issue requires merely a competent psychiatric evaluation. Legal insanity and psychiatric illness are frequently confused, resulting in the failure to provide medical assistance to those who are in desperate need of it. I wish to emphasize that neither the spirit nor the letter of the law requires such an approach, but legal strategy makes it often expedient.

In 1967 the New York Decision made a distinction between legal insanity and medical insanity. The New York Court of Appeals ruled that a convicted murderer found legally sane may still plead "medical insanity to mitigate his sentence." (People of the State of New York v. Mosley—228 N.E. 2d, N.Y., 1 June 1967.) This decision represents a procedural advance which has been characteristic of the American Criminal Law.

In the last decade the American Criminal Law has undergone changes which are described by legal scholars as revolutionary in nature. Wm. J. Curran(7) refers to the extension of the civil rights protection for those charged with crimes. These procedural mutations have attracted a great deal of attention, significantly increased expenditures connected with the administration of justice, and led to the claims that criminals are being coddled. With some reservations, the emphasis on procedure has been accepted by the American public. It is not unusual for a criminal trial to consume a few weeks of courtroom trial. Many months, at times years, elapse before the trial takes place. It has been my observation that a great many individuals, upon completion of this process, emerge with their legal rights protected but their lives ruined. For a great many people the concepts of civil rights and due process become mere principles living in legal texts but deadly to those who come in contact with them. Whether or not the American criminal is being coddled procedurally is beyond my professional competence to comment upon. I have, however, very little hesitation in asserting that the inmate of American prisons has his medical rights frequently violated without concern on anyone's part. By medical rights I am referring to the concept that every human being is entitled to be treated when sick. A man does not forfeit this right even when all the other rights have been stripped away from him by society. The state has been granted the power to deprive a citizen of such rights as liberty or pursuit of happiness. No state, however, was ever given, or even asked for, the power to take away the right to the pursuit of health.

NOTES

(1) Schachter, S., *The Psychology of Affiliation*, Stanford University Press, 1959; reprinted in *Criminal Law*, R. C. Donnelly, J. Goldstein, and R. D. Schwartz, The Free Press, New York, 1962, p. 425.

(2) Goffman, E., "Characteristics of Total Institutions," Symposium on Preventive and Social Psychiarty 1957, pp. 43-49; reprinted in *Criminal Law*, 1962, p. 429.

(3) Letter to Prison Study Committee from Inmate Connecticut State Prison, Oct. 17, 1956, in *Criminal Law*, 1962, p. 164.

(4) Roucek, J. S., *Sociology of Crime*, Philosophical Library, New York, 1961, pp. 299-328.

(5) Roucek, J. S., *Sociology of Crime*, Philosophical Library, New York, 1961, p. 303.

(6) Glueck, B. C., "Psychodynamic Patterns in the Homosexual Sex Offender," *American Journal of Psychiatry*, Vol. 112, 1956, pp. 584-589; reprinted in *Criminal Law*, 1962, p. 39.

(7) Curran, Wm. J., "The Revolution in American Criminal Law: Its Significance for Psychiatric Diagnosis and Treatment," *American Journal of Public Health*, Vol. 58, No. 12, Dec. 1968, pp. 2209-2216.

VIII

ISSUES

OF

LIFE

AND

DEATH

VIII ISSUES OF LIFE AND DEATH

INTRODUCTION

From a medicolegal point of view, death can no longer be considered a simple cessation of circulation and respiration. Life as it was generally understood, can now be revived, maintained and sustained by artificial life-saving equipment and devices. Organs can be replaced with transplants from other humans or animal cadavers, restoring disabled people to a normal life.

One of the requisites of most successful transplantations is a donated organ taken "fresh" from the donor. Because of the life-sustaining methods now available, respiration and circulation can be maintained in a patient for days, without any hope of restoring life, while at the same time the electroencephalographs and other monitors report a "brain death." It has been argued that as soon as the EEG shows no cerebral activity the patient could be declared dead, even though circulation and respiration continue to be maintained artificially.

Recent judicial decisions and statutes have endorsed this new formulation of life and death. In addition to allowing the prompt transfer of a desired organ from the "brain dead" donor to a recipient, this redefinition of death also frees hospital beds, equipment, and personnel that are often in short supply. Others however object to the "brain death" definition. Some find it objectionable because of their continuing hope for new and miraculous live-saving breakthroughs. Others fear that it places too important a life and death choice upon physicians who have to rely, in turn, on machines. Others fear that the pre-dating of death might be used as a precedent for similar action in other, less definite situations.

Other life and death issues have furnished the basis for great public interest, concern, and controversy. One of these issues is the status of the fetus and its legal rights. The Supreme Court of the United States has indicated that legal rights commence only when the fetus can maintain itself without maternal support. More fundamentalist claimants of fetal "right to life" believe that the fetus has rights at conception. Although abortion laws have been liberalized nationally, the classical controversy regarding the commencement of life continues.

An extension of this conflict is the outcry against experimentation on aborted fetuses. Related also is the need for a policy in regard to the care of the seriously handicapped and damaged newborn, whose short life will be completely useless and meaningless by our generally accepted standards of life.

Most innovative interferences with the traditional phases of reproduction are likewise subjects of heated differences of opinion. The "pill" and intrauterene devices have made contraception reasonably safe, yet they are opposed on religious, moral and ethical grounds. Sterilization as a medical procedure is opposed on the same grounds, and the issue of abortion is far from being permanently resolved.

Contemporary medicine has changed not only the quality of life but has also produced both its artificial life prolonging techniques, a renewed interest in both passive and active euthanasia. A great difference of opinion—philosophical, moral, ethical and legal—still exists about killing the hopelessly sick and injured.

New science has revived some old and has created some new issues of life and death, which must be considered as we attempt to evolve a public policy. The articles in this section represent some important, current issues of life and death.

DYING, DEATH, AND DEAD

Harold L. Hirsch

One would expect that by now "death" would be well established both as a medical status and a legal entity. The law has always accepted the criteria of death as the standard diagnosis established by medicine—the cessation of circulation and respiration without the capability of resuscitation. In the past, the function of the brain was not considered in determining death.

The situation is changing. The use of the electroencephalogram (EEG) in continued monitoring demonstrates that a flat or isoelectric pattern is evidence of cessation of cerebral activity. In some instances a gradual deterioration can be detected by the changes in the EEG. In some comatose patients with persistent respiratory and circulatory activity, the EEG may be flat. Depending on the treatment administered, these vital functions may continue for hours or even weeks after the appearance of the flat EEG. Previously, patients were considered to be alive as long as they were breathing and had a pulse. Now, a new definition for death has been proposed, "brain" or "neurologic death," considered synonymous with "death."

This concept is being accepted by the public and the medical and legal professions. In a recent Virginia case, the jury, given the choice by the judge, accepted the concept of brain death. The judgment held that the physicians were not negligent in removing the heart of a severely injured patient for the purpose of transplantation after "brain death." Recently a homicide victim in California was similarly managed. The defense now questions the crime with which the assailant has been charged. Proponents, including some physicians, have urged that brain death be legalized. Two states have adopted such statutes. The prevailing opinion is that this will result in significant problems and, when necessary, death will be established judicially on a case-to-case basis.

There is a fallacy to the concept of "brain death" being tantamount to "death" and its acceptance is now challenged. Recently there have been reports of resuscitation after a flat EEG was observed. A flat EEG depicts only "cerebral death" and not "brain death." Recently investigators reported that a flat EEG caused by hypothermia or overdoses of sedatives, tranquilizers or narcotics, by itself may not be a reliable measure of the imminence of death. A French group noted that in fatal cases they could rely on the flat EEG plus an increase in lactic dehydrogenase (type-5), transaminases and alkaline phosphatase in the spinal fluid, even though these tests pose technical and interpretive problems. Data acquired during a two-year cerebral death study indicated a chance for revival when the EEG had been flat for less than 12 hours.

Medicolegal problems may arise when the brain death theory is accepted. It may affect the criminal charge against an assailant whose victim's organs were removed for transplant purposes immediately after the diagnosis of brain death. Other problems involve the physician's duty to treat and the right of refusal of treatment by the next of kin. Many physicians maintain supportive measures until circulation and respiration cease. The question is whether treatment may be withheld or is required even though the patient's vital functions will be sustained only for a short time. It is conceivable that if the physician fails to treat, he may incur criminal liability for homicide and/or civil liability for negligence. In any event, there should be informed consent by the next of kin. If the physician's advice is refuséd, he should retire from the case. In some instances differences have resulted in court contests. Depending on such factors as the age of the patient and socioeconomic conditions, some courts have sustained the right to refuse treatment, while others have imposed treatment.

There are other objections to withholding treatment, or "pulling the plug." There is no certainty that revival is impossible in brain death situations. The possibility exists that medicine will achieve some discovery that will revive some of these patients. There is the concern that a brain death diagnosis will be used as a precedent in situations where death is less certain or as a pretext in others.

Observations indicate that transplantation is most successful when the donated organs are fresh. Brain death allows their removal immediately after the diagnosis and consideration need not be given to resuscitation of the donor. There are also such problems as cost of care, hospital beds and the anguish of the relatives. Brain death may be an important issue in the settlement of insurance claims and in probate matters.

It is obvious that these factors are not merely academic, intellectual or philosophical exercises. The concept of brain death, as evidenced by the flat EEG, has been shown to be fallible. It is not always reliable and the diagnosis of death on this basis is fraught with medicolegal consequences. As of now, the physician is best advised to rely on cessation of circulatory and respiratory functions. Although not completely problem-free, these still remain the accepted methods of ascertaining "death."

THOUGHTS ON THE ETHICS OF TREATING
OR OPERATING ON NEWBORNS AND INFANTS
WITH CONGENITAL ABNORMALITIES

H. de V. Heese

The tremendous advances in pediatrics since the Second World War, through energetic and sometimes exciting research, have undoubtedly benefited many children and their parents. For example, the survival of children after surgery for potentially lethal conditions such as atresia of the small intestine, gives joy and satisfaction to both parents and doctors.

Less publicized is the havoc caused by the short- or long-term survival of infants and children with severe physical and mental handicaps who, through the efforts of medical, nursing and para-medical personnel are a burden to themselves, their families and the community.

It may be that only in years to come will we recognize the more profound consequences of modern trends in the management of patients with inherited potentially lethal and crippling diseases or congenital malformations. A new generation of parents, saved by medical and surgical advances, is growing up—a generation which may carry a genetic predisposition to disease that may manifest itself more severely in their offspring.

In South Africa we must also face the fundamental moral question of whether the large expenditure of skilled medical, nursing, educational and rehabilitation time, as well as financial cost is justifiable even if all the infants with severe congenital abnormalities saved, grow up to be perfect and normal human beings. It has been estimated that in the USA one brain-damaged child admitted to an institution may impose a financial burden on society of $200,000 or more during his lifetime. I do not know the cost in the Republic, but it must be considerable. I also know that much still needs to be done to reduce mortality and morbidity from malnutrition, undernutrition, measles and other preventable diseases. The infant mortality rate for all races in the Cape Town municipal area alone is 50.5 per 1,000 live-births (1969), and most of these infants die of preventable conditions.

In this article I wish to discuss only one aspect of the question—the dilemma in which the doctor finds himself when he is faced with a newborn infant with congenital abnormalities or a disease known to result in severe physical or mental handicap should the child survive because of medical treatment or surgical intervention.

When faced with a foetus or newborn with an inherited potentially lethal disease or life-threatening gross congenital abnormality or with evidence of severe asphyxia or intracranial hemorrhage, the general practitioner, obstetrician, pediatrician or pediatric surgeon is faced with a number of alternatives. Should he: 1. Kill the foetus or newborn? This is an unacceptable course of action at present as far as the newborn is concerned, but permissible in the eyes of many in the case of the foetus in which cytogenic and biochemical defects can be diagnosed antenatally from the study of amniotic-fluid cells, e.g. mongolism or fibrocystic disease. 2. Actively encourage the child to die, offering no medical treatment, surgical intervention, or feeding? 3. Allow "nature to run its course," offering no treatment for complications such as pneumonia, no antibiotics, or active feeding either orally by tube or intravenous fluid therapy? The infant is simply offered a feed and allowed to take in as much orally as it can manage. 4. Actively encourage the child to live by using all means at his disposal? The doctor may follow this course of action because he believes it to be the correct one or because it is the line of least resistance. It is far easier to treat than not to treat.

In making an objective assessment of the situation the doctor may be hampered by time-honored cliches and quotations which may come to mind, including: "Our duty as doctors is crystal clear—to preserve life" and "Life is the most precious thing in the world."

These are of very little comfort to the attending medical practitioner and he must resolve important ethical and other questions such as: Should life-saving measures be instituted? And should the decision on these measures be left mainly to the parents, or be made by the doctor alone; or should the decision be made by the doctor after discussion with other colleagues and with the parents?

Answers to the above questions are likely to be based on matters of opinion, religious and moral beliefs, emotion and subconscious factors. The course of action of the medical practitioner is likely to be influenced by past personal experiences and moral convictions and to a far lesser extent by "words of wisdom" from experts.

In arriving at a decision the doctor must as far as possible satisfy himself that the institution of life-saving measures, or conversely, the withholding of active measures, will not make the situation worse by causing the survival of a child in an even more damaged or unhappy state; and that the future care of the infant is ensured, should he survive after the institution of life-saving measures.

In my opinion the responsibility for the future care of infants who survive with severe mental and physical handicaps rests with the doctor who instituted life-saving measures. He cannot escape this responsibility and he must satisfy himself, before instituting such measures, that educational or institutional facilities, community help, guidance of parents, later work opportunities, etc., will be available to the individual allowed to live through his intervention. I must stress that the situation in the Republic in this respect differs vastly from that in the United States and in Britain. I think it is true to say that parents in the higher socio-economic groups here experience many difficulties in the care of their handicapped children. In the lower socio-economic groups, life for the handicapped child can be tragic, and for responsible parents falling into this group it can be misery and catastrophe giving rise to unbearable emotional and economic stresses.

The doctor must also satisfy himself that the parents are not likely to reject the child, that the family is not likely to disintegrate because of guilt and emotional complexes engendered by the presence of the handicapped child in an already unstable family, and that siblings are not going to suffer unduly.

Parents have emotional ties and the responsibility of caring for their infant as a dependent being, and they should be informed as early as possible of the diagnosis, prognosis, and possible management of their child and have a right to express their feelings if they wish to do so. It is, however, my sincere belief that parents should never be expected to participate in the actual decision whether or not to implement treatment.

There are many good reasons for this point of view: they may make decisions contrary to their real beliefs, because they may think that their church, relatives, friends, or doctor will not approve; feelings of guilt may be aroused if they come to believe at a later stage that they made the wrong decision; and most parents have no previous experience or training with which to face these problems.

I believe that one must always be honest with parents, even if the facts pertaining to their infant at the time seem cruel and their presentation seems unnecessary.

With the years, I have come to the firm conclusion that in many instances, death with peace is preferable to the poor life that remains, if the quality of that life is so poor as to make it a burden and misery for the family and the community. In certain specific situations where gross handicap on recovery seems inevitable, I accept the responsibility for the discontinuation of active therapy which encourages the infant to stay alive.

I further believe, and here I recognize that I am on dangerous ground, that the survival of an infant may not be of equal importance when assessed in the light of different known circumstances. I am willing to manage the immature infant of less than 1.36 kg with hyaline-membrane disease by artificial means such as IPPV when it is the child of an elderly mother with a history of numerous miscarriages, but think it is wrong to do so in the case of an unwanted infant of a young unmarried mother.

The carrying out of a decision not to institute active life-saving measures may be difficult to implement and may have a demoralizing and disturbing effect on junior nursing and medical staff. It is extremely difficult to let "nature take its course" in the case of an infant with an abnormality or disease likely to give rise to death within days if left strictly alone, and not to tube-feed an obviously hungry child, although the procedure may unnecessarily prolong life and the misery of the parents.

An Editorial in the *Medical Journal of Australia*(1) suggested that many doctors over-treat patients, and tend to forget the value of death. For pediatricians dealing so much with the beginnings of life, it is perhaps even more difficult to accept death as an inevitable part of life.

It is also difficult, and sometimes impossible, in individual cases, to practice what I preach. The temptation not to accept responsibility or to take the line of least resistance by tube-feeding an infant or to "pass the buck" to a surgical colleague is always there. I must admit in all honestly that I still at times succumb to this temptation.

REFERENCE

(1) Editorial (1966): Med.J. Aust., 2, 710.

IMPACT OF THE SUPREME COURT
DECISIONS ON THE PERFORMANCE OF
ABORTIONS IN THE UNITED STATES

Harold L. Hirsh

The legal philosophy regarding abortion as enunciated by the Supreme Court has evolved over a period of nearly two years. On April 21, 1971, the United States Supreme Court rendered its first decision in the case of *The United States vs. Vuitch*(1) in which the practice of abortion in the District of Columbia was defined legally. The decision actually involved a determination of the constitutionality of the Statute governing the practice of abortion in the District of Columbia. The Statute that was subjected to interpretation declares that abortions in the District of Columbia are illegal unless done under the direction of a competent licensed practitioner of medicine and necessary for the mother's life and health. Prior to this decision the Statute had been interpreted by the courts of the District of Columbia as requiring that a legal therapeutic abortion had to be performed within rigid criteria. To qualify as a legal, therapeutic abortion, the abortion had to be performed in a hospital after consultation with and agreement by two other physicians, preferably obstetricians, approval by an appropriate hospital committee, and only if the mother's life was immediately in jeopardy. The Supreme Court held that the word "health" included psychological, emotional and mental as well as physical well-being. "Health" as employed in the District of Columbia Statute was not to be limited to physical health, but was properly defined as the "state of being sound in body and mind."

The Supreme Court did not furnish any specific guides as to the methods to be employed in determining the impact of a pregnancy on the mother's health. The Court did determine, however, that the performance of an abortion is a matter for the exercise of the physician's professional judgment. Furthermore, that abortion should be considered like any other surgical procedure. Generally, whether a particular surgical procedure is necessary for a patient's physical or mental health is a judgment that physicians are obviously called upon to make routinely whenever surgery is considered. An abortion should be no different.

Abortion is a nationwide problem. Since the District of Columbia is the nation's Capital, and the Supreme Court represents the highest legal authority in the country, I decided to explore the ramifications of the Supreme Court decision in regard to abortion as it might pertain to the judicial systems within the United States. Although the decision is applicable only to the District of Columbia because it was a review only of the District of Columbia Statute by the United States Supreme Court, the decision would undoubtedly have a great impact on the philosophy toward abortions by both the judiciary and legislatures of all the jurisdictions within the nation. This decision unquestionably would help set the legal pattern in regard to abortions nationwide.

With this concept in mind, I set out to determine the impact of the Supreme Court decision in the District of Columbia case on the performance of legal therapeutic abortions in the District of Columbia. To that end I undertook to interrogate 31 physicians who practice obstetrics and gynecology as a specialty in the District of Columbia. I also questioned the heads of the Departments of Obstetrics and Gynecology at each of the three medical schools and at each of the eleven hospitals in the District of Columbia with Obstetrics and Gynecology Departments. Also interviewed were the administrative heads of the established free-standing abortion clinics. On the law-enforcement side, I decided to talk to representatives of the U.S. Attorney's Office, charged with prosecution of offenders of the Statute, the District of Columbia Corporation Counsel's Office, the legal representatives of the city government, and of the Office of the General Counsel of the Metropolitan Police Department. Also included among the people to be interviewed was the City Councilman charged with the responsibility for health matters in the District of Columbia, and one of the Assistant Secretaries in the Department of Health, Education and Welfare concerned with this area in the national health field. I also interviewed the Judge of the District of Columbia who rendered the initial decision in the case that the District of Columbia Statute was unconstitutional on the basis of vagueness.

Over the past two years, considerable experience had been accumulated regarding the performance of legal therapeutic abortions by physicians in the District of Columbia. Statistics accumulated by the District of Columbia Government revealed that 18,897 therapeutic abortions were performed legally in the District of Columbia in 1971 since the Supreme Court decision in the District of Columbia case.(2) In 1972, 38,868 legal therapeutic abortions were performed in the District of Columbia.(3) This is in contrast to an average of less than 2500 therapeutic abortions in the five years immediately prior to this decision. Prior to 1966 there were less than 250 therapeutic abortions per year. In the period between 1966 and 1971 there was an intraprofessional liberalization of the attitude toward abortion and a relaxation of the criteria by hospitals and committees. Infected, inconplete abortions admitted to two city hospitals have fallen from about 10,000 cases a year to about 100 per year. Abortions are now being performed in all hospitals in the District of Columbia with obstetrical and gynecological facilities except for two hospitals administered by Catholic organizations. Although at that time some of the hospitals required consultations and committee review, these requirements were becoming less rigid. Under later Supreme Court decisions, these requirements were inoperative. Several of the hospitals have now established outpatient abortion services as well as inpatient facilities.

There are now ten free-standing abortion clinics that have been established and a total of nineteen facilities that are providing abortions since the Supreme Court decision in the District of Columbia. The outpatient hospital services and the free-standing clinics for the purpose of performing abortions are novel health-care establishments. They were created and developed as the result of the great need and demand for abortions at a reasonable cost in the District of Columbia. In order to obtain an abortion at a free-standing clinic, only the attending physician at the clinic is required to attest to the necessity of the procedure. In some of the clinics an evaluation by a psychologist is included preoperatively. From the start, these clinics have limited abortions to women less than ten-weeks pregnant, with complete preoperative evaluation and postoperative follow-up. In essence, an abortion is available "on demand" by the pregnant woman in the District of Columbia within the framework of the available facilities. Because of the development of the free-standing abortion clinic, the District of Columbia Council had found it necessary to regulate and license them.(4) In addition, all clinics are close geographically to a hospital and have a working arrangement with the nearby hospital for the admission of complications and emergencies. All the clinics are completely equipped to handle all problems incident to an abortion.

The interviews with the 31 obstetricians were remarkably revealing. Physicians who perform abortions now do so openly and notoriously whereas prior to the Supreme Court decision rarely was the procedure listed as such on the operation schedule. There is no longer any stigma even as compared to the most liberal attitudes toward abortions prior to the Supreme Court decision in the District of Columbia case. Only the four Catholic physicians in the group studied were irrevocably opposed to abortions. Although the other 27 physicians had performed an occasional therapeutic abortion prior to the Supreme Court decision, since this decision all of them were now performing 100 to 600 abortions per year. All were being performed in hospitals or outpatient clinics connected with a hospital. None had performed abortions in their offices and only one physician was willing to do abortions in his office.

It was amazing to learn that almost all of the physicians queried had no real understanding of the abortion statute and no true insight into the significance of the legal implications involved in the performance of therapeutic abortions in the District of Columbia. To a man they all knew that it had been illegal to perform an abortion except under very rigid hospital regulations with attesting consultations and approval by a review committee under circumstances in which the mother's life was in immediate jeopardy. Now abortion is permissible in a hospital or free-standing clinic with only a few minor regulations essentially on demand by the pregnant patient and dependent on the professional judgment of the attending physician.

Most of the queried physicians were of the opinion that there should be no statute regulating the performance of abortions. Nor should there be any regulation by any medical society. Abortions should be handled like any other medical or surgical procedure predicated on the usual and customary physician—patient relationship. None of the physicians was of the opinion that the patient should be required to be a resident where an abortion was to be performed, providing adequate pre- and postoperative care was mandatory and should be rigidly required and enforced. All of the physicians felt that any female capable of conceiving was capable of arranging for an abortion regardless of age. Parental or spousal consent should not be required, regardless of the age of the patient. All were of the opinion that abortions should not be performed after 10 weeks of pregnancy in a free-standing or outpatient clinic, and not after 20 weeks in a hospital. All but one of the physicians were opposed to abortions by paramedicals similar to midwives.

It became apparent from the questioning that the liberalizing of the performance of therapeutic abortions had come about as the result of the evolution of the rights of the individual, particularly the right to privacy and the equal status and rights of women. In addition, the decision seemed to bring into focus and crystallize the fact that the principal objections of physicians were no longer professionally valid. Dangers to the health and the life of the mother because of the surgical risks, absence of antibacterial agents to control infection, and lack of blood transfusions for hemorrhage had been almost completely overcome and crude techniques were no longer impediments to successful abortions. None of the queried physicians was opposed to the principle that abortion should be available to women essentially "on demand." They were all of the opinion that this was a reasonable prerogative of the pregnant woman and that abortion should be undertaken and performed purely and completely on the basis of the well-established physician—patient relationship.

Interviews with the various law enforcement agencies enumerated earlier revealed that there were no police investigations, grand jury presentments or criminal prosecutions since the Supreme Court decision in the District of Columbia case. This compared with 10 to 12 police investigations, 3 to 4 grand jury presentments by the prosecutor, and 2 prosecutions per year of physicians for performing abortions outside the hospital. The amount of time available to law enforcement agencies in pursuance of other criminal investigations and prosecutions was markedly increased and proved to be significant in law enforcement activities since abortions by physicians were no longer of any criminal importance and significance following the Supreme Court decision. The policy of the federal government toward abortion by the executive branch was not influenced or changed by the Supreme Court decision. The executive branch, apparently for political reasons, continued its policy of careful neglect and avoided the issue like the plague. President Nixon in his public pronouncements continued to be personally opposed to the liberalization of the abortion statutes and laws. He had not been influenced by the Supreme Court decision. The Congress has similarly avoided the issue.

It is obvious that the Supreme Court decision in the District of Columbia case has resulted in a revolution in the practice of abortion in the District of Columbia. Basically, abortion is now available "on demand" by the woman who is pregnant and does not want to continue the pregnancy. It is now, for the most part, like any other medical problem and procedure resolved on the basis of the physician—patient relationship and the medical judgment of the physician. It appears that the actual practice of abortion has gone beyond the limitations set down by the Supreme Court in its decision. Interestingly, the practice established for the performance of abortions in the District of Columbia after this initial decision anticipated later decisions of the Supreme Court in this matter.

The District of Columbia decision was only a forerunner to the latest edicts of the Supreme Court on the abortion issue. On January 22, 1973, in long-awaited decisions, the Supreme Court handed down rulings.(5, 6) which undoubtedly will affect abortion laws in almost all states and jurisdictions. The decisions are expected to result in broadly liberalized abortion practices in all but four states (New York, Hawaii, Washington and Alaska), as well as the District of Columbia. These already have essentially unrestricted laws as the result of recently enacted statutes or court decisions.

These last two Supreme Court rulings did not abolish restrictions on abortions altogether. It did lift all the restrictions on a woman's right to a physician-performed abortion during the first three months of pregnancy. For the first three months, the Supreme Court said, the decision to have an abortion lies with the woman and her physician. For the next six months, states may regulate abortion procedure in ways reasonably related to maternal health, such as licensing and regulating the persons and facilities involved. For the last ten weeks of pregnancy, when the fetus has the capability of meaningful life outside the mother's womb, states may, if they wish, prohibit abortions except where they may be necessary to preserve the life or health of the mother.

The court approaches the right of a woman to have an abortion on the legal concept of the "right of privacy." It came to the conclusion that this right, whether founded in the Fourteenth Amendment's concept of personal liberty and restrictions on state action, or in the Ninth Amendment's reservation of rights to the people, is broad enough to encompass a woman's decision of whether or not to terminate her pregnancy.

The decisions vindicate the right of the physician to administer medical treatment to a pregnant woman according to his professional judgment up to the point where important state interests provide compelling justification for intervention. Up to these points, the abortion decision in all its aspects is inherently and primarily a medical decision, and basic responsibility for it must rest with the physician. The court stressed that the ruling does not give women the right to abortion on demand in that a physician cannot be required to perform an abortion if it is against his judgment or moral principles.

The court was silent as to the requirement of a hospital to provide facilities for abortion. It would appear, based on the ruling in regard to physicians, that a hospital also does not have a duty to allow abortions to be performed in its facility if it is against its policy. However, hospitals have been required by state courts to allow sterilization procedures and abortion contrary to the hospital policy when the hospital was the only facility reasonably available to the patient.(7)

The Supreme Court noted that the medical judgment in regard to abortions should cover all relevant factors: "physical, emotional, psychological, familial and the woman's age." It also recognized such factors as "mental and physical harm" and "unwanted child" and "unwed motherhood."

The Court acknowledged the controversy over abortion and said it approached the problem free of emotion and of predilection. One of the big issues decided by the Court, however, was whether a fetus becomes a "person" upon conception and thus entitled to constitutional privileges. The Court ruled not. The Court rejected the key argument that the fetus is a person because life begins at conception, and thus is entitled to the due process and equal protection guarantees of the Constitution. The Court noted that the unborn have never been recognized in the law as persons in the whole sense and that the Constitution does not define person in so many words. Rather, the use of the word is such that it has application postnatally. The Court further held that it need not resolve the difficult question of when life begins since those trained in the respective disciplines of medicine, philosophy and theology are unable to arrive at any consensus; the judiciary at this point in the development of man's knowledge is not in a position to speculate as to the answer.

Another of the critical issues to be decided was when a state may assert its interest in safeguarding a potential life. The Court concluded that the states may properly assert important interests in safeguarding health, in maintaining medical standards, and in protecting potential life. At some point in pregnancy, these respective interests become sufficiently compelling to sustain regulation of the factors that govern the abortion decision. This compelling state interest arises first as to the pregnant woman only at the end of the first three months of pregnancy. The Court held that a state can assert protection to the potential life only during the last ten weeks of pregnancy, the time of "viability." The states may even proscribe abortions during these last ten weeks except where the abortion may be necessary to preserve the life or health of the mother after the fetus becomes viable. The Court also noted that the state may define the term physician to mean only one currently licensed and bar any abortion by a person who does not meet the qualifications.

The Supreme Court did note particularly that it had not decided in these latest cases the legal status and rights of a wife or a pregnant minor to obtain an abortion without parental consent. The legal definition of a minor and the ability of the minor to consent to an abortion is still governed by the statutes of the various states and the interpretations given to these statutes by the state courts. This major legal question left unanswered by the United States Supreme Court in its landmark abortion decisions on January 23, 1973, will soon be placed before the Court.(8) It will be asked to decide an appeal of a three-judge federal court ruling that a Florida law requiring parental or spousal consent for abortions is unconstitutional. The Florida statute required a physician to obtain the written consent of a husband or, in the case of a female under 18 years of age, the consent of a parent, custodian or legal guardian before performing an abortion. The federal panel's ruling came in a suit brought in Miami by three family physicians and two pregnant females (a married woman and an unmarried minor) who subsequently obtained abortions elsewhere.

Referring to the Supreme Court's rulings, the three-judge panel said that, since the state cannot interfere to protect the fetus' interest in its potential life until viability is reached, and cannot act to protect a pregnant woman's physical or mental health until approximately the end of the first trimester, neither can it interfere on behalf of husbands or parents to protect their interests in these matters until the "compelling points" are reached.

The federal court said that it recognized the qualitative differences in the interests of a husband or the parents within a family unit in protecting maternal health and potential life. But, the judges declared, the state may not statutorily delegate to husbands and parents an authority the state does not possess.

In an added comment, the court noted that its ruling does not limit the traditional and substantial right which husbands and parents have in asserting their respective interests within the family unit. Certainly husbands ought to participate with their wives in decisions relating to whether or not their mutual procreation should be aborted or allowed to prosper, and parents ought to advise and guide their unmarried, minor daughters in a decision of such import.

Although it does not have the effect of establishing the law for the District of Columbia, it is noteworthy that recently a United States District Court judge ordered(9) that the District of Columbia's only public hospital stop requiring the consent of the husband when a married woman applies for an abortion or sterilization. The ruling applies only to the local city hospital and not to the city's private hospitals and clinics, some of which have been requiring the husband's consent. The judge ruled that the city hospital's policy requiring the husband's consent to an abortion deprives poor married women of their right to receive needed medical care, to control their own bodies, and to choose whether to bear the greater risks of pregnancy and childbirth or the lesser risks of a therapeutic abortion.

These appeals to the Supreme Court may help to determine what rules and regulations the state may impose on the performance of abortions during the last two trimesters, particularly the last.

Since the decisions in the cases involving the Texas and Georgia statutes, the Supreme Court has refused to reconsider its decisions in cases from at least ten other states.(10) Without giving a reason, the Court declined to hear a North Carolina case involving the issue of whether a minor must have her parents' consent or whether a wife must have her husband's approval for an abortion. Because of the Florida case, which comes before it automatically, the Supreme Court will now have to decide these issues.

The Court recently returned to a lower federal court for another review of a case from New York involving the question of whether states must pay for the abortions of welfare recipients.(11) New York's highest court had ruled that a state must pay for such abortions. This decision was originally affirmed by a lower federal court and went up on appeal to the Supreme Court.

In line with the Supreme Court decision that a pregnant woman could not obtain an abortion on demand from an unwilling physician or in a hospital not providing such services, a U.S. Court of Appeals ruled(12) that a hospital that is regulated by the state and receives Hill-Burton funds may still refuse to perform abortions without violating the Civil Rights Act or be in conflict with the decision. In reversing a lower court's ruling, the appeals court in Wisconsin said that there is no constitutional objection to a state statute or policy which leaves a private hospital free to decide for itself whether or not it will admit abortion patients or to determine the conditions on which such patients will be accepted.

The Supreme Court in a brief unsigned order(13) refused to review an appeal of a state court ruling barring abortions for psychiatric reasons. This decision may be moot in view of the fact that the state of Illinois has since enacted three bills covering the practice of abortion.

Unique resolutions of the practice of abortion can be found in court rulings of several states. The Supreme Court of South Dakota ruled(14) recently that its statute enacted in 1887 forbidding the termination of pregnancy except when it is necessary to preserve the life of the mother did not interfere with a physician's right to practice medicine according to the highest professional standards.

A Michigan Court of Appeals, on the basis of the decision of the Supreme Court in the District of Columbia case, has declared(15) that a licensed physician may perform abortions in an accredited hospital although since 1864 the state has restricted abortions to save the life of the mother. The court noted that the century-old statute was enacted in an era when abortion was a risky operation often ending in the death of the mother and that modern sciences and wide use of antibiotics have made abortion a relatively safe procedure.

About one-third of the 46 states affected by the abortion rulings have introduced legislation to bring their laws into conformity with the decisions or are working on new legislation. The legislature of the state of Illinois has enacted three bills setting standards for abortions in accordance with the Supreme Court .decision.(16) The bills prohibit abortion in the third trimester except to preserve the life or health of the mother, specify that all abortions after the first trimester must be in a licensed hospital, and require that all abortions be performed by an Illinois-licensed physician affiliated with a licensed hospital and after adequate counseling has been provided for the patient and written permission has been obtained. Also approved was legislation protecting the rights of health professionals who do not wish to perform or assist in abortions. But in two state legislatures, Virginia and Maryland, bills to bring its laws into line with the Supreme Court decisions have been rejected. In more than a dozen states, attorneys general or local authorities have declared existing abortion laws invalid. However, legal or judicial authorities in at least five states have upheld the old restrictive laws.(17)

In line with the Supreme Court decisions establishing the right of women to terminate pregnancies by abortion the Massachusetts Department of Public Health induced this department to take a number of actions.(18) First of all it endorsed a statement of principles considered essential by the Abortion Advisory Committee of the Massachusetts Medical Society to maintain high standards of medical care and to safeguard the health of women undergoing abortion procedures. Moreover, it adopted, on an emergency basis, regulations for ambulatory gynecologic surgery in licensed hospitals and licensed clinics. These regulations cover a class of procedures that the American College of Obstetricians and Gynecologists believe can be safely performed on an outpatient basis. They were adopted for inclusion in the Department's proposed new regulations governing all licensed clinics, hospital-operated clinics and hospital outpatient departments. Finally, the Department determined a need for, and issued a license to, the first free-standing clinic to provide abortion services in the context of comprehensive ambulatory and gynecologic services in the Commonwealth.

The impact of the Supreme Court decisions regarding the practice of abortion has had its impact on the official policy of physicians as evidenced by the recent actions of the American Medical Association(19) at its first meeting following the Supreme Court decisions. The American Medical Association reaffirmed its 1970 policy on abortion while at the same time emphasizing the medical profession's "positive attitude toward life itself" and alternatives to abortion.

In essence, the policy requires that abortions be performed in accordance with "good medical practice"; that is, the physician must exercise sound clinical judgment, ensure there is informed patient consent, and evaluate the individual's medical and emotional needs.

Specifically, the statement says: "Abortion is a medical procedure and should be performed only by a duly licensed physician and surgeon in conformance with standards of good medical practice and that no physician or other professional personnel shall be compelled to perform any act which violated his good medical judgment. Neither physician, hospital, nor hospital personnel shall be required to perform any act violative of personally-held moral principles. In these circumstances good medical practice requires only that the physician or other professional personnel withdraw from the case so long as the withdrawal is consistent with good medical practice."

The American Medical Association also reaffirmed that the Principles of Medical Ethics do not prohibit a physician from performing an abortion in accordance with good medical practice and under circumstances that do not violate the laws of the community.

Although the American Medical Association action was labeled a "reaffirmation" of its policy, the new statement actually omits previous requirements that abortions be performed "in an accredited hospital" and "only after consultation with two other physicians." These two requirements were "edited" out by the reference committee to bring the American Medical Association policy into conformance with recent U.S. Supreme Court rulings.

In an obvious compromise move to satisfy members opposed to abortion, the American Medical Association adopted another statement: "In affirming the traditional favorable attitude of the medical profession toward pregnancy and motherhood, encourage the development of counseling programs that will offer constructive help to expectant mothers in accepting and coping with the stresses of pregnancy, offer incentives such as approval, appreciation, encouragement and emotional support for a decision to continue a pregnancy to term, assure the availability of adequate information and services regarding adoption in those cases in which the expectant mother might be unable to rear a child and educational programs on contraceptive measures appropriate for individual patients."

In several states, Oklahoma, New York, Colorado, Illinois and Maryland in particular, there are efforts to annul the convictions of physicians for performing abortions in violations of laws which are alleged to be unconstitutional under the recent Supreme Court decisions.(20)

Many local medical societies (state, county, city) have considered the problem of the performance of abortion and have issued a variety of policy statements regarding the practice: For the most part they are within the letter and spirit of the Supreme Court decisions.

A survey(21) of 33,000 physicians conducted after the Supreme Court decisions indicated that they were in favor of so-called liberalized abortion policies by 65 to 35%. Opponents were primarily Catholic and older non-Catholic physicians. Of those favoring abortion 50% thought it should be restricted to the first trimester, and 23% even in the last three months. Seventy percent of the favorable group felt there was no ethical or moral question involved. These data confirm the impression gained from my small survey of physicians in the District of Columbia.

It is worth noting that the decisions on January 23, 1973, were by 7-2 rulings. The Supreme Court's decisions were at odds with the expressed view of President Nixon, who about eight months earlier had said he opposed liberalized abortion policies and spoke out for the right to life of literally hundreds of thousands of unborn children. Interestingly, three of the four justices President Nixon appointed to the Court voted with the majority to liberalize abortion practices.(22)

The sentiment for liberalizing abortions is by no means unanimous among the voters of the various states.(23) Three-fifths of Michigan's voters and three-quarters of North Dakota's voted no to abortion-law referendums.(24) The Governors of Pennsylvania and New York have recently vetoed strict abortion bills passed by their state legislatures.(25)

It is interesting to note that, following the Supreme Court decisions, a nationwide poll showed that American public opinion in a poll taken by the Harris Survey indicated a change in the attitude of Americans.(26) A Gallup Poll(27) about a year before these Supreme Court decisions and while the highests courts of several states were invalidating their state abortion laws indicated that 64% of Americans approved "liberalized" abortions. Another poll taken six months prior to the decisions the public opposed "legalizing" abortions by 46 to 42% (12% undecided), whereas after the decision Harris found a 52-41% margin (7% undecided) in favor of the Supreme Court lifting all legal restrictions on abortions during the first three months of pregnancy. Actually, men favored abortion (56-36%) more than women (48-45%).

It is obvious that the landmark abortion decisions by the U.S. Supreme Court will have a powerful social and professional impact. The Court denied pregnant women the absolute right to have abortions, thereby protecting those physicians and hospitals who prefer not to participate in this form of medical practice. However, in most urban areas abortion requests will be honored by someone. It is only in the remote rural areas where hospitals may find themselves "forced" to accede.

In arriving at its decision to "legalize" abortions, the Supreme Court exercised simplistic reasoning, balancing the interests of the pregnant woman with the interests of the unborn child. The Court accepted the validity of both interests; yet it did not offer either the complete constitutional protection so strenuously urged by their advocates.

The unborn child is to be protected, if at all, only after it achieves the state of viability because, as the Court states, it is then that the child "presumably has the capability of meaningful life outside the mother's womb." Having acquired this status, the child's interest is greater than the mother's except when her life or health is in jeopardy. In all other situations laws can be passed to proscribe abortions after viability.

Prior to viability, the mother's interests are the greater, and abortions may not be proscribed for any reason. Existing laws forbidding pre-viable abortions are now unconstitutional. However, for all abortions performed after the first trimester, the State does have the right to regulate those procedures, provided such regulations "are reasonably related to maternal health."

Existing regulations requiring abortion committees, pre-operative consultation, or performance in the Joint Commission on Accreditation of Hospitals accredited hospitals were stricken by the Supreme Court as being unreasonable. It is clear that the Court intended to place abortions on the same footing as other surgical procedures. Therefore, while maternal welfare after the first trimester may require some regulation of abortion procedures nothing will be allowed to impede the surgeon's decision to abort.

The Supreme Court emphatically declared that abortions during the first trimester are not to be regulated, except that the State may require them to be conducted only by licensed physicians.

Therefore the Court places the first trimester abortions solely within the clinical judgment of physicians. Such a conclusion should not be construed to mean the physicians will be unfettered in performing abortions, for the Court specifically outlined the remedies if individual practitioners abused the privilege of exercising proper or acceptable medical judgment: professional censure, loss of licensure, and lawsuits. Consequently, even when doing abortions during the first trimester, physicians must consider the adequacy of their own competency, of the facilities utilized, of the availability of aftercare, and of provisions to handle whatever complications or emergencies that might arise.

Despite what some legal authorities contend are clear guidelines, the Supreme Court's decisions apparently will continue to be subject to a variety and often opposing interpretations. The only certainty is that it will be months and maybe years befory the issue is settled in all states. It does seem reasonable to expect however, that as the various states establish laws regarding the performance of abortions in conformance with the Supreme Court decisions, their experience will be similar to that witnessed in the District of Columbia. New York's experience is similar. Already the free-standing clinics and hospitals in these two jurisdictions are noting a decline in the number of abortions as out-of-state women can now get an abortion more readily at home. Some of the free-standing clinics in New York are now opening satellite clinics in other states with liberalized abortion laws because of the decrease in patient load locally.(28)

In the wake of the decisions by the Supreme Court liberalizing abortion laws in the United States, campaigns were intensified in several foreign countries—France, Belgium, The Netherlands, Italy and West Germany—to ease restrictive abortion laws there(29, 30). Despite the attempt to liberalize abortions by the French legislature, the Council of the French Order of Doctors has expressed its opposition to "on-demand" abortions, suggesting that if France liberalizes abortions physicians should not be involved with them but they should be performed by special abortion clinics. On the other hand, a number of French physicians have openly defied the above policy statement.(31) Meanwhile, El Salvador, a country predominantly Catholic, enacted a tough anti-abortion law.(32) However, a liberalized abortion law has been introduced in the Italian parliament which is also a predominantly Catholic country.(33) Federal moves to liberalize Australia's abortion laws are facing a passive defeat in the Australian parliament. Although the bill is supported by the government, opposition parties oppose it overwhelmingly, supported by one million letters from Roman Catholics.(34)

RECENT DEVELOPMENTS

The impact of the Supreme Court decisions in regard to abortion is beginning to take shape. It is becoming generally accepted across the United States that public hospitals must permit their facilities to be used for abortions. A United States District Court in Minnesota(35) recently held that a municipal hospital may not constitutionally prohibit licensed physicians on its staff from using the hospital's facilities for the performance of abortions. Furthermore, since the hospital is municipally owned its abortion policy is "state action." The court said that its decision does not require individuals to participate in abortions against their religious or moral convictions. It only requires that facilities for abortion services be provided at a public institution for physicians and their women patients who request them and legally have a right to their use. This court relied on a decision of the U.S. Court of Appeals(36) which held that once the state has undertaken to provide general short-term hospital care, it may not constitutionally draw the line at medically indistinguishable surgical procedures that impinge on fundamental rights.

A Federal District Court upheld(37) the right of private hospitals to prohibit abortions even though the facility received both federal and state funds and benefits. The court did note that there were five neighboring hospitals within 50 miles which did provide facilities for abortions. The court also held that the hospital need not appoint a physician to its staff if the physician refuses to agree to abide by the hospital rule prohibiting abortions. It may not refuse the appointment, however, if the physician performs abortions elsewhere.

A total of 39 abortion laws were enacted in 1973 in 23 of the 50 states. Ten of these states adopted two or more laws. In three states the laws basically permitted abortion only to preserve the life of the mother. Two of these have already been declared unconstitutional. Ten states have passed "comprehensive" laws which regulate the conditions under which an abortion may legally be performed. These laws plus statutes in 12 additional states contain "conscience clauses" which give hospitals and physicians the right to refuse to perform abortions. In four states only denominational or private hospitals may refuse to allow abortions to be performed. Only three of the total of 23 laws containing "conscience clauses" include provisions prohibiting discrimination against persons who do perform abortions as well as those who refuse to perform them. The laws in four states require the consent of one or both parents if the consenting pregnant female is a minor, or the consent of her husband if she is married. One state requires the consent of the father of the fetus. One state statute requires spousal consent. It was previously noted, however, that a similar statute of another state was voided by a special federal court.

It is noteworthy that a number of political subdivisions have established guidelines for abortion clinics.(38, 39) During the year ensuing the Supreme Court decisions, except for an occasional dissenting state, many state medical societies have voted for liberalized abortion practices.(40) Several large insurance companies have agreed to pay claims for abortions under provisions covering pregnancy and childbirth.(41) Suits were successfully undertaken to restore the licenses of physicians convicted over the past few years of performing abortions in contravention of state statutes which now have been declared unconstitutional.(42)

As we have noted, the change in abortion practices in the United States brought about by the Supreme Court decisions has had an international impact. Recently, the Austrian government liberalized its abortion laws so that starting in 1975 abortions will be permitted during the first three months of pregnancy for any reason. At present, abortion is legal only if the continuation of the pregnancy or childbirth is considered dangerous to the health of the mother.(43)

NOTES

(1) *United States vs. Vuitch*, 402 U.S. 62, 1971.

(2) *Abortions During 1971 in the District of Columbia*, Report, D.C., Department of Human Resources.

(3) *Therapeutic Abortions in the District of Columbia*, 1972, Report,D.C., Department of Human Resources.

(4) *Regulation Concerning Extramural Abortion Facilities,* Report, District of Columbia City Council, February 15, 1972.

(5) *Roe vs. Wade*, 93 S.Ct. 705 (1973).

(6) *Doe vs. Bolton*, 93 S.Ct. 739 (1973).

(7) *Am. Med. News*, March 12, 1973.

(8) *Am. Med. News,* September 10, 1973.

(9) *Am. Med. News,* July 10 and November 13, 1972.

(10) *Am. Med. News.* March 5, 1973.

(11) *Am. Med. News,* February 26 and June 18, 1973.

(12) *Am. Med. News*, June 18, 1973.

(13) *Am. Med. News*, December 25, 1972 and July 10, 1973.

(14) State of South Dakota *vs* Munson, 201 N.W. 2d 123 (1973).

(15) *Am. Med. News*, October 30, 1972.

(16) *Am. Med. News*, August 6, 1973.

(17) *Am. Med. News*, March 26, 1973.

(18) *New Engl. J. Med.*, 283 (1973) 686-687.

(19) *Am. Med. News*, February 19, March 12, July 2 and 9, and December 10, 1973.

(20) *Med. World News*, 14 (1973) 21, 45.

(21) 33,000 Doctors speak out on abortion, *Mod. Med.*, 41 (1973) 12, 31-35.

(22) *Am. Med. News*, May 15, 1972.

(23) *Law Week*; 72-56 Marker *vs.* Abele, 72-730 Markle *vs* Abele, Connecticut; 72-434 Byrn *vs* New York City Health and Hospital Corporation; *Am. Med. News*, January 29, 1973.

(24) *Am. Med. News*, October 23, November 13 and 20, 1972, and October 29, 1973.

(25) *Am. Med. News*, May 22 and December 11, 1972.

(26) *Am. Med. News*, March 13, 1972.

(27) *Am. Med. News*, May 13, 1972.

(28) *Med. Econ.,* April 16, 1973; *Am. Med. News*, April 2, 1973.

(29) *Am. Med. News*, February 19 and March 5, 1973.

(30) *Am. Med. News*, February 12 and June 4, 1973.

(31) *Med. World News*, 14 (1973) 9, 4-5.

(32) *Am. Med. News*, February 19, 1973.

(33) *Am. Med. News*, March 19, 1973.

(34) *Am. Med. News*, May 21, 1973.

(35) Nyberg *et al. vs* City of Virginia *et al.*, USDC, D. Minn., Fifth Div., 5-73, Civ. 72 (1973).

(36) Hathaway *vs.* Worcester City Hospital, 475 F. 2d 701 (1st Cir. 1973).

(37) Watkins *vs* Mercy Medical Center *et al.*, USDC, D. Idaho, Civil No. 1. 73-17 (1973).

(38) *Family Planning/Population Reporter*, 2, No. 6, December, 1973.

(39) *Am. Med. News*, October 29, 1973.
(40) *Am. Med. News*, May 22, June 12, July 24 and December 18, 1972; February 12, April 9, May 7, May 21, September 22 and September 29, 1973.
(41) *Am. Med. News*, March 26 and April 2, 1973.
(42) *Am. Med. News,* April 16,1973
(43) *Am. Med. News,* December 17, 1973.

VOLUNTARY EUTHANASIA

Arval A. Morris

Not many people plan or talk about death, especially their own. It is a grim topic, and that is probably why death is so little considered.(1) In our society, death is more taboo than sex. But death remains important, not only because each of us must confront it, but because death, today, has more clearly become a matter of timing.(2) Many people argue to the contrary, but they sound as though they are dealing with Gods whose only problem of choice is between eternal life or eternal death. Ordinary mortals do not confront these Olympian choices. For us, it is simply, death now, or death later. That is the only real choice we have; it is a mere matter of timing. Recognition of this simple truth implies that man *has* a choice, and makes it possible to discuss the question whether death may be preferable at some time before biological destruction of the body insures its inevitable coming.

Our choice is made poignant because modern medicine has found ways of delaying death, and prolonging life. This does not mean that modern medicine necessarily prolongs our living a full and robust life because in some cases it serves only to prolong mere biological existence during the act of dying.(3) Under these tragic circumstances a prolonged life can mean the prolongation of a heart-beat that activates the husk of a mindless, degenerating body that sustains an unknowing and pitiable life—one without vitality, health or any opportunity for normal existence—an inevitable stage in the process of dying:(4)

One day a middle-aged woman became suddenly blind in one eye. The terror of this unheralded experience was rapidly offset by recovery of vision in subsequent weeks. Attacks of giddiness and shaking of the legs and head followed, again to improve but again to reappear. This was the onset of multiple sclerosis, a disorder where disseminated foci of damage occur throughout the brain and spinal cord. Slowly but inexorably the patient was forced to bed and was ultimately unable to leave it because of paralysis of the lower limbs. Soon, control of the bladder and anal muscles led to incontinence of urine and faeces. Bed sores developed and were so large and deep that the underlying bones of the pelvis were eroded as well. This abject image of misery and pain was kept going by the frequent administration of antibiotic and pain-relieving drugs. Is it justifiable to prolong such a life, if life it be? In this question we are faced with the fundamental problem of the meaning of man's existence.

Today, death and the process of dying are being invested with new dimensions.(5) They are being forced upon us by increasing medical capacities and by increasing human sensitivity and concern about voluntary euthanasia.

That there has been an advancing public concern and sympathy for voluntary euthanasia is well-illustrated by a 1969 Chicago case.(6) One Mrs. Waskin, a hospitalized victim of terminal leukemia, had pleaded with her twenty-three-year-old son to kill her, and had herself unsuccessfully attempted to commit suicide by taking sleeping pills. Three days after she made her request for death, at a time when she was in deep pain, her son killed her by shooting her three times in the head. The son admitted killing his mother, and was arrested and charged with murder; but at trial, it took the jury only forty minutes of deliberation to find him not guilty by reason of insanity. Furthermore, the jury found that his insanity was only temporary; that it was not likely to recur, and he was released. From the facts of this case, it seems highly unlikely that the son was ever really insane. A more likely explanation is that the jury was moved by the human drama before it, and sympathized with the terrible plight of the family and that of the son. The "murder" was an excusable mercy killing, an act of compassion.(7)

As this case illustrates, the time has come for man to rethink his traditional attitudes toward death. We cannot continue to view death in every circumstance as necessarily bad, something to be avoided, or something for which punishment must necessarily follow when it is inflicted upon another. Nor can we persist in believing that any kind of life is so sanctified as to be preferred absolutely over death—rather, we must replace our neurotic attitudes toward death(8) with a more realistic view of death as a biological function.(9) Death for some persons may be a gift, and for others, a favor. Similar concern for public attitudes toward death was recently expressed by Dr. Edmund Leach:(10)

Our ordinary morality says that we must kill our neighbour if the state orders us to do so—that is to say, as a soldier in war or as an executioner in the course of his duty—but in every other case we must try to save life. But what do we mean by that? Would a headless human trunk that was still breathing be alive? And if you think that is just a fanciful question, what about a body that has sustained irreparable brain damage but still can be kept functioning by the ingenuity of modern science? It isn't so easy.

For many Americans their fear is not so much of death but of the tragic figure one might become before death. Moreover, there are many persons who refuse to outlive their usefulness and become burdens to themselves and others.(11) Suicide is an option open to those persons possessing the necessary means and the physical strength and ability to use them. It is hollow to hold that a man may, in certain circumstances, be justified in ending his life to avoid great pain and terminal suffering, but to deny justification to his call upon a willing expert for assistance in that task.(12) If we are to honor human dignity, we must not only change our attitudes toward death—we must also cease to leave the process of dying to chance and to the progressive disintegration of the body. The purpose of this article is to contribute to our necessary rethinking of death through a consideration of voluntary euthanasia.

THE PRINCIPLE OF VOLUNTARY EUTHANASIA

To avoid the possibility of confusion, it is necessary to distinguish voluntary euthanasia from other similar, but not necessarily related situations. By voluntary euthanasia I refer to one specific situation, and to no other. Any definition of the principle of voluntary euthanasia must lay emphasis on the word *"voluntary"* as it specifically applies to the right of an adult person who is in command of his faculties to have his life ended by a physician, pursuant to his own intelligent request, under specific conditions prescribed by law, and by painless means.(13) Thus, voluntary euthanasia involves at least two willing persons—a doctor and a patient. Considered solely from the perspective of its recipient, apart from its medical assistance, voluntary euthanasia is most akin to suicide.(14) Hence, with medical assistance rendered in accordance with law, the term simply refers to legally-assisted suicide.(15) But voluntary euthanasia is not subject to whim, nor indulged whenever a person may decide he would like it; rather, it is carefully controlled by statute and allowed only under rigorously defined circumstances.(16) Furthermore, voluntary euthanasia is "voluntary" on the part of the doctor as well as the patient. There is no requirement that a doctor *must* administer euthanasia to a patient. Instead, voluntary euthanasia provides a way for legalizing free choice—a liberty, and it requires a willing patient and a willing doctor, acting under law. Nothing short of that will do.

Voluntary euthanasia also involves an identifiable act of commission by the attending doctor. Thus, it is to be distinguished from somewhat similar forms of mercy-killing which involve only an omission. While a fully generalized principle of voluntary euthanasia probably includes acts of omission as well as acts of commission, I do not deal here with the problems of omissions.(17) Although the problem of omissions weighs heavily on the conscience of every sensitive doctor,(18) and certainly deserves the attention of legal scholars,(19) its passive nature places it outside the present discussion which is restricted to the affirmative act of voluntary euthanasia.

Finally, we must consider our subject matter with reference to those who may be its intended recipients. I draw sharp distinctions among the several groups who may be thought to be potential candidates for euthanasia. For reasons discussed later, I restrict my discussion and advocacy of voluntary euthanasia to only two categories of willing recipients. First among these are the incurably ill; this class is defined as including those adult persons who have a serious physical illness which is both incurable and terminal, and which is expected either to cause severe distress to the patient, or to render him incapable of leading a rational existence. The second category includes the so-called "human vegetables;" this class is defined as those adult persons who suffer a condition of irreversible brain damage or deterioration such that their normal mental faculties are so severely impaired that they are incapable of leading a rational existence. For example, a massive stroke may destroy a man's ability to move, see, and hear, and to reason or to organize his life. Other examples of permissible candidates for voluntary euthanasia may have been rendered permanently unconscious by accident or disease; and, in many cases, their biological lives may have been prolonged by artificial means.

Under my definition,(20) limiting the permissible candidates for voluntary euthanasia, there is no room for authorization of eugenics, murder, genocide, or arbitrary destruction of the sick, the deformed, the senile, or the mentally deficient. The end to be achieved is not human disposal, but, on the contrary, the enhancement of human dignity by permitting each man's last act to be an exercise of his free choice between a tortured, hideous death and a painless, dignified one.

This choice is not available under current law. Today, if a physician, motivated solely by mercy, consciously and deliberately kills his suffering patient in a painless manner at the request of the patient, his act is considered to be murder—probably, in the first degree.(21) Our current law considers whether a killing has been done with premeditation and deliberation. The motive for which a killing has been committed is otherwise irrelevant, except insofar as it might affect the sentence received upon conviction. Neither good motives, nor a request or demand by the victim that he be killed, can now function to exculpate a person charged with murder or manslaughter.(22) Nor is it a defense to such a charge that the death of the deceased was imminent, or that the deceased was incurably and terminally ill and in extreme pain. Present law forces the person who is incurably ill, or the so-called "human vegetable," to endure the physical and mental misery often accompanying the process of dying. Similarly, many doctors in such circumstances consider themselves professionally obliged to do all they can to keep the patient alive; thus, ironically, prolonging the agony of death and the misery of the patient.(23) In this way, many members of the medical profession have reinforced the steadfast refusal of our lawmakers to allow a dignified and comfortable exit from life.(24) Both professions have relied upon the assumed absolute necessity of preserving human life as the justification for a prolongation of abject indignity in order to sustain biological life alone.

One of the great tragedies that confuses almost every discussion about voluntary euthanasia is the entanglement of social and medical considerations with religion. Many among us still fail to perceive that "those who hold that Faith may follow its precepts without requiring those who do not hold it to act as if they did,"(25) and that there is a big difference between illegality and religious immorality. This confusion is peculiarly inappropriate and tragic in America where our Constitution has intentionally isolated religious affairs from secular affairs by constructing a high wall of separation between church and state. Under our Constitution a state is disabled from legislating on religion or on religious grounds; conversely legislation cannot properly be defeated solely for religious reasons. These limitations are part of a legislator's constitutional duties. Unfortunately, however, the restriction on defeating legislation for religious reasons is of that unique type of negative duty whose breach is never brought before a court for review—if, by breach of a legislator's duty, religious grounds are allowed to defeat an otherwise permissible proposed statute, the result is simply an absence of legislation which is not a legitimate subject for judicial review or redress.

The basic point is that religious grounds are constitutionally irrelevant. Mr. Justice Frankfurter has stated their irrelevancy within the context of Sunday closing laws:(26)

> To ask what interest, what objective, legislation serves, of course, is not to psychoanalyze its legislators, but to examine the necessary effects of what they have enacted. If the primary end achieved by a form of regulation is the affirmation or promotion of religious doctrine—primary, in the sense that all secular ends which it purportedly serves are derivative from, not wholly independent of, the advancement of religion—the regulation is beyond the power of the state. . . . Or if a statute furthers both secular and religious ends by means unnecessary to the effectuation of the secular ends alone—where the same secular ends could equally be attained by means which do not have consequences for promotion of religion—the statute cannot stand. A State may not endow a church although that church might inculcate in its parishioners moral concepts deemed to make them better citizens, because the very *raison d'être* of a church, as opposed to any other school of civilly serviceable morals, is the predication of religious doctrine.

The underlying constitutional foundation for this view is, of course, the language of the First Amendment prohibiting both abridgment and establishment of religion.

No question concerning abridgment of religion arises with respect to the principle of voluntary euthanasia; no one suggests that euthanasia should be mandatory, or that a doctor should be punished or otherwise officially sanctioned for not administering euthanasia. Rather, the principle of voluntary euthanasia envisions a liberty, like the First Amendment, and a legally sanctioned exercise of free choice respecting the dignity of death.

The establishment clause of the First Amendment is relevant to the discussion because it disallows the use of religious grounds to aid either the success or defeat of voluntary euthanasia legislation. As Professor Glanville Williams has convincingly illustrated, the strictly religious arguments for and against voluntary euthanasia are relatively weak and inconclusive.(27) He concludes that "if it is true that [voluntary] euthanasia can be condemned only according to a religious opinion this should be sufficient at the present day to remove the prohibition from the criminal law."(28) In addition, religious objections to voluntary euthanasia must be deemed constitutionally impermissible on the ground that state action (and inaction) based primarily upon religious grounds violates the establishment clause of the First Amendment. The meaning of this clause has often been expressed by the Supreme Court in language such as this:(29)

> [T]he "establishment of religion" clause of the First Amendment means at least this: Neither a state nor the Federal Government can set up a church. Neither can pass laws which aid one religion, aid all religions, or prefer one religion over another. Neither can force nor influence a person to go to or to remain away from church against his will or force him to profess a belief or disbelief in any religion. No person can be punished for entertaining or professing religious beliefs or disbeliefs, for church attendance or non-attendance. No tax in any amount, large or small can be levied to support any religious activities or institutions, whatever they may be called, or whatever form they may adopt to teach or practice religion. Neither a state nor the Federal Government can, openly or secretly, participate in the affairs of any religious organizations or groups and vice versa. In the words of Jefferson, the clause against establishment of religion by law was intended to erect "a wall of separation between church and State."

Thus, it is necessary to set apart and ignore all religious grounds and arguments, whether they be for or against voluntary euthanasia;(30) under our constitutional form of government, they cannot be determinative. Voluntary euthanasia legislation must stand or fall on its secular merits, not its religious acceptability or repugnance.

What then, is the secular case for voluntary euthanasia? The case is profound, yet its structure can be stated simply.(31) Voluntary euthanasia can be justified by reference to three basic values of western civilization: prevention of cruelty; allowance of liberty; and the enhancement of human dignity, an ultimate goal which is achieved by adhering to the first two values.

All civilized men will agree that cruelty is an evil to be avoided. But few people acknowledge the cruelty of our present laws which require a man be kept alive against his will, while denying his pleas for merciful release after all the dignity, beauty, promise and meaning of life have vanished, and he can only linger for weeks or months in the last stages of agony, weakness and decay.(32) In addition, the fact that many people, as they die, are fully conscious of their tragic state of deterioration greatly magnifies the cruelty inherent in forcing them to endure this loss of dignity against their will.(33) Dr. Leonard Colebrook has written that(34)

. . . in addition to pain many of the unhappy victims of cancer have to endure the mental misery associated with the presence of a four fungating growth; of slow starvation owing to difficulty in swallowing; of painful and very frequent micturition; of obstruction of the bowels; of incontinence; and of the utter prostration that makes of each day and night a "death in life" as the famous physician, the late Sir William Osler, described it.

Diseases of the nervous system in their turn lead all too often to crippling paralysis or inability to walk; to severe headaches; to blindness; to the misery of incontinence and bedsores. Distressing mental disturbances are often added to these troubles.

Bronchitis, too, with its interminable cough and progressive shortness of breath, can have its special terrors, which medical treatment in the late stages can do little to abate.

All these, and many other grievous ills which may beset the road to death, are often borne with great courage and patience—even when the burden is many times heavier by reason of loneliness and/or poverty. (It should be remembered that only about half of the dying receive skilled nursing and medical care in hospitals.) Medical progress has done much to alleviate suffering during the past century, but, in honesty, it must be admitted that the process of dying is still very often an ugly business.

Beyond such direct cruelties, our current law also indirectly results in other cruelties as well, and these must all be weighed in the balance. For example, it seems exceedingly cruel to compel the spouse and children of a dying man to witness the ever-worsening stages of his disease, and to watch the slow, agonizing death of their loved one, degenerating before their eyes, being transformed from a vital and robust parent and spouse into a pathetic and humiliated creature, devoid of human dignity.(35) The psychological trauma that comes from witnessing such a spectacle may deeply affect, or permanently impair, the mental and physical health of both children and spouse.(36) Finally, we cannot ignore the residual, indirect cruelty which survives the death of the afflicted person, and burdens the surviving family with the costs incurred in the treatment of the prolonged illness. Enormous medical debts can impair or destroy a child's educational opportunities, for example, and recognition of such gloomy prospects will undoubtedly prey heavily on the mind of the terminally-ill parent or relative, adding to the pain and suffering which he already endures.(37)

Thus, it cannot be denied that, at least in this context, our current legal system lacks compassion; it prevents the sufferer from receiving a merciful death, and forces those who care for him to watch, helplessly, as he endures his pointless pain. In these respects, ours is a very cruel law, and this fact constitutes one basic cornerstone of the case for legalizing voluntary euthanasia: it would prevent cruelty and promote human dignity by affording human beings the opportunity of escaping useless suffering by means of merciful death at their request. Of course, legalization of voluntary euthanasia will not totally eliminate all the human pain and suffering which accompanies a long terminal illness. But it will tend to eliminate the law's current indifference to human misery, and will reduce pain and suffering significantly by placing the power to terminate misery under the victim's own control. Our legal system can ill-afford to ignore this humane opportunity for reducing cruelty.

The second social value which supports the case for voluntary euthanasia, and promotes the cause of human dignity, is that of liberty. In this context, our law has got the shoe on the wrong foot from the very beginning. Why does our law provide that when a person participates in voluntary euthanasia it constitutes the crime of murder? To have fidelity to liberty, the question should be reversed. We should start from the assumption that all voluntary acts are permissible, and, in the absence of some legitimate reason to deny it, we would presume that a doctor and a patient are free to act as they wish. The question should not be: "Why should people have a legal right to voluntary euthanasia?" but rather, the appropriate question should be:"Why should our criminal law restrain the liberty of the doctor and the patient, denying them from doing what they want?" In a free society it is the restraint on liberty that must be justified, not the possession of liberty. The criminal law should not be called upon to repress an individual's conduct unless such repression is demonstrably necessary on social grounds. Further, in the case of voluntary euthanasia, this demonstrably compelling interest must be secular, not religious. Yet it is entirely unclear what secular social interest is so compelling that it justifies preventing the incurably-ill sufferer from exercising his liberty of choice to accelerate death by a few hours, days, or even months; or what interest justifies the application of criminal deterrents to a voluntary euthanasia case.

With liberty as our basic postulate, restrictions must be justified. Those persons who would deny or restrict the liberty afforded by the principle of voluntary euthanasia must sustain the burden of coming forth and clearly stating the positive, secular, social value to be achieved by maintaining the lives of incurably-ill persons, or "human vegetables," against their wills and in depredation of their human dignity. In addition, they must justify the infringement of the liberty of doctors as well. Within the limits imposed by law, a doctor's responsibility to his patient is to prolong worthwhile life, and, failing that, then to ease his passing. If a doctor, with the advice of a consultant, honestly concludes that a patient's affliction is incurable and expected to cause severe pain and distress, and genuinely believes that the best service that can be performed for the suffering patient is to grant his voluntary request for euthanasia, then what justifies the criminal law in forbidding the doctor from doing so? No rational justification appears to me, and until an adequate secular ground is advanced, there is no reason for denying voluntary euthanasia to the incurably and terminally ill, or to the so-called "human vegetables." Why should the law deny a man the ultimate decision about what to do with his life? In the final analysis, control over one's own death is a matter of human dignity, and it should not be denied without some very compelling reasons.

The chief obstacles to acceptance of voluntary euthanasia have little to do with its merits. Widespread ignorance, indifference to the plight of the dying, and misunderstanding of the implications of voluntary euthanasia, primarily account for its not having been legalized. Naturally, dying persons leave few public records of their sufferings, and because of limited experience, the living are only slightly aware of the human trials and misery involved in the process of death. Moreover, the living try to keep thoughts about death far removed from their conscious minds. And, it should be noted that the dying do not organize into lobbying groups. Thus, while the case for voluntary euthanasia is convincing, it lacks organizational backing, and finds its only potential for success in the duty of legislators to do that which is right, even though pressured in the opposite direction by vocal or influential lobbyists. At this point, it is therefore appropriate to consider the secular arguments which have been advanced in opposition to voluntary euthanasia, and which have tended to reinforce the inertia of our legislators.(38)

The major objections to legalization of voluntary euthanasia can be grouped under six headings: 1. The claim that doctors are already performing whatever mercy killings may be necessary; 2. The difficulty of ascertaining voluntary consent; 3. The risk of incorrect medical diagnosis; 4. The possibility of new medical discoveries; 5. The claim that the use of modern drugs to control pain obviates the need for resort to voluntary euthanasia; and 6. The "wedge" or "slippery-slope" objection.

1. The first objection which is sometimes advanced against legalizing voluntary euthanasia is startling indeed: it is that mercy-killing already exists among some of our most reputable medical practitioners, and that there is no remnant need for such legislation.(39) Stated so baldly, this argument is Janus-faced, holding on the one hand that doctors are to be commended for presently committing acts of voluntary euthanasia and ought to be encouraged to continue such actions, but holding on the other hand that we ought not alter our present law, but should persist in treating the doctor's act as illegal homicide if by some mischance he is investigated and brought under our system of criminal law. Thus, these persons who object to change argue simultaneously that, with respect to the same act, it is right to break the criminal law, and it is wrong to break the criminal law. Obviously, those who make this argument lack the courage of their convictions; they refuse to give the force of law to their feelings about the propriety of voluntary euthanasia; instead, they expect doctors to take heroic risks.

The extent to which doctors practice voluntary euthanasia is unknown,(40) but there is little doubt that the perpetuation of our present criminal treatment of euthanasia necessarily deters many doctors who would otherwise be willing to engage in the practice. Under this first objection to the principle of voluntary euthanasia, the achievement of non-cruelty and human dignity depend upon chance—the chance that the suffering patient has selected a doctor who is willing to risk reputation, profession, liberty and family in order to relieve his patient's pain and suffering. The objection ignores the real needs of suffering patients, and is thus not only cowardly, but inhumane as well.

2. A second common objection to voluntary euthanasia relates to the issue of voluntary consent.(41) The argument is that the afflicted patient may be so

crazed by pain or stupefied by drugs that he is incapable of giving truly voluntary consent to euthanasia. This argument must be countered. Consent to euthanasia must be voluntary.

The way to insure that a person's consent is legally "voluntary" is to require that it be given while he is rational and sane, well before he is either crazed by pain or stupefied by drugs. Thus, a statute legalizing voluntary euthanasia should require that a patient execute a formal document declaring his desire for euthanasia. This document should be attested to by two disinterested witnesses, and there should be a required thirty-day "cooling-off period" after the declaration of consent is made, before the patient becomes eligible for euthanasia. The statute should also require the attending physician, after lapse of the thirty-day period, but before administration of euthanasia to a mentally responsible patient, to affirm that the prior declaration of consent is still in accord with the ascertained desires of the patient at that time. The legislation should also provide for some protection against fraudulent statements by witnesses and doctors, and should, as a final precaution, authorize revocation of a declaration of consent at any time by any clear act by the patient, or on his order.

Obviously, only that class of persons who are incurably and terminally ill and who are expected to suffer severe distress will be sufficiently conscious and rational to satisfy statutory consent requirements beyond making the initial declaration. A requirement of repeated rational requests for euthanasia by the patient clearly will not be susceptible of fulfillment by patients in the category of so-called "human vegetables." But, as to this latter group, instead of requiring repeated requests by the patient himself to indicate continuing consent, the statute could provide that the new request be made by one of his closest relatives. But, such a provision would unwisely place a burden of guilt on any close relative, who, having been called upon to give final authorization for the death of his parent, or spouse, would have to go through life knowing that he gave the final word authorizing the death of parent or spouse. There is no reason to burden a close relative with such a load of guilt. A simple declaration of consent made by the patient well in advance, when in sound mind, can adequately demonstrate voluntariness in the case of the so-called "human vegetables."

But as to the other permissible candidates for euthanasia, the above-described statutory requirement of repeated rational requests for euthanasia would be an easily administered measure for insuring the voluntariness of the patient's consent. More extensive restrictions, designed to guarantee voluntariness further, by invoking some additional administrative or judicial machinery, or perhaps court orders, would be time-consuming, inhumane, and self-defeating—they would be cumbersome and unduly increase the time during which pain and suffering must be endured. Voluntary consent is sufficiently insured by a statute requiring repeated voluntary requests, a twice-witnessed declaration, and independent medical collaboration on the issues of necessity and consent. Finally, of course, any statute legalizing voluntary euthanasia should contain a provision allowing the revocation of a declaration at any time by the patient, or on his order.

Even so, many will be concerned about the possibility of "conspiracy" among relatives. Suppose, for example, an incurably and terminally ill person requests euthanasia in order to relieve not only his own pain but the anguish of his relatives as well. Shall a doctor consider this request to be voluntary? This dilemma can be resolved by a statutory provision requiring that the doctor determine whether the relatives are insisting on euthanasia, or whether the motivating force in fact comes from the patient and his suffering. If the patient is incurably and terminally ill and expected to suffer severe distress, and has made the necessary prior declaration, I see no reason to deny him euthanasia simply because he bases his request on his concern for relieving his family of the attendant anxieties, rather than a desire for relief from physical pains. On the other hand, of course, if pressure by relatives is the sole or primary motivating force behind the patient's request for euthanasia, then his consent is not fully voluntary, even though he may have given voluntary consent at some prior time. The risk of conspiring relatives can be moderated by appropriate statutory safeguards.

The possibility of a conspiracy against the patient by the doctor and relatives, or by several doctors, probably cannot be fully guarded against by any voluntary euthanasia statute (or any statute at all). But a properly drafted voluntary euthanasia statute can minimize these risks by requiring that the patient's declaration be witnessed, that official records be kept, and that the attending doctor's diagnosis be independently corroborated by a consulting doctor. These requirements tend to make euthanasia a public activity, thus rendering a conspiracy much more difficult. Naturally, we can conjure up horrible hypotheticals involving dishonest and unethical doctors—for example, the possibility that a doctor might keep a patient alive as long as possible in order to collect the last available penny of fees. But the important points are that voluntary euthanasia procedures will not augment the probability of such aberrance, and that a voluntary euthanasia statute will be no less successful at combating such abuse than our present malpractice regulations. Ultimately, the best protection against dishonest, conspiring doctors lies in the ethical integrity of the medical profession.

In conclusion, there is some force in the argument against voluntary euthanasia that truly voluntary consent cannot always be satisfactorily obtained, but the thrust of that objection can be met by a properly drafted statute—voluntary consent can be satisfactorily guaranteed.

3. The third objection set against legalization of voluntary euthanasia concerns the risk of mistaken medical diagnosis.(42) This objection relies for its plausibility on the assumption that euthanasia will be administered well before the patient has reached the final stages of an incurable and terminal illness—that is, before the nature of his illness becomes patently clear and death inevitable. There is no reason to indulge this assumption; euthanasia is, by principle, to be administered by physicians only as a last resort, after the final progression of the

disease has become obvious.

Naturally, doctors, being human, do make honest mistakes, and the possibility of mistaken diagnosis is present in nearly every medical case, not just those involving voluntary euthanasia. Mistaken diagnosis in "ordinary" cases can have equally lethal consequences. However, in the case of voluntary euthanasia, the risk of such mistakes can be reduced substantially if the enabling statute allows euthanasia only after two physicians (one a consultant) have certified in writing that the patient is suffering from an incurable terminal condition. Of course, each of the two doctors should be subject to criminal penalties for any intentional falsification of a diagnosis or written certification in order to bring about a patient's death.

Moreover, the risk of mistaken diagnosis is not as great with respect to the limited categories of patients who are eligible for voluntary euthanasia.(43) Such a mistake would be especially unlikely in the case of a "human vegetable" who has a condition of brain damage or deterioration which has so severely and permanently impaired his normal faculties that he is incapable of leading a rational existence, or in the case of a man afflicted with a disease which is so evidently progressing into its final stages that occasion arises for his doctor to certify that he is incurably and terminally ill.(44) In any event, if there is a question regarding the diagnosis, and irreversible euthanasia is the alternative, there is no doubt that doctors will err on the side of prolonging life rather than destroying it. Such is the tendency of their medical training and their professional obligation.

Thus, while there is always a chance of a mistaken medical diagnosis, there is every reason to believe that a well-drafted voluntary euthanasia statute can reduce the probability of such error to a level less than that confronting the average non-euthanasia patient. Although there is a slight risk, I cannot believe that the slight possibility of mistaken diagnosis is great enough to outweigh the benefits to be obtained by legalizing voluntary euthanasia.

4. A closely related objection is the possibility of future, miraculous medical discoveries.(45) The objection is that, in some future case, there will be a patient to whom euthanasia has been administered and who might have been "saved" by a subsequent medical discovery. If accepted, the theory of this objection would require that we leave to their demise all patients who are now in pain and dying from various diseases, relying on the mere chance that sometime in the future there may be some medical discovery or innovation which makes possible the cure of some fatal disease (although we do not know which one it will be).

But, in the first place, it seems obvious that, whatever force there is in this objection, it has no application to the class of so-called "human vegetables;" there can be no medical discovery that will restore or "cure" a physically destroyed or deteriorated brain. And, on examination, this objection can also be seen to have no force in its application to those persons diagnosed as incurably and terminally ill. If a new medical discovery is made, of course, it will stop administration of euthanasia in all cases to which the discovery applies. Thus, the force of this objection can apply only to those few cases where euthanasia may have been administered immediately before a new medical discovery became available. It is critical to note that the important time for consideration is not the moment at which the discovery is made, but rather the time at which it becomes available for use. Furthermore, the only cases of voluntary euthanasia which would be relevant here would necessarily involve patients who are in the final stages of an incurable illness, and these patients will neither need nor request euthanasia until they reach the final distress of their disease. Under these circumstances, the likelihood is that, by the time voluntary euthanasia is administered, the progression of the fatal disease will have so weakened or impaired the patient's body processes that any new medical discovery, even if immediately available for use, would be of little aid to him (although it might be enormously valuable to a person whose disease has not yet progressed to its terminal stages). It is improbable that a new nedical discovery would enable doctors to save patients who are actually in the final stages of terminal illness; rather, the probabilities are that any person to whom euthanasia has been administered could not have been saved.

Even if we indulge the improbable assumption that some new discovery will be useful in curing the terminal stages of a presently incurable illness, it is yet unlikely that administration of euthanasia to the patient will deprive him of the continued life which the discovery offers. Practical implementation of a new discovery is not instantaneous, no matter how rapid the word of its discovery may spread. Doctors know about a new discovery long before they are able to use it; thus, consideration of voluntary euthanasia need not take into account new medical discovereis unless they are available for use. Indeed, the lapse of time between the moment of discovery and the time its fruits are made available for use may be extreme. In the case of new drugs, there must be testing, manufacture, and distribution; in the case of new techniques for cure, information must be compiled and disseminated, and therapists must be trained. During this warning period between the time of discovery and the time of implementation, doctors will not administer euthanasia if there is any possibility of saving the patient. Thus, when the new discovery finally becomes available for use, application of the principle of voluntary euthanasia will probably not have produced any "mistakes." In the last analysis, the objection based upon the possibility of future medical discoveries has no validity.

5. The fifth objection to legalizing voluntary euthanasia relies on the pain-controlling capacities of modern drugs.(46) It asserts that these drugs can satisfy all the objectives sought to be achieved by voluntary euthanasia and, hence, the latter is irrelevant. Thus, the question is whether modern drugs do in fact achieve all that a voluntary euthanasia statute can achieve. First of all, we must again exclude from our consideration those persons—the so-called "human vegetables"—whose primary desire is not to be relieved of pain, but rather to discontinue their necessarily irrational existence, a purpose which cannot be served by use of any of our modern drugs.

In the remaining category of cases involving patients who are incurably and terminally ill, it is true that significant amounts of physical pain can sometimes (though not always— be controlled by drugs. As Glanville Williams has pointed out, drugs do save some few people from extreme physical pain, but they often fail "to save them from an artificial, twilight existence, with nausea, giddiness, and extreme restlessness as well as the long hours of consciousness of a hopeless condition."(47) Thus, many of the basic miseries of the dying can only be overcome through euthanasia. Drugs are inadequate for this purpose, and, as Professor Williams observes, we must decide "whether the unintelligent brutality of such an existence is to be imposed on one who wishes to end it. . . ." Furthermore, recent research has shown that many people are aware of their impending deaths,(48) and to the extent that such awareness produces psychological anguish and depression, it seems clear that drugs controlling physical pain alone will be of little value in comparision to the total relief afforded by voluntary euthanasia. In addition, of course, the administration of drugs to a patient cannot relieve the mental anguish suffered by a spouse or child.

Moreover, insofar as physical misery alone is concerned, there are diseases for which modern drugs fail to offer complete relief.(49) For example, a person afflicted with cancer of the throat may be able to swallow or breathe only if he is willing to endure great pain (which is present well before he reaches the final stages of the disease). Furthermore, persons dying, both at home and in the hospital, do not always receive the massive doses of drugs necessary to relieve their extreme pain. Despite the availability of non-narcotic painkillers, narcotics such as morphine are sometimes used as heavy-pain killers, and these drugs lose their effectiveness with continuous use, necessitating constantly increasing doesages.(50) This facet of drug therapy also puts our doctors in a difficult situation, because ultimately a point is reached where the needed dose of narcotic is so large that it may either considerably speed up the death of the patient, or induce it immediately. Fear of the law, religious scruples, or considerations of medical ethics, may deter a doctor from administering such massive doses of drugs in these cases, and consequently the patient and his family suffer.

In summary, while we must concede the usefulness of modern drugs in controlling pain, it is impossible to conclude that they achieve all that a voluntary euthanasia can achieve. Drugs should be looked upon as a complement to voluntary euthanasia, not as a substitute. Drugs are not equally useful in all cases, and even in cases where affective drugs are available they may have other undesirable effects. This means, not that we ought to abandon drugs, but that we ought to conjoin their use with a program of legalized voluntary euthanasia. Modern drugs are helpful, yet even with them there are people dying in grief, agony, and weakness who request a speedy end to their miseries—the need for voluntary euthanasia persists.

6. The last resort of the opponents of voluntary euthanasia is reliance on the "wedge" argument.(51) Few proposals for change in law escape criticism by some version of this—"wedge" or "slippery slope" or "camel's nose"—argument; and the more important the proposed legal change, the more vehement the

argument is likely to be. In our present context, the objection asserts that voluntary euthanasia ought not be legalized because legalization of other abhorrent practices might follow. In this view, the legalization of voluntary euthanasia is viewed as the opening wedge or precursor for the future legalization of involuntary euthanasia, murder, and perhaps even genocide. Significantly, this argument does not address itself to the merits of voluntary euthanasia, but instead conjures up a parade of horribles applicable to subjects *other than* voluntary euthanasia.

The abhorrent, genocidal practices of Nazi Germany weigh heavily upon the minds of many who advance this argument. But America is not Nazi German, and we maintain no master-race philosophy. Our American experience has been unique in precisely the contrary manner, being constitutionally founded upon beliefs in the liberty and dignity of the person. Neither the American experience, nor the Fourteenth Amendment to our Constitution, is compatible with the sort of racial laws enacted by Nazi Germany, and no state legislature will, or could constitutionally, enact legislation authorizing the extermination of any minority group, religious or racial. The American tradition presses in the opposite direction. We started with compulsory sterilization laws, for example, but have since moved away from them, toward laws allowing voluntary sterilization.(52) Anyone who seriously considers recent American history will discern our consistent and growing concern for the protection of the rights of minorities as a necessary adjunct of individual liberty.

Voluntary euthanasia should be judged on its own merits. The "wedge" argument should be dismissed because it does not address itself to the question of voluntary euthanasia. The objection serves only to confuse discussion by injecting irrelevant emotional concerns over abhorrent practices. Specifically, in this context, the "wedge" argument confuses voluntary euthanasia with involuntary euthanasia. But how would this "wedge" ever gain a foothold? Voluntary euthanasia is in principle proposed to be administered only at the express request of an adult who understands the implications of his request. There is no compulsion. Free choice is a cornerstone of voluntary euthanasia. If compulsion were a part of the principle, it would destroy its own justification, which rests on the proposition that each of us should be *free* to choose for ourselves a dignified and painless death. Thus, the "wedge" objection is both irrelevant and unsupportable, and should be dismissed.

In summary appraisal of the case in favor of legalizing voluntary euthanasia, one must conclude that it is both strong and convincing. Most objections to voluntary euthanasia fail on analysis, and those that have some force and validity can be met by a properly drafted statute. Nevertheless, legalization of voluntary euthanasia is an issue which should be judged relatively in our social context, not by reference to "absolute" religious or secular values. Increasing concern over the ugliness and human degradations of incurable suffering can no longer be dealt with solely by an unthinking reference to the "absolute sanctity" of life, requiring the prolongation of a suffering existence as long as medically possible. The agonizing aspect of some deaths requires that the sanctity of life be weighed against the competing values of compassion, liberty and human dignity. On balance, these considerations dictate that the only legally just solution is to afford our afflicted citizens the opportunity of choosing a quick and merciful death. Legalizing voluntary euthanasia is the appropriate way to make a friend of death, which need not be always an enemy. A voluntary euthanasia statute constitutes a significant step on the path toward human dignity and a more humane justice.

NOTES

(1) For scholarly comment see, A. B. Downing, Euthanasia and the Right to Death (1969) [hereinafter cited as Downing]. This fine book contains eleven essays dealing with euthanasia by commission and omission—all but one of them is favorable to reforming the law; N. St. John-Stevas, The Right to Life (1964); the excellent book by Glanville Williams, The Sanctity of Life and the Criminal Law (1957); Joseph Fletcher, Morals and Medicine (1954), and J. Sullivan, The Morality of Mercy Killing (1949). *Also see*, Sanders, *Euthanasia: None Dare Call It Murder*, 60 J. Crim. L.C. & P.S. 351 (1969); Williams, *Euthanasia and Abortion*, 38 U. Colo. L. Rev. 178 (1966); Levisohn, *Voluntary Mercy Deaths*, 8 J. For. Med. 57 (1961); Kamisar, *Some Non-religious Views Against Proposed "Mercy Killing" Legislation*, 42 Minn. L. Rev. 969 (1958) [hereinafter cited as Kamisar], the reply by Williams, *"Mercy-Killing" Legislation—A Rejoinder*, 43 Minn. L. Rev. 1 (1958) [hereinafter cited as Williams], and Silving, *Euthanasia: A Study In Comparative Criminal Law*, 103 U. Pa. L. Rev. 350 (1954).

(2) When is a person dead? Traditionally the moment of death has been determined by the moment when spontaneous heartbeat and breathing cease. These age-old criteria have become known as the signs of 'clinical' death. Throughout history there have been reports of rare individuals who returned to life after such clinical death. And in recent decades we have learned emergency measures to restore breathing and heartbeat that can bring back to life many people who in the past would have been dead permanently.

'Biological death' has been defined as the state of damage and disorganization from which, even with modern medical techniques, the whole person cannot be revived. Various organs die at different rates once heartbeat and breathing have ceased. The brain, highly vulnerable to lack of oxygen, becomes irreversibly damaged after only three to six minutes without freshly oxygenated blood, whereas other organs may survive many hours or even days depending on the conditions of the body, such as temperature and presence or absence of bacteria.

'Cellular death' is an irreversible degeneration or disorganization of the individual cell, and may precede or be delayed long after the death of the rest of the body. For example, throughout life dead skin cells over the entire body surface are constantly shed and replaced from below. On the other hand, cells from a dead person can be kept alive and growing indefinitely in a cell culture. And it is from a preserved sex cell or general body cell that, as we found earlier, a child or identical twin of a person dead for years or centuries might someday be produced. Dr. R. Gorney, *The New Biology And The Future of Man*, 15 U.C.L.A.L. Rev. 273, 311-12 (1968). Not being a unitary event, death is divided into organismal death, psychic death and vegetative death, each stage occurring at a different time, but all within 15 minutes of each other. *See*, Dr. J. W. Still, *The Three Levels of Human Life and Death, The Presumed Location of the Soul, and Some of the Implications for the Social Problems of Abortion, Birth Control, and Euthanasia*, 37 Med. Annals of D.C. 316 (1968).

(3) F. W. Reid, Jr., *Prolongation of Life or Prolonging the Act of Dying?* 202 J.A.M.A. 180 (1967), and see Dr. Joseph Fletcher, *The Patient's Right to Die,* in Downing, *supra* note 1, at 61, 63.

(4) Taken from G. A. Gresham, *"A Time To Be Born and a Time to Die,"* in Downing, *supra* note 1, at 148.

The London Times, under the caption "Doctor succumbs after eight years in coma," carried the following dispatch from its correspondent, dated Ankara, Sept. 22, 1969:

A young orthopaedic doctor was being buried in Ankara today after having lived for more than eight years in a coma, one of the longest on medical record.

On July 20, 1961, Mr. Alp Reel, then 25, was X-raying a patient at Ankara medical faculty when he received a powerful electric shock. For 3,044 days he lay in the medical faculty hospital in a specially made German bed with air mattresses.

His eyes were open, his heart beat and he breathed normally, but for all practical purposes he was dead from the moment he received the shock.

His doctor, Professor Orhan Titi, said that there had been no brain activity since the accident and that the only signs of life were an occasional reflex in his face, fingers and toes. Mr. Reel's mother and father, who had never given up hope that one day he would recover, professed to have seen an improvement over the years. Sometimes, they said, he smiled and murmured like a child.

Specialists from Britain, the United States, the Soviet Union, and Japan were consulted but none of them was able to suggest a possible cure. Mr. Reel died of inflamation of the lungs last Friday night.

(5) Although there has not yet been any definitive documentation of the view, it seems fairly apparent that Western society has gradually become increasingly humanitarian in its outlook. Suffering is no longer believed to have religious value. A decline in the belief of an afterlife has meant that the importance of *this* life is magnified. These factors have contributed to concern for the quality of both life and "dying."

There has also been a change in social attitudes toward human intervention at both the beginning and the end of life. Birth and death are now viewed as events which need not be blindly accepted by human beings. . . . Suicide and euthanasia are being tolerated to a greater extent, or at least viewed differently. Consequently, we are in the midst of developing new ethics.

D. Crane, *Social Aspects Of The Prolongation of Life* 7 (1969) (An Occasional Paper of the Russell Sage Foundation).

(6) Reported in the Chicago Tribune for Aug. 9, 1967, at 1, col. 8; Aug. 10, 1967, at 1, col. 2, and January 25, 1969, at 1, col. 8; and discussed by Sanders, *Euthanasia: None Dare Call It Murder,* 60 J. Crim. L.C. & P.S. 351 (1969), and Kutner, *Due Process of Euthanasia: The Living Will, a Proposal,* 44 Indiana L.J. 539 (1969).

(7) Public sympathy for the killer in a non-requested mercy killing has been rising. Mr. Sanders has collected the *involuntary* euthanasia cases that have led to prosecution, 60 J. Crim. L.C. & P.S. 355-56, n.36. They show a growing concern for the propriety of mercy killing, even though the victim may not have requested it:

a. Louis Greenfield chloroformed his imbecile teenage son to death. The boy reportedly had the mentality of a two-year-old. Greenfield said at the trial, "I did it because I loved him, it was the will of God." N.Y. Times, May 11, 1939, at 10, col. 2. He was acquitted of first degree manslaughter. N.Y. Times, May 12, 1939, at 1, col. 5.

b. Louis Repouille read about the Greenfield case. He said, "It made me think about doing the same thing to my boy." N.Y. Times, Oct. 14, 1939, at 21, col.

2. Repouille chloroformed his thirteen-year-old son, who had been blind for five years, bedridden since infancy and was also an imbecile, who never learned to talk. N.Y. Times, Oct. 13, 1939, at 25, col. 7. Repouille was indicted for first degree manslaughter but convicted of second degree manslaughter and freed on a suspended sentence of five to ten years. N.Y. Times, Dec. 25, 1941, at 44, col. 1.

c. John Noxon, a well-to-do lawyer, was charged with first degree murder for killing his six-month-old mongoloid son by wrapping him in a lamp cord and electrocuting him. Noxon claimed that the boy's death was an accident. N.Y. Times, Sept. 28, 1943, at 27, col. 2; N.Y. Times, Sept. 29, 1943, at 23, col. 7; N.Y. Times, Oct. 29, 1943. at 21, col. 7. Noxon was convicted of first degree murder. N.Y. Times, July 7, 1944, at 30, col. 2. His death sentence was commuted to life. N.Y. Times, Dec. 30, 1948, at 13, col. 5. Later his sentence was further reduced to six years to life to make parole possible. N.Y. Times, Dec. 30, 1948, at 5, col. 6. He was paroled shortly thereafter, N.Y. Times, Jan. 4, 1949, at 16, col. 3. The Massachusetts Supreme Court affirmed the trial court's decision and denied Noxon's request for a new trial, based on technical grounds, in Commonwealth v. Noxon, 319 Mass. 495, 66 N.E.2d 814 (1946).

d. Harry Johnson asphyxiated his cancer stricken wife. N.Y. Times, Oct. 2, 1938, at 1, col. 3. After a psychiatrist said he believed Johnson to have been "temporarily insane" the grand jury refused to indict him. N.Y. Times, Oct. 12, 1938, at 30, col. 4; N.Y. Times, Oct. 19, 1938, at 46, col. 1.

e. Eugene Braunsdorf took his 29-year-old daughter, a "spastic incapable of speech," out of a sanitorium, and shot and killed her because he feared for her future should he die. He then attempted suicide by shooting himself in the chest twice. He was found not guilty by reason of insanity. N.Y. Times, May 23, 1950, at 25, col. 4.

f. Dr. Herman Sander was acquitted of the murder of his cancer stricken patient. N.Y. Times, Mar. 10, 1950, at 1, col. 4. Dr. Sander, for some unknown reason, had written on his patient's chart that he had given her ten c.c. of air intravenously four times and she died within ten minutes. N.Y. Times, Feb. 24, 1950, at 1, col. 1. At the trial, however, his defense was that the patient was already dead at the time of the injections. N.Y. Times, Mar. 7, 1950, at 1, col. 1. The patient apparently did not request death. The case turned on the causation question and did not live up to its billing as a case to decide the legality of euthanasia.

g. Miss Carol Ann Paget, a college girl, was indicted for second degree murder (carrying a mandatory life sentence) for killing her father while he was still under anesthetic following an exploratory operation which showed him to have cancer of the stomach. The girl apparently had a cancer phobia and was acquitted on grounds of "temporary insanity." N.Y. Times, Feb. 8, 1950, at 1, col. 2.

h. Harold Mohr killed his blind, cancer stricken brother and on a conviction of voluntary manslaughter with recommendation for mercy he was sentenced to three to six years and a $500 fine. N.Y. Times, Apr. 11, 1950, at 20, col. 5. He pleaded insanity and there was testimony tending to show that his brother had repeatedly requested to die. Some of the testimony, however, tended to show that Mohr was drinking at the time and two other brothers testified against him. N.Y. Times, Apr. 4, 1950, at 60, col. 4; N.Y. Times, Apr. 8, 1950, at 26, col. 1.

i. People v. Werner. The transcript of this case is presented in Williams, *Euthanasia and Abortion*, 38 U. Colo. L. Rev. 178, 184-87 (1966). The defendant, 69, pleaded guilty to manslaughter for the suffocation of his hopelessly crippled, bedridden wife. The court found him guilty, but then after hearing testimony of the defendant's children and others showing what great devotion the defendant had shown towards his wife and that the murder had been at her request, the court allowed the guilty plea to be withdrawn and a plea of not guilty entered. Held: not guilty. For a criticism of this obviously unorthodox procedure see 34 N.D. Law 460 (1959). It is interesting to compare the events in the Werner case with article 37 of the Uruguayan Penal Code: "The judges are authorized to forego punishment of a person whose previous life has been honorable where he commits a homicide motivated by compassion, induced by repeated requests of the victim." Silving, *Euthanasia: A Study in Comparative Criminal Law*, 103 U. Pa. L. Rev. 350, 369 (1954).

    j. Mrs. Wilhelmia Langevin, 56, shot her 35-year-old son, an epileptic, with a deer rifle. The defendant was indicted for first degree murder. N.Y. Times, Nov. 2, 1965, at 26, col. 6.

    k. Robert Waskin. [The facts of this case are presented *supra*.]

    Following are the various punishments inflicted on the persons above: First Degree Murder: Noxon—4 years; Lesser Degree Homicide: Mohr and Repouille; Acquittal by Reason of Insanity: Paget, Braunsdorf, and Waskin; Acquittal: Sander, Greenfield, and Werner; Refusal to Indict: Johnson.

    (8) For discussion see, J. Mitford, The American Way of Death (1963).

    (9) *See* Slater, *Death: The Biological Aspect*, in Downing, *supra* note 1, at 49. Death performs a function for human society of incalculable value. If the aged and the sick did not die soon after they stopped being self-supporting, but lingered on, en masse, the total burden on society would be ruinous. Thus, "Death plays a wholly favourable, indeed an essential, part in human economy. Without natural death, human societies and the human race itself would certainly be unable to thrive." *Id*. at 59.

    (10) The Listener 749 (Dec. 7, 1967), and see, A. B. Downing, *Euthanasia, The Human Context*, in Downing, *supra* note 1, at 13.

    (11) The ugly truth is that sometimes patients *in extremis* try to outwit the doctors and escape from medicine's ministrations. They swallow Kleenex to suffocate themselves, or jerk tubes out of their noses or veins, in a cat-and-mouse game of life and death which is neither merciful nor meaningful. . . . Who is actually alive in these contrivances and contrapations? In such a puppetlike state most patients are, of course, too weakened and drugged to take any truly human initiative.

Dr. Joseph Fletcher, *The Patient's Right to Die*, in Downing, *supra* note 1, at 61, 65, and *see*, Exton-Smith, *Terminal Illness in the Aged*, 2 The Lancet 305 (1961).

    (12) *See*, Gillon, *Suicide and Voluntary Euthanasia: Historical Perspective*, in Downing, *supra* note 1, at 173.

    (13) *See*, Flew, *The Principle of Euthanasia*, in Downing, *supra* note 1, at 30.

    (14) *See*, Barrington, *Apologia for Suicide*, in Downing, *supra* note 1, at 152.

    (15) While suicide is not, assisting one to suicide is a crime in the great majority of American States, except Texas where, apparently, the act of providing the means of suicide is not a crime, but directly killing a sufferer is; *see*, Sanders v. State, 112 S.W. 68, 22 L.R.A. (n.s.) 243 (Tex. Crim. App. 1908), and G. Williams, The Sanctity of Life and the Criminal Law 301 (1957).

    (16) See text *infra* at note 53.

    (17) Specifically, I do not deal with the well known situation where a patient may be afflicted with a terminal illness, suffering from excruciating pain, and pleading for merciful release, every conceivable avenue of treatment having been explored with total failure. Rather than keeping the patient temporarily alive by means of inserting tubes into his stomach, veins, bladder or rectum, drugging him and then encompassing him in a cocoon of oxygen, the doctor omits to carry out these, or other actions, thereby allowing the patient to die earlier than he otherwise might.

(18) The President of the Swedish Society of Surgery, Dr. G. B. Giertz has asked: Is it in fact intended that we shall provide the medical services with resources for furnishing life-supporting measures for every individual who might qualify for it, even when the prospects of securing a recovery are negligible? The thought that we physicians should be obliged to keep a patient alive with a respirator when there is no possibility of recovery, solely to try to prolong his life by perhaps twenty-four hours, is a terrifying one. It must be regarded as a medical axiom that one should not be obliged in every situation to use all means to prolong life. . . . We refrain from treatment because it does not serve any purpose, because it is not in the patient's interest. I cannot regard this as killing by medical means: death has already won, despite the fight we have put up, and we must accept the fact. Quoted from Downing, *supra* note 1, at 15. And Dr. Gottharo Booth, a psychiatrist, suggests that if a patient is rational then his wishes should govern. *See, M.D.'s, Clergy Discuss Prolonging Life*, A.M.A. News 9 (May 9, 1966).

(19) For tentative exploration see, Fletcher, *Prolonging Life*, 42 Wash. L. Rev. 999 (1967), *reprinted in* Downing, *supra* note 1, at 71.

(20) The two categories of persons who qualify for voluntary euthanasia should be sharply distinguished from persons in other categories who may want, or be thought to need, euthanasia, but due to my imposed limitations, do not come within the two definitions. For example, infants and young children who may suffer from gross genetic physical or mental defects, and who may have only a short life expectancy, do not qualify as "adults" who can give legal consent, and consequently, do not fall within the two categories. Secondly, while adult, many old people suffering from senility, or who may be mentally ill or retarded, or who have congenital physical defects, do not have the necessarily serious, incurable and terminal physical illnesses and, consequently, do not fall within the two categories. At least these persons, and perhaps others, are excluded.

(21) *See* Wash. Rev. Code § 9.48.030 (1956). Other western countries handle mercy killings differently. Uruguay, apparently, allows good motive and a request for death, to operate as a complete defense, while in some European countries, *e.g.*, Germany, Switzerland, Norway, these factors officially function to reduce the penalty; see, Silving, *Euthanasia: A Study in Comparative Criminal Law*, 103 U. Pa. L. Rev. 350 (1954).

(22) *See, e.g.*, R. Perkins, Criminal Law 828 (2d ed. 1969); 2 W. Burdick, Law of Crime §§ 442, 447 (1946); O. Miller, Criminal Law 55, 172 (1934); Orth. *Legal Aspsects Relating to Euthanasia*, 2 Md. Med. J. 120 (1953) (Symposium); and Annot. 25 A.L.R. 1007 (1923), and see, Kalven, *A Special Corner of Civil Liberties: A Legal View I* 31 N.Y.U.L. Rev. 1223 (1956).

(23) Consider an actual case, in a top-flight hospital. After a history of rheumatic heart disease a man was admitted with both mitral and aortic stenosis—a blockage of the heart valves by something like a calcium deposit. The arts and mechanics of medicine at once went into play. First open-heart surgery opened the mitral valve; then—the patient's heart still sluggish—the operation was repeated. But the failure of blood-pressure brought on kidney failure. While the doctors weighed a choice between a kidney transplant and an artificial kidney machine, staphyloccal pneumonia set in. Next, antibiotics were tried and failed to bring relief, driving them to try a tracheotomy. Meanwhile the heart action flagged so much that breathing failed even through the surgical throat opening. The doctors then tried oxygen through nasal tubes, and failed; next, they hooked him into an artificial respirator. For a long time, technically speaking, the machine did his breathing. Then, in spite of all their brilliant efforts, he died. . . . In this case from the beginning

some of the doctors had little hope, but they felt obliged to do what they could. A few insisted that they had to do everything possible *even if they felt sure they would fail.* Where can we draw the line between prolonging a patient's life and prolonging his dying? Quoted from Downing, *supra* note 1, at 64-65.

(24) Furthermore, it seems that terminally ill, dying persons infrequently receive effective emotional support from medical personnel, probably because medical personnel prefer to treat them as though they were going to live; see, R. S. Duff & A. B. Hollingshead, Sickness and Society (1968). Moreover, of 290 physicians studied, 90 percent preferred not to tell terminal cancer patients that they had cancer, and held this preference largely on emotional grounds rather than on rational ones. Oken, *What To Tell Cancer Patients: A Study of Medical Attitudes* 175 J.A.M.A. 1120 (1961).

(25) Wechsler & Michael, *A Rationale of the Law of Homicide: I,* 37 Col. L. Rev. 701, 739-40 (1937).

(26) McGowan v. Maryland, 366 U.S. 420, 466-67 (1961) (separate opinion).

(27) G. Williams, The Sanctity of Life and the Criminal Law 311-18 (1957).

(28) *Id.* at 312. Most religious objections are based on the Fifth Commandment holding that life and body are given by God, and that therefore, only God, not man, can take them away. For sympathetic discussion see, N. St. John-Stevas, The Right to Life (1964), and J. Sullivan, The Morality of Mercy Killing (1949).

(29) Everson v. Bd. of Educ., 330 U.S. 1, 15-16 (1947). In recent years the Supreme Court has evolved a "purpose and primary effect" test of the establishment clause: "to withstand the strictures of the Establishment Clause there must be a secular legislative purpose and a primary effect that neither advances nor inhibits religion . . ." Bd. of Educ. v. Allen, 392 U.S. 236, 243 (1968) *quoting* Abington School Dist. v. Schempp, 374 U.S. 203, 222 (1963). Generally see, L. Pfeffer, Church, State and Freedom (rev. ed. 1967).

(30) It should be noted that religious opinion does not uniformly condemn euthanasia. For example:

> An interesting pronouncement, upon which there would probably be a wide measure of agreement, was made by Pope Pius XII before an international audience of physicians. The Pope said that reanimation techniques were moral, but made it clear that when life was ebbing hopelessly, physicians might abandon further efforts to stave off death, or relatives might ask them to desist "in order to permit the patient, already virtually dead, to pass on in peace." On the time of death, the Pope said that "Considerations of a general nature permit the belief that human life continues as long as the vital functions—as distinct from the simple life or organs—manifest themselves spontaneously or even with the help of artificial proceedings." By implication, this asserts that a person may be regarded as dead when all that is left is "the simple life or organs." The Pope cited the tenet of Roman Catholic doctrine that death occurs at the moment of "complete and definitive separation of body and soul." In practice, he added, the terms "body" and "separation" lack precision. He explained that establishing the exact instant of death in controversial cases was the task not of the Church but of the physician. New York Times Nov. 25, 1957, at 1, col. 3. Quoted from Williams, *supra* note 1, at 12 n.11; and see Kalish, *Some Variables in Death Attitudes,* 59 J. Social Psych. 137 (1963).

(31) Especially see, Glanville Williams, *"Mercy-Killing" Legislation—A Rejoinder,* 43 Minn. L. Rev. (1958).

(32) Consider, for example, the cruel implications of the following case

reported by Doctor Joséph Fletcher, in Downing, *supra* note 1, at 61-62: A minister pays a hospital visit to a woman in her early seventies, who has now been in the hospital for a week with what was tentatively thought to be "degenerative arthritis," but has turned out to be bone cancer. Both of her legs were already fractured when she arrived at the hospital, and little bits of her bones are now splintering all the time; occasionally, she has agonizing shaking attacks which aggravate the fracturing. She turns her face away from the minister and implores her husband: "I ought to die. Why can't I die?" Surely, it is cruel and inhumane to keep such a patient alive against her will.

(33) *See*, B. G. Glaser & A. L. Strauss, Awareness of Dying (1965). This is especially true of those who are "socially dead" which is defined as those who must live with a terminal illness because the patient perceives that "he is as good as dead" and that his social role in life has ended. *See*, Kalish, *Social Distance And The Dying*, 2 Community Mental Health J. 152 (1966) and Kalish, *Life And Death: Dividing The Invisible*, 2 Soc. Sci. & Med. 249 (1963). Most terminally ill persons have this perception and probably develop feelings of isolation, meaninglessness and acute forms of anomie; on the last see, E. Durkheim, Suicide (1951). It has been suggested that dying people may suffer as much, or more, from deprivation and abrupt emotional isolation from others than from his illness, Weisman & Hackett, *Predilection to Death: Death And Dying As A Psychiatric Problem*, 23 Psychosomatic Medicine 232 (1961). And *see*, Quint, *Mastectomy—Symbol of Cure Or Warning Sign?*, 29 Gen. Practice 119 (1964); Cappon, *The Dying*, 33 Psychiatric Q. 468 (1959), and Cappon, *Attitudes of and Toward The Dying*, 87 Canadian Med. Assoc. J. 693 (1962).

(34) Downing, *supra* note 1, at 18-19.

(35) Sir George Pickering, Regius Professor of Medicine at Oxford University holds that ". . . old people should be allowed to die as comfortably and in as dignified a way as possible," and he continues saying: "I know of nothing more tragic than the disruption of a happy and productive family life caused by an ancient, bed-ridden, incontinent and confused parent or grandparent. What might have been a happy and respectful memory becomes a nightmare and a horror. I still recoil from the sight of old people being kept alive by a constant monitoring of their heart-beat and the team of nurses and doctors ready to pounce upon them when it stops." *The Heart of the Matter: Ethical and Social Problems*, New Scientist, Jan. 18, 1968, at 125.

(36) Pathological reactions to bereavement occur fairly frequently, especially among close surviving relatives, and "the whole relationship between the dying and their partners or close relatives is falsified and distorted in a particular degrading and painful fashion." G. Gorer, Death, Grief and Mourning 17 (1965), and see, Lindemann, *Symptomatology and Management of Acute Grief*, 101 Am. J. Psychiatry 141 (1944). Some studies show that death has a higher incidence among those recently widowed, especially males, than among married persons of similar ages. *See* J. Hinton, Dying (1967) and Rees and Lutkins, *Mortality of Bereavement*, 4 British Med. J. 13 (1967). At 169 Hinton, *supra* reports irrational hostility and resentment toward doctors on the part of relatives after the death of a loved one. Furthermore, there seems to be a marked increase in physical ailments and psychiatric symptoms among persons recently widowed. *See*, Parks, *Effects of Bereavement on Physical and Mental Health—A Study of the Medical Records of Widows*, 2 British Med. J. 274 (1964).

(37) For discussion see, B. G. Glaser & A. L. Strauss, Time For Dying (1968).

(38) Professor Yale Kamisar in, *Some Non-Religious Views Against Proposed "Mercy-Killing" Legislation*, 42 Minn. L. Rev. 969 (1958), has made an excellent contribution to discussions about voluntary euthanasia. His arguments do not oppose voluntary euthanasia on its merits, but are concerned with its possible

procedural errors and abuses (which can be met by a properly drafted statute), and with the fear that legalizing voluntary euthanasia will lead on to legalizing involuntary euthanasia, and perhaps, genocide. *Cf.* Chesterton, *Euthanasia and Murder*, 8 Am. Rev. 486, 490 (1937).

(39) Stated in W.R. Matthews, *Voluntary Euthanasia: The Ethical Aspect*, in Downing, *supra* note 1, at 25, 28.

(40) Levisohn conducted a survey receiving 156 responses from Chicago surgeons and internists. He asked: " 'In your opinion do physicians actually practice euthanasia in instances of incurable adult sufferers?' Sixty-one percent agreed that physicians actually practiced it, if not in the affirmative at least in the negative or in terms of the omission to use every known medical measure to sustain life." Levisohn, *Voluntary Mercy Deaths*, 8 J. For. Med. 57, 68 (1961).

(41) Kamisar, *supra* note 1, at 978-93.

(42) *Id.* at 1005.

(43) Millard, *The Case for Euthanasia*, 136 Fortnightly Rev. 701 (1931).

(44) Medical opponents of voluntary euthanasia readily admit that the percentage or correct diagnosis is exceptionally high in cancer cases which would be the disease probably producing most euthanasia patients; see, Miller, *Why I Oppose Mercy Killings*, Woman's Home Companion, June 1950, at 38, and see, Laszlo, et al., *Errors in Diagnosis and Management of Cancer*, Part I, 33 Annals Int. Med. 670 (1950); Laszlo & Spencer, *Medical Problems in the Management of Cancer*, 37 Med. Clin. N.A. 869 (1953).

(45) Kamisar, *supra* note 1, at 998, and Williams, *supra* note 1, at 8.

(46) Kamisar, *supra* note 1, at 1008.

(47) Williams, *supra* note 1, at 8-9. He goes on to describe a "dear friend of mine, who died of cancer of the bowel, spent his last months in just this state, under the influence of morphine, which deadened pain, but vomiting incessantly, day in and day out."

(48) J. M. Hinton, Dying (1967); B. G. Glaser & A. L. Strauss, Awareness of Dying (1965), and J. M. Hinton, *The Physical and Mental Distress of Dying*, 32 Quarterly J. Med. 1 (1963).

(49) *See*, Euthanasia Society of England, A Plan for Voluntary Euthanasia 7-8 (2d rev. ed. 1962), and Downing, *supra* note 1, at 13-24.

(50) *See*, The Management of Pain in Cancer (Schiffrin ed. 1956), and Wolff, Hardy & Goodell, *Studies on Pain Measurement of the Effect of Morphine, Codeine, and other Opiates on the Pain Threshold and an Analysis of Their Relations to the Pain Experience*, 19 J. Clinical Investig. 659 (1940).

(51) Kamisar, *supra* note 1, at 1030.

(52) *See, e.g.*, Skinner v. Oklahoma, 316 U.S. 535 (1942), and Buck v. Bell, 274 U.S. 200 (1927).

SHALL WE "REPRODUCE"?

Paul Ramsey

I must judge that in vitro fertilization constitutes unethical medical experimentation on possible future human beings, and therefore it is subject to absolute moral prohibition. I ask that my exact language be noted: I said, unethical experimentation on *possible future human beings*. By this, I mean the child-to-be, the "successful" experiments when they come.

I mean to exclude three things that could be said additionally to make a showing of medical immorality and a notation of illicitness upon the trials that are currently being performed. Excluded are 1. the charge that before going to human experimentation physicians should not have omitted first proving their technique in species more closely related to man, on the primates, e.g. monkeys. This is a question of the background needed in the experimental design which an amateur cannot judge. Still I do know enough about discussions among ethical physicians concerning the need to complete the "animal work" before going to "human work" to know that this is a serious charge that requires some answer from the physicians attempting in vitro fertilization and implantation in human females—an answer which I have not seen. Excluded from my chief concern is also 2. the charge that the women "volunteers"—urged on as they are by a desperate desire to overcome their oviduct obstruction and to have a child of their own—have not given a fully understanding consent to what is being done upon them and by means of them. Clearly, the women already submitted to laparoscopy are experimental subjects, not patients who are likely to get children by this unproven technique. It is not enough to say to them, as Dr. Edwards is reported to have said, that "your only hope is to help us."(1) Now, I know that there is a spectrum and no clear lines to be drawn between pure experiment, therapeutic investigation, and proven therapy. Still, one way to make a signficant distinction along this spectrum is to suppose one of these women to ask, "Doctor, are you doing this for *me* or am I doing it for you and your research?" The answer to that question to date is that the women are undergoing surgery and other procedures for the sake of medical research; and it is a cardinal principle of medical ethics that they should have knowingly consented to that, and not primarily to a therapy they hoped would relieve their own childlessness.

Excluded also from my present concern is 3. the charge that it is immoral to discard or terminate the lives of the zygotes, the developing cluster of cells, the blastocysts, the embryos or the fetuses it will be necessary to kill in the course of developing this procedure. Persons who believe that an individual human life begins with conception, or after the time of segmentation, or at implantation, or with the morphologically human fetus, or with heartbeat or ECG readings, or self-movement (or any time before birth) must regard experiments in in vitro fertilization and artificial implantation as ab initio inherently immoral, because the physician must be willing to discard mishaps at any point in that span of time which do not come up to the standards of an acceptable human being. Make no mistake about it, this will extend, through screening by amniocentesis and fetoscopy, well into the period in which hysterotomy would have to be done if a defective result is detected, in order to abort the wrong life begun in the laboratory. I have a great deal of sympathy for the conclusion that this is, therefore, a wrong way to begin a human life. Still, when I say that in vitro fertilization followed by implantation is an immoral experiment on possible future human beings I do not assume any of these notions (for some of which there are better reasons than the socially prevailing notion) of when the possible future human being is an actual human being.

Instead, I assume the going perception of when there is a human life: when we see it before our eyes in the incubator, in a hospital nursery, in a bassinet or a playpen, playing hopscotch on the sidewalk, or going to kindergarten, and I assert that it clearly seems to me that in vitro fertilization followed by implantation is an immoral experiment on such a possible future human life.

Dr. Patrick Steptoe, Dr. Edwards' colleague, is reported(2) to have said that the decision to implant a given embryo, based on statistical evidence and hope—an embryo which cannot be karyotyped for genetic or other damage as a final procedure before implantation without too grave risk of further, more serious damage—will "call for a 'brave decision.'" Bravery, courage, used to be the word for a man's moral virtue in the fact of danger or adversity. If (as I believe) we should watch our language as we watch our morals, Dr. Steptoe seriously misused language. What he meant was "rashness" in action regardless of the consequences to another human life, and not "courage," facing one's own perils or adversities. That, in former, more moral ages of mankind, has viewed as a vice.

Dr. Daniele Petrucci of the University of Bologna is a rather discredited pioneer among these adventurers. He is discredited, however, for not having published a scientific article; his experiment was "insufficiently documented"; other scientists could not repeat his procedures or check his results, or even know his claims were not fraudulent. He was not discredited, however, for doing what he said he did to a human fetus; for what he might well have done to a possible future human life if his experiment had been continued or had that in view. In 1961, Petrucci reported that after more than forty failures he had successfully fertilized a human egg in vitro, cultured the embryo for twenty-nine days ("a heartbeat was discernible") and then destroyed it because "it became deformed and enlarged—a monstrosity." Nor, so far as I know, has Petrucci's end-in-view been generally excluded from among the possible purposes of manipulating embryos; indeed, one finds frequent mention of related designs in experimental biology: Petrucci told Italian newspapermen that he only meant to find a way to culture organs that would resist the rejection phenomenon when transplanted. With that, Petrucci yielded to his Church's condemnation of producing a human being without "the most supreme assistances of love, nature and conscience" (editorial, *L'Osservatore Romano*) and became a forgettable episode in the history of in vitro fertilization research—unless, while in Russia to receive a medal, he passed on his arts to experimental biologists there.(3)

My reason for bringing up the Petrucci episode is not, rhetorically and emotionally, to tar more responsible scientists with the damage he was willing to accept. It is rather to say simply that unless the *possibility* of such damage can be definitively excluded, in vitro fertilization is an immoral experiment on possible future human beings. And it is to say that this condition cannot be met, at least not by the first "successful" cases; and therefore that any man's or any woman's venture to begin human life in this way is morally forbidden. We cannot morally *get to know* how to perfect this technique to relieve human infertility (even if, once perfected, it would not be a disastrous further step toward the evil design of manufacturing of our posterity).

We all know from the popular and the scientific accounts that in order to accomplish in vitro fertilization, scientists must mimic nature perfectly.

> The mammalian egg has been carefully adapted over many centuries of evolution and natural selection to a very delicate balanced environment in the ovarian follicle, the fallopian tube, and the womb. Likewise, the mammalian and human sperm has been adapted through millennia by natural selection to survive in the environment of the vaginal canal and the uterus and achieve fertilization in the fallopian tubes.... The scientist must duplicate almost exactly this delicately balanced internal environment of the female reproductive tract, or fail in his attempt to achieve in vitro fertilization.

This artificial mimicry of nature has been accomplished in the matter of fertilization and the culture of human life until well beyond the time implantation would take place naturally. Along the way, the scientists have learned a great deal about duplicating the environment in which the sperm can be "capacitated"; they have learned that fertilization is not a "moment" but a process, that cells that seem to be fertilized may only be dying. (Claims to scientific fame depend on this latter point!)

The same can be said about those scientists who are at work assaulting and attempting to duplicate human gestation in the middle and later stages. They too must be able to mimic natural human gestation entirely; the slightest lapse or mistake would be disastrous to a possible future human being.

My point as an ethicist is that none of these researchers can *exclude* the possibility that they will do irreparable damage to the child-to-be. And my conclusion is that they cannot morally proceed to their first ostensibly successful achievement of the results they seek, since they cannot assuredly preclude all damage.

However much these experimental embryologists may have mimicked nature perfectly, they cannot guarantee that the last artificial procedure they carry out before implantation (or know they cannot carry through, such as karyotyping, which Dr. Steptoe cited when he erroneously spoke of "bravery") may be the important one. The last procedure may induce damage (or the last procedure known to be possibly damaging may not be able to be used although it might detect damage induced by previous procedures). Damage could be introduced during the transfer procedure, even after the last inspection is made. The last inspection may induce damage, or it may not be done because it could be fatal or damaging. For all we know, the manipulation may implant embryos that, if abnormal, will not be spontaneously aborted with the same frequency as under natural conditions. Finally, detectable natural abnormalities and detectable induced abnormalities may prove inseparable to such a degree that it will be difficult to establish exactly what are the additional risks due to this procedure. If true, that would be a limit upon experimental designs, even if one had gotten over the earlier objections that it is immoral to use the child-to-be to find out.

These are some of the reasons in vitro fertilization followed by implantation must necessarily require (by an amazing degradation of moral language) "courage" on the part of the physician-experimenter. He can never know what he is doing to a possible future human being. Even if he had not omitted experiments on monkeys first, no trial on monkeys would have told him whether he was or was not in the human case inducing mental retardation. It will not be enough to be able to discard grossly damaged embryos; there may well be damage that cannot be grossly scanned (as later on a club foot can be) and which are of crucial importance for the normal human capacity of the child-to-be. This is why experimentation on the primates could never settle the issue I am raising.

Anyone familiar with discussions of the ethics of medical experimentation knows that physicians acknowledge that the passage from "animal work" to work in the human always involves unknown risks that cannot have been tested before. Because of this fact, the move to human experimentation is made only when physicians secure the partnership of an informed, consenting volunteer for nonbeneficial investigation or when they already have a patient suffering from an illness, to cure which they need and he equally needs investigational therapy to be performed. They do not (or should not) first manipulate a patient's consent. Nor do they first manipulate a patient so that he is in some need of possibly harmful treatment. Neither of these two conditions for moving to "human work" can be met in the case of in vitro fertilization and embryo transfer. The child-to-be is not a volunteer; and before his beginning he is in no need of physicians to learn how not to harm him.

There are more cautious physicians and others who seem to believe that these obstacles and objections in the way of justifying in vitro fertilization will fall without the need for immoral experimentation on possible future human beings in the process. They have not, in my opinion, paid attention to the logic of the matter, to the unforecloseable risks involved in moving to the human work or to the necessity of bringing the first cases to term (and beyond) in order ever to learn whether the trial did harm or not. Thus, Dr. Kenneth Greet, a British Methodist, referring to criteria laid down some years ago by the British Council of Churches, stated:

> Provided the fertilization of the ovum is undertaken in order that it should be transplanted into the lining of the uterus, and provided also no harm is done at that stage which would result in malformation, then I think it is something to be welcomed.(5)

And Dr. Luigi Mastroianni, chairman of obstetrics and gynecology at the University of Pennsylvania, is reported(6) to have said,

> It is my feeling that we must be very sure we are able to produce normal young by this method in monkeys before we have the temerity to move ahead in the human. . . . In our laboratory, our position is, "Let's explore the thing thoroughly in monkeys and establish the risk to a patient and obtain truly informed consent before going ahead. We must be very careful to use patients well and not be presumptuous with human lives. We must not be just biologic technicians.(7)

Surely Dr. Mastroianni's very fine statement falls of its own weight. Because his is a splendidly articulated statement, it is clear that the conditions he lays down for not being "presumptuous with human lives" cannot be fulfilled (or that in the case of the woman's consent, they are not sufficient). One is apt to miss this when reading Dr. Greet's statement of the basic principle of medical ethics ("do no harm") which is not articulated for the case under consideration; he leaves wide open the possibility that the criteria can be met. While Dr. Mastroianni also seems to believe that this test can be met, his statement makes evident that it cannot. Work in monkeys would enable scientists to describe the risks accurately for monkeys, but not for possible deep injuries in the human case—for example, hemophilia or mental retardation or multifactoral personality and behavioral defects. These can be known only by work in humans, which, because the risks are not known, would be immoral to research by means of a possible case of embryo transplant brought to birth. Moreover, to be able to "describe the risk to a patient" (the woman, only) and to "obtain truly informed consent before going ahead" would relieve the physician of presumptuous manipulation of her consent. But that would in no way relieve the physician of complicity in such a woman's willingness to be "presumptuous" with a human life—her child-to-be—or from guilt for allowing her or enticing her to consent to any such thing, even if the risk could be exactly described from work in monkeys.

Is there any answer to this argument against in vitro fertilization—an argument which, I believe, must hold unless we are cloyed by the sentiment that a woman should be enabled to have a child by any means and if we are not simply fascinated by "advancements" in the scientific possibilities of unusual modes of human fecundity?

One answer is that after implantation, intrauterine monitoring by means of amniocentesis, or fetoscopy when it is developed, will enable physician-scientists to scan and screen their results, and by abortion discard their mishaps, i.e., any lives later discovered to have been damaged by the procedures of in vitro fertilization and implantation itself.

The proper reply to this retort is that invading the uterus to make these check-ups may itself induce additional damage to the fetus, not only to the woman. Physicians engaged in amniocentesis usually concentrate on the statistical incidence of this possibility, which is low. One or two percent, they say, which in their practice is to be compared with a like statistical risk that the fetus already conceived may be defective in one way or another. That, I would say, is a different moral problem than if human ingenuity first creates at risk the human life which must thereafter be monitored, at those additional risks, by amniocentesis with abortion as the refuge in case it is discovered that one had seriously imparied the life he meant to produce. To monitor by amniocentesis a fetus already conceived and determined to be at special risk of being genetically damaged *may* be justified by balancing that unborn child's already existent 1% or 2% risk of genetic disease against the 1% or 2% of risk that the procedure to find out may itself do damage. But even if that is an ethical practice in medicine, the cases we are discussing—in vitro fertilization and artificial implantation—do not already have a patient at risk. The possible future human being is at risk only of being created in this way, of having someone wrongly accept for him an incidence of additional risk of induced damage from the procedure chosen to be used in his creation.

Then there are those physicians who go behind the equilibration of incidence of risk, and speak frankly of the depth of what is at risk in every case in which amniocentesis is used. So we must add to the original "daring" venture to create a human life the additional risks, however small, of serious damage which monitoring what we had done itself imposes on a possible future human being. Henry Nadler, MD, of Children's Memorial Hospital, Chicago, refreshingly says that only defects established before amniocentesis is performed (12 weeks) can be excluded from its possible adverse effects.

There is no way with present studies . . . of establishing ten or fifteen years from now if these children lose 5 or 10 IQ points. We might be able to get an approximation during the first year of life if their rate of growth is significantly different. However, more subtle damage will be difficult to evaluate.

In short, if in vitro fertilization scientists appeal to intrauterine monitoring as an "out" after what they may have done by their last procedure (which by definition could not at that point be monitored), they may only be adding possible damage to possible damage that cannot be excluded and which may be brought upon a possible future human being whom they thus dare to initiate.

I see no line of moral reasoning that can justify this as an ethical practice of medicine. Nor do I see how any woman could *knowingly* consent to it. But, then, there may be depths I do not fathom in "Women's Lib"!

A negative moral verdict upon in vitro fertilization follows from right-ordered concern for the child that will be produced by the "successful" cases of these experiments. It is not a proper goal of medicine to enable women to have children and marriages to be fertile *by any means*—means which *may* bring hazard from the procedure, *any* additional hazard, upon the child not yet conceived. To suppose otherwise is to believe couples have such an absolute right to have children that this right cannot be overridden by the requirement that we should first have to exclude any incidence of *induced* risk to the child itself. This would be to adopt an extreme pronatalist assumption that an unconceived child somehow already has a title to be conceived. In such pronatalism, extremes meet: artificial modes of conception and gestation find themselves strange bedfellows with the insistence of a few uninstructed Roman Catholics that the life-giving potentiality of sperm and ovum are not artificially to be denied. (An illiterate spokesman for this point of view once told me that this was what Jesus meant when he said "Suffer the little ones to come unto me. . . !") Thus, the justification of in vitro fertilization and the prohibition of contraception both alike exalt—though in different ways—the absolute rights of "nature." The good of the possible future human being is not allowed, in the first case, to "interfere" with getting pregnant artificially, nor in the second case to interfere with natural fecundity.

The conclusion that a child should be conceived at risk of induced damage requires not only the assumption that while yet nothing, he somehow had title to be born(which, if true, might warrant our taking *his* risks in his behalf). In medical circles, this requires also the mind-boggling assumption that an unconceived child is somehow the equivalent of an existing child as already the subject of medical care and, therefore, a proper subject of investigational therapy without his consent. So only can we bring him under the ordinary categories and balancing judgments of medical treatment at risk. By first imagining the qualitative gulf separating being from nonbeing to have been traversed—and only so—can we imagine that proper treatment (of his being) means simply taking every precaution to avoid damaging him, making all possible tests, scanning and screening him to see whether anything has gone awry. By viewing the possible future child, while he is still a hypothetical nothing, as if he were already a patient needing all these precautions—and only so—can we bring ourselves to believe that minimizing the risks is enough. That *is* enough for an ordinary patient in the bush but not enough for a patient in the hand, i.e., literally, "manipulated," in vitro, before he ever was. But to manipulate a patient into being requires at least the far more stringent requirement that to do this we must know that every possibility of damage from the procedure itself has surely been foreclosed. That stipulation the manipulation of embryos is not likely to meet. Anyone familiar with discussions of the moral limits upon human experimentation would say, I think, that the stipulation cannot be met. Medicine must certainly violate it before learning how to meet it, even if the first implanted baby turns out to be a Mahalia Jackson and not a monstrosity or mentally retarded. An experiment must be moral in its inception, as Dr. Henry K. Beecher said so often—it does not become moral because it happens to produce good results.

Since medicine manipulates human beings—sometimes at great risk, always at some risk—in order to persuade ourselves that we are permitted to manipulate a baby into being, at some risk, the unmade baby must be vaguely thought of as somehow already in being. So Dr. Edwards, in a scientific (not a popular presentation of the state of the art), revealingly referred to one of his patients as "the mother."(9)

Whether physicians engaged in this practice in fact vaguely think in this way or not, they must act as if the baby already has being in order to grant themselves the permission to think it sufficient simply to do everything thereafter to minimize the risks. By the ordinary coanons of medical ethics, the unmade child has not "volunteered" to help the scientist—or even his "mother." If the possible future human being can be construed to have "volunteered," we would have first to construe him to be there, in being, or at least with a powerful title to be born, willing to suffer some induced risk in order to be manipulated to "come unto us." To construe his consent requires not only these manifest absurdities; to do so, to consent in his behalf, would also require that he be already exposed to some risk which these procedures are designed to relieve. For, again by the ordinary canons of medical ethics, we are not permitted to give proxy consent except medically in behalf of someone who may not be in a position to give expressed consent, or to impute to him a will to relieve someone else's condition—in his case "his" "mother's" infertility. We ought not to choose for another the hazards he must bear, while choosing at the same time to give him life in which to bear them and to suffer our chosen experimentations. The putative volition of such an unmade child must, anyway, be said to be negative, since researchers who work in human experimentation do not claim that they are allowed to ask volunteers to face possibly suicidal risks or to place themselves at risk of serious deformity.

It is worth calling attention to the fact that a negative moral verdict against in vitro fertilization need invoke no other standards of judgment than *the received principles of medical ethics.* I have appealed to no religious and to no other ethical criteria. Either the accepted principles of medical ethics must give way, or fabricated babies should not be ventured.

I now want to take up certain answers to my argument. From the nature of these rejoinders we can clearly see the extent to which human procreation has already been replaced by the idea of "manufacturing" our progeny. Unless and until *that* concept is reversed, mankind's movement toward Aldous Huxley's Hatcheries must surely prove irreversible.

It may be granted that the mimicry of natural fertilization, implantation, and the environment of the womb cannot be guaranteed to be perfect or without possibly harmful, induced impairments to the possible future child. It may be granted that the last possible testing procedure may itself have induced damage, or the last one—necessarily omitted (because it might damage)—could mean a *failure* to detect damage previously induced. It may be granted that subsequent screening procedures by amniocentesis or scanning by fetoscopy (when this is developed) themselves may not catch every possible earlier mishap; and that these procedures (which are only "distant" inspections in comparison with embryo manipulation) may themselves do some damage to the unborn child. In short, the facts on which my foregoing argument is based may be granted.

But then it will be said that there are advantages that can be gained for the possible future human being. While scanning for procedurally induced damage and doing everything possible to reduce any remaining incidence of mishap, we can detect naturally inborn metabolic "error" or chromosomal disorder and eliminate these before human life comes to term. Even if natural fertilization and the uterine environment have been selected over long evolutionary ages, still there are "mistakes" in nature, and the uterine environment turns out to be harsh to many. The incidence of these "natural" damages is not negligible, and the incidence of possible induced damage can be kept within acceptable bounds, it can be argued, so that the balance of added induced risks and subtracted natural risks can be (by screening, followed by abortion) to the comparative benefit of the possible future human being created by embryo implantation.

If this is said—and to be sure, it will always be said—the rebuttals are two. First, at its face value, that is no argument at all against the previously stated reasons for prohibiting in vitro fertilization and embryo transplantation. The alleged compensating advantage—the avoidance of a life of suffering from inborn errors, chromosomal disorders, or other "natural" damage—is no advantage to the individual we are talking about, because he would not have been subject to those very risks (plus the additional risks) had he not been *artifically* conceived. The rejoinder assumes his conception, and that was the issue under discussion. To obtain the avoidance of the evils which are here said to counterbalance a minimum incidence of induced risks, one has to presuppose the unconceived child has overriding title to be born, or his mother an absolute right to have a child, or that the somehow is already in the land of the living so that we should go to work on him preconceptually, applying the usual balancing medical judgments that are applicable to existing patients. Rather than rehearse that scenario, let me say simply that no one can cause an ethical conclusion justifying in vitro fertilization to bottom on its own premise, nor can he warrant doing that procedure by appeals which is mente assume it has already taken place.

My second point is the more important one. This rejoinder to my argument itself shows clearly that anyone who offers it or is persuaded by it has already in mente placed artificial fertilization and gestation on a parity with the natural processes of human procreation. He has already incipiently stated the conditions under which manufacturing *should* replace human reproduction entirely. The quality of the "product" is the overriding issue; one comparable damage is interchangeable with another whether done by men or accepted by them; one incidence of risk cancels another like incidence, whether the one or the other comes from nature or from the biological laboratory.

This is important to note here because a most important societal reason for opposing in vitro fertilization is what is called the "thin edge of the wedge" argument, the "camel's nose under the tent" argument. This is a good argument if one is concerned at all about wisdom in the practice of medicine, in public policy, or in received social outlooks. To be valid, however, the wedge argument need not, like my reasons drawn from medical ethics, attempt to show the inherent immorality of a given sort of action or practice. It need only show that if we do this particular action or permit or encourage a particular practice (perhaps because of undeniable immediate values, e.g., enabling a woman to have a child) we will influence others and cause ourselves to take following steps that in foreseeable succession add up to immense disvalue for the human community. So we shall have to assess in vitro fertilization as a long step toward Hatcheries, i.e., extracorporeal gestation, and the introduction of unlimited genetic changes into human germinal material while it is being cultured by the Conditioners and Predestinators of the future.

The truth is, however, that the reasons the wedge argument "works" are not solely extrinsic, not solely because concentration on present values causes us to forget deleterious effects on future values, not solely because we may incline ourselves and others to do things we cannot later avoid because we have lost the capacity to wish otherwise. Instead, the wedge argument "works," chiefly though not exclusively, because incipiently and intrinsically the reasoning behind the justification of a present practice already *in principle* embraces those other societal practices as well. This intrinsic connection does not compel us to take those other steps also, but the argument for so doing has already impressed itself on our minds and persuaded us in the case at hand. We will have to pull the laboring oar against our present reasons if we are not to proceed further along the line already taken.

This, I believe, is clearly the case in regard to in vitro fertilization and embryo implantation. Ostensibly, the end in view is therapeutic, the altogether praiseworthy objective of enabling a woman to have a child of her own. But when objection is raised that this should not be done *be these means*, which cannot be guaranteed not to be injurious to the child, the only possible answer is and logically must be that those who justify this procedure mean in all sorts of other ways to control and predetermine the "product." This means that in mente and in principle, human procreation has already been interchanged with manufacture, if, as, and when we can calculate that we can do so at lesser costs to the "product" than nature affords. Since under the surface this is the essence of the steps now taken, all the rest need be only technical accomplishments. When they follow it will not be because of extrinsic influences (which the wedge argument summarizes) but because our reasons here and now went wrong.

For example, apart from the needed balancing judgments about the qualifications of the product of in vitro fertilization and embryo implantation, what are we to say about the claim that this "therapy" is only devoted to curing a woman's fertility? Doctors Edwards and Sharpe(10) say that "while the physical health of the parents does not demand that their infertility be cured, still "infertility seems to be a clinical defect to be remedied if possible by medical attention." Is the "clinical defect" of infertility remedied by in vitro fertilization? I should say not! Instead, the child as a product of technology is to be brought forth, without remedying the woman's infertility. She remains as infertile as before. No wonder, then, that the chief concern about the child is whether as a product more damage from his natural genesis may be removed than may be caused by producing him in this way. If infertility is a "clinical defect" which should be remedied, that would seem to call for reconstructive surgery on the oviducts, from which 30% to 50% success has been reported. Therapy is applied directly to the defect needing remedy. The woman is made fertile, and she in her marriage transmits life to her child.

By contrast, in vitro fertilization is arguably *not* a *medical* procedure. It concentrates on the "product," not on a medical condition which itself can be cured, if at all, only in the actual patient there is. Instead, without curing that condition, in vitro fertilization concentrates on a product; it is therefore manufacture by biological technology, not medicine.(11) To construe this procudure as a practice of medicine, we have to construe medicine to be devoted to the satisfaction of desires.

Edwards and Sharpe say,(12) "the desire to have children must be among the most basic human instincts, and denying it can lead to considerable psychological and social difficulties." Alas, and of course! Still our question remains. If medicine enables a couple to have a child by menas other than endeavors to correct the woman's infertility itself, if medicine undertakes to produce the result without curing the defect, if medicine turns to doctoring *desires* instead of medical conditions, if medicine provides a woman with a child without actually curing her infertility, is there any reason for doctors to be reluctant to accede to parents' desire to have a girl rather than a boy, blond hair rather than brown, a genius rather than a clout, a Horowitz in the family rather than a tone-deaf child, or alternatively a child who because of his idiosyncracies would have a good career as a freak in the circus?

"The procedures leading to replacement and implantation *open the way* to further work on human embryos in the laboratory," [italics added] state Edwards and Sharpe.(13) In addition to the benign work of preventing the birth of children with genetic defects to which the way is open, these authors also mention cloning, and the creation of "chimeras" by adding to an embryo the precursor cells for organs from other blastocysts (perhaps from other species). For these authors, "the beginning of medical ethics . . . *primum non nocere*" permits alleviation of infertility. They note than this "*has been stretched* to cover destruction of foetuses with hereditary defects" [italics added]. Then they ask: could medical ethics be "stretched" to justify "the more remote techniques like modifying embryos?"—chimeras?(14) I suggest that the answer to that question is plainly, Yes. Not because the principles of medical ethics can be stretched so far, but because they have been *replaced* by the principles, if any, governing biological manufacture. This radical displacement happens long before we begin adding to possible future human beings organs not their own. It happens rather when we employ medical technology to "alleviate infertility" by producing the result without treating any medical condition and without alleviating any medical defect.

The point I want to make is simply that there is a correlation (which benevolent motives do not excuse) between the devotion of medical science to manufacturing the child as a "product" or to altering the child into varying products and the devotion of medical science to the treatment of human *desires* (be these desires sound, whimsical, or demonic). The important line lies between doctoring desires (which are bound to be ingenious) and seeking to correct a medical condition if it is possible to do so. Across this line, medical science has made a step—and might as well and will go further—in attempting to produce a baby without first actually curing a woman's infertility. After all, who is to say that having another wrong-gendered child is not as unacceptable a result to some parents as not having a child at all? If medical practice has an obligation to guarantee one of these wishes, it may have an obligation to guarantee the other, and many more besides. In my opinion, medical practice loses its way into an entirely different human activity—manufacture (which most wants to satisfy desires)—if it undertakes either to produce a child without curing infertility as a condition or to produce simply the desired sort of child.

Elsewhere I have pointed out(15) that a significant move toward in vitro fertilization and all the rest was made when first we began to use a manufacturing term—"reproduction"—for procreation, human parenthood, and transmission of life through life by the generating generations of mankind. Scientists working in the field of "reproductive biology" have now drawn not improper conclusions from the linguistic mistake. It is indeed possible for experimental embryologists to "conceive" of alternative modes of "reproduction"—if that, strictly, is what we mean by conception and parenthood.

What is at stake in avoiding every action or thought suggestive of manufacturing whenever we speak of parenthood has been well expressed by Dr. Leon Kass, Executive Secretary of the Committee on the Life Sciences and Social Policy, National Academy of Sciences. I cannot improve upon his reflections on this subject:

Human procreation is human partly because it is not simply an activity of our rational wills. Men and women are embodied as well as desiring and calculating creatures. It is for the gods to create in thought and by fiat (Let the earth bring forth . . .).And some future race of demigods (or demi-men) may obtain its survivors from the local fertilization and decanting station. But *human* procreation is begetting. It is a more complete human activity precisely because it engages us bodily and spiritually, as well as rationally. Is there possibly some wisdom in that mystery of nature which joins the pleasure of sex, the communication of love and the desire for children in the very activity by which we continue the chain of human existence? Is biological parenthood a built-in device selected to promote the adequate caring for children? Before embarking on New Beginnings in Life we should consider the meaning of the union between sex, love and procreation, and the meaning and consequence of its cleavage.

What is new is nothing more radical than the divorce of the generation of new life from human sexuality and ultimately from the confines of the human body, a separation which began with artificial insemination and which will finish with ectogenesis, the full laboratory growth of a baby from sperm to term. What is new is that sexual intercourse will no longer be needed for generating new life. This piece of novelty leads to two others: there is a new co-progenitor (or several such), the embryologist-geneticist-physician, and there is a new home for generation, the laboratory. The mysterious and intimate processes of generation are to be moved from the darkness of the womb to bright (fluorescent) light of the laboratory, and beyond the shadow of a single doubt.

The Hebrews, impressed with the phenomenon of transmitting life from father to son, used a word we translate "begetting" or "siring." The Greeks, impressed with the springing forth of new life in the cyclical processes of generation and decay, called it genesis, from a root meaning "to come into being." (It was the Greek translators who gave this name to the first book of the Hebrew Bible.) The pre-modern Christian English-speaking world, impressed with the world as given by a Creator, used the term Pro-creation. We, impressed with the machine and the gross national product, our own work of creation, employ a metaphor of the factory, re-production. And Aldous Huxley has provided "decantation" for that technology-worshipping Brave New World of Tomorrow.(16)

In conclusion, I now turn to the "wedge argument" and the final triumph of manufacturing over human parenthood. "Decantation" has been in our future for some time now—at least from the time we began seriously to think of children as the means by which we "reproduce."

In a 1951 pronouncement against artificial insemination as a mode of transmitting human life, Pope Pius XII said that "to reduce the cohabitation of married persons and the conjugal act to a mere organic function for the transmission of the germ of life would be to convert the domestic hearth, sanctuary of the family, into nothing more than a biological laboratory."(17) Now, since I am not a Roman Catholic, I do not believe that in that statement the Holy Father told me anything I might not have known anyway. That's different from saying that had the Pope in fact not said it, I would have had occasion actually to discern the signs of the times with wisdom enough to see the significance of the first major step taken in the 20th century which eventually will replace human procreation with laboratory manufacture. The fact is that in 1951 the Pope communicated nothing to me by that statement; I've looked it up since.

Still his warning is worthy of reexamination today as we face yet more steps—all leading with accelerated rapidity toward the same end.

The memory of the Holy See—as Lord Macauley pointed out in the last century—is very long, much longer than any other political or social body in the modern world. It is not easy to judge whether from the eminence of the Vatican and its long institutional memory there accrues to the Pontiff a prescience to see the deeper deleterious trends in present events which lesser mortals always appraise and approve in terms of their seeming immediate benefits. Still, it is worth pondering whether this may be the case or not, since teams of scientists are now hard at work assaulting the entire process of human gestation—the beginning, the middle and the end—and, now that technical possibilities and "liberal" abortion attitudes have given them free access to the uterus, they are threatening to move life's beginnings from sperm to term entirely into the laboratory. (And we can ask of that, what would the terminus be?) These developments seem likely in historical perspective to render Pius XII's 1951 statement one of the earliest and wisest warnings to humankind to be spoken by someone having some degree of moral and spiritual authority; and a call to heed the warnings of other prophetic insights and voices that are ever more muted or forgotten as our modern world, defendable step by defendable step, moves ineluctably toward the state of affairs these wise men discerned with almost unbearable dread and foreboding.

Two of these are worth mention. In 1932 Aldous Huxley published *Brave New World*, with its principal mechanisms, the pharmacological management of contentment and the Fertilizing and Decanting Rooms in the East London Hatchery. In 1947, C. S. Lewis published a book bearing the title *The Abolition of Man*. Lewis submitted man's project of gaining ever increasing power over nature to merciless analysis; his message rings as clear and true as a bell on a Sabbath morning in early New England (if anyone wants to revisit either). Since Lewis' book is less well known than Huxley's, its burden can briefly be set forth by means of the following quotations:(18)

> What we call Man's power over Nature turns out to be a power exercised by some men over other men with Nature as its instrument. . . . And all long-term exercises of power, especially in breeding, must mean the power of earlier generations over later ones. . . . If any age really attains, by eugenics and scientific education, the power to make its descendents what it pleases, all men who live after it are the patients of that power. . . . And if, as is almost certain, the age which has thus attained maximum power over posterity were also the age most emancipated from tradition, it would be engaged in reducing the power of its predecessors almost as drastically as that of its successors. . . . The last men, far from being the heirs of power will be

of all men most subject to the dead hand of the great planners and conditioners and will themselves exercise least power upon the future. . . . There neither is nor can be any simple increase of power on Man's side. Each new power won *by* man is a power *over* man as well. Each advance leaves him weaker as well as stronger. In every victory, besides being the general who triumphs, he is also the prisoner who follows the triumphal car. . . .The man-moulders of the new age . . . we shall get at last a race of conditioners who really can cut all posterity in what shape they please. . . . Nature will be troubled no more by the restive species that rose in revolt against her so many millions of years ago, will be vexed no longer by its chatter of truth and mercy and beauty and happiness. *Ferum victorem capit:* and if the eugenics are efficient enough there will be no second revolt, but all snug beneath the Conditioners, and the Conditioners beneath her, till the moon falls or the sun grows cold. . . . [We should] not do to minerals and vegetables what modern science threatens to do to man himself.

Aldous Huxley and C. S. Lewis lived and wrote during the Hitler era, soon after World War II and at the beginning of the nuclear age. It is a striking and significant fact that they did not see the abuse of political power or nuclear destruction to be the greatest threats to the humanity of man. Lesser critics did. Instead, Lewis' analysis and Huxley's bitter social satire singled out genetics, pharmacology, and experimental embryology as sources of the coming great evils. Pope Pius XII belongs at least among the minor prophets for condemning, in 1951, artificial insemination, if this was his meaning(19), as a "defendable" step (defendable only in terms of one set of immediate values, but not in a larger view) along the way toward the transformation of human procreation into manufacture in biological laboratories (and therefore undefendable).

Because of the mounting possibilities of present and future biomedical interventions and embryo manipulations, one sees frequent references to Aldous Huxley, not only by science writers in popular periodicals but also in the medical and scientific literature. Almost always it is pointed out(20) how inaccurate Huxley was in the span of time he allowed for these powers to be in the grasp of man and practically applied. *Brave New World* begins on a day in 632 AF (After Ford!). That is, about six hundred years in the future. "Let us suppose the hundredth century AD," wrote C. S. Lewis(21) when he, too, imagined the achievement of mastery over the species. Most present-day references to Aldous Huxley in the scientific literature and in the popular press forget the social criticism, the biting satire, the authors seem happy if not triumphant in fastening upon the small point that Huxley was wrong in his calendar date. It is as if the author of *A Modest Proposal* (for increasing the food supply of Ireland by having the population eat their own children) were to be mildly chided for thinking it would take some time for his proposal to be adopted!

Forgotten also is the fact that *Brave New World* depicts a frictionless society made up of entirely happy people; indeed, in essential respects a *just* society measured by the standard of proportionate justice ("to equals, the equal; to unequals, the unequal"). Evidently Huxley saw quite clearly that there can be a grossly inhumane condition of mankind characterized by the greatest happiness altogether. This needs to be noted as we consider further steps along the way Huxley foresaw, viz., the embryo transplants to be done in the next few years. It is to be expected that this sort of manipulation of embryos can be justified in terms of our present perceptions of immediate happiness. Men will not suddenly enter *Brave New World* and be happy over such institutions as the Central Hatchery and Conditioning Center without a good deal of conditioning along the way. This will be called a "demand that social attitudes are *helped to keep pace with*" the increasing tempo of scientific advancement; the right of scientists to "exercise their professional activities *to the limit that is tolerable by society,*" accepting some perhaps conservative collaboration "as *lay attitudes struggle to catch up with what the scientists can do*" [italics added] (22). Even now we can begin to learn to be happy with decantation instead of natural gestation, by stifling any moral doubts about in vitro fertilization and implantation of embryos. We should not be surprised if the value most concentrated on by most people is how happy the technique might make some people. At least, if Huxley was right in describing *Brave New World* as a happy place, we ought not to be surprised to find the way there to be a direction we are increasingly happy to take, our consciences formed exclusively by our biotechnical, pharmacological civilization as the impersonal Predestinator of our values.

The road to hell, they say, is paved with good intentions—to treat people's desires and their happiness. Thus, in reporting the plan to open commercial frozen sperm banks in New York City, *The New York Times*(23) said, in the second paragraph of the report, "That day is here now, not just as a laboratory curiosity but as a commercially available sperm banking service *that brings much closer the prospect of controlled breeding programs to produce superior members of the human species*" [italics added]. That prospect was prominently featured, not the short-range "defendable" "therapeutic" value, namely, that 85% of the clients of two sperm banks in other cities are men who have voluntarily undergone vasectomy. The name of one of the commercial firms also invoked over future possible uses, not the backstop provided by the sperm banks to men's willingness to use vasectomy for contraceptive purposes. This, too, is a part of the preconditioning by which we in the present age are persuading ourselves to be happy with Hatcheries; only the name for the institution in our future may be "Genetic Laboratories, Inc." It is clear that Huxley discerned something that (without a sea-change of values) is self-fulfilling in our culture; that indeed is the meaning of prophecy and prescience. It entails that generally we now are inclined to be persuaded of the immediate values of each step along the way to the final replacement of human procreation by laboratory manufacture. Otherwise *Brave New World* would not be the happy place it will be. Conversely, if we could not be conditioned to contentment, there would be alarms now; and a wrenching away from the strange notion that every opposing moral attitude is always retrograde and should be repressed as we "struggle to catch up with what the scientists can do."

Mr. C. S. Lewis, as we noticed, said that we should "not do to minerals and vegetables what modern science threatens to do to man himself."(24) That statement, connecting as it does with contemporary ecological awareness, may be viewed by people today as a further evidence of Lewis' remarkable prescience. The point, however, is that Lewis discerned that the last citadel from which technological applications are apt to be excluded or where we will discover limits we will agree to defend as we would defend our lives is the citadel of man's nature itself. The wounds we have inflicted upon natural objects for lack of a proper sense of the natural environment are becoming clear to us—the lashes and the ecological backlash. Today many are testifying to the spiritual autonomy of all natural objects and to arrogance over none; to the scheme of things in which man has his place. But there is as yet no discernible evidence that we are recovering a sense for man as a natural object, too, toward whom a like form of "natural piety" is appropriate.

While the leopard, the great whale, and the forests are to be protected by restoring in mankind a proper sense of things, man as a natural being is to be given no such protection. There are aspects of the cheetah's existence that ought not to be violated, but none of man's. Other species are to be protected in their natural habitat and in their natural functions, but man is not.

Today the statement of Aristotle is amply verified: it would indeed be odd if a flute-player or artisan of any kind, a carpenter or a cobbler—or the mountain goat and the falcon—"have certain works and courses of action," while "Man as Man has none, but is left by Nature without a work" of his own.(25) It may be that Aristotle's question, What is the work of man? is expressed in language that will seem too functional for the ecological ethics we need in locating man in the creation of which we are a part and toward which we should have a "natural piety." Still, his view that all things in nature "have certain works and courses of action" has enough amplitude to be helpful as we search for a sense of man as a natural object too. Procreation, parenthood, is certainly one of those "courses of action" natural to man, which cannot without violation be disassembled and put together again—any more than we have the wisdom or the right impiously to destroy the environment of which we are a part rather than working according to its lineaments, according to the functions we discover to be the case in the whole assemblage of natural objects.

If St. Francis preached to his sisters the birds, spoke of his brother fire, called the turtle doves his little sisters, and composed a canticle to his brother the sun (and for this has been proposed as the patron saint of all ecologists), what are we to say of our brother man and of ourselves? If the commandment "to subdue the earth" is a right devilish one or else sorely in need of a loose, or of another, interpretation—an interpretation properly limited by man's vocation to tend the garden of God's creation—are we then to say that man is let loose here with the proper task of disassembling his own "courses of action," making himself and his own species wholly plastic to ingenious scientific interventions and alterations?

So today we have the oddity that men are preparing to play God over the human species while many among us are denying themselves that role over other species in nature. There is a renewed sense of the sacredness of groves, of the fact that air and streams should not be violated. At the same time, there is no abatement of acceptance of the view that human parenthood can be taken apart and reassembled in Oxford, England, New York, and Washington, D.C.; and, of course, it follows that thereafter human nature has to be wrought by Predestinators in the Decanting and Conditioning Rooms of the East London Hatchery and in commercial firms bearing the name "Genetic Laboratories, Inc." in all our metropolitan centers.

I have no explanation of why there is not among medical scientists an upsurge of protest against turning the profession of medical care into a technological function; why there is not, precisely today, a strong renewal of the view that the proper objective of medicine is to serve and care for man as a natural object, to help in all our natural "courses of action," to tend the garden of our creation. (Of the two oldest helping professions, the priesthood has long since abandoned magic to bring about extraordinary interruptions of natural processes; today, the mantle of such priestly incantations seems to have fallen on a core of medical researchers.)

Still there seems to be an evident, simple explanation of why people generally in all the advanced industrial countries of the world are apt to raise no serious objection, or apt at least to yield, to what the manipulation of embryos will surely do to ourselves and our progeny. It is a final irony to realize why invasions will now be done on man that we are slowly learning not to do on other natural objects; why natural human "courses of action" will be disassembled in an age in which we have learned to deplore strip mining, why in actual practice minerals and vegetables may be more respected than human parenthood, and mankind be ushered happily into *Brave New World*.

The reason will be not only that the agents of these vast changes are authority figures in white coats promising the benefits of applied knowledge. That, in other areas, we have learned to doubt in some degree. The deeper reason is that the agents of these vast changes, defendable step by defendable step, are deemed by the public to be not researchers mainly but members of the healing profession, those who care for us, who tend the human condition.(26) Before it is realized that the objective has ceased to be the treatment of a *medical* condition, it will be too late; and Huxley will have been proved true. The people of a biomedical technical civilization, like the blind, aged Isaac, are apt to give their blessing to Jacob because of his venison and because his arms are smooth and hairy (with the skin of animals), while the voice and the future will not be those of Esau or anyone's first born (Genesis 27:19-29).

Dr. Joshua Lederberg, speaking of how public policy may be determined in regard to clonal reproduction, ventured the opinion that this would depend on "the accident of the first advertised examples . . . the batting average, or public esteem of the clonant; the handsomeness of the para-human product. . . ."(27) If Aldous Huxley had any insight into our times, perhaps one can express the paradoxical and macabre "hope" that the first example of the production of a child by in vitro fertilization and embryo transplant will prove to be a bad result—and that it will be well advertised, not hidden from view! I do not actually believe that the good to come from public revulsion in such an event would justify the impairment of that child. But then, for the same reasons, neither is the manipulation of embryos a procedure that can possibly be morally justified.

REFERENCES AND ANNOTATIONS

(1) Grossman, E.: The obsolescent mother: A scenario. *Atlantic* 227:39-50 (May) 1971. *Medical World News* (April 4, 1969, p. 27) quotes Dr. Edwards' statement in full: "We tell the women with blocked oviducts, 'Your only hope of having a child is to help us. Then maybe we can help you.' " The question is whether the single word "maybe" communicates the fact that the physicians likely did not *mean* actually to attempt to overcome childlessness in most, if any, of the cases so far. The statement that artificial fertilization is the woman's "only hope" was simply false—unless there were *medical* reasons why none of these women were patients on whom oviduct reconstruction (see below) or super-ovulation might have been tried. (In one series of 46 women, three promptly became pregnant as a result of the superovulatory drug administered as a part of the procedure to collect oocytes.) And, of course, if "hope" is a proper subject for medical treatment, adoption was also an alternative.

The question of defective consent arises in another form in the case of experiments in the 1950's performed by Dr. Landrum Shettles of Columbia University's College of Physicians and Surgeons. He was *not* trying to overcome the barrier of oviduct trouble to enable his "patients" to have a baby. Instead, as one recent account puts it: "In the course of performing various operations requiring abdominal incision into the peritoneal cavity of the female, Dr. Shettles pierced the ovaries of his patients with a syringe and aspirated . . . some of the eggs from their follicles . . . without harming the patient in any way. . . ." (Rorvik, D. M.: The test-tube baby is coming. *Look* May 18, 1971, p. 83). The question is not whether Dr. Shettles *harmed* these patients in any way, but whether they *consented* in any way to have a procedure done to them that was wholly unrelated to the condition that called for the abdominal incision to be made.

(2) Grossman, E., op cit.; also Rorvik, D. M., op cit., p. 85. Rorvik also describes Dr. Shettles as one among many "daring" experimenters who have "propelled mankind forward," and as *pressing on* in the face of criticism. This may be courage in the face of a scientist's "adversities." The question is whether this personal and professional "daring" has excluded or can exclude any possible damage to that possible future human being, before the scientist "dares" go ahead. If not, use of words like "bravery" or "courage" represents a serious degradation of our moral language.

In a scientific article published as late in the course of these advances in experimental embryology as 1970, Dr. Edwards and colleagues stated flatly that "the normality of embryonic development and the efficiency of embryo transfer *cannot* yet be assessed" [italics added]. (Edwards, R. G., Steptoe, P. C., Purdy, J. M.: Fertilization and cleavage in vitro of preovulator human oocytes. *Nature* 227:1307-1309, 1970.) That cautionary statement from the scientists is related not only to the quality of courage discussed above; on this, the question will be whether these limits can ever be overcome without actions that are irremediably rash in dealing with viable progeny. The 1970 statement is also decisive in answering the question whether all the women who to date have been experimental subjects were deceived. They were, if no more was told them than "maybe we can help you."

(3) Before desisting, Petrucci said he had maintained another fetus, a female, alive for a full 49 days before it died owing to a "technical mistake." In 1966 the Russian scientists announced they had kept 250 fetuses alive beyond the record Petrucci claimed; one lived, they said, for six months and weighed 510 gm (1 lb. 2 oz.) before dying. (Francoeur, R.T.: *Utopian Motherhood.* Garden City, N.Y., Doubleday & Co., Inc. 1970, p. 58.)

(4) Francoeur, R. T., ibid., pp. 59-69.

(5) Greet, K., quoted in Francoeur, R. T., ibid., p. 74.

(6) Cohn V: Lab growth of human embryo raises doubt of "normality." *Washington Post* March 21, 1971.

(7) Six years ago Dr. Edwards was also more cautious; indeed, he seemed to believe culturing eggs for the treatment of human infertility faced insurmountable practical and moral objections. "If rabbit and pigs eggs grown in culture can be fertilized after maturation in culture, presumably human eggs grown in culture could also be fertilized, *although obviously it would not be permissible to implant them in a human recipient.* We have therefore attempted to fertilize human eggs in vitro [italics added]." That is, in order to study the process of human fertilization and early growth, precisely *not* in order to produce a child-to-be. (Edwards, R. G.: Mammalian eggs in the laboratory. *Sci. Amer.* 215:73-81 [Aug.] 1966.)

(8) Harris, M. (ed.): *Early Diagnosis of Human Genetic Defects: Scientific and Ethical Considerations*, Symposium jointly sponsored by the John E. Fogarty International Center for Advanced Study in the Health Sciences, National Institutes of Health, Bethesda, Md., May 18-19, 1970, U.S. Government Printing Office, 1972, p. 182.

(9) Edwards, R. G., Steptoe, P. C., Purdy, J. M., op cit., pp. 1307-1309. If these women were patients for infertility, Leon Kass remarks (Hamilton, M. [ed.]: *Three Medical Futures.* Grand Rapids, Mich., Wm. B. Eerdmans Publishing Co., 1972), then "mothers" is surely the one thing they are not.

(10) Edwards, R. G., Sharpe, D. J.: Social values and research in human embryology. *Nature* 231:87-91, 1971.

(11) Anyone advancing this argument will promptly be subjected to a barrage of information he is supposed not to know about medicine's technological armamentarium. That is a very damaging defense: it reduces the baby to the status of a prothesis for the permanent cure of his mother's condition.

(12) Edwards, R. G., Sharpe, D. J., op cit., p. 87.

(13) Ibid., p. 87.

(14) Ibid., p. 89.

(15) Ramsey, P., *Fabricated Man: The Ethics of Genetic Control.* New Haven, Conn., Yale University Press, 1970, p. 137.

(16) Kass, L. R.: New beginnings in life, in Hamilton, M. (ed.): *Three Medical Futures.* Grand Rapids, Mich., Wm. B. Eerdmans Co., 1972; also: Making babies: The new biology and the "old" morality. *Public Interest*, No. 26, 1972, pp. 19-56.

(17) *Acta Apostolicae Sedis*, 43:850, 1951.

(18) Lewis, C. S.: *The Abolition of Man.* New York, Macmillan Co., 1947.

(19) See Richard A. McCormick, S.J.: Notes on moral theology: April-September 1970. *Theological Studies* 32:95-97, 1971.

(20) For example, Francoeur says that Huxley "tried to picture the world of *six hundred hence,* a world which is *already with us*" [italics added]. (Francoeur, R. T.: *Utopian Motherhood: New Trends in Human Reproduction.* Garden City, N.Y., Doubleday & Co., Inc., 1970, p. 56.

(21) Lewis, C. S., op cit., p. 37.

(22) Edwards, R. G., Sharpe, D. J., op cit., pp. 87, 90. Even so, Dr. Bentley

Glass, former president of the American Association for the Advancement of Science, regards the public utterances of Edwards and his colleagues as too cautious and conservative. "It should be obvious," Glass writes, "that the technique can be quickly and widely extended." (Glass, P.: Endless horizons or golden age? *Science* 171:23-29, 1971.)

(23) Rensberger, B.: From the day of deposit: A lien on the future., *New York Times,* Aug. 22, 1971.

(24) Lewis, C. S., op cit., p. 49.

(25) Aristotle: *Nichomachean Ethics*, 1097b.

(26) In addition to this account, there are additional specific reasons why spokesmen of Church and Synagogue, against all their former principles, are today especially vulnerable to futuristic blandishments.

(27) Lederberg, J.: Experimental genetics and human evolution. *The American Naturalists* 100:519-531, 1966; reprinted, *Bull Atomic Scientists* 22:4-11, 1966.

IX
NEW
SCIENCE,
NEW
THERAPIES,
AND
ETHICS

IX. NEW SCIENCE, NEW THERAPIES AND ETHICS

INTRODUCTION

With the development of new medical science and new therapies, there must inevitably follow a quest for new ethics to govern these innovations.

Developments in human reproduction again provide a focal point around which new ethics and public policy must evolve. New science has provided greater insights into genetics and the genetic basis of human disorders. Many genetic diseases can now be predicted by studying specimens of prospective mates. Amniocentesis allows for a diagnosis and prediction of many congenital and genetic disabilities during pregnancy.

The information gained from these new techniques has resulted in a new concern that genetic manipulation and controls might be sought under the guise of medical progress. Inherent in the reluctance to use new technologies is not only a concern with the invasion of individual autonomy and freedom of choice, but also a fear that the modification of the existing natural balance might unleash unforseen catastrophic forces.

Artificial insemination through the resources of sperm banks is now an established medical technique. The development of donor wombs—natural or artificial—is no longer inconceivable. All these radical innovations call for a new definition of marital rights and responsibilities, for a possibly new concept of the family, and a redefinition of medical duties.

Some of the problems posed by the development of life saving techniques and devices have been discussed earlier. Many of these and related scientific developments could result in a newly found concentration in potential control over the destinies not only of individual men but of society generally. Science has permitted man to control the initiation and quality of life, as well as the processes of death. We have alluded also to the control of human behavior, by chemicals, drugs and surgery. For what causes are these controls to be instituted and under whose direction?

There are already developing, in response to the new sciences, redefinitions and newer concepts of human rights, dignity and status. New sciences and new therapies develop even newer sciences, therapies, and, we hope, responsive ethics.

ETHICAL ASPECTS OF GENETIC CONTROLS:
DESIGNED GENETIC CHANGES IN MAN

Joseph Fletcher

The essential difference between science and ethics is that science is descriptive and ethics is prescriptive. Science deals with what is, in the indicative mood. Ethics deals with what ought to be, in the imperative mood. Scientific theories and statements depend for their validity upon verification (are they correct?); ethical theories and statements depend upon justification (do they conduce to the good?).

The ethical question, then, is whether we can justify designed genetic changes in man, for the sake of both therapeutic and nontherapeutic benefits. We are able to carry out both negative or corrective eugenics—for example, to obviate gross chromosomal disorders—and positive or constructive eugenics—for example, to specialize an individual's genetic constitution for a special vocation. Like all other problems in ethical analysis, the morality of genetic intervention and engineering comes down to the question of means and ends, or of acts and consequences. Can we justify the goals and the methods of genetic engineering?

Unlike many other problems, however, in this one both the means and the ends are either challenged or actually condemned. This makes it a thornier ethical issue than most others. In bacteriologic warfare, for example, the means or weaponry is sometimes opposed even by those who may morally support a war's goal—i.e., to subjugate an enemy. In education, to take a different kind of case, to have as the end or goal establishing an Orwellian group-think in the populace would be rejected by most of us, even though the means—various mass media—are regarded as morally licit and ordinarily a good thing.

Those who wish to defend or encourage genetic controls are therefore put in the position not only of having to justify such means in embryologic and genetic research as the in vitro fertilization (conception) of human organisms or the vegetative (mitotic) reproduction of human embryos by cloning, but also of having to justify the end—that is, contrived human beings psychophysically improved by biologic design and control.

The relation of means to ends is central to ethical analysis. Does a morally desirable end ever justify a bad means, on the principle of proportionate good? Could a good means ever justify an evil end or consequences—again on the principle of proportionate good? I would answer Yes to both questions, for reasons that will appear as we proceed. The phrase "good end," I shall contend, means only that the end or consequence sought is ordinarily or commonly good, not absolutely good regardless of circumstances. In the same way the phrase "good means" can mean only that this or that method of getting to the goal desired, the act, is ordinarily or commonly right, not absolutely or always right in and of itself. Furthermore, it is obvious that our values, the various elements we hold to make up goodness, must also be identified and declared in this inquiry. Altogether, this poses a complex but important bundle of questions for conscientious people.

A PRIORI VERSUS PRAGMATIC ETHICS

Moral judgments differ. Some people fear new and unexplored risks, as we can see (for example) in the debate over construction of nuclear-power plants. They prefer to forget risk-benefit calculations; they like to stay on the safe side. Others distrust any enlargement of potential powers that might give some of us some advantage over others. We are all familiar with C. S. Lewis' observation that each new power won by man is a power over man as well. Certainly, genetic design would be such a power; even though its medical aim were only to gain control over the basic "stuff" of our human constitution it could no doubt also be turned into an instrument of political power, with or without the reinforcement of Huxley's imaginary "soma." Is it possible, some wonder, echoing Henry David Thoreau, that men have become the tools of their tools?

Nobel laureate George Beadle's opinion is that "Man knows enough but is not wise enough to make man."(1) Over against his way of looking at it a Canadian biologist, N. J. Berill, says, "Sooner or later one human society or another will launch out on this adventure, whether the rest of mankind approves or not. If this happens, and a superior race emerges with greater intelligence and longer lives, how will these people look upon those who are lagging behind? One thing is certain: they, not we, will be the heirs to the future, and they will assume control."(2)

Among religionists, Canon Michael Hamilton, of the National Cathedral in Washington, approves of genetic engineering, when and if it is aimed at the personal improvement of humans.(3) At the same time a Jesuit theologian, Richard McCormick, condemns it because, he believes, only monogamously married heterosexual reproduction is morally licit.(4) Wearing his philosopher's hat, J. B. S. Haldane votes for genetic design,(5) but putting on the same hat, another biologist, Theodosius Dobshansky, votes against it.(6) Disagreement is obviously at work at all levels and in all intellectual camps, from the simplest people to scientific peers.

A careful approach to the issue will avoid what I call the capacity-fallacy—i.e., the notion that because we can do something, such as genetic control, we ought to. It does not follow that because we could, we should. There is an ethical parallel in the necessity-fallacy, the assumption by some culture analysts that because we can do something, we will. Those who are fatalists—a visceral or noncephalic condition that is fairly widespread among us—naturally do not bother to ask policy questions.

Leaving aside technical philosophical conventions, let me suggest that when we tackle right-wrong or good-evil or desirable-undesirable questions there are fundamentally two alternative lines of approach. The first one supposes that whether any acto or course of action is right or wrong depends on its consequences. The second approach supposes that our actions are right or wrong according to whether they comply with general moral principles or prefabricated rules of conduct. Kant's formula, "It is always wrong to treat people as means and not as ends," would be an example of decision by moral rules, or the pacifist's use of the fifth of the Ten Commandments, "Thous shalt not kill." The first approach is consequentialist; the second is a priori.

This is the rock-bottom issue, and it is also (I want to suggest) the definitive question in the ethical analysis of genetic control. Are we to reason from general propositions and universals to normative decisions, or are we to reason from empirical data, variable situations and human values to normative decisions? Which? One or the other.

Until modern times the most common form of a priori ethics was religious morality. It usually held in advance of any concrete or actual problem of conscience that certain kinds of acts, such as lying and stealing and fornicating, are always wrong intrinsically, in and of themselves, as such. Their inherent wrongness was believed by faith and by metaphysical opinion to be a matter of "natural" moral law or of divine revelation. They were always negatives, never affirmatives—prohibitions, not obligations. Such "moral laws" were presumably known to the moral agent—the actor or decision maker—through inner guidance or intuition, or by spirit guidance from outside, or by means of some more objective special revelation, like scriptures. In any case, right and wrong were determined by a religious or metaphysical or nonempirical kind of cognition. There is still a widespread disposition to take an ethical posture of this kind, even though it is often unconscious. It is metarational ethics.

Nonconsequentialists would say, therefore, that therapeutic or corrective goals are not enough to justify in vitro fertilization, positive eugenics or designed genetic changes, no matter how desirable they might be. It was this kind of ethics that Daniele Petrucci ran into several years ago in Bologna because of his experiments with artificial fertilization and cell divisions at preblastocyst stages. The Church forced him to stop, in a kind of modern Galileo episode.

The basic moral law here was the religious belief that "only God can make a tree" and only God should make a man. On this basis it would be wrong to use artificial fertilization, insemination or innovulation, or single cell replications in ectogenesis. And this "law" of the divine monopoly is also opposed to any human control of sexually produced conceptuses. In the same way it is believed that fertilization results directly in a "human" being or a "nascent" human being, so that the laboratory sacrifice of such zygotes, or the use of a prostaglandin, being abortifacient, would be intrinsically wrong as such—i.e., "murder."

Good consequences could not, to the a priori moralist, justify such acts or procedures since they are wrong as means, and the a priorist contends that "the end does not justify the means." The principle of proportionate good, or a balance of gains over costs, could not in their ethics make genetic intervention by laboratory reproduction morally permissible. Consequences, as they see it, do not decide what is right. At a recent discussion at Airlie House, Dr. Leon Kass, a molecular biologist working for the National Research Council, put the a priori position succinctly. "Morally," he said, "it is insufficient that your motives are good, and that your ends are unobjectionable, that you do the procedure 'lovingly' and even that you may be lucky in the result: you will be engaging in an unethical experiment upon a human subject."(7) This is also the opinion of Paul Ramsey, a Protestant moralist who, like Father McCormick, believes that such procedures as artificial insemination from a donor, artificial innovulation, cloning and other forms of asexual reproduction are wrong—wrong because morally licit reproduction must be done heterosexually by human intercourse within the context of marriage and the family.(8)

However, some a priori moral principles are not based on metaphysical grounds. One school of utilitarians, called "rule utilitarians," make moral choices on the basis of generalizations reached empirically or clinically. They might conclude that in the expectable results of laboratory reproduction and genetic engineering, the good would be outweighed by the evil, or that the attendant risks are unknown or too great, and that therefore such procedures should be disapproved as a class or category.

Here, there is no attempt to assign an intrinsic value or dis-value; it is strictly an extrinsic appraisal. Their reason for resorting to categorical principles is usually like G. E. Moore's: that they are unwilling to trust their own judgment in situations that are apparently exceptions to the general rule. They therefore simply "rule out" some class actions (such as genetic designing) universally and categorically. Outside some theological and philosophical circles, most of the opposition to designed genetic changes in man, or even to genetic intervention for therapeutic purposes, is based on rule-utilitarianism.

In this connection, by the way, it is only fair to point out that all religionists are not a prioristic; for example, Professor James Gustafson, of the Yale Divinity School, has asked if biomedical changes in man are intrinsically wrong and answered in the negative, but he then added that if its consequences were antihuman it would for that reason be wrong after all.(9) (Later, we shall have cause to return to this matter of the human and nonhuman.)

The more commonly held ethical approach is a different modality, a pragmatic one—sometimes sneered at by a priorists and called a "mere morality of goals." This ethics is my own, and I believe it is implicit in the ethics of all biomedical research and development as well as in medical care. We reason from the data of each actual case or problem and then choose the course that offers an optimum or maximum of desirable consequences.

On this basis we cannot reason deductively from a priori or predetermined rules about the moral justifiability of whole classes of acts, such as the in vitro fertilization of gametes and the experimental sacrifice of test zygotes, or the cloning of animal and human organisms. We agree with Jeremy Bentham:"If any act can with propriety be termed pernicious, it must be so by virtue of some events which are its consequences . . . no act, strictly speaking, can be evil in itself."(10)

For those whom we might call situational or clinical consequentialists results are what counts, and results are good when they contribute to human well-being. On that basis the real issue ethically is whether genetic change in man will, in its foreseeable or predictable results, add to or take away from human welfare. We do not act by a priori categorical rules nor by dogmatic principles, such as the religious-faith proposition that genetic intervention is forbidden to human initiative or the metaphysical claim that every individual has an inalienable right to a unique genotype—presumably according to however chance and the general gene pool might happen to constitute it. For consequentialists, making decisions empirically is the problem. The question becomes, "When would it be right, and when would it be wrong?"

GENETIC ENGINEERING MUST BE SELECTIVE

What, then, might be a situation in which constructive or positive eugenics would be justified because the good to be gained—the proportionate good—would be great enough? Another way of putting it is, "When would its utility justify it?" My ability to futurize, as they say nowadays, is very limited: I am not much of a seer or forecaster, and I feel uncomfortable attempting to predict shocks of the future in long time-spans. But we have to try, even though it raises our anxiety level. We owe a great obligation to the future and to our descendants, and it would be irresponsible to repudiate the problem of genetic control by either a blanket condemnation or an uncritical endorsement. As Kierkegaard said, "To venture causes anxiety, but not to venture is to lose oneself."

Take cloning of humans, for example, as a form of genetic engineering. Although Joshua Lederberg, another Nobelist in microbiology, may be correct when he says that cloning is "merely speculative" until more experimental work with animals is done, it is still possible that such science-fiction scenarios can help value analysis and ethical examination. Diderot, G. B. Shaw, H. G. Wells, Huxley, and Lederberg himself have all foretold genetic engineering. As crystal-ball gazers they have until recently been like Priam's daughter, Cassandra, doubted and pooh-poohed. But now things are different. Now not only the doomsday people but the tut-tut reactors are having a harder time.

And yet, just because cloning is defensible in asparagus or carrot growing, it does not follow that it is all right in human baby making. I respect the ethics of scientists, which is primarily a love for and search for the facts, but some scientists seem to have an almost blind faith that somehow the facts will be used to good purposes, not misused for evil. But this is too complacent as we face the wide margin of personal and social dangers in biomedical research and practice. Therefore, whether and when genetic control could be right would depend on the situation. Let's look at a few cases, both therapeutic and eugenic.

There might be a need in the social order at large for one or more people specially constituted genetically to survive long periods outside bathyspheres at great marine depths, or outside space capsules at great heights. Control of a child's sex by cloning, to avoid any one of 50 sex-linked genetic diseases, or to meet a family's survival need, might be justifiable. I would vote for laboratory fertilization from donors to give a child to an infertile pair of spouses.

It is entirely possible, given our present increasing pollution of the human gene pool through uncontrolled sexual reproduction, that we might have to replicate healthy people to compensate for the spread of genetic diseases and to elevate the plus factors available in ordinary reproduction. It could easily come about that overpopulation would force us to put a stop to general fecundity, and then, to avoid discrimination, to resort to laboratory reproduction from unidentified cell sources. If we had "cell banks" in which the tissue of a species of wild life in danger of extinction could be stored for replication, we could do the same for the sake of endangered humans, such as the Hairy Ainu in northern Japan or certain strains of Romani gypsies.

If the greatest good of the greatest number (i.e., the social good) were served by it, it would be justifiable not only to specialize the capacities of people by cloning or by constructive genetic engineering, but also to bio-engineer or bio-design parahumans or "modified men"—as chimeras (part animal) or cyborg-androids (part prostheres). I would vote for cloning top-grade soldiers and scientists, or for supplying them through other genetic means, if they were needed to offset an elitist or tyrannical power plot by other cloners—a truly science-fiction situation, but imaginable. I suspect I would favor making and using man-machine hybrids rather than genetically designed people for dull, unrewarding or dangerous roles needed nonetheless for the community's welfare—perhaps the testing of suspected pollution areas or the investigation of threatening volcanos or snow-slides.

Ours is a Promethean situation. We cannot clearly see what the promises and the dangers are. Both are there, in the biomedical potential. Much of the scare-mongering by whole-hog or a priori opponents of genetic control link it with tyranny. This is false and misleading. Their propaganda line supposes, for one thing, that a cloned person would be a "carbon copy" of his single-cell parent because the genotype is repeated, as if such genetically designed individuals would have no individuating personal histories or variable environments. Personalities are not shaped alone by genotypes.

Furthermore, they presume that society will be a dictatorship and that such designed or cloned people would not be allowed to marry or reproduce from the social gene pool, nor be free to choose roles and functions other than the ones for which they had a special constitutional capability. But is this realistic? Is it not, actually, a mood or attitudinal posture rather than a rational or problematic view of the question?

Dr. Lederberg has pointed out that although the scenario of the Brave New World has been widely advertised, emphasizing that a slave state could and probably would use genetic control, still "it could not be so without having instituted slavery in the first place." He adds, "It is indeed true that I might fear the control of my behavior through electrical impulses directed into my brain but . . . I do not accept the implantation of the electrodes except at the point of a gun: the gun is the problem."(11) I agree. The danger of tyranny is a real danger. But genetic controls do not lead to dictatorship—if there is any cause-and-effect relation between them it is the other way around—the reverse. People who appeal to Brave New World and 1984 and Fahrenheit 451 forget this, that the tyranny is set up first and then genetic controls are employed. The problem of misuse is political, not biological.

REPRODUCTION IN THE LABORATORY

The possibility of an ethical justification of genetic control, such as I have indicated, leads at once to the question of an ethical defense of its essential prerequisite—embryologic and genetic research. As I said at the outset, there are serious challenges not only to the end being sought (control) but also to the morality of the means—in vitro fertilizations, bench-made zygotes and embryos, and the entailed practice of their sacrifice in the course of investigation. If we can justify the end, can we justify the means? Does the end justify the means in this particular case? My answer is a positive Yes.

I can see only one possible objection to such research, given a humanistic and situational ethics of the sort I have explained. That objection would be that fertilizations or cloning result directly and instantly in human beings, or in creatures with nascent or proto-human status. Let me say at once that I do not believe this to be true. And that is what such a proposition calls for—belief in a faith assertion, a declaration or confession of faith. It is not in the order of either scientific or rational statements to say that such early cell tissue is human (except in the sense of the biologic specification): it is an a priori metarational opinion. It effectively excludes from its ethics all nonbelievers.

For example, a Catholic obstetrician in Washington, D.C., has complained that it is "arbitrary" to start regarding a fetus as human at the 20th week or at "viability," and yet the physician himself insists on the even more arbitrary religious doctrine that a fertilized ovum before implantation is human.(12) Granted that it is difficult to check off any specific point on the gestational continuum as the start of a human being, it is obvious that there is much more to be said for viability as that point than for fertilization.

Those who believe such things may be correct. There is no way to know whether they are or not. It follows for them deductively that abortion is wrong in any of its manifold forms, before or after nidation. It would also follow that the experimental sacrifice of zygotes and blastular embryos in the research process is the destruction of innocent human life or the "killing of unborn babies."

This rhetoric is again an instance of how a priori ethics reasons syllogistically from metaphysical and metarational premises to a normative conclusion, rather than consequentially. All the good results in the world, immediately or potentially, could not (they argue) justify what is wrong—in this case "homicide." Indeed, if anybody really believes that a zygote is a human being he or she ought not to terminate a pregnancy or engage in embryologic research, not only for the sake of ethical consistency but for the sake of their own mental and emotional balance.

But most of us do not make that faith assertion. This is precisely and basically what is at stake in the national debate about abortion laws—the fact that they rest on grounds of a private, personal religious conviction and should not therefore be established by government in violation of the Constitution's First Amendment. Obstetricians and gynecologists do not believe this doctrine, nor do surgeons nor do fetologists, nor do embryologists and geneticists—except for an atypical minority involved in certain religious groups.

There are, be it noted, additional auxiliary arguments used sometimes against the research sacrifice of embryos and other fetal life, such as the claim that "it tends to lower respect for human life." But this begs the question and is not really very convincing as a consequentialist argument (which it is) and is very likely in any case to be a cover-up for the notion that fallopian and uterine cell matter is human. There is also a "feeling" in some discussants that a conceptus somehow has a "right to be born." They would be better advised to follow the reasoning of our common and statutory law, which rejects any idea of "unborn babies" and restricts the status of "baby" to the neonate, denying that any rights at all may be assigned to a fetus.

Nevertheless, these objections to laboratory reproduction uncover two further points I feel obliged to establish. Both points are metaethical in nature or at least prenormative. The first has to do with the idea of "humanness" and the second has to do with the notion of "rights."

What does it mean to say, as Dr. Kass does, that "the laboratory reproduction of human beings is no longer human procreation"?(7) (Indeed, can he reasonably charge that laboratory reproduction is non-human and still call its products "human beings"?) Man is a maker and a selecter and a designer, and the more rationally contrived and deliberate anything is, the more human it is. Any attempt to set up an antinomy between natural and biologic reproduction, on the one hand, and artificial or designed reproduction, on the other, is absurd. The real difference is between accidental or random reproduction and rationally willed or chosen reproduction. In either case it will be biologic—according to the nature of the biologic process. If it is "unnatural" it can be so only in the sense that all medicine is.

It seems to me that laboratory reproduction is radically human compared to conception by ordinary heterosexual intercourse. It is willed, chosen, purposed and controlled, and surely these are among the traits that distinguish *Homo sapiens* from others in the animal genus, from the primates down. Coital reproduction is, therefore, less human than laboratory reproduction—more fun, to be sure, but with our separation of baby making from lovemaking, both become more human because they are matters of choice, and not chance. This is, of course, essentially the case for planned parenthood. I cannot see how either humanity or morality are served by genetic roulette.

WHAT IS HUMAN?

The fact is that most of our discourse about the ethics of biomedical innovation is a semantic swamp, because what we mean by "human" and ergo by "humanistic" usually remains vague and poorly defined. The question "What is it to be human?" is, however, no longer just an academic exercise for philosophers. Physicians and nurses, as well as geneticists and laboratory technicians, face it every day thousands of times. For them it is literally a life-and-death practical question. It arises in utero or in vitro when sacrifices are indicated, and it arises in terminus when decisions have to be made whether to go on prolonging a patient's dying. When does a fetus become human (the better term is "personal"), when is a dying patient no longer so?

Let me suggest a conceptual approach that might be adopted. In the light of medical proposals to redefine death in terms of irreversible coma or a loss of the higher brain function (what some call "cerebral")—it might be due to a massive hemorrhage, or a neoplasm, or a trauma—if such an ex-cerebral patient is no longer alive in any human sense or personal sense, would it not follow that a pre-cerebral embryo or fetus is not yet alive in any human and personal sense? This would, of course, obviate any further use of such question-begging rhetoric as "killing unborn babies."

In any case, what is called for here, for consequentialists, is a quality-of-life ethics instead of the sanctity-of-life ethics in the classical Western tradition. The metarational premise or a priori that mere life or biologic process is sacrosanct is not only neither verifiable nor falsifiable; by logical inference it is inconsistent with empirical and humanistic medicine, as well as opposed to genetic and embryologic investigation.

The uncomfortable truth is that we have not yet put our heads together in an interdisciplinary way to see if we can find some "common-ground" factors and operational terms for such synthetic concepts as "human" and "personal." Some moralists—for example, Gustafson(9)—doubt if a consensus on "humanness" is possible, but it is worth a try. This may well be the most searching and fundamental problem that faces not only ethicists but society as a whole.

It is already very late. It is urgent that scientists, philosophers, sociologists, lawyers and theologians make the attempt, especially if nondoctrinaire auspices can be found. What makes a creature human? A minimum of cerebrocortical function? Self-awareness and self-control? Memory? A sense of futurity, of time? A capacity for interpersonal relationship? Communication? Love? A minimum I.Q.? Could we add a desire to live? What else? And in what order would we rank them as priorities?

Surely Senator Mondale was on the right track in 1968 when he tried to persuade Congress to propose a National Commission on Health, Science and Society. It was obstructed by people in research medicine objecting to any outside "interference." Another effort, Senate Resolution 98, was also sidetracked, in the 91st Congress of 1969. Senator Mondale promises to try again in 1971. The alternative to such a thoughtful review of the implications of biomedical pioneering is apt to be hasty, unconsidered legislation. There is a palpable danger of a new Luddism, biologic this time instead of industrial. Little as we should like to be manipulated by what Gerald Leach has called "the biocrats,"(13) neither do we want to be paralyzed by know-nothingism.

Science deals with the possible and the probable, but ethics deals with the preferable—and it is at this level of analysis that the issue of designed genetic changes in man has at last brought us. We cannot any longer sweep it under the rug.

NEEDS FIRST, NOT RIGHTS

My second closing point has to do with what we mean by rights. Reactionaries cannot, of course, "prove" that reproduction is ethical only when it is done heterosexually within the monogamous marriage bond, or that any one set of values or any one preferential order is the correct one, or that particular "rights" alleged by this group or that are sacrosanct. None of them are. For example, we cannot establish a supposed "right to be born," to say nothing of what one theologian has called a "right to be born with a unique genotype."(14) (By this, of course, he can only mean the accidental genotype resulting from random or so-called "natural" conception, and even so, identical twins can and do occur in nature.) All alleged "rights" are at best imperfect and relative. But what is there, then, to appeal to, to validate our humanistic concerns and our person-centered values?

My answer is: needs. Needs are the moral stabilizers, not rights. The legalistic temper gives first place to rights, but the humanistic temper puts needs in the driver's seat. If human rights conflict with human needs, let needs prevail. If medical care can use genetic controls preventively to protect people from disease or deformity, or to ameliorate such things, then let so-called "rights" to be born step aside. If research with embryos and fetal tissue is needed to give us the means to cure and prevent the tragedies of "unique genotypes," even though it involves the sacrifice of some conceptuses, then let rights take a back seat.

Rights are nothing but a formal recognition by society of certain human needs, and as needs change with changing conditions so rights should change too. The right to conceive and bear children has to stop short of knowingly making crippled children—and genetics gives us that knowledge—just as the rights of parents have had to bow to required schooling and the rights of voluntary association have had to bow, in public services, to the human need to be respected regardless of ethnic and racial differences. It is human need that validates rights, not the other way around. I for one am not primarily concerned about any claimed rights to live or to die; I am first of all concerned about human needs, and whether they are met by life or by death will depend on the situation.

To speak of "needs" is to speak of human values. How shall we identify and rank-order them? Here, again, we have to have across-the-board cultural consultation. I agree with Michael Baram, of M.I.T., who says:

> I do not think scientific peer groups presently have the objectivity or capability to function as coherent and humane social controls. The members of a peer group share the narrow confines of their discipline, and individual success is measured by the degree to which one plunges more deeply into and more narrowly draws the bounds of his research. There are no peer group rewards for activities or perceptions that extend beyond the discipline or relate it to social problems. Members are therefore neither motivated nor trained to relate their peer group activity to broader social problems.
>
> Self-enclosed peer groups cannot be entrusted with self-control . . . because our educational system does not foster ethical and interdisciplinary values in professional training.(15)

Owing to the work of microbiologists and embryologists we are already able to produce babies born from parents who are separated by space or even by death; women are already able to nourish and gestate other women's children; one man can "father" thousands of children; virgin births or parthenogenesis (for that is what cloning is) are likely soon to be feasible; by genetic intervention we can shape babies, rather than only from the simple seed of our loins; artificial wombs and placentas are projected by biochemists and pharmacologists. All this means that we are going to have to change or alter our old ideas about who or what a father is, or a mother, or a family. Francis Crick, co-describer of DNA, and others are quite right to say that all this is going to destroy to some extent our traditional grounds for ethical beliefs.

But whatsoever new mental images take shape, within new reality situations, as long as they are tailored to a loving concern for human beings we need not be afraid. Fear is at the bottom of this debate—some of it the conventional wisdom's fear of change, some of it a fear of science, and some of it fear of freedom's power and creative control. It is, perhaps, the fear of fear itself that makes for a lot of hang-ups, and cop-outs. But however that may be, the historic moral order has always presupposed heterosexual coital conception as necessary for the continuance of life, and now that is no longer the case. The familiar phrase "the facts of life" is an archaism.

I agree with Roger Shinn that in the sequence or progression from aspirin to insulin to artificial kidneys to brain surgery to genetic engineering there is no point at which we can "change from a clear yes to an absolute no," even though there is a mounting difference in the complexity of the ethical issues posed.(16) We cannot accept the "invisible hand" of blind natural chance or random nature in genetics any more than we could old Professor Jevon's theory of feast and famine in 19th-century laissez-faire economics, based on sun spots and tidal movements. To be men we must be in control. That is the first and last ethical word. For when there is no choice there is no possibility of ethical action. Whatever we are compelled to do is a-moral.

The moral philosopher, sensitive to social ethics, can only echo what the biologist Robert Sinsheimer has said: "As the discoveries accumulate, as new means of biological intervention arise, we can envision such possibilities as the almost indefinite prolongation of life for at least a few, the deliberate predetermination of sex, or the design of human genetic change for varied purposes. With these will come the necessity for multiple social decisions of the most profound consequence."(17)

The pressure of social decision-making is now forcing us to dig deeper than the technical hardware sciences; we now have to grapple with the personal and human software sciences—especially biology and the crossroads it reveals to us, just ahead.

REFERENCES

(1) Britannica Book of the Year, 1964. Chicago, Encyclopaedia Britannica, Inc., 1964, pp. 499-500.

(2) Rosenfeld, A.: The Second Genesis: The coming control of life. Englewood Cliffs, New Jersey, Prentice-Hall, 1969, p. 145.

(3) Hamilton, M.: New life for old: genetic decisions. Christ Century 86:741-744, 1969.

(4) McCormick, R.: Notes on moral theology. Theologic Studies 30: 680-692. 1969.

(5) Haldane, J.B.S.: Biological possibilities for the human species in the next ten thousand years. Man and His Future. Edited by G. Wolstenholme. Boston, Little, Brown and Company, 1963, pp. 337-361.

(6) Dobzhansky, T.: Heredity and the Nature of Man. New York, Harcourt, Brace and World, 1964.

(7) Kass, L.: New beginnings in life. Three Medical Futures, Edited by M. Hamilton. Grand Rapids, Michigan, Eerdmans Publishing Company (in press).

(8) Ramsey, P.: Moral and religious implications of genetic control, Genetics and the Future of Man. Edited by J. D. Roslansky: Amsterdam. North-Holland Publishing Company, 1966, pp. 107-169.

(9) Gustafson, J.: Basic ethical issues in the biomedical fields. Soundings 52:151-180. 1970.

(10) Bentham, J.: The influence of time and place in matters of legislation. The Works of Jeremy Bentham. Vol. 1. Edited by J. Bowring, London. Simpkin, Marshall, and Company, 1843, pp. 169-194.

(11) Lederberg, J.: Genetic engineering, or the amelioration of genetic defect, Pharos 34:9-12, 1971.

(12) Helleger, A.: Letter to the editor. Washington Post, January 9, 1971, p. A21

(13) Leach, G.: The Biocrats. New York, McGraw-Hill Book Company, 1970.

(14) Ramsey, P.: Fabricated Man: The ethics of genetic control. New Haven,

Yale University Press, 1970.

(15) Baram, M. S.: Social control of science and technology. Science 172:535-539, 1971.

(16) Shinn, R.: The ethics of genetic engineering. N. D. State Univ. Bull., April 22, 1967, pp. 13-21.

(17) Sinsheimer, R.: The implications of recent advances in biology for the future of medicine. Eng. Sci. 34:6-13, 1970.

MEDICAL ETHICS AND
SOCIO-POLITICAL CHANGE

Victor W. Sidel,

At least three different historical streams, closely interrelated, have led to an increasing concern by health workers with social and political change. The first stream is the broadening concept of health, as codified in the preamble to the Constitution of the World Health Organization: "Health is a state of complete physical, mental, and social well-being and not merely the absence of disease or infirmity." There is unfortunately relatively little that can be accomplished to bring about *social* well-being by medicine when it is narrowly construed as a therapeutic art, and many would argue that the path to *physical* and *mental* well-being is also rarely within the scope of conventional medical care alone. If the medical worker is to be a promoter of health rather than simply a reactor against established disease or disability, part of his work must go beyond traditional medical care into areas of social and political change.

The second stream that forces many health workers into working for socio-political change is the changing technological nature of medical care and of preventive measures. Almost the only suggestions which Hippocrates (Sigerist, 1951) or Maimonides (1958) had to offer in the field of preventive medicine was to urge that food, sex, and other pleasures be indulged in moderation; there was then little point in engaging in other than the one-to-one relationship of physician and patient. Now many effective techniques are available—immunization, fluoridation, pre-marital or pre-natal screening for genetic defects, early detection and treatment of communicable or reversible illness—but in order to be effective many of these must be applied on a community-wide rather than on a person-to-person basis. Again the approach must be socio-political.

The third stream is the increasing recognition that the maldistribution of wealth, power, and resources—among nations and within each nation—is in itself a major root cause of poor health. While the world's have-nots fight this maldistribution—and the consequent domination of some people over other and defilement of the environment—for many reasons, health workers increasingly feel they must fight it not only as human beings but as specially-entrusted protectors of their patients' and their community's health.

HEALTH WORKERS IN SOCIAL AND POLITICAL CHANGE

Some physicians have reacted to these social forces, or to social needs, by becoming frankly political leaders. Examples within this century include such diverse figures as Dr. Sun Yat-sen (Sharman, 1968); Dr. Francois Duvalier (Latortue, 1966; Diederich et al, 1969); Dr. Ernesto (Che) Guevara (Harper, 1969; Mora, 1969; Gerassi, 1968); and Dr. Salvadore Allende (Debray, 1971: Angell, 1972). These physicians have all played important socio-political roles, but what they did had little direct connection with their training or role as health workers. They may each have learned much from their medical training or experience, and they may have done some things differently—or not done some things—because of their training. People may have even viewed them at times as different from other political leaders of their medical backgrounds, but when they acted they did so as political leaders rather than as doctors. Ethical considerations in their previous role as physicians may have led some of them to assume political roles, but once they assumed the frankly political role "medical" ethics—as opposed to ethics of other kinds—were no longer relevant. Their political activity therefore lies outside the scope of this paper.

The concern here is with physicians or other health workers who play socio-political roles while still clearly retaining their roles as health workers. Again, the list is diverse: Dr. Norman Bethune, the Canadian thoracic surgeon who provided medical services for the Loyalists against Franco in the Spanish Civil War and for Mao Tse-tung's Eighth Route Army in the war against the invading Japanese (Allan et al., 1959); Dr. Howard Levy, who refused to train Green Beret combat soldiers in medical skills which they would use along with their rifles in Indochina (Sidel 1968); Dr. Edward Annis who, as President of the American Medical Association, led its fight against national health insurance (Harris, 1969; Rayack, 1967); Dr. Jack Geiger, who among many socio-political actions in attempting to improve the quality of life for poor blacks in Mississippi, wrote prescriptions for food as a specific treatment against the social illness of malnutrition (Geiger, 1969); and the many health workers who have fought for, and against, abortion reform, the legalization of marijuana, the fluoridation of water supplies, community participation in or control of health care services, or, more broadly but argued for "health" reasons, redistribution of income or an end to American participation in the war in Indochina.

A relevant fictional example is Dr. Thomas Stockmann, in Ibsen's "Enemy of the People," who discovers and publicizes the fact that the spa on which his community's livelihood is based is contaminated, and is stoned for his "ethical" socio-political stance. In all these instances, in which a person is playing a socio-political role while being a health worker, medical ethics would appear to have considerable relevance. But how do we relate medical ethics to such situations?

PUBLISHED CODES OF MEDICAL ETHICS

Although I am aware that published codes of ethics cover only a small part of the principles of medical ethics, are often more concerned with guild rules than with values, and may not necessarily mirror practice, such codes may give us some insight into the ways in which medical ethical thought has addressed itself—or failed to address itself—to these issues. The Oath of Geneva, a "modernization" of the Hippocratic Oath drafted by the World Medical Association in 1948, is now in use in the majority of American medical schools and in many schools throughout the world (Irish *et al.*, 1965):

At the time of being admitted as a member of the medical profession:
    I solemnly pledge myself to consecrate my life to the service of humanity;
    I will give to my teachers the respect and gratitude which is their due;
    I will practice my profession with conscience and dignity;
    The Health of my patient will be my first consideration;
    I will respect the secrets which are confided in me;
    I will maintain by all the means in my power, the honor and the noble traditions of the medical profession;
    My colleagues will be my brothers;
    I will not permit considerations of religion, nationality, race, party, politics or social standing to intervene between my duty and my patient;
    I will maintain the utmost respect for human life from the time of conception; even under threat, I will not use my medical knowledge contrary to the laws of humanity,
    I make these promises solemnly, freely, and upon my honor.

A contrasting set of ethical codes is that promulgated in the Soviet Union in 1971 (*Meditsinskaya Gazeta*, 1971; Shabad, 1971).

Upon having conferred on me the high calling of physician and entering medical practice, I do solemnly swear:
    To dedicate all my knowledge and strength to the preservation and improvement of the health of mankind and to the treatment and prevention of disease, and to work in good conscience wherever it is required by society;
    To always be ready to provide medical care, to relate to the patient attentively and carefully, and to preserve medical confidences;
    To constantly perfect my medical knowledge and clinical skill and thereby in my work to aid in the development of medical science and practice;
    To refer, if the patient's better interests warrant it, for advice from my

fellow physicians, and never myself to refuse to give such advice or help;

To preserve and develop the noble traditions of Soviet medicine, to be guided in all my actions by the principles of Communist morality and to always bear in mind the high calling of a Soviet physician and my responsibility to the people and to the Soviet State.

I swear to be loyal to this oath as long as I live.

These codes have in common a number of protections for the individual patient, but the Oath of Geneva in contrast to the Soviet Oath comments little on the broader community responsibilities of the physician. In the People's Republic of China no code is published, but the communal responsibilities of the physician are constantly stressed, far more than in the United States and considerably more than in the U.S.S.R. (Sidel, 1972; Sidel et al, 1972)

It is fascinating, on the other hand, that the "Principles of Medical Ethics" adopted at the June, 1957 meeting of the House of Delegates of the American Medical Association included specific reference to this issue in Section 10 (American Medical Association, 1971):

The honored ideals of the medical profession imply that the responsibilities of the physician extend not only to the individual, but also to society where these responsibilities deserve his interest and participation in activities which have the purpose of improving both the health and the well-being of the individual and the community

In addition, Dr. Russell Roth, the Speaker of the House of Delegates, has analyzed some of the relationships between medical ethics and social needs (Roth, 1971).

Finally, as evidence for the view that many American physicians view work for socio-political change in medical ethical terms consider the action of the workshop on medical ethics at the Second National Staff Conference in Atlanta in March, 1972. After criticism of the Hippocratic Oath as "irrelevant to the moral dilemma in a revolutionary age," a set of ethical principles "as a substitute for the oath" was prepared by the workshop and approved at the plenary session of the conference. Among the principles approved, for example, were (House Physician Reporter, 1972):

Patient confidentiality must be respected, although in certain situations the responsibility of the physician to the patient and to society at large may be irreconcilable. The patient should be forewarned whenever the physician suspects that confidentiality might be violated.

The physician has an obligation to identify and oppose those social and environmental conditions that adversely affect the health of his patients, such as war, racism, and poverty.

HEALTH WORKER'S SOCIO-POLITICAL ROLE

The formulation of these codes leads to difficult questions about the socio-political role of the health worker as health worker. Are lead poisoning and rat bite the only aspects of slum housing that health workers should focus on, or are the general conditions under which people live part of our health concerns? Is the appropriate medical response to lead poisoning to a treat patients who come in for care; b. screen children in the community for lead levels; c. organize campaigns to remove or cover the lead paint; or d. fight for a fundamental change in the control and financing of housing in the United States?

As the scope of medicine is widened and the tools of medicine strengthened, and we thereby find additional arguments which force many of us into areas of social and political action, we must also be aware of concomitant dangers. Many health professionals think of themselves as a technological elite (*e.g.*, as in the phrase "No community is going to tell me how to practice medicine"), and this view persists when professionals discuss social and political issues. In certain technical areas, health workers have expertise that is most valuable, but expertise in some areas does not make the health worker an expert in all areas, not even in all health-related areas. The health worker must learn, in his socio-political as well as in his more conventionally-based medical activities, to distinguish those areas in which he has special knowledge or skill from those in which he is like all other citizens.

Where the health worker has greater expertise, the question arises whether, and when, his expertise gives that person the right to decide on a course of action or whether, and when, the community must decide. In other words, does acknowledged expertise automatically confer decision-making power? Sometimes the power clearly lies with the expert; for example, few would dispute the physician's authority, and responsibility, to act rapidly in the face of a medical emergency or to administer penicillin (with the implied or explicit permission of the patient or his family) without a community vote. (But even in such instances one can have a *socially-accountable post hoc* review mechanism, as opposed to simple peer review or no review at all.) The question becomes: what are the ground rules for distinguishing between those situations in which the health worker because of his expertise does (or should) have immediate decision-making power, and those in which he (alone) should not (Geiger, 1971).

Ibsen's Dr. Stockmann can prove bacteriologic contamination of the baths and can suggest a range of technologic solutions; those were clearly within his professional competence. However, what solution the community will follow is another problem. Dr. Stockmann may disagree with the course the community has chosen, and leave it, or—as he did—he may stay to convince people that they have taken the wrong course. However, his expertise gives him no mandate—however much we professionals may agree with him—to force his solution upon others. His most important responsibility—although it is expressed in no known written code of medical ethics—is to share his knowledge with others in his community so that all can join knowledgably in decision-making. Where this leaves the individual, standing alone with his conscience and his ethics *against* the community is not clear. But it is a problem those who would discuss medical ethics cannot evade.

The problem cannot be evaded in relation to the right of the health worker to strike, clearly a political action. Since strikes by health workers always directly or indirectly harm their patients and their communities, when are they justifiable? Again there is a spectrum. At one end are strikes in the self-interest of highly-paid and highly-privileged physicians. Further along the spectrum are strikes in the self-interest of poorly-paid hospital workers. Yet further along are strikes attempting to improve conditions of medical care by dramatizing that a community has provided inadequate resources for care. Near the other end of the spectrum are strikes against torture and concentration camps. Again, exploration of these issues lies in the areas of politics and of medical ethics, and should be included in the study of medical ethics.

Another danger of the involvement of medicine with community concerns, and therefore into social and political action, is the conflict which may arise between the physician's responsibility to his individual patient and his responsibility to his community. The classic example is that of the school bus driver with epilepsy who asks his physican to keep in confidence the danger of his having a seizure while driving a busload of children. Real choices are never quite so clearly defined as in hypothetical examples; usually alternatives are available which straddle an issue, thereby allowing the health worker to serve both patient *and* community. However numerous instances occur when physicians or other health workers must choose between patient and community. When this happens the health worker must take pains to make possible the provision of the alternative service by health workers with different views of the priorities, and not characterize by word or action his choice as the *only* choice. Both individuals and communities need medical services, and society must in great measure determine the balance. How the health worker as an individual, and health workers as a group, are to make their personal decisions on priorities and ethics—and how these "personal decisions" relate to the decisions of the community which subsidizes their training and licenses—is far from clear.

Despite the dangers, and I do not mean to minimize them, increasing numbers of health workers are beginning to believe that appropriate provision of health service forces them into social and political action. Too many problems of medicine and of the quality of life can not be solved in any other way: lead poisoning, napalm burns, Tay-Sachs disease, rat bite, veneral disease, starvation, lung cancer, drug addiction, and mass feeling of alienation and powerlessness. As the Chinese say, "Politics must be put in command." As health workers change their view of themselves and their priorities, relating in new ways to the needs of their patients and their communities and learning about and working for socio-political change as part of their medical responsibilities, medical-ethical concepts will have to be re-examined and taught so that we can keep what is useful in the old while we embrace the new.

REFERENCES

Allan, T., and S. Gordon (1952). *The Scalpel, The Sword* Boston, Little, Brown & Co.

American Medical Association (1971). *Opinion and Reports of the Judicial Council*, 56.

Angell, A. (1972) *Current Hist.* 62, 76.

Debray, R. (1971). *The Chilean Revolution: Conversations with Allende.* New York, Pantheon.

Diederich, B., and A. Burt, *Papa Doc.: The Truth about Haiti Today.* New York, Avon books.

Geiger, H. J. (1969). *Bulletin, National Tuberculosis and Respiratory Disease Association 55*, No 10, November, 1969 4.

Geiger, H. J. (1971). *Social Policy 2*, 24.

Gerassi, J., editor (1968). *Venceremos! The Speeches and Writings of Che Guevara.* New York, Simon & Schuster.

Harper, G. P. (1969). *New Eng. J. Med. 281*, 1285.

Harris, R. (1969). *The Sacred Trust.* New York, Penguin Books, Inc.

House Physician Reporter (1972). Vol. 12, No. 4, May, 1972, 7.

Irish, D. P., and D. W. McMurray (1965). *J. Chron. Dis. 18*, 275.

Latortue, G. R. *Current History 56*, 349.

Maimonides (1958). *The Preservation of Youth—Essays on Health.* New York, Philosophical Library.

Meditsinskaya Gazeta (1971). No. 32, April 20, 1971, 1.

Mora, L. O. (1969). *New Eng. J. Med. 281*, 1289.

Rayack, E. (1967). *Professional Power and American Medicine: The Economics of the American Medical Association.* New York, The World Publishing Company.

Roth, R. B. (1971). *J. Amer. Med. Assn. 215*, 1956.

Shabad, T. (1971). *N.Y. Times*, April 21, 1971, 2.

Sharman, L. (1968). *Sun Yat-Sen: His Life and Its Meaning.* Stanford, California, Stanford University Press.

Sidel, V. W. (1968). *Lancet 1*, 966.

Sidel, V. W. (1972). *The New Physician 21*, 284.

Sidel, R., and V. W. Sidel (1972). *Social Policy 2*, No. 6, March/April, 1972, 25.

Sigerist, H. (1951). *A History of Medicine: Primitive and Archaic Medicine.* New York, Oxford University Press.

SOME THINGS MEDICAL ETHICS IS NOT

K. Danner Clouser

Medical ethics has suddenly moved to center stage. It is vigorously discussed in many quarters; medical schools are in various stages of developing teaching programs dealing with these issues.

At this point in its spiraling development, it may be helpful to consider the nature of medical ethics, if only in an effort to stem conceptual sprawl. Conceptual confusion results when ethics tries to be all things to all people. It must trim down to fighting weight, refusing to encompass in its definition all that has been thrust upon it. An explication of "freedom" that included everything anyone has ever meant by the word would be meaningless by virtue of sheer generality, excluding little if anything. So too with "ethics."

My plan is to discuss some things medical ethics is not. A sheer list itemizing what is not ethics would be dictatorial and uninformative. Instead, I will guess at why some disciplines are sometimes thought appropriate housing for medical ethics, and then I will say why that view is mistaken. I will begin with the more obvious distinctions, gathering momentum for the more subtle.

One footnote about this negative approach is in order. Aside from the practical help it may afford those launching programs, there is a systematic point to be made. Determining what is not medical ethics is an important intermediary step in forging a definition of medical ethics. Leaping immediately from intuitive notion to rigid definition cuts off, by definition, consideration of borderline possibilities. The negative intermediate step is a means of reflectively zeroing in on an elusive concept, without strangling the incipient insights and fruitful observations that accrue to the open questioning search for a definition.

Of course, exclusions ought not be arbitrary; they must be justified in the usual systematic way: appeals to key concepts, to consistency, to conceptual economy, and the like. However, the goals of this article are better served by surface descriptions unencumbered by these weightier justifications.

OBVIOUS DISTINCTIONS

At this level, perhaps all we need is a list read with the ring of authority. Medical ethics is not sociology, medical ethics is not history of medicine, medical ethics is not anthropology, nor literature, nor family and community medicine. Actually, medical ethics is seldom considered synonymous with these disciplines, but these disciplines are not infrequently considered the natural home of medical ethics, or at least the executors of its estate. It is instructive to consider why responsibility for ethical deliberations might come to be located (conceptually or actually) within these disciplines. There are several possibilities.

There is a tendency to lump into one melting pot all that is not "hard" science. To the "hard" scientist all nonscience looks alike—mushy. It seems a place of rampant opinion where one such is as good as any other. If this easy categorization is simply for convenience, it is perhaps tolerable. But it is, in fact, simple-minded and terribly misleading. It ignores those pivotal areas of "hard" science that are really mushy and those critical areas of "soft" disciplines that are really hard. And to be aware of these aspects within one's own discipline is maturing.

Another underlying motivation for identifying ethics with these various camps is the "human" element they all seem to share. On the surface, literature, medical sociology, anthropology, and family and community medicine seem to have a concern with humans as whole beings that other medical sciences do not have. Whether or not this is true is not now to the point. What is to the point is "localized humanitarianism." This is the tendency of disciplines focusing on the whole human and his culture to be saddled with pushing a particular point of view—namely, humanitarianism. In effect these disciplines are forced into being the repository for all responsibility and effort on behalf of kindness, compassion, and general human concern. This does grave injustice both to these disciplines and to human compassion. It strips the disciplines of their true calling and it compartmentalizes human compassion, making it the responsibility of the few rather than the responsibility of everyone.

A subtle mistake involved in the uniting of ethics and literature may be the underlying assumption that the study of ethics should motivate one to be ethical. Everyone is aware that literature, drama, and poetry are persuasive and that they can incite to action. And if one assumes the study of ethics should convince students to be ethical, literature and ethics are apt to be coupled, if not identified.

But the validity of an ethical system cannot stand or fall on its capacity to inspire moral behavior—any more than the correctness of a medical therapy depends on its capacity to inspire a patient to follow it. Rather, the student of ethics is developing a skill in working his way through muddled ethical issues and in finding the right action amidst a morass of complicated details.

Whether or not he chooses to do the morally right action is influenced far more by the example of his medical mentor than by anything he could learn in an ethics class. And rightly so. Otherwise ethics might become a series of sermons and exhortations rather than a discipline analyzing actions, principles, and justifications as rigorously and objectively as the subject matter permits.

Related to this confusion is the tendency to regard medical ethics as synonymous with reform movements. Reform may be noble and necessary, but nevertheless it should not be confused with the study of medical ethics. Reform seldom calls for subtle clinical analysis. There is no need for intricate determination and balancing of competing rights and social effects. What is wrong is clear and obvious, and action is called for to correct it.

In short, there are clear advantages for disciplinary integrity and objectivity in keeping action groups and academic disciplines separate. It is comparable to the separation of the judicial and legislative branches of the government.

Finally, there is a subtle and mistaken belief causing and in turn strengthened by the relation of ethics with sociology and anthropology. This is the belief that ethics at its best is descriptive, that we can at most discover what things are valued by various peoples at various times and places, but that there exists no way of criticizing and analyzing these values, nor of arguing for what is morally right in current situations. This is avoided by allowing ethics to be its own discipline.

MORE DIFFICULT DISTINCTIONS

The following disciplines are more apt to be confused with ethics. I continue to present simply a sketch of how each differs from ethics. I am making suggestions and giving descriptions more than constructing arguments. If anything of value emerges, it will be as before—by the back door, that is, in saying why medical ethics should *not* be confused with these disciplines.

The relationship of law and morality has had many volumes dedicated to it. Here, as elsewhere, I simply want to give the layman an intuitive feel for the difference.

Morality is surely external to law: laws are sometimes criticized and even overturned because they are immoral or unjust; frequently laws deal with issues that simply are not moral concerns; and there are matters of morality that cannot be backed by the law because of inconvenience or impossibility of enforcement.

Yet there is overlap, as in instances where immoral behavior is proscribed by law, and becomes punishable (e.g., killing, disabling, and breaking promises of a contractual sort). This, of course, is not at all remarkable when we realize that law and morals have much the same purpose: (very roughly) a set of rules we could all agree to that would lead us to live together harmoniously, allowing each of us to achieve his aims and desires insofar as this is compatible with everyone realizing his aims and desires.

The student of medical ethics has a great deal to learn from law in terms of finely-drawn distinctions and helpful concepts. The two are, nevertheless, to be emphatically distinguished. That the law says something about death or fetuses or human experimentation is not the end of the matter. Our quest is for the moral point of view as a critique of current laws and a guide to future ones.

As with all the other possible look-alikes, the risk is not that religion and ethics might be thought completely identical. It is rather that they are frequently grouped together under the mistaken belief that they are conceptually entwined. It has often been contended that ethics is impossible without religion. I think this view incorrect, though I will not argue it here.

There are three important points to make in distinguishing religion and ethics: 1. Ethics must have universal appeal. We seek at least a basic set of rules that all rational men would agree to as moral rules and could urge everyone to follow. Religion is acceptable only to a much smaller subset of this group; we are not required by reason to accept its metaphysical bases, and it would be unjust to insist on such acceptance. Rules and principles based on special knowledge or special commitments can lead only to secret societies, whereas ethics' whole point is to be binding on all, and hence must be understandable and justifiable to everyone. 2. Usually, religion's ethics are more stringent than general ethics. That is, they not only do not go against acts of supererogation—acts above and beyond what could reasonably be *required* of all men. As such, religious ethics can count only on the voluntary commitment of a small remnant of men, whereas general ethics, being a minimal ethic (i.e., having only obligations anyone could fulfill) can count on being acceptable to all rational men. 3. Religion is very likely the motivation for many men to be moral. It may well provide impetus, inspiration, or reward for a man's morality. This is probably one reason religion and ethics are popularly lumped together. Though motivation to be moral is extremely important, I think it is not a part of the discipline of ethics, at least not such that an ethical theory would be refuted if it failed to induce moral behavior. Ethics per se should be more like principles of justice and less like political platforms. Ethics can use a sidekick like religion, but he must remain his own man for the sake of objectivity and rigor.

Counseling is apt to be regarded the home of medical ethics for a number of reasons: the personal approach, the concern for the total human, its own frequent identification with religion and thereby with ethics. Here I will comment on only two, namely, the elements of ministering and compassion. This is what many take ethics to be all about. I will briefly say why I disagree.

Comforting the bereaved, guiding the troubled, and ministering to the dying are noble endeavors. But studying ethics would not equip one for this, nor would counseling skills make one more proficient at ethics. Comforting, counseling, and ministering may well manifest ethical concern; such activity would constitute acts of supererogation for some and performance of duty for others. (For example, it is an obvious duty for counselors, and perhaps for all medical personnel.) So counseling skills are not ethical skills, yet like any other skills, counseling can be used ethically, that is, to fulfill one's moral obligations and commitments.

Compassion, closely linked with counseling and ministering, should also be distinguished from ethics as such. It has nothing to do with the study of ethics (though it might motivate one to study ethics) and it is not even a moral obligation. Insofar as compassion is a subjective state or feeling, it could not be required by ethics. But insofar as it is expressed in "compassionate behavior," such behavior may be someone's duty and hence a moral obligation (since doing one's duty is a moral obligation).

Of course, compassion may be personally very important in helping one to fulfill both ethical obligations and ethical commitments, or simply in being well-liked. It is just that ethics obligates us to certain actions (or more accurately, to refraining from certain actions) and not to a feeling or frame of mind in which the obligations should be fulfilled.

Psychiatry is much like counseling, and might be taken as intimately related to ethics for the same reasons. But I single it out in order to make a special and important point. This concerns life styles or "philosophies of life." At least some approaches in psychiatry and psychoanalysis might be seen as attempts to help the patient mold a new life style or restructure his life plan. In part, it may be this connection with "the good life" that has led people to connect ethics and psychiatry. Again, a distinction is crucial: this time between "the good life" or a "philosophy of life" and morality. Morality *proscribes* many actions (e.g., killing, breaking promises, causing pain) but it should not be expected to *prescribe* a way of life. Many styles of life are compatible with living in accord with the basic moral obligations; and many styles of life are compatible with fulfilling one's own moral commitments. Two salient points argue against making a philosophy of life a moral obligation: 1. All men could never reach agreement on a particular way of life; they could never agree on what goods life should achieve. But we could reach agreement on what men should not do to other men, and hence reach universal agreement on what actions should be forbidden. As long as a philosophy of life is in accord with those proscribed actions, ethics per se can have nothing more to say about it. (Though advice on the effectiveness and satisfaction of any such guide to life will surely flow from many other quarters!) 2. There is danger in regarding life styles as a matter of morality. It is a common practice, both dangerous and fallacious. It perpetuates moral relativity in that anyone can proclaim his life style as "his" morality and consider it a "moral obligation" to fulfill his life style and plan. His life plan might in fact be highly immoral (doing those things that would be proscribed by universal agreement). And few things are more frightening than immoral actions self-righteously supported with the rhetoric of morality.

CONCLUSIONS

Though I have had to say it in terms of what ethics is not, I have in effect been stressing three basic points: 1. That ethics is a discipline in and of itself, with its own conceptual framework, its own methods, strategies, and purposes. 2. That in studying ethics one ideally develops sensitivity to moral issues and skill in determining the morally right course of action. (The discipline itself will not provide the motivation to live by it anymore than the study of political science will motivate one to become a politician.) 3. Basic moral rules must be universal and will generally proscribe rather than prescribe.

Thus we are at the real starting point. The foregoing has only been ground-clearing, preparing the site for the construction of a definition and description of medical ethics. But that edifice must await another occasion.

INDEX